Applied Behavior Analysis Advanced Guidebook

Applied Behavior Analysis Advanced Guidebook

A Manual for Professional Practice

Edited by

James K. Luiselli

Clinical Solutions, Inc., Beverly, MA, United States

NEEDS Center, Tewksbury, MA, United States

ACADEMIC PRESS

An imprint of Elsevier

Academic Press is an imprint of Elsevier
125 London Wall, London EC2Y 5AS, United Kingdom
525 B Street, Suite 1800, San Diego, CA 92101-4495, United States
50 Hampshire Street, 5th Floor, Cambridge, MA 02139, United States
The Boulevard, Langford Lane, Kidlington, Oxford OX5 1GB, United Kingdom

Notices
Knowledge and best practice in this field are constantly changing. As new research and experience broaden our understanding, changes in research methods, professional practices, or medical treatment may become necessary.

Practitioners and researchers must always rely on their own experience and knowledge in evaluating and using any information, methods, compounds, or experiments described herein. In using such information or methods they should be mindful of their own safety and the safety of others, including parties for whom they have a professional responsibility.

To the fullest extent of the law, neither the Publisher nor the authors, contributors, or editors, assume any liability for any injury and/or damage to persons or property as a matter of products liability, negligence or otherwise, or from any use or operation of any methods, products, instructions, or ideas contained in the material herein.

British Library Cataloguing-in-Publication Data
A catalogue record for this book is available from the British Library

Library of Congress Cataloging-in-Publication Data
A catalog record for this book is available from the Library of Congress

ISBN: 978-0-12-811122-2

For Information on all Academic Press publications
visit our website at https://www.elsevier.com/books-and-journals

Working together
to grow libraries in
developing countries

www.elsevier.com • www.bookaid.org

Publisher: Nikki Levy
Acquisition Editor: Emily Ekle
Editorial Project Manager: Barbara Makinster
Production Project Manager: Sujatha Thirugnana Sambandam
Designer: Greg Harris

Typeset by MPS Limited, Chennai, India

Contents

List of Contributors xi
Preface xiii

Section I Supervision, Training, and Service Delivery 1

1 Behavior Analytic Supervision 3
Laura B. Turner
Introduction to the topic and relevance for behavioral practitioners 3
Past and current status of practitioner training in the topic 4
Research base and implications for practice 4
Practice guidelines, procedures, and implementation recommendations 7
Continuously monitor supervisory behaviors 15
Take home message of above practice guidelines 16
References 17
Appendix A Procedural checklist for first supervision meeting 19

2 Competency-Based Staff Training 21
Dennis H. Reid
Preparing behavioral practitioners to train staff 21
Behavioral research that developed evidence-based staff training
procedures 23
Research on singular staff training procedures 23
Research on staff training programs 25
Guidelines and recommendations for practice 26
Guidelines and recommendations for implementing the steps of BST 26
On-the-job component of behavioral skills training 30
Informal staff training 31
Making staff training more time efficient for practitioners 32
The critical but qualified role of staff training 35
A practice checklist for competency-based staff training 36
References 37

3 Functional Behavioral Assessments 41
Nathan A. Call, Mindy C. Scheithauer and Joanna Lomas Mevers
Status of practitioner training 43
Recommendations for practitioner training 44
Types of functional behavioral assessments 45

Indirect assessments   45
Descriptive assessments   51
Functional analyses   55
Practice guidelines checklist   62
References   63
Further reading   71

4   Social Validity Assessment   73
Eric A. Common and Kathleen Lynne Lane
Assessing social validity: A priority in the field of applied
behavior analysis   73
The relevance of social validity assessment for practicing professional   77
Practical applications of social validity   78
Summary: Essential learnings   87
References   88

5   Behavioral Risk Assessment   93
Joseph N. Ricciardi and Allison W. Rothschild
Clinical-behavioral risk in individuals with IDD   93
Applied behavior analysis in the evaluation of risk   93
Practice guidelines, procedures, and implementation recommendations   96
Conceptualizing risk and developing a mitigation plan   104
Practice guidelines, summary   109
References   109
Further reading   112
Appendix 1   113

6   Incentive-Based Performance Improvement   117
Byron Wine
Incentive-based performance improvement   117
Relevant research   120
Practice recommendations   125
Conclusion   131
Takeaways   132
References   132

7   Technology and Telehealth Applications   135
Aaron J. Fischer, Racheal Clark, Diana Askings and Erica Lehman
Technology and telehealth applications   135
Past and current status of behavior analyst telehealth training   135
Research base and implications for practice   138
Practice guidelines, procedures, and implementation recommendations   153
Conclusion   158
Practice guidelines checklist   158
References   159
Further reading   163

Section II Consultation Practices

8   Consultation Practices: School-Based Instructional Support   **167**
Brian K. Martens, Robin S. Codding and Samantha J. Sallade
Introduction   167
Foundations of effective instruction   172
Best practice recommendations for instructional intervention   179
Conclusion and practice guidelines checklist   189
References   189
Further reading   195

9   Consultation Practices: School-Based Behavior Support   **197**
*Jason C. Vladescu, Danielle L. Gureghian, April N. Kisamore
and Lauren K. Schnell*
Consultation practices: school-based behavior support   197
Functional behavior assessment: research base and implications   198
Function-based treatment: research base and implications   199
Practice recommendations   201
References   218
Further reading   226

10   Consultation Practices: Training Parents and Families   **229**
Kelly M. Schieltz, Jessica E. Graber and Jennifer McComas
Introduction   229
History of our outpatient clinics   232
Description of parent and family training approach   233
Alternative parent and family training options   241
Guidelines and recommendations for training parents and families   251
References   254

11   Consultation Practices: Organizations   **259**
Heather M. McGee
Introduction to organizational behavior management and relevance
for behavioral practitioners   259
Past and current status of practitioner training in OBM   261
OBM research base and implications for practice   263
OBM consultation practice guidelines, procedures, and implementation
recommendations   265
Summary   280
Practice guidelines checklist   280
References   281

12   Consultation Practices: Multidisciplinary Settings   **285**
Claire C. St. Peter, Sacha T. Pence and Kathryn M. Kestner
Introduction   285
Relevance for behavioral practitioners   289

Past and current practitioner training   291
Research base and implications for practice   292
Practice guidelines   295
Practice guidelines checklist   300
Acknowledgment   301
References   302
Further reading   305

Section III Professional Development   **307**

13   Continuing Education: Accessing the Peer-Reviewed Literature   309
Jennifer Gillis Mattson
Introduction to the topic and relevance for behavioral practitioners   309
Status of practitioner training   312
Research base and implications for practice   313
Practice guidelines   318
Practice guidelines checklist   322
References   324
Further reading   324

14   Practice Dissemination: Writing for Publication   325
James K. Luiselli
The appeal of writing for publication   326
Obstacles to writing for publication   327
Publication targets   329
Performance improvement guide to writing for publication   331
Summary   345
References   345

15   Practice Dissemination: Public Speaking   349
Patrick C. Friman
General suggestions   350
Suggestions for preparation   352
Suggestions for delivery of your talk   355
Concluding remarks   362
References   363
Further reading   365

16   Licensure and Certification   367
William H. Ahearn
Certification and licensure of the practice of applied behavior analysis   367
Identifying competent ABA providers   371
The essential components of the BACB credentials   375
Requirements for ABA professionals   379
A roadmap to entering the professional practice of ABA   382

Concluding remarks   384
References   385
Further reading   388

**17   Ethical and Competent Practice in Applied Behavior Analysis:
     Perspective, Requirements, and Dilemmas   389**
Raymond G. Romanczyk
Terminology   389
Historical perspective   390
Specific ethics code for behavior analysts   397
Professional and ethical compliance code for behavior analysts   399
References   407
Further reading   408

Index   409

List of Contributors

William H. Ahearn New England Center for Children, Southborough, MA, United States

Diana Askings University of Utah, Salt Lake City, UT, United States

Nathan A. Call Emory University School of Medicine and Marcus Autism Center, Atlanta, GA, United States

Racheal Clark University of Utah, Salt Lake City, UT, United States

Robin S. Codding University of Minnesota, Minneapolis, MN, United States

Eric A. Common University of Kansas, Lawrence, KS, United States

Aaron J. Fischer University of Utah, Salt Lake City, UT, United States

Patrick C. Friman Boys Town, NE, USA and The University of Nebraska School of Medicine

Jennifer Gillis Mattson Binghamton University, Binghamton, NY, United States

Jessica E. Graber University of Texas at San Antonio, San Antonio, TX, United States

Danielle L. Gureghian Garden Academy, West Orange, NJ, United States

Kathryn M. Kestner West Virginia University, Morgantown, WV, United States

April N. Kisamore Caldwell University, Caldwell, NJ, United States

Kathleen Lynne Lane University of Kansas, Lawrence, KS, United States

Erica Lehman University of Utah, Salt Lake City, UT, United States

Joanna Lomas Mevers Emory University School of Medicine and Marcus Autism Center, Atlanta, GA, United States

James K. Luiselli Clinical Solutions, Inc., Beverly, MA, United States; North East Educational and Developmental Support Center, NEEDS Center, Tewksbury, MA, United States

Brian K. Martens Syracuse University, Syracuse, NY, United States

Jennifer McComas University of Minnesota, Minneapolis, MN, United States

Heather M. McGee Western Michigan University, Kalamazoo, MI, United States

Sacha T. Pence Auburn University, Auburn, AL, United States

Dennis H. Reid Carolina Behavior Analysis and Support Center, Morganton, NC, United States

Joseph N. Ricciardi Seven Hills Foundation, Worcester, MA, United States

Raymond G. Romanczyk State University of New York at Binghamton, Binghamton, NY, United States

Allison W. Rothschild Seven Hills Foundation, Worcester, MA, United States

Samantha J. Sallade Syracuse University, Syracuse, NY, United States

Mindy C. Scheithauer Emory University School of Medicine and Marcus Autism Center, Atlanta, GA, United States

Kelly M. Schieltz University of Missouri, Columbia, MO, United States

Lauren K. Schnell Caldwell University, Caldwell, NJ, United States

Claire C. St. Peter West Virginia University, Morgantown, WV, United States

Laura B. Turner University of Saint Joseph, West Hartford, CT, United States

Jason C. Vladescu Caldwell University, Caldwell, NJ, United States

Byron Wine Florida Institute of Technology, Melbourne, FL, United States

Preface

Applied behavior analysis (ABA) has made significant contributions to education, behavioral healthcare, organizations, medicine, and society at large. ABA practitioners include licensed psychologists, board certified behavior analysts, registered behavior technicians, and other practicing professionals. Notably, there is a vast ABA research literature that documents intervention effectiveness and advances service delivery. However, most practitioners do not regularly access the extant literature in order to stay current with contemporary best practices. Most critically, research-to-practice publications typically do not inform practitioners about many of the skills they need to acquire and demonstrate proficiently at all career stages. For example, how does a senior clinician effectively supervise trainees and less experienced colleagues? What types of performance improvement tactics should a behavioral consultant recommend to service organizations? How do you speak and write persuasively, assess the social validity of your work, stay current with the published literature, and successfully achieve licensure and certification?

The *Applied Behavior Analysis Advanced Guidebook* fills a current void affecting behavioral practitioners by offering pragmatic advice, direction, and recommendations for being an effective clinician, consultant, supervisor, and performance manager. The book adopts a "how-to-do-it" perspective featuring chapter authors who are distinguished as scientist-practitioners. These authors are professionals with research expertise but equally experienced as "real world" behavior specialists. Their chapters integrate the most current evidence support with accessible tips on how to function competently and successfully among the vast population of people, settings, and systems receiving ABA services.

The primary audience for the *Applied Behavior Analysis Advanced Guidebook* is ABA practicing professionals who are licensed psychologists, board certified behavior analysts, registered behavior technicians, and behavior specialists that may not have similar credentials but nevertheless deliver related services (e.g., school psychologists, counselors, direct therapists). As well, many of the chapters in the book will apply to professionals who do not identify exclusively as ABA practitioners but are seeking empirically validated methods to fortify their work. In addition, the book will be relevant for graduate students, doctoral intern trainees, and postdoctoral fellows within education, psychology, counseling, social work, and allied disciplines. In particular, the book should have high appeal with students enrolled in course sequences approved by the Behavior Analyst Certification Board, including the faculty who teach those courses.

I wish to acknowledge the teachers, supervisors, mentors, and colleagues who shaped my understanding and practice of ABA, particularly Donald Anderson,

Gene Buchman, Van Westerveldt, Andrew Wheeler, Jerry Martin, John Lutzker, Paul Touchette, David Marholin II, David Mostofsky, Henry Marcucella, and Ron Taylor. My skills were honed at several formative service settings including the Walter E. Fernald School, Behavioral Intervention Project, Perkins School for the Blind, and Psychological and Educational Resource Associates. This book would not be possible without the kindness and support of my current associates at Clinical Solutions, Inc., and North East Educational and Developmental Support Center. Finally, I have been in the field a long time but the engine keeps running thanks to the love, inspiration, and mindful guidance from my wife, Dr. Tracy Evans Luiselli, our daughter, Gabrielle, and our son, Thomas.

James K. Luiselli
Clinical Solutions, Inc., Beverly, MA, United States;
North East Education and Developmental Support Center,
Tewksbury, MA, United States

Section I

Supervision, Training, and Service Delivery

Behavior Analytic Supervision

1

Laura B. Turner
University of Saint Joseph, West Hartford, CT, United States

Introduction to the topic and relevance for behavioral practitioners

Supervision is a needed, complex, and rewarding activity that many behavior analysts will engage in throughout their careers. Behavior analytic supervision is defined as the active process of systematically shaping the myriad skills required of individuals seeking to formally practice applied behavior analysis (ABA). In this chapter, focus is placed on the development of Board Certified Behavior Analysts (BCBA), with the eventual authority to practice independently, as well as Board Certified Assistant Behavior Analysts, who will be expected to problem solve and make decisions under the ongoing supervision of a BCBA. The term "supervisee" will be used throughout to refer to this group of individuals. Despite the focus on developing future behavior analysts, the methods, and considerations discussed in this chapter are based on empirical findings and can be applied to those being supervised across disciplines.

Shaping the skills of the next generation of behavior analysts is of crucial importance to the growth and wellbeing of the field as well as those receiving behavior analytic services [Behavior Analyst Certification Board (BACB), 2012b]. The expanding demand for ABA services worldwide has prompted a rapid growth in the number of degree and certificate programs, leading to a large increase in the number of certified practitioners. There are currently approximately 21,000 BCBAs and BCBA-Ds (Doctoral) worldwide (BACB, 2016a). Given this exciting and encouraging growth period, it is essential that supervision simultaneously function as a gatekeeper of high quality behavior analytic practice to ensure a balance of quantity and quality to prevent harm to clients, unethical behavior and a plethora of poorly trained behavior analysts (BACB, 2012b).

Despite the field's growth, behavior analysts lag far behind the number of professionals in other fields often serving similar populations. Longstanding fields such as speech and language pathology, occupational therapy, and psychology *each* have well over 100,000 practicing professionals, and there are approximately 450,000 special education teachers in the United States alone (Bureau of Labor Statistics, U.S. Department of Labor, 2015). As ABA practitioners integrate into the already established large-scale educational, organizational, and health care systems throughout the world, quality supervision may lead to effective collaboration and ensure the field grows a positive reputation among our clients and other professionals. As such, supervision is a necessary activity of BCBAs and BCBA-Ds.

Applied Behavior Analysis Advanced Guidebook. DOI: http://dx.doi.org/10.1016/B978-0-12-811122-2.00001-2

Past and current status of practitioner training in the topic

We are providing services in an era in which practitioner accountability and protection of the public are of prime importance. This emphasis has led to the development of evidence- and competency-based approaches to the training of future practitioners across multiple disciplines. A competency-based approach requires supervisees to meet predetermined standards prior to independent practice. Multiple disciplines are also placing emphasis on competency-based approaches for supervisors (e.g., American Psychological Association, 2015; BACB, 2012b; Falender et al., 2004; Kraemer-Tebes et al., 2011), in recognition that supervision is an independent area of practice requiring the development and ongoing maintenance of specific skills and the use of specific components associated with positive outcomes among supervisees. In other words, although strong behavior analytic skills are required of effective supervisors, strong behavior analytic skills do not necessarily equate to being an effective supervisor. Competency-based approaches also tend to focus on creating an individualized, collaborative environment that values frequent, bidirectional performance feedback based on observable behavior, and self-evaluation of the supervisor's behavior.

Education in effective supervision practices is becoming more common across disciplines; however, a general lack of training continues to present as a primary barrier to the widespread implementation of recommended practices. In an effort to begin the training process, the BACB recently developed a set of guidelines that outlined the core set of competencies expected of those who are providing supervision to anyone pursuing a BACB certificate or holding a certificate that requires ongoing supervision (*Supervisor Training Curriculum*, BACB, 2012b). Supervisors must receive 8 hours of competency-based instruction consistent with the curriculum prior to supervising any supervisees (BACB, 2012b). These 8 hours can be incorporated into current BACB Approved Course Sequences (e.g., in a professional development or ethics course) or supervisees can attend a postcertificate training (BACB, 2015b). Supervisors *and* supervisees must also complete a competency based online Experience Training Module prior to the start of the supervision experience to ensure both parties understand the supervision requirements and responsibilities (BACB, 2015a). Given the importance of supervision to the advancement of the field, supervisors are also required to obtain 3 hours of continuing education specifically regarding supervision practices every 2 years (BACB, 2013).

Research base and implications for practice

The organized practice of behavior analysis is a relatively new field (i.e., the BACB was established in 1998) and formal focus on supervisor behavior is a brand new initiative (i.e., supervisor training began in 2015). Empirical investigations of effective supervision practices *specifically* for future behavior analysts are thus nonexistent. However, as the ultimate responsibility of the supervisor is to *teach* a variety of skills, from simple to complex, we can use the field's foundational knowledge for effective approaches to learning to inform our supervision practices. More specifically, we can use the principles and procedures of learning and behavior (e.g., reinforcement, shaping, and generalization) as well as elements of instruction that have led to positive outcomes, such as clearly defined behavioral targets and objectives, accurate models, frequent opportunities for active responding, frequently and directly observing and measuring behavior tied to objectives, delivery of performance feedback regarding objectives, and teaching to mastery with a focus on generalized and fluent behavior (e.g., Cooper, Heron, & Heward, 2007; Moran & Mallott, 2004; Vargas, 2013).

Researchers and clinicians in the field have developed "learning packages," such as Behavioral skills training (BST), which includes several components of evidence-based instruction as described above. In BST, a competent trainer provides a rationale for the specific skill to be taught, verbally instructs the learner how to engage in the skill, models how to engage in the skill (i.e., either in vivo or video-model), allows the supervisee to practice the skill (e.g., via role play), provides performance feedback to the supervisee regarding their ability to perform the skill, and requires the supervisee practice the skill until competency has been met (see Parsons, Rollyson, & Reid, 2012 and Chapter 2: Functional Behavioral Assessments of this text). Research strongly supports BST for training nonbehavior analysts, such as parents, teachers, and paraprofessionals, how to implement behavior analytic assessment (e.g., preference assessments and functional analysis conditions) and intervention procedures (e.g., Lavie & Sturmey, 2002; Sarokoff & Sturmey, 2004; Seiverling, Williams, Sturmey, & Hart, 2012; Shayne & Miltenberger, 2013). As such, the BACB requires the use of BST to train new skills to supervisees (BACB, 2012b); however, there are no behavioral studies that have evaluated BST to teach skills (i.e., especially relatively complex skills) in the context of behavior analytic supervision.

Research also supports the effect of contingent and specific positive and corrective feedback on behavior (e.g., see Daniels & Bailey, 2014). The BACB requires supervisors to deliver timely performance feedback in various format (e.g., verbal, written, and graphic) that will improve supervisee behavior (BACB, 2012b, 2014). Performance feedback has been shown to be most effective when combined with review of data, goal setting, and modifications to antecedents and consequences (Alvero, Bucklin, & Austin, 2001; Balacazar, Hopkins, & Suarez, 1985; DiGennaro, Martens, & Kleinmann, 2007; Sanetti, Luiselli, & Handler, 2007). Similar to the research conducted on BST, research specifically evaluating the effect of performance feedback on complex behaviors relevant to supervision is lacking.

While the BST and performance feedback literature has been an invaluable and ever-increasing resource for best practices in training and providing ongoing supervision to behavioral implementers, the majority of target behaviors and skills in these studies have focused on simple, discrete, and/or step-by-step procedures requiring minimal to no variation in responding under different stimulus conditions and environmental contingencies. Teaching inflexibly, whether through rule-governance or contingency-shaping, may lead to rigid adherence to trained behavior (Hayes et al., 1986), including clinical decision-making (Follette & Callaghan, 1995). While rigid responding is often appropriate for those implementing specific procedures, practicing behavior analysts are tasked daily with the complex and dynamic responsibility of solving problems, making clinical decisions, designing programs, and mediating conflicts. In most of these situations, it is impossible to systematically teach every possible response to every possible set of stimuli. The goal is to have behavior analysts respond appropriately in situations that were never specifically trained.

Notably, the BACB lists one of the purposes of supervision as the development of problem solving and decision-making repertoires in supervisees (BACB, 2012b). There are several different areas of thought regarding problem solving and a clear and agreed upon definition is lacking, making progress in the systematic investigation of problem solving slow (e.g., see Foxx & Few, 2000). Skinner (1953) defined problem solving as "any behavior which, through the manipulation of variables, makes the appearance of a solution more probable" (p. 247). Alternatively, Nezu, Nezu, & D'Zurilla (2013) defined problem solving as "a self-directed process by which individuals attempt to identify, discover, and/or develop adaptive coping solutions for problems" (p. 8). In Nezu et al.'s (2013) framework, which is the most commonly accepted and researched form of problem solving, problem solving involves a step-by-step process that can be applied to any set of circumstances: (1) identify the problem, (2) formulate potential alternatives to solve the problem, (3) make a decision to choose one solution over others, and (4) evaluate the chosen solution.

Problem solving behaviors have been shown to be under operant control (Neef, Nelles, Iwata, & Page, 2003; Sautter, LeBlanc, Jay, Goldsmith, & Carr, 2011) and as such behavioral researchers have hypothesized several forms of problem solving that may increase the likelihood of a reinforcement. For example, teaching mediating responses, such as covert intraverbal behavior or self-instructions, is one potential method for increasing problem solving abilities (Guevremont, Osnes, & Stokes, 1988; Palmer, 1991). Although there are no published data or discussions on defining, systematically teaching, and directly measuring problem solving and decision-making abilities among behavior analytic supervisees, much of the research conducted is based on common behavioral practices (e.g., mediating generalization; Baer, 1999) and can be used to initially inform the practice of supervision until more research has been conducted. For example, rather than teaching specific rules that must be adhered to when presented with various situations (unless the rule must always be followed, such as do not have sex with your client's parents), it may be effective to teach a set of considerations, or questions supervisee's can ask themselves for different types of problems or situations, that will help them evaluate the many possible decisions they could make, each with relative risks, benefits, and differential outcomes.

Practice guidelines, procedures, and implementation recommendations

The purpose of this section is to bridge the gap between research and practice by providing a "how-to" for implementing practices consistent with a behavioral analytic and competency-based approach that focuses on complex decision-making and problem solving skills, as well as the BACB Supervision Training Curriculum Outline (BACB, 2012b) and the BACB Professional and Ethical Compliance Code ("Code"; BACB, 2014). These recommendations are summarized in Fig. 1.1. In addition, throughout this section several questions are posed to help supervisors recognize the relevant stimuli and considerations needed to make complex decisions about supervision practices.

Deciding to supervise

The first step in the supervision process, especially for novice supervisors, is making the decision to supervise. This decision should not be taken lightly as a supervisor's inability to provide an effective supervision experience may negatively impact the development of the supervisee and the field. There is often pressure to supervise, especially given the growing number of supervisees; however, committing to supervision without adequate preparation may result in harm to supervisees and their clients. If you are not yet supervising, consider asking yourself the following questions to help you gauge your preparedness for this crucial activity. Of note, your responses to these questions do not predict successful performance as a

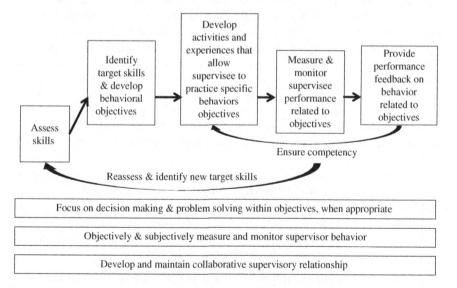

Figure 1.1 Behavior analytic practice model for supervision.

supervisor, they are simply face valid questions to ensure thoughtfulness prior to taking on such an important role.

- How much time will supervision take (think through all potential responsibilities)? Do I have the time *right now*? (See Turner, Fisher & Luiselli, 2016 for a sample time analysis.)
- Am I competent in the majority of areas on the current BACB task list? Are there any areas I need to seek further education in prior to supervising?
- Does the possibility of supervising someone else excite me?
- What feedback have I received about my ability to implement BST or deliver performance feedback?
- Am I comfortable role-playing and modeling my own behavior in front of others?
- Am I competent in, and willing to provide, corrective feedback? Do I tend to avoid providing corrective feedback?
- How often do I currently provide positive feedback to others on a daily basis?
- Do others at work approach me for behavioral advice and guidance?
- Do I have a mentor, or another colleague I have good rapport with, to provide consultation when needed?

If after asking yourself these and other related questions, you decide not to begin supervising, but you would eventually like to, you are encouraged to seek out experiences that will better prepare you to supervise, such as obtaining a mentor who is a skilled supervisor.

First meeting—Setting the stage for a positive supervision experience

Behavior analysts have discussed the importance of the initial supervision meeting (e.g., see Turner et al., 2016) as it provides an opportunity to set the stage, so to speak, for a successful supervision experience for both the supervisee and the supervisor. During the first meeting, the majority of time should be dedicated to developing a positive supervisory relationship with the supervisee and shared expectations for the supervision process (i.e., rapport). Rapport can be defined as the development of trust (i.e., say-do correspondence), mutual liking (i.e., mutual discriminative stimuli for generalized reinforcement; Carr et al., 1997, p. 111; Magito McLaughlin & Carr, 2005), and common supervision goals that are consistently worked toward in a mutually agreed upon manner (Bordin, 1983). The supervisor can also use this time to genuinely convey their commitment to the supervision process.

The thoughtful preparation of this meeting is highly encouraged as there is substantial material to cover while reviewing the required Supervision Contract (BACB, 2012b; 2014; 2015a) and discussing expectations of the supervision experience. Supervisors, especially novice supervisors, may find it helpful to make a user-friendly checklist of the following material to ensure comprehensive coverage (see sample checklist in Appendix A). Supervisors should:

1. Provide their credentials (Guideline 2.05 Rights and Prerogatives of Clients) and describe the supervisor's professional background.

2. Identify the long-term goals of the supervisee to ensure an adequate match in terms of supervisor expertise and client population.
3. Discuss the purpose and importance of supervision (BACB, 2012b). Establish a shared goal of advancing the abilities of the supervisee and convey the supervisor's commitment to the supervision process.
4. Define the nature of the supervisory relationship (see also Guideline 1.06 Multiple Relationships and Conflict of Interest and Guideline 1.07 Exploitative Relationships, BACB, 2014), including any fees for supervision. It may be beneficial to also discuss previous supervisory experiences and relationships.
5. Discuss their ethical responsibility to keep supervision material confidential (Guideline 2.06 Maintaining Confidentiality, BACB, 2014), including the use of any audio-visual recordings (also discuss client confidentiality).
6. Review the requirements of the supervision experience as established by the BACB (i.e., review the current Experience Standards, BACB, 2015a) and in this context discuss and agree upon performance expectations and evaluations of both parties.
7. Discuss the importance of feedback in supervision. Supervisees should expect frequent positive and corrective feedback regarding various basic, technical, professional and ethical behaviors (Guideline 5.06 Providing Feedback to Supervisees, BACB, 2014). Supervisors should also frequently seek feedback from the supervisee regarding their experience with supervision (BACB, 2012b).
8. Discuss outcomes of either party not abiding by shared expectations, such as the supervisor not signing off on experience hours and the supervisee having the right to lodge a complaint against the supervisor (Guideline 2.05 Rights and Prerogatives of Clients, BACB, 2014).
9. Discuss the end date of supervision and any back up plans to avoid interruption of experience (Guideline 2.15 Interrupting or Discontinuing Services, BACB, 2014).

Assessment of skills

Once expectations are established and the logistics of the experience are agreed on, the primary focus of supervision should refocus to the supervisee's acquisition of *new* behavior analytic skills (BACB, 2015a). Assessment of supervisee skills is thus of great importance and an ongoing activity. Quality and comprehensive assessment enables supervisors to select and prioritize targets for supervision that will benefit the supervisee (and ultimately clients). Supervisors should be mindful that at least 50% of a supervisee's experience hours must be *indirect* hours (BACB, 2015a), which encourages the selection of target skills outside of the procedural competencies. While comprehensive assessment is a time-consuming activity, consider the value behavior analysts place on the initial assessment of skills for a new client, especially when multiple skills need to be taught. It is logical that a similar standard be held for supervisees.

There are several methods for initially evaluating supervisee performance, such as conducting an interview and directly observing behavior (BACB, 2012b). Beginning with an interview, using the task list and code as guides, allows supervisors to narrow down areas of focus that can then be directly observed to assist with defining and measuring baseline performance. Additional information may be helpful when initially evaluating a supervisee's skillset, such as current and previous courses [request syllabi or any permanent products from courses, such as n functional behavior assessment (FBA) report] as well as content that will most likely be covered in upcoming courses.

Knowledge and performance-based assessment of *all* areas that supervisees will eventually be responsible for is key to the development of a scope and sequence as well as identifying initial behavioral targets for increase. The current practice contingencies (i.e., pass the BACB exam) encourage supervisors to ensure students *know* (i.e., knowledge-based assessments) the content on the exam, more so than be able to *perform* it (i.e., performance-based assessment); however, real world practice requires both skillsets. Supervisors may find it helpful to review the task list and code and identify knowledge vs performance-based skills, similar to the way in which the Registered Behavior Technician Competency Assessment (BACB, 2016b) is set up.

While evaluating foundational knowledge and basic skills (e.g., Sections I and III of the 4th Edition Task List, BACB, 2012a) is relatively straightforward (i.e., ask supervisees to define terms or demonstrate and/or describe procedures), the majority of skills required when overseeing services provided to a client (e.g., Section II of the BACB 4th Edition Task List) require higher level skillsets and the application of a supervisee's foundational knowledge and basic skills to solve real world problems and make clinical decisions. As assessment can be a lengthy process, use the supervisee's current foundational knowledge to inform how much detail or which areas of application to assess. For example, if the supervisee has not yet had exposure to behavioral measurement, skip the section of the task list that focuses on evaluating graphical displays and selecting appropriate measurement systems. If, however, a supervisee can adequately describe different measurement systems, it is recommended to first ask open-ended questions to evaluate their ability to directly apply their foundational knowledge (e.g., "For target behavior X, what measurement system should you choose?") as well as their *process* for making decisions (e.g., "What are the considerations when choosing a measurement system?").

Professional behavior and ethical decision-making should also be included in a comprehensive assessment. A core ethical responsibility of behavior analysts is to practice within their area of competence. Practicing behavior analysts typically provide services independently and most likely do not receive consistent feedback regarding their performance, especially if they themselves are in a lead supervisory position. As such, it is crucial that supervisors begin to develop self-evaluation repertoires in supervisees, starting with an assessment of a supervisee's ability and willingness to engage in self-evaluation (e.g., "How do you know you're competent or not yet competent in a given area?" or "How do you monitor your own behavior?").

Not only do supervisees need to learn the process and considerations for making an appropriate decision in a given situation, they also need to have the ability to implement and follow through with that decision effectively. For example, when concerned about a colleague's ethical behavior, depending on the situation, the code recommends having a direct discussion with that colleague (Guideline 7.02c; BACB, 2014). Most supervisees readily know this guideline, but they may not be able approach that colleague and raise their concerns in an appropriate and effective manner. Accordingly, when assessing, it may be helpful to identify and have the supervisee model the behaviors associated with being able to follow through with the recommendations of the code in addition to evaluating their verbal knowledge of the code and their decision-making process.

Related, behavior analysts report that they frequently need to collaborate with other professionals as part of their ongoing responsibilities; however, behavior analysts report that minimal to no formal training is often provided on effective collaboration practices (Kelly & Tincani, 2013). Rather, behavior analysts report that they more often *provide* recommendations, rather than *collaborate* in their everyday practice, suggesting that direct instruction in collaboration would be beneficial for practicing behavior analysts (Kelly & Tincani, 2013). There are several other professional behaviors required of behavioral practitioners that will influence their ability to be effective and follow the code, such as assertiveness, empathy and sensitivity to others, verbal tone & nonverbal communication (e.g., facial expressions), and flexibility/rigidity.

It is also recommended that supervisors focus on developing a supervisory skillset among, especially more advanced, supervisees. Much of a behavior analyst's professional responsibilities entail some form of training, supervision, and/or performance management, and the complex skillset required of supervisors will most likely require more than 8 hours of training.

Selecting target skills

Once an initial assessment is complete, supervisors are tasked with the challenging responsibility of selecting specific target skills among the potentially exhaustive list of supervisee needs. While it can be easy to simply address certain content areas as they arise naturally (e.g., within the context of case review), identifying and systematically teaching targeted skills is considered best practice.

Prioritization is key when initially selecting target skills. For perspective, 1500 experience hours (in the case of Supervised Independent Fieldwork) may or may not be adequate time for supervisees to meet competency with all of the required behavior analytic skills. It is recommended that prioritization be given to the development of generalized skill repertoires in certain, key areas most relevant and important to supervisees given their short and long-term goals regarding the practice of behavior analysis. If supervision is a collaborative process, supervisees will presumably identify areas of need, or skill areas they are motived to work on at the current moment.

Prioritizing certain skills does not mean supervisors should ignore other relevant skills, content, case review and/or problems that arise naturally; rather, it is recommended that supervisors dedicate *part* of every supervision period to the systematic development of a few skills at a time (e.g., through individualized and competency-based projects or assignments). Targets can be added when the supervisee reaches competency in others. As supervisors are often not able to address all skill areas, it is strongly recommended that supervisors teach supervisees how to identify their areas of weakness and seek out appropriate resources to enhance their competency in relatively less fluent areas. Supervisors can be instrumental in teaching supervisee's how to think through problems while instilling a value of lifelong learning.

Within this context, supervisors are encouraged to select targets for supervision based on the supervisee's current abilities and to ensure the supervisee has the prerequisite skills needed for targeted skill areas. A thoughtful evaluation of all the components of a target skill will allow the supervisor to teach the skill comprehensively. For example, if a supervisee expresses a desire to learn how to write a Behavior Intervention Plan (BIP), several prerequisite and component skills must be established such as (1) a clear understanding of the FBA process; (2) using nonjargon terminology; (3) writing clearly; (4) having knowledge of various antecedent and consequence procedures; (5) considerations of supervisee's work environment, resources, and skill level of the implementers; and (6) awareness of any regulations on the content to be included in a BIP. Teaching skills without a consideration of the prerequisites may lead to the rote development of a BIP rather than the ability to make an individualized BIP in consideration of all relevant variables (i.e., clinical decision-making).

While a clear sequence of skills to be acquired by a practicing behavior analyst does not exist, it can be assumed that foundational knowledge and basic skills should be acquired prior to clinical decision-making and problem solving. This assumption can be used to develop a framework for progressive goals: rather than having problem solving as a goal itself, consider integrating problem solving into specific skill areas, and using independent problem solving as an end goal. For example, work through the task list from foundational knowledge about extinction, to the skill of implementing extinction, to choosing whether or not it should be used given the current environment, target behavior, and other similar considerations. Without fluency in basic concepts, the supervisee may not be able to identify all the relevant considerations and solutions to clinical questions and problems.

Developing clearly defined and measurable behavioral objectives

At the core of behavior analytic practice is a clear definition of the behavior of interest and a measurement system that allows for tracking change in that behavior over time. Defining and measuring skills for clients is second nature for behavior analysts, and while the same logic applies to supervisees, behavior analysts rarely receive direct instruction in defining behaviors expected of supervisees. For example, the BACB Supervision Training Curriculum states that an "empathy statement" (BACB, 2012b, p. 4) should be used when delivering corrective feedback. Given supervisors will most likely be teaching supervisees how to implement BST and deliver performance feedback, it is necessary to define the behaviors that comprise empathy in order to track supervisee progress. An example definition of an empathy statement is as follows:

• A verbal statement conveying an understanding of the supervisee's current context.
    ◦ Example: "I can imagine it's hard for you to get here on time given the distance you have to travel."

• Nonexample: A positive statement about the supervisee's performance, such as, "You implemented the prompt hierarchy really well."

This clarity allows supervisors to measure the count of empathic statements and deliver specific positive and corrective feedback regarding supervisee performance. Or, in the case of a multicomponent skill, the supervisor could identify, define, and measure the percentage of correctly implemented steps of corrective feedback such as empathy statement, description of ineffective performance, rationale for desired change in behavior, instructions and demonstration of correct performance, practice opportunities, and deliver feedback (BACB, 2012b). Direct observation of the supervisee interacting with those receiving behavior analytic services must also be conducted frequently, at least every supervision period (i.e., 1−2 weeks), so supervisors have plenty of opportunities to directly measure supervisee behavior (BACB, 2015a).

It is also important to identify appropriate mastery criteria based on an evaluation of social validity and the literature. In other words, when has the supervisee reached competency for a particular skill? There are several areas in which a clear and commonly agreed upon expectation of competency does not exist. Supervisors may find answering the following questions provides support when faced with such a dilemma:

• What are the current standards in the literature?
• What are your colleagues doing?
• What laws and regulations dictate how procedures should be implemented?

Using behavioral skills training to teach objectives to competency

The BACB Supervision Training Curriculum Outline (BACB, 2012b) states that supervisors should apply BST to the various skill areas discussed previously. When teaching with BST, utilize naturally occurring or contrive activities that allow supervisees to practice the targeted skills in a variety of contexts to promote generalization (BACB, 2012b; 2015a). While behavior analytic supervisors have received instruction on the steps of BST there are minimal resources to guide supervisors on how to use this technique to teach the complex skills required of behavior analysts, such as clinical decision-making or problem solving. The following example is intended to highlight many of the recommendations discussed thus far.

Skill information:

• **Task list skill**: K-05 (advanced supervisee)—Design and use systems for monitoring procedural integrity.
• **Operational Definition of Correct Response:** The supervisee will create a procedural integrity data sheet including the following four pieces of information: general information (e.g., observer and date), specific instructions for data collection, specific implementer behavior to measure that is appropriate to the context, and a clear and organized space for recording behavior consistent with an appropriate measurement system for the context.
• **Measurement system:** Percent correct

- **Objective**: The supervisee will utilize three questions to increase her ability to accurately design systems for monitoring procedural integrity from 25% to 100% across two students with individualized BIPs.

Behavioral skills training script:

- **Supervisor**: *(Rationale & Check of Shared Goals)* "I'm excited to start working on a new goal! Procedural integrity is such a crucial component to the effectiveness of a behavior plan. Even if you have a comprehensive and function-based behavior plan, its effectiveness depends on the ability and willingness of others to implement it consistently. Now, for you we specifically decided to work on this skill because you recently discussed the concept of treatment integrity in class and you've been noticing that I come into the classrooms and collect integrity data here at school. Are you still interested in working on this skill right now?"
- **Supervisee**: "Yah! It sounds fun."
- **Supervisor**: *(Instructions with Questions)* "Ok, great. There are many variables to consider when creating a procedural integrity monitoring system. The three questions I typically ask myself are as follows: (1) What intervention and/or program components should I measure? Everything, or are there certain components that are more important to measure given the purpose of my particular clinical activity?, (2) What type of measurement system should I use for each component given the purpose of my particular clinical activity and available resources (e.g., qualitative vs quantitative direct observation, permanent product, self-monitoring)?, and (3) How often and for how long should I monitor procedural integrity in order to get a representative sample in a time frame appropriate for my current resources? Once I've answered these questions, I use the information to develop an integrity form with basic descriptive information (e.g., date and observer), clear instructions in case I'm not the one collecting the data, specific implementer behavior to measure, and a clear and organized space for recording behavior.
- **Supervisor**: *(Demonstrate)* "Let me show you what I mean." *The supervisor reviews at least one behavior plan with the supervisee and the supervisor discusses aloud the considerations and answers to the three questions. Then, the supervisor models at least one way an integrity form could be created in light of those considerations and provides answers to any questions the supervisee may have.*
- **Supervisor**: *(Practice)* "As an assignment for our next meeting, I'd like you to choose a behavior plan you are familiar with, answer the questions and create an integrity form. *(Set the expectation for performance feedback)* We'll review it together next time after we check in with your cases and I'll provide you with feedback."
- **Supervisor**: *(Next Session—Provide Positive Feedback on Assignment Completion)* "I'm glad you were able to complete the assignment as it allows us to continue moving forward with your goals. How was completing this assignment for you?"
- **Supervisee**: "I think I did ok. I just kept thinking I was missing something."
- **Supervisor**: *(Empathic statement)* "I completely understand. Thinking through all of the considerations and producing a product can be overwhelming, especially the first time you do it. Let's first start by reviewing your answers to the three questions."
- **Supervisee**: *Supervisee reviews considerations and answers to questions.*
- **Supervisor**: *(Empathic statement and description of ineffective performance)* "I can see why you thought not to include extinction on your form, as you stated that the classroom staff are currently reporting they're following through with the extinction procedure. *(Provide a rationale for desired change in performance.)* However, given this student's

behavior plan was just changed to include an extinction component, it is important to directly assess everyone's ability to follow through with this procedure as any accidental reinforcement of the behavior will produce the opposite effect that we're looking for. *(Instruction)* We had talked last week about closely monitoring procedural integrity with any new procedure given the potential impact on learning. It's also critical that we directly observe to verify the staff's say-do correspondence and to provide specific feedback, as that was one of the main purposes of collecting integrity."

- **Supervisee:** "Oh! That makes sense. I think I was getting stuck on the feasibility part, but if I, or whoever is monitoring integrity, is already observing in the classroom, collecting data on the extinction procedure won't be any more effortful or take extra time, especially if it occurs within the 30-minute observation period."
- **Supervisor:** *(Positive Feedback)* "Exactly. Good thinking. *(Empathic statement)* It's tough to feel comfortable balancing feasibility and quality of integrity. So, now that we discussed a different response to the first question, how would you answer the second question?"
- **Supervisee:** "I would record correct or incorrect use of extinction for every opportunity, or for every instance of the problem behavior."
- **Supervisor:** "Yes! And how you would add that to the form?"
- **Supervisee:** *(Practice) Supervisee demonstrates skill.*
- **Supervisor:** *(Positive feedback)* "That looks great. It's consistent with how you're recording data for other procedures as well, which you considered accurately for this assignment. *(Performance feedback + objective measure)* Overall, your form accurately included three of the four components, which is a large improvement from when we initially did this activity. Great job putting all the relevant general information on the form and I think your 30-minute daily observations are appropriate, at least until we can see staff responding consistently to problem behavior. *(Repeated Practice until competency)* Let's try this again for next week so you can get a little more practice. You can use another BIP you're familiar with from the same classroom."
- **Supervisor:** *(Next Session after reviewing the assignment with the supervisee – Provide Positive Feedback)* "Excellent progress! I agree with your considerations and you accurately included all four of the relevant components on the form. *(Assess generalization)* For next week, I'd like you to review a BIP that are you are not familiar with from Ms. Smith's classroom since you'll be transitioning to that room in a couple of weeks. If after this next assignment you feel confident with this activity, we can move onto another goal"
- **Supervisee:** "Sounds good!"

Continuously monitor supervisory behaviors

Even though we can utilize the above practices in our supervision repertoire, ultimately, the quality, and depth of our own behavioral knowledge is critical to the development of effective behavior analysts. Staying up to date with the literature, attending conferences, discussing current practice issues with peers, and seeking consultation are required activities of behavior analysts, especially those who are supervising.

In addition to participating in general continuing education activities, supervisors are expected to receive continuing education in supervision as well as monitor and evaluate their supervisory and professional behaviors. Being an accurate model of professional behavior is of crucial importance. A related statistic suggests that more than 50% of psychology supervisees perceived at least one breach of the ethics code by their supervisor over the course of training (Ladany, Lerhman-Waterman, Molinaro, & Wolgast, 1999). Supervisors are encouraged to develop their own self-monitoring forms (See Turner et al., 2016 for a sample form) and consider using a similar form to seek feedback from supervisees regarding their experience in supervision. Perhaps the most objective approach for supervisors to monitor their own supervisory behaviors is to request a mentor, or peer, directly observe and provide feedback on their behavior during a supervision meeting (if permission is granted by the supervisee). Lastly, real world variables may impact supervisors' ability to consistently implement supervision guidelines. Supervisors are encouraged to take a functional approach to understanding their own context in an effort to arrange their environments in such a way as to encourage highly effective supervisory behaviors.

To help stay up to date, supervisors are encouraged to read several articles recently published in a special issue of Behavior Analysis in Practice that offer information complimentary to the recommendations presented in this chapter:

1. Dubuque, E.M. & Dubuque, M.L. (2016). Guidelines for the establishment of a university-based practical training system. *Behavior Analysis in Practice*, 1−11. doi:10.1007/s40617-016-0154-8.
2. Hartley, B., Courtney, W.T., Rosswurm, M. & LaMarca, V.J. (2016). The apprentice: an innovative approach to meet the behavior analysis certification board's supervision standards. *Behavior Analysis in Practice*, 1−10. doi:10.1007/s40617-016-0136-x.
3. Sellers, T.P., Alai-Rosales, S. & MacDonald, R. (2016). Taking full responsibility: the ethics of supervision in behavior analytic practice. *Behavior Analysis in Practice*, 1−10. doi:10.1007/s40617-016-0144-x.
4. Sellers, T.P., LeBlanc, L.A., & Valentino, A.L. (2016). Recommendations for detecting and addressing barriers to successful supervision. *Behavior Analysis in Practice*, 1−11. doi:10.1007/s40617-016-0142-z.
5. Sellers, T.P., Valentino, A.L., & LeBlanc, L.A (2016). Recommended practices for individual supervision of aspiring behavior analysts. *Behavior Analysis in Practice*, 1−13. doi:10.1007/s40617-016-0110-7.
6. Turner, L.B., Fisher, A.J., & Luiselli, J.K. (2016). Towards a competency-based, ethical, and socially valid approach to the supervision of applied behavior analytic supervisees. *Behavior Analysis in Practice*, 1−12. doi:10.1007/s40617-016-0121-4.
7. Valentino, A.L., LeBlanc, L.A., & Sellers, T.P. (2016). The benefits of group supervision and a recommended structure for implementation. *Behavior Analysis in Practice*, 1−9. doi:10.1007/s40617-016-0138-8.

Take home message of above practice guidelines

The following five take home messages are offered in summary of the recommendations above.

1. Be prepared and have a plan for your first meeting with a supervisee.

2. Slow down and take the time to comprehensively assess supervisee baseline skills.
3. Develop specific behavioral objectives that are clearly defined, measured, and addressed frequently with BST.
4. Integrate problem solving and clinical decision-making into the objectives for specific skills.
5. Monitor your supervisory behavior, and seek out a mentor or colleague to frequently provide you with performance feedback regarding your own supervisory behavior.

References

Alvero, A. M., Bucklin, B. R., & Austin, J. (2001). An objective review of the effectiveness and essential characteristics of performance feedback in organizational settings. *Journal of Organizational Behavior Management, 21*(1), 3−29. Available from http://dx.doi.org/10.1300/J075v21n01_02.

American Psychological Association (2015). Guidelines for clinical supervision in health service psychology. *American Psychologist, 70*(1), 33−46. Available from http://dx.doi.org/10.1037/a0038112.

Baer, D. M. (1999). *How to plan for generalization* ((2nd Edition). Austin: TX: Pro-Ed.

Balacazar, F. E., Hopkins, B. L., & Suarez, Y. (1985). A critical objective view of performance feedback. *Journal of Organizational Behavior Management, 7*(3−4), 65−89. Available from http://dx.doi.org/10.1300/J075v07n03_05.

Behavior Analyst Certification Board (2012a). *Coursework requirements for BACB credentials: fourth edition task list.* Littleton, CO: Behavior Analyst Certification Board.

Behavior Analyst Certification Board (2012b). *Supervisor training curriculum outline.* Littleton, CO: Behavior Analyst Certification Board.

Behavior Analyst Certification Board (2013). *Online Newsletter, February Issue.* Littleton, CO: Behavior Analyst Certification Board.

Behavior Analyst Certification Board (2014). *Professional and ethical compliance code for behavior analysts.* Littleton, CO: Behavior Analyst Certification Board.

Behavior Analyst Certification Board (2015a). *Experience standards.* Littleton, CO: Behavior Analyst Certification Board.

Behavior Analyst Certification Board (2015b). *Online Newsletter, May Issue.* Littleton, CO: Behavior Analyst Certification Board.

Behavior Analyst Certification Board (2016a). *About the BACB.* Retrieved from http://bacb.com/about-the-bacb/.

Behavior Analyst Certification Board (2016b). *Registered behavior technician competency assessment.* Littleton, CO: Behavior Analyst Certification Board.

Bordin, E. S. (1983). A working alliance based model of supervision. *The Counseling Psychologist, 11*(1), 35−42. Available from http://dx.doi.org/10.1177/0011000083111007.

Bureau of Labor Statistics, U.S. Department of Labor. (2015), Occupational Outlook Handbook, 2016−17 Edition. Retrieved from http://www.bls.gov/.

Carr, E. G., Levin, L., McConnachie, G., Carlson, J. I., Kemp, D. C., & Smith, C. E. (1997). *Communication-based intervention for problem behavior: A user's guide for producing positive change.* Baltimore, Maryland: Paul H. Brookes Publishing Co., Inc.

Cooper, J. O., Heron, T. E., & Heward, W. L. (2007). *Applied behavior analysis.* Upper Saddle River: Pearson Education.

Daniels, A. C., & Bailey, J. S. (2014). *Performance management: changing behavior that drives organizational effectiveness (5th Edition)*. Atlanta: Aubrey Daniels International, Inc.

DiGennaro, F. D., Martens, B. K., & Kleinmann, A. E. (2007). A comparison of performance feedback procedures on teachers' treatment implementation integrity and students' inappropriate behavior in special education classrooms. *Journal of Applied Behavior Analysis, 40*(3), 447−461. Available from http://dx.doi.org/10.1901/jaba.2007.40-447.

Falender, C. A., Erickson Cornish, J. A., Goodyear, R., Hatcher, R., Kaslow, N. J., Leventhal, G., et al. (2004). Defining competencies in psychology supervision: A consensus statement. *Journal of Clinical Psychology, 60*(7), 771−785. Available from http://dx.doi.org/10.1002/jclp.20013.

Follette, W. C., & Callaghan, G. M. (1995). Do as I do, not as I say: a behavior analytic approach to supervision. *Professional Psychology: Research and Practice, 26*(4), 413−421.

Foxx, R. M., & Faw, G. D. (2000). The pursuit of actual problem-solving behavior: an opportunity for behavior analysts. *Behavior and Social Issues, 10*, 71−81.

Guevremont, D. C., Osnes, P. G., & Stokes, T. F. (1988). The functional role of preschoolers' verbalizations in the generalization of self-instructional training. *Journal of Applied Behavior Analysis, 21*, 45−55.

Hayes, S. C., Brownstein, A. J., Zettle, R. D., Rosenfarb, I., & Korn, Z. (1986). Rule-governed behavior and sensitivity to changing consequences of responding. *Journal of the Experimental Analysis of Behavior, 45*, 237−256.

Kelly, A., & Tincani, M. (2013). Collaborative training and practice among applied behavior analysts who support individuals with autism spectrum disorder. *Education and Training in Autism and Developmental Disabilities, 48*(1), 120−131.

Kraemer-Tebes, J., Matlin, S. L., Migdole, S. J., Farkas, M. S., Money, R. W., Shulman, L., et al. (2011). Providing competency training to clinical supervisors through an interactional supervision approach. *Research on Social Work Practice, 21*(2), 190−199. Available from http://dx.doi.org/10.1177/, 1049731510385827

Ladany, N., Lehrman-Waterman, D., Molinaro, M., & Wolgast, B. (1999). Psychotherapy supervisor ethical practices: adherence to guidelines, the supervisory working alliance, and supervisee satisfaction. *Counseling Psychologist, 27*(3), 443−475.

Lavie, T., & Sturmey, P. (2002). Training staff to conduct a paired-stimulus preference assessment. *Journal of Applied Behavior Analysis, 35*(2), 209−211. Available from http://dx.doi.org/10.1901/jaba.2002.35-209.

Magito-McLaughlin, D., & Carr, E. G. (2005). Quality of rapport as a setting event for problem behavior: Assessment and intervention. *Journal of Positive Behavior Interventions, 7*(2), 68−91.

Moran, D. J., & Mallott, R. (2004). *Evidence-based educational methods*. Cambridge: Academic Press.

Neef, N. A., Nelles, D. E., Iwata, B. I., & Page, T. J. (2003). Analysis of precurrent skills in solving mathematics story problems. *Journal of Applied Behavior Analysis, 36*, 21−33, 10.1901/jaba.2003.36-21

Nezu, A. M., Nezu, C. M., & D'Zurilla, T. J. (2013). *Problem-solving therapy: A treatment manual*. New York: Springer Publishing.

Palmer, D. C. (1991). A behavioral interpretation of memory. In L. J. Hayes, & P. N. Chase (Eds.), *Dialogues on verbal behavior* (pp. 261−279). Reno, NV: Context Press.

Parsons, M. B., Rollyson, J. H., & Reid, D. H. (2012). Evidence-based staff training: a guide for practitioners. *Behavior Analysis in Practice, 5*(2), 2−11.

Sanetti, L. M. H., Luiselli, J. K., & Handler, M. W. (2007). Effects of verbal and graphic performance feedback on behavior support plan implementation in a public elementary school. *Behavior Modification, 31*(4), 454−465. Available from http://dx.doi.org/ 10.1177/0145445506297583.

Sarokoff, R. A., & Sturmey, P. (2004). The effects of behavioral skills training on staff implementation of discrete-trial teaching. *Journal of Applied Behavior Analysis, 37*(4), 535−538. Available from http://dx.doi.org/10.1901/jaba.2004.37-535.

Sautter, R. A., LeBlanc, L. A., Jay, A. A., Goldsmith, T. R., & Carr, J. E. (2011). The role of problem solving in complex intraverbal repertoires. *Journal of Applied Behavior Analysis, 44*(2), 227−244. Available from http://dx.doi.org/10.1901/jaba.2011.44-227.

Seiverling, L., Williams, K., Sturmey, P., & Hart, S. (2012). Effects of behavioral skills training on parental treatment of children's food selectivity. *Journal of Applied Behavior Analysis, 45*(1), 197−203. Available from http://dx.doi.org/10.1901/jaba.2012.45-197.

Shayne, R., & Miltenberger, R. G. (2013). Evaluation of behavioral skills training for teaching functional assessment and treatment selection skills to parents. *Behavioral Interventions, 28*(1), 4−21. Available from http://dx.doi.org/10.1002/bin.1350.

Skinner, B. F. (1953). *Science and human behavior.* New York: Free Press.

Vargas, J. S. (2013). *Behavior analysis for effective teaching* (2nd Edition). London: Routledge..

Appendix A Procedural checklist for first supervision meeting

Get to know each other

- Tell the supervisee about yourself, including your credentials and professional background.
- Ask about the supervisee's professional goals, progress with graduate coursework, previous supervision experiences (e.g., how many more hours do they need?), etc.

Discuss the professional supervisory relationship

- Explain the purpose of supervision. Make it clear that you are here to support and teach the supervisee.
- Explain your role as a supervisor, including what types of interactions are appropriate and inappropriate (e.g., dual relationship).
- Explain the nature of the supervisory relationship (i.e., highly collaborative).
- Tell the supervisee that you will keep evaluative information about him/her confidential (explain any situations in which this is not the case).
- Discuss payment for supervision, if relevant.
- Discuss online, audio−visual, etc. considerations, if relevant.

Set expectations for the supervision experience

- Review BACB Experience Standards in detail.
- Ensure supervisee has completed online training module.
- Identify a clear plan and individual responsibilities for tracking supervision hours and documenting supervision activities and performance.

- Identify when supervision will end and any plans for unintended disruptions to supervision.
- Agree on consequences for not adhering to performance expectations (by *either* party).
- Discuss the conditions under which supervision will be terminated.
- Discuss importance of giving and receiving performance feedback.
- Set an established meeting time and establish best way to contact each other.
- Discuss any other expectations.
- Review, make any modifications and sign the supervision contract.

Competency-Based Staff Training

Dennis H. Reid
Carolina Behavior Analysis and Support Center, Morganton, NC, United States

A job requirement of many behavioral practitioners involves training staff in human-service agencies to apply behavior change procedures with agency clients. A prototypical example is when a behavior analyst or related clinician develops a behavior support plan to help a client overcome challenging behavior. The clinician is then expected to provide training on how to implement the plan for the client's routine support staff, such as teachers, direct support personnel in residences or adult center-based programs, and employment specialists in work situations (Reid, Parsons, & Green, 2012, Chapter 7). Behavioral practitioners are frequently expected to train human service staff in other behavior change procedures as well including, for example, how to teach people with disabilities (Catania, Almeida, Liu-Constant, & Reed, 2009), identify client preferences (Lavie & Sturmey, 2002), and help conduct functional assessments (Chok, Shlesinger, Studer, & Bird, 2012).

Staff training expectations of behavioral practitioners also go beyond behavior change procedures in human service agencies. To illustrate, depending on the specific nature of the organizations in which they work, behavioral practitioners may be involved in training staff in safe working practices (Nabeyama & Sturmey, 2010), courteous customer service (Johnson & Fawcett, 1994), or animal care skills (Howard & DiGennaro Reed, 2014). To successfully fulfill their training duties in these and numerous other areas, behavioral practitioners must be knowledgeable about effective staff training strategies and skilled in their application.

The purpose of this chapter is to describe what constitutes effective staff training. Initially, an historical overview will be provided regarding how the education and professional development of behavioral practitioners has addressed expectations for training staff. Next, research in applied behavior analysis (ABA) that has laid the foundation for what is currently considered best practices for staff training will be summarized to highlight the evidence base of recommended practices. The subsequent chapter section then summarizes these strategies with an emphasis on practical considerations for application by practitioners. Finally, the last section provides a checklist summary of effective training procedures to help guide behavioral practitioners to maximize the success of their training endeavors.

Preparing behavioral practitioners to train staff

Soon after what is generally considered the official birth of ABA as a professional discipline in 1968 (Johnston & Reid, 2015), it became apparent that there was a strong need for behavioral practitioners to train other personnel to apply

Applied Behavior Analysis Advanced Guidebook. DOI: http://dx.doi.org/10.1016/B978-0-12-811122-2.00002-4

ABA procedures (Frazier, 1972). The recognition resulted from awareness that if many people in need of supports and services were to benefit from this growing science of human behavior, their caregivers needed to be able to apply behavioral procedures during day-to-day routines. Despite this growing recognition, however, relatively little research attention focused on how to effectively train staff in the human services or other organizational settings. Due in large part to the ABA field being in its relative infancy, most early research in ABA focused on developing procedural applications of the science of human behavior to help people in need.

Commensurate with the relative lack of research on how to train staff to implement ABA procedures, there was little attention on formally preparing behavioral practitioners in methods of training staff. University and college courses that included ABA rarely emphasized how to train staff in human service and other settings. Consequently, behavioral practitioners were left to their own means of training staff as they embarked on their professional careers, often relying on what other professionals in the human services traditionally did to train staff. Usually, this consisted of practitioners meeting with staff whom they intended to train and describing the procedures staff were expected to perform (Sturmey, 1998).

Given that behavioral practitioners received little or no formal preparation on how to train staff, reliance on traditional staff training procedures involving primarily verbal instruction seemed a logical approach. However, it soon became apparent within the ABA field that such an approach to staff training was often ineffective (Gardner, 1972). Subsequently, a relatively small but significant line of ABA research began to focus on how to train staff in human service and other organizational settings.

As the ABA field continued to develop through research on applying the science of behavior to the benefit of society, investigations continued on how to effectively train staff who did not have a behavioral background in the application of the science. Although the research on training staff was small relative to research on developing and applying new behavior change procedures to help people in need of human services, over time a substantial amount of staff training research accumulated. Information resulting from this body of research was not heavily emphasized though within university and college programs designed to train ABA professionals.

It has been only recently within the almost 50-year history of the ABA field that significant attention began to be directed to formally preparing behavioral practitioners in evidence-based methods of training staff. A major impetus for the increased attention has been recognition of the importance of staff training by the Behavior Analysis Certification Board (BACB), which is the international credentialing organization for behavior analysts (Shook & Favell, 2008). The BACB includes effective staff training within its task list of required skills of behavior analysts (BACB, 2016). Correspondingly, substantially more ABA university and college programs now include course work with information about staff training.

Behavioral research that developed evidence-based staff training procedures

Behavioral research on staff training has generally occurred within two general areas. One area consists of investigations on *singular strategies* for training work skills to staff. The second area includes investigations on staff training *programs*, in which several of the individual strategies are combined together as a means of training staff. Research in both of these areas has been summarized in numerous articles (Adkins, 1996; Miller & Lewin, 1980; Oorsouw, Embregts, Bosman, & Jahoda, 2009; Parsons, Rollyson, & Reid, 2012), chapters (Reid, 2004; Reid, O'Kane, & Macurik, in press), and books (Reid & Parsons, 2006; Reid et al., 2012). Consequently, a detailed review of the staff training research in ABA will not be repeated here. Rather, a summary of the basic staff training procedures and programs that have been the focus of behavioral research will be presented.

Research on singular staff training procedures

Investigations on singular staff training procedures generally have focused on four specific strategies: instructions, modeling, performance practice, and feedback.

Instructions. Instructions refer to specifying the behaviors that trainees are expected to perform to complete a job skill that is being trained. These are most commonly presented vocally by a staff trainer describing the target behaviors for staff (Parsons, Rollyson, & Reid, 2013). Vocal instructions can likewise be presented through audiovisual media (Giannakakos, Vladescu, Kisamore, & Reeve, 2016).

Instructions are also frequently presented in written form (Parsons et al., 2013). Written instructions usually involve providing trainees with a document that describes the target behaviors (Macurik, O'Kane, Malanga, & Reid, 2008). Alternatively, written instructions can be presented through visual media in which the description is provided using a video or on-line computer format (Howard & DiGennaro Reed, 2014; Rosales, Gongola, & Homlitas, 2015).

Essentially, all behavioral approaches to staff training involve some form of vocal and/or written instruction, which is considered an essential component of effective staff training. However, although historically the traditional means through which practitioners have gone about their staff training duties, instructions alone are usually insufficient for training staff how to perform a new job skill as noted previously. Numerous investigations have demonstrated inconsistent effectiveness of relying solely on instructions to train staff (Abellon & Wilder, 2014; Alavosius & Sulzer-Azaroff, 1990; Petscher & Bailey, 2006).

Modeling

Modeling involves a trainer demonstrating how to perform a job skill for trainees. Modeling can be conducted in a live format by a trainer within the trainees' regular routine (Towery, Parsons, & Reid, 2014) and in a role-play format (Adams, Tallon, & Rimell, 1980). It is likewise becoming increasingly common for visual media to be used to provide a demonstration for trainees regarding how to perform a target skill (Catania et al., 2009; Howard & DiGennaro Reed, 2014; Rosales et al., 2015).

As with instructions, modeling in and of itself is generally considered insufficient for effectively training staff. It is currently recommended that modeling be used in conjunction with other procedures to train new work skills to staff (Parsons et al., 2012). Also as with instructions, modeling is now a standard part of evidence-based staff training approaches.

Performance practice

Performance practice refers to trainees performing the skills they are expected to acquire as part of the training process. Performance practice is also referred to as behavioral rehearsal (Parsons et al., 2012). The practice can be conducted in a live manner within the trainees' regular work situation (Towery et al., 2014) or in a role-play format (Parsons et al., 2013). Typically, performance practice is preceded by instructions and/or modeling within a staff training process. As such, although performance practice has been considered as a specific training procedure, its utility within staff training has generally been demonstrated when applied in conjunction with instructions and/or modeling. Performance practice has also been researched when applied with another procedure commonly used in staff training: performance feedback.

Performance feedback

Within a training context, feedback consists of providing a staff person with descriptive information about the individual's performance of the skill being trained. The information specifies what aspects of the skill the trainee performed correctly and incorrectly (if applicable). There are numerous formats for providing feedback including vocal (Realon, Lewallen, & Wheeler, 1983), written (Hawkins, Burgio, Langford, & Engel, 1992), graphic (Carr, Wilder, Majdalany, Mathisen, & Strain, 2013), video recorded (van Vonderen, Duker, & Didden, 2010), and self-recorded (Brackett, Reid, & Green, 2007).

Performance feedback typically has not been used as a singular strategy for training staff how to perform a new job skill but rather, as a strategy to improve or maintain staff application of a newly acquired skill during day-to-day work performance (see Alvero, Bucklin, & Austin, 2001; Balcazar, Hopkins, & Suarez, 1986, for reviews of feedback). It is noted here, however, because feedback has consistently been provided within investigations on the other staff training strategies in one format or another. Along with instructions, modeling, and performance practice, feedback is now considered a standard component of evidence-based staff training.

Research on staff training programs

Due in large part to results of early ABA research indicating the inconsistent effectiveness of singular strategies for training staff, most behavioral investigations in the staff training area have focused on evaluations of combinations of the strategies. This is particularly the case with more recent research on staff training. Various combinations of instructions, modeling, performance practice, and/or feedback have been incorporated within staff training programs to train a wide variety of work skills (e.g., Kneringer & Page, 1999; Nabeyama & Sturmey, 2010; Severtson & Carr, 2012).

Research on both singular training strategies and training programs has led to the development of an evidence-based staff training protocol. The constituent components of the protocol are presented in Table 2.1. Numerous investigations have demonstrated the effectiveness of this approach to staff training (see Parsons et al., 2012, for a summary).

The staff training protocol represented in Table 2.1 is considered *performance* and *competency based* (Reid et al., 2003). The performance aspect pertains to what both the trainer and trainees are expected to perform as part of the training process. More specifically, trainers must perform the target skill (modeling as referred to earlier) and trainees must perform the skill (performance practice). The competency aspect refers to the last step of the protocol in terms of continuing the training process until each trainee demonstrates competence in performing the target skill. Within ABA, this performance- and competency-based approach to staff training is now typically referred to as *behavior skills training* or *BST* (Miles & Wilder, 2009; Nigro-Bruzzi & Sturmey, 2010; Sarokoff & Sturmey, 2004).

BST represents what is now considered best practices for behavioral practitioners to train job skills to staff in human service and other organizational settings. As just indicated, it has a strong research base documenting its effectiveness. Being knowledgeable about BST and skilled in its application is also a BACB requirement for certified behavior analysts, with a particular emphasis on behavior analysts who function in a supervisory capacity with staff as reflected in its Supervisor Training Curriculum Outline (BACB, 2015).

Table 2.1 **Steps of performance- and competency-based staff training (behavior skills training)**

Step action
1. Provide rationale for why a skill will be trained
2. Describe the behaviors necessary to perform the skill
3. Provide a written description of the skill
4. Demonstrate the skill
5. Have staff practice performing the skill
6. Provide performance feedback
7. Repeat steps 5 and 6 until competency

Guidelines and recommendations for practice

Use of the BST protocol is most applicable when formally meeting with a group of staff for training purposes. This chapter section describes practical guidelines and recommendations for using BST in this manner. The same information is relevant, however, when formally meeting with an individual staff member for the purpose of training the staff person. Subsequently, means of training staff more informally within their regular work routine using BST as a template will be described. In addition, the utility of training other agency personnel how to use BST and applications of visual media and technology will be discussed as a means of reducing the amount of time and effort for practitioners to fulfill staff training responsibilities.

Guidelines and recommendations for implementing the steps of BST

BST step 1: Provide rationale for why a skill will be trained

Step 1 of BST involves the trainer providing a rationale or explanation regarding why staff are being requested to learn how to perform a respective work skill (Willner et al., 1977). This step is included to help make the training process acceptable to staff (Reid et al., 2012, Chapter 4). Staff are usually more accepting of having to learn a new work duty if they have an understanding of why the duty is important to perform. It is incumbent on the staff trainer to ensure the skill is indeed important for staff to acquire within their performance repertoires and then ensure staff understand its importance.

BST step 2: Describe the behaviors necessary to perform the skill

Immediately after explaining the rationale for the skill being trained, the trainer should describe the exact behaviors necessary to perform the skill for the trainees. In essence, this step requires the staff trainer to provide a behavioral definition of the target skill. It also requires specification of the sequence with which each behavior should occur to perform the skill correctly and the situation in which the skill should be applied.

BST step 3: Provide a written description of the skill

Step 3 of BST consists of providing each trainee with a written summary of the behaviors constituting the skill and the sequence in which they should be performed. The summary generally should be concise, usually involving no more than one or two pages, and focus explicitly on the behaviors to be performed. Trainees should be requested to review the summary and ask any questions they may have about the summary. This step along with the preceding BST step represents the *instruction* training strategy described previously.

Sometimes trainers provide the written summary prior to describing the skill (step 2) so that trainees can review the written information as the trainer provides the vocal description. However, experience has indicated that trainees are likely to attend more to the trainer's initial vocal description if they have not yet been provided the handout. It can also be helpful if, prior to providing the vocal description, the trainer informs the trainees that s/he will first describe the skill being trained and then provide a written description for their review.

For skills that are relatively complex in terms of requiring a number of behaviors in a particular sequence to perform, an advantageous way to provide the written summary is through a performance checklist (Casey & McWilliam, 2011). A checklist is essentially a task analysis of the work duty being trained. A sample checklist is provided in Table 2.2. This particular checklist (specifying the performance steps necessary to conduct one type of behavioral preference assessment) was developed for use when training supervisors of technicians in ABA programs serving clients with autism (Courtney, LaMarca, Hartley, Rosswurm, & Reid, in press). A practical advantage of a checklist is that it can provide trainees with a permanent guide or job aid to refer to as they perform the duty during their regular work routine.

Some trainers are reluctant to provide all trainees with a written summary of the skill being trained. The reluctance is due to having experienced situations in which staff frequently lose or otherwise discard the summary soon after the training session. Such situations can occur for certain staff. However, more conscientious staff will exert the effort to keep the summary handy and use it as a helpful reference as needed.

This step of BST is sometimes approximated by trainers in terms of making a written summary available for staff to review in a central location instead of

Table 2.2 Example of a performance checklist (conducting a multistimulus preference assessment with a client)

Step action
1. Place 3 leisure items on table in front of seated client
2. Instruct client to choose 1 item
3. Provide 1 minute for client to play with chosen item
4. Record client's choice
5. Remove chosen item
6. Repeat process for remaining two items (steps 1–5 except with just the two previously unchosen items)
7. Repeat entire process (steps 1–6) two more times
8. For each item, calculate percentage of times chosen across all opportunities (number of times item was available for choice)
9. Determine most-, second-most-, and least-preferred items based on ranking of percentage of times each item was chosen

providing the summary for each trainee. For example, when a practitioner is training staff to carry out a behavior support plan or other client treatment procedure, the practitioner may show staff the plan and then indicate where the plan will be located for their review (e.g., in the client's treatment file). The latter process is not recommended, however, for two primary reasons. First, requiring staff to go to a specific location to retrieve and review the summary necessitates extra time and effort on the part of staff. Staff, like everybody else, tend to engage in behavior that is less time consuming and effortful relative to more time consuming and effortful behavior. Consequently, staff can be more likely to actually review the summary as needed to perform a work duty on the job if they have immediate access to the summary.

The second reason the above practice is not recommended is that behavior support plans and other treatment procedures often include more information than what staff need to actually perform the target skill (e.g., background assessments and baseline data summaries). The extra information can decrease the likelihood staff can easily retrieve the exact information for actually performing the duty. It also requires increased time and effort on the part of staff to review the written information. For these reasons, it is generally recommended that each staff be provided with a concise, written summary of the behaviors in which they are being expected to engage. However, they can also be encouraged to review the entire treatment document in the central location as time permits in their schedule.

BST step 4: Demonstrate the skill

Once staff trainees have heard a description of the skill being trained and read a description, they should be provided with a demonstration of how to perform the skill. This represents application of the *modeling* training strategy. The demonstration should occur in the exact manner in which the skill was described by the trainer and as written in the summary provided to staff.

When training a group of staff, the demonstration step often occurs in a role-play situation. If the skill pertains to working directly with a client, the trainer can solicit the assistance of one of the trainees to play the role of the client (and provide explicit instructions to the assisting trainee regarding what s/he should do during the role play). Alternatively, a trainer can have someone else who is skilled in the target skill provide the demonstration or show a video or other visual recording of someone performing the skill.

Adequately performing the demonstration step of BST requires that the staff trainer him/herself be competent in performing the skill being trained. Practitioners should strongly avoid being in a situation in which they are expected to train staff when the practitioners themselves are not skilled or otherwise comfortable in performing the skill themselves. Even when someone else or a video provides the demonstration the trainer should still be skilled in performing skill as s/he will likely need to demonstrate at least some aspects of the skill during the subsequent steps of BST.

Modeling a skill being trained has several important benefits. Most notably, many people seem to learn how to do something more easily if they see how it is done relative to just hearing or reading how to do it. Experience has also indicated another more subtle but nonetheless important benefit with the use of modeling in staff training. Specifically, staff tend to appreciate the actions of their trainer more if the trainer takes the time to show them how to do something relative to just telling them how to do it (Reid et al., 2012, Chapter 4). Relatedly, by demonstrating how to perform the skill, the trainer demonstrates his/her own competency in performing the skill—an action that can enhance the credibility of the trainer among the staff trainees which in turn can further facilitate staff "buy in" to the whole training process.

BST step 5: Have staff practice performing the skill

Immediately following the demonstration, staff should be instructed to practice performing the skill (i.e., the *performance practice* training strategy). As with the demonstration step, the practice typically occurs in a role-play format. The trainer should instruct that each trainee should practice the skill, with another trainee playing the role of the client, exactly as the skill was just demonstrated. Trainees should take turns practicing the skill, using the written summary that was handed out as a guide, and playing the role of the client. It can also be helpful for trainees to observe each other (when they are not acting in the role of the person performing the skill or the client) and provide feedback to the trainee based on how accurately the trainee's practice conforms to the trainer's previous demonstration and the written summary.

BST step 6: Provide performance feedback

As trainees practice performing the skill being trained, the trainer should observe each trainee's performance and provide feedback (the performance *feedback* training strategy). The feedback should include several forms. First, the trainer should provide positive feedback in terms of specifying those aspects of the skill the trainee performed correctly and offer praise or other commendation for those actions. Second, the trainer should provide corrective feedback if necessary for any aspects of the skill the trainee performed incorrectly or omitted during the practice. Corrective feedback involves specifying what the trainee did not perform correctly *and* informing the trainee what s/he needs to do to correct the performance. The latter part of corrective feedback may consist of additional instruction and/or modeling for the trainee how to correctly perform specific aspects of the skill.

With both positive and corrective feedback it is also helpful for the trainer to specifically question a trainee whether s/he has any questions about performing the skill or about the trainer's feedback, and then respond accordingly. Such an action allows an opportunity to resolve any concerns the trainee may have. It also represents a type of *participative* action on the part of the trainer, which can enhance trainee acceptance of the training process (Reid et al., 2012, Chapter 6).

In order for a trainer to provide sufficient positive and corrective feedback, s/he must carefully observe a trainee's practice performance. The written summary of the target skill (used in BST step 3) should be used as a guide such that the trainer can observe a trainee's proficiency in performing each step constituting the skill being trained. As noted earlier, preparing the written summary in a checklist format can facilitate the trainer's observation. The trainer can observe and "check off" each step on the checklist as being correctly performed or not by each trainee.

The feedback step of BST can be time consuming to conduct, and especially if there is a large group of trainees. The trainer must spend time observing each trainee's practice and providing individualized feedback. Consequently, there is a tendency for some practitioners to only complete part of this step. That is, some practitioners generally observe the group of trainees as a whole rather than spending time observing each trainee and providing individualized feedback. Though potentially time consuming, individual feedback is critical for successfully implementing BST and should never be overlooked.

BST step 7: Repeat steps 5 and 6 until competency

The final step in conducting a BST training session is to repeat the trainee practice and feedback steps (steps 5 and 6) as necessary until *each trainee demonstrates competency performing the target skill.* Although this step also can be time consuming, and especially if respective trainees have difficulty demonstrating the target skill accurately, it is absolutely critical to the training process and must be completed. Without a trainer completing this step of BST, the training cannot be considered competency-based.

On-the-job component of behavioral skills training

As noted earlier when introducing the BST process, the steps of BST just described pertain to the common situation in which a practitioner is meeting with a group of staff for training purposes. Once all seven steps of BST have been carried out in that type of situation, the training session is then completed. However, the entire training process is not yet completed. There is one more critical step: the trainer must observe each trainee complete the skill that was targeted during the training session in a competent manner during the trainee's regular work routine.

Following the BST session, the trainer must go to each trainee's routine work setting at a time when the trainee would be expected to perform the skill that was addressed during the session. The trainer should then follow BST steps 5, 6, and 7 to ensure the trainee generalizes what was learned during the session to his/her usual work routine. That is, the trainer should observe the trainee performing the newly acquired skill and provide positive and if necessary, corrective feedback. The process should be continued until the trainer observes the trainee competently perform the skill at that point. In short, training should never be considered completed or successful until the trainer observes the trainee perform the skill competently on the job.

As with ensuring competent trainee performance during a formal training session, ensuring competent performance on the job can be time consuming for the trainer. Nonetheless, again as with this step in a formal BST session, ensuring competent on-the-job performance of each trainee is a critical requirement of staff training. The latter step can be facilitated in this regard if the former step is adequately carried out by the trainer. When trainees demonstrate competence in a role-play situation during a formal BST session, the likelihood of them demonstrating competence on the job is enhanced relative to a trainer not ensuring competence in the former situation. This is a primary reason why the critical nature of step 7 of BST was highlighted earlier. By taking the time to ensure trainee competence during a BST session, the trainer can reduce his/her time to carry out the on-the-job component of the training.

Informal staff training

A practitioner's training responsibilities with staff can also be fulfilled in many cases in an *informal* manner. Informal staff training usually involves a trainer conducting the training with a staff person within the individual's regular work setting during ongoing work activities. This type of staff training is generally applicable whenever a practitioner observes a staff person having difficulty performing a particular skill on the job. Although the training is informal in terms of occurring in an on-the-job manner in contrast to a formally scheduled meeting away from a staff member's usual work site, the training should still be evidence based.

Conducting informal staff training in an evidence-based manner involves the staff trainer implementing certain steps of BST with the staff member in the latter's work site. Specifically, BST steps 2, 4, 5, 6, and 7 should be carried out. The trainer first describes what the staff person should do to perform the duty of concern, models the relevant skills, has the staff person perform (practice) the duty again and provides feedback, and then repeats the practice and feedback as necessary until the trainer observes the staff person perform the duty correctly.

Notice that BST steps 1 and 3 are usually not included with informal, on-the-job staff training. Step 1, or providing a rationale for the skill, is typically not necessary as the staff person is already attempting to complete a duty such that the importance of the duty is likely already apparent to the staff person. Providing a written summary of the skill (step 3) typically is not applicable because the training occurs in an impromptu manner whenever a practitioner observes a need for training such that a written summary would likely not be readily available.

Practitioners must decide if various staff training responsibilities should be fulfilled in a formal or informal manner. Experience suggests several guidelines that can be helpful for practitioners in making such a decision (see Table 2.3). First, informal training is usually most applicable when a practitioner needs to train one

Table 2.3 Guidelines for conducting informal, on-the-job training

Guideline action
1. Use when only one or a very small number of staff require training
2. Use when training can be conducted in a brief period of time, generally no more than 10 min
3. Use when training can be conducted without leaving clients unsupervised or otherwise placing clients in a potentially unsafe situation

or a very small number of staff. If more than two or three staff require training on a respective skill, it is usually more efficient to train the group of staff in a formal manner. Second, informal on-the-job training should generally be conducted only if the training is likely to require a relatively brief amount of time, usually less than 10 minutes or so. Otherwise, the informal training may cause too much of a disruption in the staff person's fulfillment of ongoing work expectations.

A related consideration for the appropriateness of informal training is the welfare of the clients whom the staff person supports. Informal training requires the staff person to stop whatever work activity is ongoing and attend to the trainer. If such a process is likely to leave one or more clients unattended that could result in a potentially unsafe situation, then the on-the-job approach to training should not be implemented at that point.

Making staff training more time efficient for practitioners

As noted earlier, being knowledgeable about BST and skilled in its application is a professional expectation of behavioral practitioners. This approach to training staff is not only effective, it is also usually well received by staff trainees (Reid & Parsons, 2000). In contrast to these important advantages of BST, however, there is one noted disadvantage—that of time efficiency.

The time efficiency issue pertains to the amount of time required to train staff with BST. A noted concern with BST is that it can be time consuming for practitioners to carry out appropriately (Parsons et al., 2013). The features of BST that can be most time consuming have already been noted in terms of the repeated practice and feedback steps during both a formal training session and on-the-job, informal training.

The time commitment for implementing BST is one reason that staff training in many settings continues to occur in a traditional manner with a focus on instruction as the training strategy (Reid, 2004). However, as repeatedly emphasized (see also Casey & McWilliam, 2011; Clark, Cushing, & Kennedy, 2004), it has been well documented that sole reliance on instruction is usually an ineffective means of training staff how to perform work duties. Consequently, instead of conducting staff training in a manner that is less time consuming than BST but has little likelihood of success, attention is warranted on how to make effective training with BST less time consuming for practitioners.

Research in ABA has been addressing ways of making BST more time efficient. Results of the research to date have indicated two general means of reducing the amount of trainer time to conduct staff training in an effective manner. These include *pyramidal training* and use of *visual media and technology*.

Pyramidal staff training

Pyramidal training involves a practitioner training a small group of agency staff who in turn train a larger group of staff (Page, Iwata, & Reid, 1982). When the staff who are trained then train other staff who hold similar positions in an agency as the former individuals, the approach is also referred to as *peer training* (Finn & Sturmey, 2009). Most investigations on pyramidal training have involved one trainer training other personnel to function as trainers for teaching one particular skill set to other staff (Demchak, Kontos, & Neisworth, 1992; Green & Reid, 1994; Haberlin, Beauchamp, Agnew, & O'Brien, 2012; Kuhn, Lerman, & Vorndran, 2003; Neef, 1995; Page et al., 1982; Pence, St. Peter, & Tetreault, 2012). A more robust use of pyramidal training has involved training a small group of staff to use BST to train a variety of work skills to other staff (Parsons et al., 2013). In the latter situation, BST is used to train selected staff in turn how to apply BST for multiple training purposes.

Pyramidal training can offer a number of advantages for practitioners who have staff training responsibilities. A primary advantage is that this approach to training typically reduces the amount of time required of a given practitioner to train staff—the staff training duty is shared across several agency personnel (Parsons et al., 2013). A second advantage is that once a select group of agency personnel have been trained in BST, they can assist a practitioner when new staff training responsibilities arise such as training staff in new behavior support plans (Parsons et al., 2013). The latter advantage can reduce the amount of time for a practitioner to fulfill staff training responsibilities on a long-term basis. An additional advantage is that when the personnel who are trained to conduct BST are indigenous to an agency, such as staff supervisors, their functioning as staff trainers can enhance maintenance of the staffs' newly trained skills (Demchak et al., 1992). The latter outcome can occur because the new trainers are often present in the staffs' regular work site more frequently than a respective practitioner and the routine presence can facilitate implementation of maintenance procedures.

There are also some potential disadvantages with pyramidal training. First, although the amount of time required of one practitioner to train staff is reduced, the total amount of training time across all trainers and staff trainees is not reduced and may even be increased (Parsons et al., 2013). Second, some staff prefer not to function as a staff trainer and choose not to assume such a responsibility when given the opportunity (van den Pol, Reid, & Fuqua, 1983). The apparent dislike of functioning as a staff trainer can be due to the extra work required of personnel who assume staff training duties (Parsons et al., 2013). The dislike can also be due

Table 2.4 **Guidelines for using pyramidal staff training**

Guideline action

1. Most efficient when at least one of the following conditions is met
  a. large numbers of staff need to be trained
  b. staff are spread across geographical locations
  c. additional skills will likely need to be trained in the future.
2. Arrange with agency management to allow new staff trainers to have time built into their work schedules for training staff
3. Question individuals before being trained as staff trainers to assess their willingness to function in the future in a staff training capacity

to the new training status of the staff trainer being negatively received by staff trainees when the process involves peer training (Finn & Sturmey, 2009).

In light of the advantages and potential disadvantages of pyramidal training, several guidelines have been offered regarding use of this approach for staff training (Parsons et al., 2013). These are summarized in Table 2.4. The first guideline focuses on when pyramidal training is likely to be most practical or time efficient for a practitioner. Specifically, pyramidal training is most helpful if there are large numbers of staff to be trained, the staff are spread across different geographical settings, and/or it is likely that a number of new skills will need to be trained to staff over time. If at least one of these conditions is not met, then the practical advantage of pyramidal training is reduced or eliminated (with the exception of the potential maintenance benefit of the staff trainer being indigenous to the staffs' work site as referred to above).

The second guideline pertains to a likely source of discontent among agency personnel in terms of functioning in a staff training capacity. Specifically, it is recommended that prior to training certain staff to be trainers, negotiations be conducted with agency management to ensure such personnel are aware of the new (training) duties expected of the selected staff. Effort is also warranted to try to solicit management action to possibly relieve the new trainers of other work responsibilities in order to have available time within their regular work routines to train staff. The intent would be to ensure the new training requirements occur in lieu of some of the trainers' existing duties in contrast to being added on to current duties.

The third guideline pertains to apparent dislike among some agency personnel of being placed in the new role with their colleagues of being a peer trainer. It is recommended that practitioners question potential trainers to assess their willingness to function as a peer trainer. The intent in this case, again where possible, would be to involve agency personnel in pyramidal or peer training only if they express a willingness to function in such a role.

Use of visual media and technology in staff training

Information dissemination has been revolutionized in recent years. Internet access, training videos and DVDs, and interactive software, for example, are now readily available to many organizations including human service agencies (Severtson & Carr, 2012). Correspondingly, there has been an increasing amount of research attention directed to evaluating and demonstrating the utility of visual media and technology within staff training programs (e.g., Catania et al., 2009; Moore & Fisher, 2007; Rosales et al., 2015; Weldy, Rapp, & Capocasa, 2014).

New information technologies offer a number of attractive features for practitioners who conduct staff training. To illustrate, training DVDs can represent a means of providing relevant information and procedural demonstrations that reduce a practitioner's time for training staff relative to BST conducted entirely in a face-to-face manner (Macurik et al., 2008). However, caution is also warranted based on what research has shown to represent effective training of staff job skills. Much of the information technologies still rely heavily on dissemination of verbal information, with the addition of performance-based modeling in many cases (Reid et al., in press). This may explain why there has been some inconsistency regarding the effectiveness of this technology when training staff (e.g., Digennaro-Reed, Codding, Catania, & Maguire, 2010; Neef, Trachtenberg, Loeb, & Sterner, 1991).

Assuming ready access to visual media and technology along with the growing body of research supporting its use—albeit with some inconsistency—it can be helpful for practitioners to consider technological applications in staff training programs. It is recommended, however, that when employing visual media and technology, practitioners ensure that each of the steps of BST are still incorporated within the training. Particular attention is warranted to ensure that the performance practice and feedback steps are implemented to ensure trainee competency. The latter steps may be included, for example, through interactive software involving real time applications or other types of interactive computer training (Pollard, Higbee, Akers, & Brodhead, 2014). Another approach is to use visual media and technology for carrying out some of the steps of BST (e.g., the rationale, instructions, and modeling) and then implementing the remaining practice and feedback steps in an on-the-job format (Macurik et al., 2008).

The critical but qualified role of staff training

The importance of staff training for behavioral practitioners was emphasized in the introductory comments to this chapter. Staff training by practitioners is frequently necessary to help staff fulfill behavior change duties with clients as well as other performance expectations. However, although often necessary for helping staff perform job duties in a quality manner, staff training is rarely sufficient in this regard.

It has been very well established in ABA research that staff training endeavors must be followed by specific supervisory or performance management procedures to promote and maintain quality work behavior. It is beyond the scope here to discuss effective supervision and performance management. However, there is a large behavioral literature available on this topic (see Daniels, 1994; Harchik & Campbell, 1998; Reid & Parsons, 2006; Reid et al., 2012, for reviews and summaries) as well as a curriculum for training supervisors in evidence-based supervision

(Reid, Parsons, & Green, 2009). The point of concern here is that practitioners should be prepared to promote follow-up supervision of staff application of newly trained skills to ensure their training endeavors significantly affect day-to-day work performance.

A practice checklist for competency-based staff training

Fig. 2.1 provides a practice checklist for use by behavioral practitioners to guide their actions for effectively training work skills to staff in human service and other organizations. The checklist summarizes the main points discussed in the preceding chapter section, **Guidelines and Recommendations for Practice**. The checklist

Practice Guidelines Checklist

Competency-Based Staff Training

1. For formally training a group of staff or a staff member individually, use the steps of Behavior Skills Training (BST):

    a. Provide rationale for skill being trained

    b. Describe behaviors constituting the skill

    c. Provide written summary of the skill

    d. Demonstrate the skill

    e. Have staff practice the skill

    f. Provide performance feedback

    g. Repeat above to steps until competency

2. For informally training an individual staff member on the job, use BST steps b, d, e, f, and g above if the training:

    a. Can be conducted briefly, usually in less than 10 minutes

    b. Can be conducted without putting clients in unsupervised or otherwise potentially un safe situation

3. Whether training formally or informally, always observe trainee(s) competently perform the skill being trained on the job during routine work situation before completing the training.

4. Arrange for follow-up supervision to support staff application and maintenance of the skill on the job.

Figure 2.1 Practice guidelines checklist for competency-based staff training.

focuses on use of the steps of BST when training staff in a formal manner, when selected steps of BST are most applicable for training staff in an informal or on-the-job manner, the importance of training not being considered complete until the staff trainer observes trainees competently perform the skill being trained effectively during routine work situations, and arranging for follow-up supervision of newly trained skills during staffs' day-to-day job performance.

References

Abellon, O. E., & Wilder, D. A. (2014). The effect of equipment proximity on safe performance in a manufacturing setting. *Journal of Applied Behavior Analysis, 47*, 628–632.

Adams, G. L., Tallon, R. J., & Rimell, P. (1980). A comparison of lecture versus role-playing in the training of the use of positive reinforcement. *Journal of Organizational Behavior Management, 2*, 205–212.

Adkins, V. K. (1996). Discussion: Behavioral procedures for training direct care staff in facilities serving dependent populations. *Behavioral Interventions, 11*, 95–100.

Alavosius, M. P., & Sulzer-Azaroff, B. (1990). Acquisition and maintenance of health-care routines as a function of feedback density. *Journal of Applied Behavior Analysis, 23*, 151–162.

Alvero, A. M., Bucklin, B. R., & Austin, J. (2001). An objective review of the effectiveness and essential characteristics of performance feedback in organizational settings. *Journal of Organizational Behavior Management, 21*(1), 3–29.

BACB (2015). *Supervisor training curriculum outline*. Retrieved from bacb.com/wp-content/uploads/2015/05/supervisor_curriculum.pdf.

BACB (2016). *Fourth Edition task list*. Retrieved from bacb.com/fourth-edition-task-list/.

Balcazar, F., Hopkins, B. L., & Suarez, Y. (1986). A critical, objective review of performance feedback. *Journal of Organizational Behavior Management, 7*(3/4), 65–89.

Brackett, L., Reid, D. H., & Green, C. W. (2007). Effects of reactivity to observations on staff performance. *Journal of Applied Behavior Analysis, 40*, 191–195.

Carr, J. E., Wilder, D. A., Majdalany, L., Mathisen, D., & Strain, L. A. (2013). An assessment-based solution to a human-service employee performance problem: An evaluation of the *Performance Diagnostic Checklist—Human Services. Behavior Analysis in Practice, 6*, 16–32.

Casey, A. M., & McWilliam, R. A. (2011). The impact of checklist-based training on teachers' use of the zone defense schedule. *Journal of Applied Behavior Analysis, 44*, 397–401.

Catania, C. N., Almeida, D., Liu-Constant, B., & Reed, F. D. D. (2009). Video modeling to train staff to implement discrete-trial instruction. *Journal of Applied Behavior Analysis, 42*, 387–392.

Chok, J. T., Shlesinger, A., Studer, L., & Bird, F. L. (2012). Description of a practitioner training program on functional analysis and treatment development. *Behavior Analysis in Practice, 5*, 25–36.

Clark, N. M., Cushing, L. S., & Kennedy, C. H. (2004). An intensive onsite technical assistance model to promote inclusive educational practices for students with disabilities in middle school and high school. *Research & Practice for Persons with Severe Disabilities, 29*, 253–262.

Courtney, T., LaMarca, V.J., Hartley, B., Rosswurm, M., & Reid, D.H. (in press). The Training Curriculum for Supervisors of ABA Technicians in Autism Programs. Cornwall-on-Hudson, NY: Sloan Publishing.

Daniels, A. C. (1994). *Bringing out the best in people: How to apply the astonishing power of positive reinforcement.* New York: McGraw-Hill.

Demchak, M., Kontos, S., & Neisworth, J. T. (1992). Using a pyramid model to teach behavior management procedures to childcare providers. *Topics in Early Childhood Special Education, 92,* 458−478.

Digennaro-Reed, F. D., Codding, R., Catania, C. N., & Maguire, H. (2010). Effects of video modeling on treatment integrity of behavioral interventions. *Journal of Applied Behavior Analysis, 43,* 291−295.

Finn, L. L., & Sturmey, P. (2009). The effect of peer-to-peer training on staff interactions with adults with dual diagnoses. *Research in Developmental Disabilities, 30,* 96−106.

Frazier, T. W. (1972). Training institutional staff in behavior modification principles and techniques. In R. D. Ruben, H. Fensterheim, J. D. Henderson, & L. P. Ullmann (Eds.), *Advances in behavior therapy: Proceedings of the fourth conference of the Association for Advancement of Behavior Therapy* (pp. 171−178). New York: Academic Press.

Gardner, J. M. (1972). Teaching behavior modification to nonprofessionals. *Journal of Applied Behavior Analysis, 5,* 517−521.

Giannakakos, A. R., Vladescu, J. C., Kisamore, A. N., & Reeve, S. A. (2016). Using video modeling with voiceover instruction plus feedback to train staff to implement direct teaching procedures. *Behavior Analysis in Practice, 9,* 126−134.

Green, C. W., & Reid, D. H. (1994). A comprehensive evaluation of a train-the-trainers model for training education staff to assemble adaptive switches. *Journal of Developmental and Physical Disabilities, 6,* 219−238.

Haberlin, A. T., Beauchamp, K., Agnew, J., & O'Brien, F. (2012). A comparison of pyramidal staff training and direct staff training in community-based day programs. *Journal of Organizational Behavior Management, 32,* 65−74.

Harchik, A. E., & Campbell, A. R. (1998). Supporting people with developmental disabilities in their homes in the community: The role of organizational behavior management. *Journal of Organizational Behavior Management, 18(2/3),* 83−101.

Hawkins, A. M., Burgio, L. D., Langford, A., & Engel, B. T. (1992). The effects of verbal and written supervisory feedback on staff compliance with assigned prompted voiding in a nursing home. *Journal of Organizational Behavior Management, 13(1),* 137−150.

Howard, V. J., & DiGennaro Reed, F. D. (2014). Training shelter volunteers to teach dog compliance. *Journal of Applied Behavior Analysis, 47,* 344−359.

Johnson, M. D., & Fawcett, S. B. (1994). Courteous service: Its assessment and modification in a human service organization. *Journal of Applied Behavior Analysis, 27,* 145−152.

Johnston, J. M., & Reid, D. H. (2015). Applied behavior analysis: A science-based technology of behavior change. In J. M. Johnston, & D. H. Reid (Eds.), *The promise of behavioral services for people with intellectual disabilities* (pp. 93−107). Cornwall on Hudson, NY: Sloan Publishing.

Kneringer, M., & Page, T. J. (1999). Improving staff nutritional practices in community-based group homes: Evaluation, training, and management. *Journal of Applied Behavior Analysis, 32,* 221−224.

Kuhn, S. A., Lerman, D. C., & Vorndran, C. M. (2003). Pyramidal training for families of children with problem behavior. *Journal of Applied Behavior Analysis, 36,* 77−88.

Lavie, T., & Sturmey, P. (2002). Training staff to conduct a paired-stimulus preference assessment. *Journal of Applied Behavior Analysis, 35,* 209−211.

Macurik, K. M., O'Kane, N. P., Malanga, P., & Reid, D. H. (2008). Video training of support staff in intervention plans for challenging behavior: Comparison with live training. *Behavioral Interventions, 23*, 143–163.

Miles, N. I., & Wilder, D. A. (2009). The effects of behavioral skills training on caregiver implementation of guided compliance. *Journal of Applied Behavior Analysis, 42*, 405–410.

Miller, R., & Lewin, L. M. (1980). Training and management of the psychiatric aide: A critical review. *Journal of Organizational Behavior Management, 2*, 295–315.

Moore, J. W., & Fisher, W. W. (2007). The effects of videotape modeling on staff acquisition of functional analysis methodology. *Journal of Applied Behavior Analysis, 40*, 197–202.

Nabeyama, B., & Sturmey, P. (2010). Using behavioral skills training to promote safe and correct staff guarding and ambulation distance of students with multiple physical disabilities. *Journal of Applied Behavior Analysis, 43*, 341–345.

Neef, N. A. (1995). Research on training trainers in program implementation: An introduction and future directions. *Journal of Applied Behavior Analysis, 28*, 297–299.

Neef, N. A., Trachtenberg, S., Loeb, J., & Sterner, K. (1991). Video-based training of respite care providers: An interactional analysis of presentation format. *Journal of Applied Behavior Analysis, 24*, 473–486.

Nigro-Bruzzi, D., & Sturmey, P. (2010). The effects of behavioral skills training on mand training by staff and unprompted vocal mands by children. *Journal of Applied Behavior Analysis, 43*, 757–761.

Oorsouw, W. M. W. J. V., Embregts, P. J. C. M., Bosman, A. M. T., & Jahoda, A. (2009). Training staff serving clients with intellectual disabilities: A meta-analysis of aspects determining effectiveness. *Research in Developmental Disabilities, 30*, 503–511.

Page, T. J., Iwata, B. A., & Reid, D. H. (1982). Pyramidal training: A large-scale application with institutional staff. *Journal of Applied Behavior Analysis, 15*, 335–351.

Parsons, M. B., Rollyson, J. H., & Reid, D. H. (2012). Evidence-based staff training: A guide for practitioners. *Behavior Analysis in Practice, 5*, 2–11.

Parsons, M. B., Rollyson, J. H., & Reid, D. H. (2013). Teaching practitioners to conduct behavioral skills training: A pyramidal approach for training multiple human service staff. *Behavior Analysis in Practice, 6*, 4–16.

Pence, S. T., St. Peter, C. C., & Tetreault, A. S. (2012). Increasing accurate preference assessment implementation through pyramidal training. *Journal of Applied Behavior Analysis, 45*, 345–359.

Petscher, E. A., & Bailey, J. S. (2006). Effects of training, prompting, and self-monitoring on staff behavior in a classroom for students with disabilities. *Journal of Applied Behavior Analysis, 39*, 215–226.

Pollard, J. S., Higbee, T. S., Akers, J. S., & Brodhead, M. T. (2014). An evaluation of interactive computer training to teach instructors to implement discrete trials with children with autism. *Journal of Applied Behavior Analysis, 47*, 765–776.

Realon, R. E., Lewallen, J. D., & Wheeler, A. J. (1983). Verbal feedback vs. verbal feedback plus praise: The effects on direct care staff's training behaviors. *Mental Retardation, 21*, 209–212.

Reid, D. H. (2004). Training and supervising direct support personnel to carry out behavioral procedures. In J. L. Matson, R. B. Laud, & M. L. Matson (Eds.), *Behavior modification for persons with developmental disabilities: Treatments and supports* (pp. 73–99). Kingston, NY: NADD Press.

Reid, D.H., O'Kane, N.P., & Macurik, K.M. (in press). Staff training and management. In W. W. Fisher, C. C. Piazza, & H. S. Roane (Eds.), *Handbook of applied behavior analysis, 2nd Edition.* New York: Guilford Press.

Reid, D. H., & Parsons, M. B. (2000). Organizational behavior management in human service settings. In J. Austin, & J. E. Carr (Eds.), *Handbook of applied behavior analysis* (pp. 275−294). Reno, NV: Context Press.

Reid, D. H., & Parsons, M. B. (2006). *Motivating human service staff: Supervisory strategies for maximizing work effort and work enjoyment* (2nd Edition). Morganton, NC: Habilitative Management Consultants, Inc.

Reid, D. H., Parsons, M. B., & Green, C. W. (2009). *The supervisor training curriculum: Evidence-based ways to promote work quality and enjoyment among support staff.* Washington, DC: American Association on Intellectual and Developmental Disabilities.

Reid, D. H., Parsons, M. B., & Green, C. W. (2012). *The supervisor's guidebook: Evidence-based strategies for promoting work quality and enjoyment among human service staff.* Morganton, NC: Habilitative Management Consultants.

Reid, D. H., Rotholz, D. A., Parsons, M. B., Morris, L., Braswell, B. A., Green, C. W., & Schell, R. M. (2003). Training human service supervisors in aspects of PBS: Evaluation of a statewide, performance-based program. *Journal of Positive Behavior Interventions, 5,* 35−46.

Rosales, R., Gongola, L., & Homlitas, C. (2015). An evaluation of video modeling with embedded instructions to teach implementation of stimulus preference assessments. *Journal of Applied Behavior Analysis, 48,* 209−214.

Sarokoff, R. A., & Sturmey, P. (2004). The effects of behavioral skills training on staff implementation of discrete-trial teaching. *Journal of Applied Behavior Analysis, 37,* 535−538.

Severtson, J. M., & Carr, J. E. (2012). Training novice instructors to implement errorless discrete-trial teaching: A sequential analysis. *Behavior Analysis in Practice, 5,* 13−23.

Shook, G. L., & Favell, J. E. (2008). The Behavior Analyst Certification Board and the profession of behavior analysis. *Behavior Analysis in Practice, 1,* 44−48.

Sturmey, P. (1998). History and contribution of organizational behavior management to services for persons with developmental disabilities. *Journal of Organizational Behavior Management, 18*(2/3), 7−32.

Towery, D., Parsons, M. B., & Reid, D. H. (2014). Increasing independence within adult services: A program for reducing staff completion of daily routines for consumers with developmental disabilities. *Behavior Analysis in Practice, 7,* 61−69.

van den Pol, R. A., Reid, D. H., & Fuqua, R. W. (1983). Peer training of safety-related skills to institutional staff: Benefits for trainers and trainees. *Journal of Applied Behavior Analysis, 16,* 139−156.

van Vonderen, A., Duker, P., & Didden, R. (2010). Instruction and video feedback to improve staff's trainer behaviour and response prompting during one-to-one training with young children with severe intellectual disability. *Research in Developmental Disabilities, 31,* 1481−1490.

Weldy, C. R., Rapp, J. T., & Capocasa, K. (2014). Training staff to implement brief stimulus preference assessments. *Journal of Applied Behavior Analysis, 47,* 214−218.

Willner, A. G., Braukmann, C. J., Kirigin, K. A., Fixsen, D. L., Phillips, E. L., & Wolf, M. M. (1977). The training and validation of youth-preferred social behaviors of childcare personnel. *Journal of Applied Behavior Analysis, 10,* 219−230.

Functional Behavioral Assessments

3

Nathan A. Call[1,2], Mindy C. Scheithauer[1,2] and Joanna Lomas Mevers[1,2]
[1]Emory University School of Medicine, Atlanta, GA, United States, [2]Marcus Autism Center, Atlanta, GA, United States

Individuals with developmental disabilities and their caregivers face many challenges: for example, postsecondary educational, employment, and residential opportunities are frequently limited for these individuals (Billstedt, Gillberg, & Gillberg, 2005; O'Brien & Daggett, 2006), and social stigma can prevent social integration (Hayman, 1990). Although the factors that contribute to these challenges are many and varied, individuals who engage in problem behavior tend to experience the greatest constraints on opportunities for integration and independence (Hall, Bouldin, Andresen, & Ali, 2012). Furthermore, in addition to the negative effects for the individual who exhibits problem behavior, caregivers are also challenged (Davis & Gavidia-Payne, 2009). That is, behaviors such as aggression, noncompliance, and emotional outbursts negatively affect caregivers' quality of life, including decreased marital satisfaction (Hall et al., 2012) and diminished employment opportunities (Hartley, Barker, Baker, Seltzer, & Greenberg, 2012).

Fortunately, the literature on interventions for this population has, for some time, been replete with examples of successful behavioral treatments for problem behaviors (Corte, Wolfe, & Locke, 1971; Jones, Simmons, & Frankel, 1974; Lovaas & Simmons, 1969; Tate, 1972; Weiher & Harman, 1975). In a seminal paper, Carr (1977) summarized much of the research at the time by juxtaposing several of the prominent theories regarding the etiology of self-injurious behavior with a behavior analytic perspective. He noted that a number of studies showed that self-injurious behavior (SIB) was sensitive to reinforcement in the form of caregiver/therapist attention, access to preferred leisure items/activities, and escape from nonpreferred demands. Furthermore, many of the studies Carr reviewed demonstrated successful interventions that discontinued these consequences for SIB (i.e., extinction; Bucher & Lovaas, 1967; Ferster, 1964; Hamilton, Stephens, & Allen, 1967; Jones et al., 1974; Lovaas & Simmons, 1969; Wolf, Risley, Johnston, Harris, & Allen, 1967; Wolf, Risley, & Mees, 1964) or delivered them contingent upon the absence of SIB (Corte et al., 1971; Repp, Dietz, & Dietz, 1976). That is, these studies demonstrated that SIB could be successfully treated when an intervention is based upon an understanding of the reinforcers maintaining the behavior (i.e., its *function*).

To base a treatment on a problem behavior's function, it is necessary to accurately identify the reinforcer(s) that maintain it (Mace, 1994). Carr (1977) raised the possibility of identifying the function of a given individual's SIB experimentally

Applied Behavior Analysis Advanced Guidebook. DOI: http://dx.doi.org/10.1016/B978-0-12-811122-2.00003-6

by arranging conditions likely to evoke it and then delivering the hypothesized functional reinforcer contingent upon the occurrence of SIB. Shortly thereafter, Iwata, Dorsey, Slifer, Bauman, and Richman (1982) conducted this type of analysis. The experimenters arranged antecedents and consequences for SIB within discrete test conditions, each of which served as an analog to a situation in which SIB might occur in the natural environment. For example, in the social disapproval test condition, a therapist ignored the participant but delivered a mild reprimand if SIB occurred. Similarly, in the academic demand test condition, the therapist presented instructions to complete a task, but provided a break if the participant engaged in SIB. Elevated rates of SIB in a test condition relative to a control condition that included access to attention and no demands suggested that the corresponding consequence functioned as a reinforcer capable of maintaining SIB. Conversely, consistently elevated rates in an alone condition devoid of programmed consequences indicated the SIB was insensitive to environmental consequences and suggested that SIB instead produced its own source of reinforcement (i.e., *automatic* reinforcement). Subsequent extensions to this methodology added a test condition to evaluate whether problem behavior is maintained by access to preferred tangible items or activities (Day, Rea, Schussler, Larsen, & Johnson, 1988). The methodology described by Iwata et al., which is known as a *functional analysis* (FA), has been replicated numerous times since its introduction and is now broadly accepted as a best practice in the treatment of problem behavior (Beavers, Iwata, & Lerman, 2013; Hanley, Iwata, & McCord, 2003). Supporting this view are findings from research that function-based treatments are more effective than those that are not based upon the results of a functional behavioral assessment (FBA) (Campbell, 2003; Didden, Korzilius, van Oorsouw, & Sturmey, 2006; Heyvaert, Saenen, Campbell, Maes, & Onghena, 2014). There is even some evidence that the advent of these assessment methods have led to decreased reliance on the use of punishment-based interventions for problem behavior (Pelios, Morren, Tesch, & Axelrod, 1999).

The FA methodology introduced by Iwata et al. (1982) has undergone numerous extensions since its inception. For example, it has been adapted to a wide range of behaviors, including aggression (Derby et al., 2000; Mace, Page, Ivancic, & O'Brien, 1986), property destruction (Fisher, Lindauer, Alterson, & Thompson, 1998), bizarre vocalizations (Durand & Crimmins, 1987), selective mutism (Mace & West, 1986), vocal tics (Carr, Taylor, Wallander, & Reiss, 1996), stereotypy (Mace, Browder, & Lin, 1987), hand mouthing (Goh et al., 1995), breath holding (Kern, Mauk, Marder, & Mace, 1995), pica (Call, Simmons, Mevers, & Alvarez, 2015; Piazza, Hanley, & Fisher, 1996), noncompliance (Reimers et al., 1993; Rodriguez, Thompson, & Baynham, 2010; Wilder Harris, Reagan, & Rasey, 2007), elopement (Call et al., 2015; Call, Pabico, Findley, & Valentino, 2011), and many others. Other modifications include evaluating less common reinforcers (Falcomata, Roane, Muething, Stephenson, & Ing, 2012; Hausman, Kahng, Farrell, & Mongeon, 2009; O'Reilly, 1997) or the role of particular antecedent variables (Carr, Yarbrough, & Langdon, 1997; Huete & Kurtz, 2010; McAdam, DiCesare, Murphy, & Marshall, 2004). It has also been adapted to address constraints imposed by various settings, such as outpatient clinics (Wacker et al., 1994), homes (Harding, Wacker, Berg, Lee, & Dolezal, 2009), schools (Moore et al., 2002; Sterling-Turner, Robinson, & Wilczynski, 2001), or using a telehealth approach (Wacker et al., 2013). In addition, recognition of the value of identifying the function of problem behavior has led to the development of other assessment methods that do not involve direct manipulation of consequences, including descriptive observations (Anderson & Long, 2002; Touchette, MacDonald, & Langer, 1985) and indirect measures such as surveys or questionnaires (Matson & Vollmer, 1995; O'Neill et al., 1997).

Such proliferation highlights the need to define and categorize these various methods. Any procedure designed to identify the function of problem behavior is referred to as a *FBA*. These fall into three broad categories. *Indirect assessments* (IAs) involve those methods in which the function of an individual's problem behavior is determined based on sources of information other than direct observation. Examples of IAs include surveys, questionnaires, and structured/unstructured interviews. In contrast, *descriptive assessments* (DAs) involve determining function based on direct observation, but without any manipulation of the consequences for problem behavior. Examples of DAs include structured and unstructured observations in the natural environment and collection of data on environmental events correlated with the occurrence of problem behavior. Finally, FAs are FBAs in which a causal relationship is demonstrated between problem behavior and environmental antecedents and consequences through the direct manipulation of those events. For example, the methodology demonstrated by Iwata et al. (1982), and many of the refinements since then, fall into this category.

Status of practitioner training

FBA methodologies are included in the most recent version of the Board Certified Behavior Analyst (BCBA) Task List, which is a guide for training behavior analysts, including content for formal course work and practical experiences. Specifically, candidates for board certification should be able to "design and implement the full range of functional assessment procedures" (Behavior Analyst Certification Board, 2012a,b). In addition, the Behavior Analyst Certification Board (BACB) further delineates that course work must cover at least 30 hours of problem identification and assessment (Behavior Analyst Certification Board, 2012a,b). The BACB Guidelines for Responsible Conduct for Behavior Analysts (Behavior Analyst Certification Board, 2014) also stipulates that this process should include FBA strategies when problem behavior is the primary presenting concern. Together, these guidelines demonstrate that the BACB considers it important for behavior analysts to be well versed in, and capable of implementing, the full array of measures described in this chapter.

Acquisition of training in FBA methods is also endorsed by clinicians already credentialed as BCBAs. That is, in a survey of 724 behavioral practitioners (71.7%

Masters and 18.5% PhD levels) the vast majority of participants reported that they had received training in FBA strategies (Oliver, Pratt, & Normand, 2015). Results from the same survey indicated that almost all respondents had received formal training such as course work in the use of DAs (93%), followed by IAs (83%). Although still common, the fewest respondents received formal training in the use of FAs (77%). Fewer individuals reported obtaining practical experience in conducting each type of FBA (77% for DAs, 70% for IAs, and only 50% for FAs), suggesting that a sizeable portion of behavioral clinicians are receiving training on some FBA strategies through didactic training only. This limited access to direct experience with FBA methods may be a barrier to consumers receiving the most appropriate assessment methodology called for by each clinical situation.

Perhaps unsurprisingly, given the data on training in the various FBA methods, DAs and IAs are reportedly used most often by behavior analysts. Specifically, 93.6% of clinicians surveyed by Oliver et al. reported always or almost always utilizing DAs when targeting problem behavior, whereas only 36.3% of this sample endorsed always or almost always utilizing FAs. The researchers also asked respondents about barriers to implementation of FAs. Common themes included a lack of time, insufficient space, administrative policies, and lack of assistance from well-trained individuals (Oliver et al., 2015).

Recommendations for practitioner training

Although it is important that FBA methodologies are reviewed in a didactic format during training, it is equally important that trainees acquire hands-on experience with these methodologies through well-supervised practicum and field work. These experiences should encompass the full array of complexity and severity of problem behavior. Although some of the less intensive types of FBAs may be sufficient and appropriate for some individuals, it is likely that a practitioner will encounter a client at some point who will require a more in depth assessment, such as an FA. Acquiring hands-on experience with this type of assessment allows the clinician to determine if the assessment can be implemented in a particular setting, and if it cannot, then to understand when to refer to a provider who has the means to conduct the necessary assessment.

A secondary recommendation may be to address some of the misconceptions about the burden of conducting FAs during the training process. Functional analyses can indeed be more difficult to conduct than many IAs and DAs. However, if an FA is required to accurately identify the function of an individual's problem behavior, then doing so is likely to save time and resources, as treatment development is likely to be more efficient after accurately identifying the function. In addition, with appropriate modifications, FAs have been conducted in a variety of settings including schools, outpatient clinics, and community settings (Beavers et al., 2013). There are also several modifications that can be made to save time when conducting an FA (Neidert, Iwata, Dempsey, & Thomason-Sassi, 2013; Wilder, Chen, Atwell, Pritchard, & Weinstein, 2006). Given that a lack of resources is commonly presented as a reason for not conducting an FA, it may be important to focus on these modifications during training to highlight the feasibility of FAs.

Types of functional behavioral assessments

Each FBA method possesses relative advantages and disadvantages that may make them particularly well suited to a given behavior, individual, or clinical situation (Fig. 3.1). Thus, selecting the optimal methodology for a given clinical situation is one of the principle challenges for practitioners. Iwata and Dozier (2008) identified several factors that can be important to consider when selecting a specific FBA methodology, including the time available for assessment, risk of harm to people or property as a result of problem behavior, and the extent to which it is possible to exert control over the environment. In addition to these factors, the relative importance of demonstrating experimental control is an important consideration. For example, if treatments have been attempted unsuccessfully based upon results of a less rigorous model of FBA, a version capable of a more rigorous demonstration of experimental control may be needed. Also, strong demonstrations of experimental control may be important for certain groups of consumers, such as school systems or a skeptical parent. Finally, FBA methods can vary in the degree to which they incorporate input from the natural environment. Although some formats of FBA will intrinsically reflect naturally occurring contingencies, without taking precautions it is possible for others to demonstrate that problem behavior can be evoked and maintained by variables that are distinct from those that occur naturally. Although the number of specific FBA methods prohibits a comprehensive review of all of their relative advantages and disadvantages, the remainder of this chapter will attempt to highlight some of the approaches most commonly used.

Indirect assessments

As described above, IAs identify the function of problem behavior without direct observation by a clinician. Instead, the clinician relies on the report of caregivers who regularly interact with the individual whose behavior is being assessed (e.g., parents and teachers). IAs can be divided into two categories: interviews and questionnaires.

In many instances, useful information regarding the function of problem behavior can be gathered by interviewing caregivers. Interviews exist along a continuum from structured to unstructured formats. Structured interviews follow a fixed sequence of scripted questions that the clinician asks to gather information about common antecedents and consequences to problem behavior (e.g., Functional Analysis Interview; O'Neill et al., 1997). Common questions in these types of interviews include:

- What is happening when the behavior occurs?
- Where is the behavior most likely to occur?
- When is the behavior most likely to occur?
- Is problem behavior likely when you present the child with a difficult task?
- Is problem behavior likely when the child wants something?

Unstructured formats are open-ended and guided by the clinician. There are some published examples of this type of interview; however, little research has been conducted to validate these methodologies.

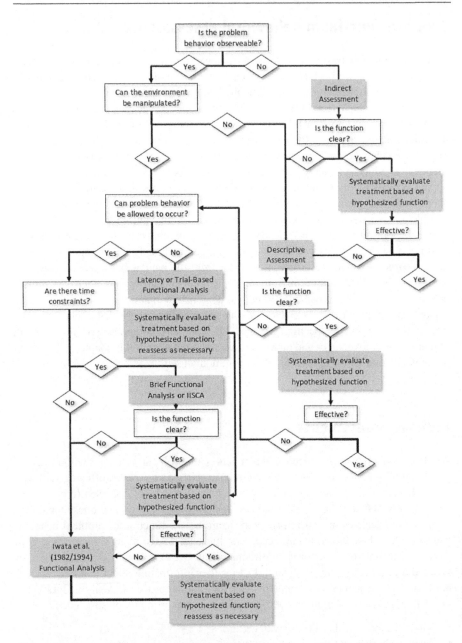

Figure 3.1 A potential decision-making process for selecting a Functional Behavioral Assessment methodology. If problem behavior is severe or the clinician has evidence of complexity (e.g., resistant to change from past quality interventions) all assessment methods should be used with direct and indirect being used to inform the functional analysis. If the setting does not allow the type of FBA suggested, clinicians should consider referring to centers where such an assessment is possible.

In contrast to interviews, which generally require clinicians to use their clinical judgment to interpret caregiver responses, questionnaires utilize some method of scoring their responses to reach a conclusion about the likely function of an individual's problem behavior. Some of the most common questionnaires include the Questions About Behavioral Function (QABF; Matson & Vollmer, 1995), Motivation Assessment Scale (MAS; Durand & Crimmins, 1988), and the Functional Assessment Screening Tool (FAST; Iwata, DeLeon, & Roscoe, 2013). When completing each of these measures, a caregiver responds to questions about the individual's problem behavior using a Likert-scale or yes/no format. The clinician then sums the scores from various items to determine the hypothesized function of problem behavior. For example, several items on each measure ask whether the individual is likely to engage in the targeted problem behavior when asked to do something he/she does not want to do. Consistently endorsing items from this category would result in an elevated score for escape, suggesting that the individual's problem behavior is maintained by this class of reinforcer. Similarly, several items address times when the problem behavior in question occurs when attention is diverted or a caregiver is busy. Frequently endorsing these items suggests that the problem behavior is maintained by access to attention.

Research base—Indirect assessments

The primary advantage of IAs is ease of implementation. Unlike direct measures, which can require significant time and resources to conduct observations, the measures listed above usually take less than 30 minutes to complete and can be filled out by a parent, teacher, or other individual who regularly interacts with the person whose problem behavior is being assessed. Scoring of IAs is also straightforward and does not require complex algorithms or norming, making them easily interpretable by clinicians with minimal training. Finally, when compared to FAs and DAs, IAs may be deemed more acceptable by stakeholders for three major reasons. First, these assessments do not require problem behavior to occur, eliminating concerns about safety or property destruction that may be raised with FBAs that base determinations of function on observing actual instances of the behavior in question. Second, the fact that IAs do not require direct observation of problem behavior also makes them well-suited to assessing problem behavior that occurs infrequently or by individuals who exhibit reactivity to observers. Third, they do not require any manipulation or modification of the natural environment, nor insertion of an observer into the natural environment. Thus, completing an IA has minimal disruption of ongoing activities. Finally, by their very nature, IAs have a high potential to reflect the contingencies maintaining problem behavior in the natural environment because conclusions about function are based upon caregivers descriptions of problem behavior as it occurs in daily life. However, the extent to which this is the case depends upon the accuracy of the caregiver's depiction.

The major disadvantage of IAs is their weak internal validity compared to other forms of FBAs. This is largely due to the fact that they demonstrate correlational rather than causal relationships between the problem behavior and environmental events. IAs are also limited by the challenges caregivers may face when attempting to identify events correlated with instances of problem behavior. In the natural environment, problem behavior is frequently preceded or followed by several antecedent and consequence events. For example, it is not uncommon for access to preferred items to also be restricted when a caregiver makes a demand, such as when a parent tells a child who is watching television to go brush his teeth. In this example, noncompliance on the part of the child may produce both escape from brushing his teeth and continued access to the television. Similarly, attention is a common consequence for problem behavior because it naturally produces a reaction from caregivers in most settings (St. Peter et al., 2005; Thompson & Iwata, 2007). That is, without training, caregivers are likely to either deliver a reprimand or attempt to calm a child engaging in problem behavior. Thus, caregivers may struggle to correctly identify all of the relevant antecedents and consequences of problem behavior when completing indirect IAs.

IAs also have the potential to incorporate any biases held by the individual completing the measure. For example, a caregiver's responses may be influenced by the most extreme or recent episodes of problem behavior, rather than typical instances, leading the individual to endorse items associated with outliers rather than more common episodes (Paulhus & Vizire, 2007). For example, if a child's most severe tantrum was related to removal of a toy, his caregiver may strongly endorse items from the IA associated with a tangible function, even if that tantrum was actually an outlier and other antecedents and consequences are more strongly correlated with tantrums.

Interpretation of IAs can also be challenging. For example, most IAs consistently produce a result suggesting that the problem behavior in question is maintained by one of the more commonly evaluated functions (e.g., escape, attention, tangible, and automatic/sensory). However, there is ample evidence that problem behavior can be maintained by idiosyncratic functions (Carr et al., 1997; Schlichenmeyer, Roscoe, Rooker, Wheeler, & Dube, 2013) that are typically not assessed by these measures. Similarly, there is clear evidence that problem behavior can serve multiple functions, especially when targeting multiple topographies of problem behavior (Beavers & Iwata, 2011). However, because several of the most commonly used IAs are interpreted by placing scores for each function in a hierarchy, it is not clear whether potential functions with elevated scores that are not the highest should be interpreted as an indication that the individual's problem behavior serves a second function.

To evaluate the internal validity of an IA, it is important to test a variety of psychometric properties, including reliability and validity. Several such aspects of IAs have been evaluated in the literature (e.g., Koritsas & Iacono, 2013; Shogren & Rojahn, 2003; Zaja, Moore, van Ingen, & Rojahn, 2010). Results from several of these studies are presented in Table 3.1. The structure of each instrument is determined by the number of unique factors the measure represents and the internal consistency within each factor. The QABF and MAS have each generally shown strong internal consistency within factors, whereas the FAST has variable consistency across factors. Second, test–retest reliability has been consistently reported for each of these measures. That is, when the same informant completes the assessment

Table 3.1 Psychometric properties of indirect measures—When more than one study assessed the same property of an indirect assessment this table reflects findings from the most recent and/or representative studies.

Measure	Number of items	Factors	Internal consistency (Cronbach's alpha)	Test–retest (intraclass correlation)	Interrater reliability (intraclass correlation)	Agreement with FA on identified functions
QABF	25 Likert-scale[a]	5 factors (attention, escape, nonsocial, tangible, and physical)[a]	.78–.90[c] .92–.96[i]	.61–.91[b] .76–.85[i]	59% agreement on identified functions[d] ICC = .56–.91[c] ICC = 53–.60[b] ICC = 51–.73[i]	56.3%[e]
MAS	16 Likert-scale[f]	4 factors (sensory, escape, attention, tangible, and physical)[f]	.73–.87[c]	.71–.88[b]	29% agreement on identified functions[g] ICC = .88–.91[c] ICC = .52–.73[b]	43.8%[e]
FAST	16 yes/no[h]	4 scales (attention/preferred items, escape from tasks/activities, sensory stimulation, and pain attenuation)[h]	.05–.77[i]	.57–.71[i]	64.8% agreement on identified function[h] ICC = .50–.63[i]	63.8%[h]

[a]Paclawskyj, Matson, Rush, Smalls, and Vollmer (2000).
[b]Shogren and Rojahn (2003).
[c]Koritsas and Iacono (2013).
[d]Nicholson, Konstantinidi, and Furniss (2006).
[e]Paclawskyj et al. (2001).
[f]Durand and Crimmins (1988).
[g]Zarcone et al. (1991).
[h]Iwata et al. (2013).
[i]Zaja, Moore, van Ingen, & Rojahm (2010).

at different times, the QABF, MAS, and FAST each produce moderate-to-high agreement between administrations.

The validity and reliability of these measures is not as strong when interrater reliability and agreement with FA procedures are assessed. Agreement across informants appears to differ depending on the methodology of assessing interrater agreement. Evaluations of intraclass correlations have generated only moderate agreement for all three measures (Shogren & Rojahn, 2003; Zaja et al., 2010), with the exception of the initial study evaluating the MAS (Durand & Crimmins, 1988), which reported high agreement. Although these IAs differed in terms of whether they identified the same function when completed by different respondents, with the MAS producing the worst (Zarcone, Rodgers, Iwata, Rourke, & Dorsey, 1991) and the FAST producing the best agreement (Iwata et al., 2013; 64.8%), all were generally poor. Finally, studies have evaluated the agreement between IAs and FAs (Iwata et al., 2013; Paclawskyj, Matson, Rush, Smalls, & Vollmer, 2001). Each of these studies demonstrated relatively poor agreement between the IA and FA, suggesting that they are unlikely to produce the same results as a FA. Given that FAs are generally regarded as the "gold-standard" against which other FBA formats are compared, such low agreement has led several to question the validity of results from these IAs (Hanley, 2012).

Implications for practice—Indirect assessments

Results from the research generate several clear implications for practice. First, IAs should always be considered for use in situations in which the setting precludes the use of more direct measures. For example, an IA may be most appropriate if stakeholders deem it unsafe or unacceptable to purposely evoke problem behavior or if the clinician does not have sufficient time to obtain a representative observation of problem behavior. However, it may be most appropriate to adopt a conservative approach to interpreting results from an IA. That is, results may be best viewed as suggesting the reinforcer(s) that are most likely to maintain problem behavior, but not as definitively ruling in or out any potential functions.

If a clinician must rely solely on the results of an IA, it is best practice to obtain information from multiple sources (e.g., parents, school personnel, respite care providers, siblings, etc.) to ensure that the most representative and thorough information is obtained. It can also be beneficial to have caregivers complete multiple forms of IAs (e.g., interview and more than one structured questionnaire). Identifying common themes when using a multisource and multimethod approach is ideal. If a clinician is confident of the results of an IA, he/she can begin treatment sooner, as opposed to taking the time to conduct a DA or FA. However, such a treatment should be systematically evaluated to ensure that it is based upon the correct function. If the intervention proves to be ineffective, one of the earliest considerations should be whether the results of the IA were inaccurate.

When more direct methods are possible, IAs can still serve a useful purpose as a means of obtaining information to guide direct assessments. For example, they can provide information about a caregiver's perceptions of problem behavior. This information can be used to increase the social validity of the intervention by ensuring that the behaviors targeted for intervention are those of greatest concern. They can also help to decrease the probability of a false negative finding from a FA by guiding the inclusion of idiosyncratic variables associated with the child's problem behavior that may not be included otherwise. For example, if IAs are completed prior to a FA and the results strongly suggest an escape function that is subsequently not identified in the FA, the IA can be revisited to determine whether an important aspect of demands was potentially missed in the FA. If this is not the case, it can also provide an important opportunity to debrief with caregivers about potential causes for the inconsistent results. For example, a caregiver may overestimate the degree to which demands consistently evoke problem behavior when completing the IA because they consistently accompany restriction of a preferred tangible item, which is actually serving as the antecedent that evokes the problem behavior in question. A clinician in this scenario could then use the results of the IA to guide a conversation on the relative role of demands. In another example, the caregiver may be referring to demands that are different from those included in the initial FA. In this situation, the clinician may be inclined to repeat the FA using different demands. In other words, IAs can serve as a useful compliment to direct assessments as a means of helping design direct assessments and engage stakeholders in the FBA process.

Descriptive assessments

A *DA* is a FBA that consists of direct observation of the interactions of the individual and the environment without systematic manipulation of antecedents or consequences. Common examples of DAs include collection of antecedent–behavior–consequence (ABC) data, scatterplots, and structured DAs. In addition, analyses of the conditional probability of consequences are a topic of relatively recent research.

DAs can be an important tool for: (1) developing hypotheses about the function of specific problem behaviors (Anderson & Long, 2002; English & Anderson, 2006); (2) obtaining information that can be important in the design of FAs (Anderson & Long, 2002; Tiger, Hanley, & Bessette, 2006); (3) providing an estimate of the frequency of problem behavior that can be used as a baseline for treatment in the natural environment (Rooker, Deleon, Borrero, Frank-Crawford, & Roscoe, 2015); and (4) helping caregivers better understand the relationship between problem behavior and the environment (Frea & Hepburn, 1999). However, DAs do not systematically manipulate potential consequences, and generally do not establish experimental control. Thus, similar to IAs, they demonstrate correlational rather than causal relationships between the problem behavior and the consequences that are maintaining it. As a result, conclusions about the function of problem behavior derived from DAs are considered less definitive than those that demonstrate a causal relationship (i.e., FAs).

ABC recording typically includes observation of the individual in his/her natural environment without arranging any specific antecedent events. Similarly, consequences for problem behavior are not programmed. Rather, the data-collector records the natural antecedents (e.g., location, individuals present, activities occurring, time of day, etc.), any relevant dimensions of the problem behavior (e.g., topography, duration, target, etc.), and the consequence(s) of the problem behavior (e.g., caregiver attention, a break from demands, access to a preferred toy, etc.) (Fig. 3.2). This approach can be helpful in detecting patterns that can be used to develop specific hypotheses about the function of the problem behavior. For example, after a week of ABC recording, it may become clear that the individual only engages in problem behavior when academic demands are placed and that breaks from those demands are the most common consequence. Such a result may lead a clinician to hypothesize that the problem behavior is likely to be maintained by negative reinforcement in the form of escape from demands. However, it is important to note that in this example only one antecedent and one consequence are described. Yet, as described above, in the natural environment there are often multiple types of antecedents and consequences correlated with problem behavior, making it more difficult to reach a definitive conclusion regarding function based upon results of ABC data alone.

A scatterplot is a graphic display of data that depicts the relationship between two variables (Pigott, Fantuzzo, & Gorsuch, 1987). Arranging data collected on

Setting/Time *Where/when did the behavior happen?*	Antecedent *What happened right before the behavior?*	Behavior *What was the behavior and what did it look like?*	Consequence *What happened right after the behavior?*
___/___/___ ___:___ am/pm Setting:	☐ Demand/work/chore ☐ Alone ☐ Denied access/told "no" ☐ Attending to other(s) ☐ Unknown ☐ Other Describe:	☐ Tantrum ☐ Self-injury ☐ Aggression ☐ Other: ____ Describe: How long did the behavior last? ☐ 0-15 min ☐ 15-30 min ☐ 30-60 min ☐ 60+ min	☐ Talk to/reprimand ☐ Demand removed ☐ Demand cont'd ☐ Item/toy given ☐ Didn't respond ☐ Other Describe:
___/___/___ ___:___ am/pm Setting:	☐ Demand/work/chore ☐ Alone ☐ Denied access/told "no" ☐ Attending to other(s) ☐ Unknown ☐ Other Describe:	☐ Tantrum ☐ Self-injury ☐ Aggression ☐ Other: ____ Describe: How long did the behavior last? ☐ 0-15 min ☐ 15-30 min ☐ 30-60 min ☐ 60+ min	☐ Talk to/reprimand ☐ Demand removed ☐ Demand cont'd ☐ Item/toy given ☐ Didn't respond ☐ Other Describe:
___/___/___ ___:___ am/pm Setting:	☐ Demand/work/chore ☐ Alone ☐ Denied access/told "no" ☐ Attending to other(s) ☐ Unknown ☐ Other Describe:	☐ Tantrum ☐ Self-injury ☐ Aggression ☐ Other: ____ Describe: How long did the behavior last? ☐ 0-15 min ☐ 15-30 min ☐ 30-60 min ☐ 60+ min	☐ Talk to/reprimand ☐ Demand removed ☐ Demand cont'd ☐ Item/toy given ☐ Didn't respond ☐ Other Describe:
___/___/___ ___:___ am/pm Setting:	☐ Demand/work/chore ☐ Alone ☐ Denied access/told "no" ☐ Attending to other(s) ☐ Unknown ☐ Other Describe:	☐ Tantrum ☐ Self-injury ☐ Aggression ☐ Other: ____ Describe: How long did the behavior last? ☐ 0-15 min ☐ 15-30 min ☐ 30-60 min ☐ 60+ min	☐ Talk to/reprimand ☐ Demand removed ☐ Demand cont'd ☐ Item/toy given ☐ Didn't respond ☐ Other Describe:

Figure 3.2 An example of an ABC data sheet.

problem behavior according to the time it occurred, or the status of some other environmental event, can be a helpful way to identify patterns that suggest the behavior's function. Scatterplots are most commonly used to evaluate the temporal distribution of a target behavior (Houlihan, Sloane, Jenson, & Levine, 1991; Kahng & Iwata, 1998; Persel, Persel, Ashely, & Krych, 1997; Symons, McDonald & Wehby, 1998; Touchette et al., 1985). To do so, instances of the targeted problem behavior are recorded, as well as the time it occurred, either within set intervals (e.g., 8:00—8:30 a.m.) or according to the individual's schedule (e.g., "Free Time"). For example, a preschool teacher could use a scatterplot to identify that problem behavior only occurred in the afternoon. Such a result would suggest potential antecedents or consequences that are correlated with that time of day, such as being tired, or a certain class activity that always happens in the afternoon (e.g., packing up to go home).

More complex analyses of data from DAs have also been used to determine the type and magnitude of the relationship between problem behavior and consequences. For example, the conditional probability of a particular consequence following problem behavior can be determined by dividing the number of times that sequence of events occurred by the total number of instances of the behavior (Schachtman & Reed, 1998). Thus, if a parent delivers attention following aggression 10 times, but there were an additional 20 instances of problem behavior that did not result in parental attention, the conditional probability of attention given aggression would be .33 (i.e., 10 divided by the total number of behaviors, or 30). The consequence(s) with the highest conditional probability can be considered most likely to function as a reinforcer that maintains the problem behavior (Lalli, Browder, Mace, & Brown, 1993; Mace & Lalli, 1991; Repp & Karsh, 1994). A slightly more sophisticated analysis involves comparing the probability of a consequence given the problem behavior of interest to the base rate or "background" probability of each consequence (McKerchar & Thompson, 2004; Vollmer et al., 2001). For example, if the conditional probability of attention following aggression is .33, but the probability of attention at any given moment is .45, then there is a negative contingency between aggression and parental attention, meaning aggression actually decreases the probability of attention from the parent (McKerchar & Thompson, 2004; Vollmer et al., 2001).

Several quantitative methods have been developed to calculate the probability of environmental events given problem behavior (McComas et al., 2009), some of which may be too complicated or time intensive for regular use in clinical settings. However, Martens et al. (2008) developed a relatively straightforward methodology for evaluating a "contingency space" by scoring each interval of time for the presence/absence of the problem behavior of interest, as well as each of the consequences being evaluated. The conditional probability of that consequence is calculated by dividing the number of times that consequence was delivered in the same interval that the target behavior occurred by the overall number of intervals in which the target behavior was present (see the equation below). This number can then be compared to the same calculation for the absence of target behavior (i.e., number of intervals with the consequence but no problem behavior divided by the total number of intervals with no problem behavior occurred) to establish the relative strength of the contingency. In case examples, Martens et al. showed that an intervention based on this type of DA was effective and that the measure was sensitive to detect changes in the caregiver's to problem behavior following parent training.

# of times the target behavior and consequence occur in the same interval

---

Total # of intervals in which target behavior occurred

Research base—Descriptive assessments

In general, research on DAs has not demonstrated strong correspondence with more well-controlled methodologies. For example, studies by Tarbox et al. (2009) and Thompson and Iwata (2007) both demonstrated poor correspondence between DAs and FAs. Not only did the results of the DA not correspond with those of the FA in these studies, the DAs frequently did not produce a clear determination of function. There are several potential explanations for these inconclusive results. For one, data collection during a DA frequently occurs in a manner that can produce reactivity on the part of the individual whose problem behavior is being targeted, as well as those who may be delivering consequences. For example, a teacher whose student is being observed may have a tendency to respond to problem behavior in the manner they believe they should, rather than in the manner they typically do. As a result, it may be difficult to identify the consequences typically produced in the natural environment. Kazdin (1979) provides several strategies for reducing such reactivity during direct observation. One such strategy is to contrive the situation in a manner that makes the caregiver less aware of being observed (e.g., observation occurs during an initial interview). The low correspondence between DA and FA results reported in the literature may also have to do with the duration of the observations conducted in the DAs in those studies. At least two studies have empirically evaluated the impact of the duration of observations necessary to obtain a good representation of problem behavior during a DA. Mudford, Beale, and Singh (1990) evaluated data collected using an interval data collection system in observations that ranged from 15 to 135 minutes in duration. They found that 30 minutes observations were sufficient to obtain a representative sample of problem behavior when it occurred at a relatively high rate (i.e., $\geq 50\%$ of intervals). However, lower rate behaviors (i.e., occurred in 10%−25% of intervals) required observations of up to 105 minutes for an accurate sample. In a follow-up study conducted by Tiger et al. (2013), the authors found that 10 minutes observation intervals are sufficient to get an accurate estimate of behavior when there was little variability in the rate of problem behavior. However, observation intervals of 60 minutes were necessary when there was greater variability in order to obtain representative data. This study provides some guidance to clinicians on the appropriate duration of observations conducted as part of a DA.

Another consideration when analyzing results of a DA is the likelihood of identifying an attention function. Because attention tends to be delivered frequently regardless of whether problem behavior preceded it (St. Peter et al., 2005), DAs may have a tendency to overestimate the prevalence of attention functions. For example, Tarbox et al. (2009) identified an attention function for 75% of cases when function was determined using a DA. In contrast, an attention function was only identified for 16.7% of those cases when using a FA.

Implications for practice—Descriptive assessments

DAs can be a useful form of FBAs, particularly to identify less common antecedents and consequences or as a tool to help inform FAs. In situations when the problem behavior is relativity straightforward, in that it only occurs in a limited number of contexts, a DA in conjunction with IAs may be sufficient to develop a hypothesis regarding the function of a particular behavior. DAs can also help gather information necessary to design a FA. Data collected via a DA can be used to develop specific conditions that would otherwise not be included in a standard FA. For example, a DA may suggest that social attention is aversive, leading a therapist to include a social avoidance condition (see Harper, Iwata, & Camp, 2013) in the initial FA that would otherwise not be included. Information from a DA can also be used to eliminate unnecessary conditions saving time and resources. For example, if results from a DA suggest that problem behavior never occurs when academic demands are presented, but frequently does when preferred items are restricted, a clinician may elect to save time in a subsequent FA by either not conducting an escape condition, or running fewer escape sessions compared to those for the tangible condition.

In many ways, DAs represent a middle ground between IAs and FAs. As described above, DAs can be as brief as 10 minutes, representing a significant time savings over most formats of FAs, but still more time intensive than most IAs. Similarly, as is true of IAs, DAs do not require a clinician to exert control over the environment. Yet, as with FAs, it is still necessary to be able to observe the target behavior. Therefore, DAs may not be advised if there are concerns about harm to the individual, caregivers, or the environment. However, DAs may be the FBA method most likely to generate results that reflect the natural environment because problem behavior and related environmental variables can be directly observed within the context of regular daily activities. Furthermore, although it cannot be said that a DA demonstrates experimental control because there is no manipulation of an independent variable, the fact that results are based upon multiple direct observations alleviates concerns of IAs being overly reliant on caregiver report.

Functional analyses

The FA methodology developed by Iwata et al. is the most rigorously evaluated FBA procedure, and is considered the gold-standard (Beavers, Iwata et al., 2013; Hanley, Iwata, & McCord, 2003). However, some procedural variability is common within the framework of this methodology. Beavers et al (2013) conducted a review of 435 FAs appearing in the literature and found that 90.1% of published accounts of FAs included a condition to test for social negative reinforcement. In these conditions, a therapist typically presents some potentially aversive stimulus (frequently a demand to complete a nonpreferred activity), with a brief break from that stimulus contingent upon problem behavior. Similarly, 86.2% of the FAs reviewed by Beavers et al. included a condition designed to test for a positive reinforcement function in the form of attention. Although less common, FAs also frequently included a test for a social positive reinforcement in the form of preferred tangible items (40.1% of published accounts). In these conditions, a therapist typically creates an establishing operation for the relevant reinforcer by providing brief presession access to the potential reinforcer before restricting it as the session commences (O'Reilly et al., 2009). If the targeted problem behavior occurs, the reinforcer is delivered for some fixed duration (Fisher, Piazza, & Chaing, 1996), typically 20 or 30 seconds. Rates of problem behavior in the test conditions are compared with those of a control condition, most often within a multielement design (80.5% of published FAs). The control is commonly a play condition in which the individual is provided with either continuous, or fixed-time delivery of attention and or preferred items and no demands are placed.

Beavers et al. (2013) also reported that 55.9% of published FAs included a test condition for automatic reinforcement. Typically, this consists of either an alone condition (Iwata et al., 1982/1994) in which the individual is observed without the presence of a therapist, or an ignore condition (Bloom, Iwata, Fritz, Roscoe, & Carreau, 2011) that includes the presence of a therapist who continuously restricts their attention. Regardless of which condition is included, neither includes programmed consequences for problem behavior. The ignore condition includes the benefit that an individual can intervene quickly if problem behavior reaches dangerous levels. However, the presence of a therapist may also signal the availability of attention, making it harder for the individual to differentiate between the ignore and attention conditions. Finally, when problem behavior is consistently elevated in an alone/ignore condition, or elevated in all conditions, it is common to confirm that problem behavior is maintained by automatic reinforcement using an extended series of alone sessions (Vollmer, Marcus, Ringdahl, & Roane, 1995). If the problem behavior gradually decreases across successive alone sessions, it can be concluded that the behavior is sensitive to extinction from a social reinforcer. However, the persistence of problem behavior across sessions suggests that the behavior is insensitive to social consequences.

Beavers found that 78.5% of the published examples of FAs occurred in inpatient or outpatient clinical settings. Such settings may afford the greatest possibility of exerting the kind of control necessary to regularly conduct FAs. However, outside of these settings, a number of pragmatic barriers, including time and space constraints or the lack of a setting in which problem behavior can be allowed to occur safely, can prevent some clinicians from utilizing this method. As a result, researchers and clinicians have developed a number of variations of this methodology that may be considered, depending on the circumstances.

One of the simplest variations on the Iwata et al. (1982/1994) FA methodology, which can reduce the time required to complete the analysis, is to only test for one function. Some of the earliest forms of FAs used this methodology to identify the function of problem behavior by comparing the rate of problem behavior in a single test condition to that observed in a control condition (Corte et al., 1971; Jones et al., 1974; Lovaas & Simmons, 1969). Because the assessment only evaluates one potential function, the control condition need only control for one antecedent and consequence. This method may be most appropriate when a clinician has a clear hypothesis regarding the function of the target behavior based on indirect or descriptive sources of information.

As with the single-function test, the brief functional analysis (BFA) also reduces the time required to conduct a FA. Although there are several versions of BFAs in the literature, the methodology that best typifies the BFA format (i.e., Northup et al., 1991) included only a few sessions, each with a decreased duration (e.g., 5 minutes). Northup et al. employed an experimental design, later described as a brief multielement (Wacker, Berg, Harding, & Cooper-Brown, 2004), in which the sequence of test and control conditions was based upon hypotheses from prior indirect or DAs rather than a random or fixed order. In addition, the authors demonstrated experimental control, in part through the inclusion of a contingency reversal phase in which the reinforcer shown to maintain problem behavior was delivered contingent upon an alternative behavior (e.g., mands).

Other modifications encompassed by the BFA methodology include having caregivers conduct sessions (Cooper, Wacker, Sasso, Reimers, & Donn, 1990; Derby et al., 1992; Harding, Wacker, Cooper, Millard, & Jensen-Kovalan, 1994). In addition to requiring fewer clinical personnel to conduct the BFA, having caregivers act in the role of therapist has the potential to decrease the time required to conduct a BFA if their presence serves as a discriminative stimulus. That is, because the individual whose behavior is being assessed is unlikely to have a prior history with a novel therapist, their presence is usually not associated with the availability of reinforcement for problem behavior. Although some individuals' problem behavior has generalized sufficiently to occur regardless of who plays the role of the therapist, for others problem behavior tends to be infrequent until it has repeatedly contacted the relevant contingencies. This fact is highlighted by a study by Kurtz, Fodstad, Huete, and Hagopian (2013) in which caregiver-conducted FAs identified the function of problem behavior for 52 participants when staff-conducted FAs were undifferentiated. Thus, using caregivers as therapists may decrease the length of the BFA or the probability of a false negative result if rates of problem behavior would otherwise remain low or not occur at all while such a history is established with a novel therapist. However, increasing the probability of evoking problem behavior quickly in this way comes at the expense of a possible reduction in procedural fidelity. In contrast to clinical staff who can be trained to implement the conditions of a BFA with high fidelity, caregivers may be more likely to commit fidelity errors.

Problem behavior is frequently part of a response class, in which several topographies of behavior (both appropriate and problematic) are maintained by the same functional reinforcer (Harding et al.,2001; Lalli, Mace, Wohn, & Livezey, 1995;

Richman, Wacker, Asmus, Casey, & Andelman, 1999). The risk of harm from problem behavior that occurs during a FA can potentially be reduced by shifting the focus to identifying the function of the less destructive behaviors that are part of this response class. Doing so requires identifying behaviors that reliably precede the targeted topography of problem behavior. For example, if aggression consistently follows yelling, then a clinician may elect to conduct an FA of yelling because it is less likely to cause harm. If the FA of yelling shows that the behavior is maintained by access to preferred tangible items, then by inference, the aggressive behavior likely serves the same function. Fritz, Iwata, Hammond, and Bloom (2013) developed a methodology for identifying precursors to severe problem behavior within discrete trials that included antecedent conditions hypothesized to evoke the targeted topography of problem behavior. After 10 trials in which the targeted problem behavior occurred, therapists scored videos to identify behaviors that reliably preceded the problem behavior. For seven of the eight participants that received a subsequent FA, the same reinforcer maintained problem behavior for both the identified precursor and target topography.

Most FAs make determinations about function based on the relative rate of problem behavior in test and control conditions. However, there can be situations in which latency to the first instance of problem behavior can have some advantages as a dependent variable (Thomason-Sassi, Iwata, Neidert, & Roscoe, 2011). For example, latency has the advantage of decreasing the number of instances of problem behavior that must be observed as part of the assessment. Also, latency may be better suited as a unit of analysis when conducting FAs of certain behaviors, such as elopement, pica, or disrobing, which alter the environment or cannot be easily repeated.

Literature reviews have shown that most FAs appearing in the literature have been conducted in well-controlled clinical settings (Hanley et al., 2003). However, the advantages of such settings are generally not available to all clinicians (Ervin, Radford, Bertsch, & Piper, 2001; Sterling-Turner et al., 2001). To address this limitation, several researchers have evaluated whether FAs can be conducted under naturalistic conditions. Similarly, Sigafoos and Saggers (1995) introduced a method that takes advantage of ongoing activities by embedding a FA into a classroom setting using 2-minute probes. Each probe included a 1-minute test segment in which the individual was exposed to the antecedent event hypothesized to evoke problem behavior (i.e., the establishing operation present phase). For example, if testing for an escape function, the therapist presented demands to complete nonpreferred work. The therapist then delivered access to the corresponding reinforcer (e.g., breaks) contingent upon problem behavior. The subsequent minute comprised an establishing operation absent control segment, in which the hypothesized antecedent (e.g., demands) was removed by providing continuous access to the hypothesized reinforcer (e.g., a continuous break). The experimenters terminated either segment if problem behavior occurred. The function of problem behavior was determined by comparing the likelihood of the behavior occurring in the establishing operation (EO) present phase to the EO absent phase for each reinforcer evaluated.

More recently, Hanley, Jin, Vanselow, and Hanratty (2014) described a FA methodology that selected potential antecedents and consequences for inclusion based on the results of an open-ended IA. Thus, the experimenters referred to this form of FA as an interview informed structured contingency analysis (IISCA). The IISCA also differed from a more typical FA in that a single test condition included simultaneous presentation of all of the antecedents hypothesized to evoke problem behavior. Similarly, problem behavior resulted in delivery of all of the associated consequences together. The control condition delivered these same reinforcers continuously. Differentiation in the rate of problem behavior observed in the test and control condition was interpreted as each of the consequences included in the test condition serving as functional reinforcers for the problem behavior. Treatments that included functional communication training in which problem behavior was on extinction and requests produced all of the consequences evaluated in the IISCA effectively reduced each participant's problem behavior. The authors suggested that the IISCA has the potential to dramatically decrease the amount of time required to complete a FA, and can detect instances in which interactions between reinforcers play an important role in the maintenance of problem behavior.

Research base—Functional analysis

There have been numerous demonstrations and replications of FAs and treatment analyses using small-n methods (Beavers et al., 2013; Hanley, Iwata, & McCord, 2003). Thus, FAs are generally regarded as the most valid form of FBA. Although each of the variations to the typical FA methodology presented above (e.g., BFA, latency-based FAs) have some empirical support, none have undergone the same degree of replication and evaluation as the methodology originally described by Iwata et al. (1982/1994). Thus, evaluating the validity or utility of these variations for a particular clinical application should be based upon the amount of systematic evaluation it has undergone in the research literature, the degree to which it differs from the original methodology, its feasibility given the particulars of the clinical context, and the presence of viable alternatives for the clinical application in question.

For several of the variations presented above, results have been compared to those of a FA that adhered to the methods of Iwata et al (1982/1994). For example, in a comparison of separate FAs that used either the rate of problem behavior or latency to problem behavior as the dependent measure, results corresponded for nine of 10 participants (Thomason-Sassi et al., 2011). Similarly, in an initial study on precursor behavior, results of FAs of precursors resulted in identifying the same function as a FA of the problem behavior targeted for intervention for all four participants (Smith & Churchill, 2002). In a subsequent follow-up study, a comparison of FAs of precursor behaviors identified using the methodology proposed by Fritz et al. (2013) and a subsequent FA found that the same reinforcer maintained problem behavior in both FAs for seven of eight participants. However, although such favorable preliminary evidence likely justifies the use of these variations in situations where the methodology described by Iwata et al. (1994) are not viable, additional study is likely important prior to widespread adoption.

Other variations to FA methodology, such as the BFA, have undergone more replication and evaluation. For example, in two separate studies comparing results from BFAs and FAs with three and two participants respectively, results matched across FA type for all participants (Tincani, Castrogiavanni, & Axelrod, 1999; Wallace & Knights, 2003). Derby et al. (1992) summarized the results from 79 BFAs conducted with individuals with developmental disabilities. Problem behavior was observed in 66% of the cases. Of those who exhibited problem behavior during the BFA, a function was identified for 75%. In other words, the BFA was able to identify a functional reinforcer for half of the participants. Given these results, the propensity to produce false negative results has emerged as a potential limitation of the BFA format (Wacker et al., 2004).

Other studies have evaluated the correspondence between FAs and simulated BFAs that were produced by truncating data from a more typical FA to evaluate one of the ways in which the BFA departed from typical FA methodology. For example, Kahng and Iwata (1999) evaluated the impact of basing a determination of function on a limited number of sessions by comparing the results of a "BFA" that was constructed from the first session of each condition from a typical FA to the results of the full FA. Results of the two methods corresponded for 66% of the participants. In a similar study, results from 15 minutes FA sessions were reanalyzed using only the first 5 or 10 minutes to compare the impact of using shorter sessions in a BFA (Wallace & Iwata, 1999). For 46 participants, the comparisons of the 5 and 15 minutes sessions resulted in only three disagreements. Although these studies showed moderate correspondence between assessments, they should be interpreted with caution because they isolated the impact of only one of the several factors that are typically manipulated in a BFA. Additionally, these did not always manipulate these factors in the same manner as is customary in a BFA. For example, in the study by Kahng et al., the BFA only included a single session from each condition, and the sequence of conditions was randomized. In contrast, BFAs often include repetition of certain conditions, and the sequence is frequently arranged based on results of indirect or DAs to maximize the probability of determining the function.

The trial-by-trial format of FA has also undergone several replications. In a study that employed procedures similar to those of Sigafoos and Saggers (1995) in a vocational setting, Wallace and Knights (2003) found that the trial-based FA produced the same results as a FA that employed the methodology described by Iwata et al. (1982/1994) for two of their three participants. More recently, LaRue et al. (2010) also replicated the trial-based FA methodology, but used latency to the first instance of maladaptive behavior as an alternative measurement. These authors showed correspondence between the trial-based FA using latency to first response and the traditional FA for four of five participants, with partial correspondence for the remaining participant. Significantly, for both of these studies, the trial-based FA required considerably less time than the traditional FA (88.4% reduction for Wallace & Knights and 84.8% for LaRue et al.).

As one of the newer variations on FA methodology, the IISCA has undergone less replication than some of the other variations. However, Jessel, Hanley, and Ghaemmaghami (2016) presented 30 replications of the IISCA, showing that a function could be identified in an average duration of 25 minutes. Within subject data analysis also suggested that the first session could be used to determine the function of problem behavior in 80% of cases (EO present vs EO absent). Although these results are promising, to date the IISCA has almost exclusively been replicated by the group of researchers that first presented it in the literature. In the one replication by an outside group of researchers the findings were not as favorable. Fisher, Greer, Romani, Zangrillo, and Owen (2016) compared results from an IISCA with those of a typical FA and found that one participant did not engage in problem behavior in either assessment, but the results for the remaining four participants' were better accounted for by the FA than the IISCA. That is, these participants' problem behavior was maintained by individual contingencies and did not show any evidence that problem behavior was sensitive to interactions between reinforcers. This result suggests that, for these participants, the IISCA may have produced a false positive result by implicating the presence of a function that was not identified in the FA. The implication is that the IISCA may increase the probability of including extraneous treatment components unnecessarily. However, despite these findings, there is evidence that interactions between reinforces can occur (Call & Lomas Mevers, 2014), even if they did not do so for these five participants. Furthermore, it is also true that the IISCA required significantly less time to complete in the study by Fisher et al. Thus, the potential for a false positive finding, and the clinical implications thereof, may need to be balanced against the time required to complete a typical FA. Finally, as with most of the other variations to FA methodology presented here and elsewhere in the literature, additional research is necessary to replicate and validate these procedures, as well as determine the clinical applications for which they are best suited.

Implications for practice—Functional analyses

As mentioned above, FAs are considered more rigorous than other formats of FBAs because they can demonstrate causal relationships between problem behavior and consequences. Thus, they hold the potential to produce meaningful results when clinicians are able to conduct them safely and with good fidelity. Yet, a wealth of research has explored the utility of alternative formats of FAs that can be adopted when circumstances make it impossible to do so. Each of the FA variations presented in this section possesses relative strengths and weaknesses that make them better suited to address different limitations of the typical FA methodology. For example, the single function test, BFA, trial-based, and IISCA have all attempted to decrease the time commitment required by a typical FA. In addition, replacing rate measures with latency to the first instance of problem behavior as a dependent variable may be a means of decreasing the number of instances of problem behavior that must be allowed to occur. Finally, although FAs have been conducted in a wide range of settings, all of the variations presented here require the ability to exercise control over the environment in order to establish the relevant antecedents and consequences for each condition. Environments that do not allow for this kind of environmental manipulation may not be suited to conducting an FA, and another form of FBA should be considered.

Although each of the FA variations presented here as alternatives to the method described by Iwata et al. (1982/1994) have a distinct profile of advantages and disadvantages, they also share some commonalities. For example, most have not been shown to consistently be able to determine whether problem behavior is maintained by automatic reinforcement. Results of a FA suggest that problem behavior is automatically-maintained if it occurs across all conditions or persists despite the absence of any programmed consequences (Vollmer et al., 1995). Thus, FAs frequently require additional time, or separate confirmatory analyses, to conclude that problem behavior serves an automatic function. Given that a central purpose of most of the FA variations described above is to decrease time, they may not be well suited for this purpose. If a clinician suspects problem behavior is maintained by automatic reinforcement, they may be best served to either conduct a traditional FA or beginning with the confirmatory analysis (Vollmer et al., 1995).

Several of the FA variations described above manipulate more than one element of the traditional FA methodology. Although they are presented as a "package" in the literature, clinicians may wish to consider implementing separate variations, or even novel combinations, depending on clinical circumstances. For example, several of the FA variations described above use the results of a previous indirect or DA to inform the selection or sequence of test conditions (e.g., single-function test, BFA, and IISCA). However, even when implementing a more traditional FA, there are many potential benefits to conducting a prior IA or DA: such assessments can provide useful information regarding the quality of certain reinforcers, or idiosyncratic reinforcers that are delivered in the natural environment. Similarly, although caregivers served as therapists in several studies on BFAs, incorporating this element into a more traditional FA may be appropriate if there are concerns that problem behavior may not generalize to a novel therapist (Kurtz et al., 2013).

Of all of the formats of FBAs, FAs are clearly best equipped to demonstrate experimental control. However, certain procedural details can affect the extent to which findings from a FA are relevant to the natural environment. That is, it is possible to demonstrate that problem behavior is maintained by a particular type of reinforcer, but if that reinforcer bears little resemblance to those delivered in the natural environment, treatments based on its results may not be very effective. Similarly, failure to include specific qualities of reinforcers that maintain problem behavior in the natural environment may lead to a false negative finding in a FA (Kodak, Northup, & Kelley, 2007). Thus, taking care to make a FA representative of the contingencies that may be in place in the natural environment is an important step, regardless of the FA format employed.

Practice guidelines checklist

Indirect assessments

- When relying solely on IAs, it is important to get information from multiple sources and to systematically evaluate your hypothesis by measuring treatment success.

- If treatment is not successful, the clinician should make accommodations to conduct a more intensive FBA, including direct observations or functional analyses. If this is not feasible within the available setting, it may be necessary to refer the client to another clinician/setting in which a more thorough FBA is feasible.
- If the setting allows for direct assessment of function, IAs should be utilized to guide the format of direct assessments and engage caregivers in the FBA process.

Descriptive assessments

- Observation intervals should be sufficiently long to obtain a representative sample of the target behavior.
- Observations should be conducted in a manner that minimizes reactivity.
- Consider conducting a more thorough FBA (e.g., a FA) if treatment based upon a DA fails to achieve a clinically significant reduction in problem behavior.

Functional analyses

- Precede a FA with indirect and/or DAs whenever possible to identify specific types and qualities of potential reinforcers delivered in the natural environment so that they can be evaluated systematically.
- In certain clinical settings, it may be necessary to alter one or more properties of the traditional FA methodology to decrease the time, increase safety, or evaluate certain topographies or functions.

References

Anderson, C. M., & Long, E. S. (2002). Use of structured descriptive assessment methodology to identify variables affecting problem behavior. *Journal of Applied Behavior Analysis*, *35*(2), 137−154. Available from http://dx.doi.org/10.1901/jaba.2002.35-13.

Beavers, G. A., & Iwata, B. A. (2011). Prevalence of multiply controlled problem behavior. *Journal of Applied Behavior Analysis*, *44*(3), 593−597. Available from http://dx.doi.org/10.1901/jaba.2011.44-593.

Beavers, G. A., Iwata, B. A., & Lerman, D. C. (2013). Thirty years of research on the functional analysis of problem behavior. *Journal of Applied Behavior Analysis*, *46*(1), 1−21. Available from http://dx.doi.org/10.1002/jaba.30.

Behavior Analyst Certification Board (2012a). Coursework requirements for BACB credentials: 4th ed. Task List. Retrieved from http://bacb.com/wp-content/uploads/2015/05/BACB_CourseContentAllocation.pdf.

Behavior Analyst Certification Board (2012b). Fourth Edition Task List. Retrieved from http://bacb.com/wp-content/uploads/2016/03/160101-BCBA-BCaBA-task-list-fourth-edition-english.pdf.

Behavior Analyst Certification Board (2014). Professional and Ethical Compliance Code for Behavior Analysts. Retrieved from http://bacb.com/wp-content/uploads/2016/03/160321-compliance-code-english.pdf.

Billstedt, E., Gillberg, C., & Gillberg, C. (2005). Autism after adolescence: Population-based 13-to 22-year follow-up study of 120 individuals with autism diagnosed in childhood. *Journal of Autism and Developmental Disorders*, *35*(3), 351−360.

Bloom, S. E., Iwata, B. A., Fritz, J. N., Roscoe, E. M., & Carreau, A. B. (2011). Classroom application of a trial-based functional analysis. *Journal of Applied Behavior Analysis*, *44*(1), 19−31.

Bucher, B., & Lovaas, O. I. (1967). *Use of aversive stimulation in behavior modification. Miami symposium on the prediction of behavior*. Coral Gables, FL: University of Miami Press.

Call, N. A., & Lomas Mevers, J. E. (2014). The relative influence of motivating operations for positive and negative reinforcement on problem behavior during demands. *Behavioral Interventions*, *29*(1), 4−20.

Call, N. A., Pabico, R. S., Findley, A. J., & Valentino, A. L. (2011). Differential reinforcement with and without blocking as treatment for elopement. *Journal of Applied Behavior Analysis*, *44*(4), 903−907.

Call, N. A., Simmons, C. A., Mevers, J. E. L., & Alvarez, J. P. (2015). Clinical outcomes of behavioral treatments for pica in children with developmental disabilities. *Journal of Autism and Developmental Disorders*, *45*(7), 2105−2114.

Campbell, J. M. (2003). Efficacy of behavioral interventions for reducing problem behavior in persons with autism: A quantitative synthesis of single-subject research. *Research in Developmental Disabilities*, *24*(2), 120−138.

Carr, E. G. (1977). The motivation of self-injurious behavior: A review of some hypotheses. *Psychological bulletin*, *84*(4), 800.

Carr, E. G., Yarbrough, S. C., & Langdon, N. A. (1997). Effects of idiosyncratic stimulus variables on functional analysis outcomes. *Journal of Applied Behavior Analysis*, *30*(4), 673−686. Available from http://dx.doi.org/10.1901/jaba.1997.30-673.

Carr, J. E., Taylor, C. C., Wallander, R. J., & Reiss, M. L. (1996). A functional-analytic approach to the diagnosis of a transient tic disorder. *Journal of Behavior Therapy and Experimental Psychiatry*, *27*(3), 291−297.

Cooper, L. J., Wacker, D. P., Sasso, G. M., Reimers, T. M., & Donn, L. K. (1990). Using parents as therapists to evaluate appropriate behavior of their children: Application to a tertiary diagnostic clinic. *Journal of Applied Behavior Analysis*, *23*(3), 285−296.

Corte, H. E., Wolf, M. M., & Locke, B. J. (1971). A comparison of procedures for eliminating self-injurious behavior of retarded adolescents. *Journal of Applied Behavior Analysis*, *4*, 201−213.

Davis, K., & Gavidia-Payne, S. (2009). The impact of child, family, and professional support characteristics on the quality of life in families of young children with disabilities. *Journal of Intellectual and Developmental Disability*, *34*(2), 153−162.

Day, R. M., Rea, J. A., Schussler, N. G., Larsen, S. E., & Johnson, W. L. (1988). A functionally based approach to the treatment of self-injurious behavior. *Behavior Modification*, *12*(4), 565−589.

Derby, K. M., Hagopian, L., Fisher, W. W., Richman, D., Augustine, M., Fahs, A., et al. (2000). Functional analysis of aberrant behavior through measurement of separate response topographies. *Journal of Applied Behavior Analysis*, *33*, 113−117.

Derby, K. M., Wacker, D. P., Sasso, G., Steege, M., Northup, J., Cigrand, K., & Asmus, J. (1992). Brief functional assessment techniques to evaluate aberrant behavior in an outpatient setting: A summary of 79 cases. *Journal of Applied Behavior Analysis*, *25*(3), 713−721.

Didden, R., Korzilius, H., van Oorsouw, W., & Sturmey, P. (2006). Behavioral treatment of challenging behaviors in individuals with mild mental retardation: Meta-analysis of single-subject research. *American Journal on Mental Retardation, 111*(4), 290−298.

Durand, V. M., & Crimmins, D. B. (1987). Assessment and treatment of psychotic speech in an autistic child. *Journal of Autism and Developmental Disorders, 17*(1), 17−28.

Durand, V. M., & Crimmins, D. B. (1988). Identifying the variables maintaining self-injurious behavior. *Journal of Autism and Developmental Disorders, 18*(1), 99−117. Available from http://dx.doi.org/10.1007/BF02211821.

English, C. L., & Anderson, C. M. (2006). Evaluation of the treatment utility of the analog functional analysis and the structured descriptive assessment. *Journal of Positive Behavior Interventions, 8*(4), 212−229. Available from http://dx.doi.org/10.1177/10983007060080040401.

Ervin, R. A., Radford, P. M., Bertsch, K., & Piper, A. L. (2001). A descriptive analysis and critique of the empirical literature on school-based functional assessment. *School Psychology Review, 30*(2), 193.

Falcomata, T. S., Roane, H. S., Muething, C. S., Stephenson, K. M., & Ing, A. D. (2012). Functional communication training and chained schedules of reinforcement to treat challenging behavior maintained by terminations of activity interruptions. *Behavior Modification, 36*(5), 630−649.

Ferster, C. B. (1964). *Positive reinforcement and behavioral deficits of autistic children. Conditioning techniques in clinical practice and research* (pp. 255−274). Springer Berlin Heidelberg.

Fisher, W. W., Greer, B. D., Romani, P. W., Zangrillo, A. N., & Owen, T. M. (2016). Comparisons of synthesized and individual reinforcement contingencies during functional analysis. *Journal of Applied Behavior Analysis,* .

Fisher, W. W., Lindauer, S. E., Alterson, C. J., & Thompson, R. H. (1998). Assessment and treatment of destructive behavior maintained by stereotypic object manipulation. *Journal of Applied Behavior Analysis, 31*(4), 513−527.

Fisher, W. W., Piazza, C. C., & Chiang, C. L. (1996). Effects of equal and unequal reinforcer duration during functional analysis. *Journal of Applied Behavior Analysis, 29*(1), 117−120.

Frea, W. D., & Hepburn, S. L. (1999). Teaching parents of children with autism to perform functional assessments to plan interventions for extremely disruptive behaviors. *Journal of Positive Behavior Interventions, 1*(2), 112.

Fritz, J. N., Iwata, B. A., Hammond, J. L., & Bloom, S. E. (2013). Experimental analysis of precursors to severe problem behavior. *Journal of Applied Behavior Analysis, 46*(1), 101−129.

Goh, H. L., Iwata, B. A., Shore, B. A., DeLeon, I. G., Lerman, D. C., Ulrich, S. M., & Smith, R. G. (1995). An analysis of the reinforcing properties of hand mouthing. *Journal of Applied Behavior Analysis, 28*(3), 269−283.

Hall, A. G., Bouldin, E. D., Andresen, E. M., & Ali, A. K. (2012). Maintaining employment among caregivers of individuals on a medicaid waitlist for services. *Journal of Disability Policy Studies, 23*(2), 121−128.

Hanley, G. P. (2012). Functional assessment of problem behavior: Dispelling myths, overcoming implementation obstacles, and developing new lore. *Behavior Analysis in Practice, 5*(1), 54−72, Retrieved from file:///C:/Users/Scheithauer/Downloads/i1998-1929-5-1-54.pdf.

Hanley, G. P., Iwata, B. A., & McCord, B. E. (2003). Functional analysis of problem behavior: A review. *Journal of Applied Behavior Analysis, 36*(2), 147−185.

Hanley, G. P., Jin, C. S., Vanselow, N. R., & Hanratty, L. A. (2014). Producing meaningful improvements in problem behavior of children with autism via synthesized analyses and treatments. *Journal of Applied Behavior Analysis, 47*(1), 16−36.

Hamilton, J., Stephens, L., & Allen, P. (1967). Controlling aggressive and destructive behavior in severely retarded institutionalized residents. *American Journal of Mental Deficiency, 1967*(71), 852−856.

Harding, J. W., Wacker, D. P., Berg, W. K., Barretto, A., Winborn, L., & Gardner, A. (2001). Analysis of response class hierarchies with attention-maintained problem behaviors. *Journal of Applied Behavior Analysis, 34*(1), 61−64.

Harding, J. W., Wacker, D. P., Berg, W. K., Lee, J. F., & Dolezal, D. (2009). Conducting functional communication training in home settings: A case study and recommendations for practitioners. *Behavior Analysis in Practice, 2*(1), 21.

Harding, J., Wacker, D. P., Cooper, L. J., Millard, T., & Jensen-Kovalan, P. (1994). Brief hierarchical assessment of potential treatment components with children in an outpatient clinic. *Journal of Applied Behavior Analysis, 27*(2), 291−300.

Harper, J. M., Iwata, B. A., & Camp, E. M. (2013). Assessment and treatment of social avoidance. *Journal of Applied Behavior Analysis, 46*(1), 147−160.

Hartley, S. L., Barker, E. T., Baker, J. K., Seltzer, M. M., & Greenberg, J. S. (2012). Marital satisfaction and life circumstances of grown children with autism across 7 years. *Journal of Family Psychology, 26*(5), 688.

Hausman, N., Kahng, S., Farrell, E., & Mongeon, C. (2009). Idiosyncratic functions: Severe problem behavior maintained by access to ritualistic behaviors. *Education and Treatment of Children, 32*(1), 77−87.

Hayman, R. L., Jr (1990). *Presumptions of justice: Law, politics, and the mentally retarded parent. Harvard Law Review* (pp. 1201−1271).

Heyvaert, M., Saenen, L., Campbell, J. M., Maes, B., & Onghena, P. (2014). Efficacy of behavioral interventions for reducing problem behavior in persons with autism: An updated quantitative synthesis of single-subject research. *Research in Developmental Disabilities, 35*(10), 2463−2476.

Houlihan, D., Sloane, H. N., Jenson, W. R., & Levine, H. D. (1991). Treating preschool children with multiple behavior problems: Testing for the response covariation phenomenon. *Behavioral Residential Treatment, 6*(5), 321−340. Available from http://dx.doi.org/10.1002/bin.2360060503.

Huete, J. M., & Kurtz, P. F. (2010). Therapist effects on functional analysis outcomes with young children. *Research in Developmental Disabilities, 31*(3), 804−810.

Iwata, B. A., DeLeon, I. G., & Roscoe, E. M. (2013). Reliability and validity of the functional analysis screening tool. *Journal of Applied Beahvior Analysis, 46*(1), 271−284. Available from http://dx.doi.org/10.1002/jaba.31.

Iwata, B. A., Dorsey, M. F., Slifer, K. J., Bauman, K. E., & Richman, G. S. (1982). Toward a functional analysis of self-injury. *Analysis and Intervention in Developmental Disabilities, 2*(1), 3−20.

Iwata, B. A., Dorsey, M. F., Slifer, K. J., Bauman, K. E., & Richman, G. S. (1994). Toward a functional analysis of self-injury. *Journal of Applied Behavior Analysis, 27*(2), 197−209.

Iwata, B. A., & Dozier, C. L. (2008). Clinical application of functional analysis methodology. *Behavior Analysis in Practice, 1*(1), 3−9.

Jessel, J., Hanley, G. P., & Ghaemmaghami, M. (2016). Interview-informed synthesized contingency analyses: Thirty replications and reanalysis. *Journal of Applied Behavior Analysis, 49*(3), 576−595.

Jones, F. H., Simmons, J. Q., & Frankel, F. (1974). An extinction procedure for eliminating self-destructive behavior in a 9-year-old autistic girl. *Journal of Autism and Childhood Schizophrenia, 4*, 241−250.

Kahng, S., & Iwata, B. A. (1998). Play versus alone conditions as controls during functional analyses of self-injurious escape behavior. *Journal of Applied Behavior Analysis, 31*(4), 669−672.

Kahng, S., & Iwata, B. A. (1999). Correspondence between outcomes of brief and extended functional analyses. *Journal of Applied Behavior Analysis, 32*(2), 149−160.

Kazdin, A. E. (1979). Unobtrusive measures in behavioral assessment. *Journal of Applied Behavior Analysis, 12*(4), 713−724.

Kern, L., Mauk, J. E., Marder, T. J., & Mace, F. C. (1995). Functional analysis and intervention for breath holding. *Journal of Applied Behavior Analysis, 28*(3), 339−340.

Kodak, T., Northup, J., & Kelley, M. E. (2007). An evaluation of the types of attention that maintain problem behavior. *Journal of Applied Behavior Analysis, 40*(1), 167−171.

Koritsas, S., & Iacono, T. (2013). Psychometric comparison of the Motivation Assessment Scale (MAS) and the Questions about Behavioral Function (QABF). *Journal of Intellectual Disability Research, 57*(8), 747−757. Available from http://dx.doi.org/10.1111/jir.12022.

Kurtz, P. F., Fodstad, J. C., Huete, J. M., & Hagopian, L. P. (2013). Caregiver- and staff-conducted functional analysis outcomes: A summary of 52 cases. *Journal of Applied Behavior Analysis, 46*(4), 738−749.

Lalli, J. S., Browder, D. M., Mace, F. C., & Brown, D. K. (1993). Teacher use of descriptive analysis data to implement interventions to decrease students' problem behaviors. *Journal of Applied Behavior Analysis, 26*(2), 227−238.

Lalli, J. S., Mace, F. C., Wohn, T., & Livezey, K. (1995). Identification and modification of a response-class hierarchy. *Journal of Applied Behavior Analysis, 28*(4), 551−559.

LaRue, R. H., Lenard, K., Weiss, M. J., Bamond, M., Palmieri, M., & Kelley, M. E. (2010). Comparison of traditional and trial-based methodologies for conducting functional analyses. *Research in Developmental Disabilities, 31*(2), 480−487.

Lovaas, O. I., & Simmons, J. Q. (1969). Manipulation of selfdestruction in three retarded children. *Journal of Applied Behavior Analysis, 2*, 143−157.

Mace, F. C. (1994). The significance and future of functional analysis methodologies. *Journal of Applied Behavior Analysis, 27*(2), 385−392.

Mace, F. C., Browder, D. M., & Lin, Y. (1987). Analysis of demand conditions associated with stereotypy. *Journal of Behavior Therapy and Experimental Psychiatry, 18*(1), 25−31.

Mace, F. C., & Lalli, J. S. (1991). Linking descriptive and experimental analyses in the treatment of bizarre speech. *Journal of Applied Behavior Analysis, 24*(3), 553−562.

Mace, F. C., Page, T. J., Ivancic, M. T., & O'Brien, S. (1986). Analysis of environmental determinants of aggression and disruption in mentally retarded children. *Applied Research in Mental Retardation, 7*(2), 203−221.

Martens, B. K., DiGennaro, F. D., Reed, D. D., Szczech, F. M., & Rosenthal, B. D. (2008). Contingency space analysis: An alternative method for identifying contingent relations from observational data. *Journal of Applied Behavior Analysis, 41*(1), 69−81.

Mace, F. C., & West, B. J. (1986). Analysis of demand conditions associated with reluctant speech. *Journal of Behavior Therapy and Experimental Psychiatry*, *17*(4), 285−294.

Matson, J. L., & Vollmer, T. R. (1995). *User's guide: Questions about behavioral function (QABF)*. Baton Rouge, LA: Scientific Publishers, Inc.

McAdam, D. B., DiCesare, A., Murphy, S., & Marshall, B. (2004). The influence of different therapists on functional analysis outcomes. *Behavioral Interventions*, *19*(1), 39−44.

McComas, J. J., Moore, T., Dahl, N., Hartman, E., Hoch, J., & Symons, F. (2009). Calculating contingencies in natural environments: Issues in the application of sequential analysis. *Journal of Applied Behavior Analysis*, *42*(2), 413−423.

McKerchar, P. M., & Thompson, R. H. (2004). A descriptive analysis of potential reinforcement contingencies in the preschool classroom. *Journal of Applied Behavior Analysis*, *37*(4), 431−444.

Moore, J. W., Edwards, R. P., Sterling-Turner, H. E., Riley, J., DuBard, M., & McGeorge, A. (2002). Teacher acquisition of functional analysis methodology. *Journal of Applied Behavior Analysis*, *35*(1), 73−77.

Mudford, O. C., Beale, I. L., & Singh, N. N. (1990). The representativeness of observational samples of different durations. *Journal of Applied Behavior Analysis*, *23*(3), 323−331.

Neidert, P. L., Iwata, B. A., Dempsey, C. M., & Thomason-Sassi, J. L. (2013). Latency of response during the functional analysis of elopement. *Journal of Applied Behavior Analysis*, *46*(1), 312−316. Available from http://dx.doi.org/10.1002/jaba.11.

Nicholson, J., Konstantinidi, E., & Furniss, F. (2006). On some psychometric properties of the questions about behavioral function (QABF) scale. *Research in Developmental Disabilities*, *27*(3), 337−352. Available from http://dx.doi.org/10.1016/j.ridd.2005.04.001.

Northup, J., Wacker, D., Sasso, G., Steege, M., Cigrand, K., Cook, J., & DeRaad, A. (1991). A brief functional analysis of aggressive and alternative behavior in an outclinic setting. *Journal of Applied Behavior Analysis*, *24*(3), 509−522.

O'Brien, M., & Daggett, J. A. (2006). *Beyond the autism diagnosis: A professional's guide to helping families* (p. 21285). Baltimore, MD: Brookes Publishing Company. PO Box 10624.

Oliver, A. C., Pratt, L. A., & Normand, M. P. (2015). A survey of functional behavior assessment methods used by behavior analysts in practice. *Journal of Applied Behavior Analysis*, *48*(4), 817−829. Available from http://dx.doi.org/10.1002/jaba.256.

O'Neill, R. E., Horner, R. H., Albin, R. W., Sprague, J. R., Storey, K., & Newton (1997). *Functional assessment and program development for problem behavior: A practical handbook* (2nd ed.). Belmont, CA: Wadsworth.

O'Reilly, M., Lang, R., Davis, T., Rispoli, M., Machalicek, W., Sigafoos, J., ... Carr, J. (2009). A systematic examination of different parameters of presession exposure to tangible stimuli that maintain problem behavior. *Journal of Applied Behavior Analysis*, *42* (4), 773−783.

O'Reilly, M. F. (1997). Functional analysis of episodic self-injury correlated with recurrent otitis media. *Journal of Applied Behavior Analysis*, *30*(1), 165−167.

Paclawskyj, T., Matson, J., Rush, K., Smalls, Y., & Vollmer, T. R. (2001). Assessment of the convergent validity of the Questions About Behavioral Function scale with analogue functional analysis and the Motivation Assessment Scale. *Journal of Intellectual Disability Research*, *45*(6), 484−494. Available from http://dx.doi.org/10.1046/j.1365-2788.2001.00364.x.

Paclawskyj, T. R., Matson, J. L., Rush, K. S., Smalls, Y., & Vollmer, T. R. (2000). Questions about behavioral function (QABF): A behavioral checklist for functional assessment of aberrant behavior. *Research in Developmental Disabilities, 21*(3), 223−229. http://dx.doi.org/10.1016/S0891-4222(00)00036-6.

Paulhus D.L. and Vazire S., The self-report method. In R.W. Robins, R. C. Fraley, & R. F. Krueger (Eds.), Handbook of research methods in personality psychology (pp. 224−239). New York: Guildford.

Pelios, L., Morren, J., Tesch, D., & Axelrod, S. (1999). The Impact of functional analysis methodology on treatment choice for self-injurious and aggressive behavior. *Journal of Applied Behavior Analysis, 32*(2), 185−195.

Persel, C. S., Persel, C. H., Ashley, M. J., & Krych, D. K. (1997). The use of noncontingent reinforcement and contingent restraint to reduce physical aggression and self−injurious behaviour in a traumatically brain injured adult. *Brain Injury, 11*(10), 751−760. Available from http://dx.doi.org/10.1080/026990597123124.

Piazza, C. C., Hanley, G. P., & Fisher, W. W. (1996). Functional analysis and treatment of cigarette pica. *Journal of Applied Behavior Analysis, 29*(4), 437−450.

Pigott, H. E., Fantuzzo, J. W., & Gorsuch, R. L. (1987). Further generalization technology: Accounting for natural covariation in generalization assessment. *Journal of Applied Behavior Analysis, 20*(3), 273−278. Available from http://dx.doi.org/10.1901/jaba.1987.20-273.

Reimers, T. M., Wacker, D. P., Cooper, L. J., Sasso, G. M., Berg, W. K., & Steege, M. W. (1993). Assessing the functional properties of noncompliant behavior in an outpatient setting. *Child & Family Behavior Therapy, 15*(3), 1−15.

Repp, A. C., Deitz, S. M., & Deitz, D. E. D. (1976). Reducing inappropriate behaviors in classrooms and in individual sessions through DRO schedules of reinforcement. *Mental Retardation, 14*, 11−15.

Repp, A. C., & Karsh, K. G. (1994). Hypothesis-based interventions for tantrum behaviors of persons with developmental disabilities in school settings. *Journal of Applied Behavior Analysis, 27*(1), 21−31.

Richman, D. M., Wacker, D. P., Asmus, J. M., Casey, S. D., & Andelman, M. (1999). Further analysis of problem behavior in response class hierarchies. *Journal of Applied Behavior Analysis, 32*(3), 269−283.

Rodriguez, N. M., Thompson, R. H., & Baynham, T. Y. (2010). Assessment of the relative effects of attention and escape on noncompliance. *Journal of Applied Behavior Analysis, 43*(1), 143−147.

Rooker, G. W., DeLeon, I. G., Borrero, C. W., Frank-Crawford, M. A., & Roscoe, E. M. (2015). Reducing ambiguity in the functional assessment of problem behavior. *Behavioral Interventions, 30*(1), 1−35. Available from http://dx.doi.org/10.1002/bin.1400.

Schachtman, T. R., & Reed, P. (1998). Optimization: Some factors that facilitate and hinder optimal performance in animals and humans. In W. O'Donohue (Ed.), *Learning and behavior* (pp. 301−333). Needham Heights, MA: Allyn & Bacon.

Schlichenmeyer, K. J., Roscoe, E. M., Rooker, G. W., Wheeler, E. E., & Dube, W. V. (2013). Idiosyncratic variables affecting functional analysis outcomes: A review (2001−2010). *Journal of Applied Behavior Analysis, 46*(1), 339−348. Available from http://dx.doi.org/10.1002/jaba.12.

Shogren, K. A., & Rojahn, J. (2003). Convergent reliability and validity of the Questions about Behavioral Function and the Motivation Assessment Scale: A replication study. *Journal of Developmental & Physical Disabilities, 15*(4), 367. Available from http://dx.doi.org/10.1023/A:1026314316977.

Sigafoos, J., & Saggers, E. (1995). A discrete-trial approach to the functional analysis of aggressive behaviour in two boys with autism. *Australia and New Zealand Journal of Developmental Disabilities*, *20*(4), 287–297.

Smith, R. G., & Churchill, R. M. (2002). Identification of environmental determinants of behavior disorders through functional analysis of precursor behaviors. *Journal of Applied Behavior Analysis*, *35*(2), 125–136.

Symons, F. J., McDonald, L. M., & Wehby, J. H. (1998). Functional assessment and teacher collected data. *Education and Treatment of Children*, *21*, 135–159.

St. Peter, C. C., Vollmer, T. R., Bourret, J. C., Borrero, C. S., Sloman, K. N., & Rapp, J. T. (2005). On the role of attention in naturally occurring matching relations. *Journal of Applied Behavior Analysis*, *38*(4), 429–443. Available from http://dx.doi.org/10.1901/jaba.2005.172-04.

Sterling-Turner, H. E., Robinson, S. L., & Wilczynski, S. W. (2001). Functional assessment of distracting and disruptive behaviors in the school setting. *School Psychology Review*, *30*(2), 211.

Tarbox, J., Wilke, A. E., Najdowski, A. C., Findel-Pyles, R. S., Balasanyan, S., Caveney, A. C., ... Tia, B. (2009). Comparing indirect, descriptive, and experimental functional assessments of challenging behavior in children with autism. *Journal of Developmental and Physical Disabilities*, *21*(6), 493–514. Available from http://dx.doi.org/10.1007/s10882-009-9154-8.

Tate, B. G. (1972). Case study: Control of chronic self-injurious behavior by conditioning procedures. *Behavior Therapy*, *3*, 72–83.

Thompson, R. H., & Iwata, B. A. (2007). A comparison of outcomes from descriptive and functional analyses of problem behavior. *Journal of Applied Behavior Analysis*, *40*(2), 333–338. Available from http://dx.doi.org/10.1901/jaba.2007.56-06.

Thomason-Sassi, J. L., Iwata, B. A., Neidert, P. L., & Roscoe, E. M. (2011). Response latency as an index of response strength during functional analyses of problem behavior. *Journal of Applied Behavior Analysis*, *44*(1), 51–67.

Tiger, J. H., Hanley, G. P., & Bessette, K. K. (2006). incorporating descriptive assessment results into the design of a functional analysis: A case example involving a preschooler's hand mouthing. *Education and Treatment of Children*, *29*, 107–124.

Tiger, J. H., Miller, S. J., Mevers, J. L., Mintz, J. C., Scheithauer, M. C., & Alvarez, J. (2013). On the representativeness of behavior observation samples in classrooms. *Journal of Applied Behavior Analysis*, *46*(2), 424–435.

Tincani, M. J., Castrogiavanni, A., & Axelrod, S. (1999). A comparison of the effectiveness of brief versus traditional functional analyses. *Research in Developmental Disabilities*, *20*(5), 327–338.

Touchette, P. E., MacDonald, R. F., & Langer, S. N. (1985). A scatter plot for identifying stimulus control of problem behavior. *Journal of Applied Behavior Analysis*, *18*(4), 343–351.

Vollmer, T. R., Borrero, J. C., Wright, C. S., Camp, C. V., & Lalli, J. S. (2001). Identifying possible contingencies during descriptive analyses of severe behavior disorders. *Journal of Applied Behavior Analysis*, *34*(3), 269–287.

Vollmer, T. R., Marcus, B. A., Ringdahl, J. E., & Roane, H. S. (1995). Progressing from brief assessments to extended experimental analyses in the evaluation of aberrant behavior. *Journal of Applied Behavior Analysis*, *28*(4), 561–576.

Wacker, D. P., Berg, W. K., Cooper, L. J., Derby, K. M., Steege, M. W., Northup, J., & Sasso, G. (1994). The impact of functional analysis methodology on outpatient clinic services. *Journal of Applied Behavior Analysis*, *27*(2), 405–407.

Wacker, D. P., Lee, J. F., Dalmau, Y. C. P., Kopelman, T. G., Lindgren, S. D., Kuhle, J., Pelzel, K. E., & Waldron, D. B. (2013). Conducting functional analyses of problem behavior via telehealth. *Journal of Applied Behavior Analysis, 46*(1), 31−46.

Wacker, D., Berg, W., Harding, J., & Cooper-Brown, L. (2004). Use of brief experimental analyses in outpatient clinic and home settings. *Journal of Behavioral Education, 13*(4), 213−226.

Wallace, M. D., & Iwata, B. A. (1999). Effects of session duration on functional analysis outcomes. *Journal of Applied Behavior Analysis, 32*(2), 175−183.

Wallace, M. D., & Knights, D. J. (2003). An evaluation of a brief functional analysis format within a vocational setting. *Journal of Applied Behavior Analysis, 36*(1), 125−128.

Weiher, R. G., & Harman, R. E. (1975). The use of omission training to reduce self-injurious behavior in a retarded child. *Behavior Therapy, 6*, 261−268.

Wilder, D. A., Chen, L., Atwell, J., Pritchard, J., & Weinstein, P. (2006). Brief functional analysis and treatment of tantrums associated with transitions in preschool children. *Journal of Applied Behavior Analysis, 39*(1), 103−107. Available from http://dx.doi.org/10.1901/jaba/2006.66-04.

Wilder, D. A., Harris, C., Reagan, R., & Rasey, A. (2007). Functional analysis and treatment of noncompliance by preschool children. *Journal of Applied Behavior Analysis, 40*(1), 173−177.

Wolf, M., Risley, T., Johnston, M., Harris, F., & Allen, E. (1967). Application of operant conditioning procedures to the behavior problems of an autistic child: A follow-up and extension. *Behaviour Research and Therapy, 5*(2), 103−111.

Wolf, M. M., Risley, T., & Mees, H. (1964). Application of operant conditioning procedures to the behavior problems of an autistic child. *Behaviour Research and Therapy*, 305−312.

Zaja, R. H., Moore, L., Van Ingen, D. J., & Rojahn, J. (2010). Psychometric comparison of the functional assessment instruments QABF, FACT, and FAST for self-injurious, stereotypic and aggressive/destructive behaviour. *Journal of Applied Research in Intellectual Disabilities, 24*(1), 18−28. Available from http://dx.doi.org/10.1111/j.1468-3148.2010.00569.x.

Zarcone, J. R., Rodgers, T. A., Iwata, B. A., Rourke, D. A., & Dorsey, M. F. (1991). Reliability analysis of the Motivation Assessment Scale: A failure to replicate. *Research in Developmental Disabilities, 12*(4), 349−360. http://dx.doi.org/10.1016/0891-4222(91)90031-M.

Further reading

Alter, P. J., Conroy, M. A., Mancil, G. R., & Haydon, T. (2008). A comparison of functional behavior assessment methodologies with young children: Descriptive methods and functional analysis. *Journal of Behavioral Education, 17*(2), 200−219. Available from http://dx.doi.org/10.1007/s10864-008-9064-3.

McCord, B. E., Thomson, R. J., & Iwata, B. A. (2001). Functional analysis and treatment of self-injury associated with transitions. *Journal of Applied Behavior Analysis, 34*(2), 195−210.

Piazza, C. C., Hanley, G. P., Bowman, L. G., Ruyter, J. M., Lindauer, S. E., & Saiontz, D. M. (1997). Functional analysis and treatment of elopement. *Journal of Applied Behavior Analysis, 30*(4), 653−672.

Social Validity Assessment

Eric A. Common and Kathleen Lynne Lane
University of Kansas, Lawrence, KS, United States

4

Wolf (1978) described social validity as how the field of applied behavior analysis (ABA) found its heart. In the introductory issue of the *Journal of Applied Behavior Analysis* (JABA), Don Baer indicated the purpose of JABA was "... for the publication of applications of the analysis of behavior to problems of social importance" (as cited in Wolf, 1978, p. 203): the very essence of social validity.

In this chapter, we define the term *social validity* and address the important topic of social validity assessment. Specifically, the intent is to provide behavioral practitioners with pragmatic direction and recommendation regarding social validity assessment. We begin by introducing the relevance of social validity assessment for practicing professionals such as school psychologists, board certified behavior analysts, registered behavior technicians, and behavior specialists. Here, we provide a concise discussion of the history of social validity, explaining how the assessment of social validity (both pre- and postintervention efforts) became—and continues to be—a priority in the field of ABA. We discuss the relation between social validity, fidelity of implementation (e.g., treatment integrity), and generalization and maintenance (e.g., performance outcomes). Then, we focus on practical applications of social validity: (1) the importance of assessing social validity at each level of prevention, (2) the importance of assessing social validity from all stakeholders involved in any intervention effort, and (3) the range of methods for measuring social validity. Finally, we conclude with a summary of practical guidelines, noting salient essential learning from this chapter.

Assessing social validity: A priority in the field of applied behavior analysis

Baer, Wolf, and Risley (1968) published a seminal article, "Some Current Dimensions of Applied Behavior Analysis," in *JABA*. In this article, Baer et al. discussed important features of ABA:

> *Thus, the evaluation of a study which purports to be an applied behavior analysis ... must be* applied, behavioral, *and* analytic; *in addition, it should be* technological, conceptually systematic, *and* effective, *and it should display some* generality *(Baer et al., 1968, p. 92).*

Applied Behavior Analysis Advanced Guidebook. DOI: http://dx.doi.org/10.1016/B978-0-12-811122-2.00004-8

The content of this article had such a profound impact on the field, 20 years later Baer, Wolf, and Risley (1987) published an update on behavioral research, "Some Still-Current Dimensions of Applied Behavior Analysis." In this later publication, they indicated social validity (the extent to which all the consumers of an intervention like it; Baer et al., 1987, p. 322), should serve as a secondary measure of intervention effectiveness.

Considering ABA is the application of behavioral science in real-world settings such as schools, community, and industry to address socially important issues, social validity is a keystone variable of inquiry theoretically grounded in ABA (Lane, Oakes, Lusk, Cantwell, & Schatschneider, 2016). Namely, the field of ABA introduced social validity to describe such notions of social and cultural importance, relevance, significance, and validity. The secondary focus on social validity in intervention research reflects ABA's commitment to effecting desired changes in behaviors to enhance and improve people's lives by selecting behaviors to change that are socially significant.

Social validity is not one person's opinion; rather researchers, practitioners, and families must select behaviors to change while weighing the consideration of one' child, client, student, or subject (Kazdin, 1977). Specifically, the construct of social validity refers to the (1) social significance of treatment or intervention goals, (2) social acceptability of treatment or intervention procedures, and (3) social importance of effects resulting from treatment or intervention (Kazdin, 1977; Wolf, 1978).

Social significance of the goals

Validating the social significance of behavior change goals begins with a clear description of those goals, including selecting and defining socially important target behaviors and performance criterion. Fawcett (1991) recommended social validation of the goals occurs at three levels when assessing the importance of goals: (1) the broad social goal (e.g., improved teaching, enhanced social competencies, and decreased at-risk behavior), (2) the categories of behavior hypothesized to be related to the broad social goal (e.g., teaching—provide frequent opportunities to respond, reinforcement), and (3) the responses constituting the behavior category of interest (e.g., reinforcement—using behavior specific praise). To ensure correct intervention goals are identified and agreed upon prior to treatment design and implementation, the behavior analyst and relevant stakeholders are encouraged to assess social validity prior to treatment design and implementation. Implicit to selecting socially important goals in applied settings, goals should focus on socially important outcomes such as improving one's quality of life, social status, or educational experience (Lane & Beebe-Frankenberger, 2004).

In some instance, the behavior analysts, the client, and/or additional relevant stakeholders will have conflicted opinions when establishing goals. For example, a parent may want the behavior analyst to develop goals around decoding for reading, a teacher may prioritize decreasing elopement behavior outside of the classroom. A multidisciplinary team with the support of a strong behavior analyst can assess social validity by rating goals from each stakeholders' perspective to help home in on what target behavior to prioritize. Cooper, Heron, and Heward (2007) recommend one way to minimize and resolve conflicts such as these is to obtain participation of all relevant stakeholders in the goal determination process, including short- and long-term goals. For example, Dardig and Heward (1981) offer a systematic approach for prioritizing Individual Education Program goals across stakeholders. This process includes: (1) introducing stakeholders, (2) brainstorming possible goals, (3) determining criterion for prioritizing goals, (4) rating of goals individually and independently using a five-point Likert-type scale across relevant stakeholders (0 = no or never to 4 = yes or always), (5) aggregating individual responses across raters, and (6) prioritizing list of annual goals. Facilitators of this process should not commit a priori to whichever goal is top ranked, rather this process can be viewed as a heuristic to identify areas of agreement and disagreement which can lead to further discussion. In the example posed, the team may prioritize the student's academic engagement inside the classroom which is incompatible with elopement behavior and can work toward academic tasks related to decoding.

Social significance of the intervention goals should be assessed prior to treatment to determine whether the intervention is addressing an important or keystone behavior to solve a problem or promote desired outcomes. This should occur again after the intervention, to determine if the goals were indeed pivotal, producing meaningful and lasting behavior changes (Lane & Beebe-Frankenberger, 2004), and behavioral cusps, a special type of behavior change providing the learner with new opportunities to access other behaviors, contingencies, environments, and reinforcers (Rosales-Ruiz & Baer, 1997).

Social acceptability of intervention procedures

Validating the social acceptability of intervention procedures involves obtaining input from stakeholders regarding the procedures proposed to attain intervention goals. Relevant, efficient, positive intervention procedures that minimize disruption to the environment are more likely to achieve desired levels of social acceptability than more cumbersome intervention procedures. Prevention and intervention efforts with high levels of social acceptability increase the likelihood intervention agents and relevant stakeholders will sustain a strong commitment toward implementation and continued treatment until the goal is achieved (Gresham, 1998; Hanley, 2010; Kazdin, 1981; Reimers, Wacker, & Koeppl, 1987). In the consultation literature, social acceptability of procedures is known as treatment acceptability (Carter, 2007, 2008a, 2008b), defined by Kazdin (1980) as judgment of treatments by actual or potential stakeholders, including potential consumers of the treatment (hereby referred to as participant).

Lennox and Miltenberger (1990) conceptualized treatment acceptability across 12 critical indicators grouped into four different factors: efficacy considerations, secondary effects, social/legal implications, and practical considerations. More recently, Carter (2008b) recommended future work in conceptualizing treatment acceptability across four emerging issues: (1) assessment procedures related to evaluation of treatment acceptability, (2) consideration for both the immediacy of treatment effects and potential for aversive effects, (3) treatment precedence in consideration of treatment effectiveness and topography of behavior, (4) potential participant preference for treatments that do are not considered least restrictive, and (5) the potential for the practitioner to have influence on the participant in an interactive relationship across parties (Carter, 2008a).

Social acceptability of the intervention procedures should be assessed preceding treatment to ensure all relevant stakeholders agree the procedures are reasonable for the intervention setting (e.g., home, classroom, and/or clinic). Gresham and Lopez (1996) suggested social acceptability is likely to influence treatment integrity. Namely, if intervention procedures are viewed as socially acceptable, intervention agents will be more likely to follow its procedures with integrity. In turn, higher rates of treatment integrity will be more likely to yield desirable interventions outcomes (e.g., meaningful changes in behavior that sustain over time and context) than interventions implemented with lower rates of integrity (Lane & Beebe-Frankenberger, 2004; Wolf, 1978; Wood, Umbreit, Liaupsin, & Gresham, 2007). Social acceptability of actual procedures should be assessed again after the intervention to determine if procedures were practical, cost-effective and had habilitative validity (defined as consumer satisfaction in terms of maximizing overall benefit to treatment while minimalizing the overall cost of treatment; Hawkins, 1991)

Social importance of effects

Validating the social importance of effects is the extent treatment agents, relevant stakeholders, and participants view the intervention as producing socially important outcomes. *Proximal effects* are direct and immediate outcomes of the intervention. Notably, after selecting an appropriate target for change and identifying a desired performance goal, intervention agents must identify an appropriate measurement system to monitor the intervention with data produced prior to, during, and after the intervention. *Collateral effects* are indirect outcomes of an intervention and are changes in levels of associated skills or behaviors resulting from the proximal effects of an intervention. For example, Ms. Timek, a sixth-grade teacher may implement a new program to promote math fact fluency during her daily 60 minutes of core math instruction. The proximal effect for math fact fluency was met, demonstrated by 95% her students reaching their performance goal. As their mastery of math facts increased, there was a collateral effect of decreasing rates of off-task behavior during independent math (e.g., less walking around the room, throwing objects given the student was now capable of engaging in the assigned tasks). Finally, *distal effects* of treatment refer to the long-term outcomes produced from the behavior change associated with intervention procedures. For instance, resulting from Ms. Timek's instruction, more students from her class engaged in school-wide academic enrichment activities in comparison to students from other classrooms. Note that distal effects are not always easily measured by observation or permanent products.

We reiterate that social importance of the intervention's effects should be assessed prior to implementation of the intervention to clarify anticipated outcomes and to facilitate stakeholders having parallel expectations for what they hope the intervention will achieve. Social importance of the effects should again be assessed at the conclusion of the intervention to (1) achieve consensus across stakeholders regarding intervention outcomes, (2) evaluate the extent to which the goals were attained, and (3) evaluate consumer satisfaction with the immediate and potential long-term positive consequences associated with intervention outcomes (Lane & Beebe-Frankenberger, 2004).

The relevance of social validity assessment for practicing professional

Social validity is a priority in practice and in research. Assessing social validity attempts to ask and provides answers to questions such as "Are we focusing on the right thing? Is what we are doing or recommending okay with you? Is this type or amount of change sufficient; are you satisfied with the effects?" (Hanley, 2010, p. 13). Following the Behavior Analysis Certification Board (BACB) (2014), *Professional and Ethical Compliance Codes*, behavior analysts have the responsibility to operate and advocate in the best interests of their client(s). Social validity is an important component in aiding behavior analysts in objectively and subjectively measuring what is of social important to facilitate the interests of their clients. For examples, behavior analysts are expected to clearly define and describe goals, and to the extent possible, conduct risk-benefit analyses of the procedures selected to achieve objectives. When designing, implementing, and evaluating an intervention, including identifying goals, behavior analysts are trained, and expected to select strategies based in part, on the social validity of the intervention [Behavior Analysis Certification Board (BACB), 2012]. Further, social validity has become a priority when using core quality indicators (e.g., Council for Exceptional Children, 2014; Gersten et al., 2005; Horner et al., 2005). For example, Horner et al. (2005) proposed social validity to be satisfied when a study met four components: (1) the dependent variable (DV) was considered socially important (e.g., surveys or interviews; Sreckovic, Common, Knowles, & Lane, 2014); (2) the magnitude change resulting in the intervention DV indicated changes that were socially importance; (3) the intervention was practical and cost-effective in terms of time, materials, and other resources (e.g., materials typical in environmental context; Sreckovic et al., 2014); and (4) the intervention was implemented over extended time periods, by typical intervention agents, and in typical environments.

Social validity is important because it values the extent to which students, parents, teachers, and professionals view a behavior intervention as addressing socially significant goals, socially acceptable treatment procedures, and socially important intervention outcomes. The adoption of effective practices and teaching is largely influenced by the extent to which stakeholders find the procedures effective and appropriate (Hanley, 2010).

Stakeholders' views can be assessed using various methods to subjectively and objectively measure social validity, and ideally should be assessed before intervention onset and immediately following intervention completion (Lane & Beebe-Frankenberger, 2004). We recommend assessing social validity prior to and after intervention for several reasons: (1) to identify and agree on the target area (e.g., target behavior) for the behavior change procedure and the discrepancy (e.g., goal) between the current and desired level of performance, (2) to identify meaningful, yet reasonable focus areas to guide prevention and intervention efforts, (3) to facilitate discussion among all relevant stakeholders to the student's context while identifying environmental/cultural supports that will provide programed and natural contingencies and reinforcement to facilitate the new skill/behavior, (4) to facilitate a greater probability of intervention agents to implement and continue the treatment through intervention and generalization, and (5) to evaluate intervention outcomes and the likelihood the behavior change procedures or change itself will maintain over time (Lane & Beebe-Frankenberger, 2004). Assessing social validity, both before and after the intervention, helps answer what did stakeholders think about the social significance of the intervention goals, the social acceptability of the intervention procedures, and (anticipated) effects of the intervention after concluding the intervention and how those opinions shifted. Answer to these questions helps assess whether the goals, procedures, and effects of the intervention met, exceeded, or failed to meet the expectations from the onset to the conclusion of the intervention (Lane, Oakes, Cantwell, & Royer, 2016).

Practical applications of social validity

In the following sections, we discuss assessing social validity at each level of prevention, involving input from key stakeholders, and using a range of measures. These applications are relevant across real-world settings including schools, clinics, community, and industry.

Assessing social validity at each level of prevention

Across the United States, many school systems design, implement, and evaluate comprehensive, integrated, three-tiered (Ci3T) models of prevention to prevent the development of learning and behavior challenges and respond efficiently when such challenges arrive. These activities are designed so that general and special educators are able to work with a range of professionals (e.g., school psychologists, behavior analysts, and social workers) to meet students' academic, behavioral, and social needs in an integrated fashion. These and other tiered systems with origins in public health involve a continuum of supports ranging from *primary* (Tier 1) prevention efforts for all students, *secondary* (Tier 2) prevention efforts to reduce risk factors, and *tertiary* (Tier 3) prevention efforts to ameliorate existing concerns about individual students (Walker et al., 1996). Multiple sources of data are used to inform decision-making as to which students require more than primary prevention efforts.

These models are theoretically grounded in ABA (Horner & Sugai, 2015), with careful attention to measuring not only student performance and treatment integrity (the extent to which intervention efforts are implemented as designed; Gast & Ledford, 2014), but also social validity. For example, Lane, Oakes, Menzies, and colleagues have developed a systematic approach for building Ci3T models of prevention that explicitly involves measuring social validity at each level for prevention (Lane et al., 2016). During the formal training process, faculty and staff complete the Primary Intervention Rating Scale (PIRS, Lane, Robertson, & Wehby, 2002; an adapted version of the Intervention Rating Profile Scale—15, Witt & Elliott, 1985), to provide input on the goal, procedures, and intended outcomes of primary prevention efforts. PIRS mean scores have been shown to predict treatment integrity of primary prevention efforts during the first year of implementation (Lane et al., 2009), offering evidence of a positive relation between social validity and treatment integrity. Then, as part of implementation procedures, faculty and staff complete social validity and treatment integrity measures in fall and spring each year and examine these data in tandem with behavioral and academic screening scores, attendance, and office discipline referral data to answer questions regarding stakeholders' views, the level of treatment integrity, and shifts in student performance. Collectively this information is used to inform (1) school-wide implementation of Tier 1 and connect students to Tiers 2 and 3 supports and (2) inform annual revisions to their primary prevention efforts (Oakes, Lane, & Germer, 2014).

Similarly, social validity data are assessed prior to and following Tier 2 (e.g., self-monitoring interventions; Menzies, Lane, & Lee, 2009) and Tier 3 (e.g., functional assessment-based intervention; Lane, Oakes, Ennis, & Hirsch, 2014; Umbreit, Ferro, Liaupsin, & Lane, 2007) intervention. Information collected as part of preintervention social validity measures are used to ensure stakeholders prioritize shared intervention goals, view the intervention procedures as not too time consuming or involving materials unreasonable for the given context and, if implemented with integrity, are likely to achieve the desired outcomes. If social validity data suggest there are challenges in one or more of these areas, treatment integrity is likely to be low, and consequently student performance goals are less likely to be achieved (Lane & Beebe-Frankenberger, 2004). In these instances, it is important to work with involved stakeholders to revise the intervention or provide additional learning. This work will help stakeholders to better understand the rationale for the intervention as proposed to increase social validity prior to beginning intervention efforts. Following intervention testing using an appropriate design (e.g., A-B-A-B withdrawal or multiple baseline design) social validity is again assessed to determine if the intervention met expectations. For example, did the intervention target socially significant goal(s), were the intervention procedures socially acceptable (and used as designed), and did the intervention yield socially importance effects (ideally sustaining over time)? Given the goal of treatment-outcome studies and programs is to produce meaningful, lasting change, social validity is truly at the heart of this work (Wolf, 1978). We encourage the interested reader to visit www.ci3t.org for free-access social validity measures as well as illustrations on how to assess social validity at each level of prevention.

Assessing social validity from stakeholders involved

Just as it is important to assess social validity before and after intervening at each level of prevention (Tiers 1, 2, and 3), it is also important to assess social validity from multiple stakeholders. Specifically, we encourage assessing social validity from intervention agents which can include behavior specialists, teachers, family members, parents and/or caregivers, and students or other clients. Given each stakeholder plays different roles in the intervention process, try to obtain each of their views about intervention goals, procedures, and outcomes (Lane & Beebe-Frankenberger, 2004).

Intervention agent

When conducting any intervention, assess social validity from each stakeholders' perspectives, who often come from richly diverse trainings and cultural perspectives prior to conducting the intervention. Specifically, nearly 30 years of inquiry has suggested various intervention features influence views regarding treatment acceptability (Cooper et al., 2007; Gresham & Kendell, 1987). For example, interventions requiring substantial time and effort, involving materials typically not founded in the proposed intervention setting, involving complex or cumbersome procedures, and those incorporating negative techniques (e.g., reductive techniques such as extinction) are likely to be rated as less socially valid and are less likely to be implemented with integrity relative to interventions requiring less effort, featuring more feasible intervention materials and procedures, and involving more positive techniques (e.g., behavior specific praise and precorrection). However, the more severe the target behavior and the more the target negatively impacts the environment (e.g., verbal or physical aggression in a classroom), the more acceptable any proposed intervention, even complex interventions, will likely be perceived. Finally, it is also important to assess social validity from the intervention agents' view following an empirical test of the intervention to see if the intervention met expectations as well as inform future intervention efforts. It is a delicate, but important balance to design and implement interventions that are both effective and feasible for use in the context of interest (Lane & Beebe-Frankenberger, 2004).

Parents and caregivers

When working with youth and other individuals supported by parents and caregivers, it is critical to involve them in the intervention efforts. It also equally important to involve parents in school-based interventions that support the goal of meaningful, lasting changes in behavior generalizing and maintaining over time

(Wolf, 1978). Parents and caregivers can provide critical information to enhance the intervention process. It is important not to assume family social constructions and ecocultural circumstances are consistent within a given community (Keogh & Weisner, 1993).

Students or clients

Finally, assessing social validity from the student or client's perspective is also important but often overlooked. Preintervention assessments enable students to have a voice in establishing shared goals, procedures likely to be implemented, and interventions likely to yield the desired outcomes. For example, if during the planning process of a functional assessment-based intervention, the student indicates it would be embarrassing to have a self-monitoring form tapped to a desk, this intervention component is unlikely to be implemented as planned. Obtaining this information preceding intervention would suggest a more socially valid intervention.

Keeping in mind the range of stakeholders to be involved in the assessment of social validity, the next step is to determine the appropriate method of measurement. In the following section, we present a range of options for assessing social validity. Although more subjective social validity measures may hold some value as described above, there are challenges of using self-report measures (e.g., social desirability effects; Ledford, Wolery, & Gast, 2014). As such, we encourage practitioners and researchers to explore the full scope of tools available, including objective measures such as normative comparisons, blind ratings, substance use, and client preference (Ledford et al., 2014).

Assessing social validity using a range of methods

We indicated previously that measuring social validity has been at the heart of ABA while simultaneously being a thorny and potentially problematic construct given its subjective dimension which at times contrasts the field's naturalistic roots (Ledford et al., 2014; Wolf, 1978). For example, Van Houten (1979) and Hawkins (1991) advocated use of objective methods of measurement when assessing social validity. Examples of objective measures include social comparison and direct observation. Conversely, Schwartz and Baer (1991) argued that social validity assessment was never intended to be objective. To date, social validity has primarily been assessed using subjective measures such as self-reported satisfaction (Hurley, 2012). We agree with Ledford et al.'s (2014) call for more research to examine the extent to which subjective and objective measures of social validity are correlated and result in similar conclusions regarding outcome measures, procedural fidelity, and continued use of procedures.

In the subsequent section, we describe four common methods of assessment to measure social validity. These methods are self-report rating scales, interviews, direct techniques (normative comparisons, participant preference assessments, and sustained use), and external evaluation (content expert, blind rating).

Self-report rating scales

Social validity assessment with stakeholders has typically used rating scales, surveys, and questionnaires that focus primarily on treatment acceptability (Finn & Sladeczek, 2001). The first measure of treatment acceptability was the Treatment Evaluation Inventory (TEI; Kazdin, 1980). The TEI and the Intervention Rating Profile-20 (IRP-20; Witt, Martens, & Elliott, 1984) are the two earliest and most commonly used treatment acceptability measures (Calvert & Johnston, 1990; Miltenberger, 1990). To date, several empirically validated measurement tools have been developed building off both the TEI and IRP-20. When examining the empirical validity of measurement tools, internal consistency and factor structures are two important considerations. Factor structures describe how well indicators (i.e., question items) vary and form unidimensional (single factor) or multidimensional (multiple factor) constructs. Internal consistency is a statistical measure based on the correlation between different items on the same test or subscale of a larger test. Some examples of empirically validated social validity measures grounded in the TEI and IRP-20 are the Treatment Acceptability Rating Form (Reimers & Wacker, 1988). Children's Intervention Rating Profile (Witt & Elliott, 1985), and PIRS (Lane et al., 2002; see Table 4.1 for a brief description of TEI and IRP-20-related measures).

In addition to empirically validated measures to assess participant opinions, it is also possible to use nonempirically validated measures. Researchers and practitioners may design new or use previously developed rating scales to address the social significance of the problem by asking questions about the cause of the problem, ability, and/or willingness to change, and how the area of concern influences the individual in his or her environment (Lane & Beebe-Frankenberger, 2004). Likewise, acceptability of treatment procedures and the importance of intervention outcomes can be similarly assessed. Ideally, these dimensions of social validity would be assessed from multiple perspectives at the onset and at the conclusion of the intervention as explained previously.

Interviews

Another method of social validity assessment is conducting semistructured interviews with adults (Gresham & Lopez) and children (Lane, 1997). For example, Carter, Moss, Hoffman, Chung, and Sisco (2011) interviewed classroom teachers, paraprofessionals, students with disabilities, and peer partners to evaluate their perceptions of the feasibility and acceptability of a peer support to promote participation of students with severe disabilities, and its impact. Unfortunately, participant opinions of acceptability as a social validity measure are less common than assessing the opinions of other stakeholders (e.g., parents, teachers; Hurley, 2012).

Table 4.1 Social validity rating scales: overview

Instrument	Description	Scoring and interpretation
Treatment Evaluation Inventory related measures		
Treatment Evaluation Inventory (TEI; Kazdin, 1980)	The TEI was developed to measure treatment recommendations for children with emotional and behavior disorders. TEI is a single factor structure (accounting for 51.4% of the variance) with internal consistency ranging from .35 to .96.	15 items are rated using a seven point Likert-type scale, descriptive anchor points vary depending on item. Total scores are summed wither higher scores indicating greater levels of acceptability.
Treatment Acceptability Rating Form (TARF; Reimers & Wacker, 1988)	The TARF was developed from the TEI for use with parents to measure the acceptability of treatments devised within clinical settings. It also added items addressing effectiveness and cost of treatment. The TARF includes five composites (disruption, time, effectiveness, willingness, and acceptability) with internal consistency ranging from .80 to .91.	15 items are rated using a seven point Likert-type scale, descriptive anchor points vary depending on item, with lower scores equaling negative ratings. Total scores are summed wither higher scores indicating greater levels of acceptability.
Treatment Evaluation Inventory-Short Form (TEI-SF; Kelley, Heffler, Gresham, & Elliott, 1989)	The TEI-SF is shortened revised version of the TEI, focusing on shortening completion time. The TEI-SF is a two-factor structure: acceptability (accounting for 57% of variance) and discomfort (accounting for 12% of the variance) with internal consistency of .85).	9 items are rated using a five-point Likert-type scale, with ranges from 1 (*strongly disagree to*) to 5 (*strongly agree*). Total scores are summed with higher scores indicating greater levels of acceptability.
Treatment Acceptability Rating Form-Revised (TARF-R; Reimers, Wacker, & Cooper,1991)	The TARF-R is a revised version of the TARF to include items addressing problem severity and understanding of treatment TARF-R and to measure a single dimension—acceptability with an internal consistency ranging from .90 to .92).	20 items are rated using a seven point Likert-type scale, descriptive anchor points vary depending on item. Total scores are summed with higher scores indicating greater levels of acceptability.

(Continued)

Table 4.1 (Continued)

Instrument	Description	Scoring and interpretation
Intervention Rating Profile related measures		
Intervention Rating Profile-20 (IRP-20; Witt et al., 1984)	The IRP-20 was developed to measure educational treatments and make practitioners more aware of intervention's acceptability from educators' perspectives. It includes a single factor (with loadings ranging between .71 and .93) with an internal consistency of .91.	20 items are rated using a six point Likert-type rating scale with ranges from 1 (*strongly disagree to*) to 6 (*strongly agree*). Total scores are summed and higher scores indicate grater levels of acceptability.
Intervention Rating Profile-15 (IRP-15; Martens, Witt, Elliott, & Darveaux, 1985)	The IRP-15 was a shortened instrument to the IRP-20 to measure educational interventions and included eight new items and removed others to increase internal consistence from the original IRP-20. IRP-15 is a single factor structure (with loadings ranging between .82 and .95) with an internal consistency of .98.	15 items are rated using a six point Likert-type rating scale with ranges from 1 (*strongly disagree to*) to 6 (*strongly agree*). Total scores are summed and higher scores indicate greater levels of acceptability.
Abbreviated Acceptability Rating Profile (AARP; Tarnowski & Simonian, 1992)	The AARP is a shortened instrument to the IRP-15 by eliminating seven items and maintain eight reworded items to improve readability and shorten completion time. The AARP is a single factor structure (accounting for 84.9%–90.3% of the variance) with an internal consistency of .95–.98.	8 items are rated using a six point Likert-type rating scale with ranges from 1 (*strongly disagree to*) to 6 (*strongly agree*). Total scores are summed and higher scores indicate greater levels of acceptability.
Children's Intervention Rating Profile (CIRP; Witt & Elliott, 1985)	The CIRP is a parallel version of the IRP-15 designed for use with school-age children. Items are written at a fifth-grade level and modified versions have been developed for use with younger children (Lane, 1997). The CIRP	7 items are rated using a seven point Likert-type rating scale with ranges from 1 (*I do not agree*) 6 (*I agree*) to. Negatively worded items are then reverse scored. Total scores are summed and

		higher scores indicate greater levels of acceptability.
Behavior Interventions Rating Scales (BIRS; Von Brock & Elliott, 1987)	is a single-factor structure (accounting for 79% of the variance) with internal consistency ranging from .75 to .89 (Carter, 2007). The BIRS is modified version of the IRP-15 written for school settings and includes nine new items to operationalize treatment effectiveness. The BIRS is a three-factor structure. Including acceptability (accounting for 63% of variance), effectiveness (additional 6% of variance), and time of effectiveness (additional 4.3% of variance) with internal consistency of .97.	24 items are rated using a six point Likert-type scale with ranges from 1 (*strongly disagree to*) to 6 (*strongly agree*). Total scores are summed and higher scores indicate greater levels of acceptability.
Primary Intervention Rating Scale (PIRS; Lane et al., 2002)	The PIRS is an adopted version of the IRP-15 to measure and monitor teachers' opinions about a school's school-wide program. It consists of 17 items regarding the primary plan and four open-ended questions regarding (1) suggestions for changes to the primary plan, (2) perceptions of student performance resulting from implementation of the primary plan, and (3) perceptions of least and most beneficial components of primary plan. The PIRS is a single-factor structure [accounting for 70.47% (elementary school), 72.41% (middle school), and 70.47% (high school) of the variance) with internal consistencies of .97 (elementary school), .98 (middle school), and .97 (high school; Lane et al., 2009).	17 items are rated using a six point Likert-type rating scale with ranges from 1 (*strongly disagree to*) to 6 (*strongly agree*). Total scores are summed across the 17 items and higher scores indicate greater levels of acceptability. Open-ended can be summarized and shared back along with the numerical data to support decision-making processes.

Note: AARP = Acceptability Rating Profile, BIRS = Behavior Interventions Rating Scales, CIRP = Children's Intervention Rating Profile, IRP = Intervention Rating Profile, PIRS = Primary Intervention Rating Scale, R = Revised, SF = Short Form, TARF = Treatment Acceptability Rating Form, TEI = Treatment Evaluation Inventory.

Direct techniques

Normative comparison

Direct technique can be used to assess social validity as well. Direct observation employs behavior measurement procedures (e.g., duration recording) to discern the present levels of behavior of individuals in the same environment (e.g., peer comparison) of the client. This information can be used to identify goal levels (e.g., optimal behavior) prior to implementation, as well as following intervention to assess social important changes have occurred following intervention (Cooper et al., 2007; Kazdin, 1977). In peer comparisons, the behavior analyst identifies peers who are either (1) highly competent in the skill area or (2) representative of environmental context. Social comparisons are not without limitations. Misalignment between clinically significant levels to produce change and identified levels through normative criterion may not achieve habilitative validity. This occurs when normative comparison do not identify levels of performance which would lead to goal associated with the desired changes in behavior. For example, a behavior analyst may work with a student who is underachieving academically and displaying low rates of on-task behavior (approximately 45% engagement). The goal may be to increase this student's on-task behavior at a level commensurate with their classmates' level of engagement (approximately 75% engagement). After successfully designing and implementing an intervention to increase this student's time on-task to 70% or higher, the behavior analyst finds that although the student achieved the desired behavior change (on-task 70% or more of the time), she/he did not achieve the desired academic benefit thought to be associated with being on-task. Likewise, it is possible that the normative sample and the environment may not reflect optimal levels of performance. For example, the behavior analyst may observe the on-task behavior of other students in the class and find students are on-task less than 65% of the time, which is below optimal levels of academic engagement (70%–80%; Kauchak & Eggan, 1993; Reavis et al., 1996). Fawcett (1991) suggested one way to remedy normative social comparisons is to establish proficiency levels for a behavior or skill (e.g., ideal, normative, and deficient prior to an intervention). This method quantifies whether a behavior change is warranted and/or was achieved by assessing shifts in the individual's performance before and after the intervention.

Participant preference assessment

Direct observations can also be used to assess participant preference toward intervention procedures. Preference assessments can be used across a diverse range of learners, and are both possible and preferable particularly for young children or individuals who have significant language or cognitive impairments (Hanley, 2010). Preference assessment technology includes procedures to identify objects and activities that may function as reinforcement (Pace, Ivancic, Edwards, Iwata, &

Page, 1985) as well as selecting interventions. For example, Heal and Hanley (2011) assessed a 4-year-old typically developing girl's preference for three teaching strategies by allowing them to choose (1) instruction embedded in play, (2) presession modeling then play, and (3) presession direct instruction then play, each teaching strategy was associated with one of three colored cards.

Sustained use

The measurement of continued use of interventions by professionals and caregivers is an important measure of social validity to assess how acceptable and feasible they judge the procedures (Ledford et al., 2014). Continued implementation can serve as behavioral marker for acceptability because routine use of procedures suggests that they are socially valid (Gresham & Lopez, 1996).

External evaluation

Content experts can be recruited to evaluate the social validity of a behavior change program. For example, a classroom teacher might be introduced to three classroom management strategies and based on his or her expertise of classroom procedures and common problem behaviors, asked to select the most socially acceptable classroom management program to receive further training. Similarly, blind raters can be used to objectively determine whether a participant's behaviors are rated as different before, during, and/or after an intervention to evaluate the social importance of its effect. Sometimes, content experts may or may not be blind to experimental conditions. To illustrate, a behavior analyst implementing compliance training with a toddler may ask a parent to rate their child's engagement, disruptive behavior, and happiness during baseline and postintervention phases. The parent did not know which of 3-minute video segments were associated with the phases. In this example, the mother may be considered a content expert but was blind to experimental conditions. The behavior analysts may have used these procedures to facilitate the parent's social validity toward her child's home ABA program.

Summary: Essential learnings

Wolf (1978) described social validity as how the field of ABA found its heart. Assessing social validity documents the social significance of intervention goals, social acceptability of intervention procedures, and social importance of effects (Kazdin, 1977; Wolf, 1978). With the introduction of JABA, the field placed a priority on social validity and a journal committed to rigorous scientific inquiry of ABA principals to address socially significant challenges. In this chapter, we defined the term *social validity*, addressed the important topic of social validity assessment, and provided a brief discussion of the history of social validity. We focused on practical applications of social validity, emphasizing the importance of assessing social validity in each level of prevention within tiered systems and from multiple stakeholders' perspectives. We also introduced a range of methods for measuring social validity, emphasizing the importance of objectives approaches (Ledford et al., 2014).

Moving forward, we encourage behavioral practitioners to retain these essential learnings:

- Social validity is a keystone variable of inquiry theoretically grounded in ABA (Cooper et al., 2007) and committed to the application of behavioral science in real-world settings such as schools, community, and industry to address socially important issues.
- Social validity refers to the (1) social significance of treatment or intervention goals, (2) social acceptability of treatment or intervention procedures, and (3) social importance of effects resulting from treatment or intervention (Kazdin, 1977; Wolf, 1978).
- Social validity should be assessed before, during, and after testing a given intervention. The assessment will inform current and future interventions, develop interventions likely to be implemented integrity, and yield socially important outcomes that generalize and maintain (Lane & Beebe-Frankenberger, 2004).
- Social validity should be addressed at each level of prevention (e.g., Tiers 1, 2, and 3) and with multiple stakeholders.
- Social validity can be assessed using subjective (e.g., rating scales and interviews) as well as objective techniques (e.g., normative comparisons, participant preference assessment, sustained use, and external evaluation). The combination of subjective and objective measures is recommended.

References

Baer, D. M., Wolf, M. M., & Risley, T. R. (1968). Some current dimensions of applied behavior analysis. *Journal of Applied Behavior Analysis, 1,* 91−97. Available from http://dx.doi.org/10.1901/jaba.1968.1-91.

Baer, D. M., Wolf, M. M., & Risley, T. R. (1987). Some still-current dimensions of applied behavior analysis. *Journal of Applied Behavior Analysis, 20,* 313−327.

Behavior Analysis Certification Board (BACB) (2012). Behavior Analysis Certification Board fourth edition task list. Retrieved from: http://bacb.com/fourth-edition-task-list/.

Behavior Analysis Certification Board (BACB) (2014). Professional and ethical compliance code for behavior analysts. Retrieved from: http://bacb.com/ethics-code/.

Calvert, S. C., & Johnston, C. (1990). Acceptability of treatments for child behavior problems: Issues and implications for future research. *Journal of Clinical Child Psychology, 19,* 61−74. Available from http://dx.doi.org/10.1207/s15374424jccp1901_8.

Carter, E. W., Moss, C. K., Hoffman, A., Chung, Y. C., & Sisco, L. (2011). Efficacy and social validity of peer support arrangements for adolescents with disabilities. *Exceptional Children, 78*(1), 107−125.

Carter, S. L. (2007). Review of recent treatment acceptability research. *Education and Training in Developmental Disabilities, 42,* 301−316.

Carter, S. L. (2008a). A distributive model of treatment acceptability. *Education and Training in Developmental Disabilities, 43,* 411−420.

Carter, S. L. (2008b). Further conceptualization of treatment acceptability. *Education and Training in Developmental Disabilities, 43,* 135−143.

Cooper, J. O., Heron, T. E., & Heward, W. L. (2007). *Applied behavior analysis (2nd ed.)*. Upper Saddle River, NJ: Pearson Merrill Prentice Hall.

Council for Exceptional Children (CEC) (2014). *CEC standards for evidence-based practices in special education.* Arlington, VA: Author.

Dardig, J. C., & Heward, W. L. (1981). A systematic procedure for prioritizing IEP goals. *The Directive Teacher, 3*, 6–8.

Fawcett, S. (1991). Social validity: A note on methodology. *Journal of Applied Behavior Analysis, 24*, 235–239. Available from http://dx.doi.org/10.1901/jaba.1991.24-235.

Finn, C. A., & Sladeczek, I. E. (2001). Assessing the social validity of behavior interventions: A review of treatment acceptability measures. *School Psychology Quarterly, 16*, 176–206.

Gast, D. L., & Ledford, J. R. (Eds.), (2014). *Single case research methodology: Applications in special education and behavioral sciences* Baltimore, MD: Paul H. Brookes.

Gersten, R., Fuchs, L. S., Compton, D., Coyne, M., Greenwood, C., & Innocenti, M. S. (2005). Quality indicators for group experimental and quasi-experimental research in special education. *Exceptional Children, 71*(2), 149–164. Available from http://dx.doi.org/10.1177/001440290507100202.

Gresham, F. M. (1998). Designs for evaluating behavioral change: Conceptual principles of single case methodology. In. In T. Watson, & F. Gresham (Eds.), *Handbook of child behavior therapy*. New York: Plenum Press.

Gresham, F. M., & Kendell, G. K. (1987). School consultation research: Methodological critique and future directions. *School Psychology Review, 16*, 306–316.

Gresham, F. M., & Lopez, M. F. (1996). Social validation: A unifying construct for school-based consultation research and practice. *School Psychology Quarterly, 11*, 204–227. Available from http://dx.doi.org/10.1037/h0088930.

Hanley, G. P. (2010). Toward effective and preferred programming: A case for the objective measurement of social validity with recipients of behavior-change programs. *Behavior Analysis in Practice, 3*(1), 13–21.

Hawkins, R. (1991). Is social validity what we are interested in? Argument for a functional approach. *Journal of Applied Behavior Analysis, 24*, 205–213. http://dx.doi.org/10.1901/jaba.1991.24-205.

Heal, N. A., & Hanley, G. P. (2011). Embedded prompting may function as embedded punishment: Detection of unexpected behavioral processes within a typical preschool teaching strategy. *Journal of Applied Behavior Analysis, 44*, 127–131. Available from http://dx.doi.org/10.1901/jaba.2011.44-127.

Horner, R. H., Carr, E. G., Halle, J., McGee, G., Odom, S., & Wolery, M. (2005). The use of single-subject research to identify evidence-based practice in special education. *Exceptional Children, 71*, 165–179. Available from http://dx.doi.org/10.1177/001440290507100203.

Horner, R. H., & Sugai, G. (2015). School-wide PBIS: An example of applied behavior analysis implemented at a scale of social importance. *Behavior Analysis in Practice, 8*(1), 80–85. Available from http://dx.doi.org/10.1007/s40617-015-0045-4.

Hurley, J. J. (2012). Social validity assessment in social competence interventions for preschool children: A review. *Topics in Early Childhood Special Education, 32*, 164–174. Available from http://dx.doi.org/10.1177/0271121412440186.

Kauchak, D., & Eggen, P. (1993). *Learning and teaching*. Boston, MA: Allyn and Bacon.

Kazdin, A. E. (1977). Assessing the clinical or applied importance of behavior change through social validation. *Behavior Modification, 1*, 427–452. Available from http://dx.doi.org/10.1177/014544557714001.

Kazdin, A. E. (1980). Acceptability of alternative treatments for deviant child behavior. *Journal of Applied Behavior Analysis*, *13*, 259–273. Available from http://dx.doi.org/10.1901/jaba.1980.13-259.

Kazdin, A. E. (1981). Acceptability of child treatment techniques: The influence of treatment efficacy and adverse side effects. *Behavior Therapy*, *12*, 493–506. http://dx.doi.org/10.1016/s0005-7894(81)80087-1.

Kelley, M., Heffer, R., Gresham, F., & Elliott, S. (1989). Development of a modified treatment evaluation inventory. *Journal of Psychopathology and Behavioral Assessment*, *1*, 235–247. Available from http://dx.doi.org/10.1007/bf00960495.

Keogh, B. ,K., & Weisner, T. (1993). An ecocultural perspective on risk and protective factors in children's development: Implications for learning disabilities. *Learning Disabilities Research & Practice*, *8*, 3–10.

Lane, K.L. (1997). Students at-risk for antisocial behavior: The Utility of Academic and Social Skills Interventions. Doctoral dissertation.

Lane, K. L., & Beebe-Frankenberger, M. E. (2004). *School-based interventions: The tools you need to succeed*. Boston, MA: Allyn & Bacon.

Lane, K. L., Oakes, W. P., Cantwell, E. D., & Royer, D. J. (2016). *Building and installing comprehensive, integrated, three-tiered (Ci3T) models of prevention: A practical guide to supporting school success*. Phoenix, AZ: KOI Education, (Interactive eBook).

Lane, K. L., Kalberg, J. R., Bruhn, A. L., Driscoll, S. A., Wehby, J. H., & Elliott, S. (2009). Assessing social validity of school-wide positive behavior support plans: Evidence for the reliability and structure of the Primary Intervention Rating Scale. *School Psychology Review*, *38*, 135–144.

Lane, K. L., Oakes, W. P., Ennis, R. P., & Hirsch, S. E. (2014). Identifying students for secondary and tertiary prevention efforts: How do we determine which students have Tier 2 and Tier 3 needs? *Preventing School Failure*, *58*, 171–182. Available from http://dx.doi.org/10.1080/1045988X.2014.895573.

Lane, K. L., Oakes, W. P., Lusk, M. E., Cantwell, E. D., & Schatschneider, C. (2016). Screening for intensive intervention needs at the secondary level: Directions for the future. *Journal of Emotional and Behavioral Disorders*, *24*, 159–172. Available from http://dx.doi.org/10.1177/1063426615618624.

Lane, K.L., Robertson, E.J., & Wehby, J.H. (2002). *Primary Intervention Rating Scale*. Unpublished rating scale.

Ledford, J. R., Wolery, M., & Gast, D. L. (2014). Controversial and critical issues in single case research. In D. L. Gast, & J. R. Ledford (Eds.), *Single case research methodology: Applications in special education and behavioral sciences* (pp. 377–396). Baltimore, MD: Paul H. Brookes.

Lennox, D. B., & Miltenberger, R. G. (1990). On the conceptualization of treatment acceptability. *Education and Training in Mental Retardation*, *25*(3), 211–224.

Martens, B. K., Witt, J. C., Elliott, S. N., & Darveaux, D. X. (1985). Teacher judgments concerning the acceptability of school-based interventions. *Professional Psychology: Research and Practice*, *16*, 191–198. Available from http://dx.doi.org/10.1037//0735-7028.16.2.191.

Menzies, H. M., Lane, K. L., & Lee, J. M. (2009). Self-monitoring strategies for use in the classroom: A promising practice to support productive behavior for students with emotional or behavioral disorders. *Beyond Behavior*, *18*(2), 27–35.

Miltenberger, R. G. (1990). Assessment of treatment acceptability: A review of the literature. *Topics in Early Childhood Special Education*, *10*(3), 24–38. Available from http://dx.doi.org/10.1177/027112149001000304.

Oakes, W. P., Lane, K. L., & Germer, K. A. (2014). Developing the capacity to implement tier 2 and tier 3 supports: How do we support our faculty and staff in preparing for sustainability? *Preventing School Failure: Alternative Education for Children and Youth, 58*(3), 183−190. Available from http://dx.doi.org/10.1080/1045988X.2014.89557.

Pace, G. M., Ivancic, M. T., Edwards, G. L., Iwata, B. A., & Page, T. J. (1985). Assessment of stimulus preference and reinforcer value with profoundly retarded individuals. *Journal of Applied Behavior Analysis, 18*(3), 249−255. Available from http://dx.doi.org/10.1901/jaba.1985.18-249.

Reavis, H., Kukic, S., Jenson, W., Morgan, D., Andrews, D., & Fisher, S. (1996). *BEST practice: Behavioral and Educational Strategies for Teachers.* Longmont, CO: Sopris West.

Reimers, T. M., & Wacker, D. P. (1988). Parents' rating of the acceptability of behavioral treatment recommendation made in an outpatient clinic: A preliminary analysis of the influence of treatment effectiveness. *Behavioral Disorders, 14,* 7−15.

Reimers, T. M., Wacker, D. P., & Cooper, L. J. (1991). Evaluation of the acceptability of treatments for their children's behavioral difficulties: Ratings by parents receiving services in an outpatient clinic. *Child & Family Behavior Therapy, 13*(2), 53−71. Available from http://dx.doi.org/10.1300/j019v13n02_04.

Reimers, T. M., Wacker, D. P., & Koeppl, G. (1987). Acceptability of behavioral treatments: A review of the literature. *School Psychology Review, 15,* 212−227.

Rosales-Ruiz, J., & Baer, D. M. (1997). Behavioral cusps: a developmental and pragmatic concept for behavior analysis. *Journal of Applied Behavior Analysis, 30,* 533−544. Available from http://dx.doi.org/10.1901/jaba.1997.30-533.

Schwartz, I. S., & Baer, D. M. (1991). Social validity assessment: Is current practice state of the art? *Journal of Applied Behavior Analysis, 24,* 189−204. Available from http://dx. doi.org/10.1901/jaba.1991.24-189.

Sreckovic, M. A., Common, E. A., Knowles, M. M., & Lane, K. L. (2014). A review of self-regulated strategy development for writing for students with EBD. *Behavioral Disorders, 39*(2), 56−77.

Tarnowski, K. J., & Simonian, S. J. (1992). Assessing treatment acceptance: The abbreviated accept ability rating profile. *Journal of Behavior Therapy &? Experimental Psychiatry, 23,* 101−106. http://dx.doi.org/10.1016/0005-7916(92)90007-6.

Umbreit, J., Ferro, J., Liaupsin, C., & Lane, K. (2007). *Functional behavioral assessment and function-based intervention: An effective, practical approach.* Upper Saddle River, NJ: Prentice-Hall.

Van Houten, R. (1979). Social validation: The evolution of standards of competency for target behaviors. *Journal of Applied Behavior Analysis, 4,* 581−591. Available from http://dx.doi.org/10.1901/jaba.1979.12-581.

Von Brock, M., & Elliott, S. (1987). Influence of treatment effectiveness information on the acceptability of classroom interventions. *Journal of School Psychology, 25,* 131−144. . http://dx.doi.org/10.1016/0022-4405(87)90022-7.

Walker, H. W., et al. (1996). Integrated approaches to preventing antisocial behavior patterns among school-age children and youth. *Journal of Emotional and Behavioral Disorders, 4,* 194−209.

Witt, J. C., & Elliott, S. N. (1985). Acceptability of classroom intervention strategiesIn T. Kratochwill (Ed.), *Advances in school psychology* (4, pp. 251−288). Hillsdale, NJ: Erlbaum.

Witt, J. C., Martens, B. K., & Elliott, S. N. (1984). Factors affecting teachers' judgments of the acceptability of behavioral interventions: Time involvement, behavior problem severity, and type of intervention. *Behavior Therapy, 15,* 204−209. http://dx.doi.org/10.1016/s0005-7894(84)80022-2.

Wolf, M. M. (1978). Social validity: The case for subjective measurement or how applied behavior analysis is finding its heart. *Journal of Applied Behavior Analysis, 11*, 203−214. Available from http://dx.doi.org/10.1901/jaba.1978.11-203.

Wood, B. K., Umbreit, J., Liaupsin, C. J., & Gresham, F. M. (2007). A treatment integrity analysis of function-based intervention. *Education and Treatment of Children, 30*, 105−120. Available from http://dx.doi.org/10.1353/etc.2007.0035.

Behavioral Risk Assessment

Joseph N. Ricciardi and Allison W. Rothschild
Seven Hills Foundation, Worcester, MA, United States

5

Clinical-behavioral risk in individuals with IDD

Problematic beahviors are prevalent in individuals with intellectual and developmental disabilities (IDD) (Emerson et al., 2001). Some forms of challenging behvaiors such as aggression, property destruction, and self-injury place them at risk for harming themselves and others (Crocker et al., 2006; Crotty, Doody, & Lyons, 2014). Behavioral challenges that bring harm to self or others can lead to a host of secondary complications with health, placement restrictions, employment, housing, and the judicial system (Lowe et al, 2007). Some people with IDD present forms of dangerous behaviors that are highly unusual in almost any other clinical population, and would be considered indicative of mental illness in typically developing individuals. Examples include copraphagia (Ing, Roane, & Venstra, 2011), pica of dangerous items (Matson, Hattier, Belva, & Matson, 2013), and inserting objects into bodily orifices (Lowe et al., 2007; Waite et al., 2014). In the IDD population, challengeing behaviors may be independent of co-occuring psychiatric disorders (Ricciardi, 2013). Still, people with IDD can suffer from psychiatric disorders and exhibit the full range of dangerous behaviors associated with mental illness such as suicidal behavior (Dodd, Doherty, & Guerin, 2016; Mollison, Chaplin, Underwood, & McCarthy, 2014), nonsuicidal self-injury behavior (Brown & Beail, 2009), homicidal ideation (Hurley & Moore, 1999), erotomania (Hurley & Moore, 1999), and elopement from care settings (Kiely, Migdal, Vettam, & Adesman, 2016). Other problem behaviors that are dangerous to self and others, and often require specialized clinical approaches have been reported as well; for example, fire-setting (Alexander, Chester, Green, Gunaratna, & Hoare, 2015) and sexually inappropriate behaviors (Crotty et al., 2014).

These findings suggest that practitioners responsible for assessment and intervention planning for people with IDD who are referred for an intial presentation of "problem behavior" should employ a comprehensive approach to evaluation of many behavioral topographies and potentially harmful variations.

Applied behavior analysis in the evaluation of risk

Applied behavior analysis (ABA) is a well-established clinical approach to probelm behavior in individuals with intellectual disabilities (Didden, Korzilius, van Oorsouw, & Sturmey, 2006; Harvey, Boer, Meyer, & Evans, 2009). It has been

Applied Behavior Analysis Advanced Guidebook. DOI: http://dx.doi.org/10.1016/B978-0-12-811122-2.00005-X

demonstrated that ABA may be more effective than medication alone for these problems (Hassiotis et al., 2009) and behavioral intervention has been argued by some
as a first choice over medication treatments (Grey & Hastings, 2005). Assessment
strategies and interventions have been employed for many forms of behavioral problems that incur a risk to self or others, such as aggression (Brosnan & Healy,
2011) and self-injury (Kurtz et al., 2003; Oliver & Richards, 2010). For these reasons, behavior analysts are often the first specialists asked to assess challenging
behavior and assume clinical leadership roles in the safe management of at risk
individuals.

The prevailing thinking is that behavioral problems in people with IDD are most
often functional—they are learned responses that serve as adaptations to cognitive
and communication limitations. According to this model, problem behaviors compensate for deficits in communicating needs or solving problems and are reinforced
by the events that follow. For example, a form of severe aggression that harms
others is learned by a man with severe intellectual disability and communication
disorder as a way to avoid unpleasant tasks. The underying principle is "negative
reinforcement" where the behavior results in avoidance or termination of an
unpleasant stimulus (the task, demanding staff interactions, etc.). Under different
circumstances, another man may display aggressive behavior that is positively reinforced: following exhibition of the challenging behavior, staff provide comfort or
the offer of favorite foods or activities often as ways to help the person calm down.
It is now well-established that health problems can influence problem behavior and
the reinforcement process, as well, so behavior analysts now assess for this influence and incorporate findings in intervention designs (May & Kennedy, 2010).

Typically, a clinical-behavioral case formulation focuses on functional relationships between environmental variables and topographies of behavior. Interventions
are designed based on the function of the problem behavior, ideally, targeting resolution of contributing health problems, establishing preventative practives (also
called, "antecedent intervention"), elimination of sources of reinforcement, and
development of an adaptive skill to replace challenging behaviors (e.g., teaching
functionally equivalent communication skills, see Kurtz, Boelter, Jarmolowicz,
Chin, & Hagopian, 2011). The functional hypothesis of behavior disorders is standard practice in ABA and interventions developed based on a functional assessment
are considered highly effective (Ingram, Lewis-Palmer, & Sugai, 2005).

However, the understanding of function does not provide sufficient information
about the level of risk to self or others posed by challenging behavior. Behavior
analysts do not usually engage in a comprehensive examine of risk, though they are
often the ideal practitioner to do so. Assessment of risk would require (1) the identification of other possible topographies of risk, beyond those provided as the "presenting concern;" (2) evaluation of intensity of identified challenging behaviors
(e.g., frequency, specific targets, capacity to injure self or others, etc.); (3) identifying high-risk settings where problem behaviors may occur; and (4) identification of
possible secondary consequences, such as health complications due to the behaviors
of concern. In addition, a comprehensive review by a behavior analyst should identify the need for consultation by specialists such as medical doctors, psychiatrists,

speech pathologists, and others. We review the components of comprehensive assessment, below.

Identification of multiple topographies

Often a small set of current, specific presenting problem behaviors is provided as the basis for a referral to a behavior analyst. However, as we have reviewed, individuals with intellectual disability are a risk for a spectrum of risk behaviors: multiple topographies of aggressive behaviors to self or others, many behaviors often seen in individuals with mental illness, and a number of unusual behavior topographies that pose risk to themselves or others (Crocker et al., 2006; Crocker, Mercier, Allaire, & Roy, 2007). This is a challenge as it is easy to be focused on what is presented and not consider the unmentioned. However, given the risks in the population, an ideal approach would identify behavioral markers of risk *before* they are exhibited in the treatment setting using a comprehensive process intended to identify possible risk topographies. For example, although "Dave" is referred for evaluation of aggression, it is prudent to ask, "In addition to aggression, does Dave exhibit any inappropriate sexual behaviors?" The cost of decision-making errors is too great to omit a good question.

Identification of intensity and targets. A comprehensive assessment of risk should consider intensity of behavior topographies as the topography "physical aggression toward others" does not convey sufficient information to evaluate risk. Intensity could be estimated by the history of impact of the problem behavior on others (injuries and their severity) and the environment (economic and functional impact of property destruction). For example, a man with aggression may strike with limited ability to orchestrate a coordinated, forceful attack; another may do the same, with no motor skill deficits, and with a history of causing severe injury to caregivers and peers. Or, a person with IDD who shows self-injury may bang his hand to his head leaving redness; another might do so causing tissue damage requiring medical attention and risk for long-term brain trauma (Oliver & Richards, 2010). The targets of problem behavior would need to be considered in an assessment of risk: a history of targeting the most vulnerable would indicate greater risk than targeting trained staff only.

Identification of settings

The degree of risk to self and others is affected by the settings where problematic behaviors might occur. For example, masturbation displayed in common areas of a group home as a consequence of social skills deficits presents less risk for an individual than the same behavior exhibited in a community mall or in the presence of children (Ward, Trigler, & Pfeiffer, 2001). Similarly, aggressive behavior in a public location increases the risk for injury to the untrained public and legal consequences. A comprehensive assessment of behavioral risk would need to include the settings where at risk topographies might occur.

Identification of secondary consequences

Risk is also affected by any secondary physical consequences of the behavioral topography. These consequences include increased risk for irreparable tissue damage, loss of functional abilities (i.e., blindness and hand movement), exposure to infectious materials, poisoning, among other possibilities. Some topographies carry an immediate, direct risk, such as coprophagia (Anna, Roane, & Veenstra, 2011), pica (Ali, 2001), and self-injurious behavior (SIB) (head banging, biting, and skin scratching). Others present risk when the behavior is repeated over a period of time: for example, neurologic sequelae followed prolonged head banging, or esophageal erosion following recurrent functional vomiting (Böhmer, Klinkenberg-Knol, Niezen-de Boer, & Meuwissen, 2000). Some topographies might increase risk to self or others circumstantially, such as property destruction of large furnishings, or breaking glass or walls with bare hands. In these cases, a behavior analyst conducting a risk assessment would assess the presence of these specific forms and features and clinically consider the potential for immediate and long-term risk with repeated exhibitions of the topography.

Identifying the need for specialist involvement

The training and scope of practice of behavior analysis is different from mental health and medical specialists. Yet, medical and mental health problems may contribute to the occurrence of problem behavior in the population. For example, recurrent vomiting may indicate a primary medical problem not functional behavior disorder (Böhmer et al., 2000). Allergies, ear infections, and constipation are among numerous illnesses that interact with reinforcement contingencies in functional behavior problems (May & Kennedy, 2010). Untreated chronic pain may be associated with SIB in nonverbal individuals with IDD (Symons, Harper, McGrath, Breau, & Bodfish, 2009). Presentations which include topographies indicating health risks or possible health problems require consultation by a medical specialist as well.

In addition, suicidal behaviors, nonsuicidal self-injury, and a diagnosis of a major mental illness would require specialist consultation as part of a comprehensive risk-management approach. Some forms of challenging behaviors such as sexual offending behavior and fire-setting are typically evaluated by other disciplines. Identifying these topographies and seeking consultation from other disciplines would aid in reduction of risk to the individual, caregivers, and the community.

Practice guidelines, procedures, and implementation recommendations

We recommend a comprehensive strategy for gathering information about possible topographies of risk in cases of behavior disorder in people with IDD. The approach helps a clinician form a structured, clinical judgement about risk for harm to self or others on the basis of behavioral topography. From identified topographies, behavior analysts inquire about dynamic factors such as illnesses and evocative antecedents that might be resolved, mitigting risk. Information about intensities and setting risks unique to a topography might argue for the use of protective equipment (Urban, Luiselli, Child, & Parenteau, 2011), environmental modificaitons, or restrictions from certain settings until treatment can progress.

For this purpose, we have developed the Screening Tool for Behaviors of Concern (Ricciardi & Weiss, 2014; Ricciardi, 2004) (see Appendix 1). The Screening Tool for Behaviors of Concern, Adult Risk Version, is a 34 item semi-structured interview tool. The items are common behavioral topographies of risk within the adult IDD population and using the tool aides the clinician in a comprehensive assessment. In addition, it includes prompts for detailed questioning regarding specific behavioral features including frequency, intensity, targets, settings, and clinical features requiring a specialized clinical consult. The tool is organized alphabetically, which eases implementation. There is an option for other behaviors of risk to be added by the evaluating clinician.

For each of the 34 risk items, the clinician is asked to code the item as either a *present* area of risk (i.e., the behavior has occurred in the last 12 months), a *past* area of risk (i.e., the behavior has not been observed in over 12 months), or *never* (there is no known history of the behavior in question, per record and informant). There is also the option of indicating "unknown" when record or informant does not permit any rating. Throughout the interview, the evaluating clinician makes notes of other specific information that is shared regarding the behavior of concern. This information will help to form the basis of any necessary safety protocols.

Topographies are quite specific. For example, aggression can be evaluated for actual physical aggression, threats, and the use of objects as weapons. Sexually inappropriate can be evaluated as inappropriate actions toward adults, interest in children or adolescents, inappropriate use of pornography. Other distinctions include bolting/elopement (impulsive or planned/opportunistic) versus wandering (apparently tied to poor safety skills, inattention). Suicidal behaviors (ideation, threats, and actual attempts) are distinguished from nonsuicidal self-harm (American Psychiatric Association, 2013), and stereotyped SIB more typical in the IDD population. The list of topographies is not exhaustive so clinicians may find themselves adding additional items during an interview.

Other clinical-behavioral problems are asked about as well, though they may fall outside of the scope of practice of behavior analysts. Yet, when evaluating a case of behavior disorder, the presence of these conditions could influence frequency and intensity of a functional behavior problem, so the behavior analyst is advised to ask about their presence, and then seek specialist consultation for any finding that falls outside of scope of practice. These clinical-behavioral problems include substance abuse, sexually offending behavior, fire-setting, and major mental illnesses.

Many of the risk domains include a list of guided follow up questions to be asked following an indication of risk preceded by a prompt to "check." For example, if an interviewer endorses aggression, then follow-up checks should include targets (staff, peers, strangers in the community), resultant injuries, and use of weapons. Not all follow-up questions can be predicted, so a clinician may need to invent follow up questions to clarify risk.

There are some guidelines for best clinical interviewing practices included later in this chapter, but it is expected that any clinician who chooses to administer the tool will already have some familiarity with clinical interviewing techniques. In the event that the evaluating clinician does not have strong clinical interviewing skill, it is recommended that the tool is completed under the supervision of a practitioner who has the requisite skills.

When to use the screening tool for behaviors of concern

The screening tool was originally developed as an intake screening protocol (1) to determine if the case includes features that might exclude entrance to the program and (2) to assist clinicians with identification of risky behaviors and to prepare for a safer entry into a program. The authors have since used the tool with cases already admitted to a program. In this case, its use is part of a comprehensive strategy for reassessing a case that is presenting chronic complexities that remain severe and concerning. All three uses are described below.

Determining appropriateness for admission to a setting

Consider a young man with a diagnosis of ASD and a history of aggression directed at others. It may initially seem that a certain day setting is appropriate for this individual as the program serves many individuals who engage in aggression. Use of the screening tool reveals that this individual's aggression has included the use of objects in the environment as weapons, resulting in injuries to others. If this day program includes access to potentially dangerous items that cannot be secured, then this placement may no longer be deemed appropriate. In this way, the screening tool allows providers to make better informed intake decisions. Similarly, an individual referred to a secure, applied setting, who presents with aggression and self-injury, is also discovered only through the use of the comprehensive screening process, which the individual targets small children with aggression and sexual advances. As the setting shares space with a program serving youth with IDD, an admission may create too great a risk for this individual and others. The authors have considerable experience with referrals for admission that do not provide a comprehensive list of problem behaviors "other than" the primary referral concerns.

Preparing for safer entry into a program

The tool can also be used to help prepare for an individual's transition into a new program. An individual's history of challenging and risk behaviors and comprehensive list of current and past topographies aids clinicians in designing risk mitigation plans prior to entry. Consider the example of the man who uses objects in aggressive episodes, above. If the day program admits him, there may be certain activities that are too high risk for the individual, such as a janitorial task involving chemical cleaners or tools that might be used as weapons. Aware of this in advance, the clinician can develop initial programing that minimizes exposure to high-risk situations.

The screening process can help clinicians to identify triggers and warning signs for specific risk behaviors, and to understand risk behaviors as part of a behavioral chain. For example, a woman with an IDD diagnosis who makes frequent statements of suicidal ideation but has never acted on these statements may require a different intervention than another individual who makes similar statements preceding actual attempts at self-harm. Identifying these different behavioral chains surrounding at risk behavior allows for an individualized intervention plan (Hart, Sturmey, Logan, & McMurran, 2011), than simply viewing suicidal ideation as a general risk factor. When a clinician learns that a soon to be admitted man reportedly displays yelling and banging objects prior to dangerous property destruction, there is an option of a deescalation strategy to be designed and trained to staff in anticipation of the purported behavioral chain. Direct observation will be required to confirm the reported chain, once the individual is on site, or options for fading the strategy can be developed after a safe transition period.

Reassessment of chronic complexities

The screening tool is also appropriate to use as part of a comprehensive reassessment of cases already in the system. The purpose is to carefully describe areas of risk for individuals who are particularly challenging to the system, to confirm or disconfirm the previous case formulation, identify any missed information, establish a new preliminary hypothesis, and eventually to design a new approach to treatment. The strategy has been mentioned in other disciplines, particularly emergency medicine for complex cases where uncertainty is high: the clinician begins anew with an exhaustive search, sifting through all information available to mitigate biases and any prior, erroneous judgments (Croskerry, 2002).

Preparation

The screening tool is intended to be used as part of a comprehensive assessment process. In order to maximize the utility of the tool, clinicians will need to (1) review the available record, (2) select appropriate informants, and (3) attend to a range of "other considerations" (such as setting, timing, etc.).

Comprehensive record review

Prior to administering the tool, the clinician should first complete a comprehensive record review for the individual. It is the responsibility of the clinician to be aware of all of the information related to risk referenced in the record. The tool can help the clinician organize information from the record around the 34 risk topographies. The clinician can begin to populate the tool with indications of past or current risk and can make notes within the tool for follow-up questions to ask or areas in need of clarification, during the informant interview phase.

Some of the most important forms of documentation that should be reviewed include testing reports, service-delivery documents from past providers, behavioral data, and medical records. Testing reports include psychological evaluations, educational reports, and other specialist evaluations. They usually provide a history which can be reviewed with an informant for verification, and they often contain descriptions of serious concerns and incidents, as this is often the reason why a specialist report or consult is sought.

Service-delivery documents include incident reports, shift notes, or daily communication logs. Often, these include descriptions of concerning behaviors or incidents which an informant can be asked about for additional information and can help aid the clinician to develop a preliminary functional hypothesis. Working from documented, specific incidents, speeds along the interview process as well.

The record may contain behavioral data (i.e., data recording sheets) or behavior graphs. The reviewing clinician cannot know the integrity of these data. However, they are nonetheless valuable to work from the following: (1) they establish best estimates of frequency in cases soon to be entering the system, which will guide development of a plan for safe entry to the program and (2) the variability of data should lead clinicians to questions about function, again to form a preliminary hypothesis for later, direct testing in the new setting.

Finally, a record may include highly significant medical reports such as records of emergency room visits, psychiatric-behavioral hospitalizations, doctor's notes from primary care and specialist appointments, and hospital discharge reports. These reports must all be reviewed, as they often include specific incidents, reports of injury to the individual or others, and reference to medical conditions that may affect a behavioral presentation. Again, they will help a thorough clinician inquire more specifically about events and medical influences on behavior during the informant interview phase.

Client records are often incomplete. Whenever a clinician suspects that a specific document or a prior provider's records are missing from the file, it is useful for the clinician to request these documents to be reviewed as part of the record review. Once the clinician has available to them as much of the record as possible, the clinician should then carefully review all of the documents included in the record and keep a list of all documents reviewed.

Choosing informants

Choosing the right person to interview is critical for an effective process. Informants can be primary (the best source of information) or secondary (time permitting, used to corroborate information, or provide clarifying details). Primary informants are met for face-to-face interview, whenever possible.

An ideal informant is a person who has known the individual for a long time, across settings, and has worked closely and directly with the individual. Parents or other close family members are often the best choice for an interview informant;

however, a family member who is believed to minimize or deny the individual's challenging behaviors may not be the best choice as the primary informant. As individuals age, there are often fewer family members who have direct, recent experience working closely with the individual.

State-agency case workers may also be a good choice for an interview informant, as they frequently work with the same individuals over the course of several years and have access to information across a range of settings. Unfortunately, case workers often do not have experience working directly with the individual in question, and therefore, they cannot provide first-hand information to help clarify areas of risk and behavioral patterns.

Another option is a treatment provider who worked closely with the individual in a recent treatment setting. Providers are often the best informants in that they have a wealth of direct experience working with the individual, and may be less prone to underreporting challenging behavior. However, most providers will only be able to report on the individual's behavior in one specific setting, and only for the duration of the placement. This is problematic for individuals who engage in a constellation of high-risk behaviors, as these individuals are more prone to frequent disrupted placements, resulting in no one provider having extensive experience working with the individual.

There are pros and cons to each type of interview informant. Review of the record along with the considerations of potential informant biases help guide the clinician to choose the most appropriate person. When opportunity and resources allow, it is often beneficial to choose more than one informant, with each interview conducted separately.

Other considerations

There are a few additional considerations that can help the clinician to maximize the effectiveness of the interview. Central to the success of any clinical interview, is to arrange for an appropriate interview setting. This should be a private, comfortable setting, which encourages the informant to speak freely. This is particularly important with family member informants, as they may experience a range of emotions when discussing their loved one's challenging behaviors. Whenever possible the interview should occur in a face-to-face meeting, although phone or video conferencing may serve as a substitute if necessary and is valuable when interviewing for highly specific follow-up information and clarifications.

It is also useful to prepare the informant's expectations for the interview prior to the actual meeting including how much time it will take and the nature of topics to be discussed. Typically, the interview lasts between 60 and 90 minutes with an experienced interviewer, longer for someone new to the protocol. Many factors, including the number and extent of risk behaviors, can impact this estimate. In addition, as the assessment tool asks about many topics that are sensitive in nature, it is helpful to prepare the informants for this ahead of time, so as not to "blindside" the informant with difficult questions during the actual interview. Again, this may be most relevant for family members who are more likely to have an emotional response to discussing their relative's challenges. The authors routinely introduce the protocol by showing the list of items on the tool itself, explaining, "This is a list of common problem behaviors we sometimes see in the people we work with. We like to ask about these in advance so we can train staff, and begin our treatment work right away. Many of these won't apply, but we ask them anyway, just to be sure."

One final decision that the clinician must consider in advance is whether to include the individual in the interview process. This needs to be an individualized decision, specific to the needs and risks of each situation. There are some key factors that may impact this decision including the individual's developmental level, communication skills, ability to accept responsibility for past behaviors, and behavioral reactivity (i.e., the likelihood of evoking a behavioral episode upon mention of challenging behaviors). It is often useful for the clinician to ask the informant at the time the interview is scheduled whether the informant believes it is appropriate for the referred individual to participate in the interview. This in itself can provide valuable information about severity, stimulus control of informants, and the capacity of the individual to collaborate on their treatment plan. Regardless of the individual's participation in the interview, whenever possible, it is always recommended that the clinician also conducts an observation of the referred individual in a natural setting.

Administering the screening tool

As mentioned earlier in this chapter, there are several clinical interview strategies that are helpful to ensure that the interview tool elicits the necessary information from the informant. It is recommended that any clinician who is inexperienced in clinical interviewing conduct initial administrations of the tool under the supervision of a more experienced clinician. Some basic clinical interviewing strategies are outlined here.

Building rapport

The most important aspect of any clinical interview is building rapport with the interview respondent. A good rapport helps the informant to feel more at ease during the interview, which will likely encourage the informant to be more forthcoming and honest in their responses. An intriguing experiment illustrates the impact of rapport and semistructured interviewing (as is used in the method present here) on interview outcome. Collins, Lincoln, and Frank (2002) randomly assigned research participants to "rapport, neutral, or abrupt" interviewer styles, and then free narrative or semistructured interview methods. After watching video of an event, they interviewed participants. Results suggested that the combination of rapport plus semistructured interview produced more correct and fewer incorrect recollections by subjects.

Building rapport requires good listening and speaking skills on the part of the interviewer. Some of the most basic listening skills include maintaining eye contact and using active listening, as well as ensuring that the questions asked are cogent to the informant. Additional skills include the interviewer's ability to summarize what the informant has said, and to diplomatically redirect the informant when the conversation has moved too far from the topic of interest.

Sometimes, it will be appropriate to convey empathy and concern, especially with family caregivers. Interview rapport is directly affected by empathic statements from the clinician. Practitioner empathy lowers interviewee anxiety, leading to better information, and results in better treatment outcomes (Derksen, Bensing, & Lagro-Janssen, 2013). These statements can be simple reassurances, "It's been really hard for your family" or affirmations, "It's been really challenging, but you seem to have a good sense of what John needs to do well." What is important is that they be made in response to interviewee distress, be it sadness, guilt, worry, or anger.

Avoiding tangents

It is important for the interviewer to avoid conversational tangents that are irrelevant to the informant. Tangents may take the form of "war stories" documenting the clinician's own experience with a particular challenging behavior or well-meaning but out of context clinical guidance. The interview should be focused and brief, without being abrupt. A good interviewer should be able to control the pace politely, and stick with the planned content of an interview, ensuring that the discussion is progressing without feeling rushed, and the topic is pursued logically to its end.

Using understandable language

In addition, the interviewer should speak in a language that is professional, but not overly technical, to ensure that the conversation is spoken in language that the informant can understand. An effective interviewer is willing to accommodate less professional and technical language from the informant. The clinician should not attempt to relabel the informant's words with technical terminology unless it is necessary for the clinician to understand the point the informant is attempting to make. For example, a clinician may need to clarify what a respondent means if they say the individual has a "blow up" (e.g., does this mean yelling, physical aggression, or property destruction?), but likely does not need to reframe "trigger" as "antecedent stimuli."

The general-to-specific strategy

One additional interviewing skill that is helpful to use with this tool is a purposeful questioning technique, moving from open-ended and general questions toward more closed-ended and specific questions. Starting with open-ended questions invites broad commentary and free flow of information, and can also help to build rapport with the respondent. Examples of these types of questions include things like,

"What's it like working with John?" or "Has John ever become aggressive?" or "Can you tell me what his aggression looks like?" The informant's answers to these early questions will often lead the interviewer to several specific questions to follow up on, which often takes the form of "yes or no" questions, or "closed-ended" questions. Suppose the informant responds to "Tell me what John's aggression looks like?" by saying "He yells, throws things, and hits people." Some of the follow up questions might include "Does he throw items at people?" and "Has he ever caused a serious injury to someone?" and "Are there certain items that he tends to throw, small items, or big items like furniture?" Notice that the effective progression begins with the item in the tool: "Aggression" and then moves toward more and more specifics as the conversation is progressing. We call this the "general-to-specific" strategy.

This example is clearly not exhaustive, and the interviewer may generate other follow up questions derived from an initial broad question. However, once the interviewer feels that there has been sufficient discussion of the topic, then it is time for the interviewer to summarize the informant's responses, in order to move on to the next topic of concern. This allows the interviewer to control the pace of the interview and to ensure that there is time to work through the entire tool. With experience, the clinician's information gathering will become more economical and effectively directive without losing rapport.

Conceptualizing risk and developing a mitigation plan

We have conceptualized risk on the basis of topography of concerning behaviors and associated, idiosyncratic features such as unique intensities, settings, and targets. Less frequently, risk is based on specific diagnoses. As others have argued, psychiatric diagnoses shed limited light on risk because the classifications often overlap, lack sufficient inter-rater agreement, are theoretical not empirical, and neglect unusual features unique to the case being assessed (Burch, 2015). However, when an informant reports that the person exhibits aggression targeting caregivers that includes hiding objects to be used as weapons during later aggressive acts, then risk is no longer theoretical, but possible and concerning. It remains to be seen if aggression with objects as weapons will occur in the next setting, but aware of the potential, a clinician can prepare the setting and caregivers.

As we have argued, a topography-based assessment approach seems especially applicable to people with IDD as the occurrence of problem behavior is often part of a clinical presentation. Risk assessment is about individual case features, observations, and history that must be discovered and evaluated, and where all relevant data are integrated into a meaningful picture (Burch, 2015). For example, SIB in the form of skin picking and gouging is a risk to the health and safety of any individual, yet risk is increased when the case history includes extended periods of tissue damage, open wounds, and recurrent infections. A diagnosis of depression may be uncovered as well, and if depressed mood is judged to increase the rate or intensity of SIB, then episodes of depression increase risk. In this example, topography is the primary concern given the individual features, medical complications must be managed, and depression is a contributing factor. A similar demonstration of an integrated case formulation is O'Reilly's (1997) case of SIB that was functional (operant), yet driven by chronic recurrences of a medical problem.

A risk mitigation plan is the clinician's recommendations for prevention, preparation, and initial management. Tom is a young man with moderate intellectual disability. During preadmission evaluation caregivers report that in the past year, there have been three occasions where he attempted to leap from a moving van during arguments with peers. He has not exhibited this as a locking safety belt was added to his van, though caregivers report he continues to make unsuccessful attempts to remove the locked belt when bickering with peers. He is moving into a new residential program and will be living with peers he has never met. Because we cannot predict his ability to navigate the social demands in his new setting, he is at risk for harming himself during van transportation. A risk reduction plan may include seating next to staff who can block access to the van door, or a locking seat belt, or no transport with peers until the quality of their relationship can be established. Each of these has merits, and limitations, but all would in some way reduce risk.

In addition, during interviews it was determined that Tom may exhibit aggressive threats, but no actual aggression. Caregivers report that in the past, he brandished a broom handle in an aggressive manner while arguing with peers. He has also thrown objects at peers including kitchen utensils and pans. Clearly, part of the plan will be to advise staff of this possibility, perhaps secure items he commonly throws for a short period until his adjustment to the setting appears positive and stable.

A risk mitigation plan might also direct staff to introduce him to peers for several days after his arrival, arrange opportunities to engage in preferred activities with peers, and arrange opportunities for Tom to learn domestic routines in the kitchen and clean-up chores with a 1:1 staffing ratio and without peers nearby. In addition, the clinician may assess prosocial habits, assertiveness behaviors, and conflict resolution skills, in preparation for a treatment plan for social skills development.

There are several core principles when designing a risk mitigation plan: (1) preparation, (2) prevention, (3) protection, (4) contingent response, (5) consultation, (6) treatment planning, and (7) documentation. Each is explained, below.

Preparation of caregivers

Preparation encompasses sharing history and case formulation with caregivers and training. Having identified topographies of concern and their history, this information must be shared with caregivers along with the recommendations for risk reduction and safer management. The sharing of information raises awareness of the possibility of at risk behaviors and explains the seriousness of the situation. All caregivers must be "on the same page." Indeed, it is difficult to imagine working safely and effectively with an individual who is at risk for harming self or others if caregivers dispute the risks. So, the clinician must first share information, check-on agreement, and work through any disagreements. The general advice would be to be honest about what is known and not known, explore everyone's understanding and reactions, and discuss differing opinions openly (Thomson, Edwards, & Grey, 2005).

There is likely to be a need for staff training as part of preparation. Evidence-based methods for training and strategies for increasing intervention implementation integrity are well-established in the applied behavior analytic literature. They range from simple delineations of procedural steps in written plans, verbal reviews, and demonstrations; to competency-based checklists and ongoing consultation and problem-solving (Minor, DuBard, & Luiselli, 2014; Parsons, Rollyson, & Reid, 2012). Given the need for accurate and consistent implementation of risk-management protocols, clinicians should train caregivers according to these best practices.

Preventive approaches

The clinician should ask, "What can be done so the problem is less likely to occur?" The clinician should consider eliminating or minimizing exposure to likely antecedents and access places where the problem might represent a high risk (certain activities, community settings, proximity to vulnerable individuals, etc.). The clinician might consider modifying unavoidable, recurrent antecedents so they are less likely to evoke the topography, or increasing supervision in high-risk situations. The intent of the strategy is immediate safety, not punishment or restriction. For a new case, the strategy is used to gain immediate risk reduction, allowing time for a safer adjustment to the setting, and to develop a case formulation based on direct assessment. After achieving these aims, the clinician is in a position to develop a planned approach to fading any restrictive practices and increasing alternative behaviors and skills.

Numerous preventative options exist, primarily designed to reduce exposure to eliciting stimuli, or eliminate associated conditions that increase the motivation for problem behavior. The efficacy of the antecedent approach is well-established (Luiselli, 2006). One common area for consideration is medical problems. Medical problems which may contribute to problem behavior should be evaluated by the appropriate professional, and direct caregivers should be aware of signs of emergent medical problems and how to respond if they should occur. For example, Carr, Smith, Giacin, Whelan, and Pancari (2003) trained caregivers to identify signs of pain in individuals with pain-related challenging behaviors, and to implement a range of pain management options as a preventive strategy. Demand fading is also commonly employed. For example, Piazza, Moes, and Fisher (1996), reduced exposure to demands and then systematically faded them while reinforcing alternative behaviors. In an at risk case, the value of eliminating intense, at risk behaviors outweighs the value of engagement in habilitative activities at least initially, with a plan for increasing participation over time, as in this study. Other options include noncontingent reinforcement, establishing predictable schedules and routines, and dense reinforcement of alternative behaviors (Luiselli, 2006).

Protecting people and settings

The clinician should ask, "Can anything be done to minimize harm if the at risk behavior were to occur?" This question leads to consideration of protective equipment or modifications to the facilities. Protective equipment is widely available and can be used to protect individuals from self-directed harmful behaviors, aggression toward others, and severe property destruction that may harm themselves, or the facilities. Significant research has demonstrated significant reductions in injury to individuals with IDD and the staff who support them when protective equipment is used (Fisher, Rodriguez, Luczynski, & Kelley, 2013; Urban et al., 2011). In addition, strategies for fading, reducing, and eliminating use have been developed (Fisher et al., 2013).

Setting preparation should be considered as well: modifying facility features such as locks or door alarms, reinforcing windows, adding locking seat belts, and any other alterations that may reduce risk of harm to self or others based on identified topographies. There are risks and benefits to any modifications; there are considerations for loss of freedoms and normalization, versus safety as well. Clinical judgment, regulatory restrictions, and agency philosophy will need to be considered.

Contingent response protocols

Caregivers will need specific response protocols if a high-risk behavior were to occur. Clinicians should prepare protocols for the question caregivers will be asking: "So what should I do if the topography were to occur?" These approaches often include specific strategies for "deescalation" which have been behaviorally conceptualized as extinction, shaping, and differential reinforcement (Lennox, Geren, & Rourke, 2011). In some cases, it may be sufficient to refer staff to implement these default procedures, whereas in other cases, an individualized contingent response protocol will need to be developed.

Staff in applied settings may be trained to implement a standard packaged of therapeutic or protective holding techniques for the safe management of problem behavior, many of which are commercially available (Reed, Luiselli, Miller, & Kaplan, 2013). Numerous studies have shown that restrictive interventions such as therapeutic holding can be implemented safely, while minimizing restrictiveness and reducing implementation over time (Luiselli, 2009), and with positive ratings of social validity (Luiselli, Sperry, & Draper, 2015). Where risk is high, or staff expertise is limited, clinicians should consider retraining in these procedures as part of a risk mitigation plan.

Seeking consultation

High-risk behaviors often involve complexities beyond the scope of the behavior analyst. Behavior analysts evaluating high-risk topographies should consider specialist consultation and advocate for care recommendations that might mitigate risk.

Cases that may require consultation from other disciplines include medical complications and behaviors more commonly seen by mental health specialists such as suicidal statements, nonsuicidal self-harm, fire-setting, and sexual offending. Other indications for consultation are behaviors that may suggest unique problems requiring continuous oversight by another specialist. For example, dysphagia contributing to ruminative vomiting or food refusals should be monitored by a speech pathologist. A chronic psychiatric condition and multiple psychiatric medications should be followed by a psychiatrist. There are other indications as well.

Medical approaches compliment behavioral intervention (May & Kennedy, 2010), and other clinical specialties would be considered to serve the same role. Furthermore, in high-risk cases, the involvement of other disciplines challenges the clinical biases of a single discipline.

Treatment planning considerations

In addition to a risk mitigation plan, the behavior analyst should map out a systematic approach to assessment and treatment planning. Having identified at risk behaviors through the process, the clinician is in a position to begin baseline data recording immediately and proceed through direct observations and the entire functional assessment process.

At risk, cases will demonstrate at risk behaviors while in treatment. The ethical and professional expectation is that the clinician approaches the reality of risk while doing what a similarly trained professional would do under similar circumstances. Working with high-risk cases requires that clinicians carefully meet the standard of practice for behavior analysis, which is presently described as evidence-based practice (Slocum et al., 2014). In a high-risk case, the clinician will need to oversee a thorough yet expedited evidence-based process strongly tied to the clinical research literature.

The interview process for the screening tool for behaviors of concern may assist with this. The interview should include questions about probable antecedents and consequences leading to the identification of highly individualized stimuli. Designing assessment conditions around interview-informed contingencies been shown to improve efficacy of functional analyses (Jessel, Hanley, & Ghaemmaghami, 2016). In addition, hypothesized contingencies discovered during the interview can be monitored, probed, and evaluated directly in the care setting.

Documenting your work

In high-risk cases, clinical and professional risk is managed by a careful and comprehensive approach as we have been emphasizing. Documentation is valuable for ensuring a detailed, comprehensive clinical and professional approach, and being able to explain this approach to others. Documentation prepares the clinician for participation in a peer review process. Peer review is strongly recommended for complex cases as a strategy for increasing access to consultation and adding effective oversight to restrictive procedures (Luiselli & Russo, 2005).

Practice guidelines, summary

This chapter described a comprehensive approach to the evaluation of clinical-behavioral risk specific for individuals with IDD. A topogrpahy-based approach was described, using a semistructured interview tool, the Screening Tool for Behaviors of Concern (Ricciardi & Weiss, 2014; Ricciardi, 2004). The tool is structured around 34 behavioral risk topographies seen in individuals with IDD, though clinicians should consider the possibility of additional, unlisted behaviors. The tool is used to guide a semistructured clinical-behavioral interview with a well-selected informant, and aid the clinician with development of a risk mitigation plan and initial assessment/treatment steps.

Below we present an abbreviated listing of the core tasks for using this strategy:

* *Review the clinical record.* Begin with review of record, using the screening tool as a guide to organize findings and prepare follow-up questions.
* *Conduct the interview.* Identify an informant with direct knowledge of problem behvaiors likely to be exhibited. Plan for a conducive setting for the interview with suffficient time and opportunity for follow-up. Arrange for direct observation as part of the process.
* *Design a risk mitigation plan.* Components of the plan should include: (1) preparing caregivers; (2) preventing at risk behaviors; (3) adding protections for the person and caregivers, adding modifications to the treatment settings to mitigate risk; (4) developing case specific, contingent response protocols; (5) seeking consultation from other disciplines and practices outside the scope of ABA; and (6) beginning assessment/treatment right away.
* *Document your work.* Document your approach to the case from initial screening, assessment, and ideally, into a peer-review process. The ethical and professional requirement is to adhere to the current "standard of practice" for ABA.

References

Alexander, R. T., Chester, V., Green, F. N., Gunaratna, I., & Hoare, S. (2015). Arson or fire setting in offenders with intellectual disability: Clinical characteristics, forensic histories, and treatment outcomes. *Journal of Intellectual and Developmental Disability, 40,* 189−197.

Ali, Z. (2001). Pica in people with intellectual disability: A literature review of aetiology, epidemiology and complications. *Journal of Intellectual and Developmental Disability, 26,* 205−215.

American Psychiatric Association (2013). *Diagnostic and statistical manual of mental disorders* (5th ed.). Arlington, VA: American Psychiatric Publishing.

Anna, D., Roane, H. S., & Veenstra, R. A. (2011). Functional analysis and treatment of coprophagia. *Journal of Applied Behavior Analysis, 44,* 151−155.

Böhmer, C. J. M., Klinkenberg-Knol, E. C., Niezen-de Boer, M. C., & Meuwissen, S. G. M. (2000). Gastroesophageal reflux disease in intellectually disabled individuals: How often, how serious, how manageable? *The American Journal of Gastroenterology, 95,* 1868−1872.

Brosnan, J., & Healy, O. (2011). A review of behavioral interventions for the treatment of aggression in individuals with developmental disabilities. *Research in Developmental Disabilities, 32,* 437−446.

Brown, J., & Beail, N. (2009). Self-harm among people with intellectual disabilities living in secure service provision: A qualitative exploration. *Journal of Applied Research in Intellectual Disabilities, 22*, 503−513.

Burch, M. (2015). The development of case formulation approaches. In M. Burch (Ed.), *Beyond diagnosis: Case formulation in cognitive behavioural therapy* (2nd Edition). Chichester: John Wiley & Sons, Ltd.

Carr, E. G., Smith, C. E., Giacin, T. A., Whelan, B. M., & Pancari, J. (2003). Menstrual discomfort as a biological setting event for severe problem behavior: Assessment and intervention. *American Journal on Mental Retardation, 108*, 117−133.

Collins, R., Lincoln, R., & Frank, M. G. (2002). The effect of rapport in forensic interviewing. *Psychiatry, Psychology & Law, 9*, 69−78.

Crocker, A. G., Mercier, C., Allaire, J. F., & Roy, M. E. (2007). Profiles and correlates of aggressive behaviour among adults with intellectual disabilities. *Journal of Intellectual Disability Research, 51*, 786−801.

Crocker, A. G., Mercier, C., Lachapelle, Y., Brunet, A., Morin, D., & Roy, M.-E. (2006). Prevalence and types of aggressive behaviour among adults with intellectual disabilities. *Journal of Intellectual Disability Research, 50*, 652−661.

Croskerry, P. (2002). Achieving quality in clinical decision making: Cognitive strategies and detection of bias. *Academic Emergency Medicine, 9*, 1184−1204.

Crotty, G., Doody, O., & Lyons, R. (2014). Aggressive behavior and its prevalence within five topographies. *Journal of Intellectual Disabilities, 18*, 76−89.

Derksen, F., Bensing, J., & Lagro-Janssen, A. (2013). Effectiveness of empathy in general practice: A systematic review. *British Journal of General Practice, 63*, e76−e84.

Didden, R., Korzilius, H., van Oorsouw, W., & Sturmey, P. (2006). Behavioral treatment of challenging behaviors in individuals with mild mental retardation: Meta-analysis of single-subject research. *American Journal on Mental Retardation, 111*, 290−298.

Dodd, P., Doherty, A., & Guerin, S. (2016). A systematic review of suicidality in people with intellectual disabilities. *Harvard Review of Psychiatry, 24*, 202−213.

Emerson, E., Kiernan, C., Alborz, A., Reeves, D., Mason, H., Swarbrick, R., ... Hatton, C. (2001). The prevalence of challenging behaviors: A total population study. *Research in Developmental Disabilities, 22*, 77−93.

Fisher, W. W., Rodriguez, N. M., Luczynski, K. C., & Kelley, M. E. (2013). The use of protective equipment in the management of severe behavior disordersIn D. D. Reed, F. DiGennaro Reed, & J. K. Luiselli (Eds.), *Handbook of crisis intervention and developmental disabilities* (2013, pp. 87−105). New York: Springer.

Grey, I. M., & Hastings, R. P. (2005). Evidence-based practices in intellectual disability and behaviour disorders. *Current Opinion in Psychiatry, 18*, 469−475.

Hart, S., Sturmey, P., Logan, C., & McMurran, M. (2011). Forensic case formulation. *International Journal of Forensic Mental Health, 10*, 118−126.

Harvey, S. T., Boer, D., Meyer, L. H., & Evans, I. M. (2009). Updating a meta-analysis of intervention research with challenging behaviour: Treatment validity and standards of practice. *Journal of Intellectual and Developmental Disability, 34*, 67−80.

Hassiotis, A., Robotham, D., Canagasabey, A., Romeo, R., Langridge, D., Blizard, R., ... King, M. (2009). Randomized, single-blind, controlled trial of a specialist behavior therapy team for challenging behavior in adults with intellectual disabilities. *American Journal of Psychiatry, 166*, 1278−1285.

Hurley, A., & Moore, C. (1999). A review of erotomania in cases of developmental disabilities and a new case report. *Mental Health Aspects of Developmental Disabilities, 2*, 1−10.

Ing, A. D., Roane, H. S., & Veenstra, R. A. (2011). Functional analysis treatment of coprophagia. *Journal of Applied Behavior Analysis, 44*, 151–155.

Ingram, K., Lewis-Palmer, T., & Sugai, G. (2005). Function-based intervention planning comparing the effectiveness of FBA function-based and non-function-based intervention plans. *Journal of Positive Behavior Interventions, 7*, 224–236.

Jessel, J., Hanley, G. P., & Ghaemmaghami, M. (2016). Interview-informed synthesized contingency analyses: Thirty replications and reanalysis. *Journal of Applied Behavior Analysis, 49*, 576–595.

Kiely, B., Migdal, T. R., Vettam, S., & Adesman, A. (2016). Prevalence and correlates of elopement in a nationally representative sample of children with developmental disabilities in the United States. *PLoS ONE, 11*(2), e0148337. Available from http://dx.doi.org/10.1371/journal.pone.0148337.

Kurtz, P. F., Boelter, E. W., Jarmolowicz, D. P., Chin, M. D., & Hagopian, L. P. (2011). An analysis of functional communication training as an empirically supported treatment for problem behavior displayed by individuals with intellectual disabilities. *Research in Developmental Disabilities, 32*, 2935–2942.

Kurtz, P. F., Chin, M. D., Huete, J. M., Tarbox, R. S., O'Connor, J. T., Paclawskyj, T. R., & Rush, K. S. (2003). Functional analysis and treatment of self-injurious behavior in young children: A summary of 30 cases. *Journal of Applied Behavior Analysis, 36*, 205–219.

Lennox, D., Geren, M., & Rourke, D. (2011). Emergency physical restraint: considerations for staff training and supervision. In J. K. Luiselli (Ed.), *The handbook of high-risk challenging behaviors in people with intellectual and developmental disabilities* (pp. 271–292).

Lowe, K., Allen, D., Jones, E., Brophy, S., Moore, K., & James, W. (2007). Challenging behaviours: Prevalence and topographies. *Journal of Intellectual Disability Research, 51*, 625–636.

Luiselli, J. K. (2006). *Antecedent assessment and intervention: Supporting children and adults with developmental disabilities in community settings*. Baltimore: Brookes.

Luiselli, J. K. (2009). Physical restraint of people with intellectual disability: A review of implementation reduction and elimination procedures. *Journal of Applied Research in Intellectual Disabilities, 22*, 126–134.

Luiselli, J. K., & Russo, D. C. (2005). Clinical peer review description of a comprehensive model in behavioral healthcare. *Behavior Modification, 29*, 470–487.

Luiselli, J. K., Sperry, J. M., & Draper, C. (2015). Social validity assessment of physical restraint intervention by care providers of adults with intellectual and developmental disabilities. *Behavior Analysis in Practice, 8*, 170–175.

Matson, J. L., Hattier, M. A., Belva, B., & Matson, M. L. (2013). Pica in persons with developmental disabilities: Approaches to treatment. *Research in Developmental Disabilities, 34*, 2564–2571.

May, M. E., & Kennedy, C. H. (2010). Health and problem behavior among people with intellectual disabilities. *Behavior Analysis in Practice, 3*, 4–12.

May, M. E., & Kennedy, C. H. (2010). A review of health conditions contributing to problem behavior in people with intellectual/developmental disabilities. *Behavior Analysis in Practice, 3*, 1–9.

Minor, L., DuBard, M., & Luiselli, J. K. (2014). Improving intervention integrity of direct-service practitioners through performance feedback and problem solving consultation. *Behavioral Interventions, 29*, 145–156.

Mollison, E., Chaplin, E., Underwood, L., & McCarthy, J. (2014). A review of risk factors associated with suicide in adults with intellectual disability. *Advances in Mental Health and Intellectual Disabilities, 8*, 302–308.

Oliver, C., & Richards, C. (2010). Self-injurious behaviour in people with intellectual disability. *Current Opinion in Psychiatry, 23*, 412–416.

O'Reilly, M. F. (1997). Functional analysis of episodic self-injury correlated with recurrent otitis media. *Journal of Applied Behavior Analysis, 30*, 165–167.

Parsons, M. B., Rollyson, J. H., & Reid, D. H. (2012). Evidence-based staff training: A guide for practitioners. *Behavior Analysis in Practice, 5*, 2.

Piazza, C., Moes, D. R., & Fisher, W. W. (1996). Differential reinforcement of alternative behavior and demand fading in the treatment of escape-maintained destructive behavior. *Journal of Applied Behavior Analysis, 29*, 569–572.

Reed, D. D., Luiselli, J. K., Miller, J. R., & Kaplan, B. A. (2013). Therapeutic restraint and protective holding. In D. D. Reed, F. DiGennaro Reed, & J. K. Luiselli (Eds.), *Handbook of crisis intervention and developmental disabilities* (pp. 107–120). New York: Springer.

Ricciardi, J.N. (2004). Clinical interviewing for behavior analysts. Workshop presented at the meeting of the Berkshire Association for Behavior Analysis and Therapy, Amherst, MA.

Ricciardi, J. N. (2013). Co-occurring psychiatric disorders in individuals with developmental disabilityIn D. D. Reed, F. DiGennaro Reed, & J. K. Luiselli (Eds.), *Handbook of crisis intervention and developmental disabilities* (2013, pp. 213–243). New York: Springer.

Ricciardi, J.N., Weiss, A. (2014). Clinical risk assessment and management of children and adolescents with intellectual and developmental disabilities. Workshop presented at the annual conference of the Berkshire Association for Behavior Analysis and Therapy, Amherst, MA.

Slocum, T. A., Detrich, R., Wilczynski, S. M., Spencer, T. D., Lewis, T., & Wolfe, K. (2014). The evidence-based practice of applied behavior analysis. *The Behavior Analyst, 37*, 41–56.

Symons, F. J., Harper, V. N., McGrath, P. J., Breau, L. M., & Bodfish, J. W. (2009). Evidence of increased non-verbal behavioral signs of pain in adults with neurodevelopmental disorders and chronic self-injury. *Research in Developmental Disabilities, 30*, 521–528.

Thomson, R., Edwards, A., & Grey, J. (2005). Risk communication in the clinical consultation. *Clinical Medicine, 5*, 465–469.

Urban, K. D., Luiselli, J. K., Child, S. N., & Parenteau, R. J. (2011). Effects of protective equipment on frequency and intensity of aggression-provoked staff injury. *Journal of Developmental and Physical Disabilities, 23*, 555–562.

Waite, J., Heald, M., Wilde, L., Woodcock, K., Welham, A., Adams, D., & Oliver, C. (2014). The importance of understanding the behavioural phenotypes of genetic syndromes associated with intellectual disability. *Paediatrics and Child Health, 24*, 468–472.

Ward, K. M., Trigler, J. S., & Pfeiffer, K. T. (2001). Community services, issues, and service gaps for individuals with developmental disabilities who exhibit inappropriate sexual behaviors. *Mental Retardation, 39*, 11–19.

Further reading

Allen, D. (2000). Recent research on physical aggression in persons with intellectual disability: An overview. *Journal of Intellectual and Developmental Disability, 25*, 41–57.

Appendix 1

Screening Tool for Behaviors of Concern—ADULT RISK VERSION

Individual _____   Informant _____

Date(s) _____   Clinician _____

This is not a questionnaire. It is a guide to a semi-structured clinical interview. This should be used by a clinician with a qualified informant to rate each item as follows:

☐ Present: Reported to occur within the past year
☐ Past: Reported to occur, but more than 1-year ago
☐ Never: No known history per record and informant
☐ Unknown: Insufficient information to know

Behaviors of Concern	Finding
1. **Aggression (actual physical aggression):** Strikes and grabs, including weak attempts. **Check for:** Biting? ☐ Yes ☐ No **Check:** Targets staff? ☐ Yes ☐ No **Check:** Targets other individuals? ☐ Yes ☐ No **Check:** Targets strangers (visitors, persons in community)? ☐ Yes ☐ No **Check:** Injuries to others? ☐ Yes* ☐ No *Describe in your notes	☐ Present ☐ Past ☐ Never ☐ Unknown
2. **Aggression (threat of physical aggression):** Verbal or gestural threat to aggress, with or without actual aggression. **Check:** Followed by actual aggression? ☐ Yes ☐ No	☐ Present ☐ Past ☐ Never ☐ Unknown
3. **Aggression (uses object as weapon):** Uses item during aggressive episode, either threatens with object or actually uses object. **Check:** Securing or fabricating then hiding object for use as weapon at an opportunistic time? ☐ Yes* ☐ No *Describe **Check:** Targets staff? ☐ Yes ☐ No **Check:** Targets other individuals? ☐ Yes ☐ No **Check:** Targets strangers (visitors, persons in community)? ☐ Yes ☐ No **Check:** Injuries to others? ☐ Yes* ☐ No *Describe	☐ Present ☐ Past ☐ Never ☐ Unknown
4. **Bolting/Elopement:** Will impulsively run away from assigned area; runs from caregivers. Or, will make attempts to leave or escape a setting if not closely supervised. (Differentiated from "Wandering"). **Identify specific form and settings** **Check:** Is 1:1 staffing required for safety? ☐ Yes ☐ No **Check:** Does individual bolt into unsafe settings/situations? ☐ Yes ☐ No	☐ Present ☐ Past ☐ Never ☐ Unknown
5. **Climbing:** Will climb on furniture despite warnings or reprimands; will climb trees or other high places that may be dangerous. **Specify what he/she climbs**	☐ Present ☐ Past ☐ Never ☐ Unknown
6. **Day services refusal:** Refuses to attend an appropriately identified day program consistently. **Check:** What is actual attendance: ☐ Never ☐ Sometimes/Partial* *Describe	☐ Present ☐ Past ☐ Never ☐ Unknown
7. **Disrobing:** Removes clothing in inappropriate settings. **Identify specific settings** **Check:** Does behavior occur in community/public setting? ☐ Yes ☐ No	☐ Present ☐ Past ☐ Never ☐ Unknown
8. **Eating difficulties (choking hazard):** Gorges on food, swallowing difficulties, other possible choking hazards while eating. **Describe** **Check:** Is there a dysphagia diagnosis? ☐ Yes ☐ No **Check:** Risk of aspiration reported and/or suspected: ☐ Yes ☐ No **Check:** Are there any special food presentation (pre-cut foods, ground, avoidances), supervision needs, or feeding plans? ☐ Yes* ☐ No *Describe	☐ Present ☐ Past ☐ Never ☐ Unknown
9. **Eating difficulties (refusals):** Refuses to eat for extended periods; refuses to eat many meals. **Check for weight loss:** ☐ Yes* ☐ No *Describe	☐ Present ☐ Past ☐ Never ☐ Unknown
10. **Exits moving vehicle:** Attempts or actual leaving a moving vehicle; opening door of moving vehicle and gestures to exit. **Check:** Use of physical restraint during transport: ☐ Yes ☐ No **Check:** Supportive/protective devices for van safety: ☐ Yes* ☐ No *Describe	☐ Present ☐ Past ☐ Never ☐ Unknown

Behaviors of Concern	Finding
11. Fire setting/fire interest: History of intentionally setting fires; suspected fire setting incidents. OR, unusual interest in fire. **Describe reported events** **Check:** Any injuries as a result? □ Yes* □ No *__Describe__ **Check:** Any substantial property damage as a result? □ Yes* □ No *__Describe__ **Check:** Special restrictions/precautions in place? □ Yes* □ No *__Describe__	□ Present □ Past □ Never □ Unknown
12. Inserting objects into self: Will insert small objects into orifices (not mouth): nose, ears, rectum, urethra. **Describe form and stimuli** **Check:** Has this problem led to any health threats (emergency extractions required; bodily injuries as a result): □ Yes* □ No *__Describe__	□ Present □ Past □ Never □ Unknown
13. Legal involvement: History of involvement with criminal justice system (arrests, convictions, restraining orders, etc.). *__List all involvement__ **Check:** Is the person presently on parole? □ Yes* □ No *__Describe requirements__ **For sexual offenses:** Is the person registered? □ Yes* □ No *__Describe__ **For sexual offenses:** Are there any court mandated treatment or monitoring requirements? □ Yes* □ No *__Describe__	□ Present □ Past □ Never □ Unknown
14. Major mental illness: Has a diagnosis of a major mental illness, or mental illness with psychotic features: schizophrenia, bipolar disorder, major depression, psychotic disorder. **List diagnoses** **Check:** Are there any risk behaviors that worsen or emerge during an acute phase of the mental illness? □ Yes* □ No *__Describe__ **Check:** Refusal to take prescribed psychiatric medicines? □ Yes* □ No *__Describe__ **Check:** History of psychiatric hospitalization? □ Yes* □ No *__List history of hospitalizations, emergency evaluations__	□ Present □ Past □ Never □ Unknown
15. Masturbation (in an inappropriate location): Touches genitals in a self-stimulating manner other than in private location (unoccupied bedroom, bathroom) or other and/or times/places where this is inappropriate. **Identify specific settings** **Check:** Rubbing self over clothing? □ Yes □ No **Check:** Hands in pants, touching genitals? □ Yes □ No **Check:** Exposes genitals? □ Yes □ No **Check:** Does behavior occur in community or public setting? □ Yes □ No	□ Present □ Past □ Never □ Unknown
16. Non-compliance with medical treatments: A pattern of refusal (verbal) or resistance (overt behavior) to medical treatments requiring special strategies or approaches to overcome. (E.g. medication refusal, refusal to wear AFO's, etc.) **Describe medical treatment, and topography of non-compliance** **Describe strategies required to ensure compliance, if any:** □ None **Check:** Has this problem led to any health threats? □ Yes* □ No *__Describe__ **Check:** Any pre-sedating medications used for medical appointments? □ Yes* □ No *__Describe__	□ Present □ Past □ Never □ Unknown
17. Non-compliance with transitions from UNSAFE LOCATIONS: A pattern of refusing to step away from unsafe settings, places, activities. **Describe typical eliciting situations**	□ Present □ Past □ Never □ Unknown
18. Pica: Puts inedible objects in his/her mouth and attempts to ingest. Distinguished from mouthing objects by attempt to swallow or masticate/swallow. **Identify typical stimuli** **Check:** Has this problem led to any health threats (consuming poison, dangerous objects, blockages, ER evaluations)? □ Yes* □ No *__Describe__ **Check:** Are there any specific environmental protections or restrictions in place to prevent occurrences? □ Yes* □ No *__Describe__	□ Present □ Past □ Never □ Unknown
19. Property destruction: Deliberately damages property of others or self. Includes throwing school materials, tearing papers, etc. **Describe** **Check:** Unusually large, heavy objects (furnishings, etc.) □ Yes □ No **Check:** Throws unusually large items directly at others □ Yes □ No **Check:** Form of behavior could harm self □ Yes □ No **Check:** Extreme expense associated with property destruction □ Yes □ No **Check:** Community/public property target □ Yes □ No	□ Present □ Past □ Never □ Unknown
20. Rectal digging or finger insertion: Digs fingers into rectum. **Check:** Has this problem led to any health problems? □ Yes* □ No *__Describe__	□ Present □ Past □ Never □ Unknown

Behaviors of Concern	Finding
21. Rumination: Regurgitates and re-ingests food. May attempt to play with vomitus. **Check:** Has this problem led to any health threats? ☐ Yes* ☐ No *Describe	☐ Present ☐ Past ☐ Never ☐ Unknown
22. Self-harming/self-mutilation behavior (Nonsuicidal self-injury, NOT SIB): Deliberate, non-accidental cutting, scratching, burning, skin. **Describe specific topography and typical implements** **Check:** Has this problem led to any health threats (tissue damage, infections, serious injuries, other problems)? ☐ Yes* ☐ No *Describe	☐ Present ☐ Past ☐ Never ☐ Unknown
23. Self-injurious behavior (SIB, NOT Nonsuicidal self-injury): Hits, bites, scratches self in a stereotypic manner. May resist attempts to interrupt. **Check:** Has this problem led to any health threats (tissue damage, infections, serious injuries, other problems)? ☐ Yes* ☐ No *Describe **Check:** Supportive/protective devices for in use: ☐ Yes* ☐ No *Describe	☐ Present ☐ Past ☐ Never ☐ Unknown
24. Sexually inappropriate (actions toward adults): Unwelcome sexual advances toward others; unwelcome sexual touch to others. Sexualized speech in inappropriate setting. (FOR adjudicated sexual offender, go to "Legal Involvement" as well) *Describe **topography and any pattern of targets** **Check:** Targets staff? ☐ Yes ☐ No **Check:** Targets other individuals? ☐ Yes ☐ No **Consensual, with others:** Is there evidence of safety skills: ☐ Yes ☐ No **Check:** Any reports of forceful sexual contact? ☐ Yes ☐ No *Describe **Check:** Have there been any investigations, arrests, or convictions? ☐ Yes* ☐ No ***List incidents leading to investigations**	☐ Present ☐ Past ☐ Never ☐ Unknown

25. Sexually inappropriate (interest in children/adolescents): Evidence of child or adolescent sexual interest or suspected interest in sexual contact with children or adolescents. **Describe pattern of targets**
Check: Have there been any investigations, arrests, or convictions? ☐ Yes* ☐ No
***List incidents leading to investigations**
  Check: Sexual offender registration requirement? ☐ Yes* ☐ No
***Describe requirements**
  Check: Has he/she received sexual offender treatment? ☐ Yes* ☐ No
***List treatment history**
	☐ Present
	☐ Past
	☐ Never
	☐ Unknown

26. Sexually inappropriate (pornography): Uses pornography in indiscrete locations; uses excessively with interference with important life goals and activities; or seeks inappropriate content. **Check:** Accesses in non-private, residence locations? ☐ Yes ☐ No **Check:** Accesses in public locations? ☐ Yes ☐ No **Check:** Seeks child pornography content? ☐ Yes ☐ No **Check:** Seeks sexually violence content? ☐ Yes ☐ No **Check:** Frequency interferes with life goals, quality of life? ☐ Yes* ☐ No *Describe	☐ Present ☐ Past ☐ Never ☐ Unknown
27. Smearing feces or eating feces: Touches, plays with, smears fecal matter. Occurs during toileting and/or occurs during other occasions; or eats feces. *Describe **Check:** Has this problem led to any health threats (Eats feces, hepatitis risk or history, or other communicable diseases). ☐ Yes* ☐ No *Describe	☐ Present ☐ Past ☐ Never ☐ Unknown
28. Spits at others: Expels saliva to person. **Targets other individuals?** ☐ Yes ☐ No **Check:** Hepatitis risk or history, or other communicable diseases. ☐ Yes* ☐ No ***Describe**	☐ Present ☐ Past ☐ Never ☐ Unknown
29. Substance use/abuse: Uses alcohol and/or illegal substance. **Uses alcohol** ☐ Yes* ☐ No *Describe pattern of use **Uses illegal substance(s)** ☐ Yes* ☐ No *Describe types/pattern of use **History of substance abuse treatment** ☐ Yes* ☐ No *List **Check:** Are there any risk behaviors that worsen or emerge when actively using substances? ☐ Yes* ☐ No *Describe	☐ Present ☐ Past ☐ Never ☐ Unknown
30. Suicidal statements or activities: Verbalizes "I am thinking of killing myself", makes threatening statements to kill self, or similar direct statements of killing self. OR, has made attempts, or excessive risk taking/may be suicidal. **Describe** **Check:** Is there a history of attempts? ☐ Yes* ☐ No *List actual attempts and **methods employed**	☐ Present ☐ Past ☐ Never ☐ Unknown

Behaviors of Concern	Finding
31. Unsafe attraction: Is attracted to object, item, or area that is possibly unsafe for the person. May try to overcome attempts to block access to objects or areas. Must be carefully supervised near these items or areas. **Describe** **Check:** May lead to violation of trespassing restrictions or other laws while in community: ☐ Yes* ☐ No ***Describe**	☐ Present ☐ Past ☐ Never ☐ Unknown
32. Volitional elimination (urinating or defecating intentionally): Attempts/actual to urinate or defecate at inappropriate times and places, with indications of intentionality. **Check:** Has this problem led to any health threats (hepatitis risk or history, or other communicable diseases). ☐ Yes* ☐ No ***Describe**	☐ Present ☐ Past ☐ Never ☐ Unknown
33. Volitional vomiting: Attempts/actual self-induced vomiting. **Check:** a) Has a medical cause been <u>ruled out</u>? b) Any health complications? ☐ Yes* ☐ No ***Describe**	☐ Present ☐ Past ☐ Never ☐ Unknown
34. Wandering: Will leave staff presence and supervision without continuous visual monitoring. **Describe form and examples of occurrences**	☐ Present ☐ Past ☐ Never ☐ Unknown
35. OTHER—Describe any other identified behaviors of concern:	

Incentive-Based Performance Improvement

6

Byron Wine
Florida Institute of Technology, Melbourne, FL, United States

Incentive-based performance improvement

Organizational Behavior Management (OBM) might be simply defined as the application of behavior analysis to business—as such OBM represents a subdiscipline of applied behavior analysis (ABA) as the targets selected for change in organizations are always socially significant. As in all applications of ABA, the main goal is to predict and control socially significant behavior to improve the lives of the clients. In OBM, the clients are both the stakeholders and the employees of the organization. Over the years, OBM has proven effective in numerous industries with a variety of targets. OBM has grown so large that several subspecialties such as safety and systems analysis have been developed. Practicing clinicians are most likely interested in the specialty of OBM called performance management (PM), which focuses on the behavior of individuals or small groups.

Almost all practicing clinicians rely to some degree on other employees to complete clinical work. In many settings, these employees are referred to as technicians, line staff, direct-care professionals, or registered behavior technicians. Often times after clinicians conduct assessments and write plans, they must rely on therapists to provide the bulk of the therapy hours. However, employees also assist with nonclinical tasks such as interviewing potential staff members, cleaning therapy rooms, and tracking accounts receivable, among countless other tasks that are essential in maintaining an effective practice. Any master's-level clinician therefore has a significant stake in PM. For those who aspire to own an organization or rise to senior management, a more robust understanding of all areas of OBM is required.

Thanks to sophisticated verbal repertoires and a long-learning history, employee behavior may be more complex than many of the clients behavior analysts serve, and yet a number of empirically validated strategies have been developed to improve employee performance. A primer on PM in general would require book length treatment (for such a treatment see Daniels & Bailey, 2014). This chapter will focus primarily on consequences, specifically financial compensation. Compensation and other forms of tangible delivery seem to be widely acknowledged as the "reason" people go to work instead of allocated responding elsewhere during the week. So, it is not surprising that when management in organizations seeks to motivate employees, they favor manipulating compensation in some form. For example, it has been suggested that up to 75% of US companies attempt to

Applied Behavior Analysis Advanced Guidebook. DOI: http://dx.doi.org/10.1016/B978-0-12-811122-2.00006-1

connect employee performance to their pay, typically in the form of a bonus or annual salary increase (Webb & Blandin, 2006).

All employees in organizations, aside from volunteers, must be compensated in some fashion for their efforts. Most often the method used is a pay-for-time (PFT) scheme in which employees spend 40 hours per week (for a full-time job) in one or more specific locations and engage in work related tasks. In exchange, the employee receives a salary at fixed-time intervals. As behavior analysts this scheme creates problems in that the pay, or any other benefit such as matching retirement contributions, are often not specifically tied to performance. That is, as long as an employee shows up to work when scheduled and engages in enough behavior to avoid termination she will receive a paycheck. From a behavior analytic perspective, the relationship between performance and paychecks (i.e., the performance and consequences) is tenuous at best.

As pointed out by Bill Abernathy in his seminal text, PFT is also conceptually problematic (Abernathy, 1996). According to Dr. Abernathy, paying a fixed salary to employees is often associated with an annual increase in salary that results in an ever increasing cost to the organization. If turnover remains relatively low, employee cost will continually rise over time. All businesses can expect fluctuations in income, and the increasing cost of employee salaries can become especially problematic when there is a temporary downturn in business, likely resulting in lay-offs or decreased hours. To stay profitable over the long term in such a paradigm, organizations must constantly grow or continually cut expenses. An additional complication in fixed salary situations is how to reward employees who perform well. In order to justify an increase in salary or reward exceptional performance, an employee often must be promoted, whether it is the best thing for that employee or not. Steadily promoting individuals based on current achievement might lead to an untenable situation; employees who are promoted as a reward will eventually be promoted to a job where they fail. Laurence Peter identified the Peter Principle in which employees are promoted based upon current success instead of what will be required (Peter & Hull, 1969). In short, the Peter Principle describes situations in which employees are moved out of jobs in which they excel until they reach a level in which they cannot perform; so even though promotions are a form of organizational reward, such promotions may have deleterious effects on the employee and possibly the organization itself.

Many researchers and practitioners have augmented PFT by adding additional, response-contingent consequences. In terms of incentives, these might be considered intangibles (e.g., praise, feedback, and celebrations) or tangibles such as extra pay. From a conceptual standpoint, this may be viewed as superimposing a consequence system onto an existing fixed-time delivery of pay such that a response-reward contingency is created. This method may improve performance but does not directly address the conceptual concerns raised in Abernathy (1996) unless the improvement in employee performance decreases organizational cost (decreased material usage) and/or increases revenue (decreasing transition time allowing more clients to be served).

The complement to a PFT is pay-for-performance (PFP). Generally speaking, PFP is a system in which employees earn money based purely on performance or can earn money in addition to a salary based upon performance (Long III, Wilder, Betz, & Dutta, 2012). This definition allows for many different permutations of PFP. For example, an individual may earn all of her pay in the PFP scheme as in piece rate work where an employee is paid only for the number of items generated or sold. Other systems have employees earning a base salary with an ability built in to earn another 20% contingent upon performance. No matter what percentage of pay can be earned through performance, the performance in question may be based on individuals alone, or subject to group performance. An example of a group contingency can be found in jobs that require teams to work on large projects. Often, a reward is delivered if the project is delivered early or under budget. PFP has also been used to describe interventions in which savings or increased revenue due to improved employee performance is paid out. Essentially, PFP programs treat compensation as a production cost that makes the relationship between pay and productivity salient to organizational stakeholders by objectively tying pay to the performance of employees (Honeywell-Johnson & Dickinson, 1999).

To further complicate the term, PFP has been used to refer to one of several alternative compensation strategies that are tied to organizational financial measures. Financial incentive plans provide money to employees based upon profit (profit sharing) or improvements in cost or production (gainsharing). Profit sharing typically involves annual payouts to employees based upon how successful the company was during the year. Gainsharing typically pays quarterly or yearly when departments, sectors, or even the company itself meets a stated goal. The data concerning the effectiveness of these types of plans are extensive, mixed, and largely from fields not behavior analytic in nature (e.g., Barnes, Hollenbeck, Jundt, DeRue, & Harmon, 2011). However, given that the payouts in both gainsharing and profit sharing are temporally removed from behavior, and that it is entirely possible for an organization to be profitable or meet goals despite the behavior of some individuals, it seems unlikely that these programs strongly influence employee behavior. For this reason, I will not consider these alternative compensation strategies and readers are encouraged to read Abernathy (1996) for a more detailed discussion. To allow for a general discussion of the research any system that allows employees to earn additional money beyond a set salary for responding will be considered a PFP system. However, it seems reasonable to distinguish between interventions that simply add consequences to improve performance to those that have a specific earning ability for employees based upon increased fiscal health of the organization.

PFP seems intuitive in that it links performance directly to the amount of money an employee receives. Consider a salesperson who receives 100% of his salary from sales. The cars sold are the result of his "selling" behavior and chances are you have seen that behavior if you have ever stepped foot on a car lot. When behavior is linked directly to responding relatively little other intervention may be necessary as the responding is directly maintained by the consequences. Several different lines of research have investigated the benefits of various PFP programs in organizations.

Relevant research

Several demonstrations have concluded that PFP, in its various forms, are superior to PFT (e.g., George & Hopkins, 1989). In a review of individual incentive programs, Bucklin and Dickinson (2001) concluded that PFP improved performance relative to PFT. In addition, researchers have manipulated several parameters in individual PFP arrangements. The most salient variable appears to be the ratio schedule relationship between performance and pay. That is, the contingency between the work completed and the money earned is the key in these arrangements. Somewhat surprisingly, levels of performance were not related to the actual money earned per piece of work completed or the total amount of money earned. Moreover, other variables such as the percent of a participant's paycheck available for PFP (e.g., 3%–100%), the specific ratio of reinforce delivery, or whether piece rate pay was accelerating, decelerating, or linear also did not have a significant impact on the effectiveness of the evaluated PFP systems. Although research is needed for more conclusive results, it suggests that if the contingency between performance and pay is strong, other variables may not have a significant impact on performance.

With this perspective in mind, many common organizational practices that attempt to motivate individual employees by implementing programs that do not align employee behavior with consequences should be viewed skeptically. For example, it was long hypothesized by thought leaders in the field of OBM that employee-of the-month (EOM) programs were given to too few people, and likely too far removed from behavior to be of much help to organizations (Daniels, 2000). EOM does not create a strong contingency between performance and reward. Recently, the relative ineffectiveness of EOM (that included recognition only, or recognition and a financial reward) to improve performance was demonstrated empirically (Johnson & Dickinson, 2010). Another common practice, providing year-end bonuses to employees, suffers the same conceptual problems. Several months to a year is likely too long for a reward to be effective. In addition, most employees would likely have trouble identifying why, exactly, they are receiving a bonus.

An empirical example of an individual incentive system was demonstrated in LaMere, Dickinson, Henry, Henry, and Poling (1996). The study was initiated by a request to increase waste disposal drivers' productivity without increasing accidents or employee dissatisfaction. Employees could earn incentive pay when weekly performance exceeded baseline, but the incentives were lost if there was a chargeable accident. A complex point system was developed to allow for different values to be assigned to job components of varying difficulty. Points earned were divided by the hours worked. Using a formula generated for this setting, points per hour were calculated that accounted for the miles driven (i.e., miles had to be accounted for, otherwise more points could be earned by employees that drove fewer miles between jobs). The intervention was successful in increasing the performance of the drivers but also highlights the difficulty in creating systems when there are multiple variables such as job difficulty and miles between jobs influencing employee performance. Clinicians may encounter similar problems when assigning staff to clinical cases. For example, some clients may engage in problematic behavior that interferes with instruction. Even a relatively straightforward target such as number of discrete trials delivered per session could become complex if a clinician must also account for how the disruptive behavior of specific clients should factor into employee performance. To account for client difficulty, a clinician may need to develop a system, wherein technicians are rotated equally among the clients throughout the week, adding strain to what is typically an already daunting scheduling task.

Incentive programs can be individualized to each employee or presented as a group contingency. An example of a group PFP system is a human services organization that sets aside a sum of money based upon cost savings from effective scheduling of clients. This money could then be paid out to the members of the scheduling team who contributed to the improvement. In a comprehensive review, Honeywell-Johnson and Dickinson (1999) evaluated group PFP contingencies. The group contingencies typically performed as well as individual incentives, both of which outperformed PFT. However, most of the group research included teams of 2−12 members, leading to questions of group incentives in larger groups.

An empirical demonstration of a group incentive plan was demonstrated by Austin, Kessler, Riccobono, and Bailey (1996). Austin et al (1996) evaluated labor cost as a percentage of estimated (derived from a bid accepted by the contractor) cost for a roofing crew. Seven employees received small rewards daily if the previous day's goal, which involved completing a portion of the job, was completed ahead of schedule. The crew also received a paid lunch when they accumulated three days saved. The main component of the intervention was an incentive system. The system was designed such that each week the daily savings were summed. Then, 40% of the savings were divided amongst the crew. The system allocated the savings relative to labor costs. The example of the system provided by Austin et al. (1996) stated that if the estimated cost was $1000 and the actual labor cost was $900, then $40 (100*.4) would be split amongst the crew. In terms of labor cost, if the foreman of the crew accounted for 20% of the wages then he received 20% of the cost savings. This program was so effective in increasing productivity that a second study to increase employee safety behavior was implemented. The earlier clinical example where technicians needed to be rotated to account for varying degrees of problem behavior might be remedied by the implementation of group contingencies. If a specific number of trials needed to be conducted across all clients so that a sum of money is shared amongst the employees, there may be less need to rotate all of the employees.

Honeywell-Johnson and Dickinson (1999) also note that group contingencies that have competitive contingencies may occasionally be more effective than equally distributed rewards. An example of the different group contingencies can be seen in Allison, Silverstein, and Galante (1992) where three pay systems were evaluated. In the cooperative contingency each participant could receive a portion of allocated funds based upon the performance of a group. In the competitive condition only the three best performers received the allocated funds. Lastly, in the independent conditions, each participant could earn a portion of the allotted funds based on her or his performance alone. Although in this particular study, there was no difference between the incentive conditions participants preferred the cooperative condition. It has been cautioned that competitive group contingencies may allow for exemplar performers to repeatedly obtain the rewards; if this happens many employees will not contact reinforcers and the intervention may not be effective. Even worse, employees may begin to sabotage others to gain the top financial incentives (Honeywell-Johnson & Dickinson, 1999).

Abernathy (2011) presents a system that does not contain a competitive component and ties the incentives to the profitability of the company. Essentially, employee profits increase individually along with performance, but the incentives are only delivered if the organization is profitable. The individual performance of employees is linked to cascading organizational objectives, and so although employees are paid for individual performance, they are encouraged to work together to make the organization profitable. The system developed by Abernathy (2011) is likely the most comprehensive and generalizable PFP system to date but it is complex, and although he provides several case examples, it has yet to be empirically validated.

It should be noted that simply arranging a PFP system does not guarantee success. Bateman and Ludwig (2004) evaluated a PFP system in a food distribution warehouse. When the researchers began collecting data, an existing PFP involved incentive pay, 1.6 cents per case selected, and loss of incentive pay for errors was in-place. That is, correct orders were incentivized, and shorts (omitting an item from an order) and mispicks (placing an incorrect item in an order) were deincentivized through a $.50 and $1.50 fine, respectively. At the outset of the study weekly feedback on productivity and errors along with the incentive program was not effective in maintaining employee behavior at desired levels. The intervention employed by the researchers involved more detailed feedback and tiered goals to allow for shaping. In addition, an "earn-back" component was developed wherein if the errors for the week were below the current goal of errors per 1000, then the employee would avoid the $.50 per short and $1.50 per mispick penalties. If the errors for an employee were 7 per 1000 cases and the current goal was set at 1 per 1000, then she would not lose the earned incentive money for the mistakes. The modified intervention was effective in decreasing employee errors.

As related to practice there are several considerations that should be noted in the available research on PFP. Long et al. (2012) compared PFP ($0.02 for each check completed in an analog check entering task) to a PFT (fixed pay no matter how many checks were completed) condition. The PFP condition did increase performance relative to both baseline and PFT conditions. However, when the authors allowed participants to select whether they complete work in PFT or PFP conditions, selection varied both between and within participants. In a social validity measure one of the three participants called the PFP "stressful." Although this was a single analog study, the implications of employees choosing PFT schedules should not be overlooked. It seems possible that if these research results generalize to work environments some employees may elect to work in settings without PFP, or tenure of existing employees may be impacted if PFP is introduced.

As noted earlier, although not separated in many reviews, there appears to be a difference between comprehensive PFP systems where employees earn more money contingent upon performance that decreases organizational cost (or increases revenue) and the simple addition of consequences to modify behavior. The addition of performance-based contingencies not directly related to organizational savings/ gains is likely less complicated than comprehensive PFP and improves employee performance. An additional benefit of these systems is that they do not require an overhaul of the pay system as required in some forms of PFP, but rather may be presented as an adjunct to current pay. Numerous investigations can be found in the OBM literature where incentives have been added to existing pay structures to improve employee performances (Bourdon, 1977; Orpen, 1978; Slowiak, 2014). Slowiak (2014) used a package intervention consisting of goal setting, feedback, job aides, task clarification and contingent incentives (twice-weekly preferred items for meeting goals) to improve customer service in a medical clinic. This study demonstrated a relatively straightforward addition of consequences to an intervention package to influence performance. Other examples from this literature include more complex interventions such as token economies.

In a seminal study on safety, Fox, Hopkins, and Anger (1987) demonstrated a comprehensive system to decrease injuries in an open-pit mining operation. A token economy was implemented across two sites wherein employees earned tokens (stamps) redeemable for valuable back-up reinforcers for safety related behavior and lost stamps for injuries, accidents, and failing to report accidents. Not only did the reductions in costs exceed the cost of the program but the program maintained for years. In this example, the intervention targeted safety behavior which resulted in fewer injuries and thus saved the company money. It may be that some incentive programs, especially in human services, may need to target employee behavior which will not save money, at least in any easily measurable manner (e.g., the quality of discreet trials may have a long-term impact on the financial health of an organization but it would be difficult to quantify). So, interventions that do not directly, or quickly, impact the profitability of an organization must be considered carefully for cost.

Lotteries, or raffles, are a consequence intervention widely used in the OBM literature (Cook & Dixon, 2006; Evans, Kienast, & Mitchell, 1988; Miller, Carlson, & Sigurdsson, 2014). Lotteries typically involve one of many permutations in which meeting performance goals results in an opportunity, but not a guarantee, of contacting a back-up reward. Back-up rewards are often money, gift certificates, or other items with financial value. This intervention has the advantages of allowing for conditioned reinforcers, in the form of entry tickets, to be delivered close in time to employee performance, whereas the back-up rewards are only delivered to the lottery winners. Given that the back-up reinforcer represent the only significant cost and a small number of staff win the drawings the intervention is likely affordable for many human service organizations.

Several investigations have used lottery procedures to directly impact clinically significant targets. Miller et al. (2014) evaluated the effects of a combination goal setting, feedback, and weekly lottery system on integrity of discrete trial implementation. The participants in this study were one-on-one aides in a special education classroom. The lottery in this study consisted of drawings for a $25 gift certificate to a retail store of the winners choosing. The intervention was successful at increasing treatment integrity of discrete trial training (DTT).

In addition to implementation of learning trials, direct-care staff are often also tasked with completing paperwork that is required by funding agencies. Cook and Dixon (2006) recruited three supervisors in an agency providing group homes to adult with developmental disabilities. The dependent variable was the percent of subordinate paperwork completed. This study also implemented a lottery system for the supervisors but added to the literature separating out the effects of on-going feedback and feedback plus a lottery. Feedback first was effective in isolation, but became even more effective when combined with the lottery.

In addition to straightforward clinical applications, lotteries have also been used in human service settings to impact business operations. Luiselli et al. (2009) noted that absenteeism of direct-care staff is especially problematic as employees are required to provide supports. Luiselli et al. (2009) implemented a lottery system with public feedback in the form of daily and weekly rates of employee absenteeism and a prelottery informational brochure. The lottery consisted of a single weekly drawings of a significant financial incentive ($1000) for employees who met the attendance requirements. The intervention was successful in maintaining low rates of employee absences for 10 months.

The existing research of lotteries in human services applications suggests that they are effective across a variety of targets, especially when combined with feedback (Cook & Dixon, 2006). As a robust consequence intervention, lotteries also allow for customization to the specific work environment—often in empirical applications aspects such as the number of drawings, time of drawings, and value of back up rewards vary significantly. The potential customization not only makes it flexible for various environments, but also allows for employees to provide input into the design of the intervention which may increase the social validity of the intervention.

Only recently has research started examining specific characteristics that make lotteries effective. Gravina, Wilder, White, and Fabian (2005) examined a lottery in which the odds of winning were systematically varied. Depending upon the condition, odds of winning were 75%, 50%, or 25%. The authors found no significant difference between the conditions. Despite the variation in procedures, lotteries appear effective in various formats for improving employee performance when presented along with performance goals and objective feedback. Although there is not yet much research on this topic, it appears that lotteries may need to only payout a quarter of the time for entrants to be effective. This lends support to the idea that lotteries may be especially useful for practicing clinicians in that they may decrease the financial burden of a sustained consequence intervention.

In addition, although research has yet to evaluate this aspect of lotteries, conducting drawings frequently in group settings may allow for the supervisor to hold a celebration. In his classic text, Daniels (2000) recommends that behavior be reinforced often and that achievements, what the behavior resulted in, should be celebrated. Daniels recommends that in celebrations employees relive the achievement and management should encourage employees to tell stories about success. Tangibles, according to Daniels, should be designed to allow the employees to relive the experience. For example, a shift of workers who achieved a goal by working late several nights in a row may receive coffee cups with the slogan "The late night crew" emblazoned on the side. A lottery system may be embedded into such an arrangement wherein entry tickets and praise are delivered periodically for target behavior and the drawings are turned into celebrations of achievement. The implication of Daniels' recommendations is that to be most effective celebrations should be tied to organizational success. That is, the hard work of employees led to an accomplishment that can now be celebrated. Provided that the correct targets were selected, success in organizations will be achieved if employee performance improves. The focus for many clinicians will likely be clinical outcomes of clients and so the target behavior of employees should be selected carefully to improve clinical outcomes. If the goal of a clinician is to improve organizational profitability employee targets must be selected that will impact the finances which may, or may not, impact clinical outcomes. Although we are discussing improving employee performance, the development of an organization-wide improvement plan often necessary to significantly impact the financial well-being is beyond the scope of this paper.

Daniels (2000) also cautions against the delivery of tangibles per se. The caution being: if organizational achievement is celebrated and the organization realizes significantly increased revenue a $25 lottery drawing may be seen as insulting. This problem is avoided according to Daniels (2000) by customizing the reward so when people see the tangible item they are reminded of their success. Improvements in clinical behavior in employees should result in improvements in clinical outcomes which can be celebrated. By drawing attention away from financial indicators, the concerns outlined by Daniels may be avoided. However, this does not mean that clever clinicians cannot customize back-up rewards along with lottery drawings to increase customization and the chance that the item will represent employee success. Daniels (2000) is comprised of practice recommendations from one of the most experienced OBM practitioners, but nevertheless many of the specific claims have yet to be empirically validated. As such, his recommendations, although intuitive, should be considered cautiously until data are available.

Practice recommendations

It seems prudent to recommend against wholesale adoption of PFP for most readers. First, as seen in Long III et al (2012), not all employees prefer working under PFP systems and some human service agencies find it difficult to hire enough employees without turning away qualified applicants. In addition, state employment laws like those involved in independent contractors may make it difficult to implement such plans (it is advisable to consult an attorney before making changes to compensation). I will also assume that many readers are not in a position to recommend and implement a complete PFP system, and even if they were, PFP can be quite complex. For example, earlier in the chapter, I described a car salesperson on a type of PFP known as commission. At the same time that we may marvel at the degree to which they work long hours without direct supervision, we also know that many people have stories of being misled by salespersons who were powerfully motivated to sell a car. Prendergrast (1999) noted that employees will shift their responding towards tasks that are incentivized at the cost of others. For salespersons, if selling is incentivized whereas customer service is not, you may not get the strong customer-oriented interactions that lead to repeat customers over time.

Well-constructed PFP systems require careful analysis and implementation and even so, are not guaranteed to be immediately successful (Bateman & Ludwig, 2004). Also, if implemented incorrectly, employees may feel cheated or they may perform well, and if their ability to earn is not held in check by an organizational success index, they may earn more money than an organization can afford to pay. For those fully committed to realizing the benefits of a well-constructed PFP plan provide, I encourage you to carefully study a book length treatment of the subject such as Abernathy (2011).

As identified by Arco (1993), tangibles, intangibles, and client outcomes maintain staff behavior in human services organizations. Intangibles likely come primarily in the form of feedback on performance. This might be conceptualized as practices where employees who perform well receive regular praise for meeting goals, and corrective feedback when the occasional mistakes are made. However, a manager should not wander about aimlessly delivering praise to employees she catches working; it is possible to be caught working by a manager when one has been largely inactive most of the day. Although the occasional reinforcement error will not significantly impact an organization and may even aid in pairing the manager with reinforcement, it could appear unfair to employees who are meeting goals.

Before any incentive systems are considered, make sure that a fair and balanced observation tool is in-place and is used frequently, weekly is likely a good interval for many organizations to generate graphed data. Supervisors can use these data to provide timely feedback. Measuring employee performance is a difficult task but there are some general recommendations to follow. Limit yourself to a few targets that will have the greatest impact on the outcome. Selecting too many targets will create a measurement tool that is cumbersome and confusing. When setting up a measurement system, it is certainly possible to measure and graph several different aspects of employee performance separately, but it is often easier to collapse several measures together onto one tool that generates a single graph. The tool that allows for multiple measures to be evaluated together is called a point system. I recommend a specific point system called a performance matrix for employees (see

Daniels & Bailey, 2014 for guidance) but I will present a simplified version of the point system below to present the concept.

Fig. 6.1 represents a hypothetical point system for a direct-care staff member working in an early intervention center. On the left-hand side of the figure, there are five targets for the employees. All of these targets would need to be operationally defined and reviewed with the employees prior to data collection. Targets are located vertically on the left of the data sheet. The targets have been calibrated to weekly observations. "Observations with all elements" refers to quality checks (in this case perhaps two clinical checks are conducted per day by a clinician). The number of observations where all elements of the behavior plan are being followed are recorded and added up each week. The next three targets, "Rooms clean," "copies made," and "days on-time" refer to the number of days per week where technicians cleaned therapy rooms, made copies of data sheets for binders, and arrived to work on-time. The final target "trials per week" refers to the summed trials recorded by the technician each week. As all targets are not of equal importance, in point systems each target is assigned a number of points. In Fig. 6.1, "observations" and "trials" have been allocated 35 and 45 points, respectively, whereas the other targets are worth less. As all of the targets added together are worth 110 points, it is clear that observations and trials are considered the most important targets. However, as long as the total point value remains the same, the points that each target is worth can be changed to reflect changes in priorities without compromising the point system. To the right of each target are two numbers. The observed behavior can be seen across the top and the relative point values are found under the behavior. For "observations" if two integrity checks are conducted by clinicians 5 days per week, 10 observations would be the maximum number of correct demonstrations, and thus worth the most points. Note that the measure begins at four per week for the 'observations' target. The measurement tool can be designed to fit the needs of the practitioner, and in practice a score below four correct observations

Observations with all elements	Data	4	5	6	7	8	9	10
	Points	5	10	15	20	25	30	35
Rooms clean	Data			1	2	3	4	5
	Points			1	2	3	4	5
Copies made	Data			1	2	3	4	5
	Points			1	2	3	4	5
Days on-time	Data			1	2	3	4	5
	Points			0	0	10	15	20
Trials per week	Data	6000	6500	7000	7500	8000	8500	9000
	Points	15	20	30	30	35	40	45

Employee Name: B. Wine   Goal: 100

Week starting: 8/15   Total: 100

Figure 6.1 Weekly point system for a hypothetical employee with five measurement targets.

per week might never occur, or would trigger corrective actions, but in either case it is not worth any points.

All of the targets combined are worth a possible 110 points and the goal is 100 points. The system is calibrated to allow for employees to beat the goal (in this case by 10-points) to allow for achievement beyond the goal but it is not necessary. To make it easier for staff to orient to the data sheet a goal for each target has been bolded to allow for easier reference. By identifying a goal for each target it is abundantly clear what is expected of the employees. By way of example if B. Wine for the week beginning on August 15th achieves the following: 10 observations with correct implementation, 5 days with rooms clean and copies made, 4 days on-time, and 8621 trials recorded then a total of 100 points would be recorded. Note that for trials per week the score of 8621 exceeded the value for 40 points but did not meet the goal for 45 points and so 40 points were awarded. In addition to points being changed to match shifting priorities, targets can be added or removed from the data sheet, making for a flexible measurement tool.

A point system allows for easy goals setting and graphing, which are the two prerequisite components for any consequence-based intervention. Goals inform employees about what is required and should always be in-place. In general goals should be difficult but attainable for employees, but for clinicians the goals should be set so that the outcomes they are trying to receive will be influenced by the increase in performance. Graphing the data from points system can be accomplished simply (i.e., number of points earned) and should be tracked individually for each employee. In some settings these data may be publicly posted, and in others only group data are publicly posted. This is an individualized decision as having data on performance publicly posted for all to see might be problematic in some settings. In general, individual employees should be shaped with sincere feedback until they are continually meeting the goals and then groups of employees meeting the goal should be praised and occasionally celebrations should be held to recognize achievement.

Arco (1993) also suggested that seeing client progress motivates some employees. While certainly informal measures can influence client behavior (i.e., this child interacts with her peers now, and she did not do that a month ago) client data should be graphed and accessible to employees. Supervisors can also show improvements in client performance in addition to employee performance to demonstrate how their work is impacting the clients, thus allowing employees to most directly observe client outcomes. Fig. 6.2 presents a dual axis graph where employee performance, as captured in a hypothetical points system, is mapped on to the number of programs the client masters per week. Graphs of this type are also valuable tools for clinicians to see if the targets they selected are impacting the clients. In Fig. 6.2, it does appear that increase in the point system is impacting the number of programs the client is mastering. If the employee's performance improves in clinical targets and the client's behavior did not change, then it would suggest that the clinician did not select the correct targets, or that there are other variables in-place. If multiple employees work with a client, then measures can also be plotted per classroom for groups of employees to see the impact on other clients.

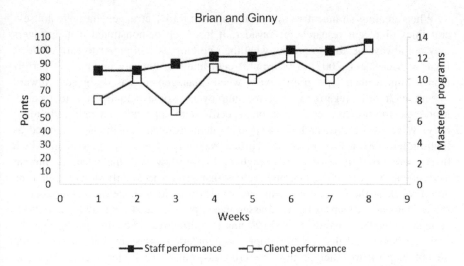

Figure 6.2 Sample performance data for an employee graphed with the results of instruction for a client.

Other client variables can be measured (again, for simplicity larger variables such as organizational profitability are not presented here, but are in the end, critical for organizational success) such as number of trial required to meet mastery, problem behavior, or milestones met. Assuming that a measurement system is in-place, goals are set, and regular feedback is delivered to employees we can now turn to the specifics of implementing tangible incentives.

When employees do not meet the goal we must first conduct an assessment of why they are faltering. Organizational assessment is complex and several tools and methodologies exist, but practitioners have several basic interview assessments at their disposal. Tools such as the performance diagnostic checklist (PDC) for general business environments (Austin, 2000), and PDC-human services (PDC-HS) (Ditzian, Wilder, King, & Tanz, 2015) have been empirically validated and can be used to assess performance problems so that specific treatment can be implemented. These tools use an interview format to identify problems with antecedents, training, processes, and consequences. Typically, a clinician interviews several relevant employees, tallies up the survey results and looks for areas where employees identify the greatest concern. For the purposes of this discussion, only consequences will be discussed.

Insufficient consequences are disastrous for anyone attempting to maintain performance. Daniels (2000) recommends using tangibles only as back-up reinforcement for social reinforcement. However, although we wait for research to answer questions about specific applications, it seems likely that tangibles are required in certain circumstances such as brief periods where extra effort is required or if feedback, praise, and client achievement is insufficient in maintaining performance.

When creating an incentive system to augment a PFT arrangement there are several lines of recent research to consider. It has been demonstrated that managers may not always be able to predict what their employees will prefer to earn (Wilder, Rost, & McMahon, 2007). This would seem intuitive but any number of "performance improvement" programs exists where management has designed a reward system with little regard to what the employees would actually like to receive. Moreover, the preferences for any one specific item appears to change fairly regularly. Wine, Kelley III, and Wilder (2014) demonstrated that items designated as high-preference or low-preference shifted regularly. The only interval at which there were no shifts from low-to-high or high-to-low was the smallest interval assessment, 1 week. One interpretation is that preferences shift slowly over time and 1 week is the longest interval one would want to wait before reassessing. If more than a week elapses between assessments preference shifts may become large enough to render existing reward systems less effective. It could also be that the both the items, and the specific employee population assessed yielded results that do not map on to other groups. Nevertheless, employee preferences change and these shifts need to be accounted for by reassessing preferences or having many reward options available.

Although minor shift in preference may decrease the relative efficacy of tangibles somewhat, these changes may not be large enough to truly impinge upon a reward system. It is important to note that one study suggests even a relatively low chance of receiving a nonpreferred item for completing work (i.e., 25%) negatively impacted the amount of work employees were willing to complete (Wine & Axelrod, 2014).

A common solution to the tangible preference problem could be to just use money to motivate employees. Wine, Gugliemella, and Axelrod (2013) found that money was not always the most preferred option amongst rewards of similar value. This would seem counterintuitive given that money can be used to obtain nearly all items an employee could desire, but one would do well to remember that there are items you cannot buy (taking an extra break) and that even an equivalent amount of money in gift certificates for example may have its advantages. To illustrate, imagine receiving a gift certificate to a coffee shop. Given that you cannot exchange the gift certificate, you almost have to spend it on a pleasurable item whereas cash could be spent on a pleasurable item, or it could be used to pay for an upcoming field trip for your third grader. If employees would prefer to earn items that are cheaper or more readily available than a financial incentive, the program may endure inflated costs.

Given that there is a need, how do we assess preferences? Although there are several different options available, one method seems especially useful. Reinforcer surveys involve listing several potential rewards and having employees assess each item individually. Typically, employees assess each option in terms of how much work they are willing to complete to earn the item. For example, an employee may give a score of 0 (not willing to complete any work at all) to 4 (willing to complete very much work) based on her or his interest in earning that item. Generally, a score of "3" or "4" would indicate highly preferred, and "0" or "1" would indicate nonpreferred items (Wine, Reis, & Hantula, 2014). Reinforcer surveys are effective at identifying potential rewards and do not have the drawback of forcing a distribution of items, as in ranking assessments. A ranking assessment that requires items to be organized from most to least preferred may suggest that some items at the bottom of the list are not preferred even if that is not the case. In light of recent research preference assessments may be useful not only in determining what an employee would prefer to earn but also what items an employee would not like to earn (items marked as "0" or "1"); should they receive these items for their efforts the results could be harmful to incentive systems (Wine & Axelrod, 2014).

There are a number of consequence interventions that can be used by clinicians to modify employee performance. Although it is possible for clinicians to track employee preferences and implement a specific tangible system for each employee this would seem to be both expensive and time consuming. Lotteries may be the most useful strategy for applying tangible consequences to improve employee performance. Lotteries allow for incentives to be added in a manner that may decrease the cost of traditional incentive programs, and allow for public celebrations of achievement.

Conclusion

When developing incentive programs there are many choices. As discussed above, you may elect to implement a comprehensive PFP system where employee performance is directly related to performance and the amount of money earned is tied to organizational effectiveness. However, these programs are complex and require substantial expertise and organizational control. There are alternatives that many could use to enhance employee performance.

First, assuming that employee problems are not a result of topics omitted in this chapter (training, or poorly constructed processes), managers should ensure that employees are being measured fairly and openly, using objective measures. Next, goals should be set that are fair and challenging to obtain and maintain. Also, feedback, should be delivered to employees frequently. Without fair measurement, feedback, and goals it is unlikely other interventions will be effective. Many texts discuss how to implement these components in great detail (Daniels & Bailey, 2014). A lottery system may be considered as a consequence intervention if needed. Lotteries will vary across implementation but a few guidelines are suggested. Employees should earn entry at least once weekly for meet predetermined goals. The number of entries may be augmented to provide for more reinforcement opportunities but one must be careful to keep this fair across all employees. Hold drawings at least weekly and make sure that the prizes available are large enough to motivate employees; if the reward is not cash it should be access to a catalogue of items for the participant to select that is generated from preference assessments. Hold the weekly drawings publicly and use them as an opportunity to genuinely praise those that met the entry criteria. To help develop the lottery it may be advisable to obtain employee input (i.e., should we have tiered goals, should the drawings be on Friday afternoons, etc.). Once the lottery is in-place, monitor it closely and consider changes as needed. Possible modifications include additional entries, increased number of drawings, and altering the value of back-up rewards. An additional benefit of lotteries may be realized if specific employees continually fail to earn entry into the lottery this may suggest that additional problems may need to be addressed. In this manner the lottery, if properly designed, may also help to identify employees with skill deficits, or identify other issues that have gone unnoticed.

Takeaways

1. Incentives are not likely to be effective if there is not a strong contingency between employee performance and the incentive.
2. Pay-for-performance creates a strong link between incentives and performance but can be complex to implement.
3. Fair and objective measurement of behavior, goal setting, and feedback should be in-place before any other intervention is attempted in an organization.
4. Lotteries are a financially viable intervention that can be tailored to organizations.
5. Any intervention in organizations must be evaluated not only for its effectiveness in changing employee behavior, but also in terms of an organizational outcomes. In human service setting typical outcomes are clinical effectiveness, increased revenue, and decreased cost.

References

Abernathy, W. B. (1996). *The sin of wages*. Memphis, TN: Perfsys Press.
Abernathy, W. B. (2011). *Pay for profit: Designing an organization-wide performance-based compensation system*. Atlanta, GA: Performance Management Publications, Inc.
Allison, D. B., Silverstein, J. M., & Galante, V. (1992). Relative effectiveness and cost-effectiveness of cooperative, competitive, and independent monetary incentive systems. *Journal of Organizational Behavior Management, 13*, 85–112.
Arco, L. (1993). A case for researching performance pay in human service management. *Journal of Organizational Behavior Management, 14*, 117–136.
Austin, J. (2000). Performance analysis and performance diagnostics. In J. Austin, & J. E. Carr (Eds.), *Handbook of Applied Behavior Analysis* (pp. 321–349). Reno, Nevada: Context Press.
Austin, J. A., Kessler, M. L., Riccobono, J. E., & Bailey, J. S. (1996). Using feedback and reinforcement to improve the performance and safety of a roofing crew. *Journal of Organizational Behavior Management, 16*, 49–75.
Barnes, C. M., Hollenbeck, J. R., Jundt, D. K., DeRue, D. S., & Harmon, S. J. (2011). Mixing individual incentives and group incentives: Best of both worlds or social dilemma? *Journal of Management, 37*, 1611–1635.

Bateman, M. J., & Ludwig, T. D. (2004). Managing distribution quality through an adapted incentive program with tiered goals and feedback. *Journal of Organizational Behavior Management, 23,* 33—55.

Bourdon, R. D. (1977). A token economy application to management performance improvement. *Journal of Organizational Behavior Management, 1,* 23—37.

Bucklin, B. R., & Dickinson, A. M. (2001). Individual monetary incentives: A review of different types of arrangements between performance and pay. *Journal of Organizational Behavior Management, 21,* 45—136.

Cook, T., & Dixon, M. R. (2006). Performance feedback and probabilistic bonus contingencies among employees in a human service organization. *Journal of Organizational Behavior Management, 25,* 45—63.

Daniels, A. C. (2000). *Bringing out the best in people: How to apply the astonishing power of positive reinforcement.* New York, New York: McGraw-Hill.

Daniels, A. C., & Bailey, J. S. (2014). *Performance Management: Changing behavior that drives organizational effectiveness* (5th ed.). Atlanta, GA: Performance Management Publications.

Ditzian, K., Wilder, D. A., King, A., & Tanz, J. (2015). An evaluation of the performance diagnostic checklist—human services to assess an employee performance problem in a center-based autism treatment facility. *Journal of Applied Behavior Analysis, 48,* 199—203.

Evans, K. M., Kienast, P., & Mitchell, T. R. (1988). The effects of lottery incentive programs on performance. *Journal of Organizational Behavior Management, 9,* 113—135.

Fox, D. K., Hopkins, B. L., & Anger, W. K. (1987). The long-term effects of a token economy on safety performance in open-pit mining. *Journal of Applied Behavior Analysis, 20,* 215—224.

George, J. T., & Hopkins, B. L. (1989). Multiple effects of performance-contingent pay for waitpersons. *Journal of Applied Behavior Analysis, 22,* 131—141.

Gravina, N., Wilder, D. A., White, H., & Fabian, T. (2005). The effect of raffle odds on signing in at a treatment center for adults with mental illness. *Journal of Organizational Behavior Management, 24,* 31—42.

Honeywell-Johnson, J. A., & Dickinson, A. M. (1999). Small group incentives. *Journal of Organizational Behavior Management, 19,* 89—121.

Johnson, D. A., & Dickinson, A. M. (2010). Employee-of-the-month programs: Do they really work? *Journal of Organizational Behavior Management, 30,* 308—324.

LaMere, J. M., Dickinson, A. M., Henry, M., Henry, G., & Poling, A. (1996). Effects of a multicomponent monetary incentive program on the performance of truck drivers. *Behavior Modification, 20,* 385—405.

Long, R. D., III, Wilder, D. A., Betz, A., & Dutta, A. (2012). Effects of and preference for pay for performance: An analogue analysis. *Journal of Applied Behavior, 45,* 821—826.

Luiselli, J. K., DiGennaro-Reed, F. D., Christian, W. P., Markowski, A., Rue, H. C., St., Amand, C., & Ryan, C. J. (2009). Effects of an informational brochure, lottery-based financial incentive, and public posting on absenteeism of direct-care human services employees. *Behavior Modification, 33,* 175—181.

Miller, M. V., Carlson, J., & Sigurdsson, S. O. (2014). Improving treatment integrity in a human service setting using lottery-based incentives. *Journal of Organizational Behavior Management, 34,* 29—38.

Orpen, C. (1978). Effects of bonuses for attendance on the absenteeism of industrial workers. *Journal of Organizational Behavior Management, 1,* 118—124.

Peter, L. J., & Hull, R. (1969). *The peter principle: Why things always go wrong.* New York, New York: Harper Collins Publishers.

Prendergrast, C. (1999). The provision of incentives in firms. *Journal of Economic Literature, 37,* 7−63.

Slowiak, J. M. (2014). "How may I help you?" Improving telephone customer service in a medical clinic setting. *Journal of Organizational Behavior Management, 34,* 39−51.

Webb, N. J., & Blandin, J. S. (2006). Evaluating executive performance in the public sector. *International Public Management Review, 7,* 98−117.

Wilder, D. A., Rost, K., & McMahon, M. (2007). The accuracy of managerial prediction of employee preference. *Journal of Organizational Behavior Management, 27,* 1−14.

Wine, B., & Axelrod, S. (2014). The effects of progressively thinning high-preference stimulus delivery on responding in employees. *Journal of Organizational Behavior Management, 34,* 291−299.

Wine, B., Gugliemella, C., & Axelrod, S. (2013). An analysis of generalized conditioned reinforcers in preference assessments. *Journal of Organizational Behavior Management, 33,* 244−251.

Wine, B., Kelley, D. P., III, & Wilder, D. A. (2014). An initial assessment of effective preference assessment intervals among employees. *Journal of Organizational Behavior Management, 34,* 188−195.

Wine, B., Reis, M., & Hantula, D. A. (2014). An evaluation of preference assessment methodology in organizational behavior management. *Journal of Organizational Behavior Management, 34,* 7−15.

Technology and Telehealth Applications

7

Aaron J. Fischer, Racheal Clark, Diana Askings and Erica Lehman
University of Utah, Salt Lake City, UT, United States

Technology and telehealth applications

Telehealth, as it pertains to behavioral health services, and specifically applied behavior analysis, is comprised of contemporary technology including telecommunication (i.e., videoconferencing and phone conversations), email, and short message service (i.e., text message), among others. Overall, services provided through technology, including telehealth, aim to increase the efficiency of tasks, while improving client access to services. As cutting edge hardware (e.g., smartphones, tablet computers, laptops, and smart watches) has become ubiquitous in our society, and related software that operate on those devices enable user access to a variety of valuable applications, behavioral analysts are able to use technology to enhance their service provision and improve outcomes for their clients.

This chapter discusses the application of technology, specifically telehealth, during behavior analytic practice, by presenting the past and current status of behavior analytic practitioner training in telehealth, the research base and implications for practice, and practice guidelines, procedures, and implementation recommendations.

Past and current status of behavior analyst telehealth training

As the demand for behavior analysts in a range of diverse settings continues to grow (Burning Glass Technologies, 2015), it is important to ensure that preservice and practicing providers aim to reduce service gaps and improve access to behavioral health services. Utilizing innovative technologies for service delivery provides one viable, immediate solution to help current and future practitioners work toward this goal. To this end, behavior analysts should gain the requisite skills and knowledge to appropriately incorporate service delivery through technology-based platforms into their practice. Although many training programs in behavior analysis operate through online platforms and utilize distance education, the following section will singularly focus on practitioner training in *the use of* technology and telehealth applications rather than receiving behavior analytic training *through* a web-

Applied Behavior Analysis Advanced Guidebook. DOI: http://dx.doi.org/10.1016/B978-0-12-811122-2.00007-3

based distance program [e.g., board certified behavior analyst (BCBA) approved course sequence].

Despite the inherent need for training in this topic, the rapid speed of technological advancement and the alluring convenience of its usage, as well as the recent proliferation of applied research in this area, have eclipsed the emergence of formal training and supervision for service providers. In behavior analysis, practitioner training in technology and telehealth applications can be categorized as two broad domains: a modality for service delivery or an intervention component. In professional practice, each application domain calls for a unique set of specific procedures, skills and competencies to obtain, and ethical considerations. For this reason, practitioners should receive didactic and experiential training in evidence-based practices specific to the integration of technology in service delivery and interventions. This preparation will ensure that program graduates can effectively integrate these contemporary tools as they enter professional practice. At present, practitioner training in the former domain remains highly variable and largely dependent upon the training experiences pursued independent of formal program requirements, while training in the latter domain is more commonly included.

Need for formal telehealth training

A comprehensive search through the course sequences of 30 on-campus master's level applied behavior analysis programs through The Association for Behavior Analysis International (ABAI) yielded no course titles or descriptions that pertained to technology and telehealth applications, and no reference was made to alternative modalities for service delivery (ABAI Training Directory, 2016). The material delivered in listed core and elective courses may indeed include information on applying technology to service delivery, though it is difficult to determine the extent to which these courses mention or emphasize technology and telehealth in either domain of application. This determination becomes even more difficult when considering supervised experiential training.

For university or other supervised practicum experiences, it is often the case that if current program research or practice involves technology or telehealth applications, preservice behavior analysts might be exposed to training around the integration of technology within behavior analysis outside of core coursework. Some behavior analytic training programs have developed a telehealth emphasis and have generated multiple studies examining the feasibility and efficacy of behavioral assessment and interventions delivered through telehealth. In these training programs many preservice behavior analysts receive training in telehealth service provision. On the other hand, without a preexisting program focus or faculty interest in this area, such opportunities are much less likely, and students would be required to independently explore this contemporary modality of service delivery without any form of training. In regard to the intervention component domain, if preservice behavior analysts are currently receiving any education or training in technology during coursework and practicum, it will most likely pertain to intervention applications.

Along these lines, a growing body of research has demonstrated a functional link between the application of technology-dependent behavioral interventions and changes in behavior (Gardner & Wolfe, 2015; Legge, DeBar, & Alber-Morgan, 2010; Lindhiem, Bennett, Rosen, & Silk, 2015). Although interventions using technology is not the primary focus of the present chapter, some examples of these intervention components include video modeling, electronic devices such as the MotivAider, and digital forms of the Picture Exchange Communication System. Computer and mobile device applications (i.e., apps) have also made significant contributions, especially in the area of electronic behavioral measurement (e.g., Decibel 10th and BehaviorSnap). These tools have been effectively used to enhance previously existing interventions based on behavior analytic principles to create a more robust behavioral intervention. For this reason, some of the tools have been cited in one of the leading comprehensive behavior analytic texts (Cooper, Heron, & Heward, 2006) and may be included in didactic and practicum training offered as part of behavior analytic training programs.

Telehealth training recommendations

As this service-delivery modality continues to become more prevalent in the broader psychological field as a means of improving access to mental health services (Fortney et al., 2015; Gray et al., 2015), it is important to consider incorporating more standardized training opportunities into supervised practicum experience and coursework for pre service behavior analysts. To this end, recommendations for training have been provided by other researchers and providers in the broad field of mental health and education who already work with telehealth technology. These general suggestions might serve as helpful guidelines for behavior analysts in training or who are already in practice and wish to initiate and sustain the provision of behavioral assessment and intervention services through telehealth (Dart, Whipple, Pasqua, & Furlow, 2016). Referring to the delivery of mental health services via telehealth, Barnett and Kolmes (2016) have established the goals of best practices in practitioner training by first defining two primary areas—*technological competence* and *clinical competence*. This division creates a helpful framework to conceptualize what best practice training in this novel modality of service delivery would look like for behavior analysts.

Technological competence, as defined by Barnett and Kolmes, refers to the knowledge base and procedural skills required to obtain and properly utilize all hardware and software, initiate and sustain connectivity, and ensure the protection of privacy. This knowledge base would include information about the available technological devices, and an understanding of which platforms would be best for individual client needs and other contextual factors. Barnett and Kolmes also pointed out that this knowledge and skillset must not only be sufficient for effective use on the practitioner's side, but also, at a level that will allow the practitioner to provide a brief training or information session to the client who will be receiving services through telehealth. This briefing would pave the way for smooth service delivery despite inevitable connectivity, audio, or visual problems. The authors also made the important point that use of this technology in a practitioner's personal life is not sufficient to be able to competently employ the devices in professional practice in the absence of explicit training regarding usage in this context. Ideally, a course on appropriate telehealth applications would cover this technological aspect of service delivery as well as the clinical competence component.

Barnett and Kolmes conceptualized clinical competence in telehealth service delivery would necessitate an ability to utilize careful clinical judgment in the consideration of whether or not telehealth service delivery would be an appropriate option to address the wide variation of needs across and within each client. Practitioners interested in providing services through telehealth should take coursework or professional training that reviews the research base of telehealth treatment outcomes, practical applications, and legal and ethical considerations.

Research base and implications for practice

In recent years, research on the feasibility, acceptability, and efficacy of technology and telehealth applications in behavior analysis has grown due to the rising demand for behavior analytic services, lack of behavior analytic professionals available in rural and underserved locations, and increased efficiency of service delivery. Aiming to bridge these service gaps and develop empirical support for this contemporary service-delivery modality, researchers have sought to examine the effectiveness and acceptability of using technology throughout the assessment and intervention process; from psychoeducation for caregivers to procedural integrity of a teacher's intervention implementation. Research has also been conducted to address similar questions pertaining to telehealth applications during more indirect service provision such as consultation and performance feedback.

These studies often have two primary goals: to determine the feasibility and efficacy of the specific technology mediated intervention implemented and to emphasize procedures and methods to establish practice guidelines and implications for appropriate use within the field. In fact, behavior analysts are leading the charge in many school- and clinic-based applications of telehealth (Barretto, Wacker, Harding, Lee, & Berg, 2006; Fischer et al., 2016b). Although a substantial amount of studies have explored this topic in recent years, the effectiveness and generalization of telehealth as a service-delivery model is still being evaluated following promising initial support. The subsequent section will describe the current state of research that uses technology and telehealth applications in behavior analytic practice during direct (i.e., assessment, intervention, progress monitoring) and indirect (i.e., consultation and feedback) service delivery. A table of the articles included in this section is shown in Table 7.1, which describes the goal of each article, the technology used, and a summary of results.

Table 7.1 **Review of behavior analytic telehealth studies**

Article	Goal	Reported technology used	Summary of results
Alnemary et al. (2015)	Training teachers to conduct FAs	Skype, laptop, web camera, PowerPoint	Participants met mastery criteria for correct FA implementation across at least two conditions
Ashburner et al. (2016)	Evaluating the feasibility of an intervention program delivered through telehealth	Article did not specify	Participants rated the telehealth service delivery as socially valid
Bahrav and Reiser (2010)	Parent training to support reciprocal communication skills of children with ASD	Skype, laptop computer, bluetooth wireless headset	Skills acquired following in vivo therapy were maintained using a combination of in vivo and telehealth treatment
Barretto et al. (2006)	Conducting FAs via telehealth	Television monitors, camera, microphone, multimedia projectors, and PowerPoint	FAs were performed through telehealth with an acceptable levels of procedural integrity
Breitenstein and Gross (2013)	Examining the feasibility and acceptability of a web-based parent training program	Android tablet, videotaped vignettes	The intervention was feasible and acceptable for families of low SES
Davis et al. (2013)	Examining the efficacy of a telemedicine intervention for pediatric obesity in rural areas	Article did not specify	The improvement in the behavioral telemedicine group was not significantly different from the in vivo physician care group
Fischer et al. (2016a)	Evaluating the effectiveness and acceptability of teleconsultation in schools	Vsee, digital video cameras, and box	Teleconsultation resulted in improved student outcomes, and was an acceptable medium for service delivery

(Continued)

Table 7.1 **(Continued)**

Article	Goal	Reported technology used	Summary of results
Fisher et al. (2014)	Evaluating knowledge and correct implementation following a virtual Registered Behavior Technician training program	Blackboard website, GoToMeeting, webcam, Bluetooth headset, and Ethernet connection cord	Participants demonstrated statistically significant gains in implementation, and rated the program highly in terms of acceptability and social validity
Fischer et al. (2016b)	Evaluating the acceptability of videoconferencing in schools	FaceTime, tablet	Teachers found teleconsultation acceptable
Frieder et al. (2009)	Examining the feasibility of web-based teleconsultation in school settings	Two cameras, a digital video recorder (DVR), a monitor for the DVR, and a remote access software program	School staff implemented FA procedures with high levels of procedural fidelity
Funderburk et al. (2015)	Comparing outcomes following the provision of live and remote parent training intervention	Internet-based encrypted audio-visual technology, live video consultation equipped room, working internet connection	Service provision through teleconsultation increased efficiency and potentially maximized outcomes
Gibson et al. (2010)	Using videoconferencing to deliver behavioral interventions	laptop, webcam, and skype	Problem behavior decreased
Hay-Hansson & Eldevik (2013)	Comparing the efficacy of in person and telehealth discrete trial training	Laptop, external web camera, Movi, and external speakers	There were no significant differences in fidelity between on site-and telehealth training program outcomes

(Continued)

Table 7.1 **(Continued)**

Article	Goal	Reported technology used	Summary of results
Heitzman-Powell et al. (2014)	Evaluating the feasibility of delivering an ABA parent training program remotely	Password protected online learning management system, Polycom videoconferencing, telemedicine rooms with microphones and a television monitor	Parents reached mastery criteria of implementation fidelity of evidence-based interventions with their children
Ingersoll et al. (2016)	Comparing outcomes from a self-directed and therapist-led web-based parent training intervention	Article did not specify	Parents that received coaching via telehealth in addition to the web-based training modules made greater gains compared to parents who only received the modules
Lindgren et al. (2016)	Determining the efficacy of a parent-training telehealth intervention	Video recording equipment, windows-based laptops, webcams, and Ethernet cables	Implementation fidelity did not significantly differ across clinic telehealth, home telehealth, and in-home therapy service-delivery models
Machalicek et al. (2009)	Conducting FAs through videoconferencing and developing behavior support plans	Laptop computers, web cameras, iChat videoconferencing software, and a broadband internet connection	FAs were feasible, and function-based interventions reduced challenging behavior
Machalicek et al. (2010)	Providing feedback via telehealth immediately after FA implementation	Laptop computer, web camera, desktop computer with a built-in camera, iChat videoconferencing software	Procedural fidelity improved, and participants reported that the intervention was socially acceptable

(Continued)

Table 7.1 (**Continued**)

Article	Goal	Reported technology used	Summary of results
Machalicek et al. (2016)	Teaching parents to implement FAs through telehealth	Laptop computer, web camera, USB cable, iChat, eCamm call recording software	Function-based intervention strategies taught to parents following the FA, which reduced challenging behaviors
McCarty et al. (2015)	Determining the feasibility of a telehealth parent training intervention	Article did not specify	Parents demonstrated improved knowledge and rated the intervention as highly acceptable
McCulloch and Noonan (2013)	Effectiveness of online training program for increasing manding	Article did not specify	Implementation integrity and spontaneous manding increased
Myers et al. (2015)	Evaluating the efficacy of a multicomponent intervention program delivered through telehealth	Article did not specify	Individuals receiving the multicomponent intervention had superior outcomes compared to those in primary care
Neely et al. (2016)	Evaluation of a telehealth training model for practitioners	Tablet with built in microphone and camera, external hard drive, Vsee, desktop computer, and laptop computers	Practitioners reached and maintained high levels of fidelity
Reese et al. (2012)	Evaluating the efficacy of a parent training program delivered through telehealth	Camera, microphone, speaker, monitor, and network connection	Parents reported improved child behavior and reduced parental stress
Reese et al. (2015)	Evaluating the efficacy of a parent training program provided through telehealth	Web camera, microphone, speaker, monitor, network connection, HDTV monitors, a desktop computer, and overhead microphones	Rural families received higher quality diagnostic services, children received diagnosis earlier, and older children were identified

(*Continued*)

Table 7.1 (Continued)

Article	Goal	Reported technology used	Summary of results
Sourander et al. (2016)	Determining the efficacy of a web-based parent training program combined with telephone coaching	Article did not specify	Participation in the intervention improved and disruptive child behaviors decreased
Suess et al. (2014)	Evaluating the fidelity of functional communication interventions delivered via telehealth	Laptop, webcam, Ethernet cable, and used Skype	Interventions were delivered with high levels of fidelity and problem behaviors were decreased
Suess, Wacker, Schwartz, Lustig, and Detrick (2016)	Feasibility of telehealth service delivery in an outpatient behavior clinic	Desktop computers, webcams, and headsets	Problem behavior was decreased
Taylor et al. (2008)	Evaluating the efficacy of a web-based delivery and consultation with the Incredible Years program	Hard drives and dial up internet service	Participants reported high levels of acceptability with the program and
Taylor et al. (2015)	Comparing the efficacy of in-person and web-based delivery of a parent training program	Article did not specify	Significant reductions in parenting stress were found for both groups, however the in-person group showed greater levels of improvement
Tse et al. (2015)	Comparing the efficacy of in-person and teletherapy delivery of a parent training program	Administrative web portal, real-time data management system	There were no significant differences between in-person service delivery and teletherapy service delivery

(*Continued*)

Table 7.1 **(Continued)**

Article	Goal	Reported technology used	Summary of results
Vismara et al. (2013)	Evaluating the efficacy of parent training program delivered via telehealth	Website portal with many interactive features	Parent knowledge, parent skills, and child skills reportedly improved
Wacker et al. (2013a)	Conducting FAs of problem behavior via telehealth	Desktop computers, webcams, and headsets	FAs were successfully implemented by parents
Wacker et al. (2013b)	Comparing the efficacy of in-person and telehealth functional communication training	Desktop computers, webcams, and headsets	In-person and telehealth service-delivery modalities significantly reduced problem behavior
Wainer and Ingersoll (2015)	Evaluating the efficacy of a parent training imitation intervention provided through telehealth	Article did not specify	Participants showed significant improvements after receiving the self-directed modules and remote coaching
Xie et al. (2013)	Evaluating the efficacy of a parent training intervention provided via teleconsultation	University provided videoconferencing system	Acceptability and child outcomes were not significantly different for the in-vivo and telehealth group

Technology and telehealth applications in behavioral assessment

Technology can be used to provide various professionals, school personnel, and families with the training (i.e., information and skills) required to perform behavioral assessment procedures. For example, indirect and direct assessment may take place via prerecorded videos or real time interaction through videoconferencing. As part of the assessment process, behavior analysts typically integrate information obtained from a host of possible sources: caregivers, client family members, systematic data collection, and experimental procedures. This information gathering process is time intensive, although necessary, to gain sufficient understanding of the target behavior in order to provide appropriate interventions that are functionally linked to the presenting problem. In describing the role of telehealth applications in behavioral assessment, we will first address indirect forms of assessment before moving on to more direct and experimental methods.

During the indirect assessment process, the behavior analyst may need to interview the caregivers or other individuals that have observed the target behavior. This is traditionally done in person; however, various technological devices now allow behavior analysts to interview an individual, or group of individuals, in different locations that may not otherwise be easily accessible. There are many ways to collect indirect assessment data such as correspondence over email, record reviews using cloud storage, interviews through videoconferencing, video recordings, and even conversations over the telephone. By conducting these indirect assessment methods through remote communication, the clinician is able to access individuals that may be difficult to reach in person and eliminate significant travel and overhead costs. For example, if a school, treatment facility, or individual caregiver in a rural location does not have access to a BCBA, they may consult with a professional over the phone or use videoconferencing software to discuss their behavioral concerns and set up initial data collection systems to gain more information that will ultimately inform intervention plans.

Using technology, behavior analysts may also collect direct and experimental assessment data, or train and coach caregivers and educational personnel to do so. Practitioners may conduct live observations over videoconferencing software and video recordings of the target behavior occurring in the natural environment may be collected and sent to the behavior analyst to evaluate the target behavior. Even functional analyses (FA) can be conducted over live videoconferencing with procedural information provided to the clinician, teacher, or caregiver using "bug in the ear" coaching. However, this procedure requires the behavior analyst to provide in-depth training to the assessor prior to the FA sessions in order to ensure that the assessor will be able to properly manipulate the environment.

Research on conducting behavioral assessments using telehealth in clinical, school, and residential settings

In 1997, the Biobehavioral Service (BBS) clinic at the University of Iowa began using videoconferencing over a statewide telehealth network to provide behavioral services to families throughout Iowa (Barretto et al., 2006). Due to the rural environment and lack of locally trained professionals, Barretto and colleagues provided brief FAs for children with developmental and behavioral disorders using telehealth. In a case study example, they were able to successfully train local individuals without prior formal training to conduct FAs and determine the function of two children's behaviors (Barretto et al., 2006). Between 1997 and 2000, the BBS clinic completed more than 75 assessments using videoconferencing technology, thus leading the field in telehealth models of behavioral assessment.

As the inception of technological modalities in behavioral assessment, there have been multiple studies outlining the various applications of technology as a platform through which training in assessment procedures may be delivered. For instance, Alnemary, Wallace, Symon, and Barry (2015) successfully provided functional behavior assessment (FBA) and FA training to four special education teachers, on a different continent, who lacked the resources and access to professionals necessary to conduct FBAs or FAs. The teachers had no previous experience with FBA procedures and were trained over videoconferencing in a group format with individualized feedback provided. The results indicated that all four teachers mastered the skills taught across at least two of four training conditions. This study provided evidence of the feasibility of training behavioral assessment procedures to individuals that did not have access to services otherwise in distant locations.

Interestingly, Lambert, Lloyd, Staubitz, Weaver, and Jennings (2014) found that an automated training program on teaching trial-based FA procedures improved preservice behavior analyst's performance when conducting FAs; however, the participants were unable to consistently reach acceptable levels of fidelity when attempting to implement the procedures. Similarly, Trahan and Worsdell (2011) found that participants who interacted with a training DVD on FAs could not effectively teach FA procedures to 90% mastery criteria, and all participants required feedback to meet the performance criterion. These studies suggest that training in behavioral assessment procedures through current web-based and DVD modalities may not alone be sufficient to adequately train individuals and may require supplemental training components such as live practice with a trained professional or performance feedback as described in the study by Alnemary et al. (2015) for best practice implementation.

Behavioral assessment and training has also been provided to parents and caregivers within residential settings. For example, Machalicek et al. (2016) provided behavioral consultation to the parents of three children with autism spectrum disorder (ASD) using telehealth applications over desktop computers in the client's home. In order to inform the interventions, the parents conducted Fas, and they were interviewed by the researchers to provide information for FBAs. The parents were trained on each FA condition prior to the session, and they were also coached through the procedure as they were conducting the FA over videoconferencing. The results of the parent implemented FA informed function-based interventions that were effective in reducing the challenging behavior of each child. Furthermore, Lee et al. (2015) used telehealth in residential settings to train parents to conduct FAs and provide functional communication training (FCT) for children with ASD to decrease problem behavior. The article also described general guidelines and considerations for telehealth practice with caregivers in home settings. The researchers recommended that when providing telehealth behavioral services in residential settings, it is important to consider the equipment necessary for telehealth implementation (e.g., internet connection, hardware, and software) including ongoing technical support and troubleshooting. Overall, both of these studies suggest that the telehealth model can also be applied to home settings by conducting behavioral assessments that inform function-based interventions.

Intervention and consultation

Following a comprehensive direct or indirect assessment of the presenting concerns, behavior analysts are charged with developing, implementing, and collecting a substantial amount of data to develop a function-based intervention. Due to the distance between the behavior analyst and the client, telehealth interventions are typically conducted using a triadic model of consultation. In this indirect service-delivery model, the behavior analyst (i.e., consultant) will collaborate with a consultee (e.g., parent, school personnel, or clinicians) over a telehealth application in order for the consultee to provide the intervention to the client. Often, the interventions that practitioners develop may be targeted to address a specific area (e.g., feeding, toileting, or self-injurious behavior) or the intervention might be intended to address more broadly defined challenging behaviors such as with FCT. In either case, the behavior analyst must program for generalization and ensure that the skills acquired will be employed in the wide variety of settings the client may encounter following intervention. However, it isn't feasible for the behavior analyst to directly ensure the maintenance of skills across this wide range of settings for each client. Instead, parent and caregiver training, school consultation, and clinical consultation with interventionists are important components of any behavioral intervention that is implemented using telehealth (Fischer et al., 2016b; Murphy & Zlomke, 2016; Preece, 2014).

Intervention and consultation in home settings

It is important to ensure that intervention outcomes are sustained in a variety of environments. To this end, technology and telehealth applications are especially helpful for a number of reasons: remote service provision increases the efficiency of provision by eliminating travel time for the family to the clinic or the clinician to the family's home, treatment can be conducted in the naturalistic environment that contains the discriminative stimulus for the problem behavior to occur, and data collection will be significantly less reactive for the family. Considering this logic, researchers have designed studies in which parents are trained via telehealth to implement behavioral interventions in the home setting, while simultaneously receiving coaching and feedback from the behavior analyst. In some cases, these studies also included technology mediated training materials that caregivers were instructed to view prior to implementation.

One such study implemented a hybrid self-directed and coaching intervention designed to increase imitation skills among children with ASD (Wainer & Ingersoll, 2015). Using a multiple baseline design, each of five parent–child dyads received access to a slideshow with built in audio which taught the intervention and then received three sessions of coaching and feedback via videoconferencing. During both conditions (i.e., self-directed and coaching), the researchers measured implementation integrity by rating the parents on the extent to which they correctly followed the intervention protocol. The results showed that two participants were able to achieve sufficient integrity after completing the online training modules, and the other participants considerably improved following the coaching condition. By the conclusion of the study, parents were generally able to implement the intervention as intended following the delivery of a technology-based intervention package that entirely circumvented travel time and taught skills in a naturalistic setting. In addition, parents found the intervention to be acceptable. Similarly, Vismara, McCormick, Young, Nadhan, and Monlux (2013) provided videoconferencing and web-based training to parents of children with ASD using a single-case, multiple baseline design. Eight child−parent dyads were provided information and training on the Early Start Denver Model intervention using laptops and web-cameras. The intervention lasted for 12 weeks and all parents found the website acceptable. More importantly, the parents found that the consultation (i.e., coaching and feedback) provided over videoconferencing was a vital component necessary to properly implement the intervention. Furthermore, all of the children who participated in the study increased the frequency of their functional vocal utterances, although they did not make significant gains in joint attention.

Another study by Heitzman-Powell et al. (2014) examined an intervention package also intended to improve access to behavioral services, especially for individuals living in rural areas. However, rather than presenting the online modules and live coaching as separate conditions to be delivered sequentially, each of eight modules was presented to seven families of children with ASD through videoconferencing, immediately followed by a coaching session that allowed parents to practice the behavioral skills just taught with their children. For the videoconferencing sessions, parents traveled to a nearby school, hospital, or clinic. The results of the study found that the parents increased their knowledge of behavioral skills by an average of 39% and their implementation of behavioral skills improved by an average of 41% after the training. Furthermore, the parents found the training acceptable. However, like most studies in this area, the article concluded with a call for additional research with larger groups of participants to provide further evidence of the intervention's effectiveness.

Intervention and consultation in school settings

In school settings, FBAs can be conducted using technology to observe in the classroom, inform behavioral intervention plans, collect intervention data, monitor intervention fidelity, and provide feedback to the consultee. In particular, the United States Federal Law, Individuals with Disabilities Education Act (IDEA; IDEA Improvement Act, 2004), mandates that behavioral intervention plans are informed by FBAs for students with disabilities who also exhibit behavioral problems in schools. With the need for behavioral assessments and intervention plans in schools, behavior analysts are increasingly working with student and teacher populations. Telehealth is helping these behavior analysts consult with school districts that lack the access to, but are in great need of, behavioral health services.

Frieder, Peterson, Woodward, Crane, and Garner (2009) consulted with and trained teachers in a rural school to conduct FAs and function-based interventions, with fidelity, for students using web-based technologies. In this study, the teachers were provided with an initial face-to-face training on FAs. Once trained, cameras captured the FA conditions implemented by the teachers, and both web-based and phone communication were used to provide coaching and feedback. Around this same time, Machalicek et al. (2009) used videoconferencing to consult with untrained special education graduate students in conducting FAs and developing behavioral support plans for two students with ASD. Instead of using expensive and highly sophisticated equipment, researchers used laptop computers and basic web-cameras. The interventions selected were informed by the FAs conducted via live coaching over videoconferencing and resulted in decreased problem behavior and increased academic engagement of the students. Expanding on their own research, Machalicek et al. (2010) also trained teachers to conduct FAs with their students using performance feedback by videoconferencing over laptops and web-cameras. The researchers found that upon receiving performance feedback through videoconferencing, the teachers were able to conduct FAs with high levels of fidelity; however, the teacher's performance declined during the maintenance phase. This finding suggests that ongoing consultation support and feedback is likely necessary to implement FAs and interventions with fidelity and is echoed in other teleconsultation studies (Frieder et al., 2009; Lambert et al., 2014; Machalicek et al., 2009, 2010; Trahan & Worsdell, 2011; Vismara et al., 2013; Wainer & Ingersoll, 2015).

Further providing evidence of the effectiveness of telehealth applications in school settings, Fischer et al. (2016a) provided behavioral consultation to three teacher-student dyads located in different States. Using laptop computers, classroom video recordings, and videoconferencing, the consultants collected indirect and direct data on the target behaviors in order to provide function-based interventions. All three teachers implemented the interventions with greater than 80% procedural integrity and the behavior of all three students improved, suggesting that using tele-health in school settings for consultation is an effective service-delivery model (Fischer et al., 2016a). The teachers also found both the intervention and the service-delivery method to be highly acceptable and easy to use. Furthermore, in order to compare the acceptability of in-person consultation and teleconsultation in school settings, Fischer et al. (2016b) conducted a study on the acceptability of the initial interview conducted within a behavioral consultation framework (Frank & Kratochwill, 2014). Sixty teachers participated in interviews and experienced interviews in both formats. Prior to the interviews, teachers rated teleconsultation as an acceptable service-delivery modality, and they reported higher ratings of acceptability after experiencing the teleconsultation interview (Fischer et al., 2016b).

Although the research on teleconsultation often includes the use of laptop computers and web-cameras, new devices such as telepresence robots (e.g., Kubi and Double (images shown in Figs. 7.1 and 7.2)) are breaking further barriers in consultation by allowing remotely located consultants to physically move and look around the environment they are viewing. For example, the Kubi is a desktop robot that integrates with many tablet computers. The consultant can tilt and turn the robot using a web based application, and although the robot is stationary, the consultant is able to look around the room. This allows consultants to be able to follow a moving client around a room during observations more easily. The Double is another

Figure 7.1. Double robot.

device that allows a remote consultant to view and move around an environment. Unlike the Kubi, the Double can be driven, which allows mobility and access to many locations without the assistance of other staff members. Both the Kubi and the Double robots were used in three studies conducted by Thompson et al. (2016). In these studies, conjoint behavioral consultation (Sheridan & Kratochwill, 2008) was provided to special education teachers, paraprofessionals, and parents. The first study examined the use of 3-step prompting procedure to increase the compliance of three students with ASD at school and at home using a multiple baseline design. The researchers found increases in compliance, high levels of procedural integrity, and high acceptability rates across all participants. In the second study, researchers coached teachers and paraprofessionals to conduct brief FAs on students in their classroom. The results demonstrated that FAs using mobile telepresence robots were feasible and that they could be efficiently conducted in a special education classroom setting without disrupting instruction. The last study used a concurrent multiple baseline with a changing criterion design to teach a student to identify numbers by systematically fading number opacity. This academic intervention taught the student to independently recognize three numbers at least 80% across

Figure 7.2. Kubi robot.

trials. The results further indicated that teleconsultation through telepresence robots was an effective modality to provide consultation for an academic intervention.

Intervention and consultation in clinical settings

Telehealth provided interventions have also been effectively demonstrated in clinical settings. For example, Neely, Rispoli, Gerow, and Hong (2016) found that interventionists could be trained to implement incidental teaching with fidelity for preschool students with ASD using an online module, self-evaluation, and performance feedback over videoconferencing. In this study, iPads were used to communicate with the interventionists over VSee, a HIPPA compliant videoconferencing platform. Another study conducted by Suess et al. (2016) further supported the use of telehealth consultation and intervention in outpatient clinical settings. The researchers provided FA coaching to the parents of five children located in a separate clinic over Skype using laptop computers and web-cameras. The results of the FA informed a targeted FCT intervention to be used for each of the families. The results found that there was an average 65.1% reduction in the target problem behaviors and an increase in independent task completion and manding across all participants (Suess et al., 2016). Similarly, Wacker et al. (2013a, b) trained parents to implement a FCT intervention to reduce the problem behavior of 17 children with ASD. Although the intervention was provided to the parents, they traveled to regional clinics to receive coaching over a telehealth network. The FCT interventions, informed by FAs conducted by their parents also trained over the telehealth network, reduced the children's problem behavior an average of 93.5%.

The studies cited above provide initial evidence of the usefulness of telehealth as a service-delivery system for behavior analysts; however, it is important to note that many of these studies did not use manualized procedures (e.g., problem-solving consultation (Frank & Kratochwill, 2014)). Behavior analysts should be applying evidence-based procedures when using telehealth, and future research should be conducted on various manualized procedures and interventions to make the literature more robust and inform best-practice for home, clinical, and school settings.

Implications and future directions

Overall, the research suggests that telehealth may successfully be utilized as a service-delivery model for a variety of populations and to address numerous behavioral applications. It is important, however, to consider the features of the device or program (e.g., confidentiality, ease of use, cost, etc.) and the unique needs of the client (e.g., familiarity and comfort using technology, access to technology, etc.) when using telehealth as a service-delivery modality. There are three main benefits to consider when using technology to provide assessment, intervention, and consultation for clients: ease of access to services, increased flexibility in the provision of services, and reduced cost.

Many rural and underserved communities lack access to psychological and behavioral health services. Prior to the use of telehealth, many behavior analysts had to physically travel expansive distances to provide consultation or the burden of access was placed on the client to find and travel to clinics while spending many resources, including time and money, in order to access services. Otherwise, many families and schools lacked the ability to assess and provide appropriate interventions for individuals in need of behavioral health services. Now, with the application of telehealth, it is much easier to provide services in rural and underserved areas.

Telehealth is a flexible service-delivery model not only due to its capacity to reach individuals in remote or underserved locations, but in its ability to meet with multiple individuals in different locations and to alleviate scheduling concerns. For instance, a behavior analyst could simultaneously meet with a student's teachers while they are in a classroom, their parents while they are at their home, and the school principal who is out of town for a conference all in their respective locations. The behavior analyst may also be able to view the client in a variety of natural environments where the behavior is emitted rather than in clinical settings. Furthermore, telehealth provides flexibility in schedule changes and instantly accessing information. For example, during a formal observation, the target behavior might not be emitted, but the behavior may occur once the behavior analyst is not available. In this case, the individual could be recorded and viewed at a later time by the professional.

Lastly, when providing services to clients in rural areas, it can be incredibly costly to travel and meet in person. This does not even include the amount of time lost traveling, in which the behavior analyst could be consulting with other clients. By using telehealth for service delivery, the travel costs and amount of time needed to reach clients are dramatically decreased. Lindgren et al. (2016) found that there was no significant difference in the quality of services provided or behavioral outcomes between telehealth and traditional in-person behavioral services in reducing problem behavior, but there was a significantly reduced cost for implementing interventions using telehealth compared to in-person services. Providing services over telehealth platforms allow for the behavior analyst to more efficiently spend their time and resources. However, it is important to consider the client's access to electronic devices necessary for telehealth services to be implemented. The initial cost of such devices, software, and internet connectivity may indeed be a considerable cost and require training and troubleshooting in the use of the device.

Despite the growing research and popularity of using various applications of telehealth in behavioral practice, there is still a need for more research on the appropriate use of technology to provide ethical and best-practice services to clients. Future research should continue to evaluate the effectiveness of various electronic devices in the assessment, intervention, and consultation of behavioral health services. Due to the novelty of applying technology to behavioral health services and the rapid pace of technological innovations, it may be difficult for early career and even seasoned behavior analysts to know which programs or electronic devices to use. To further complicate the matter, technology is continually updating with new versions of hardware and software constantly being released. Due to these challenges, researchers should continue to evaluate the generalizability of services provided through telehealth platforms and compare systems in order to inform practitioners on which platforms should or should not be considered for specific uses. Furthermore, various behavioral health services should be formally evaluated to understand the scope and limitations of this delivery model.

Practice guidelines, procedures, and implementation recommendations

Whether behavioral health services are provided via telehealth or in person, practitioners are required to comply with a number of guidelines that are in place, legally and ethically. These rules, regulations, and guidelines also depend upon the setting in which services are being provided, therefore, practitioners need to become familiar with the relevant stipulations. Within the services that are provided using technology, it is important to understand how these regulations apply and what further consideration is necessary to practice professionally. Furthermore, there are multiple sources of outlined and enforced procedures with entities overlapping and expanding upon one another, thus causing practitioners to be highly vigilant about staying up to date on each of the governing bodies.

Legal and ethical considerations

The Health Insurance Portability and Accountability Act (HIPAA) of (1996), Public Law 104-191, outlines the United States Federal privacy and security standards that apply to most providers delivering telehealth services. In addition to the Federal standards, there may also be state privacy and security standards. HIPAA most typically applies when patients' health information is electronically communicated for purposes regarding insurance payments and other third party reimbursement. Under HIPAA there are two central rules: the Privacy Rule and the Security Rule.

The primary goal of the Privacy Rule is to assure that individuals' health information is properly protected while also allowing health information to be shared among providers who are involved. The Privacy Rule requires that providers also use reasonable safeguards to avoid unauthorized or unintended parties to gain access to an individual's protected health information (PHI; HIPAA Administrative Simplification Rules, 2003). Although this rule outlines using reasonable safeguards, it is important to note that no specific actions or practices are mandated to comply with the safeguard requirement. The Privacy Rule applies to all forms of PHI—electronic, paper, and verbal information. Under the Privacy Rule individuals have rights over their health information where they can request a copy of their medical records and request corrections.

The Security Rule is specific to electronic PHI, and aims to protect against unintended disclosure, alteration, or loss of electronic PHI. One important clarification about the Security Rule is that it only applies to providers who store or transmit electronic PHI; this does not include communication with individuals by videoconferencing, telephone, or fax. Similar to the Privacy Rule, the Security Rule does not outline specific security measures or technology that should be used to comply with the rule, such as encryption or password protection.

Providers are given the responsibility to implement policies and practices that are most appropriate for the size, function, and needs of the provider or organization. Large institutions and large-scale health care delivery systems most typically have private secure networks (i.e., virtual private networks) to receive, communicate, and store PHI. Therefore, the conscience and careful research and development of safeguard and security practices falls to providers who are independent of such large healthcare networks (i.e., independent practice). Under the Federally established HIPAA regulations, the Health and Human Services Office of Civil Rights is charged with enforcing HIPAA. Providers are also advised to familiarize themselves with the state rules and regulations regarding electronic PHI storage and transmission as well as potential guidelines for providing telehealth services.

In addition to HIPAA regulations, the Health Information Technology for Economic and Clinical Health (HITECH) Act (2009) was adopted to strengthen the privacy, security, and enforcement rules under HIPAA. The HITECH Act outlines procedures and consequences for the privacy and enforcement regulations of HIPAA. More specifically the HITECH Act addresses the practitioner's legal obligations in the event of an improper disclosure as well as the full extent of the consequences that will follow proper and improper procedures. Although HIPAA and the HITECH Act are Federally enforced procedures, the Family Educational Rights and Privacy Act (FERPA) is yet another Federal stipulation that provides further guidelines for school-based professionals and contracted consultants (34 C.F.R. § 99, 2011). In addition to the legal obligations associated with technology use, practitioners are also obligated to uphold the professional and ethical rules of their respective licensure boards.

The Behavior Analyst Certification Board (BACB) released the Professional and Ethical Compliance Code for Behavior Analysts, which is an update and replacement of a previous version, which went into effect on the first of January 2016 (Behavior Analyst Certification Board, 2014). This code incorporates 10 sections that are relevant to every BCBAs' professional and ethical conduct in relation to responsibilities, research, assessment, treatment, and supervision. Although the full extent of the code should be taken into consideration when using technology as it would be without technology, those parts of the code that outline technology use will be discussed.

Initiation of services

First, the primary responsibility of a BCBA is the benefit and well-being of the client. With the use of technology, most services are provided using a consultation model, given that all parties will benefit from the services, a hierarchy needs to be established in order to better define who the BCBA's primary obligation is to. Upon establishing services, the BCBA needs to gain appropriate consent for all parties involved. For example, if working within a school setting, teacher and parent consent, and potentially student assent is required to provide services. The consent process needs to include explicit permission for electronic recording, if indicated. Consent must be gained when using information for multiple purposes, separately and in explicit terms (e.g., research, instructional or training purposes, etc.). In addition, the scope of services and involved parties' rights (e.g., access to service records and data) need to be outlined so that all parties involved have a full understanding of the services.

Confidentiality

When providing services, the behavior analyst needs to consider the location in which sessions are conducted or observed. Sessions and recordings need to be viewed where PHI can be protected. Upon beginning services, the behavior analyst needs to disclose the limits of confidentiality and that as a BCBA they are mandated to report any suspected abuse with persons they work with. This is especially important when considering that services may take place in the home, school, or clinical setting. In addition, extra attention needs to be paid to the storage methods of electronic files. The BACB requires that records be maintained for seven years. There are a number of ways that these files can be stored including secure cloud storage, external sources (e.g., external hard drive or flash drive) maintained with the same security as paper records, or password protected on an electronic device such as a personal computer.

Assessment and intervention

When employing technology during behavioral assessment and intervention, remote observations will be a key component of the services. With remote observations, the practitioner needs to be aware of the variance in the environment and instruct the implementer to arrange the environment properly. The variables present in the environment are important to identify and account for throughout services, the behavior analyst needs to adequately train the implementer. The implementer's knowledge and subsequent control over the environment becomes a point of emphasis in order to uphold the integrity and efficacy of the services. In addition to environmental factors that may impose upon services, medical and other possible biological factors should be ruled out before proceeding, or if additional variables are present, treatment should incorporate consultation with pertinent outside providers, if necessary.

In relation to supervisory responsibilities when using technology, a BCBA supervisor should maintain the same capacity when using technology. If providing supervision using teleconferencing, feedback that is given based on recorded treatment time should be provided on a consistent basis in order to fully support the supervisee. If a supervisor is planning to observe a live session from a different location than the supervisee, all parties should be notified and all observers need to do so from a secure location.

Implementation recommendations

Although there are legal and ethical guidelines set forth for behavior analysts, there are no guidelines specific to the use of technology for BCBAs. As mentioned earlier, the Federal regulation (i.e., HIPAA) does not present specific requirements for the types of technology, however, the American Telemedicine Association (ATA) has specified a number of technical guidelines for practitioners using telehealth service options (American Telemedicine Association, 2014). The following implementation recommendations outline communication applications, equipment, connectivity, and privacy.

First, the applications used in telehealth services need to have proper verification, confidentiality, and security criterion. At present, available platforms that maintain the necessary components include, but are not limited to, Adobe Connect, Polycom, TruClinic, Vidyo, and VSee. All data transmission need to be secure through the use of encryption that meets recognized standards (e.g., National Institute of Standards and Technology).

In order to ensure the adequacy of services, devices and equipment should use high quality cameras, audio, and transmission. When providing services, the latest version of the software should be used and maintenance procedures, including frequent update checks, should be completed in order to maintain the safety and security of the software. When using technology, a protocol should be in place in case of a security breach or software failure. This protocol needs to be reviewed and updated routinely, especially considering the ever-changing components of technology. With regard to internet connectivity, the bandwidth needs to be at least 384 kbps (.384 mbps) for both upload and download speeds (ATA, 2014). Different technologies will yield different video quality results at the same bandwidths, this emphasizes the importance of testing and adjusting bandwidth when possible in order to maximize quality, and in turn maximize the adequacy of services.

In addition, providers should be familiar with the technologies available that employ adequate computer and mobile device security, and individuals receiving services should be educated regarding privacy and security options. The provider and client should have access to specific privacy features of videoconferencing including audio and video muting and the option to switch from private to public audio mode (i.e., using headphones). If recording any portion of the services, behavior analysts need to discuss what will be recorded, how the recording will be stored, and what steps will be taken to ensure privacy. As mentioned earlier, clients are legally entitled to their records and data, it is also important to discuss a provider's policy regarding the sharing of information with the public. A written agreement outlining this issue can be used to protect all involved parties.

When the use of a mobile device is employed, special attention should be placed on the relative privacy of information that is communicated. Contact information that the provider retains on any device needs to be sufficiently restricted; in other words, devices need to require a passphrase or equivalent security feature, and when multifactor authentication is available it is recommended. In addition, automatic device locking functions should be incorporated in order to minimize the risk of security breaches. The ATA recommends that a time lapse is implemented, and that, this device "timeout" should be activated after 15 minutes of inactivity, if not less (American Telemedicine Association, 2014). Practitioners should also sustain the whereabouts of all devices that hold sensitive information at all times. In the case of a lost or stolen device, the practitioner needs to have the ability to remotely deactivate or delete the stored information. Those entities providing and storing information electronically should consider procedures for routine consolidation and clean-up of all electronic healthcare records and forms with consideration of legally outlined timelines.

Finally, when using videoconferencing software, procedural safeguards need to be in place to restrict more than one session from being opened at any time by a provider, although the session may include more than two relevant parties. The use of multiple cameras during the same session is permitted given the secure transmission and storage of the recordings. All PHI and other confidential information needs to be stored in secure locations, this includes cloud storage. It is important to recognize that all forms of information and data need secure storage locations, cloud storage should meet HIPAA/HITECH standards. The transmission and storage of confidential information can be monitored on both the provider's and client's computer hard drives. All teleconferencing software and cloud storage software should be decided upon prior to initiating any services provided with technology. There are a number of preferred and recommended components of such software that enables services to be provided via telehealth and with the sole use of technology.

Features important for behavior analysts

It is important to discuss what features of a teleconferencing software are most important to behavior analytic work. Fischer et al. (2016a) identified six features that include onscreen document sharing, group videoconferencing, instant messaging, recording capabilities, integrated cloud storage, and legal compliance. Onscreen document sharing is important when providing behavioral services, this enables the BCBA to share and review data, provide graphing assistance, and watching video together in order to directly provide feedback or give specific procedural examples. Group videoconferencing is an important means of full inclusion, if there are multiple disciplines or parties in different locations, having software that can fully integrate a team promotes a more supportive environment. Instant messaging within the videoconferencing software can be utilized in many helpful ways including providing feedback during an observation that is not disruptive to the client and documenting ideas and plans in the same application. The capability to record a session or meeting eliminates the need for a second camera, which also promotes the feature of integrated cloud storage in order to cut down on the number of secure storage locations. The teleconferencing software that is legally compliant with the rules and regulations makes it possible to safely use and store information when using these features. Overall, these important features create an environment that is similar to in person services, they also provide the means to execute effective and increase fidelity of the behavioral services.

Conclusion

This chapter discussed the application of technology and telehealth during the practice of applied behavior analysis, while identifying legal, ethical, and practical considerations. At present, there is a strong foundation supporting the use of telehealth during the practice of applied behavior analysis; however, more research needs to be conducted to expand the breadth and depth services. In addition, as novel technology becomes readily available, researchers should take the initiative to conduct studies using that technology and share with the behavior analytic community through conference proceedings and publications. The practice of behavior analysis can be highly accessible and efficient when technology is integrated into research and practice, and as such, telehealth technology should be considered when it is possible, and empirical support. Finally, although contemporary technology is at times readily accessible and exciting due to their novelty, practitioners and researchers should only use technology when it helps solve a practical problem in research or practice.

Practice guidelines checklist

1. Use HIPAA and FERPA compliant software during research and practice.
2. Using technology and telehealth during research and practice can be exciting—remember to be familiar with practice guideless and ethical considerations.
3. Learn how to troubleshoot the technology before you provide services through telehealth.
4. Before providing telehealth services, conduct trainings with clients teaching them how to use telehealth software and applications.
5. Only use technology when it increases the efficiency to solve socially valid problems.

References

34 C.F.R. § 99. (2011). Family Educational Rights and Privacy Act (FERPA). Retrieved from http://www2.ed.gov/policy/gen/guid/fpco/ferpa/index.html.

Alnemary, F. M., Wallace, M., Symon, J. G., & Barry, L. M. (2015). Using international videoconferencing to provide staff training on functional behavioral assessment. *Behavioral Interventions*, *30*(1), 73−86. Available from http://dx.doi.org/10.1002/bin.1403.

American Telemedicine Association. (2014). Core operational guidelines for telehealth services involving provider-patient interactions. Retrieved from http://www.americantelemed.org/resources/telemedicine-practice-guidelines/telemedicine-practice-guidelines/core-operational-guidelines-for-telehealth-services-involving-provider-patient-interacti ons#.V9v_WmWhTnQ.

Ashburner, J., Vickerstaff, S., Beetge, J., & Copley, J. (2016). Remote versus face-to-face delivery of early intervention programs for children with autism spectrum disorders: Perceptions of rural families and service providers. *Research in Autism Spectrum Disorders*, *23*, 1−14. Available from http://dx.doi.org/10.1016/j.rasd.2015.11.011.

Association for Behavior Analysis International, Behavior Analysis Training Directory (2016). *Searchable Database.* Retrieved from https://www.abainternational.org/accreditation/training-directory.aspx.

Bahrav, E., & Reiser, C. (2010). Using telepractice in parent training in early autism. *Telemedicine & E-Health*, *16*(6), 727−731.

Barretto, A., Wacker, D. P., Harding, J., Lee, J., & Berg, W. K. (2006). Using telemedicine to conduct behavioral assessments. *Journal of Applied Behavior Analysis*, *39*(3), 333−340.

Barnett, J. E., & Kolmes, K. (2016). The practice of tele-mental health: Ethical, legal, and clinical issues for practitioners. *Practice Innovations*, *1*(1), 53−66. Available from http://dx.doi.org/10.1037/pri0000014.

Behavior Analyst Certification Board (BACB). (2014). Behavior Analyst Certification Board guidelines for responsible conduct for behavior analysts. Retrieved from http://bacb.com/wp-content/uploads/2016/03/160321-compliance-code-english.pdf.

Breitenstein, S. M., & Gross, D. (2013). Web-based delivery of a preventive parent training intervention: A feasibility study. *Journal of Child & Adolescent Psychiatric Nursing*, *26*(2), 149−157. Available from http://dx.doi.org/10.1111/jcap.12031.

Burning Glass Technologies. (2015). US Behavior Analyst Workforce: Understanding the National Demand for Behavior Analysts 2015.

Cooper, J. O., Heron, T. E., & Heward, W. L. (2006). *Applied behavior analysis* (2nd ed.). Upper Saddle River, NJ: Pearson/Merrill-Prentice Hall.

Dart, E. H., Whipple, H. M., Pasqua, J. L., & Furlow, C. M. (2016). Legal, regulatory, and ethical issues in telehealth technology. In J. K. Luiselli, & A. J. Fischer (Eds.), *Computer-assisted and web-based innovations in psychology, special education, and health* (pp. 339−363). San Diego, CA, US: Elsevier Academic Press.

Davis, A. M., Sampilo, M., Gallagher, K. S., Landrum, Y., & Malone, B. (2013). Treating rural pediatric obesity through telemedicine: Outcomes from a small randomized controlled trial. *Journal of Pediatric Psychology*, *38*(9), 932−943. Available from http://dx.doi.org/10.1093/jpepsy/jst005.

Fischer, A. J., Dart, E. H., Radley, K. C., Richardson, D., Clark, R., & Wimberly, J. (2016a). Evaluating the effectiveness of videoconferencing as a behavioral consultation medium. *Journal of Educational and Psychological Consultation*, 1−22. doi:10.1080/10474412.2016.1235978.

Fischer, A. J., Dart, E. H., Leblanc, H., Hartman, K. L., Steeves, R. O., & Gresham, F. M. (2016b). An investigation of the acceptability of videoconferencing within a school-based behavioral consultation framework. *Psychology in the Schools*, *53*(3), 240–252.

Fisher, W. W., Luczynski, K. C., Hood, S. A., Lesser, A. D., Machado, M. A., & Piazza, C. C. (2014). Preliminary findings of a randomized clinical trial of a virtual training program for applied behavior analysis technicians. *Research in Autism Spectrum Disorders*, *8*(9), 1044–1054. Available from http://dx.doi.org/10.1016/j.rasd.2014.05.002.

Fortney, J. C., Pyne, J. M., Turner, E. E., Farris, K. M., Normoyle, T. M., Avery, M. D., & Unützer, J. (2015). Telepsychiatry integration of mental health services into rural primary care settings. *International Review of Psychiatry*, *27*(6), 525–539. Available from http://dx.doi.org/10.3109/09540261.2015.1085838.

Frank, J. L., & Kratochwill, T. R. (2014). School-based problem-solving consultation: Plotting a new course for evidence-based research and practice in consultation. In W. P. Erchul, S. M. Sheridan, W. P. Erchul, & S. M. Sheridan (Eds.), *Handbook of research in school consultation* (2nd ed, pp. 18–39). New York, NY: Routledge/Taylor & Francis Group.

Frieder, J. E., Peterson, S. M., Woodward, J., Crane, J., & Garner, M. (2009). Teleconsultation in school settings: Linking classroom teachers and behavior analysts through web-based technology. *Behavior Analysis In Practice*, *2*(2), 32–39.

Funderburk, B., Chaffin, M., Bard, E., Shanley, J., Bard, D., & Berliner, L. (2015). Comparing client outcomes for two evidence-based treatment consultation strategies. *Journal of Clinical Child and Adolescent Psychology*, *44*(5), 730–741. Available from http://dx.doi.org/10.1080/15374416.2014.910790.

Gardner, S. J., & Wolfe, P. S. (2015). Teaching students with developmental disabilities daily living skills using point-of-view modeling plus video prompting with error correction. *Focus On Autism & Other Developmental Disabilities*, *30*(4), 195–207.

Gibson, J. L., Pennington, R. C., Stenhoff, D. M., & Hopper, J. S. (2010). Using desktop videoconferencing to deliver interventions to a preschool student with autism. *Topics in Early Childhood Special Education*, *29*(4), 214–225.

Gray, M. J., Hassija, C. M., Jaconis, M., Barrett, C., Zheng, P., Steinmetz, S., & James, T. (2015). Provision of evidence-based therapies to rural survivors of domestic violence and sexual assault via telehealth: Treatment outcomes and clinical training benefits. *Training and Education in Professional Psychology*, *9*(3), 235–241. Available from http://dx.doi.org/10.1037/tep0000083.

Hay-Hansson, A. W., & Eldevik, S. (2013). Training discrete trials teaching skills using videoconference. *Research in Autism Spectrum Disorders*, *7*(11), 1300–1309. Available from http://dx.doi.org/10.1016/j.rasd.2013.07.022.

Health Information Technology for Economic and Clinical Health (HITECH) Act. (2009). Title XIII of Div. A and Title IV of Div. B of the American Recovery and Reinvestment Act of 2009, Public Law. No. 111–5.

Health Insurance Portability and Accountability Act (HIPAA). (1996). Public Law No. 104-191, 110 Stat. 1936. The Individuals with Disabilities Education Improvement Act of 2004, Public Law No. 108-446, §101, 118 Stat. 2647 (2004).

Heitzman-Powell, L. S., Buzhardt, J., Rusinko, L. C., & Miller, T. M. (2014). Formative evaluation of an ABA outreach training program for parents of children with autism in remote areas. *Focus on Autism & Other Developmental Disabilities*, *29*(1), 23–38.

HIPAA Administrative Simplification Regulation Text (2003). 45 C.F.R. § 160, 162, and 164.

Individuals with Disabilities Education Act (2004). 20 U.S.C. § 1400.

Ingersoll, B., Wainer, A. L., Berger, N. I., Pickard, K. E., & Bonter, N. (2016). Comparison of a self-directed and therapist-assisted telehealth parent-mediated intervention for children with ASD: A pilot RCT. *Journal of Autism and Developmental Disorders, 46*(7), 2275—2284. Available from http://dx.doi.org/10.1007/s10803-016-2755-z.

Lambert, J. M., Lloyd, B. P., Staubitz, J. L., Weaver, E. S., & Jennings, C. M. (2014). Effect of an automated training presentation on pre-service behavior analysts' implementation of trial-based functional analysis. *Journal of Behavioral Education, 23*(3), 344—367.

Lee, J. F., Schieltz, K. M., Suess, A. N., Wacker, D. P., Romani, P. W., Lindgren, S. D., & Dalmau, Y. P. (2015). Guidelines for developing telehealth services and troubleshooting problems with telehealth technology when coaching parents to conduct functional analyses and functional communication training in their homes. *Behavior Analysis in Practice, 8*(2), 190—200. Available from http://dx.doi.org/10.1007/s40617-014-0031-2.

Legge, D. B., DeBar, R. M., & Alber-Morgan, S. R. (2010). The effects of self-monitoring with a MotivAider[R] on the on-task behavior of fifth and sixth graders with autism and other disabilities. *Journal of Behavior Assessment and Intervention in Children, 1*(1), 43—52.

Lindgren, S., Wacker, D., Suess, A., Schieltz, K., Pelzel, K., Kopelman, T., & Waldron, D. (2016). Telehealth and autism: Treating challenging behavior at lower cost. *Pediatrics, 137*, S167—S175.

Lindhiem, O., Bennett, C. B., Rosen, D., & Silk, J. (2015). Mobile technology boosts the effectiveness of psychotherapy and behavioral interventions: A meta-analysis. *Behavior Modification, 39*(6), 785—804. Available from http://dx.doi.org/10.1177/0145445515595198.

Machalicek, W., Lequia, J., Pinkelman, S., Knowles, C., Raulston, T., Davis, T., & Alresheed, F. (2016). Behavioral telehealth consultation with families of children with autism spectrum disorder. *Behavioral Interventions, 31*(3), 223—250. Available from http://dx.doi.org/10.1002/bin.1450.

Machalicek, W., O'Reilly, M., Chan, J. M., Lang, R., Rispoli, M., Davis, T., & Didden, R. (2009). Using videoconferencing to conduct functional analysis of challenging behavior and develop classroom behavioral support plans for students with autism. *Education and Training in Developmental Disabilities, 44*(2), 207—217.

Machalicek, W., O'Reilly, M. F., Rispoli, M., Davis, T., Lang, R., Franco, J. H., & Chan, J. M. (2010). Training teachers to assess the challenging behaviors of students with autism using video tele-conferencing. *Education and Training in Autism and Developmental Disabilities, 45*(2), 203—215.

McCarty, C., Vander Stoep, A., Violette, H., & Myers, K. (2015). Interventions developed for psychiatric and behavioral treatment in the children's ADHD telemental health treatment study. *Journal of Child & Family Studies, 24*(6), 1735—1743.

McCulloch, E. B., & Noonan, M. J. (2013). Impact of online training videos on the implementation of mand training by three elementary school paraprofessionals. *Education and Training in Autism and Developmental Disabilities, 48*(1), 132—141.

Murphy, J., & Zlomke, K. R. (2016). A behavioral parent-training intervention for a child with avoidant/restrictive food intake disorder. *Clinical Practice in Pediatric Psychology, 4*(1), 23—34. Available from http://dx.doi.org/10.1037/cpp0000128.

Myers, K., Stoep, A. V., Zhou, C., McCarty, C. A., & Katon, W. (2015). Effectiveness of a telehealth service delivery model for treating attention-deficit/hyperactivity disorder: A community-based randomized controlled trial. *Journal of The American Academy of Child & Adolescent Psychiatry, 54*(4), 263—274. Available from http://dx.doi.org/10.1016/j.jaac.2015.01.009.

Neely, L., Rispoli, M., Gerow, S., & Hong, E. R. (2016). Preparing interventionists via tele-practice in incidental teaching for children with autism. *Journal of Behavioral Education*. Available from http://dx.doi.org/10.1007/s10864-016-9250-7.

Preece, D. (2014). Providing training in positive behavioural support and physical interventions for parents of children with autism and related behavioural difficulties. *Support for Learning*, *29*(2), 136−153.

Reese, R. J., Slone, N. C., Soares, N., & Sprang, R. (2012). Telehealth for underserved families: An evidence-based parenting program. *Psychological Services*, *9*(3), 320−322. Available from http://dx.doi.org/10.1037/a0026193.

Reese, R. J., Slone, N. C., Soares, N., & Sprang, R. (2015). Using telepsychology to provide a group parenting program: A preliminary evaluation of effectiveness. *Psychological Services*, *12*(3), 274−282.

Sourander, A., McGrath, P. J., Ristkari, T., Cunningham, C., Huttunen, J., Lingley-Pottie, P., & Unruh, A. (2016). Internet-assisted parent training intervention for disruptive behavior in 4-year-old children: A randomized clinical trial. *JAMA Psychiatry*, *73*(4), 378−387. Available from http://dx.doi.org/10.1001/jamapsychiatry.2015.3411.

Suess, A. N., Romani, P. W., Wacker, D. P., Dyson, S. M., Kuhle, J. L., Lee, J. F., & Waldron, D. B. (2014). Evaluating the treatment fidelity of parents who conduct in-home functional communication training with coaching via telehealth. *Journal of Behavioral Education*, *23*(1), 34−59.

Sheridan, S. M., & Kratochwill, T. R. (2008). *Conjoint behavioral consultation: Promoting family−school connections and interventions*. New York, NY: Springer.

Suess, A. N., Wacker, D. P., Schwartz, J. E., Lustig, N., & Detrick, J. (2016). Preliminary evidence on the use of telehealth in an outpatient behavior clinic. *Journal of Applied Behavior Analysis*, . Available from http://dx.doi.org/10.1002/jaba.305.

Taylor, L., Leary, K., Boyle, A., Bigelow, K., Henry, T., & DeRosier, M. (2015). Parent training and adolescent social functioning: A brief report. *Journal of Child & Family Studies*, *24*(10), 3030−3037. Available from http://dx.doi.org/10.1007/s10826-014-0106-2.

Taylor, T. K., Webster-Stratton, C., Feil, E. G., Broadbent, B., Widdop, C. S., & Severson, H. H. (2008). Computer-based intervention with coaching: An example using the Incredible Years program. *Cognitive Behaviour Therapy*, *37*(4), 233−246. Available from http://dx.doi.org/10.1080/16506070802364511.

Thompson, M.C., Clark, R.R., Bloomfield, B.S., Askings, D.C., McClelland, A.L., Lehman, E., & Erchul, W.P. (2016). *Conjoint behavioral teleconsultation for special education teachers*. Poster presentation at the 2016 Annual American Psychological Association Conference in Denver, CO.

Trahan, M. A., & Worsdell, A. S. (2011). Effectiveness of an instructional DVD in training college students to implement functional analyses. *Behavioral Interventions*, *26*(2), 85−102.

Tse, Y. J., McCarty, C. A., Stoep, A. V., & Myers, K. M. (2015). Teletherapy delivery of caregiver behavior training for children with attention-deficit hyperactivity disorder. *Telemedicine and E-Health*, *21*(6), 451−458. Available from http://dx.doi.org/10.1089/tmj.2014.0132.

Vismara, L. A., McCormick, C., Young, G. S., Nadhan, A., & Monlux, K. (2013). Preliminary findings of a telehealth approach to parent training in autism. *Journal of Autism and Developmental Disorders*, *43*(12), 2953−2969.

Wainer, A., & Ingersoll, B. (2015). Increasing access to an ASD imitation intervention via a telehealth parent training program. *Journal of Autism & Developmental Disorders, 45* (12), 3877–3890. Available from http://dx.doi.org/10.1007/s10803-014-2186-7.

Wacker, D. P., Lee, J. F., Dalmau, Y. P., Kopelman, T. G., Lindgren, S. D., Kuhle, J., Pelzel, K. E., & Waldron, D. B. (2013a). Conducting functional analyses of problem behavior via telehealth. *Journal of Applied Behavior Analysis, 46*(1), 31–46. Available from http://dx.doi.org/10.1002/jaba.29.

Wacker, D. P., Lee, J. F., Dalmau, Y. P., Kopelman, T. G., Lindgren, S. D., Kuhle, J., Pelzel, K. E., Dyson, S., Schieltz, K. M., & Waldron, D. B. (2013b). Conducting functional communication training via telehealth to reduce the problem behavior of young children with autism. *Journal of Developmental and Physical Disabilities, 25*(1), 35–48. Available from http://dx.doi.org/10.1007/s10882-012-9314-0.

Xie, Y., Dixon, J. F., Yee, O. M., Zhang, J., Chen, Y. A., DeAngelo, S., & Schweitzer, J. B. (2013). A study on the effectiveness of videoconferencing on teaching parent training skills to parents of children with ADHD. *Telemedicine and E-Health, 19*(3), 192–199. Available from http://dx.doi.org/10.1089/tmj.2012.0108.

Further reading

Carr, J. E., & Fox, E. J. (2009). Using video technology to disseminate behavioral procedures: A review of functional analysis: A guide for understanding challenging behavior (DVD). *Journal of Applied Behavior Analysis, 42*(4), 919–923. Available from http://dx.doi.org/10.1901/jaba.2009.42-919.

Fischer, A .J., Schultz, B. K., Collier-Meek, M. A., Zoder-Martell, K., & Erchul, W. P. (2016c). A critical review of videoconferencing software to support school consultation. *International Journal of School & Educational Psychology*. doi:10.1080/21683603.2016.1240129.

Section II

Consultation Practices

Consultation Practices: School-Based Instructional Support 8

Brian K. Martens[1], Robin S. Codding[2] and Samantha J. Sallade[1]
[1]Syracuse University, Syracuse, NY, United States, [2]University of Minnesota, Minneapolis, MN, United States

Introduction

The need for instructional consultation in schools

Data from the National Center for Education Statistics (NCES, 2015) show that approximately a third of all 4th graders nationwide (31%) continue to perform below the basic level in reading, with about 1 in 5 children scoring below the basic levels in math (18%) and writing (20% of 8th graders in 2011). In all content areas, these numbers are even higher for African-American children and those who qualify for free or reduced-price lunch. Nationwide, for example, nearly half (48%) of African-American 4th graders and 44% of children receiving free or reduced-price lunch scored below the basic level in reading (NCES, 2015).

To reduce the large numbers of children at risk for academic failure, the Individuals with Disabilities Education Improvement Act (IDEA) of (2004) encouraged schools to adopt a data-based systems approach for identifying children with learning disabilities. This approach, known as *response to intervention* (RtI), allowed local education agencies to "use a process that determines if the child responds to scientific, research-based intervention as a part of the evaluation procedures" (Part B, Section 614, [b], 6, B). In addition, IDEA 2004 encouraged schools to make use of a comprehensive *school-wide positive behavior support* (SWPBS) system in which the strength of intervention for children's classroom behavior problems was matched to the size and need of the population being served (Daly, Martens, Barnett, Witt, & Olson, 2007; Erchul & Martens, 2010).

RtI models for children's learning problems and SWPBS models for children's behavior problems are organized similarly, and include school-wide universal interventions at Tier 1, small-group standard protocol interventions at Tier 2, and individualized intensive interventions at Tier 3. Children who show inadequate RtI at each level receive more intensive intervention, and data from the child's cumulative intervention history are used to make high-stakes diagnostic and eligibility decisions (Daly et al., 2007).

For children who are at risk for academic problems, school-based consulting teams are responsible for implementing instructional interventions at Tiers 2 and 3 of an RtI model. Toward this goal, consulting teams make use of a systematic problem solving process to identify an academic area of concern, define a target

Applied Behavior Analysis Advanced Guidebook. DOI: http://dx.doi.org/10.1016/B978-0-12-811122-2.00008-5

academic skill or set of skills within this area, assess the child's level of proficiency in executing the skill, and select an appropriate evidence-based instructional intervention to teach the skill (Erchul & Martens, 2010). The NCES data suggest that in some schools large numbers of children may require Tier 2 or Tier 3 instructional intervention services. This need was anticipated by IDEA 2004 which also mandated that school-based consulting teams receive high-quality intensive preparation and training to ensure they have the skills and knowledge necessary to address children's academic problems (Part A, Section 601, C,[5], E).

Differences between children's academic and behavior problems

Children's academic problems are different from classroom behavior problems in several ways, and these differences have important implications for designing instructional interventions (Martens, Daly, & Ardoin, 2015). First, many behavior problems are learned through interaction with direct care providers and occur as behavioral *excesses* (e.g., Beavers, Iwata, & Lerman, 2013). As such, behavior problems are often maintained by one or more sources of socially mediated reinforcement (e.g., allowing the child to escape academic demands), the value of which is established in part by ineffective teaching and classroom management practices (e.g., assigning work that is too difficult; Mueller, Nkosi, & Hine, 2011; Witt, VanDerHeyden, & Gilbertson, 2004). Second, both the establishing and reinforcing variables for children's behavior problems are discoverable in the sense that their operation in the classroom can be revealed by conducting a functional behavior assessment (Martens & Lambert, 2014; Martens et al., 2015). Once identified, these controlling variables can be eliminated, reversed, or weakened by implementing a reinforcement-based intervention matched to the function of problem behavior (e.g., Martens, Witt, Daly, & Vollmer, 1999). In contrast, academic problems are skills that have not been learned and therefore occur as behavioral *deficits*. Behavioral deficits are academic responses (e.g., math computation) that have not been brought under stimulus control of curriculum materials (e.g., addition problems with sums to 20) and therefore have no, too weak, or too few controlling variables in the classroom (Martens et al., 2015). Unlike behavioral intervention, the fundamental goals of instructional intervention are to establish, strengthen, and diversify stimulus control over academic responding so children can meet increasingly more difficult academic demands in school and beyond.

Accomplishing the goal of instructional intervention poses challenges to school-based consulting teams who must work with limited time and resources. For example, instructional interventions are often implemented for relatively short periods of time (e.g., 2−3 times a week for a portion of the school year), and it is impossible to reteach an entire curriculum of basic skills concurrent with grade-level instruction. These limitations mean that consulting teams must decide where in a curriculum sequence to begin instruction, which skills are most important or pivotal to teach, and what is the most efficient way to teach them. The goals of this chapter are to contrast historical and current approaches to designing school-based instructional interventions, describe the behavioral principles underlying effective instruction, and present best practice recommendations to help consulting teams select and implement evidence-based instructional interventions and monitor student progress.

The past and present of school-based instructional intervention

It has long been axiomatic in education and psychology that instruction should be tailored to the needs of individual students. How to accomplish this goal in a public education system that currently serves over 50 million children (National Center for Educational Statistics, 2016) has been a source of considerable debate since the middle of the 20th century (Reschly, 2004). Stemming from this debate, efforts to accommodate children who fail to benefit from regular class instruction have gone through at least two major eras; the era of special education reform (1975–97) and the era of early intervention (1997 to the present).

Beginning with the passage of PL94–142 The Education for All Handicapped Children's Act of 1975, children who did not make adequate progress in their regular class placements were mandated to receive individualized instruction through a process known as the *refer–test–place* model. The process was initiated when a regular education teacher identified a chronically low achieving student relative to other children in the classroom and referred this student for a psychoeducational evaluation. Upon receiving the referral, a multidisciplinary team of support personnel evaluated the student in all areas related to her suspected disability and determined the student's eligibility for special education services. Pending a positive eligibility determination, the student was placed with a special education teacher who provided individualized instruction for part or all of the school day (Erchul & Martens, 2010; Martens & Mullane, in press). In short, PL94–142 mandated a continuum of instructional services in special education for those children who failed academically in regular education.

Within the refer–test–place model, psychologists and other support personnel assisted in the design of instructional interventions through a *diagnostic-prescriptive approach* in which the referred child was compared to same age or grade peers on standardized tests of achievement and abilities correlated with achievement (e.g., receptive vocabulary, simultaneous processing; Reschly, 2004). In his presidential address to the American Psychological Association, Cronbach (1957) referred to this approach as *aptitude–treatment interaction* (ATI) and outlined its application to instructional intervention. Specifically, ATI rested on the assumptions that (1) student aptitude levels moderated the effects of instruction, (2) student aptitude levels could be reliably measured using standardized tests, and (3) selecting instructional methods that remediated aptitude weaknesses or capitalized on aptitude strengths would maximize student learning (Reschly, 2004; Ysseldyke & Marston, 1990).

Despite the initial promise of an ATI approach, a considerable amount of research has failed to show that latent student abilities or aptitudes actually moderate the effects of instruction, but rather that some instructional methods are simply more effective on average than others (Cronbach, 1975; Kavale, 1990; Ysseldyke &

Marston, 1990). Although the need to individualize instruction continued to make intuitive sense, the failure of ATI was attributed largely to its focus on latent abilities as moderating variables and problems with their measurement (Ysseldyke & Marston). Even Cronbach (1957) anticipated this problem when he warned, "... persons should be allocated on the basis of those aptitudes which have the greatest interaction with treatment variables. I believe we will find these aptitudes to be *quite unlike our present aptitude measures* [italics added] chosen to predict differences within highly correlated treatments" (p. 681).

The refer—test—place model was criticized on grounds other than the lack of support for ATI. Lengthy delays often occurred before children received special education services or fell far enough below their peers to qualify for such services (what Vaughn & Fuchs, 2003 referred to as a "wait-to-fail" model). With the cost of special education nearly twice that of regular education (Reschly, 1988) and with increasing numbers of children qualifying for special class placement, special education became financially unsustainable as the primary solution to children's failure in regular education.

Based on these criticisms along with the effectiveness of prereferral intervention programs at reducing the number of children placed in special education (e.g., Fuchs, Fuchs, & Bahr, 1990; McDougall, Clonan, & Martens, 2000), the era of early intervention began in the late 1990s. Perhaps, the most significant advancement in intervention research that helped usher in the early intervention era was the development of curriculum-based measurement (CBM) for assessing student progress (McIntosh, Martinez, Ty, & McClain, 2013; Shinn, 1989; Ysseldyke & Marston, 1990). CBM probes are rate measures of important academic responses (e.g., oral reading fluency) that are inexpensive, quick and easy to administer, can be administered repeatedly, and are sensitive to short-term instructional gains. As such, CBM probes can be used to model academic growth, inform instructional planning, and evaluate instructional outcomes for individual students. Moreover, CBM data can be aggregated to evaluate student gains at the classroom, school, or district levels, thereby leading to increased accountability for intervention services (Ardoin, Christ, Morena, Cormier, & Klingbeil, 2013; Good, Simmons, & Kame'enui, 2001).

In one of the most widely cited articles in school psychology, Fuchs and Fuchs (1986) conducted a meta-analysis examining the effects of collecting at least twice weekly CBM data on students' academic achievement in the areas of reading, math, spelling, and writing. Termed *systematic formative evaluation*, this practice involved the ongoing evaluation of student progress to inform changes in instructional programming. Results from 21 studies indicated that collecting CBM data at least twice weekly, graphing these data, and applying decision rules to these data to make instructional changes (e.g., comparing a trend line to a goal line) increased student achievement by an effect size of .91 over control group participants. This effect size was larger than many instructional programs currently being used in special education (Kavale, 1990) and was similar regardless of student age, disability status, or length of instructional program.

As an *inductive* approach to program development based on the ongoing monitoring of student skills, systematic formative evaluation contrasted sharply with the *deductive* approach of ATI which focused on the pretreatment diagnosis of inferred learner characteristics (Fuchs & Fuchs, 1986). Given its greater effectiveness, systematic formative evaluation was critical to development of the data-based problem-solving model as an alternative to ATI for instructional intervention, and prompted legislation calling for outcomes-based education [e.g., Individuals with Disabilities Education Improvement Act (IDEA) of, 2004; No Child Left Behind (NCLB), 2001]. The use of CBM probes to evaluate instructional interventions is now a key component of RtI models (Ardoin et al., 2013) and has helped to change the role of psychologists and other support personnel from that of diagnostician to intervention agent.

Applied behavior analysis as an evidence-based practice

Although systematic formative evaluation provides a basis for revising instructional programs, it provides no guidance for selecting such programs in the first place. For this reason and others (e.g., to increase schools' accountability for services), No Child Left Behind (NCLB) (2001) required the use of science-based instructional and intervention strategies in the prevention and early identification of children's academic problems (Erchul & Martens, 2010). Among the most effective science-based practices for academic instruction and instructional intervention are those based on applied behavior analysis (ABA; Alberto & Troutman, 2013). ABA combines behavior analytic principles (e.g., reinforcement, extinction, stimulus control) and procedures (e.g., frequent opportunities to respond with modeling, prompting, and feedback) with the ongoing measurement of student progress (Wolery, Bailey, & Sugai, 1988). Instructional strategies based on ABA are effective evidence-based practices for teaching academic, social, and vocational skills to individuals with autism spectrum disorder (e.g., Roth, Gillis, & DeGennaro Reed, 2014). These strategies have also been shown to improve children's academic skills when used as instructional interventions (e.g., Hier & Eckert, 2016; Jaspers et al., 2012; Martens et al., 2007; McCallum, Skinner, Turner, & Saecker, 2006) or within more comprehensive instructional programs (e.g., direct instruction; Adams & Engelmann, 1996; Helping Early Literacy with Practice Strategies; Begeny, Braun, Lynch, Ramsay, & Wendt, 2012).

Despite the demonstrated effectiveness of ABA principles and procedures for academic instruction, results of practitioner surveys and large-scale evaluation studies suggest that these procedures may not be used widely or when used, may not be matched to students' instructional needs (Balu et al., 2015; Begeny & Martens, 2006; Burns & Ysseldyke, 2009). For example, Burns and Ysseldyke asked a sample of 174 special education teachers to rate how often they used seven evidence-based instructional practices for children with disabilities (1 = almost never, 5 = almost every day). Three of the practices were considered effective (e.g., direct instruction, effect size = .84), one moderately effective (systematic formative evaluation, effect size = .70), and four ineffective (e.g., modality instruction, effect size = .14) based on results of meta-analytic reviews. Although the vast majority of respondents reported using the effective practice of direct instruction at least once a week or every day (89.6%), between 32% and 80% of respondents also reported using the four ineffective practices at least once a week or every day.

In a large-scale impact study of RtI models, Balu et al. (2015) evaluated the effects of Tier 2 interventions on the achievement of first, second, and third grade students in 146 schools across 13 states. Outcomes were compared for students just above and just below the cut score for receipt of Tier 2 services. Results indicated that 45% of schools provided Tier 2 services to all students who were referred to school-based consulting teams whether they qualified or not, and 67% of schools replaced rather than supplemented students' core reading instruction with Tier 2 intervention. For the vast majority of students reading below level (90%), Tier 2 intervention consisted only of systematic phonics instruction regardless of the students' needs. Tier 2 intervention and core instruction had a small negative impact on two measures of reading at Grade 1 (effect sizes of $-.17$ and $-.11$), a small positive impact at Grade 2 (effect size of $.10$), and a negligible impact on state-wide tests at Grade 3 (effect size of $-.01$). Across schools, the average effect sizes of Tier 2 interventions were more variable than beneficial (range $= -1.18$ to $+.53$). The authors cited three reasons for the low and variable effectiveness of Tier 2 services in their sample including (1) incorrect identification of students for Tier 2 intervention, (2) mismatch between the type of reading intervention and students' instructional needs, and (3) poor alignment between Tier 2 intervention and core reading instruction.

Findings such as these suggest that school-based consulting teams may be selecting instructional interventions on the basis of conventional wisdom or anecdotal information rather than scientific evidence (Burns & Ysseldyke, 2009) and may need additional training in how to match interventions to students' instructional needs (Balu et al., 2015). These findings also suggest the need for simple, practical models of instructional intervention that teachers and support personnel can use to guide intervention selection (Erchul & Martens, 2010). Toward these goals, the next section describes the principles that underlie ABA approaches to skill instruction and presents a conceptual model for intervention design known as the learning/instructional hierarchy (IH) (Martens, Daly, Begeny, & Sullivan, in press).

Foundations of effective instruction

Academic responding as the index of learning

ABA principles and procedures focus on what we can observe children can do rather than what we can infer about what they know (Martens, Daly, et al., in press). As noted before, children's academic problems can be viewed as behavioral deficits with no, too weak, or too few controlling variables in the academic curriculum. To identify these deficits, it is important to first determine what children can and cannot do, how well they can do it, and when (i.e., under what conditions) they will do it.

Repeated measures of academic responding are the first and most important feature of effective instructional intervention. Repeated measures allow teachers to pinpoint what a child can do accurately and fluently, and what skills a child needs additional help with to master. Repeated measures also allow instructors to determine if and how rapidly academic performance is improving and make instructional changes accordingly. Understanding what a child will correctly respond to allows one to identify the academic skills that an intervention should target. Establishing this starting point in turn allows for the reinforcement of desired responding which is a key ingredient for establishing stimulus control.

CBM is a particularly well-developed and scientifically supported technology for collecting repeated measures of academic responding (Fuchs & Fuchs, 1999; Shinn, 1989). CBM probes are brief, repeated, rate measures of production responses in foundational academic skills (e.g., reading aloud from passages, writing the answers to math computation problems). CBM probes target a variety of content areas including early literacy, early numeracy, math computation, reading, spelling, and writing. In addition, CBM probes are sensitive to differences in students' academic growth (Ardoin et al., 2013) which means they can be used to model student progress and inform instructional decisions. As a result, published sets of CBM reading (CBM-R) probes [e.g., Dynamic Indicators of Basic Early Literacy Skills (DIBELS; Good & Kaminski, 2001) or AIMSweb] are widely used in RtI models for universal screening, progress monitoring, and program evaluation.

Regardless of academic content area, all CBM probes are scored similarly by counting the number of correct and incorrect responses made within a brief time period (Shinn, 1989). As such, CBM probes assess fluency or rate of correct responding in a given content area. For example, CBM-R probes are scored by calculating the number of words read correctly per minute (WRCM), curriculum-based measures in mathematics (CBM-M) are scored for digits correct per minute (DCPM), and curriculum-based measures in written expression (CBM-WE) are scored for total words written per minute.

CBM probes are time efficient, while remaining reliable and valid measures of student performance (e.g., Fuchs & Fuchs, 1999). Specifically, CBM-R probes require 1 minute of passage reading, CBM-M probes require 2 minutes of math computation, and CBM-WE probes require 3 minutes of writing from a story starter. CBM-R probes are reliable measures of student reading ability. In a study conducted by Howe and Shinn (2002), researchers found that alternate form reliability estimates for a single CBM-R probe ranged from .79 to .92. Furthermore, Howe and Shinn examined the reliability between alternate forms within the same grade level for grades 1−8. When the scores on three probes were averaged for each grade, the correlation between CBM-R alternate forms ranged from .92 to .97. When used for monitoring student progress over time, sets of CBM-R probes are compiled at each grade level and equated for difficulty (e.g., Christ & Ardoin, 2009). Research has shown that the standard error of measurement for CBM-R probes will typically range from 5 to 9 WRCM depending on the equating procedure used (e.g., Christ & Silberglitt, 2007). Although a given student may score somewhat differently across probes within grade levels, scores can be reliability rank ordered across students, making CBM-R probes particularly useful for universal screening (Ardoin & Christ, 2009).

CBM-WE is scored by calculating total words written, words spelled correctly, or correct word sequences when given a story starter. In a study conducted by Gansle, VanDerHeyden, Noell, Resetar, and Williams (2006), test–retest reliability over a one-week period was .80 for total words written, .82 for words spelled correctly, and .78 for correct word sequence for a sample of 190 students in grades 1–5. With respect to validity estimates for CBM-M probes, the AIMSweb Technical Manual (2012) reported that scores on the CBM-M were highly correlated with ($r = .73–.84$) scores on the Group Mathematics Assessment and Diagnostic Evaluation. Furthermore, when CBM-M alternate form reliability was calculated, the median correlation was .88 for Grades 1–8 (AIMSweb Technical Manual, 2012). The reliability and validity for probes in all CBM content areas allows school-based consulting teams to obtain an accurate snapshot of student performance and use these data to make decisions about instructional intervention.

Stimulus control as the process of learning

Stimulus control provides the process through which appropriate academic responding occurs (Daly et al, 2007). That is, stimulus control is the reason why a student will respond with the answer "42" but not "43" when a flash card is presented with the problem "7 × 6." Likewise, a student is expected to say "bat" but not "bet" when presented with a flash card with the letters "b-a-t." For each of these examples, if the academic stimuli (i.e., the math fact "7 × 6" and the letters "b-a-t") elicit the correct responses (i.e., "42" and "bat") from a student, then the student's response is said to be signaled or controlled by the academic stimuli. When a student is first acquiring a skill, inconsistent responding might be observed. When presented with the letter sequence "b-a-t" a student may sometimes say the word "bat" but other times say the word "bet" or "cat." In order for academic responding to come under control of the correct stimuli, a three-term contingency relating the (A)ntecedent stimuli, student (B)ehavior, and a reinforcing (C)onsequence for behavior (ABC) must be operating. The antecedent event that occasions student academic responding can be an instructional task or verbal directive from the teacher. In the example that we have been using, the antecedent is the letter sequence "b-a-t." Saying "bat," represents the academic behavior that is appropriate in response to the antecedent. Finally, the consequence is the reinforcement (e.g., praise) provided by the teacher or other instructional specialist confirming to the student that "b-a-t" is indeed "bat" (Alberto & Troutman, 2013). This sequence, comprised of the antecedent (i.e., "what word does b-a-t make?"), the behavior (i.e., saying "bat") and the consequence (i.e., "Terrific work—b-a-t is bat!"), is also referred to as a *learning trial*. Application of the three-term contingency or learning trial forms the basis of all teacher-directed instruction: (1) ask a question, (2) observe the response, and (3) provide feedback (praise or error correction).

In order to ensure that the response "bat" is under stimulus control of the letter sequence "b-a-t," the student must be able to discriminate "b-a-t" from other letter sequences. If a student's responding is under stimulus control s/he will not say "bat" when presented with any other letter sequence. In order for a student to discriminate the appropriate response when presented with different letter sequences, the teacher must provide *differential reinforcement*. In the most simplistic form differential reinforcement occurs when a student receives teacher praise for saying the word "bat" when presented with the letter sequence "b-a-t" but no praise when the student says the word "cat." Instead the teacher provides error correction when "b-a-t" is followed by a student response of "cat." Learning occurs when these trials are repeated frequently. Modeling (e.g., teacher demonstrates the response), prompting (e.g., teacher provides verbal, visual, or physical cues that increase the probability the student will provide the correct response to the stimuli), and fading (gradual removal of the verbal, visual, or physical cue) are instructional techniques designed to facilitate stimulus control (Alberto & Troutman, 2013).

Although learning trials are very useful to help students acquire discrete skills, it is difficult and inefficient for teachers to directly instruct all combinations of letter sequences or all multiplication facts (Alberto & Troutman, 2013; Skinner & Daly, 2010). Instead, students might be taught all the "at" words as a group. The "at" words represent a class of stimuli (words) that have the last two letter sequences in common. This is an example of concept formation. By recognizing the characteristics that stimuli have in common, such as words that end with "at," students should be able provide the appropriate response to all members of the same stimulus class. As learning continues to become more complex as students' progress through schooling, discrete skills are combined or performed in sequence.

These discrete foundational skills, such as letter–sound correspondence and basic math facts, might be considered component skills. Component skills might be thought of as the building block for more complex skills, and for these basic skills it is usually the case that only one response is correct (Daly et al., 2007). Two or more component skills can be combined into complex response sequences called composite skills (Johnson & Layng, 1992; Lin & Kubina, 2005). For example, basic multiplication facts represent a component skill necessary to solve multiple-digit multiplication problems. Curricular scope and sequence charts can help guide instructors by identifying the order in which component skills need to be addressed and how those component skills link into composite skills.

The learning/instructional hierarchy as a model for strengthening stimulus control

Stimulus control, discrimination training, and understanding the relationship between critical component skills and more complex composite skills are necessary but not sufficient conditions for learning. These tactics help to establish students' skill accuracy. That is, students will consistently provide the correct response in the presence of a stimulus ($7 \times 6 =$ ___) and this response will not be provided in the presence of a different stimulus ($5 \times 3 =$ ___). However, some evidence suggests that if instruction is provided on composite skills prior to achieving sufficient levels of fluency with component skills, students' learning on composite skills may plateau (Johnson & Layng, 1992; Lin & Kubina, 2005). Targeting the fluency of a component skill may also impact performance on composite skills. For example, Codding, Archer, and Connell (2010) taught a sixth grade student basic multiplication facts to a specified fluency criterion and the student's performance generalized to simple one step word and fraction problems involving multiplication. It is likely that this student already had established the procedural and conceptual knowledge necessary to solve the word and fraction problems; however, the lack of fluent performance with basic multiplication facts hindered the student's ability to perform sufficiently with composite tasks (Skinner & Daly, 2010).

Fluency refers to the rate of performance, or, the extent to which a skill is performed accurately and quickly. Fluency has been described as a stage of skill development that facilitates remembering and retention of learning. A metaanalysis by Driskell, Willis, and Copper (1992) demonstrated that overlearning (i.e., training beyond an established accuracy criterion) resulted in the retention of performance on both physical and cognitive tasks. Results indicated that that the degree of overlearning, 50%, 100%, and 150%, corresponded to small, moderate, and large effect sizes, respectively; providing evidence that as the degree of overlearning increased, retention also increased. These authors postulated that additional opportunities to practice an established skill lead to greater retention of that skill over time. These data suggest that in order for a skill to be considered fluent the definition of fast and accurate may be too simplistic if responding is expected to be maintained and to generalize to composite skill performance.

Johnson and Layng (1996) proposed that the following elements, known as RESAA, describe proficient academic responding: (1) retention, (2) endurance, (3) stability, (4) application, and (5) adduction. Retention occurs when students perform the skill at the expected criterion level after a period of time without intervention or practice. Endurance refers to the ability of students to continue engaging in an instructional task for increasingly longer periods of time than practiced. Stability is similar to endurance in that the skill will continue to be performed over longer periods of time but without deviating from the task despite the presence of potential distractors. Application is when accurate and fast performance on component skills facilitates learning on composite response classes as in Codding et al. (2010). Response adduction refers to the fact that fluent component learning can lead to rapid acquisition of composite skills without instruction (Binder, 1996). The notion behind RESAA is that once component behaviors fall under stimulus control and are also practiced to fluency, then it is easier for students to link component skills together and engage in composite tasks. An important aspect of component skill development is that foundational skills are organized and learned in a meaningful and hierarchical sequence.

In order to promote proficient performance, it is useful to consider how to evaluate responding according to the stage of skill development a student is operating within. The learning/IH provides a heuristic within which instructors can identify a students' stage of skill development and then vary the instructional techniques accordingly in order to promote accurate, rapid, sustained, and then generalized responding (Haring, Eaton, 1978). Fig. 8.1 summarizes the various stages of the IH (boxes), how each is related to stimulus control over responding (ovals), performance goals for the learner (first row), instructional strategies for the teacher (second row), and the instructional arrangement used at each stage (bottom row). As shown in the figure, the IH is comprised of four stages: (1) acquisition, (2) fluency/ maintenance, (3) generalization, and (4) adaption. Student responding in the acquisition stage is characterized by slow and inaccurate performance as stimulus control is still being established. When in the fluency stage of skill development, students display accurate responding, but responding is slow, inefficient, and tentative when presented with a stimulus. When in the generalization stage of skill development, students display accurate and fast responding when presented with a stimulus; however, students might not respond accurately or quickly over time (retention), in the classroom environment when distractors are present (stability), or be able to apply component skills such as reading a word or solving a basic math fact to composite skills such as reading the word in text or a solving a basic fact embedded within a word problem (application). When a student is in the final stage of skill development, adaption, s/he is working on integrating known component skills in novel ways when presented with novel instructional tasks. When the IH is combined with frequent progress monitoring data (e.g., twice weekly CBM probes), instructors can determine which stage of skill development a student falls within (Burns, Codding, Boice, & Lukito, 2010; Chafouleas, Martens, Dobson, Weinstein, & Gardner, 2004). Instructional goals for students and instructional plans for teachers can be made according to these data.

Measurement goals for students will vary depending on their level of skill proficiency (Daly et al., 2007). For students who are working on establishing a skill and

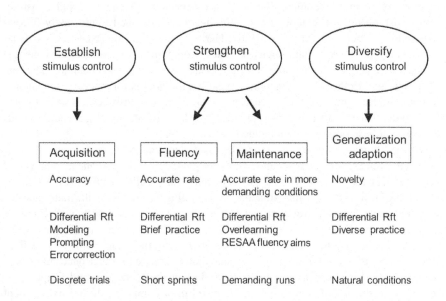

Figure 8.1 An overview of the learning/instructional hierarchy. *Rft*, reinforcement.

are in the acquisition stage of development, the primary outcome measures are percentage accuracy or the number of correct and incorrect responses. The objective is to improve accurate responding such that stimulus control is observed. For students in the fluency stage of skill development outcomes that can assess rate of performance are most useful. CBM probes are commonly used for this purpose (Shapiro, 2011). The objective for the fluency stage of skill development is for performance to be fast and accurate. For students in the generalization phase of skill development, a number of different goals could be arranged including: (1) reaching a fluency criterion that is linked to generalized responding, (2) displaying accurate and fast performance on a task that requires the component skill (e.g., high word overlap reading passages or word problems containing known basic facts), (3) maintaining high levels of performance at expected rates over time, (4) sustaining performance during longer intervals of engagement (endurance), and (5) displaying high levels of performance even within highly distractible environments (stability; Daly et al., 2007; Johnson & Layng, 1996). It is imperative that teachers and consulting teams frequently monitor student progress toward these specific instructional goals in order to make frequent instructional changes that will promote skill proficiency.

Instructional planning for teachers also varies according to the stage of skill proficiency a student is determined to be operating within. Each stage of skill development is associated with different types and levels of teacher assistance and different considerations when developing the instructional materials that students will access. In the acquisition stage, more teacher assistance is required for the student to produce accurate responding. Typically, this takes the form of teacher modeling, demonstration, teacher directed opportunities for guided practice, the provision of cues or prompts to signal the appropriate response expected of students, explicit instruction, and high rates of elaborate corrective feedback provided immediately following student responses (Daly et al., 2007; Haring, Eaton, 1978). Teacher's curricular goals are more narrow and focused. Instructional materials should also be: (1) aligned with the curricular objective; (2) clear, consistent, and unambiguous; and (3) absent of extraneous information. Given that the goal is for students' responding to come under control of the instructional stimuli, it may also be necessary to provide students with opportunities to practice the skill in isolation (e.g., reading words on flash cards as opposed to embedded in text).

In the fluency stage of skill development, less teacher-directed assistance is required. Rather, the focus of instruction is providing brief, frequent, and varied opportunities for students to engage in meaningful practice with a skill (Martens et al., 2007). It is critical that students are engaging in practice with materials that match each student's instructional level (can engage in the task with a minimum of 80% accuracy). Practice activities can occur in isolation, but are more likely to be embedded in the natural context such as reading text rather than word cards or lists. Practice activities are typically brief, sequentially arranged so that once mastery is achieved then practice ensues on the next skill in the hierarchy, and frequent (at least daily). Practice activities can be arranged on a computer, during independent seatwork, or even provided through class-wide peer tutoring. Unfortunately, typical classroom instruction often does not include enough opportunities for productive practice (Daly et al., 2007). It is useful to keep in mind that some experts suggest that 70% of instructional time be devoted to practice (Johnson & Layng, 1996). Teacher feedback and reinforcement continue to be important at this stage of skill development; however, feedback is typically directed at students' rate of performance rather than accuracy. The immediacy of feedback can also be faded. In addition teachers might provide students with specific fluency aims and teach students to monitor their own progress toward these goals through graphing and charting. To increase students' motivation on practice activities, teachers might also construct materials that contain interspersed easier items (Billington, Skinner, & Cruchon, 2004).

Generalized responding is a critical instructional objective. Although this stage of development is conceptually organized following the fluency stage of skill development, activities that promote generalization can be arranged by teachers within the acquisition and fluency stages of development. For example, in the acquisition stage of skill development students should produce accurate responding across a variety of contexts. By providing students with many different practice examples that are promoted initially through guided practice, students are more likely to exhibit accurate responding that can be maintained. In the fluency stage of skill development, students should be practicing skills within the natural context. For example, although initially it might be useful to provide students with practice reading words in isolation, the goal is for students to read text. Therefore, more opportunities for practice should be provided for reading connected text. Practice opportunities might also be arranged so that they are cumulative in nature and therefore contain a broader set of instructional objectives and component skills. Instructional tasks might incorporate games whereby students have to apply learned skills to novel situations. Teacher support is faded and the schedule of feedback and/or reinforcement is also thinned. Instead students may monitor their own progress toward goal attainment and teachers might provide prompts and cues for generalization.

Best practice recommendations for instructional intervention

Assessing student skills and skill deficits

Measuring a student's skills and skill deficits allows consulting teams to identify what an instructional intervention should target. When used to measure students' basic academic skills, scores on CBM probes are typically categorized within three proficiency levels; *frustrational, instructional, or mastery*. Research has shown better generalization of academic skills (i.e., children maintain similar levels of performance on untrained material) when academic tasks are matched to the child's instructional level (Daly, Martens, Kilmer, & Massie, 1996). Thus, the first step of academic assessment using CBM probes is to identify the student's current instructional level. This can be accomplished by administering three CBM probes from the student's current grade level, and comparing the median WRCM to normative standards provided for the probe set (e.g., Shinn, 1989). For example, Shapiro (2011) recommended that, when given passages from grades 3−6, students' oral reading fluency levels be categorized as frustrational at 69 WRCM or less, instructional at 70−100 WRCM, and mastery at over 100 WRCM. At present, both DIBELS and AIMSweb report screening benchmarks for making instructional placement decisions (e.g., Good & Kaminski, 2001). If the child scores in the frustrational range for the current grade level, probes are administered from one grade lower. Consecutively easier probes are administered (i.e., "slicing back" in difficulty) until the child's instructional level is identified. It may be appropriate in some cases to skip multiple grade levels if the child continues to score in the frustrational range.

When monitoring student progress in an RtI model, it is common for intervention to be applied to lower grade instructional-level passages, whereas gains in oral reading fluency are measured on a different, standardized set of current-grade CBM-R passages as global outcome measures (Ardoin & Christ, 2009). Standardized CBM-R probes are representative of most basal curricula and therefore serve as global indicators of reading competence (Good et al., 2001). CBM-R global outcome measures also make it easier for intervention teams to monitor long-term student progress as the same pool of equivalent, grade-level passages can be used at different sites throughout the school year without adjusting passage difficulty. When used as global outcome measures, CBM-R passages assess *generalized oral-reading fluency* because they differ from the passages on which students are trained (Hintze & Silberglitt, 2005). As generalization probes, the effects of supplemental instruction on CBM-R global outcome measures will be a function of the type and difficulty of the passages administered as well as the strength of students' response to intervention.

Once progress-monitoring data have been collected, the second step of a systematic formative evaluation model is to graph the data in time-series fashion. Graphing academic performance data allows consulting teams to make decisions about whether to terminate, continue, or modify an instructional intervention by comparing the student's slope of progress to an aim line (Shinn, 1989). Establishing a goal or aim line also allows one to track student progress in comparison to the rate of growth required for students to catch up with typical peers over a set period of time (e.g., by the end of the year; Deno, Fuchs, Marston, & Shinn, 2001). As an example, Fig. 8.2 shows sample data from twice weekly CBM-R progress monitoring for a student who received a standard protocol, Tier 2 intervention starting at Week 8 to increase oral reading fluency. The student's progress with regular classroom instruction was an increase in rate of .5 words per week. At the start of intervention, an aim line was set for a desired increase in rate of 2 words per week. The data show that this goal was met following implementation of the Tier 2 intervention, with no data points consistently above or below the aim line.

Wolery et al. (1988) listed eight different instructional decisions that can be made from the visual inspection of graphed progress monitoring data. The first

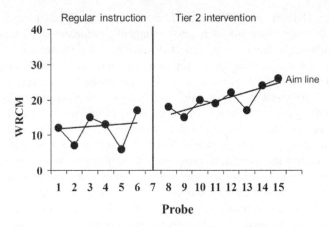

Figure 8.2 Sample data from twice-weekly CBM-R progress monitoring showing .50 words gained per week with regular instruction and an aim line of 2 words gained per week that was met with Tier 2 intervention.

decision is to "make no change" when the student is progressing satisfactorily or in a manner consistent with the aim line (i.e., no data points consistently above or below the aim line). The second decision is to "raise the goal or aim line." This decision should be made when the child's progress exceeds expected growth (e.g., four consecutive data points above the aim line; Fuchs, Fuchs, Hamlett, & Allinder, 1991). If four consecutive data points fall below the aim line, decisions three and four are to "try a different instructional procedure" or to "slice back" and teach the same skill using less difficult material or briefer tasks (Fuchs et al.). If slicing back is still too difficult or the child's data show a lack of success with the current skills being trained, the fifth decision is to "step back." A decision to step back would be indicated by few or no accurate responses with a high number of errors. Stepping back requires teaching component skills that are prerequisite to the composite skill that was originally targeted. When a child consistently exhibits high accuracy but fluency is not increasing, a sixth decision is to "add rate contingent reinforcement." Once accuracy and fluency have both met expected levels, the seventh decision is to "move to a new skill." Finally, if a student shows considerable variability in performance, the eighth decision is to "add a reinforcement program" in which highly preferred attention, tangible, or activity reinforcers are given contingent on exceeding a specified performance goal.

Another method for determining whether additional instruction or a simple reinforcement program is required to improve performance is to conduct a *performance-deficit analysis* (PDA; Daly, Martens, Dool, & Hintze, 1998). A PDA allows consulting teams to differentiate between skill and performance deficits, and is considered a "best practice" in selecting instructional interventions (Jones et al., 2009). Another name for a PDA is a "Can't do/Won't do" analysis. This analysis is conducted by experimentally comparing the effects of rate-contingent reinforcement to various instructional strategies on WRCM using different but equivalent CBM-R probes (e.g., Daly et al., 1998). A different probe is assigned to each condition beginning first with baseline then rate-contingent reinforcement and then one or more instructional strategies [e.g., repeated readings (RR), phrase drill error correction]. Once an effective strategy is identified (i.e., WRCM for that condition shows a clear increase above all prior conditions), a one-session mini-reversal to baseline is conducted followed by replication of the most effective strategy. If fluency increases with rate-contingent reinforcement using highly preferred items, it can be concluded that the child is failing to show expected levels of performance due to a lack of motivation or a performance deficit (a "Won't do" problem). If this occurs, a more structured reinforcement program can be implemented during classroom instructional time to increase performance. If fluency does not improve with rate-contingent reinforcement alone but only when one or more instructional strategies are implemented, this indicates the presence of a skill deficit (a "Can't do" problem). In this case, the instructional procedure that improved performance during the PDA is then implemented over a longer period of time as a Tier 2 or Tier 3 intervention.

Fig. 8.3 shows data from a sample PDA in which the effects of rate-contingent reinforcement were compared to two instructional procedures. The first procedure, RR, required the student to reread the same passage three times with the third reading being timed (a practice procedure). The second procedure involved modeling and practice of unknown words via a combination of two intervention components. For the first component, listening passage preview (LPP), the instructor read the passage aloud, whereas the student followed along reading the words to herself. The second component, phrase drill error correction (PD), involved the instructor modeling the correct reading of any three-word phrase that contained a word the

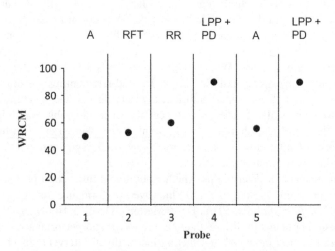

Figure 8.3 Sample data from a performance-deficit analysis. *A*, baseline;
RFT, rate-contingent reinforcement; *RR*, repeated readings; *LPP*, listening passage preview;
PD, phrase drill error correction.

student missed and then the student reading each phrase correctly three times. As shown in the figure, the student's oral reading fluency did not increase with either the reinforcement contingency or practice via RR. Fluency did increase when the instructor modeled unknown words via LPP and PD. Fluency decreased during the mini-reversal to baseline, but increased again when LPP and RR were implemented for a second time on a different passage, thereby increasing confidence in the effectiveness of the procedure.

Selecting instructional interventions

Daly, Witt, Martens, and Dool (1997) described five reasons why students may be exhibiting academic problems that can be used to diagnose instruction and select an appropriate intervention. These reasons are based on ABA principles and emphasize the importance of academic responding on instructionally matched materials with reinforcement and feedback. Consistent with a "Won't do" problem in a PDA, the first reason for children's academic problems is that "they don't want to do it." When this occurs, an instructional intervention matched to the student's needs would require that correct responding be reinforced. The second reason for children's academic deficits is that "it's too hard," meaning that the instructional material is too difficult for the student's skill level. To address this issue, the student's instructional level would need to be reevaluated using CBM levels testing and adjusted downward into the student's instructional range. The third reason is that "they haven't had enough help to do it" or the student has not received sufficient instruction with modeling, prompting, and error correction to accurately perform the skill. In this case, direct instruction of the skill or set of skills would be required to bring accurate responding under stimulus control of the curriculum materials. Once children are responding accurately (i.e., have achieved acquisition-level goals of the IH), a fourth reason for performance deficits is that "they haven't spent enough time doing it." If the child has not been given sufficient opportunities to practice a newly learned skill, additional practice would be needed to build fluency and strengthen stimulus control. The fifth reason for children's academic problems is that "they haven't done it that way before," or that the way a skill is assessed (e.g., the materials used, format, or response requirements) differs from the way it was taught. If this is the case, the instructor would need to vary the instructional materials or formats to create a better test—teach overlap thereby addressing generalization-level goals of the IH.

For consulting teams, the task of selecting an evidence-based instructional intervention that is matched to a student's needs can be daunting. Both the IH and the five reasons described by Daly et al. (1997) can help consulting teams select appropriate interventions based on each procedure's active instructional components (e.g., modeling and prompting, opportunities to respond, rate-contingent reinforcement). Table 8.1 lists 24 evidence-based instructional interventions mapped to Daly et al.'s five reasons. Another tool that can help support personnel identify and select evidence-based interventions is the website Intervention Central (www.interventioncentral.org). Intervention Central is a user-friendly, free resource that describes evidence-based academic and behavioral interventions for use in schools. Instructional interventions on the website are categorized by content area, and the website also provides users with helpful tools such as protocols and online applications that might be beneficial for students.

Designing instructional sessions

Once a consulting team selects an evidence-based intervention matched to a student's proficiency level of the IH (e.g., cover-copy-compare for acquisition-level training), they must gather the necessary materials and make a number of decisions about how to implement the procedure during each intervention session. Regardless of the skill (e.g., word list reading) or response dimension (e.g., accuracy) being targeted, all intervention sessions have several elements in common. These elements stem from the ABA principles of skill instruction discussed previously in the chapter, namely, that (1) academic responding should be continuously monitored, (2)

Table 8.1 Instructional interventions mapped to Daly et al.'s (1997) five reasons for academic problems

Reason (instructional change)	Instructional intervention
They don't want to do it (reinforcement program)	Goal setting and charting
	Offer highly preferred reinforcers
	Classwide point or token systems
	Offer choice of assignments
It's too hard (instructional match)	Slice back to CBM instructional range
	Step back and teach prerequisite skills
	Shorten the task
They haven't had enough help to do it (acquisition-level training)	Discrete trial training
	Cover-copy-compare
	Taped problems
	Listening passage preview
	Taped stories
	Phrase drill error correction
	Self-regulated strategy development
	Quickwrite
They haven't spent enough time doing it (fluency-level training)	Brief practice opportunities or sprints
	Rate-contingent reinforcement
	Drill sandwich
	Incremental rehearsal
They haven't done it that way before (generalization-level training)	High word overlap passages
	Common word rimes
	Multiple exemplar words
	Multiple exemplar passages
	Train phoneme blending
	Train to functional fluency aims

instructional stimuli always occasion academic responding, (3) desired academic responding should be reinforced, and (4) desired academic responding should change as the student's proficiency level increases.

Given these principles and prior to implementing any instructional intervention, instructors must collect several sets of materials. First, the instructor must assemble a set of stimulus materials to which the student can respond. These materials constitute the curriculum that will be "taught" during each intervention session, and might include, for example, word lists, grade-level reading passages, or math computation worksheets. As students are taught new skills during acquisition-level training (i.e., how to respond correctly to the stimuli presented), materials at stage are comprised of mostly unknown items. With that said, including a mix of known and unknown items or interspersing already mastered or easy items among more difficult items has been shown to increase task engagement (e.g., McCurdy, Skinner, Grantham, Watson, & Hindman, 2001).

When providing opportunities for students to practice and build fluency on skills they can already perform accurately, it is important to select material matched to the students' instructional level. Selecting instructional-level material for fluency building helps ensure that students practice and strengthen stimulus control over only correct responses. Once students reach a fluency criterion on currently instructed material (e.g., reading 3rd grade passages over 100 WRCM), instructors should gradually increase the difficulty level to ensure a consistent instructional match.

When providing practice opportunities that help prepare students for situations that differ from training (i.e., generalization programming), instructors should select curricular materials that are more diverse than the narrow range of stimuli used for acquisition-level training (Martens et al., 2015). Efforts to diversify the curricular materials for generalization programming have involved (1) exemplars of stimulus variations that the student will encounter later (i.e., multiple exemplar training; Silber & Martens, 2010), (2) incorporating stimuli that are common to both the intervention and generalization setting (Mesmer et al., 2010), or (3) simply having the student respond to a wide variety of materials over a longer intervention trial (i.e., "training loosely"; Stokes & Baer, 1977).

Second, based on results of a reinforcer preference assessment (e.g., Fisher et al., 1992) or survey (Northup, George, Jones, Broussard, & Vollmer, 1996), instructors should collect highly preferred attention, tangible, or activity reinforcers that will be provided to the student for desired responding. Changing the pool of reinforcers periodically or offering students a choice of items can reduce the chances of satiation over time.

Third, instructors must decide how to monitor student progress and graph the resulting data. For example, the direct effects of intervention can be monitored by scoring and graphing performance on the same materials that are used for teaching. Alternatively, the generalized effects of intervention require that instructors periodically monitor performance using materials different from those on which the student was instructed (i.e., CBM goal-level or global outcome measures; Ardoin & Christ, 2009).

Once instructors have assembled the necessary instructional materials and reinforcers, they must decide what dimension of responding to target and how best to provide the student with frequent opportunities to emit the desired academic response. First, in order to reinforce desired responding, instructors must determine what dimension of responding they want to increase (i.e., accuracy, fluency, or novelty), and establish a performance criterion for determining when to introduce new material from the curriculum (e.g., 90% correct responses ever three consecutive sessions). Second, instructors must decide whether to structure intervention sessions (i.e., provide students with opportunities to respond) using a discrete trial or free operant format (Johnson & Layng, 1996). A discrete trial is an opportunity to emit a single response that this controlled by the trainer. Discrete trials are commonly used during acquisition-level training to establish stimulus control over accurate responding. In a discrete trial format, instructors present stimulus items in isolation, prompt or guide the correct response, and reinforce correct responding or correct errors prior to presenting the next discrete trial (Smith, 2001). A number of procedures exist for prompting and then fading prompts for correct responses during discrete trail training (e.g., progressive time delay, system of decreasing assistance), and instructors should select a procedure that is appropriate for the skill being taught (Alberto & Troutman, 2013).

In a free operant format, the learner is "free" to emit a number of academic responses at her own rate over a specified period of time as with CBM probes (e.g., reading a 150-word passage aloud for 1 minute). As accurate rate is the response dimension targeted during fluency and maintenance training, instructors must use a free operant format during these stages of the IH. To build fluency but avoid fatigue or boredom, instructional interventions are typically formatted as brief, repeated opportunities for skill practice (e.g., 3 minutes of writing practice twice a day with rate-contingent reinforcement).

Providing implementation support to teachers

Selecting an intervention often consists of surveying effective interventions that match the reason for the academic problem as in Table 8.1 (Daly et al., 1996). However, Yeaton and Sechrest (1981) suggested that there are two other dimensions that also need to be considered: (1) treatment integrity and (2) treatment intensity. Treatment integrity refers to the consistent and comprehensive implementation of essential treatment components (Schulte, Eaton, & Parker, 2009). Changes in student behavior will not be observed even if the most effective and well-matched intervention is not implemented correctly or often enough. Therefore, an important aspect of the implementation planning process is to determine how treatment integrity will be monitored. Treatment intensity refers to the form within which the intervention will work (Codding & Lane, 2015). Common dimensions of treatment intensity that have been described in the literature include the dose of the intervention required to observe an effect, total treatment duration, delivery format (e.g., small group, individualized), treatment cost (the materials or resources required to deliver the intervention), and treatment complexity (the number of intervention components; Yoder & Woynaroski, 2015).

In-service teachers report limited exposure to coursework or applied training on many aspects of behavioral instructional techniques and concepts including Direct Instruction, strategies to promote generalization, and the importance of timed trials to promote fluent performance (Begeny & Martens, 2006). Therefore, it is essential for school-based consulting teams to support teacher implementation of evidence-based instructional practices through ongoing support. An essential element of promoting implementation integrity is to provide teachers with a written protocol that details the active treatment ingredients. Inclusion of only the essential treatment steps that a teacher needs to perform is an important consideration because an overly comprehensive or complex written protocol is unlikely to be used or followed by teachers (Codding, Sanetti, & DiGennaro Reed, 2014). However, a script that details the quality aspects of intervention delivery or an intervention manual that provides more comprehensive explanations and examples of the intervention components can be generated as supplemental resources. Although a written protocol is a necessary aspect of treatment implementation, without ongoing follow-up support it is unlikely that teachers will successfully and consistently implement an intervention (Noell et al., 2014). In order to provide accurate feedback to teachers, it is necessary to monitor treatment implementation. Although treatment integrity is a multidimensional construct, adherence, or accurate implementation of the treatment steps, is the most commonly monitored aspect (Sanetti & Kratochwill, 2009). Treatment integrity is often measured using systematic direct observation of treatment implementation or by reviewing permanent products affiliated with the intervention (Barnett et al., 2014; Sanetti & Collier-Meek, 2014).

There are several strategies that facilitate teachers' intervention implementation including: (1) performance feedback, (2) directed rehearsal, and (3) self-monitoring. Performance feedback has been extensively researched as a form of follow-up support provided to teachers and accordingly has been described in the literature as an evidence-based practice (Fallon, Collier-Meek, Maggin, Sanetti, & Johnson, 2015). Performance feedback is commonly delivered verbally during individual meetings with a teacher or through written notes distributed to teachers' mailboxes or through email (Fallon et al., 2015). Regardless of delivery format, performance feedback includes review of the treatment plan as well as the integrity data (which are often provided graphically), praise for intervention steps implemented as intended, and corrective feedback for steps omitted or implemented incorrectly (Noell et al., 2014). A variation of this performance feedback procedure includes the use of directed rehearsal. Directed rehearsal is added to the performance feedback procedure when treatment adherence is less than desirable, and requires teachers to rehearse omitted or inaccurate intervention components in the presence of a consultant. Contingent upon high rates of accurate treatment implementation, directed rehearsal meetings with the consultant can be avoided or canceled (e.g., DiGennaro, Martens, & McIntyre, 2005; DiGennaro, Martens, & Kleinmann, 2007). Self-monitoring, despite a smaller literature base, also yields considerable support as a promising option for supporting teachers' treatment implementation (Noell et al., 2014). Self-monitoring requires that teachers monitor their own implementation of an intervention using a checklist of steps; however, a number of supports are provided to facilitate accurate self-monitoring. For example, a pager can be used to signal teachers when to engage in a specific intervention step and subsequent to delivery teachers complete a checklist on the accuracy of implementation (Petscher & Bailey, 2006). Video self-monitoring requires that teachers watch a video of themselves implementing the intervention and subsequently record their performance on the checklist (Belfiore, Fritts, & Herman, 2008). It is possible that performance feedback is necessary to promote accurate implementation, but self-monitoring can be used to fade the intensity of follow-up support once implementation with performance feedback occurs at high rates (Mouzakitis, Codding, & Tryon, 2015).

There is no agreed upon definition of treatment intensity (Codding & Lane, 2015; Yoder & Woynaroski, 2015). A more precise definition of treatment intensity is likely conflated with the use of intensity within multitiered systems of service delivery to refer to modifications in time allocated to treatment, treatment cost, and delivery format (i.e., class-wide, small group, individual) made according to student needs (Batsche et al., 2006). Yoder and Woynaroski suggest that variables associated with treatment intensity are exclusively related to the number of learning trials per session (dose), the number of sessions offered (dose frequency), and the total sessions, days, or weeks the treatment (total treatment duration) is provided. These authors suggest that these variables are closely tied to treatment effectiveness albeit there is limited empirical evidence that carefully manipulates these variables. Considerations of these aspects of treatment intensity are potentially important when student progress is slow or at lower than expected levels. For example, if an intervention delivered twice weekly is not yielding the expected success, then one potential manipulation in practice would be to increase the dose frequency to three, four, or five times weekly. Another option would be to extend the number of total weeks the intervention is provided if student performance is progressing and the aim line and trend lines are anticipated to intersect with a few more weeks of performance. Finally, the number of complete learning trials or even opportunities to respond within a session might be considered. It is possible that a given instructional intervention provides too few opportunities to respond each session and could be altered accordingly. When and how to make these adjustments according to student responding is an area of needed future research.

Another conceptualization of treatment intensity is defined by Yoder and Woynaroski (2015) as treatment complexity. Barnett, Daly, Jones, and Lentz (2004) describe a model of treatment complexity for which the goal is to identify the most parsimonious treatment package necessary to improve student outcomes. Increasing intensity designs are those intervention packages or components that initially do not show the expected gains in student performance. As a result, a subsequent treatment element is added and this results in changes in the student's behavior as expected. For example, when provided with a RR intervention a student's WRCM may not exceed baseline. However, when goal setting is added the student's performance reaches mastery levels. In contrast, a decreasing intensity design begins with a multicomponent treatment package (e.g., RR + goal setting) and then is revised to eliminate one treatment element (e.g., goal setting). This latter type of treatment design is applicable when a student does display desirable responding to expected rates of performance and the treatment needs to be gradually faded to evaluate whether performance will be maintained or endure over time.

Conclusion and practice guidelines checklist

The goals of this chapter were to describe the behavioral principles and strategies that constitute evidence-based instructional interventions for children's academic problems. In so doing, we highlighted the importance of monitoring student performance, presented several practical models for diagnosing instruction (i.e., the IH, the five reasons for academic performance problems by Daly et al., 1997), and described "best practices" in selecting, implementing, and evaluating school-based instructional interventions within an RtI model. We conclude the chapter by listing these "best practices" as guidelines for school-based consulting teams. Our hope is that consulting teams find the material presented in the chapter and the list of practice guidelines helpful in their efforts to match instructional procedures to students' individual needs and that their students benefit as a result.

1. Intervention sessions with as many learning trials per session (dose), number of sessions per week (dose frequency), and total number of sessions, days, or weeks of treatment (total treatment duration) as is practical.
2. Differential reinforcement of desired responding using highly preferred attention, tangible, or activity reinforcers identified from a reinforcer preference assessment.
3. Target accuracy of responding using complete learning trials for acquisition-level training.
4. Target accurate rate of responding using brief, repeated practice opportunities on instructionally matched material during fluency-level training.
5. Target accurate rate of responding to RESAA fluency aims during maintenance-level training.
6. Target accurate rate of responding in conditions that differ from those of training or novel forms of responding during generalization- and adduction-level training.
7. Monitor direct effects of intervention on trained materials and generalized effects of intervention on untrained, global outcome measures.
8. Support teachers' efforts to implement instructional interventions with integrity by providing step-by-step protocols and using performance feedback, directed rehearsal, or self-monitoring.

References

Adams, G. L., & Engelmann, S. (1996). *Research on direct instruction: 25 years beyond.* Seattle, WA: Educational Achievement Systems, *DISTAR*.

Aimsweb Technical Manual (2012). Pearson. Retrieved February 11, 2017 from the Web site: http://www.aimsweb.com/wp-content/uploads/aimsweb-technical-manual.pdf.

Alberto, P. A., & Troutman, A. C. (2013). *Applied behavior analysis for teachers* (9th edition). Upper Saddle River, NJ: Pearson.

Ardoin, S. P., & Christ, T. J. (2009). Curriculum-based measurement of oral reading: Standard errors associate with progress monitoring outcomes from DIBELS, AIMSweb, and an experimental passage set. *School Psychology Review*, *38*, 266−283.

Ardoin, S. P., Christ, T. J., Morena, L. S., Cormier, D. C., & Klingbeil, D. A. (2013). A systematic review and summarization of the recommendations and research surrounding curriculum-based measurement of oral reading fluency (CBM-R) decision rules. *Journal of School Psychology*, *51*, 1−18.

Balu, R., Zhu, P., Doolittle, F., Schiller, E., Jenkins, J., & Gersten, R. (2015). *Evaluation of response to intervention practices for elementary school reading: Executive summary*. Retrieved January 12, 2016 from the Institute of Education Sciences Web site: http://ies.ed.gov/ncee/pubs/20164000/.

Barnett, D. W., Daly, E. J., III, Jones, K. M., & Lentz, F. E., Jr. (2004). Response to intervention: Empirically based special service decisions from single-case designs of increasing and decreasing intensity. *Journal of Special Education*, *38*, 66−79.

Barnett, D., Hawkins, R., McCoy, D., Wahl, E., Shier, A., Denune, H., et al. (2014). Methods used to document procedural fidelity in school-based intervention research. *Journal of Behavioral Education*, *23*, 89−107.

Batsche, G., Elliott, J., Graden, J. L., Grimes, J., Kovaleski, J. F., Prasse, D., et al. (2006). *Response to intervention: Policy considerations and implementation*. Alexandria, VA: National Association of State Directors of Special Education.

Beavers, G. A., Iwata, B. A., & Lerman, D. C. (2013). Thirty years of research on the functional analysis of problem behavior. *Journal of Applied Behavior Analysis*, *46*, 1−21.

Begeny, J. C., & Martens, B. K. (2006). Assessing pre-service teachers' training in empirically-validated behavioral instruction practices. *School Psychology Quarterly*, *21*, 262−285.

Begeny, J. C., Braun, L. M., Lynch, H. L., Ramsay, A. C., & Wendt, J. M. (2012). Initial evidence for using the HELPS reading fluency program with small instructional groups. *School Psychology Forum: Research in Practice*, *6*, 50−63.

Belfiore, P. J., Fritts, K. M., & Herman, B. C. (2008). The role of procedural integrity: Using self-monitoring to enhance discrete trial instruction (DTI). *Focus on Autism and Other Developmental Disabilities*, *23*, 95−102. Available from http://dx.doi.org/10.1177/1088357607311445.

Billington, E. J., Skinner, C. H., & Cruchon, N. M. (2004). Improving sixth-grade students perceptions of high-effort assignments by assigning more work: Interaction of additive interspersal and assignment effort on assignment choice. *Journal of School Psychology*, *42*(6), 477−490. Available from http://dx.doi.org/10.1016/j.jsp.2004.08.003.

Binder, C. (1996). Behavioral fluency: Evolution of a new paradigm. *The Behavior Analyst*, *19*, 163−197.

Burns, M., Codding, R. S., Boice, C., & Lukito, G. (2010). Meta-analysis of acquisition and fluency math interventions with instruction and frustration level skills: Evidence for a skill-by-treatment interaction. *School Psychology Review*, *39*, 69−83.

Burns, M. K., & Ysseldyke, J. E. (2009). Reported prevalence of evidence-based instructional practices in special education. *The Journal of Special Education*, *43*, 3−11.

Chafouleas, S. M., Martens, B. K., Dobson, R. L., Weinstein, K. S., & Gardner, K. B. (2004). Fluent Reading as the improvement of stimulus control: Additive effects of performance-based interventions to repeated reading on students' reading and error rates. *Journal of Behavioral Education*, *13*, 67−81.

Christ, T. J., & Ardoin, S. P. (2009). Curriculum-based measurement of oral reading: Passage equivalence and probe-set development. *Journal of School Psychology*, *47*, 55−75.

Christ, T. J., & Silberglitt, B. (2007). Estimates of the standard error of measurement for curriculum-based measures of oral reading fluency. *School Psychology Review, 36,* 130−146.

Codding, R. S., & Lane, K. L. (2015). A spotlight on treatment intensity: An important and often overlooked component of intervention inquiry. *Journal of Behavioral Education, 24,* 1−10.

Codding, R. S., Archer, J., & Connell, J. (2010). A systematic replication and extension of using incremental rehearsal to improve multiplication skills: An investigation of generalization. *Journal of Behavioral Education, 19,* 93−105.

Codding, R. S., Sanetti, L., & DiGennaro Reed, F. (2014). Best practices in facilitating teacher/administrator collaboration and consultation. In A. Thomas, & P. Harrison (Eds.), *Best Practices in school psychology Data-based and collaborative decision making* (pp. 525−540). Washington, DC: National Association of School Psychologists.

Cronbach, L. J. (1957). The two disciplines of scientific psychology. *American Psychologist, 12,* 671−684.

Cronbach, L. J. (1975). Beyond the two disciplines of scientific psychology. *American Psychologist, 30,* 116−127.

Daly, E. J., Martens, B. K., Barnett, D., Witt, J. C., & Olson, S. C. (2007). Varying intervention delivery in response-to-intervention: Confronting and resolving challenges with measurement, instruction, and intensity. *School Psychology Review, 36,* 562−581.

Daly, E. J., Martens, B. K., Dool, E. J., & Hintze, J. M. (1998). Using brief functional analysis to select interventions for oral reading. *Journal of Behavioral Education, 8,* 203−218.

Daly, E. J., Martens, B. K., Kilmer, A., & Massie, D. R. (1996). The effects of instructional match and content overlap on generalized reading performance. *Journal of Applied Behavior Analysis, 29,* 507−518.

Daly, E. J., Witt, J. C., Martens, B. K., & Dool, E. J. (1997). A model for conducting a functional analysis of academic performance problems. *School Psychology Review, 26,* 554−574.

Deno, S. L., Fuchs, L. S., Marston, D., & Shin, J. (2001). Using curriculum-based measurement to establish growth standards for students with learning disabilities. *School Psychology Review, 30,* 507−524.

DiGennaro, F. D., Martens, B. K., & McIntyre, L. L. (2005). Increasing treatment integrity through negative reinforcement: Effects on teacher and student behavior. *School Psychology Review, 34,* 220−231.

DiGennaro, F. D., Martens, B. K., & Kleinmann, A. E. (2007). A comparison of performance feedback procedures on teachers' implementation integrity and students' inappropriate behavior in special education classrooms. *Journal of Applied Behavior Analysis, 40,* 447−461.

Driskell, J. E., Willis, R. P., & Copper, C. (1992). Effect of overlearning on retention. *Journal of Applied Psychology, 77,* 615−622.

Erchul, W. P., & Martens, B. K. (2010). *School consultation: Conceptual and empirical bases of practice* (3rd ed). New York: Springer.

Fallon, L. M., Collier-Meek, M. A., Maggin, D. M., Sanetti, L. H., & Johnson, A. H. (2015). Is performance feedback for educators an evidence-based practice? A systematic review and evaluation based on single-case research. *Exceptional Children, 81,* 227−246. Available from http://dx.doi.org/10.1177/0014402914551738.

Fisher, W., Piazza, C. C., Bowman, L. G., Hagopian, L. P., Owens, J. C., & Slevin, I. (1992). Comparison of two approaches for identifying reinforcers for persons with severe and profound disabilities. *Journal of Applied Behavior Analysis, 25,* 491−498.

Fuchs, D., Fuchs, L. S., & Bahr, M. W. (1990). Mainstream assistance teams: A scientific basis for the art of consultation. *Exceptional Children*, *57*, 128−139.

Fuchs, L. S., & Fuchs, D. (1986). Effects of systematic formative evaluation: A meta-analysis. *Exceptional Children*, *53*, 199−208.

Fuchs, L. S., & Fuchs, D. (1999). Monitoring student progress toward the development of reading competence: A review of three forms of classroom-based assessment. *School Psychology Review*, *28*, 659−671.

Fuchs, L. S., Fuchs, D., Hamlett, C. L., & Allinder, R. M. (1991). Effects of expert system advice within curriculum-based measurement on teacher planning and student achievement in spelling. *School Psychology Review*, *20*, 49−66.

Gansle, K. A., VanDerHeyden, A. M., Noell, G. H., Resetar, J. L., & Williams, K. L. (2006). The technical adequacy of curriculum-based and rating-based measures of written expression for elementary school students. *School Psychology Review*, *35*(3), 435−450.

Good, R.H., & Kaminski, R.A. (2001). Dynamic indicators of basic early literacy skills (5th ed.). Eugene, OR: Institute for the Development of Educational Achievement. Retrieved February 6, 2017 from the Website: http://dibels.uoregon.edu/.

Good, R. H., Simmons, D. C., & Kame'enui, E. J. (2001). The importance and decision-making utility of a continuum of fluency-based indicators of foundational reading skills for third-grade high-stakes outcomes. *Scientific Studies of Reading*, *5*, 257−288.

Haring, N. G., & Eaton, M. D. (1978). Systematic procedures: An instructional hierarchy. In N. G. Haring, T. C. Lovitt, M. D. Eaton, & C. L. Hansen (Eds.), *The fourth R: Research in the classroom* (pp. 23−40). Columbus, OH: Merrill.

Hier, B. O., & Eckert, T. L. (2016). Programming generality into a performance feedback writing intervention: A randomized controlled trial. *Journal of School Psychology*, *56*, 111−131.

Hintze, J. J., & Silberglitt, B. (2005). A longitudinal examination of the diagnostic accuracy and predictive validity of R-CBM and high-stakes testing. *School Psychology Review*, *34*, 372−386.

Howe, K. B., & Shinn, M. M. (2002). *Standard reading assessment passages (RAPs) for use in general outcome measurement: A manual describing development and technical features*. Eden Prairie, MN: Edformation.

Individuals with Disabilities Education Improvement Act (IDEA) of (2004). *Public Law*, 108−446.

Jaspers, K. E., Williams, R. L., Skinner, C. H., Cihak, D., McCallum, R. S., & Ciancio, D. J. (2012). How and to what extent do two cover, copy, and compare spelling interventions contribute to spelling, word recognition, and vocabulary development. *Journal of Behavioral Education*, *21*, 80−98.

Johnson, K. R., & Layng, T. J. (1992). Breaking the structuralist barrier. *American Psychologist*, *47*(11), 1475.

Johnson, K. R., & Layng, T. V. J. (1996). On terms and procedures: Fluency. *The Behavior Analyst*, *19*, 281−288.

Jones, K. M., Wickstrom, K. F., Noltemeyer, A. L., Brown, S. M., Schuka, J. R., & Therrien, W. J. (2009). An experimental analysis of reading fluency. *Journal of Behavioral Education*, *18*, 35−55.

Kavale, K. (1990). Effectiveness of special education. In T. B. Gutkin, & C. R. Reynolds (Eds.), *Handbook of school psychology* (2nd ed., pp. 868−898). New York: John Wiley.

Lin, F., & Kubina, R., Jr. (2005). A preliminary investigation of the relationship between fluency and application for multiplication. *Journal of Behavioral Education*, *14*, 73−87. Available from http://dx.doi.org/10.1007/s10864-005-2703-z.

Martens, B. K., Eckert, T. L., Begeny, J. C., Lewandowski, L. J., DiGennaro, F., Montarello, S., et al. (2007). Effects of a fluency-building program on the reading performance of low-achieving second and third grade students. *Journal of Behavioral Education, 16*, 39–54.

Martens, B. K., & Lambert, T. L. (2014). Conducting functional behavior assessments for students with emotional/behavioral disorders. In H. M. Walker, & F. M. Gresham (Eds.), *Handbook of evidence-based practices for emotional and behavioral disorders: Applications in schools* (pp. 243–257). New York: Guilford.

Martens, B.K., & Mullane, M.P. (in press). Prediction versus control: Influences of applied behavior analysis on school psychology practice. In M. Burns (Ed.), *Introduction to school psychology: Controversies and current practice*. New York; Oxford University Press.

Martens, B. K., Daly, E. J., & Ardoin, S. P. (2015). Applications of applied behavior analysis to school-based instructional intervention. In H. S. Roane, J. L. Ringdahl, & T. S. Falcomata (Eds.), *Clinical and organizational applications of applied behavior analysis* (pp. 125–150). New York: Elsevier.

Martens, B.K., Daly, E.J., Begeny, J.C., & Sullivan, W.E. (in press). Behavioral approaches to education. In W. Fisher, C. Piazza, & H. Roane (Eds., 2nd ed.), *Handbook of applied behavior analysis*. New York: Guilford.

Martens, B. K., Witt, J. C., Daly, E. J., & Vollmer, T. (1999). Behavior analysis: Theory and practice in educational settings. In C. R. Reynolds, & T. B. Gutkin (Eds.), *Handbook of school psychology* (3rd ed, pp. 638–663). New York: John Wiley & Sons.

McCallum, E., Skinner, C., Turner, H., & Saecker, L. (2006). The taped-problems intervention: Increasing multiplication fact fluency using a low-tech, classwide, time-delay intervention. *School Psychology Review, 35*, 419–434.

McCurdy, M., Skinner, C. H., Grantham, K., Watson, T. S., & Hindman, P. M. (2001). Increasing on-task behavior in an elementary student during mathematics seatwork by interspersing additional brief problems. *School Psychology Review, 1*, 23–32.

McDougal, J. L., Clonan, S. M., & Martens, B. K. (2000). Using organizational change procedures to promote the acceptability of prereferral intervention services: The school-based intervention team project. *School Psychology Quarterly, 15*, 149–171.

McIntosh, K., Martinez, R. S., Ty, S. V., & McClain, M. B. (2013). Scientific research in school psychology: Leading researchers weigh in on its past, present, and future. *Journal of School Psychology, 51*, 267–318.

Mesmer, E. M., Duhon, G. J., Hogan, K., Newry, B., Hommema, S., Fletcher, C., & Boso, M. (2010). Generalization of sight word accuracy using a common stimulus procedure: A preliminary investigation. *Journal of Behavioral Education, 19*, 47–61.

Mouzakitis, A., Codding, R. S., & Tryon, G. (2015). The effects of self-monitoring and performance feedback on the treatment integrity of behavior intervention plan implementation and generalization. *Journal of Positive Behavior Interventions, 17*, 223–234. Available from http://dx.doi.org/10.1177/1098300715573629.

Mueller, M. M., Nkosi, A., & Hine, J. F. (2011). Functional analysis in public schools: A summary of 90 functional analyses. *Journal of Applied Behavior Analysis, 44*, 807–818.

National Center for Educational Statistics (2015). *The nation's report card: Mathematics and reading assessments*. Retrieved January 24, 2017 from the Web site: http://www.nationsreportcard.gov/reading_math_2015/#?grade=4.

National Center for Educational Statistics (2016). *Public school enrollment*. Retrieved January 24, 2017 from the Institute of Education Sciences Web site: https://nces.ed.gov/programs/coe/indicator_cga.asp.

No Child Left Behind Act of 2001, 20 U.S.C.6301 (2002).

Noell, G., Gansle, K., Mevers, J., Knox, R. R., Mintz, J., & Dahir, A. (2014). Improving treatment plan implementation in schools: A meta-analysis of single subject design studies. *Journal of Behavioral Education*, *23*, 168−191. Available from http://dx.doi.org/10.1007/s10864-013-9177-1.

Northup, J., George, T., Jones, K., Broussard, C., & Vollmer, T. (1996). A comparison of reinforcer assessment methods: The utility of verbal and pictorial choice procedures. *Journal of Applied Behavior Analysis*, *29*, 201−212.

Petscher, E. S., & Bailey, J. S. (2006). Effects of training, prompting, and self-monitoring on staff behavior in a classroom for students with disabilities. *Journal of Applied Behavior Analysis*, *39*, 215−226. Available from http://dx.doi.org/10.1901/jaba.2006.02-05.

Reschly, D. J. (1988). Special education reform: School psychology revolution. *School Psychology Review*, *17*, 459−475.

Reschly, D. J. (2004). Commentary: Paradigm shift, outcomes criteria, and behavioral interventions: Foundations for the future of school psychology. *School Psychology Review*, *33*, 408−416.

Roth, M. E., Gillis, J. M., & DiGennaro Reed, F. D. (2014). A meta-analysis of behavioral interventions for adolescents and adults with autism spectrum disorders. *Journal of Behavioral Education*, *23*, 258−286.

Sanetti, L. M. H., & Kratochwill, T. R. (2009). Toward developing a science of treatment integrity: Introduction to the special series. *School Psychology Review*, *38*, 445−459.

Sanetti, L., & Collier-Meek, M. (2014). Increasing the rigor of procedural fidelity assessment: An empirical comparison of direct observation and permanent product review methods. *Journal of Behavioral Education*, *23*(1), 60−88. Available from http://dx.doi.org/10.1007/s10864-013-9179-z.

Schulte, A. C., Eaton, J. E., & Parker, J. (2009). Advances in treatment integrity research: Multidisciplinary perspectives on the conceptualization, measurement, and enhancement of treatment integrity. *School Psychology Review*, *38*, 460−475.

Shapiro, E. S. (2011). *Academic skills problems: Direct assessment and intervention*. New York: Guilford Press.

Shinn, M. R. (1989). *Curriculum-based measurement: Assessing special children*. New York: Guilford.

Silber, J. M., & Martens, B. K. (2010). Programming for the generalization of oral reading fluency: Repeated readings of entire text versus multiple exemplars. *Journal of Behavioral Education*, *19*, 30−46.

Skinner, C., & Daly, E. (2010). Improving generalization of academic skills: Commentary on the special issue. *Journal of Behavioral Education*, *19*(1), 106−115. Available from http://dx.doi.org/10.1007/s10864-010-9100-y.

Smith, T. (2001). Discrete trial training in the treatment of autism. *Focus on Autism and Other Developmental Disabilities*, *16*, 86−92.

Stokes, T. F., & Baer, D. M. (1977). An implicit technology of generalization. *Journal of Applied Behavior Analysis*, *10*, 349−367.

Vaughn, S., & Fuchs, L. S. (2003). Redefining learning disabilities as inadequate response to instruction: The promise and potential problems. *Learning Disabilities Research & Practice*, *18*, 137−146.

Witt, J. C., VanDerheyden, A. M., & Gilbertson, D. (2004). Troubleshooting behavioral interventions: A systematic process for finding and eliminating problems. *School Psychology Review*, *33*, 363−383.

Wolery, M., Bailey, D.B., & Sugai, G.M. (1988). Effective teaching: Principles and procedure of applied behavior analysis with exceptional students. (Chapter 8) Boston: Allyn
and Bacon.

Yeaton, W. H. , Y., & Sechrest, L. (1981). Critical dimensions in the choice and maintenance
of successful treatments: Strength, integrity, and effectiveness. *Journal of Consulting &
Clinical Psychology*, *49*, 156–167.

Ysseldyke, J. E., & Marston, D. (1990). The use of assessment information to plan instructional
interventions: A review of the research. In T. B. Gutkin, & C. R. Reynolds (Eds.), *The
handbook of school psychology, second edition* (pp. 661–682). New York: John Wiley.

Yoder, P., & Woynaroski, T. (2015). How to study the influence of intensity of treatment on
generalized skill and knowledge acquisition in students with disabilities. *Journal of
Behavioral Education*, *24*(1), 152–166. Available from http://dx.doi.org/10.1007/
s10864-014-9216-6.

Further reading

Intervention Central (2017). Retrieved February 7, 2017 from the Website: http://www.inter-
ventioncentral.org/.

Consultation Practices: School-Based Behavior Support

9

Jason C. Vladescu[1], Danielle L. Gureghian[2], April N. Kisamore[1] and Lauren K. Schnell[1]

[1]Caldwell University, Caldwell, NJ, United States, [2]Garden Academy, West Orange, NJ, United States

Consultation practices: school-based behavior support

Challenging behaviors (e.g., aggression, noncompliance) emitted by students are considered a barrier to making educational progress (Lloyd, Weaver, & Staubitz, 2016) and may lead to long-term academic and social difficulties (Agostin & Bain, 1997; Ledingham & Schwatzman, 1984). [Clinicians and researchers have used a variety of terms to refer to behavior that is undesirable in the school setting (i.e., problem behavior, aberrant behavior, inappropriate behavior). To increase clarity, we will refer to such behavior as *challenging behavior*. We will not differentiate challenging behavior based on topography and our discussion is limited to challenging behavior that is sensitive to socially mediated reinforcement contingencies. A discussion of consultation approaches relative to behaviors sensitive to automatic reinforcement contingencies is beyond the scope of this chapter.] In fact, teachers rank challenging behavior as the most significant classroom barrier to teaching students (Harrison, Vannest, Davis, & Reynolds, 2012). To address this issue, there is a need for qualified professionals to provide behavior consultation to school staff to increase the likelihood of student success (DiGennaro-Reed & Jenkins, 2013).

Overall, teachers have reported that consultation is effective and improves student performance in the classroom (MacLeod, Jones, Somers, & Havey, 2001). This consultation, typically delivered by a behavior analyst or behavioral expert, involves providing support and assistance to school staff with the goal of improving student performance. [There are a number of individuals (e.g., teachers, paraprofessionals, administrators, school psychologists) in a school who may be involved in and receive services from a consultant. We will refer to such individuals collectively as *school staff*.] The consultant collaborates with the school staff, usually through a series of face-to-face interviews and direct observations and the school staff is then expected to be primarily responsible for implementing the consultant's suggestions (Erchul & Martens, 2010). The role of the consultant is to influence the school staff's behavior by facilitating communication, formulating assessments that identify variables maintaining the student's behavior, designing interventions that change the behavior of the student, and providing training to improve the skills of the school staff. Ultimately, the goal of the consultation process is to ensure that school staff are equipped to address future instances of challenging behavior independent of the

Applied Behavior Analysis Advanced Guidebook. DOI: http://dx.doi.org/10.1016/B978-0-12-811122-2.00009-7

consultant (Putnam, Handler, Rey, & McCarty, 2005). Along these lines, the primary purposes of the current chapter are to provide consultants a broad review of the extant literature related to the function-based assessment and treatment of challenging behavior and provide recommended practice guidelines for consultants to consider when providing professional services to public and private school staff.

Functional behavior assessment: research base and implications

Consultants should be aware that schools are required to conduct a functional behavior assessment (FBA) in situations in which a student's challenging behavior results in a change of educational placement (Individuals with Disabilities Education Act; P.L. 101–476). Further, board certified behavior analysts are required to use FBAs as per the Behavior Analyst Certification Board *Guidelines for Responsible Conduct for Behavior Analysts*. Broadly speaking, the goal of FBA is to gather information about the topography of challenging behaviors and identify variables (antecedents and consequences) related to the occurrence of these behaviors. FBA encompasses a range of procedures, typically grouped as indirect assessments, descriptive assessments, and functional analysis (FA).

Indirect assessments do not involve observation of the challenging behavior, but rather include rating scales, questionnaires, and interviews. This type of assessment is considered to have poor reliability and validity (Duker & Sigafoos, 1998; Paclawskyj, Matson, Rush, Smalls, & Vollmer, 2001; Shogren & Rojahn, 2003; Sigafoos, Kerr, & Roberts, 1994; Zarcone, Rodgers, Iwata, Rourke, & Dorsey, 1991). Yet, despite their poor technical adequacy, practitioners report commonly using indirect assessments (Ellingson, Miltenberger, & Long, 1999; Oliver, Pratt, & Normand, 2015).

Descriptive assessments involve direct observation, which may produce *correlational* information regarding the occurrence of challenging behavior and certain antecedent and consequent events. Similar to indirect assessments, descriptive assessments are thought to produce information that is of limited validity (Hall, 2005; Lerman & Iwata, 1993; Pence, Roscoe, Bourret, & Ahearn, 2009; Thompson & Iwata, 2007). Despite this, survey research has consistently reported descriptive assessments to be the most used FBA procedure (Ellingson et al. 1999; Oliver et al. 2015; Roscoe, Phillips, Kelly, Farber, & Dube, 2015).

Originally described by Iwata, Dorsey, Slifer, Bauman & Richman, 1994), the standard FA involves the measurement of challenging behavior during the experimental manipulation of antecedents (e.g., motivating operations, discriminative stimuli) and putative reinforcing consequences. This manipulation allows for the demonstration of causal (i.e., functional) relationships between the challenging behavior and environmental variables. The standard FA includes three (attention, demand, alone/ignore) or four (plus tangible) distinct test conditions and one control condition (toy play). Test and control conditions are rapidly alternated in a multielement design until higher and stable levels of challenging behavior occur in one or more test conditions as compared to the control condition. A description of the substantial empirical support for the standard FA and its generality is beyond the scope of this chapter, but see Hanley, Iwata, and McCord (2003) and the *Journal of Applied Behavior Analysis* special issue (2013, Vol. 46) on the FA for excellent reviews and discussion of the FA as it relates to challenging behavior.

Historically, researchers have considered the FA to be the *gold standard* in identifying functional relations. Yet, the FA is reportedly used less frequently than indirect and descriptive assessments, and over half (60%) of survey respondents indicated they almost never or never use an FA (Oliver et al., 2015). These results suggest that the FA is in fact *not* the gold standard in practice. When considering why practitioners may not employ FA procedures, common barriers have included lack of time, space, materials, trained staff, approval, and funding; prohibitive administrative policies; and a belief that FAs are not informative (Hanley, 2011; Oliver et al., 2015).

Function-based treatment: research base and implications

Following the FBA, consultants are required to design, implement, and evaluate a function-based treatment. The goal of a function-based treatment is to (1) disrupt the contingency between the challenging behavior and functional reinforcer by weakening the EO, (2) arrange the functional reinforcer for a socially acceptable response (or providing the reinforcer noncontingently), and (3) eliminate reinforcement for challenging behavior (Geiger, Carr, & LeBlanc, 2010). We will review three types of function-based treatments: extinction, noncontingent reinforcement (NCR), and differential reinforcement.

Extinction

Extinction (EXT) involves withholding reinforcement for a previously reinforced response that leads to a decrease in responding. Procedurally, EXT involves *withholding* the reinforcer (e.g., attention) contingent on challenging behavior maintained by social positive reinforcement, and the *continued presentation* (i.e., nonremoval) of an event contingent on challenging behavior maintained by social negative reinforcement. Research indicates that using a contraindicated form of EXT is counter therapeutic; thus, highlighting the importance of conducting an FBA to inform a function-matched intervention (Iwata, Pace, Cowdery, & Miltenberger, 1994).

Noncontingent reinforcement

NCR involves the time-based delivery of a functional reinforcer, independent of the occurrence of challenging behavior. This should have two effects: result in a weakening of the contingency between the challenging behavior and serve as an abolishing operation (AO) for challenging behavior (Carr, Severtson, & Lepper, 2009). These effects have the outcome of producing rapid decreases in the frequency of challenging behavior. This effect means NCR is particularly beneficial in situations in which immediate reductions in challenging behavior are desired (Fischer, Iwata, & Mazaleski, 1997; Vollmer, Iwata, Zarcone, Smith, & Mazaleski, 1993), the school staff does not have complete control of the functional reinforcer (e.g., peer attention; Jones, Drew, & Weber, 2000), EXT is dangerous due to the severity of the challenging behavior, and a student is unable to be continuously monitored. These potential benefits are not without drawback, as NCR does not involve explicit reinforcement of an alternative response (the student does not learn a socially appropriate functional response), may function as an AO for an alternative response, may result in the continuation of the challenging behavior as a result adventitious reinforcement (Vollmer, Ringdahl, Roane, & Marcus, 1997), and long-term use may be cumbersome and considered unfair by others students.

Differential reinforcement

We limit our discussion of differential reinforcement (DR) to the application of differential reinforcement of alternative behavior to functional communication training. It is common for other authors (e.g., Hanley, 2011) to expand their discussion of DR to include differential reinforcement of other behavior (DRO). However, we selected not to include DRO in our discussion as this procedure does not result in the explicit reinforcement of an alternative, socially appropriate response. This is not surprising considering DRO may be conceptualized as a punishment contingency, wherein the occurrence of challenging behavior prevents access to a functional reinforcer (Malott & Sloane, 2014).

Functional communication training (FCT) is composed of two components: differential reinforcement of alternative behavior (DRA) and EXT. More specifically, FCT involves a student making an alternative response that serves the same function as the challenging behavior and extinction for the challenging behavior. FCT offers several attractive features. First, FCT provides an opportunity to teach a socially appropriate response and increased opportunities for social exchanges. Second, the initial stages of FCT include high rates of reinforcement that may serve as an AO for challenging behavior. Third, FCT has been shown to have high generality (e.g., FCT has been successfully used with individuals with and without disabilities and in the treatment of many topographies of challenging behavior; Hagopian, Fisher, Sullivan, Acquisto, & LeBlanc, 1998; Kurtz, et al., 2003; Rooker, Jessel, Kurtz, & Hagopian, 2013). Last, FCT has shown to be preferred by teachers relative to extinction alone (McConnachie & Carr, 1997) and by children relative to NCR and EXT (Hanley, Piazza, Fisher, Contrucci, & Maglieri, 1997). Given these features it is not surprising that FCT is the most commonly used function-based treatment for challenging behavior maintained by social positive and negative reinforcement (Tiger, Hanley, & Bruzek, 2008).

Practice recommendations

Recommended practice guideline 1: be analytical

We recommend the consultant to be first and foremost analytical (Baer, Wolf, & Risley, 1987). That is, we recommend the consultant to adopt assessment and treatment practices with the goal of demonstrating a functional relationship between behavior (the challenging behavior and the appropriate behavior) and environmental variables. This skill set not only involves employing best practices with respect to behavior analytic assessment and treatment procedures, it involves proper data collection and analysis, on-going evaluation, and effective training and supervision. Analytical decision-making should guide the consultant throughout the consultation process. We would be remiss not to mention proper consideration of *all* the dimensions of applied behavior analysis (Baer et al., 1987); however, an in-depth description of these is beyond the scope of the chapter.

Recommended practice guideline 2: employ a functional analysis

Use open-ended indirect and direct assessments to inform the functional analysis, not replace it

The extant literature is clear: indirect and descriptive assessments produce information that is of poor reliability and validity (e.g., Thompson & Iwata, 2007). Therefore, we recommend that consultants not rely solely on indirect and direct assessments to identify functions of challenging behavior (Hanley, 2012; Iwata & Dozier, 2008). Rather, we recommend the consultant use open-ended indirect and direct assessments to inform and refine hypotheses that will be tested in an FA (Fisher, Greer, Romani, Zangrillo, & Owen, 2016; Hanley, 2012). We are in good company for such a recommendation, as Hanley (2012) suggests using open-ended interviews and brief observations as the *initial* step in the FA process. Others have also suggested using these strategies to develop additional hypotheses when undifferentiated responding is observed during the initial FA iteration (Fisher et al., 2016). For example, open-ended narrative recording can be utilized to clarify operational definitions and obtain details on idiosyncratic antecedent and consequent events that may not have been revealed during the interview process or initial FA. Consultants who use open-ended indirect and direct assessments should develop and refine, rather quickly, appropriate hypotheses regarding function of challenging behavior without having to conduct potentially labor-intensive (e.g., antecedent—behavior—consequence recordings) or unreliable assessments (e.g., closed-ended indirect rating scales).

Consider potential barriers to conducting an FA, and select the FA format that reduces these potential barriers

Practical barriers, such as time, risk, and dangerous challenging behaviors, have been discussed extensively in the research literature. This discussion has led to a number of procedural variations in the standard FA methodology (Hanley, 2012; Iwata & Dozier, 2008; Lloyd et al., 2016). To address the concern that standard FAs (the standard FA as described by Iwata et al., 1982/1994 included 15 minutes sessions) take too much time, researchers have shown that relatively brief (e.g., 5 minutes) sessions can readily identify function (Hanley et al., 2003).

Latency- and trial-based FAs offer the consultant an efficient alternative to the standard FA. Measuring latency (i.e., onset of a stimulus and time to the first instance of challenging behavior) as an index of response strength has been shown to identify functions of elopement and other common challenging behaviors (Neidert, Iwata, Dempsey, & Thomason-Sassi, 2013; Thomason-Sassi, Iwata, Neidert, & Roscoe, 2011). Trial-based FAs (e.g., Kodak, Fisher, Paden, & Dickes, 2013; Sigafoos & Saggars, 1995) involve brief 1-minute trials in which the relevant establishing operation (EO) and putative reinforcer are arranged (test trial) and are followed by a trial in which the EO is absent and the reinforcer is freely available (control trial). For example, when testing for challenging behavior maintain by escape from instructional activities, the school staff asks a student to complete an activity at her desk (test). Contingent on challenging behavior, the school staff removes the activity and allows a break (control). Trial-based FAs provide an ecologically valid alternative to the standard FA because this type of assessment is easily incorporated into on-going classroom activities thereby mitigating the need to conduct the assessment in an isolated setting.

Dangerous challenging behavior can pose considerable concern to the consultant and school staff. To address this concern, researchers have evaluated the extent to which reinforcement of precursors to challenging behavior reliably identify function of the target behavior (Smith & Churchill, 2002). Precursors are behaviors that occur prior to and are functionally related to the challenging behavior. In addition, precursors tend to be less intense behaviors, thus could be considered less dangerous to target during assessment and treatment. If the topography of challenging behavior is of concern for the school staff, we recommend the consultant take steps to identify precursors to target during the FA. The consultant could identify precursors through school staff report (Hanley, 2010a; Herscovitch, Roscoe, Libby, Bourret, & Ahearn, 2009) or through an experimental method (a description of which is beyond the scope of this chapter, for details see Fritz, Iwata, Hammond, & Bloom, 2013; Borlase, Vladescu, Kisamore, Reeve, & Fetzer, 2017).

We recommend the consultant consider several additional recommendations from Hanley (2012) that may minimize risk during an FA. First, the materials used in the FA should be considered. Hard objects and furniture should be avoided if students are likely to engage in property destruction or bang their heads or body parts on them. If a student engages in aggression, the consultant and school staff may consider wearing protective equipment (e.g., padded arm guards, helmets; see Fisher, Rodriguez, Luczynski, & Kelley, 2013) to decrease the risk of injury. The putative reinforcer should be arranged for each occurrence of the challenging behavior such that it results in its cessation. Similarly, consultants should clearly signal contingencies (e.g., the consultant and school staff can wear different colored shirts for each condition) and structure control conditions to include dense delivery of the reinforcer to increase the likelihood of eliminating the EO for the challenging behavior. For further discussion on overcoming barriers to implementing FAs we recommend the consultant read Hanley (2012) and Iwata and Dozier (2008).

Be prepared to clarify undifferentiated responding in the FA through design variations and procedural modifications

Rooker, DeLeon, Borrero, Frank-Crawford, and Roscoe (2015) reported that 4% to 15% of FAs to be inconclusive (based on published data). Because identification of the reinforcement contingency (or contingencies) that maintain challenging behavior is paramount to treatment success, the consultant will likely have to make informed decisions regarding inconclusive FA outcomes. Thus, the consultant must engage in effective problem solving to clarify inconclusive FA results. Fortunately, Vollmer, Marcus, Ringdahl, and Roane (1995) outlined a model that provides recommendations for implementing FA procedural refinements in the presence of undifferentiated responding that we recommend consultants follow.

Consider a synthesized contingency analysis

We provide a relative longer description and discussion of the synthesized contingency analysis because this approach to an FA appeared recently in the literature. As such, it may be possible that consultants have contacted this literature to a lesser extent than the standard FA literature.

Hanley (2010b, 2011, 2012) have described and evaluated (e.g., Ghaemmaghami, Hanley, Jessel, 2016; Hanley, Jin, Vanselow, & Hanratty, 2014; Jessel, Hanley, & Ghaemmaghami, 2016; Santiago, Hanley, Moore, & Jin, 2016) an alternative approach, referred to as an interview-informed synthesized contingency analysis (IISCA), to the standard FA in an attempt to increase the efficiency of identifying variables controlling challenging behavior. This analysis involves comparing the occurrence of challenging behavior during a control condition to a *single* test condition. The test condition involves multiple reinforcement contingencies (i.e., synthesized contingencies; e.g., escape *to* attention) identified through an open-ended interview. The control condition differs from the test condition in only one-way: the synthesized contingency is removed, and all putative reinforcers are provided noncontingently during the session. This assessment process represents a fairly substantial deviation from the procedures included in a standard FA, namely the exclusion of closed-ended indirect and descriptive assessments, multiple test conditions that each includes only a *single* reinforcement contingency, and a control condition that differs in multiple ways from the test conditions. In addition, whereas the standard FA was designed to be conducted in an analogue setting, the IISCA was designed to be more easily transportable to nonanalog settings. We would be remiss not to mention the disagreement that exists in the behavior analytic community regarding adaptation of the IISCA given the limited demonstrations and lack of independent replications (for further discussion of some of these issues see Fisher et al., 2016; Jessel et al., 2016).

We recommend consultants consider conducting an IISCA, which involves the following components. When planning to conduct an IISCA, the consultant begins by conducting an open-ended functional assessment interview with school staff who knows the student well. From the consultant's perspective, the purposes of the interview are to identify and define the challenging behavior, identify, and define precursors to the challenging behavior, identify the putative reinforcers maintaining the challenging behavior, and identify the EOs related to these putative reinforcers. This interview should be expected to last approximately 40 minutes (Jessel et al., 2016). Next, the consultant casually interacts with the student during a 10 to 20 minutes period. This observation period may serve to reduce reactivity due to the consultant's presence and provide supplemental information to that obtained during the interview. Following the interview and observation, the consultant designs the IISCA. More specifically, it would be important to identify data collection procedures, who will conduct the assessment sessions, where the assessment sessions will be conducted, and what materials should be present during assessment sessions. This information should be used to create test and control conditions. Again, the distinction between these conditions is that the test condition involves arrangement of the evocative variables and the delivery of the putative synthesized reinforcers contingent on the occurrence of precursors or the challenging behavior. The control condition ensures that no evocative variables are present and putative synthesized reinforcers are available noncontingently. Last, the consultant and school staff conduct the IISCA. The IISCA should consist of a minimum of two control condition sessions and three test condition sessions conducted in a control—test—control—test—test sequence (Jessel et al., 2016).

Hanley et al. (2014) provided the initial demonstration that information obtained from an IISCA could be used as the basis from which to design an effective treatment. [The functional analysis conducted was not referred to as an IISCA by Hanley, Jin, Vanselow, and Hanratty (2014). The IISCA terminology was adapted later, but we will use it throughout for ease.] Three children, aged 3-, 8-, and 11-year-old with an autism spectrum disorder participated. The experimenters conducted an open-ended interview (Hanley, 2009) with each participant's parents. The results of these interviews suggested that each participant's problem behavior was sensitive to multiple reinforcement contingencies, and the results of synthesized contingency analyses supported this conclusion. Subsequently, the experimenters devised a comprehension treatment for each participant based on the results of their individual IISCA. Broadly speaking, the experimenters implemented FCT and denial- and delay-tolerance training (the specific details of the treatment are beyond the scope of this chapter) over the course of 8 to 14 weeks. Following this intervention, the participants engaged in zero levels of problem behavior.

Recently, Santiago et al. (2016) replicated and extended Hanley et al. (2014). Most notably, the IISCA and treatment were successfully carried out in naturalistic settings (i.e., school classroom, bedroom). The results of Santiago et al. provide promising information regarding the generality of the IISCA. In another recent extension, Jessel et al. (2016) described the results of 30 IISCAs. This data set revealed several interesting findings. First, the average IISCA duration was

25 minutes. This suggests the IISCA can yield useful outcomes rapidly. Second, in approximately 73% of cases, differentiation (i.e., high rates of challenging behavior during the test condition relative to the control condition) was observed during the first IISCA iteration. Even though subsequent iterations may have been required, differentiation was achieved in 1 hour for 90% of total cases. No treatment data were included, which limits the conclusions that can be drawn regarding the predictive validity of the IISCA. Nonetheless, these data are encouraging as they provide information regarding IISCA efficiency. When combined with the results of Santiago et al., these outcomes provide initial support for the applicability of the IISCA in nonanalogue settings such as schools.

See Table 9.1 for a summary of considerations when creating and conducting a FA.

Table 9.1 **Considerations for conducting a functional analysis (FA)**

Practice recommendation	Considerations
Use open-ended indirect and direct assessments to *inform* the functional analysis, not replace it	• Use open-ended interviews and observations to inform the hypothesis to be tested in the FA • Use open-ended interviews and observations to develop additional hypotheses, clarify operational definitions, and obtain details on idiosyncratic antecedent and consequent events
Consider potential barriers to conducting an FA, and select the FA format that reduces these potential barriers	• To address time, consider brief sessions, IISCA, latency- and trial-based FAs • To address dangerous behavior, consider latency-based and precursor FAs • To minimize risk, consider using soft materials, wearing protective equipment, arranging the reinforcer for every challenging behavior, signaling contingencies, and arranging dense delivery of reinforcement in the control condition
Be prepared to clarify undifferentiated responding in the FA through design variations and procedural modifications	• Consult Vollmer and colleagues model on refining FA procedures
Consider a synthesized contingency analysis	• Conduct open-ended interviews • Conduct brief observations • Combine contingencies into a single test condition and provide putative reinforcers noncontingently into the control condition • For further resources, see www.practicalfunctionalassessment.com

Recommended practice guideline 3: employ skill- and function-based treatments

Use FCT

We recommend consultants design their treatment around the use of FCT. The rationale behind this specific recommendation is that FCT is not only function-based, but results in an increase in socially appropriate skills while decreasing challenging behavior. There are several guidelines to consider when designing an FCT-based treatment.

First, the consultant should select an appropriate response [i.e., the functional communicative response (FCR)] that is simple, easily acquired, low effort, and recognized by the student's verbal community (Fisher & Bouxsein, 2011; Hanley, 2011; Tiger et al., 2008). For example, the consultant could select the simple FCR to be a single-word response (e.g., "toys," "break"). Once the student has acquired the initial, simple FCR, the consultant can build more complex appropriate responses by teaching the student to emit additional collateral behaviors and longer vocal utterances (e.g., student must obtain eye contact, and state, "May I have a break, please?" or "Can I play with my toys?"; see Hanley et al., 2014). Second, the consultant should consider using transfer of stimulus control technologies (e.g., prompt delay, most-to-least prompting) to teach the FCR (e.g., Shirley, Iwata, Kahng, Mazaleski, & Lerman, 1997). The goal of these prompt and prompt-fading procedures is to transfer the control of the prompt to the relevant evocative condition. Third, we recommend the consultant implement the initial stages of FCT to ensure proper implementation and careful arrangement of EOs, prompts, prompt-fading techniques, and consequences. Once the FCR is taught, the consultant should train relevant school staff to implement the FCT-based treatment to enhance generalization. Fourth, the FCT procedure should be initially taught in a safe environment, especially for those students with severe challenging behavior (Tiger et al., 2008). Fifth, the consultant should initially contrive learning opportunities that sample the likely conditions under which the FCR will be expected to occur and to prompt and reinforce the FCR as a means to increase exposure to the FCT contingencies. Sixth, the consultant should ensure a continuous schedule of reinforcement is in place for the FCR during the initial stages of FCT. Once the FCR occurs reliably and challenging behavior is low, the schedule of reinforcement can be thinned (see below on recommendations for creating practical treatments). Last, if the immediate goal is rapid behavior reduction with a secondary goal of increasing appropriate behavior the consultant should use NCR. Once, NCR has resulted in the elimination of challenging behavior, the consultant can systematically thin NCR and simultaneously begin FCT (see Goh, Iwata, & DeLeon, 2000 for an excellent example of how this may be achieved).

Consider extinction

The extant literature demonstrates FCT is most effective when paired with EXT or punishment as compared to FCT alone (e.g., Zarcone, Iwata, Smith, Mazaleski, & Lerman, 1994). As such, we recommend consultants use EXT to facilitate reductions in challenging behavior. However, EXT alone is not recommended (Hanley, 2011) and is more effective when paired with reinforcement-based procedures (Vollmer & Athens, 2011). The consultant should be aware of the potential unwanted side effects of EXT (e.g., extinction bursts, aggression, emotional responding, and spontaneous recovery; Lerman & Iwata, 1996), and plan for them accordingly through use of reinforcement-based procedures (Lerman & Iwata, 1995). It is beyond the scope of this chapter to provide a thorough description of each of these side effects; therefore, we refer the readers to Vollmer and Athens (2011).

In situations in which EXT is not a viable treatment option due to the severity of challenging behavior or the effort required to implement the procedure with high integrity, we recommend consultants consider manipulating parameters of reinforcement available for the FCR and the challenging behavior. The consultant should consider manipulation of one or more of the following reinforcement parameters: quality, magnitude, delay, and schedule (e.g., Athens & Vollmer, 2010; Worsdell, Iwata, Hanley, Thompson, & Kahng, 2000). When manipulating reinforcement parameters, consultants could provide higher quality, larger magnitude, shorter delays, or denser schedules of reinforcement for the FCR; and lower quality, smaller magnitude, longer delays, and leaner schedules of reinforcement for the challenging behavior. The hope of doing so is that the student allocates their responding to the FCR as this response maximizes reinforcement (Matching Law; Herrnstein, 1961).

Create a practical treatment via reinforcement schedule thinning

One potential limitation of FCT-based treatments is that it becomes impractical for school staff to reinforce every FCR, once this response is acquired. If the FCR is not reinforced, this EXT may weaken the contingency between the newly acquired FCR and the reinforcer and can result in the reemergence of challenging behavior (Fisher, Thompson, Hagopian, Bowman, & Krug, 2000). To address this limitation, we recommend consultants take active steps to thin the schedule of reinforcement available for the FCR. Along this line, researchers have identified a number of potential procedures that may be used to thin reinforcement and increase the practicality of FCT. These procedures include delay schedules, multiple schedules, chained schedules, and response restriction (Greer, Fisher, Saini, Owen, & Jones, 2016; Hagopian, Boelter, & Jarmolowicz, 2011). A comprehensive review of these procedures is beyond the scope of this chapter, but we refer to the reader to Greer et al. (2016) and Hagopian et al. (2011) for excellent reviews and guidelines, as well as Hanley et al. (2014) for a methodology to include a tolerance response during schedule thinning. In addition, we also recommend consultants consider arranging the availability of alternative reinforcers during reinforcement schedule thinning, as these may function as AOs for the FCR and challenging behavior (e.g., Hagopian, Contrucci-Kuhn, Long, & Rush, 2005).

Consider antecedent strategies for escape-maintained problem behavior

A recent literature review indicated that challenging behavior sensitive to negative reinforcement (i.e., escape) was most common in public school settings (Lloyd et al., 2016). As such we recommend the consultant be well prepared to develop function-based treatments for challenging behavior sensitive to escape.

A limitation of FCT unique to escape is it may not be practical to deliver any amount of instruction due to severity of challenging behavior, which is necessarily required during FCT. Thus, we recommend the consultant consider demand fading as an appropriate function-based alternative to FCT. Demand fading initially involves the removal of all demands, which are then gradually reintroduced (Pace, Iwata, Cowdery, Andree, & McIntyre, 1993). This should result in the removal of the EO for challenging behavior and an immediate reduction in challenging behavior (Geiger et al., 2010). However, the primary drawback of demand fading is loss of instruction time, which is not practical in certain classroom environments and limits the amount of learning opportunities for the student. An additional consideration for the consultant is that demand fading requires expertise and close oversight, which may not be possible during some consultation processes (Geiger et al., 2010).

In addition to demand fading, we recommend the consultant consider additional antecedent-based strategies that have been shown to be effective in reducing escape-maintained challenging behavior. Antecedent strategies involve modifying some aspect of the instructional context such that it reduces the value of escape as a reinforcer (Smith, 2011). For example, researchers have shown that modifications to materials (e.g., using a computer to write instead of a pencil; Ervin, DuPaul, Kern, & Friman, 1998) or the instructional context (e.g., embedding instruction within preferred activities; Carr & Carlson, 1993) served as an AO for escape-maintained challenging behavior. Additional antecedent-based strategies include providing choice of activities (Dyer, Dunlap, & Winterling, 1990; Kern et al., 1998; Vaughn & Horner, 1997) and revising curricula (Dunlap, Kern-Dunlap, Clarke, & Robbins, 1991).

The consultant should not overlook the importance of appropriate individualized curriculum. Curricula revision involves a comprehensive assessment of a student's curriculum to ensure it is appropriate to her current skill set. Subsequently, necessary changes are made based on the outcomes of the assessment. Examples of curricula revision include modifying curriculum that is too easy or too hard (Dunlap et al., 1991), modifying the length of instructional time (Kern, Childs, Dunlap, Clarke, & Falk, 1994), modifying types of prompts (Munk & Repp, 1994), and increasing the rate of positive reinforcement for compliance (Ingvarsson, Hanley, & Welter, 2009; Lalli et al., 1999). Interestingly, positive reinforcement has been shown to be effective in reducing escape-maintained challenging behavior suggesting that positive reinforcement may serve to decrease the aversive instructional contexts (Ingvarsson et al., 2009; Lalli et al., 1999).

Conduct a treatment analysis before recommending a long-term intervention

We recommend the consultant conduct a treatment analysis. A treatment analysis is an evaluation of the consultant's proposed treatment to evaluate its effectiveness prior to recommending long-term adaption. The treatment analysis can be conducted in brief sessions multiple times a day using within-subject designs (see Mueller & Nkosi, 2009). In addition, the consultant should consider using the data from the relevant test condition in the FA (i.e., the test condition that identified the functional reinforcer) as the baseline level of student responding from which to evaluate the treatment's effectiveness.

Conducting a treatment analysis has practical advantages. The consultant should be able to evaluate the effects of the treatment analysis rather quickly as compared to evaluating the treatment over the course of an entire school day. The treatment analysis can allow the consultant to make relevant modifications quickly, avoid unnecessary training on ineffective treatment components, and ultimately make better treatment recommendations. An additional advantage is that the consultant can use treatment analysis data to obtain buy-in from the school staff and other relevant constituents (Mueller & Nkosi, 2009). Buy-in is particularly important as we think it has direct implications for treatment integrity.

See Table 9.2 for a summary of considerations when creating and implementing a skill- and function-based treatment.

Table 9.2 Considerations when creating and implementing a skill- and function-based treatment

Practice recommendation	Considerations
Use FCT	• Select simple, recognizable, easily acquired, low effort FCR • Increasing complexity of the FCR • Use prompt and prompt-fading procedures • Initiated by a highly trained professional • Teach in a safe environment • Contrive learning opportunities • Arrange a dense schedule of reinforcement • Consider using NCR first then transition to FCT
Consider extinction	• Consider extinction and be prepared to address potential side effects • Consider manipulating parameters of reinforcement when extinction is not viable
Create a practical treatment via reinforcement schedule thinning	• Consider using multiple schedules, chained schedules, response restriction, and delay schedules • Consider training a tolerance response • Consider using alternative reinforcers
Consider antecedent strategies for escape-maintained challenging behavior	• Consider demand fading when it is impractical to initially deliver any amount of instruction • Consider modifying materials, instructional context, and providing choice • Consider curricula revision
Conduct a treatment analysis before recommending a long-term intervention	• Evaluate the proposed treatment prior to recommending long-term use

Recommended practice guideline 4: prevent the development of challenging behavior

Foxx (1996a,b) noted that educational systems typically employ a reactive model to addressing challenging behavior. That is, challenging behavior is targeted for intervention only after its occurrence. This is juxtaposed to a proactive model where the prevention of challenging behavior is the target of intervention. It seems unlikely that all instances of challenging behavior are preventable, but surely some are. To the extent possible, we recommend consultants urge schools to adapt a proactive stance related to challenging behavior and train school staff to implement strategies that may prevent challenging behavior. One recommended curriculum is the Preschool Life Skills program (Hanley, Heal, Tiger, & Ingvarsson, 2007). (Dr. Hanley has made the Preschool Life Skills curriculum manual available for free at www.practicalfunctionalassessment.com. The manual includes data sheets, lesson plans, and teaching stimuli.) Hanley et al. (2007) evaluated the effectiveness of a class wide approach to teach preschool children of typical development to engage in appropriate behaviors [referred to as preschool life skills (PLS)] when presented with situations that might typically lead to (i.e., evoke) challenging behavior. The PLS domains included instruction following (e.g., the student should look at the teacher and say "yes" when name is called), how to solicit attention and items (e.g., the student should say "help me please" when completing a difficult task), tolerating delays (e.g., the student should say "okay" and wait quietly when told to wait following a request), and friendship skills (e.g., the student should say "hello" when a new individual comes into their play area). The experimenters measured the occurrence of these PLS and challenging behaviors under several evocative conditions. Following baseline, the experimenters sequentially taught 13 PLS using behavior skills training (BST) over the course of 15 weeks. Across participants, the intervention lead to a 400% increase in the use of PLS and a 74% decrease in challenging behavior. Similar results were obtained in a systematic replication (Hanley et al., 2014).

Individualize training as needed

One advantage of adapting a proactive model is that class- or school-wide adoption is possible. However, similar to other educational practices, not all students will respond sufficiently when exposed to broad, large-scale interventions (Hanley et al., 2014). In fact, several participants from Hanley et al. (2014) did not acquire all PLS through the class wide teaching approach. As such, we recommend consultants monitor implementation and assist school staff in arranging supplemental modifications. There is precedent for such an approach, as supplemental small group and individual PLS instruction has proven effective (Francisco & Hanley, 2012; Luczynski & Hanley, 2013).

Additionally, special care may be needed to adopt the PLS program for use with individuals with disabilities. Specific recommendations for modification are threefold. First, consultants should consider the use of a performance- rather than time-based criterion for teaching subsequent skills. Hanley et al. (2014) taught each PLS over a 2-day time period. For some students, this teaching period may not be sufficient to establish the desired stimulus control. As such, a specific PLS should be trained until the consumer independently demonstrates the skill a number of times. Second, the topography of each PLS may need to be modified to meet the needs of individual students. Many of the PLS taught by Hanley et al. required the participant to provide a vocal response. This will be impractical for students who have unestablished vocal verbal behavior repertoires, and alternative topographies may be taught (e.g., sign language). Third, consultants may need to arrange individualized teaching components and contrived reinforcement. Hanley et al. employed BST to train all PLS. Some students may require individualized prompt, prompt-fading, and reinforcement strategies to ensure appropriate stimulus control is achieved.

See Table 9.3 for a summary of considerations when implementing challenging behavior prevention programs.

Recommended practice guideline 5: train and supervise staff well

The role of school staff in the consultation process is quite important as these individuals provide valuable information to the consultant during the initial stages of assessment, collect data throughout assessment and intervention, and directly implement the skill- and function-based treatment. Ultimately, the degree to which the treatment produces a robust behavioral change is tied to the degree to which it is implemented as designed (i.e., treatment integrity). We recommend treatments be implemented with high treatment integrity (Vollmer, Sloman, & Peter Pipkin, 2008) throughout the day, to reap the benefits of the procedures (DiGennaro, Martens, & Kleinmann, 2007; Wilder, Atwell, & Wine, 2006). This is easier said than done, as school staff behavior is likely to be influenced by variables outside of those controlled by the consultant. The consultant should be aware of these variables, understand how they may influence treatment integrity, and take steps to minimize their influence.

Table 9.3 **Considerations for preventing the development of challenging behavior**

Practice recommendation	Considerations
Adopt a proactive stance to challenging behavior Individualize training	• Consider class-wide intervention • Consider using Preschool Life Skills • Consider small group or individualized instruction • Make adaptations for individuals with disabilities

Consider variables that may influence integrity

Allen and Warzak (2000) noted that behavior analysts focus a good deal of attention on assessing function and developing function-based interventions for children, but are not as vigilant when it comes to addressing parental adherence to implementing the interventions. They identified four main variables that may affect parent behavior: EOs, skill acquisition, generalization, and consequences. These same variables likely affect school staff behavior, and we recommend the consultant consider them from the onset of the consultative relationship. That is, the consultant should take a proactive, rather than a reactive stance, to increase the likelihood of acceptable school staff integrity from the onset of the consultative relationship.

Consider establishing operations

EOs are variables that momentarily alter the value of a stimulus as a reinforcer and momentarily alter the behavior associated with that particular stimulus (Michael, 1993). School staff behavior is controlled by a number of EOs at any given time. The consultant's job is to identify EOs that might interfere with implementation of behavioral technologies. For example, when implementing a treatment, it is unlikely that the student's challenging behavior will immediately conform to the new contingencies, and if the reinforcer that maintains the challenging behavior is withheld for the first time, there might even be an extinction burst. School staff might see the slow decrease or the increase in challenging behavior as failure of the treatment and might not continue to implement it. To prepare school staff for the likelihood that the treatment will not result in the immediate elimination of challenging behavior, the consultant might need to establish intermediate outcomes as reinforcers (Allen & Warzak, 2000). This could be achieved by providing instructions about expected slow decreases in the challenging behavior and the possibility of an extinction burst. In addition, the consultant can help the school staff identify smaller successes that might be evident along the way such that their behavior of implementing the intervention contacts reinforcement more quickly (e.g., challenging behavior still occurs, but for a shorter duration).

The consultant might also need to extinguish competing social approval as a reinforcer. This may be indicated in situations that involve (1) school staff implementing an intervention in the presence of individuals who might not be familiar with the procedures and clearly state their disapproval of them, (2) other staff might have had a bad experience with a consultant in the past and might state their current disapproval of consultant behavior in general, or (3) poor school staff treatment integrity might be maintained by attention in the form of commiserating about how difficult it is to work with students who have challenging behavior. In this instance, one potentially useful strategy is for the consultant to explain the rationale for the selected treatment, have the school staff practice providing an explanation, and provide feedback on how the school staff could improve their explanation of the treatment.

Use effective staff training approaches

Behavior analysts pride themselves on their use of effective, evidence-based skill acquisition procedures. However, when it comes to skill acquisition of staff, effective procedures might not be used due to a lack of knowledge by consultants regarding evidence-based staff training procedures (Reid, Parsons, Lattimore, Towery, & Reade, 2005). One reason for this might be that consultants have little time or resources to contact staff training research (Carr & Briggs, 2010). Another reason that effective, evidence-based procedures might not be used to train school staff, is that training can be a time consuming endeavor that requires a substantial response effort on part of school staff and the consultant (Phillips, 1998). As such, there is a need to consider not only the effectiveness of staff training procedures, but the efficiency as well (Reid et al., 2005). We recommend consultants use behavioral skills training (BST) and video modeling (VM) as both have strong empirical support (Karsten, Axe, & Mann, 2015).

BST involves instructions, modeling, rehearsal, and performance feedback and has been used to train a number of behavioral technologies, including FA procedures (e.g., Iwata et al., 2000; Lambert, Bloom, Kunnavatana, Collins, & Clay, 2013; Moore et al., 2002; Roscoe & Fisher, 2008; Ward-Horner & Sturmey, 2012). This training approach provides school staff an opportunity to observe and practice the desired behavior, and to receive positive and corrective feedback with respect to their performance (Reid & Fitch, 2011). Performance feedback that includes graphic presentations of treatment integrity and student performance has been shown to be particularly beneficial for maintaining behavior of school staff (Noell, Duhon, Gatti, & Connell, 2002). The efficiency of BST might be enhanced if it is conducted with a group rather than individually because instructions and modeling can be presented to multiple school staff simultaneously. In addition, a group format may enhance the rehearsal and feedback components of BST if staff observe feedback provided to colleagues or take part in evaluating colleague performance. School staff who are present during BST might assist with the generalization of skills because they can assist in programming for common stimuli and mediation of generalization.

VM involves showing a staff trainee a video demonstrating a trained individual implementing a behavioral technology with a simulated or actual student. Following the viewing, scenarios are arranged to evaluate the extent to which the staff trainee can implement the procedure depicted in the video. Some researchers have noted that VM might reduce the need to have a trained consultant present for all aspects of training; thus, it might be more convenient and less costly than the traditional BST approach (Karsten et al., 2015). To increase the saliency of aspects of the video, components such as voiceover instruction and on-screen text should be considered (e.g., Giannakakos, Vladescu, Kisamore, & Reeve, 2016). In addition, all necessary components of desired skills can be shown (Moore & Fisher, 2007), and staff can see how actors respond to student errors (Catania, Almeida, Liu-Constant, & DiGennaro-Reed, 2009). VM can also be used to train a number of staff at one time, and the videos can be shown to new staff at later dates; thus, potentially requiring less training time from the consultant. VM has been used to teach a range of behavioral technologies, including FA procedures and behavior intervention plan components (e.g., DiGennaro-Reed, Codding, Catania, & Maguire, 2010; Lavie & Sturmey, 2002; Moore & Fisher, 2007). Although the goal of VM might be to limit the need for a trained consultant, it appears that performance feedback (DiGennaro-Reed et al., 2010; Giannakakos et al., 2016) or video-based feedback (Nosik & Williams, 2011) is sometimes necessary to achieve the desired outcomes. Video-based feedback might be useful for consultants who cannot be present at all implementations of the intervention and might be useful for providing feedback to a large number of people in an efficient manner (Karsten et al., 2015).

Regardless of the training procedures used, consultants should consider the complexity of their assessments and treatments in light of the resources available to school staff. Such consideration is important, as it is unlikely that school staff will implement assessments and interventions regularly and with integrity if they do not have the necessary time or resources (e.g., additional staff). We recommend consultants consider modifying procedures as needed to increase integrity. For example, it may be possible to increase data collection integrity by decreasing response effort (e.g., create a table where all data can easily be tallied and analyzed).

Plan for generalization

Although consultants may often take a "train and hope" approach to staff training, the same strategies used to program for and assess generalization of student behavior can be applied to staff training. Some of these include training sufficient exemplars, programming common stimuli, and mediating generalization (Stokes & Baer, 1977). To train with sufficient exemplars, consultants should provide opportunities for school staff to experience a wide and varied range of possible student responses (e.g., errors of commission and omission, challenging behavior, correct responses, appropriate behavior). Consultants can program common stimuli by conducting training in the classroom, playground, or with relevant school staff present. To mediate generalization, the consultant might pay close attention to the language she uses to explain procedures and be careful to repackage her language so that it is less technical and more user-friendly. In addition, the consultant might use words and examples that are highly valued by society (e.g., focus on the student's success and achieving the student's best behavior).

Manipulate consequences

Consequent events likely have the largest impact on school staff behavior. This is one reason why providing performance feedback is likely so effective. When thinking of how to program for effective consequent events, consultants need to consider competing contingencies that punish school staff treatment integrity (Allen & Warzak, 2000). For example, school staff might implement a treatment and the student's challenging behavior might worsen. If school staff provide escape following this worsening, the student's worsening challenging behavior is reinforced. Escape is relevant in this situation not only to the student's behavior, but to the behavior of school staff as well. That is, the staff experience an aversive condition (worsening of challenging behavior) and their behavior (removing the treatment) is reinforced when the challenging behavior returns to its previously inappropriate, but tolerable level. Scenarios such as this have been called negative reinforcement traps

(Patterson, 1982, 2002; Stocco & Thompson, 2015). The consultant must intervene on the negative reinforcement contingencies that act on school staff by providing regular and structured feedback and establishing intermediate outcomes as reinforcers (Allen & Warzak, 2000). In addition, the consultant may proactively discuss the implications of negative reinforcement traps with the school staff to increase awareness of their own implementation.

Consultants also need to consider competing contingencies that reinforce behaviors incompatible with treatment integrity such as the presence of other students in the classrooms, limited support from other staff, mandatory school staff behavior (e.g., union mandates regarding work hours), time management difficulties, and complex data collection procedures. The consultant might focus on creating intermediate reinforcing social contingencies that do not involve changes in the student's behavior. For example, the consultant might attempt to establish himself as a conditioned reinforcer or mediator of social consequences by taking the time to build rapport with the school staff. Some strategies that might assist in this include showing interest and concern in the school staff by giving eye contact and making reflective comments during conversations, being supportive by praising past behavior, and taking care to be empathetic and nonjudgmental. The goal is to build and foster a strong relationship between the consultant and school staff.

Some barriers that might impede relationship building include poor interpersonal skills on the part of school staff or difficulty accepting/applying feedback (Putnam et al., 2005; Sellers, LeBlanc, & Valentino, 2016). In addition, behavior analysts are often seen as arrogant and abrasive (Foxx, 1996a,b) because we use technical language that is not easily understood or digested by the general public (Foxx, 1990). It is also possible that school staff have a poor history with other consultants. The consultant's job is not to erase this history, but to gain insight and get valuable information about this history so that she might give the school staff new experiences with a consultant that are positive (Sellers et al, 2016). To do this, consultants must be "behavioral ambassadors and translators" (Foxx, 1996a, p. 154) who are considerate of their audiences and modify their language to ensure that their behavior has the desired effect on the school staff. Consultants should also engage in good consultant behavior that includes providing clear expectations; providing positive feedback to increase acceptance of feedback (Reid & Parsons, 2006; Reid, Parsons, & Green, 2012); giving corrective feedback for lower stakes behaviors initially; avoiding punishment, coercion, or harsh feedback; and being understanding of limitations related to the school staff knowledge and skill repertoires.

See Table 9.4 for a summary of considerations when training school staff.

Recommended practice guideline 6: assess social validity

It is the responsibility of the consultant to ensure that school staff are satisfied and approve of the services provided. The importance of this cannot be understated, as satisfied school staff will be more likely to employ the consultant's services in the future. Therefore, we recommend consultants validate the social significance of goals, procedures, and outcomes (Wolf, 1978).

Table 9.4 **Considerations for training and supervising staff**

Practice recommendation	Considerations
Consider establishing operations	• Identify EOs that may interfere with implementation of treatment • Consider establishing smaller treatment successes as reinforcers • Consider extinguishing competing social approval as a reinforce
Use effective staff training approaches	• Consider using behavioral skills training • Consider using video modeling • Consider the complexity of the assessment and treatment process in light of available resources • Consider modifying procedures as needed to increase social validity
Plan for generalization	• Use strategies outlined by Stokes and Baer (1977) to program for generalization
Manipulate consequences	• Provide regular and structured feedback • Consider competing contingencies that reinforce behaviors incompatible with treatment integrity • Consider establishing oneself as a conditioned reinforcer • Develop strong interpersonal skills and create positive experiences for the staff • Avoid punishment, coercion, and harsh feedback

Target socially significant challenging behavior

Often when a consultant provides services, there are numerous challenging behaviors that need to be addressed. In these cases, we recommend the consultant work with school staff to prioritize the challenging behavior to treat first. This should occur during the early components of the assessment phase, when initially gathering information about the challenging behavior. For example, a student may engage in both task refusal and aggression directed towards school staff. In these cases, we recommend the consultant treat the aggressive behavior as a priority as these occurrences may pose an immediate threat to the staff and other students in the classroom. Cooper, Heron, and Heward (2007) offer a worksheet for evaluating the social significance of potential target behaviors (p. 57). The authors suggest, for example, the consultant consider whether the changing the behavior is likely to produce reinforcement in the student's natural environment after the treatment ends or whether the behavior is a necessary prerequisite for a more complex skill.

Evaluate practical significance of behavior change

As behavior analysts, we are concerned with practical changes in behavior, specifically whether the change in behavior is useful in the student's environment or in the real world and whether the change is of social importance (Kirk, 1996). The consultant may want to ask, "Does the quantity or quality of behavior change make a difference in the student's overall functioning in life?" For example, reducing a student's tantrum behavior from 90% of the school day to 30% of the school day may result in an observable change in behavior rate; however, this behavior decrease may not be considered practical. In this example, the continued high rates of challenging behavior make it likely that the student will miss important academic and social learning opportunities.

Evaluate acceptability of assessment and treatment procedures

We recommend consultants evaluate the extent to which school staff find the assessment and treatment procedures selected for use and implemented acceptable. Consultants should consider using a published acceptability scale for this purpose, and modifying the scale as needed. One such scale is the Intervention Rating Profile-15 (IRP-15; Martens, Witt, Elliott, & Darveaux, 1985). The IRP-15 involves having a rater (i.e., any school staff who implemented procedures at the consultant's direction) score 15 items using a Likert-type scale. The IRP-15 produces a score that ranges from 15 to 90, and those above 52.50 are considered to reflect acceptability (Von Brock & Elliott, 1987). The consultant should use the acceptability information obtained to inform changes to the assessment and treatment recommendations that may increase their acceptability without impacting effectiveness. In addition, consultants should use acceptability information to modify future consultation services provided.

Consider student preferences

In addition to measuring the acceptability of goals, outcomes, and procedures by those in the target student's community, consultants have a responsibility to take into account the student's own preference for a given treatment (Hanley, 2010b). We recommend that consultants measure whether the student receiving treatment actually prefers the intervention. In some cases, if several interventions have been successful in decreasing challenging behavior, it may be appropriate to have the student select which of the interventions they prefer most. This can be done using questionnaires, interviews, or more objective ways, such as a concurrent chain procedure as described in the behavior analytic literature (Hanley, 2010b).

Evaluate acceptability of the consultation process

We recommend consultants evaluate the school staff's acceptability of the broader consultation process. This type of evaluation should provide information above and beyond that provided when assessing the school staff's acceptability of the assessment and treatment. One published acceptability scale that could be used for this purpose is Sheridan's (1992) modified Behavior Interventions Rating Scale-Revised (BIRS-R; Von Brock & Elliott, 1987). The BIRS-R involves having a rater score 26 items using a 6-point Likert-type scale. The consultant should use information obtained about consultation acceptability to inform their future consultation efforts.

Table 9.5 Considerations when assessing social validity

Practice recommendation	Considerations
Target socially significant challenging behavior	• Work with school staff to prioritize challenging behavior • Conduct a social significance analysis to determine what challenging behavior to target first
Evaluate practical significance of behavior change	• Evaluate whether the reductions in challenging behavior are socially meaningful
Evaluate acceptability of assessment and treatment procedures	• Administer socially acceptability rating scales • Use outcomes of rating scales to inform potential modifications to assessment and treatment process without impacting effectiveness
Consider student preferences	• Consider students' preferences for treatment options • Consider measuring student preference
Evaluate acceptability of the consultation process	• Evaluate the staff's acceptability of the broader consultation process • Use outcome measures to inform future consultation efforts

For example, if the rater indicates they were not pleased with the consultation and gives a low likelihood of referring the consultant to other school staff, the consultant should consider developing better rapport with consultees and take the steps to establish to establish themselves as a reinforcer in the future.

See Table 9.5 for a summary of considerations when evaluating social validity. Practice Guidelines Checklist:

1. Be analytical (Baer et al., 1987) by adopting assessment and treatment practices that demonstrate a functional relationship between the challenging behavior and manipulated environmental variables.
2. When training staff consider EOs, evidence-based training approaches, generalization, and consequences.
3. Evaluate the school staffs' satisfaction with and acceptability of services and recommendations.
4. Help schools adopt a proactive stance by training school staff to implement strategies that may prevent challenging behavior.

References

Agostin, T. M., & Bain, S. K. (1997). Predicting early school success with developmental and social screeners. *Psychology in the Schools, 34*, 219–228.

Allen, K. D., & Warzak, W. J. (2000). The problem of parental nonadherence in clinical behavior analysis: Effective treatment is not enough. *Journal of Applied Behavior Analysis, 33*, 373–391.

Athens, E. S., & Vollmer, T. R. (2010). An investigation of differential reinforcement of alternative behavior. *Journal of Applied Behavior Analysis, 43*, 569−589. Available from http://dx.doi.org/10.1901/jaba.2010.43-569.

Baer, D. M., Wolf, M. M., & Risley, T. R. (1987). Some still-current dimensions of applied behavior analysis. *Journal of Applied Behavior Analysis, 20*, 313−327. Available from http://dx.doi.org/10.1901/jaba.1987.20-313.

Borlase, M.A., Vladescu, J.C., Kisamore, A.N., Reeve, S.A., & Fetzer, J.L. (2017). Analysis of precursors to multiply controlled problem behavior: A replication. *Journal of Applied Behavior Analysis*, doi: 10.1002/jaba.398.

Carr, E. G., & Carlson, J. I. (1993). Reduction of severe behavior problems in the community using a multicomponent treatment approach. *Journal of Applied Behavior Analysis, 26*, 157−172. Available from http://dx.doi.org/10.1901/jaba.1993.26-157.

Carr, J. E., & Briggs, A. M. (2010). Strategies for making regular contact with the scholarly literature. *Behavior Analysis in Practice, 3*, 13−18.

Carr, J. E., Severtson, J. M., & Lepper, T. L. (2009). Noncontingent reinforcement is an empirically supported treatment for problem behavior exhibited by individuals with developmental disabilities. *Research in Developmental Disabilities, 30*, 44−57.

Catania, C. N., Almeida, D., Liu-Constant, B., & DiGennaro-Reed, F. D. (2009). Video modeling to train staff to implement discrete-trial instruction. *Journal of Applied Behavior Analysis, 42*, 387−392. Available from http://dx.doi.org/10.1901/jaba.2009.42-387.

Cooper, J. O., Heron, T. E., & Heward, W. L. (2007). *Applied behavior analysis* (2nd ed.). Upper Saddle River, NJ: Pearson Prentice Hall.

DiGennaro, F. D., Martens, B. K., & Kleinmann, A. E. (2007). A comparison of performance feedback procedures on teachers' treatment implementation of integrity and students' inappropriate behavior in special education classrooms. *Journal of Applied Behavior Analysis, 40*, 447−461.

DiGennaro Reed, F. D., Codding, R., Catania, C. N., & Maguire, H. (2010). Effects of video modeling on treatment integrity of behavioral interventions. *Journal of Applied Behavior Analysis, 43*, 291−295. Available from http://dx.doi.org/10.1901/jaba.2010.43-291.

DiGennaro Reed, F. D., & Jenkins, S. R. (2013). Consultation in public school settings. In D. D. Reed, F. D. DiGennaro Reed, & J. K. Luiselli (Eds.), *Handbook of crisis intervention and developmental disabilities* (pp. 317−329). New York: Springer.

Duker, P. C., & Sigafoos, J. (1998). The motivation assessment scale: Reliability and construct validity across three topographies of behavior. *Research in Developmental Disabilities, 19*, 131−141.

Dunlap, G., Kern-Dunlap, L., Clarke, S., & Robbins, F. R. (1991). Functional assessment, curricular revision, and severe behavior problems. *Journal of Applied Behavior Analysis, 24*, 387−397. Available from http://dx.doi.org/10.1901/jaba.1991.24-387.

Dyer, K., Dunlap, G., & Winterling, V. (1990). Effects of choice making on the serious problem behaviors of students with severe handicaps. *Journal of Applied Behavior Analysis, 23*, 515−524. Available from http://dx.doi.org/10.1901/jaba.1990.23-515.

Ellingson, S. A., Miltenberger, R. G., & Long, E. S. (1999). A survey of the use of functional assessment procedures in agencies serving individuals with developmental disabilities. *Behavioral Interventions, 14*, 187−198.

Erchul, W. P., & Marten, B. K. (2010). *School consultation: Conceptual and empirical bases of practice* (3rd ed.). New York, NY: Springer. Available from http://dx.doi.org/10.1007/978-1-4419-5747-4.

Ervin, R. A., DuPaul, G. J., Kern, L., & Friman, P. C. (1998). Classroom-based functional and adjunctive assessments: Proactive approaches to intervention selection for adolescents with attention deficit hyperactivity disorder. *Journal of Applied Behavior Analysis, 31*, 65−78. Available from http://dx.doi.org/10.1901/jaba.1998.31-65.

Fischer, S. M., Iwata, B. A., & Mazaleski, J. L. (1997). Noncontingent delivery of arbitrary reinforcers as treatment for self-injurious behavior. *Journal of Applied Behavior Analysis, 30*, 239−249.

Fisher, W. W., & Bouxsein (2011). Developing function-based reinforcement procedures for problem behavior. In W. W. Fisher, C. C. Piazza, & H. S. Roane (Eds.), *Handbook of applied behavior analysis* (pp. 335−347). New York, NY: Guilford Press.

Fisher, W. W., Greer, B. D., Romani, P. W., Zangrillo, A. N., & Owen, T. M. (2016). Comparisons of synthesized and individual reinforcement contingencies during functional analysis. *Journal of Applied Behavior Analysis, 49*, 596−616. Available from http://dx.doi.org/10.1002/jaba.314.

Fisher, W. W., Rodriguez, N. M., Luczynski, K. C., & Kelley, M. E. (2013). Protective equipment. In D. D. Reed, F. D. DiGennaro Reed, & J. K. Luiselli (Eds.), *Handbook of crisis intervention and developmental disabilities* (pp. 87−105). New York: Springer.

Fisher, W. W., Thompson, R. H., Hagopian, L. P., Bowman, L. G., & Krug, A. (2000). Facilitating tolerance of delayed reinforcement during functional communication training. *Behavior Modification, 24*, 3−29.

Foxx, R. M. (1990). Suggested common North American translations of expressions in the field of operant conditioning. *The Behavior Analyst, 13*, 95−96.

Foxx, R. M. (1996a). Translating the covenant: The behavior analyst as ambassador and translator. *The Behavior Analyst, 19*, 147−161.

Foxx, R. M. (1996b). Twenty years of applied behavior analysis in treating the most severe problem behavior: Lessons learned. *The Behavior Analyst, 19*, 225−235.

Francisco, M. T., & Hanley, G. P. (2012). An evaluation of progressively increasing intertrial intervals on the acquisition and generalization of three social skills. *Journal of Applied Behavior Analysis, 45*, 137−142. Available from http://dx.doi.org/10.1901/jaba.2012.45-137.

Fritz, J. N., Iwata, B. A., Hammond, J. L., & Bloom, S. E. (2013). Experimental analysis of precursors to severe problem behavior. *Journal of Applied Behavior Analysis, 46*, 101−129. Available from http://dx.doi.org/10.1002/jaba.27.

Geiger, K. B., Carr, J. E., & LeBlanc, L. A. (2010). Function-based treatments for escape-maintained problem behavior: A treatment-selection model for practicing behavior analysts. *Behavior Analysis in Practice, 3*, 22−23.

Ghaemmaghami, M., Hanley, G. P., & Jessel, J. (2016). Contingencies promote delay tolerance. *Journal of Applied Behavior Analysis, 49*, 548−575. Available from http://dx.doi.org/10.1002/jaba.333.

Giannakakos, A., Vladescu, J. C., Kisamore, A. N., & Reeve, S. (2016). Using video modeling with voiceover instruction plus feedback to train staff to implement direct teaching procedures. *Behavior Analysis in Practice, 9*, 126−134, doi: 10.1007/s40617-015-0097-5.

Goh, H. L., Iwata, B. A., & DeLeon, I. G. (2000). Competition between noncontingent and contingent reinforcement schedules during response acquisition. *Journal of Applied Behavior Analysis, 33*, 195−205.

Greer, B. D., Fisher, W. W., Saini, V., Owen, T. M., & Jones, J. K. (2016). Functional communication training during reinforcement schedule thinning: An analysis of 25 applications. *Journal of Applied Behavior Analysis, 49*, 1−17. Available from http://dx.doi.org/10.1002/jaba.265.

Hagopian, L. P., Boelter, E. W., & Jarmolowicz, D. P. (2011). Reinforcement schedule thinning following functional communication training: Review and recommendations. *Behavior Analysis in Practice, 4*, 4−16.

Hagopian, L. P., Contrucci-Kuhn, S. A., Long, E. S., & Rush, K. S. (2005). Schedule thinning following communication training: Using competing stimuli to enhance tolerance to decrements in reinforcer density. *Journal of Applied Behavior Analysis, 31,* 211−235.

Hagopian, L. P., Fisher, W. W., Sullivan, M. T., Acquisto, J., & LeBlanc, L. A. (1998). Effectiveness of functional communication training with and without extinction and punishment: A summary of 21 inpatient cases. *Journal of Applied Behavior Analysis, 31,* 211−235.

Hall, S. S. (2005). Comparing descriptive, experimental and informant-based assessment of problem behaviors. *Research in Developmental Disabilities, 26,* 514−526.

Hanley, G. P. (2010a). Prevention and treatment of severe problem behavior. In E. Mayville, & J. Mulick (Eds.), *Behavioral foundations of effective autism treatment* (pp. 233−256). New York, NY: Sloan.

Hanley, G. (2010b). Toward effective and preferred programming: A case for the objective measurement of social validity with recipients of behavior-change programs. *Behavior Analysis and Practice, 3,* 13−21.

Hanley, G. P. (2011). Functional analysis. In J. Luiselli (Ed.), *Teaching and behavior support for children and adults with autism spectrum disorder: A "how to" practitioner's guide* (pp. 22−29). New York, NY: Oxford University Press.

Hanley, G. P. (2012). Functional assessment of problem behavior: Dispelling myths, overcoming implementation obstacles, and developing new lore. *Behavior Analysis in Practice, 5,* 54−72.

Hanley, G. P., Fahmie, T. A., & Heal, N. A. (2014). Evaluation of the preschool life skills program in head start classrooms: A systematic replication. *Journal of Applied Behavior Analysis, 47,* 443−448. Available from http://dx.doi.org/10.1002/jaba.132.

Hanley, G. P., Heal, N. A., Tiger, J. H., & Ingvarsson, E. T. (2007). Evaluation of a classwide teaching program for developing preschool life skills. *Journal of Applied Behavior Analysis, 40,* 277−300. Available from http://dx.doi.org/10.1901/jaba.2007.57-06.

Hanley, G. P., Iwata, B. A., & McCord, B. E. (2003). Functional analysis of problem behavior: A review. *Journal of Applied Behavior Analysis, 36,* 147−185.

Hanley, G. P., Jin, C. S., Vanselow, N. R., & Hanratty, L. A. (2014). Producing meaningful improvements in problem behavior of children with autism via synthesized analyses and treatments. *Journal of Applied Behavior Analysis, 47,* 16−36. Available from http://dx.doi.org/10.1002/jaba.106.

Hanley, G. P., Piazza, C. C., Fisher, W. W., Contrucci, S. A., & Maglieri, K. A. (1997). Evaluation of client preference for function-based treatment packages. *Journal of Applied Behavior Analysis, 30,* 459−473.

Harrison, J. R., Vannest, K., Davis, J., & Reynolds, C. (2012). Common problem behaviors of children and adolescents in general education classrooms in the United States. *Journal of Emotional and Behavioral Disorders, 20,* 55−64. Available from http://dx.doi.org/10.1177/1063426611421157.

Herrnstein, R. J. (1961). Relative and absolute strength of response as a function of frequency of reinforcement. *Journal of Experimental Analysis of Behavior, 4,* 267−272. Available from http://dx.doi.org/10.1901/jeab.1961.4-267.

Herscovitch, B., Roscie, E. M., Libby, M. E., Bourret, J. C., & Ahearn, W. H. (2009). A procedure for identifying precursors to problem behavior. *Journal of Applied Behavior Analysis, 42,* 697−702. Available from http://dx.doi.org/10.1901/jaba.2009.42-697.

Ingvarsson, E. T., Hanley, G. P., & Welter, K. M. (2009). Treatment of escape-maintained behavior with positive reinforcement: The role of reinforcement contingency and density. *Education and Treatment of Children, 32,* 371−401.

Iwata, B. A., Dorsey, M. F., Slifer, K. J., Bauman, K. E., & Richman, G. S. (1994). Toward a functional analysis of self-injury. *Journal of Applied Behavior Analysis, 27*, 197—209, (Reprinted from *Analysis and Intervention in Developmental Disabilities, 2*, 3-20, 1982)

Iwata, B. A., & Dozier, C. L. (2008). Clinical application of functional analysis methodology. *Behavior Analysis in Practice, 1*, 3—9.

Iwata, B. A., Pace, G. M., Cowdrey, G. E., & Miltenberger, R. G. (1994). What makes extinction work: An analysis of procedural form and function. *Journal of Applied Behavior Analysis, 27*, 131—144.

Iwata, B. A., Wallace, M. D., Kahng, S., Lindberg, J. S., Roscoe, E. M., Conners, J., . . . Worsdell, A. S. (2000). Skill acquisition in the implementation of functional analysis methodology. *Journal of Applied Behavior Analysis, 33*, 181—194. Available from http://dx.doi.org/10.1901/jaba.2000.33-181.

Jessel, J., Hanley, G. P., & Ghaemmaghami, M. (2016). Interview-informed synthesized contingency analyses: Thirty replications and reanalysis. *Journal of Applied Behavior Analysis, 49*, 576—595. Available from http://dx.doi.org/10.1002/jaba.316.

Jones, K. M., Drew, H. A., & Weber, N. L. (2000). Noncontingent peer attention as treatment for disruptive classroom behavior. *Journal of Applied Behavior Analysis, 33*, 343—346.

Karsten, A. M., Axe, J. B., & Mann, C. C. (2015). Review and discussion of strategies to address low trainer-to-staff ratios. *Behavioral Interventions, 30*, 295—313.

Kern, L., Childs, K. E., Dunlap, G., Clarke, S., & Falk, G. D. (1994). Using assessment-based curricular intervention to improve the classroom behavior of a student with emotional and behavioral challenges. *Journal of Applied Behavior Analysis, 27*, 7—19. Available from http://dx.doi.org/10.1901/jaba.1994.27-7.

Kern, L., Vorndran, C. M., Hilt, A., Ringdahl, J. E., Adelman, B. E., & Dunlap, G. (1998). Choice as an intervention to improve behavior: A review of the literature. *Journal of Behavioral Education, 8*, 151—169. Available from http://dx.doi.org/10.1023/A:1022831507077.

Kirk, R. E. (1996). Practical significance: A concept whose time has come. *Educational and Psychological Measurement, 56*, 746—759.

Kodak, T., Fisher, W. W., Paden, A., & Dickes, N. (2013). Evaluation of the utility of a discrete-trial functional analysis in early intervention classrooms. *Journal of Applied Behavior Analysis, 46*, 301—306.

Kurtz, P. F., Chin, M. D., Huete, J. M., Tarbox, R. S., O'Connor, J. T., Paclawskyj, T. R., & Rush, K. S. (2003). Functional analysis and treatment of self-injurious behavior in young children: A summary of 30 cases. *Journal of Applied Behavior Analysis, 36*, 205—219.

Lalli, J. S., Vollmer, T. R., Progar, P. R., Wright, C., Borrero, J., Daniel, D., et al. (1999). Competition between positive and negative reinforcement in the treatment of escape behavior. *Journal of Applied Behavior Analysis, 32*, 285—296. Available from http://dx.doi.org/10.1901/jaba.1999.32-285.

Lambert, J. M., Bloom, S. E., Kunnavatana, S. S., Collins, S. D., & Clay, C. J. (2013). Training residential staff to conduct trial-based functional analyses. *Journal of Applied Behavior Analysis, 46*, 296—300.

Lavie, T., & Sturmey, P. (2002). Training staff to conduct a paired-stimulus preference assessment. *Journal of Applied Behavior Analysis, 35*, 209—211. Available from http://dx.doi.org/10.1901/jaba.2002.35-209.

Ledingham, J. E., & Schwartzman, A. E. (1984). A 3-year follow-up of aggressive and withdrawn behavior in childhood: Preliminary findings. *Journal of Abnormal Child Psychology, 12*, 157—168.

Lerman, D. C., & Iwata, B. A. (1993). Descriptive and experimental analyses of variables maintaining self-injurious behavior. *Journal of Applied Behavior Analysis, 26,* 293−319.

Lerman, D. C., & Iwata, B. A. (1995). Prevence of the extinction burst and its attenuation during treatment. *Journal of Applied Behavior Analysis, 28,* 93−94.

Lerman, D. C., & Iwata, B. A. (1996). Developing a technology for the use of operant extinction in clinical settings: An examination of basic and applied research. *Journal of Applied Behavior Analysis, 29,* 345−382.

Lloyd, B. P., Weaver, E. S., & Staubitz, J. L. (2016). A review of functional analysis methods conducted in public school classroom settings. *Journal of Behavioral Education, 25,* 324−356. Available from http://dx.doi.org/10.1007/s10864-015-9243-y.

Luczynski, K. C., & Hanley, G. P. (2013). Prevention of problem behavior by teaching functional communication and self-control skills to preschoolers. *Journal of Applied Behavior Analysis, 46,* 355−368. Available from http://dx.doi.org/10.1002/jaba.44.

MacLeod, I. R., Jones, K. M., Somers, C. L., & Havey, J. M. (2001). An evaluation of the effectiveness of school-based behavioral consultation. *Journal of Educational and Psychological Consultation, 12,* 203−216. Available from http://dx.doi.org/10.1207/S1532768XJEPC1203_02.

Malott, R., & Sloane, J. T. (2014). *Principles of behavior (7th ed.).* Upper Saddle River, NJ: Pearson.

Martens, B. K., Witt, J. C., Elliott, S. N., & Darveaux, D. (1985). Teacher judgments concerning the acceptability of school-based interventions. *Professional Psychology: Research and Practice, 16,* 191−198. Available from http://dx.doi.org/10.1037/0735-7028.16.2.191.

McConnachie, G., & Carr, E. G. (1997). The effects of child behavior problems on the maintenance of intervention fidelity. *Behavior Modification, 21,* 123−158.

Michael, J. (1993). Establishing operations. *The Behavior Analyst, 16,* 191−206.

Moore, J. W., Edwards, R. P., Sterling-Turner, H. E., Riley, J., DuBard, M., & McGeorge, A. (2002). Teacher acquisition of functional analysis methodology. *Journal of Applied Behavior Analysis, 35,* 73−77. Available from http://dx.doi.org/10.1901/jaba.2002.35-73.

Moore, J. M., & Fisher, W. W. (2007). The effects of videotape modeling on staff acquisition of functional analysis methodology. *Journal of Applied Behavior Analysis, 40,* 197−202. Available from http://dx.doi.org/10.1901/, jaba.2007.24-06

Mueller, M. M., & Nkosi, A. (2009). *Behavior analytic consultation to schools.* Marietta, Georgia: Stimulus Publications.

Munk, D. D., & Repp, A. C. (1994). The relationship between instructional variables and problem behavior: A review. *Exceptional Children, 60,* 390−402.

Neidert, P. L., Iwata, B. A., Dempsey, C. M., & Thomason-Sassi, J. L. (2013). Latency of response during the functional analysis of elopement. *Journal of Applied Behavior Analysis, 46,* 312−316.

Noell, G. H., Duhon, G. J., Gatti, S. L., & Connell, J. E. (2002). Consultation, follow-up, and behavior management intervention implementation in general education. *School Psychology Review, 31,* 217−234.

Nosik, M. R., & Williams, W. L. (2011). Component evaluation of a computer based format for teaching discrete trial and backward chaining. *Research in Developmental Disabilities, 32,* 1694−1702. Available from http://dx.doi.org/10.1016/j.ridd.2011.02.022.

Oliver, A. C., Pratt, L. A., & Normand, M. P. (2015). A survey of functional behavior assessment methods used by behavior analysts in practice. *Journal of Applied Behavior Analysis, 48,* 817−829. Available from http://dx.doi.org/10.1002/jaba.256.

Pace, G. M., Iwata, B. A., Cowdery, G. E., Andree, P. J., & McIntyre, T. (1993). Stimulus (instructional) fading during extinction of self-injurious escape behavior. *Journal of Applied Behavior Analysis, 26*, 205–212. Available from http://dx.doi.org/10.1901/jaba.1993.26-205.

Paclawskyj, T., Matson, J., Rush, K., Smalls, Y., & Vollmer, T. R. (2001). Assessment of the convergent validity of the Questions About Behavioral Function scale with analogue functional analysis and the Motivation Assessment Scale. *Journal of Intellectual Disability Research, 45*, 484–494.

Patterson, G. R. (1982). *Coercive family process*. Eugene, OR: Castalia Press.

Patterson, G. R. (2002). Etiology and treatment of child and adolescent antisocial behavior. *The Behavior Analyst Today, 3*, 133–144.

Pence, S. T., Roscoe, E. M., Bourret, J. C., & Ahearn, W. H. (2009). Relative contributions of three descriptive methods: Implications for behavioral assessment. *Journal of Applied Behavior Analysis, 42*, 424–446.

Phillips, J. F. (1998). Applications and contributions of organizational behavior management in schools and day treatment settings. *Journal of Organizational Behavior Management, 18*, 103–129.

Putnam, R. F., Handler, M. W., Rey, J., & McCarty, J. (2005). The development of behaviorally based public school consultation services. *Behavior Modification, 29*, 521–538. Available from http://dx.doi.org/10.1177/0145445504273286.

Reid, D. H., & Fitch, W. H. (2011). *Training staff and parents: Evidence-based approaches. International Handbook of Autism and Pervasive Developmental Disorders* (pp. 509–519). New York: Springer.

Reid, D. H., & Parsons, M. B. (2006). *Motivating human service staff: Supervisory strategies for maximizing work effort and work enjoyment*. Morganton: Habilitative Management Consultants, Inc.

Reid, D. H., Parsons, M. B., & Green, C. G. (2012). *The supervisor's guidebook: Evidence based strategies for promoting work quality and enjoyment among human service staff*. Morganton: Habilitative Management Consultants, Inc.

Reid, D. H., Parsons, M. B., Lattimore, L. P., Towery, D. L., & Reade, K. K. (2005). Improving staff performance through clinician application of outcome management. *Research in Developmental Disabilities, 26*, 101–116.

Rooker, G. W., DeLeon, I. G., Borrero, C. S., Frank-Crawford, M. A., & Roscoe, E. M. (2015). Reducing ambiguity in the functional assessment of problem behavior. *Behavioral Interventions, 30*, 1–35.

Rooker, G. W., Jessel, J., Kurtz, P. F., & Hagopian, L. P. (2013). Functional communication training with and without alternative reinforcement and punishment: An analysis of 58 applications. *Journal of Applied Behavior Analysis, 46*, 708–722.

Roscoe, E. M., & Fisher, W. W. (2008). Evaluation of an efficient method for training staff to implement stimulus preference assessments. *Journal of Applied Behavior Analysis, 41*, 249–254. Available from http://dx.doi.org/10.1901/, jaba.2008.41-249

Roscoe, E. M., Phillips, K. M., Kelly, M. A., Farber, R., & Dube, W. V. (2015). A statewide survey assessing practitioners use and perceived utility of functional assessment. *Journal of Applied Behavior Analysis, 48*, 830–844.

Santiago, J. L., Hanley, G. P., Moore, K., & Jin, C. S. (2016). The generality of interview-informed functional analyses: Systematic replications in school and home. *Journal of Autism and Development Disorders, 46*, 797–811. Available from http://dx.doi.org/10.1007/s10803-015-2617-0.

Sellers, T. P., LeBlanc, L. A., & Valentino, A. L. (2016). Recommendations for detecting and addressing barriers to successful supervision. *Behavior Analysis in Practice, 9*, 271–273.

Sheridan, S. (1992). Consultant and client outcomes of competency-based behavioral consultation training. *School Psychology Quarterly, 7,* 245–270.

Shirley, M. J., Iwata, B. A., Kahng, S., Mazaleski, J. L., & Lerman, D. C. (1997). Does functional communication training compete with ongoing contingencies of reinforcement? An analysis during response acquisition and maintenance. *Journal of Applied Behavior Analysis, 30,* 93–104.

Shogren, K. A., & Rojahn, J. (2003). Convergent reliability and validity of the Questions About Behavioral Function and the Motivation Assessment Scale: A replication study. *Journal of Developmental and Physical Disabilities, 15,* 367–375.

Sigafoos, J., Kerr, M., & Roberts, D. (1994). Interrater reliability of the Motivation Assessment Scale: Failure to replicate with aggressive behavior. *Research in Developmental Disabilities, 15,* 333–342.

Sigafoos, J., & Saggers, B. (1995). A discrete-trial approach to the functional analysis of aggressive behaviour in two boys with autism. *Journal of Intellectual and Developmental Disability, 20,* 287–297.

Smith, R. G. (2011). Developing antecedent interventions for problem behavior. In W. W. Fisher, C. C. Piazza, & H. S. Roane (Eds.), *Handbook of applied behavior analysis* (pp. 297–316). New York, NY: Guilford Press.

Smith, R. G., & Churchill, R. M. (2002). Identification of environmental determinants of behavior disorders through functional analysis of precursor behaviors. *Journal of Applied Behavior Analysis, 35,* 125–136.

Stocco, C. S., & Thompson, R. H. (2015). Contingency analysis of caregiver behavior: Implications for parent training and future directions. *Journal of Applied Behavior Analysis, 48,* 1–19.

Stokes, T. ,F., & Baer, D. M. (1977). An implicit technology of generalization. *Journal of Applied Behavior Analysis, 10,* 349–367. Available from http://dx.doi.org/10.1901/jaba.1977.10-349.

Tiger, J. H., Hanley, G. P., & Bruzek, J. (2008). Functional communication training: A review and practical guide. *Behavior Analysis in Practice, 1,* 16–23.

Thompson, R. H., & Iwata, B. A. (2007). A comparison of outcomes from descriptive and functional analyses of problem behavior. *Journal of Applied Behavior Analysis, 40,* 333–338.

Thomason-Sassi, J. L., Iwata, B. A., Neidert, P. L., & Roscoe, E. M. (2011). Response latency as an index of response strength during functional analyses of problem behavior. *Journal of Applied Behavior Analysis, 44,* 51–67.

Vaughn, B. J., & Horner, R. H. (1997). Identifying instructional tasks that occasion problem behaviors and assessing the effects of student verse teacher choice among these tasks. *Journal of Applied Behavior Analysis, 30,* 299–312. Available from http://dx.doi.org/10.1901/jaba.1997.30-299.

Vollmer, T. R., & Athens, E. (2011). Developing function-based extinction procedures for problem behavior. In W. W. Fisher, C. C. Piazza, & H. S. Roane (Eds.), *Handbook of applied behavior analysis* (pp. 317–334). New York, NY: Guilford Press.

Vollmer, T. R., Iwata, B. A., Zarcone, J. R., Smith, R. G., & Mazaleski, J. L. (1993). The role of attention in the treatment of attention-maintained self-injurious behavior: Noncontingent reinforcement and differential reinforcement of other behavior. *Journal of Applied Behavior Analysis, 26,* 9–21.

Vollmer, T. R., Marcus, B. A., Ringdahl, J. E., & Roane, H. S. (1995). Progressing from brief assessments to extended experimental analyses in the evaluation of aberrant behavior. *Journal of Applied Behavior Analysis, 28,* 561–576. Available from http://dx.doi.org/10.1901/jaba.1995.28-561.

Vollmer, T. R., Ringdahl, J. E., Roane, H. S., & Marcus, B. A. (1997). Negative side effects of noncontingent reinforcement. *Journal of Applied Behavior, 30*, 161−164.

Vollmer, T. R., Sloman, K. N., & St. Peter Pipkin, C. (2008). Practical implications of data reliability and treatment integrity monitoring. *Behavior Analysis in Practice, 1*, 4−11.

Von Brock, M. B., & Elliott, S. N. (1987). Influence of treatment effectiveness information on the acceptability of classroom interventions. *Journal of School Psychology, 25*, 131−144.

Ward-Horner, J., & Sturmey, P. (2012). Component analysis of behavior skills training in functional analysis. *Behavioral Interventions, 27*, 75−92.

Wilder, D. A., Atwell, J., & Wine, B. (2006). The effects of varying levels of treatment integrity on child compliance during treatment with a three-step prompting procedure. *Journal of Applied Behavior Analysis, 39*, 369−373.

Wolf, M. M. (1978). Social validity: The case for subjective measurement or how applied behavior analysis is finding its heart. *Journal of Applied Behavior Analysis, 11*, 203−214. Available from http://dx.doi.org/10.1901/jaba.1978.11-203.

Worsdell, A. S., Iwata, B. A., Hanley, G. P., Thompson, R. H., & Kahng, S. (2000). Effects of continuous and intermittent reinforcement for problem behavior during functional communication training. *Journal of Applied Behavior Analysis, 33*, 167−179.

Zarcone, J. R., Iwata, B. A., Smith, R. G., Mazaleski, J. L., & Lerman, D. C. (1994). Reemergence and extinction of self-injurious escape behavior during stimulus (instructional) fading. *Journal of Applied Behavior Analysis, 27*, 307−316.

Zarcone, J. R., Rodgers, T. A., Iwata, B. A., Rourke, D. A., & Dorsey, M. F. (1991). Reliability analysis of the Motivation Assessment Scale: A failure to replicate. *Research in Developmental Disabilities, 12*, 349−360.

Further reading

Ducharme, J. M., & Feldman, M. A. (1992). Comparison of staff training strategies to promote generalized teaching skills. *Journal of Applied Behavior Analysis, 25*, 165−179. Available from http://dx.doi.org/10.1901/, jaba.1992.25-165

Ducharme, J. M., Williams, L., Cummings, A., Murray, P., & Spencer, T. (2001). General case quasi- pyramidal staff training to promote generalization of teaching skills in supervisory and direct-care staff. *Behavior Modification, 25*, 233−254. Available from http://dx.doi.org/10.1177/0145445501252004.

Fisher, W. W., Kuhn, D. E., & Thompson, R. H. (1998). Establishing discriminative control of responding using functional and alternative reinforcers during functional communication training. *Journal of Applied Behavior Analysis, 31*, 543−560.

Jarmolowicz, D. P., Kahng, S. W., Ingvarrsson, E. T., Goysovich, R., Heggemeyer, R., Gregory, M. K., ... Taylor, S. J. (2008). Effects of conversational versus technical language on treatment preference and integrity. *Intellectual and Developmental Disabilities, 46*, 190−199. Available from http://dx.doi.org/10.1352/2008.46.190-199.

Jenkins, S. R., & DiGennaro-Reed, F. D. (2016). A parametric analysis of rehearsal opportunities on procedural integrity. *Journal of Organizational Behavior Management, 36*, 255−281.

Lerman, D. C., Iwata, B. A., & Wallace, M. D. (1999). Side effects of extinction: Prevalence of bursting and aggression during the treatment of self-injurious behavior. *Journal of Applied Behavior Analysis, 32*, 1−8.

Mortenson, B. P., & Witt, J. C. (1998). The use of weekly performance feedback to increase teacher implementation of a prereferral academic intervention. *School Psychology Review*, *27*, 613–627.

Noell, G. H., & Witt, J. C. (1999). When does consultation lead to intervention implementation? Critical issues for research and practice. *The Journal of Special Education*, *33*, 29–35. Available from http://dx.doi.org/10.1177/, 002246699903300103

Noell, G. H., Witt, J. C., Gilbertson, D. N., Ranier, D. D., & Freeland, J. T. (1997). Increasing teacher intervention implementation in general education settings through consultation and performance feedback. *School Psychology Quarterly*, *12*, 77–88.

Noell, G. H., Witt, J. C., LaFleur, L. H., Mortenson, B. P., Ranier, D. D., & LeVelle, J. (2000). A comparison of two follow-up strategies to increase teacher intervention implementation in general education following consultation. *Journal of Applied Behavior Analysis*, *33*, 271–284.

Noell, G. H., Witt, J. C., Slider, N. J., Connell, J. E., Gatti, S. L., Williams, K. L., Koenig, J. L., Resetar, J., & Duhon, G. J. (2005). Treatment implementation following behavioral consultation in schools: A comparison of three follow-up strategies. *School Psychology Review*, *34*, 87–106.

Nosik, M. R., Williams, W. L., Garrido, N., & Lee, S. (2013). Comparison of computer based instruction to behavior skills training for teaching staff implementation of discrete-trial instruction with an adult with autism. *Research in Developmental Disabilities*, *34*, 461–468. Available from http://dx.doi.org/10.1016/j.ridd.2012.08.011.

Parsons, M. B., Rollyson, J. H., & Reid, D. H. (2012). Evidence-based staff training: A guide for practitioners. *Behavior Analysis in Practice*, *5*, 2–11.

Pelletier, K., McNamara, B., Braga-Kenyon, P., & Ahearn, B. A. (2010). Effect of video self-monitoring on procedural integrity. *Behavioral Interventions*, *25*, 261–274. Available from http://dx.doi.org/10.1002/bin.316.

Reed, F., & Jenkins, S. (2013). *Handbook of crisis intervention and developmental disabilities*. New York: Springer Science + Business Media New York.

Reimers, T. M., & Wacker, D. P. (1988). Parents' ratings of the acceptability of behavior treatment recommendations made in an outpatient clinic: A preliminary analysis of the influence of treatment effectiveness. *Behavioral Disorder*, *14*, 7–15.

Rispoli, M., Neely, L., Healy, O., & Gregori, E. (2016). Training public school special educators to implement two functional analysis models. *Journal of Behavioral Education*, *25*, 249–274. Available from http://dx.doi.org/10.1007/s10864-016-9247-2.

Sarakoff, R. A., & Sturmey, P. (2004). The effects of behavioral skills training on staff implementation of discrete-trial teaching. *Journal of Applied Behavior Analysis*, *37*, 535–538.

Vladescu, J. C., Carroll, R., Paden, A., & Kodak, T. M. (2012). The effects of video modeling with voiceover instruction on accurate implementation of discrete-trial instruction. *Journal of Applied Behavior Analysis*, *45*, 419–423. Available from http://dx.doi.org/10.1901/jaba.2012.45-419.

Witt, J. C., & Martens, B. K. (1983). Assessing the acceptability of behavioral interventions used in class-rooms. *Psychology in the Schools*, *20*, 510–517.

Consultation Practices: Training Parents and Families

10

Kelly M. Schieltz[1], Jessica E. Graber[2] and Jennifer McComas[3]
[1]University of Missouri, Columbia, MO, United States, [2]University of Texas at San Antonio, San Antonio, TX, United States, [3]University of Minnesota, Minneapolis, MN, United States

Introduction

Although parents and families interact with and address their children's problem behavior on a daily basis, they also often do so with a very limited amount of training. A large proportion of behavior analytic assessment and treatment evaluations, including several conducted within our own services, continue to rely on therapist implementation, whereas parents and families often fulfill the role of observer until just before discharge from the service. At that point, they are briefly trained to implement the treatment that was shown to be effective at reducing the child's problem behavior with therapist implementation. There are several potential problems with this scenario, with the most obvious one being limited parent/family training (e.g., because all of the available time is devoted to the therapist conducting assessment/treatment). Even if the parent/family is trained on the specific procedures used by the therapist, there is almost never time to teach the parent/family how to generalize or maintain the treatment in other settings, situations, or with other tasks or people. Thus, even when parents are trained to implement the specific treatment, the brief training may be a necessary but not sufficient condition for durable success with the parent at home.

An equally significant problem is that behavior analytic assessments and treatments conducted by therapists may result in false negative findings. Schlichenmeyer, Roscoe, Rooker, Wheeler, and Dube (2013) conducted a review of idiosyncratic variables that affected functional analysis (FA) outcomes and found over 30 variables that influenced responding. One of the variables that may contribute to a lack of problem behavior during therapist-led behavioral evaluations is the absence of the parents and family members during those evaluations.

Differences in child behavior during therapist-led versus family-led assessments may be relatively common. For example, in a study conducted by Kurtz, Fodstad, Huete, and Hagopian (2013), FAs were conducted by therapists as well as by primary caregivers to determine if caregiver-conducted analyses resulted in conclusive results when the therapist-conducted analyses yielded either undifferentiated (i.e., low rates, zero rates, or undifferentiated) or questionable (i.e., inconsistent with other sources of information) results. Of the 52 cases evaluated, results showed that the rates of problem behavior were higher in all caregiver-conducted analyses, and

Applied Behavior Analysis Advanced Guidebook. DOI: http://dx.doi.org/10.1016/B978-0-12-811122-2.00010-3

in all but one case, caregiver-conducted analyses provided interpretable results when therapist-conducted analyses did not. Similarly, Derby et al. (1992) showed that approximately 37% of clinic patients did not engage in problem behavior within the clinical evaluation, even though they were referred specifically for an evaluation of problem behavior.

A treatment evaluation in which the child does not engage in problem behavior with the therapist results in a lack of opportunities for the parents and family to observe how individual treatment components (e.g., extinction, response blocking) are conducted when problem behavior occurs. False negative findings can occur for several reasons associated with motivating operations (MOs; Laraway, Snycerski, Michael, & Poling, 2003; Michael, 1982). MOs are those variables that establish a consequence as either being or not being reinforcing, and may be inadvertently altered when therapists versus parents/family members conduct assessment and treatment procedures. For example, parent attention may be a more potent reinforcer than therapist attention, in which case, an analysis may identify attention as a reinforcer only when the parent conducts the assessment (Ringdahl & Sellers, 2000). Similarly, the style of task presentation, rather than the task itself, may be the aversive stimulus that evokes escape-maintained problem behavior. For example, Gardner, Wacker, and Boelter (2009) showed that when nonpreferred demands were paired with high quality attention, children who engaged in escape-maintained problem behavior often chose to complete the tasks they had previously attempted to escape. Thus, if therapists tend to provide high quality attention during a demand, but parents provide low quality attention, this may lead to a false negative finding when therapists conduct the assessment of demands. Similarly, in Thomason-Sassi, Iwata, and Fritz (2013), the problem behavior displayed by a 6-year-old boy with an autism spectrum disorder was shown to only occur in the presence of his mother. That is, when his mother conducted the evaluation, he displayed problem behavior when instructed to complete demands. In contrast, when the therapist conducted the same condition, no problem behavior was observed. These results suggest that this boy's mother served as a discriminative stimulus (a signal for reinforcement) for the availability of escape as a reinforcer, and she likely obtained those stimulus control properties by historically providing escape contingent on his problem behavior.

If problem behaviors are not observed during the assessment (false negative), a level of inference, based on indirect measures, is often utilized to provide treatment recommendations, increasing the potential for prescribing ineffective or counter-therapeutic treatments (Wacker, Berg, Harding, & Cooper-Brown, 2004). In addition, the failure of problem behavior occurring during treatment (lack of opportunities to demonstrate all treatment components), may lead to poor treatment fidelity, which has been shown to result in resurgence of the problem behavior (St. Peter Pipkin, Vollmer, & Sloman, 2010; Volkert, Lerman, Call, & Trosclair-Lasserre, 2009).

Given the relevant role parents and families play in the behavior analytic assessments and treatments provided to their child(ren), our clinical teams decided to maximally include parents/family throughout our assessment and treatment process. One of our initial questions was related to the parents' acceptance of conducting all of the procedures rather than watching trained therapists conduct the procedures. Throughout our clinical projects we have assessed the acceptability of the procedures [primarily FA and functional communication training (FCT)] and the parents have rated the procedures as highly acceptable (Wacker et al., 1998; Wacker et al., 2011). High levels of acceptability are important for several reasons, but one practical reason is that high levels of social acceptability may lead to higher treatment adherence (Reimers, Wacker, Cooper, & DeRaad, 1992). Treatment adherence, which is defined as the extent to which parents/families implement the treatment recommendations as prescribed (Allen & Warzak, 2000), is important because, as mentioned earlier, poor fidelity of implementation may lead to the recurrence of problem behavior (St. Peter Pipkin et al., 2010). However, when parents/families are trained to implement treatment with good fidelity, research has shown that the fidelity with which parents/families implement treatment components when a therapist is not present is similar to their implementation when the therapist is present (Suess et al., 2014b). Suess et al. worked with families via telehealth, with parents/families conducting the treatments in their homes and the therapists working at a tertiary-level hospital. Thus, the therapists never worked directly with the children; all procedures were conducted by the parents. The results of this study strongly suggest that when parents/families are involved in the training process and they receive coaching, they can accurately implement treatment strategies independently.

To increase treatment fidelity and treatment adherence, Allen and Warzak (2000) discussed four areas that therapists should consider and include in their practice: (1) MOs, (2) generalization, (3) response acquisition, and (4) consequence events. With MOs, therapists may increase parent/family treatment adherence by explaining what is likely to happen with problem behavior, thereby establishing that result as a reinforcer. For example, explaining that problem behavior needs to become worse (extinction burst) before it gets better may increase the likelihood that parents/families will follow through with the treatment recommendation rather than "give up" because they were prepared for the increase in problem behavior. In the area of generalization, training multiple exemplars (e.g., different tasks required of the child) and increasing salient visual stimuli (e.g., providing visual schedules and word cards) may make treatment more clear to both the child and parent. Similarly, reducing the complexity of the treatment when possible, and providing models, rehearsal, and feedback, may improve the fluency with which parents deliver treatment. For consequence events, considering the competing reinforcers for the parents/family and the response effort required to carry out the treatment may be dimensions of reinforcement that potentially disrupt long-term treatment.

In the remainder of this chapter, we focus on how we train parents and families on behavior analytic procedures conducted within our behavioral services for problem behavior displayed by children with and without disabilities (Wacker et al., 2015; Wacker, Berg, Schieltz, Romani, & Padilla Dalmau, 2013; Wacker, Schieltz, & Romani, 2015). We begin with a brief historical overview of our outpatient clinics at the University of Iowa Children's Hospital. Then we discuss the training approach we use and its benefits and limitations in our one-time 90-minute outpatient clinics. To address the limitations of our one-time 90-minute outpatient clinics, we next describe two alternative clinic models we use for training: (1) in-person Day Treatment service, and (2) in-home service, either conducted in-person or via telehealth. We conclude this chapter with guidelines and recommendations for therapists on how to train parents and families.

History of our outpatient clinics

Our outpatient clinical practice began in the 1980s and consisted of indirect measures (i.e., interviews, checklists, surveys) during 90-minute clinical evaluations (Wacker & Steege, 1993). This practice was not satisfying to us, which led to an evolution of services (Wacker et al., 1994) following the development of the FA (Iwata, Dorsey, Slifer, Bauman, & Richman, 1982/1994). Given the constraints imposed by our clinical service (90-minute clinical evaluations), we began to modify our assessment procedures based on the FA methodology. Our initial modifications, as described by Cooper, Wacker, Sasso, Reimers, and Donn (1990) and Northup et al. (1991) included a two-phase assessment in which antecedent variables (Cooper et al., 1990) or consequence variables (Northup et al., 1991) were evaluated to determine the effects on appropriate (Cooper et al., 1990) or problem (Northup et al., 1991) behavior. Following the results of the first phase, behaviors were further evaluated under either the "best" and "worst" conditions (Cooper et al., 1990) or the contingencies for an appropriate alternative behavior, versus problem behavior (Northup et al., 1991). In addition to the variables evaluated, sessions were 5 to 10 minutes in length, and parents conducted all procedures, as described by Cooper et al. With these modifications, the evaluations were often successful in identifying the functional reinforcers related to problem behavior displayed by children with and without developmental disabilities.

As these initial demonstrations of how the FA methodology can be successfully modified and applied to 90-minute clinical evaluations, we have continued to evolve our assessments while maintaining the integrity of the basic assessment method. Our evolution of assessments has broadened from exclusive implementation of the FA to conducting other evaluations, such as choice assessments and treatment evaluations (Wacker et al., 2015, 2013). This broadening to other evaluations occurred for at least two reasons. First, when problem behaviors did not occur or were anticipated to not occur in the clinic (false negative), we sought alternative direct behavioral assessment methodologies to provide some level of direct evidence for treatment recommendations so as to avoid recommending ineffective or counter-therapeutic treatments (see Wacker et al., 2013, for example). Second, we began modifying our assessments to systematically evaluate the idiosyncratic variables that were influencing responding to provide more individualized treatment recommendations (e.g., see Wacker et al., 2015).

Throughout the history of our clinical services, parents and families have been the cornerstone of our practice, in which they are fully incorporated into the assessment and treatment evaluations. We believe that by fully integrating parents and families into our evaluations, we obtain a better understanding of the variables influencing the occurrence of problem behavior, and the parents and families obtain a level of training that is useful when generalizing from the clinic to other settings such as their homes. For example, when parents/families conduct an FA, they see that the change in conditions is correlated with changes in problem behavior. As an illustration, in one of our in-home projects (Wacker et al., 1998), "Bobby" displayed severe self-injury, which his mother believed was out of his control. During the FA, as "Bobby's" problem behavior always got worse during the attention condition, and was always fine during all other conditions, she looked right into the camera that was recording the session and said, "He has been fooling me, hasn't he?" At that point in our analysis, we did not need to have any further discussion regarding the attention function of his problem behavior because his mother had helped us to identify it.

Description of parent and family training approach

Outpatient clinic description

We have two outpatient clinics at the University of Iowa Children's Hospital that provide single 90-minute behavioral evaluations. The Biobehavioral Outpatient Service serves individuals with developmental disabilities who engage in severe problem behavior, whereas the Behavioral Pediatrics Clinic serves typically developing children, between the ages of 2 and 10 years, who engage in severe problem behavior. For both clinics, individuals are typically referred by their primary care physician for consultation regarding behavior management strategies to address the problem behaviors displayed at home, school, and in the community. Both clinics utilize an interdisciplinary team including applied behavior analysts, physicians, nurse practitioners, speech and language pathologists, and social workers. Four to six children are evaluated per clinic day.

The general procedures conducted by the behavior analytic team consists of a four-step process: (1) referral, (2) preparation for the evaluation, (3) conducting the evaluation, and (4) follow-up after the evaluation. Throughout each step, parents and families are involved in various ways. For each service delivery model, we describe how they are involved and how training occurs in each step of the process. We then illustrate the benefits of our training approach through a case illustration, followed by a brief discussion of the clinic's limitations related to parent/family training. Table 10.1 provides a summary of the specific procedures we use and their rationales for training parents/families across each step of our clinical process.

Step one: Referral

Following a referral to one of our clinics, a questionnaire and daily behavior record are sent to the parents/family of the scheduled patient. Parents are instructed to fill

Table 10.1 Summary of the 4-step clinical process used within our 90-minute outpatient clinic, Day Treatment clinic, and in-home service, including our specific activities and procedures, and the purposes of those activities from a clinical and parent/family training perspective

4-Step clinical process	Specific activities & procedures	Purpose of the activities	
		Clinical perspective	*Parent/family training perspective*
Referral	Questionnaire Daily behavior record	Gather information to guide development of the assessment plan	Introduce the idea that behavior can be predicted and is controllable (*MOs*)
Preparation prior to evaluation	Review record ABC interview (*telephone or in-person*) Parent/family (*all services*) Referring provider (*Day Treatment only*) Overview on function-based evaluations	Gain understanding of history of problem behavior, formulate hypotheses, and develop assessment plan	Begin to establish that there is a correlation between the environment and occurrence of behavior (*MOs*)
During the evaluation	Staffing	Identify assessment plan based on the obtained information	Consider the specific role of the parents (*response acquisition*)
	Assessment Coach (*e.g., explaining procedures & results providing praise & feedback*)	Identify the function of and variables related to problem behavior; increase procedural fidelity to increase likelihood of valid results	Demonstrate and then provide experience for how behavior can be controlled and predicted (*MOs*)
	Treatment Coach (*e.g., modeling & explaining procedures, assisting with implementation of procedures, providing feedback and praise*)	Demonstrate effects of treatment	Develop and improve procedural skills toward accurate independence (*response acquisition*)
	Wrap-Up Discuss recommendations, provide handouts	Provide individualized description of results and recommendations	Continue to develop skills (*response acquisition & generalization*)
Follow-up	Follow-up initiated by parents/families Interview, consult, & schedule, as needed	Obtain information to guide further consultation	Improve skills (*response acquisition, generalization, & consequence events*)

Note: MO, motivating operations.

out and return these forms prior to the child's evaluation. The questionnaire asks about basic patient demographics, the referral question, behaviors of concern, and communication. Specifically, for behaviors of concern, parents/families are asked about the topography of behavior, the frequency with which the behavior occurs, the severity of the behavior, and how long the behavior has been occurring. The daily behavior record (refer to Fig. 10.1 for a sample form) asks the parent/family to record specific instances of the occurrence of the target behavior over a 2-week period, including the date and time when the behavior occurred, the activity involved (antecedent), the behavior displayed, the parents'/family's responses to the behavior (consequence), and how long the behavior occurred (duration). From a clinical perspective, the purpose of these forms is to gather information about the behaviors of concern to guide the development of the clinic assessment plan. From a parent/family training perspective, the daily behavior record begins to introduce the notion that behavior is often controlled by the environment and that its occurrence can be predicted. For example, by completing this form over a 2-week period, a parent may begin to notice that his or her child engages in problem behavior frequently when he or she is asked to pick up toys. Seeing that the behavior is not random may increase the parents' motivation to implement a behavioral treatment at home or to stop using an approach that may be counter-therapeutic.

Step two: Preparation prior to the evaluation

A few days before the scheduled evaluation, clinic therapists prepare by reviewing the child's medical record, including the questionnaire and daily behavior record filled out by the parent/family, and conducting a telephone antecedent-behavior-consequence (ABC) interview with the parent/family. Clinically, the review of records allows the clinic therapist to understand the history of the patient and his or her problem behaviors, and to begin formulating hypotheses of why the current concerns may be occurring. The ABC interview (Bijou, Peterson, & Ault, 1968) is then conducted with the parent/family to clarify information from the medical record and to gain a more thorough understanding of the behaviors of concern, including specific and recent examples, in terms of the ABC sequence. Synthesizing this information leads to an assessment plan for the clinic evaluation. For parent/family training, the ABC interview builds upon the introduction that behavior is predictable by gathering recent ABC examples of the occurrence of problem behavior and describing how the function of problem behavior is assessed in a clinical evaluation. During the ABC interview, a clinic therapist describes the purpose of the clinic, ensures that the parent/family goal(s) aligns with the objectives of the clinic, describes what a typical assessment looks like, and how the results of the assessment guide the treatment recommendations.

Step three: During the evaluation

On the day of clinic and prior to the evaluation, the entire clinic team meets to discuss the information obtained by the therapists with a specific focus on the ABC

Daily behavior record

Child_____

Date_____

Time of day	How often?	What activity was involved	What did your child do?	What did you do about your child's behavior?
Morning				
5:00-5:30 am				
5:30-6:00 am	_____			
6:00-6:30 am	_____			
6:30-7:00 am	_____			
7:00-7:30 am	_____			
7:30-8:00 am	_____			
8:00-8:30 am	_____			
8:30-9:00 am	_____			
9:00-9:30 am	_____			
9:30-10:00 am	_____			
10:00-10:30 am	_____			
10:30-11:00 am	_____			
11:00:11:30 am	_____			
11:30-12:00 pm	_____			
Afternoon				
12:00-12:30 pm	_____			
12:30-1:00 pm	_____			
1:00-1:30 pm	_____			
1:30-2:00 pm	_____			
2:00-2:30 pm	_____			
2:30-3:00 pm	_____			
3:00-3:30 pm	_____			
3:30-4:00 pm	_____			
4:00-4:30 pm	_____			
4:30-5:00 pm	_____			
5:00-5:30 pm	_____			
5:30-6:00 pm	_____			
Evening				
6:00-6:30 pm	_____			
6:30-7:00 pm	_____			
7:00-7:30 pm	_____			
7:30-8:00 pm	_____			
8:00-8:30 pm	_____			
8:30-9:00 pm	_____			
9:00-9:30 pm	_____			
9:30-10:00 pm	_____			
10:00-10:30 pm	_____			
10:30-11:00 pm	_____			

This record will help us understand the times and situations in which your child is having problems. Here is a sample entry:

Time of day	How often?	What activity was involved	What did your child do?	What did you do about your child's behavior?
3:30-4:00 pm	_____	Picking up toys	Refused to pick up, screamed, bit hand	Gave up, picked up toys myself

Figure 10.1 Sample daily behavior record that is sent to parents/families prior to a clinic evaluation.

interview information. Based on this "morning staffing," the clinic team designs the individualized assessment procedures for each scheduled evaluation. Our clinic evaluations often start with an assessment such as an FA, with the order of conditions based on the ABC interview. We most often begin with a free play condition, followed by the condition in which our team anticipates problem behavior is most likely to occur. In most cases, parents/families conduct all assessment sessions with coaching from a clinic therapist.

We do not train parents/families on how to conduct the assessment because our goal is not for parents/families to routinely conduct assessment conditions outside of the clinic setting. Rather, our goals are to identify why the problem behaviors are occurring and to demonstrate to the parents/family that these behaviors can be controlled by the environment. Therefore, prior to each assessment session, a clinic therapist instructs the parent/family on what to do during that session. For example, if the next session to be conducted is a free play, the therapist instructs the parents/family to play with their child, ignore problem behavior, and avoid asking the child to do something in any particular way. Further, the clinic therapist explains that the purpose of the condition is to determine how the child acts when he or she has access to toys and attention, and is not being asked to do anything he or she does not want to do. If a preference assessment has not been conducted prior to the FA, then the first free play session is conducted as a free operant preference assessment (Roane, Vollmer, Ringdahl, & Marcus, 1998). If the clinic team continued to have questions regarding the child's preferences following this initial free play, the free operant preference assessment is either repeated or a more structured preference assessment is conducted (e.g., DeLeon & Iwata, 1996; Fisher et al., 1992).

Following each parent/family-conducted session, the clinic therapist reviews with the parent/family what occurred during the prior session and provides instructions for the next session. Reviewing what occurred in the prior session meets two goals. First, the therapist acknowledges what was observed during the session and clarifies whether the occurrence or nonoccurrence of problem behavior in that situation is typical for the child. Second, the therapist explains what the observations suggest regarding the child's problem behavior. For example, following an escape session in which mild problem behavior occurred, the parents may indicate that the task/escape situation is one in which the child typically engages in more severe or frequent problem behavior. In response, the clinic therapist acknowledges that often in an outpatient clinic, milder forms of the behavior are observed, but that observing even the mild form of the behavior is an indication that the child is engaging in the problem behavior because it tends to result in the ability to avoid or escape nonpreferred tasks. Further, the clinic therapist may point out that the problem behavior stopped when the parents/family removed the demand, and resumed each time the demand was presented to the child, demonstrating that the problem behavior can be controlled by the parent changing the environment. Finally, the clinic therapist might remind the parent/family that these sessions are for assessment purposes only, and that the procedures they are conducting in assessment are not the procedures they will implement during treatment.

After briefly reviewing the observations from the previous session, instructions are provided for the next session. If a similar session was conducted earlier, the therapist provides praise for components that were implemented well and provides corrective feedback for components that were viewed as needing improvement. For example, if the parent/family responded to appropriate communication during an FA session that was only targeting problem behavior, the therapist clarifies and reinstructs the parents/family to only respond to problem behavior while ignoring all appropriate communication.

At the end of the 90-minute clinic evaluation, a brief treatment evaluation is often conducted, in which we conduct as least one treatment session so that parents/families can, at the very least, observe the primary recommendation for addressing their child's problem behavior. We begin our treatment evaluations with a clinic therapist demonstrating the treatment procedures, whereas the parent/family observes in the clinic room. During this demonstration, a second therapist is often in the clinic room explaining the procedures to the parent/family and pointing out various aspects related to the treatment, such as when particular components should be implemented, how the child is responding, and what behavioral effects are expected. After the therapist demonstrates the treatment a couple of times, the therapist coaches the parent/family through the implementation of treatment. During this coaching, the therapist again explains how and when to conduct the procedures. The parents/family are praised for components implemented well and provided with corrective feedback for components that need improvement. If extensive feedback is needed, we try to schedule the parents to either return to our clinic, or meet with a local behavior analyst to continue to work on their delivery of the treatment. If parents/families return to our clinic, we most often devote the entire 90 minutes to coaching the parent/family in conducting treatment.

At the end of the clinic evaluation, we wrap-up with the parents/family. Our wrap-up consists of reviewing the results of the evaluation and discussing recommendations for preventing and addressing the problem behaviors at home. Typically, this discussion reiterates the various messages described throughout our evaluation process. However, other aspects of addressing problem behavior may also be described such as what parents/families should expect with these problem behaviors when returning home. For example, because extinction is frequently a component of the treatment package, parents/families should expect an increase in problem behavior (extinction burst) when implementing most treatment strategies, but, if they remain consistent and follow through with the treatment recommendation, problem behaviors should then decrease.

The treatment recommendations, which were demonstrated in clinic and discussed during the wrap-up, are provided to the parents/families in a variety of formats including handouts and a clinic report. Handouts are general, but provide step-by-step instructions on how to implement the treatment procedures and/or answer common questions related to behavior change programs (e.g., what a parent should do if behavior gets worse), and are sent home with the parents/family on the day of the evaluation. Clinic reports are sent to parents/families by the hospital several weeks after the clinic evaluation. For this reason, we provide our email addresses to each parent/family, and indicate that if they send us an email request for the clinic recommendations, we can provide those recommendations within a couple days of the evaluation. Although clinic report recommendations cover the same information as the handouts, the step-by-step instructions on how to implement the treatment procedures are individualized for each parent/family (e.g., examples or materials are specified). In addition to the handouts and specific clinic report recommendations, we also provide parent/family-friendly literature surrounding specific recommendations. For example, when recommending FCT (Carr & Durand, 1985) as a treatment procedure, we often provide parents/families with a copy of Wacker, Berg, and Harding (2002), which summarizes the use of FCT.

Step four: Follow-up after the evaluation

We explain to the parents/families that the "real" evaluation will occur at home, because the clinic cannot account for all of the variables that may be influencing responding. Given that problem behaviors may occur at different levels at home than observed in clinic, or that parents/families might struggle more with implementing the treatment strategies in the home setting, we recommend that parents/families follow-up with us so that we can provide further consultation. Given the staff constraints and clinical load of our clinic, we do not routinely initiate follow-up with parents/families. Rather, we ask parents/families to contact us via telephone or email when questions or concerns arise. When parents/family contact us, we are able to follow-up with them in a variety of ways, including telephone, email, and video conferencing software (i.e., telehealth).

During the follow-up, a clinic therapist obtains information about the reason for follow-up and reviews how the treatment is being implemented as well as its effectiveness on reducing the occurrence of problem behavior. After obtaining this information, the clinic therapist may either troubleshoot areas that need to be adjusted with the treatment or schedule a return visit to the clinic for further evaluation.

Case illustration and benefits of the 90-minute outpatient clinic

Adam was a 6-year-old boy with Sotos syndrome and mild to moderate intellectual disability. His communication consisted of a few single words (e.g., "more," "mama," "ball"), gestures (e.g., bringing items to someone), and the use of an augmentative communication device that was currently "lost or stolen." He was referred to our clinic to address his aggression (e.g., hitting, biting). Following the referral to our clinic, parents were asked to fill out our questionnaire and the daily behavior record. During the ABC interview, Adam's mother indicated that he engaged in aggression, in general, when he "struggles to communicate" with specific examples being to get attention, and when he is asked to stop a preferred activity or transition to a less preferred activity. The aggressive behavior was typically preceded by screaming, and occurred across home and school settings. At home, parents responded to aggression by placing him in his bedroom, which was

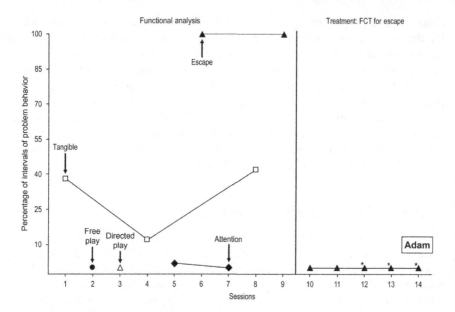

Figure 10.2 Results of Adam's outpatient clinic evaluation. *FCT*, functional communication training; * indicates parent implemented treatment sessions.
Parents implemented all functional analysis sessions.

typically effective at calming him down. An FA was conducted to determine the reinforcer(s) maintaining his problem behavior.

During the outpatient clinic evaluation, Adam's mother conducted all FA sessions with coaching from a clinic therapist. Results (Fig. 10.2; left panel) indicated that Adam's problem behaviors were maintained by access to tangible items and escape from demands. From the parent/family training perspective, Adam's parents directly observed Adam engage in problem behavior every time he was instructed to complete a task, and rarely engage in problem behavior when his parents ignored him. Thus, his parents demonstrated to themselves that they could turn Adam's problem behaviors off and on.

To address the occurrence of Adam's problem behavior during situations in which he was instructed to leave his preferred items and complete a nonpreferred task, a treatment package was implemented that included gaining access to preferred items and a break for completing a portion of the task and appropriately requesting a break to play. Initially, the clinic therapist modeled and explained how to implement the treatment package. Following this demonstration, Adam's parents conducted the treatment with coaching from the clinic therapist (sessions 12—14). As his parents showed independence with implementing the treatment package, the clinic therapist faded the amount of coaching she provided and increased the amount of praise provided to the parents. The results of the treatment evaluation (Fig. 10.2, right panel) showed that the treatment package was effective at decreasing the occurrence of Adam's problem behavior. By modeling the treatment and then coaching both of Adam's parents to implement the treatment procedures, we attempted to increase the parents' accuracy and generalization of how to implement the treatment. Only one follow-up evaluation occurred and focused on continuing to implement the treatment at home.

Limitations of the 90-minute outpatient clinic

One major limitation to the 90-minute outpatient clinic is that there is often insufficient time to conduct a full treatment evaluation, limiting time available for parents/families to obtain the skills needed to carry out the treatment at home. If there is time to conduct a treatment evaluation, typically there is only time for one or two sessions to be conducted. This time limitation is problematic because parents/families who do not observe the treatment being implemented may not implement the treatment at all or might do so with poor treatment fidelity. This same issue applies to parents/families who have the opportunity to observe but may not have the opportunity to practice the treatment strategy while receiving therapist feedback. Each of these examples increases the likelihood of a lack of response acquisition and generalization by the parents/family.

Alternative parent and family training options

If acquisition or generalization are a problem, we have two alternative services that we provide that are each associated with much more extensive parent training: (1) Day Treatment service, and (2) in-home service. Both alternatives have been shown to be effective at identifying the functional relations between problem behavior and environmental events, and demonstrating that problem behavior can be reduced and more appropriate behaviors increased with the implementation of treatment recommendations (Asmus et al., 2004; Lindgren et al., 2016).

Day Treatment clinic description

The Day Treatment clinic is an outpatient service that provides more in-depth behavioral evaluations for children and adults whose severe problem behavior (1) failed to reduce to acceptable levels following recommendations provided by the outpatient team or other community- and school-based behavior analysts, or (2) is determined by the outpatient team to need such services to further clarify the function(s) of the problem behavior, identify the appropriate treatment components, and/or to provide additional training to parents/families on how to implement the treatment recommendations. Referrals to the Day Treatment service are typically made by the outpatient team or community-based behavior analysts. Day Treatment evaluations are scheduled and conducted over the course of 10 consecutive half-days, which requires families to either travel daily to the clinic or stay in a hotel close to the hospital for the duration of the service.

Steps one (referral) and two (preparation prior to the evaluation)

After receiving a referral to Day Treatment, the same steps described for our outpatient clinics are followed. The ABC interview includes questions related to behavioral strategies that have been tried, effectiveness of those strategies, and the extent to which the parents/family were able to implement behavioral recommendations. For example, the therapist may ask the parent/family to describe (1) the recommendations provided by the outpatient clinic, (2) how often those recommendations were tried, (3) which strategies, if any, were most helpful, and (4) the biggest challenges in implementing the recommendations.

Because individuals referred to Day Treatment have typically received some level of behavioral services elsewhere, Day Treatment therapists attempt to consult with the referring provider prior to the patient's evaluation to obtain the referring provider's clinical impressions, review results of the data collected, and identify specific questions or concerns to be addressed during the Day Treatment evaluation. Clinically, these preparation activities serve the same purpose as they did for the outpatient service, which is to understand the patient's history and to develop an assessment plan based on hypotheses. Similarly, for parent/family training, the information obtained is reviewed with the parent/family early in the Day Treatment service to facilitate discussions about the ways in which environmental variables may be maintaining problem behavior.

Step three: During the evaluation

An FA is conducted over several days to identify the function(s) of problem behavior(s). Other analyses, such as preference assessments, may be conducted to answer additional questions (e.g., relative preferences between competing reinforcers; Harding et al, 1999) related to the patient's problem behavior or potential treatment plans. Parent/family involvement in the assessment process can range from a lead role to a support role, and is dependent on a variety of factors, such as the preferences of the parent, the occurrence of a false negative finding during the initial sessions, and the severity of the problem behavior.

During assessment, therapists teach parents about the assessment procedures and the rationale for those procedures prior to asking them to conduct the assessment. In this situation, clinic therapists conduct the assessment procedures with the patient, whereas the parents/family observe either in the clinic room or in an adjacent room via video-monitoring. During this time, other clinic therapists describe the procedures, explain the results, and answer any questions posed by the parents/family. Following this training, the parents/family conduct the remainder of the assessment sessions with clinic therapist coaching.

Next, the goal shifts to assisting the parents/family in becoming independent with the treatment procedures. The parents/family initially observe the therapists conducting the treatment procedures, which allows for the parents/family to (1) receive instruction and a rationale on the procedures (e.g., how time-out can inadvertently reinforce problem behavior maintained by escape from demands), and (2) observe how various procedures are implemented under specific situations. For example, it is not uncommon for an extinction burst to occur early in treatment that involves differential reinforcement; therefore, by having the parents/family observe how therapists respond to this increase in behavior, other clinic therapists can explain to the parent what is happening, why the procedures being implemented are important to carry out with fidelity, and what the expected long-term results will be following implementation of these procedures.

As problem behaviors begin to decrease with the therapist implementing all treatment procedures, therapists begin to directly coach the parents on how to conduct the treatment procedures with their child(ren). The therapist explains how and when to conduct the procedures and provides praise and corrective feedback. For example, if a burst in problem behavior occurs when the parents/family begin implementing the treatment (not an uncommon occurrence), the therapist may provide coaching to ensure procedural fidelity, while also providing praise for implementing components with good fidelity. As the parents/family demonstrate increasing independence with the treatment procedures, the therapist fades his/her support which allows the parents/family to practice the treatment procedures independently in a controlled environment. When the parents/family have independently and successfully implemented the treatment procedures across several consecutive sessions with the patient displaying little to no problem behavior and increased levels of appropriate behaviors, programming for generalization and maintenance occurs. Although we try to program and assess for generalization and maintenance of the patient's behaviors, we are often unable to do more than a rudimentary job due to time pressures and a limited ability to incorporate the natural stimuli from the setting in which the problem behavior typically occurs (e.g., home). Examples of programing and assessing for generalization and maintenance of the patient's behaviors within Day Treatment include conducting the treatment in untrained locations or with untrained people (stimulus generalization; Stokes & Baer, 1977) and probing for fidelity errors, such as intermittently withholding a treatment component, and/or gradually increasing the delay to reinforcement (maintenance; Nevin & Wacker, 2013). Each of these procedures assists the parents in learning how to generalize the treatment, and what to do if generalization or maintenance do not occur.

Step four: Follow-up after the clinic evaluation

The follow-up model for Day Treatment is consistent with the model described for the outpatient clinics, with ongoing support available via telephone or email.

Case illustration and benefits of the Day Treatment clinic

Sasha was a 3-year-old girl with an autism spectrum disorder, mild intellectual disability, mixed receptive-expressive language disorder, macrocephaly, and focal epilepsy. She had no vocal communication. She was referred to Day Treatment by a community provider for the assessment and treatment of severe problem behavior including self-injury (e.g., head and leg hitting, head banging, hair pulling), aggression (e.g., hitting, pinching, biting, throwing items at others), and property destruction (e.g., throwing items, dumping food or drinks on the floor). In the past year, behavioral services included two outpatient clinic evaluations and ongoing consultation from applied behavior analysts working in the school. The outpatient clinic evaluations suggested that Sasha's problem behavior was maintained by escape from demands and access to preferred items. Based on these results, treatment recommendations consisted of a structured work/break routine with FCT for "play." During the interview, Sasha's mother reported difficulty implementing the outpatient clinic recommendations because of the severity of Sasha's problem behaviors, which led to her discontinuing the use of this treatment (lack of acquisition and generalization). In addition, she believed that the high levels of Sasha's problem behaviors were related to Sasha's inability to calm down and "self-soothe." The first goal of the Day Treatment evaluation was to verify the results obtained during the outpatient evaluations and to further demonstrate to Sasha's mother the functional relations between Sasha's problem behavior and environmental events.

An FA was conducted jointly by the clinic therapists and Sasha's mother. Initially, Sasha's mother observed the assessment sessions in an adjacent room via live video, whereas clinic staff explained the assessment procedures. During subsequent sessions, Sasha's mother conducted sessions with therapist coaching, which consisted of the therapist modeling the procedures across several trials and then coaching the mother on how to conduct the procedures. When problem behavior escalated to levels that could cause harm to Sasha or others, the clinic therapist resumed control of the FA procedures, whereas Sasha's mother observed and assisted. The results of the FA, conducted across three days, are depicted in Fig. 10.3 (left panel), and showed that Sasha's problem behavior was maintained by escape from demands and access to preferred items, which was consistent with the results obtained during her 90-minute outpatient evaluations. Sasha's mother now had multiple opportunities to learn about, observe, and directly experience how specific environmental variables influenced the occurrence and nonoccurrence of her child's problem behaviors, which potentially increased the likelihood that she would be motivated to generalize the use of the treatment procedures to her home.

Treatment for Sasha was conducted in two phases. Phase 1 consisted of FCT for preferred items and activities, and was conducted over the course of three days. With this treatment, Sasha was taught to hand a picture card to her mother which produced access to preferred items, snacks, or play. During the first day of treatment, a clinic therapist modeled the procedures for Sasha's mother, while explaining each step and having her assist with providing reinforcement to her daughter. As Sasha began to demonstrate success with the treatment, we observed the interactions between Sasha and her mother become increasingly enthusiastic during reinforcement, which resulted in Sasha's mother becoming excited to take a more active role in conducting the treatment procedures. The therapist gradually faded her support as Sasha's mother became increasingly independent with conducting the procedures. Results of Treatment Phase 1 (Fig. 10.3, middle panel) showed that Sasha's problem behavior gradually decreased.

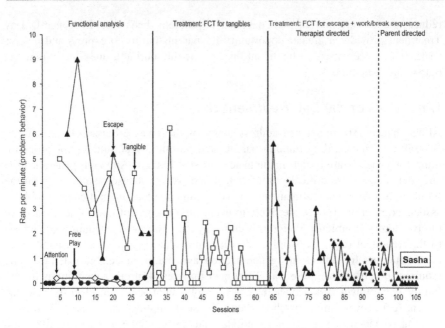

Figure 10.3 Results of Sasha's Day Treatment evaluation. *FCT*, functional communication training; * indicates parent implemented treatment: FCT for Escape + Work/Break Sequence sessions.
Parents implemented all Treatment: FCT for Tangibles sessions.

To address the escape function of Sasha's problem behavior, a second treatment was implemented during the last four days of her evaluation (Fig. 10.3, right panel). Phase 2 consisted of FCT for escape plus a work-break sequence. During this phase, Sasha's mother observed (in the clinic room) the therapist implement the procedures during the first five sessions (sessions 64−68) because it was anticipated that Sasha would engage in high levels of problem behavior. This occurred, but as problem behavior began to decrease, her mother implemented the treatment with therapist coaching (sessions 69 and 70). For the next 11 sessions, Sasha's mother observed the treatment being implemented by a therapist, whereas other clinic therapists discussed with the mother strategies for implementing the treatment in the home setting following discharge from the clinic. During session 82, Sasha's mother returned to the clinic room and conducted all remaining treatment sessions with therapist support fading over time. Beginning in session 95, Sasha's mother conducted the treatment independently, whereas the therapist observed from an adjacent room. Overall, results showed that Sasha's problem behavior reduced to zero levels with her mother implementing all procedures independently (Fig. 10.3).

These results show the benefits of extended services such as Day Treatment. Sasha's mother learned through observation and discussion of the treatment procedures, including understanding the rationale for those specific procedures. In addition, she had multiple opportunities to successfully implement the treatment to reduce the occurrence of her daughter's problem behavior. In general, Day Treatment provides a greater opportunity for parents/family to express and resolve issues and concerns with a treatment than is possible during a one-time, 90-minute outpatient evaluation.

Limitations of the Day Treatment clinic

Although Day Treatment can address many of the areas discussed by Allen and Warzak (2000) regarding training parents and families, opportunities for programming for generalization and maintenance are still limited. Although generalization and maintenance are critically important, often we are focused exclusively on the problem behavior and refinements in the treatment plan. In particular, problems associated with resurgence are likely to occur after the parent returns home, and we rarely address resurgence directly in clinic by, for example, scheduling challenges to the treatment (e.g., the word card is not immediately available). In addition to the limitations for addressing generalization and maintenance, the extended time required to participate in the Day Treatment may result in other disruptions for the family (e.g., travel distance, hotel costs, employment leave, meal costs) and the patient (e.g., several missed school days). These disruptions can impact the overall training provided to parents and families, and can continue to be disruptive even when the family returns home. For example, after spending 10 days working on a treatment, a parent may try to reduce the time spent with the child to devote time to others in the home. This may lead to a resurgence of problem behavior, and if not anticipated, may lead to treatment relapse.

In-home service (in vivo and via telehealth) description

The in-home service we provide has always been a part of federally-funded research projects (Wacker & Berg, 1992; Wacker, Berg, & Harding, 1996, 2000, 2004) because of a lack of funding for these services. Our first in-home service began in the early 1990s because there was a paucity of evidence suggesting that FAs and FCT could be effectively conducted by parents in the home environment. Results have routinely shown that functional relations between problem behavior and environmental events could often be identified and that FCT was effective at reducing problem behaviors and increasing more appropriate behaviors when parents conducted all procedures within the home (e.g., Wacker et al., 1998, 2017). In addition, other positive findings have been shown in relation to generalization (Berg, Wacker, Harding, Ganzer, & Barretto, 2007) and maintenance (Wacker et al., 2011), as well as when the services have been conducted via telehealth (Lindgren et al., 2016).

The in-home service is provided in-person as well as via telehealth for young children (up to age 6 years) with developmental disabilities who engage in severe problem behavior. Evaluations are typically conducted during 1 hour weekly visits, for up to 2 years. Similar to Day Treatment, children are referred for in-home services by the outpatient clinic team, Day Treatment clinic team, or other healthcare professionals who are familiar with the in-home service. In contrast to our other two services, applied behavior analysts are the only practitioners providing services within this model. Please refer to Harding, Wacker, Berg, Lee, and Dolezal (2009), Lee et al. (2015), Suess et al. (2014a), Wacker et al. (2013a,b, 2016) for specific details relating to the specific procedures conducted throughout this service.

Step one: Referral

Following a referral to the in-home service, the parents/family are asked to complete a daily behavior record in the same manner as outlined for the outpatient clinics.

Step two: Preparation prior to the evaluation

During the first evaluation of the in-home service, the therapist conducts an ABC interview with the parents/family. In addition, during this interview, the therapist reviews the daily behavior record filled out by the parents/family, obtains information about the child's preferences for leisure activities, and conducts additional interviews using a behavior rating scale. The behavior rating scale facilitates obtaining information about various contexts in which problem behavior occurs (e.g., grocery store, asked to brush teeth). Clinically, this information assists the therapist with developing hypotheses regarding the antecedents and consequences that occasion and maintain problem behavior. From a parent/family training perspective, these interviews begin to introduce the parents/family to how we think about behavior (e.g., what happens right before the behavior, and how do others respond to the behavior), and it begins to demonstrate the patterns related to problem behavior (e.g., always occurs at the grocery store, never occurs on the playground). In addition to gathering information from the parents/family, the therapist describes the history of the clinics and research projects and provides an overview on function-based evaluations. These activities further serve the purpose of introducing the parents/family to the idea that behavior is lawful and responsive to the environment.

Step three: During the evaluation

We begin our assessment with an extended preference assessment and then conduct an FA across a number of weeks. Assessment is conducted over a longer period of time during the in-home service because sessions are conducted across consecutive weeks (1 hour evaluation per week) rather than across consecutive days, as is done in Day Treatment. All assessment sessions are conducted by the parents/family with coaching from the therapist. Coaching is conducted in a similar manner to the way it was described for the outpatient and Day Treatment clinics. However, because the therapist is present at each session, the therapist also provides ongoing coaching (e.g., when to give a task instruction, when to provide attention, etc.) and praise throughout the session, rather than waiting until the end of the session to provide corrective feedback. Following the conclusion of the assessment, the therapist reviews the results with the parents/family and answers their questions. Throughout the assessment phase of the in-home service, the goal is for parents/families to understand why their child's problem behavior is occurring and that it can be controlled by altering the environment.

After the FA, a treatment goal, based on the results of the analysis, is established by the parents/family and the therapist. Similar to the other clinics, the parents/family are coached on how to implement the treatment. However, with the in-home service, especially if conducted via telehealth, the therapist only coaches the parents/family vocally, meaning that the therapist does not routinely model how to implement the procedures. For example, during initial treatment sessions when extinction procedures often need to be implemented, the therapist vocally instructs the parents/family to ignore the problem behavior, remove items and people for safety reasons, etc. Similar to the assessment process, treatment procedures are practiced with coaching from the therapist across a number of weeks. As the parents/family demonstrate independence with the treatment procedures, the therapist begins to fade the amount of coaching provided. Typically, coaching and feedback occur at the beginning, middle, and end of all early treatment sessions. Over time, therapist coaching in the middle of sessions reduces, wherein all feedback and praise are provided at the end of treatment sessions. In addition to therapist coached sessions, the parents/family are asked to record treatment practice sessions in the absence of the therapist. When parents complete these recordings, the therapist reviews them for procedural fidelity errors and provides additional coaching, corrective feedback, and praise during the next scheduled evaluation, as needed.

Step four: Follow-up after the evaluation

Given that the in-home service is provided over the course of several months to years, follow-up tends to occur on a weekly basis when the therapist and parents/family meet for the regularly scheduled evaluation. For example, upon discussing with the parents/family about the past week, the parents/family may bring up an issue that occurred in the last week, and the therapist may offer suggestions for addressing the issue. Similar to the outpatient and Day Treatment clinics, when the in-home service is completed, the parents/family are encouraged to contact us via telephone or email when additional concerns or questions arise. Options for follow-up are the same as the other clinics: brief consultation via telephone or email, return visit to one of the in-person clinics, or return in-home visit (typically conducted via telehealth).

Case illustration and benefits of the in-home service

Bruce was a 4-year-old male diagnosed with an autism spectrum disorder, mixed receptive-expressive language disorder, and cognitive developmental delay. He was referred to the in-home telehealth service (Lindgren & Wacker, 2015) by the outpatient clinic for noncompliance (e.g., refusing to follow adult directives, yelling "no" or running away when instructed to complete a task), property destruction (e.g., throwing, hitting, kicking, pushing, biting, scratching objects), and aggression (e.g., hitting, kicking, pushing, biting, scratching, throwing items toward a person), which were shown to be maintained by escape from demands and access to preferred items. Besides the outpatient clinic evaluation, Bruce had not received previous behavioral treatments or related supports. However, his problem behaviors resulted in termination of his enrollment in a daycare center, and his parents were concerned that he would be asked to leave a second daycare because of similar concerns.

Following the initial interview and preference assessment, an FA was conducted in the home via telehealth. Both of Bruce's parents were present for all assessment sessions, with his mother implementing the majority of the procedures, whereas his father assisted. Results of the FA (Table 10.2) showed that Bruce's problem behavior was multiply maintained by escape from task demands and access to attention and preferred items. These results were obtained during 4, 1 hour visits, in which the parents were coached by the therapist on how to conduct the procedures. In addition, the therapist discussed the implications of the observed behavior throughout the assessment with the parents. For example, the therapist pointed out that Bruce calmed down immediately when he received what he wanted (i.e., break from demands, attention after it had been diverted, preferred items when access had been removed).

Before beginning treatment, an extinction baseline was conducted to determine the strength of Bruce's problem behavior. From a clinical perspective, this procedure helps us determine the need for treatment. That is, if problem behavior reduces and remains low within 5 minutes of being under extinction, other treatment components may not be necessary. However, if problem behavior escalates and maintains at similar levels, additional treatment components may be needed to mitigate the side effects

Table 10.2 Summary of Bruce's in-home service (via telehealth) evaluation results

Functional analysis results		
Condition	*Average rate per min*	*Range*
Free play	.03	0−.4
Tangible	.43	0−.8
Attention	.67	.4−1
Escape	.40	0−1
Treatment results		
Extinction	1.53	.2−3.4
Treatment 1	.33	0−2.1
Final 3 sessions	.13	0−.4
% Reduction	92%	
Treatment 2	.33	0−3.2
Final 3 sessions	0	0
% Reduction	100%	

of extinction. From a parent training perspective, this procedure allows us to describe and explain extinction and its side effects. In Bruce's case, extinction bursts were described to his parents, using Bruce's behavior during those sessions as the example. For Bruce's parents, this may have increased their understanding of why and how they had "given in" to Bruce's problem behavior in the past, and how far his behavior would escalate because in the past it had, at least on occasion, produced that reinforcer. These extinction sessions also provided an opportunity for the therapist to begin discussing the importance of treatment fidelity.

Treatment consisted of two phases: (1) FCT for items and activities; and (2) FCT for escape plus a work-break sequence. Results (Table 10.2) showed that Bruce's problem behavior reduced to zero or near zero levels during both Phases, which were conducted entirely by his parents. By having the parents/families conduct all procedures from the beginning of treatment, including ones that a therapist may typically conduct at the onset (i.e., extinction), response acquisition may be further facilitated because the parents/family are required, especially via telehealth, to work through the initial extinction bursts. Their success then may lead to greater motivation to implement the behavioral treatment.

Over the course of several weekly visits, in-home therapists often observe that specific components of the treatment are not consistently implemented, and provide feedback to the parents/family to improve treatment implementation. For example, during one of the final weeks of the Phase 2 treatment for Bruce, the therapist observed an increase in Bruce's problem behavior, as well as a decrease in the parents' fidelity of treatment implementation compared to previous weeks. Following a discussion of fidelity and problem behavior, substantial improvement occurred in Bruce's behavior and his parents' implementation of the treatment (refer to Table 10.3 for a task analysis of how we measure parent treatment fidelity and the

Table 10.3 Treatment fidelity task analysis and results of Bruce's parents' treatment fidelity across selected treatment sessions

	Specific procedural component	Percentage of opportunities correct
1	**Establish MO**—Demand presented	20/20 = 100%
2	Model and physical prompt for demand, if needed	10/10 = 100%
3	**Restrict high preferred tangibles, attention, and other activities** (within 10 seconds) until task completion and appropriate mand completed	13/20 = 65%
4	When task is completed, **present mand opportunity**	17/17 = 100%
5	**Require correct target mand** from child	19/19 = 100%
6	Model and physical prompt for mand, if needed	2/3 = 67%
7	Task ended, provide **praise and high preferred tangibles post mand**	19/19 = 100%
8	Reset MO if target behavior occurs	3/5 = 60%
9	**Ignore all behavior other than target behavior**	11/16 = 69%

Note: MO, motivating operations.

results of Bruce's parents' fidelity across selected treatment sessions). This relationship between fidelity and behavioral improvements may establish parents' motivation for implementing the treatment correctly. The discussion of factors that influence fidelity (in this case, the behavior of other care providers), permits the therapist to address naturally occurring contingencies. In addition, because treatment during the in-home service is conducted within the natural environment, parents may be more successful in generalizing the strategies across various situations. For example, parents/family routinely set up separate areas for "work" and "play" during treatment, and these areas can be used to replicate treatment across various activities and demands within the home. Finally, the in-home service decreases some of the limitations noted for Day Treatment (e.g., travel and lodging expenses, missed school, etc.) because all services are provided directly in the home.

Limitations of the in-home service

Not all families are comfortable inviting other people into their homes, and with our home-based services, substantial time is needed over the course of months or years. Telehealth is relatively new and some families do not have the equipment needed for efficient use of telehealth and others may experience technological problems. Following vocal-only instructions may be difficult for some parents/families, and attempting to keep the child in view of the webcam can be a challenge. Finally, some families live in very tight quarters and there can be problems with what to do with other children or adults living in the home during sessions.

Guidelines and recommendations for training parents and families

Training parents and families on functions of behavior and function-based treatment strategies is important, regardless of the setting in which training occurs, because parents/families are arguably the most important behavior change agents in their child's life. Training should occur at various stages of the assessment and treatment process to increase the likelihood of high fidelity and treatment adherence when services provided by applied behavior analysts are discontinued. We provide three recommendations that have been successful for us in training parents/families.

First, we suggest that applied behavior analysts consider which direct experiences are possible for parents/families, given both the strengths and limitations of the service delivery model. As outlined in Table 10.1, we directly train parents/families at each stage of our clinical process. For example, we introduce the concept of function and correlations between behavior and the environment by having parents/families complete daily behavior records and provide recent ABC examples of the behaviors of concern, whereas the clinic therapist explains how we assess function. After this introduction, we have the parents conduct many of the assessment and treatment procedures, which is followed by additional resources such as handouts designed to support parents/families in implementing treatment in the home.

Second, we suggest that applied behavior analysts consider strategies that may promote generalization and maintenance of the recommended treatment strategies, because these factors may impact parent/family treatment adherence and long-term treatment outcomes. Table 10.4 provides examples of the strategies we use across our clinic services to promote generalization and maintenance.

Third, we suggest that, when choosing between various clinic services, applied behavior analysts determine the clinical purpose of the evaluation and the specific parent/family training goals. Each service delivery model we have described has its own benefits and limitations (see Table 10.5 for a summary). For example, the 90-minute outpatient clinic is quick and may be the best way to introduce the concept of function to parents/families. In contrast, the Day Treatment clinic may be best

Table 10.4 **Examples of techniques to promote or assess for generalization and maintenance across the outpatient, Day Treatment, and in-home services to improve parent/family training during the evaluation**

Step of clinical process	Techniques to promote or assess for generalization and maintenance	Examples from our clinics
During the evaluation	Sufficient exemplars	1. Multiple people (therapists, parent/family) implement the treatment procedures 2. Implement treatment procedures across a variety of stimuli (e.g., tasks, items)
	Programming common stimuli	1. Separate work and play areas so child knows what is expected 2. Incorporate picture cues 3. Signal when reinforcement is available (e.g., timers, picture cards)
	Natural contingencies	1. Fade treatment components toward what typically occurs in the natural environment (e.g., increase demand requirements, increase delays to reinforcement)
	Maintenance	1. Conduct baseline extinction sessions to determine strength of the behavior & whether treatment is needed 2. Return to extinction to determine if behavior persists in the absence of treatment

Table 10.5 Summary of the positive and negative impacts of each service relative to parent/family training

	90-minute outpatient clinic	Day Treatment	In-home service	
			In vivo	*Via telehealth*
Benefits	1. Quick 2. Experience behavior function	1. Extended observations and discussions regarding specific procedures and the rationales for selection 2. Multiple opportunities to successfully implement the treatment procedures 3. Directly address issues and concerns raised by parents 4. Practice generalization 5. Assess and treat multiply controlled behavior	1. Assess and treat in naturally occurring MOs, S^Ds, reinforcement, and routines 2. Multiple opportunities to discuss assessment and treatment implications across weeks 3. Parents/families conduct all procedures with little to no direct therapist involvement (primarily vocal instructions) 4. Travel to evaluations not required	1. Assess and treat in naturally occurring MOs, S^Ds, reinforcement, and routines 2. Multiple opportunities to discuss assessment and treatment implications across weeks 3. Parents/families conduct all procedures without direct therapist involvement (vocal instructions only) 4. Travel to evaluations not required 5. Presence of therapist is virtual 6. Reduced costs
Limitations	1. Often insufficient time to learn and master treatment procedures	1. Often insufficient time to systematically address generalization and maintenance 2. Extended time and travel for parents/families to participate in the service	1. High cost of the therapist's travel 2. Potential discomfort of inviting others into the home 3. Time commitment across months/years 4. Potentially invasive to other people within the home	1. Lack of in-person therapist support when needed 2. Time commitment across months/years 3. Lack of equipment for efficient use 4. Technology problems 5. Difficult to keep child in view of webcam 6. Potentially invasive to other people within the home

Note. MO, motivating operations; S^D, discriminative stimuli.

when the goal is for parents/families to learn how to implement treatment or practice generalization in a highly controlled setting. Finally, the in-home service may be best when looking to implement treatment under naturally occurring conditions. A final consideration when choosing between clinic services is parent/family preference, especially in regards to the continuum of least-to-most intrusive; however, what qualifies as "intrusive" may vary across parents/families and lies within the eye of the beholder.

References

Allen, K. D., & Warzak, W. J. (2000). The problem of parental nonadherence in clinical behavior analysis: Effective treatment is not enough. *Journal of Applied Behavior Analysis, 33*, 373−391. Available from http://dx.doi.org/10.1901/jaba.2000.33-373.

Asmus, J. M., Ringdahl, J. E., Sellers, J. A., Call, N. A., Andelman, M. S., & Wacker, D. P. (2004). Use of a short-term inpatient model to evaluate aberrant behavior: Outcome data summaries from 1996 to 2001. *Journal of Applied Behavior Analysis, 37*, 283−304. Available from http://dx.doi.org/10.1901/jaba.2004.37-283.

Berg, W. K., Wacker, D. P., Harding, J. W., Ganzer, J., & Barretto, A. (2007). An evaluation of multiple dependent variables across distinct classes of antecedent stimuli pre and post functional communication training. *Journal of Early and Intensive Behavior Intervention, 3-4*, 305−333. Available from http://dx.doi.org/10.1037/h0100346.

Bijou, S. W., Peterson, R. F., & Ault, M. H. (1968). A method to integrate descriptive and experimental field studies at the level of data and empirical concepts. *Journal of Applied Behavior Analysis, 1*, 175−191. Available from http://dx.doi.org/10.1901/jaba.1968.1-175.

Carr, E., & Durand, V. (1985). Reducing behavior problems through functional communication training. *Journal of Applied Behavior Analysis, 18*, 111−126. Available from http://dx.doi.org/10.1901/jaba.1985.18-111.

Cooper, L. J., Wacker, D. P., Sasso, G. M., Reimers, T. M., & Donn, L. K. (1990). Using parents as therapists to evaluate appropriate behavior of their children: Application to a tertiary diagnostic clinic. *Journal of Applied Behavior Analysis, 23*, 285−296. Available from http://dx.doi.org/10.1901/jaba.1990.23-285.

DeLeon, I. G., & Iwata, B. A. (1996). Evaluation of a multiple-stimulus presentation format for assessing reinforcer preferences. *Journal of Applied Behavior Analysis, 29*, 519−533. Available from http://dx.doi.org/10.1901/jaba.1996.29-519.

Derby, K. M., Wacker, D. P., Sasso, G., Steege, M., Northup, J., Cigrand, K., & Asmus, J. (1992). Brief functional assessment techniques to evaluate aberrant behavior in an outpatient setting: A summary of 79 cases. *Journal of Applied Behavior Analysis, 25*, 713−721. Available from http://dx.doi.org/10.1901/jaba.1992.25-713.

Fisher, W., Piazza, C. C., Bowman, L. G., Hagopian, L. P., Owens, J. C., & Slevin, I. (1992). A comparison of two approaches for identifying reinforcers for persons with severe and profound disabilities. *Journal of Applied Behavior Analysis, 25*, 491−498. Available from http://dx.doi.org/10.1901/jaba.1992.25-491.

Gardner, A. W., Wacker, D. P., & Boelter, E. W. (2009). An evaluation of the interaction between quality of attention and negative reinforcement with children who display escape-maintained problem behavior. *Journal of Applied Behavior Analysis, 42*, 343−348. Available from http://dx.doi.org/10.1901/jaba.2009.42-343.

Harding, J. W., Wacker, D. P., Berg, W. K., Cooper, L. J., Asmus, J., Mlela, K., & Muller, J. (1999). An analysis of choice making in the assessment of young children with severe behavior problems. *Journal of Applied Behavior Analysis, 32,* 63−82. Available from http://dx.doi.org/10.1901/jaba.1999.32-63.

Harding, J. W., Wacker, D. P., Berg, W. K., Lee, J. F., & Dolezal, D. (2009). Conducting functional communication training in home settings: A case study and recommendations for practitioners. *Behavior Analysis in Practice, 2,* 21−33.

Iwata, B. A., Dorsey, M. F., Slifer, K. J., Bauman, K. E., & Richman, G. S. (1994). Toward a functional analysis of self-injury. *Journal of Applied Behavior Analysis, 27,* 197−209, (Reprinted from *Analysis and Intervention in Developmental Disabilities, 2,* 3-20, 1982). doi: 10.1901/jaba.1994.27-197.

Kurtz, P. F., Fodstad, J. C., Huete, J. M., & Hagopian, L. P. (2013). Caregiver- and staff-conducted functional analysis outcomes: A summary of 52 cases. *Journal of Applied Behavior Analysis, 46,* 738−749. Available from http://dx.doi.org/10.1002/jaba.87.

Laraway, S., Snycerski, S., Michael, J., & Poling, A. (2003). Motivating operations and terms to describe them: Some further refinements. *Journal of Applied Behavior Analysis, 36,* 407−414. Available from http://dx.doi.org/10.1901/jaba.2003.36-407.

Lee, J. F., Schieltz, K. M., Suess, A. N., Wacker, D. P., Romani, P. W., Lindgren, S. D., & Padilla Dalmau, Y. C. (2015). Guidelines for developing telehealth services and troubleshooting problems with telehealth technology when coaching parents to conduct functional analyses and functional communication training in their homes. *Behavior Analysis in Practice, 8,* 190−200. Available from http://dx.doi.org/10.1007/s40617-014-0031-2.

Lindgren, S., & Wacker, D. (2015). *Comparing behavioral assessments using telehealth for children with autism.* Washington, DC: Department of Health and Human Services, National Institute of Mental Health.

Lindgren, S., Wacker, D., Suess, A., Schieltz, K., Pelzel, K., Kopelman, T., & Waldron, D. (2016). Telehealth and autism: Treating challenging behavior at lower cost. *Pediatrics, 137,* S167−S175. Available from http://dx.doi.org/10.1542/pedds.2015-2851O.

Michael, J. (1982). Distinguishing between discriminative and motivational functions of stimuli. *Journal of the Experimental Analysis of Behavior, 37,* 149−155. Available from http://dx.doi.org/10.1901/jeab.1982.37-149.

Nevin, J., & Wacker, D. (2013). Response strength and persistenceIn G. J. Madden, W. V. Dube, T. D. Hackenberg, G. P. Hanley, & K. A. Lattal (Eds.), APA handbook of behavior analysis *(Translating principles into practice* (2, pp. 109−128). Washington: American Psychological Association. Available from http://dx.doi.org/10.1037/13938-005.

Northup, J., Wacker, D., Sasso, G., Steege, M., Cigrand, K., Cook, J., & DeRaad, A. (1991). A brief functional analysis of aggressive and alternative behavior in an outclinic setting. *Journal of Applied Behavior Analysis, 24,* 509−522. Available from http://dx.doi.org/10.1901/jaba.1991.24-509.

Reimers, T. M., Wacker, D. P., Cooper, L. J., & DeRaad, A. O. (1992). Acceptability of behavioral treatments for children: Analog and naturalistic evaluations by parents. *School Psychology Review, 21,* 628−643.

Ringdahl, J. E., & Sellers, J. A. (2000). The effects of different adults as therapists during functional analyses. *Journal of Applied Behavior Analysis, 33,* 247−250. Available from http://dx.doi.org/10.1901/jaba.2000.33-247.

Roane, H. S., Vollmer, T. R., Ringdahl, J. E., & Marcus, B. A. (1998). Evaluation of a brief stimulus preference assessment. *Journal of Applied Behavior Analysis, 31,* 605−620. Available from http://dx.doi.org/10.1901/jaba.1998.31-605.

Schlichenmeyer, K. J., Roscoe, E. M., Rooker, G. W., Wheeler, E. E., & Dube, W. V. (2013). Idiosyncratic variables that affect functional analysis outcomes: A review (2001–2010). *Journal of Applied Behavior Analysis*, *46*, 339–348. Available from http://dx.doi.org/10.1002/jaba.12.

Stokes, T., & Baer, D. (1977). An implicit technology of generalization. *Journal of Applied Behavior Analysis*, *10*, 349–367. Available from http://dx.doi.org/10.1901/jaba.1977.10-349.

St. Peter Pipkin, C., Vollmer, T. R., & Sloman, K. N. (2010). Effects of treatment integrity failures during differential reinforcement of alternative behavior: A translational model. *Journal of Applied Behavior Analysis*, *43*, 47–70. Available from http://dx.doi.org/10.1901/jaba.2010.43-47.

Suess, A. N., Kopelman, T. G., Wacker, D. P., Lindgren, S. D., Lee, J. F., Romani, P. W., & Schieltz, K. M. (2014a). Orienting caregivers to conduct in-home functional analyses via telehealth. *Association of Professional Behavior Analysts Reporter, 50.*

Suess, A. N., Romani, P. W., Wacker, D. P., Dyson, S. M., Kuhle, J. L., Lee, J. F., & Waldron, D. B. (2014b). Evaluating the treatment fidelity of parents who conduct in-home functional communication training with coaching via telehealth. *Journal of Behavioral Education*, *23*, 34–59. Available from http://dx.doi.org/10.1007/s10864-013-9183-3.

Thomason-Sassi, J. L., Iwata, B. A., & Fritz, J. N. (2013). Therapist and setting influences on functional analysis outcomes. *Journal of Applied Behavior Analysis*, *46*, 79–87. Available from http://dx.doi.org/10.1002/jaba.28.

Volkert, V. M., Lerman, D. C., Call, N. A., & Trosclair-Lasserre, N. (2009). An evaluation of resurgence during treatment with functional communication training. *Journal of Applied Behavior Analysis*, *42*, 145–160. Available from http://dx.doi.org/10.1901/jaba.2009.42-145.

Wacker, D. P., & Berg, W. K. (1992). *Inducing reciprocal parent/child interactions*. Washington, DC: Department of Health and Human Services, National Institute of Child Health and Human Development.

Wacker, D. P., Berg, W. K., Bassingthwaite, B. J., Kopelman, T. G., Schieltz, K. M., Padilla Dalmau, Y. C., & Lee, J. F. (2015). Conducting functional analyses of behavior. In R. L. DePry, F. Brown, & J. Anderson (Eds.), *Individual positive behavior supports: A standards-based guide to practices in school and community-based settings* (pp. 295–313). Baltimore, MD: Paul H. Brookes..

Wacker, D. P., Berg, W. K., Cooper, L. J., Derby, K. M., Steege, M. W., Northup, J., & Sasso, G. (1994). The impact of functional analysis methodology on outpatient clinic services. *Journal of Applied Behavior Analysis*, *27*, 405–407. Available from http://dx. doi.org/10.1901/jaba.1994.27-405.

Wacker, D. P., Berg, W. K., & Harding, J. W. (1996). *Promoting stimulus generalization with young children*. Washington, DC: Department of Health and Human Services, National Institute of Child Health and Human Development.

Wacker, D. P., Berg, W. K., & Harding, J. W. (2000). *Functional communication training augmented with choices*. Washington, DC: Department of Health and Human Services, National Institute of Child Health and Human Development.

Wacker, D. P., Berg, W. K., & Harding, J. W. (2002). Replacing socially unacceptable behavior with acceptable communication responses. In J. Reichle, D. R. Beukelman, & J. C. Light (Eds.), *Exemplary practices for beginning communicators: Implications for AAC* (pp. 97–121). Baltimore, MD: Paul H. Brookes Publishing Co.

Wacker, D. P., Berg, W. K., & Harding, J. W. (2004). *Maintenance effects of functional communication training.* Washington, DC: Department of Health and Human Services, National Institute of Child and Human Development.

Wacker, D., Berg, W., Harding, J., & Cooper-Brown, L. (2004). Use of brief experimental analyses in outpatient clinic and home settings. *Journal of Behavioral Education, 13,* 213−226. Available from http://dx.doi.org/10.1023/B:JOBE.0000044732.42711.f5.

Wacker, D. P., Berg, W. K., Harding, J. W., Derby, K. M., Asmus, J. M., & Healy, A. (1998). Evaluation and long-term treatment of aberrant behavior displayed by young children with disabilities. *Journal of Developmental and Behavioral Pediatrics, 19,* 260−266. Available from http://dx.doi.org/10.1007/s10882-012-9314-0.

Wacker, D. P., Berg, W. K., Schieltz, K. M., Romani, P. W., & Padilla Dalmau, Y. C. (2013). Outpatient units. In D. D. Reed, F. D. DiGennaro-Reed, & J. K. Luiselli (Eds.), *Handbook of crisis intervention and developmental disabilities* (pp. 409−422). New York, NY: Springer..

Wacker, D. P., Harding, J. H., Berg, W. K., Lee, J. F., Schieltz, K. M., Padilla, Y. C., & Shahan, T. A. (2011). An evaluation of persistence of treatment effects during long-term treatment of destructive behavior. *Journal of the Experimental Analysis of Behavior, 96,* 261−282. Available from http://dx.doi.org/10.1901/jeab.2011.96-261.

Wacker, D. P., Lee, J. F., Padilla Dalmau, Y. C., Kopelman, T. G., Lindgren, S. D., Kuhle, J., & Waldron, D. B. (2013a). Conducting functional communication training via telehealth to reduce the problem behavior of young children with autism. *Journal of Developmental and Physical Disabilities, 25,* 35−48. Available from http://dx.doi.org/10.1007/s10882-012-9314-0.

Wacker, D. P., Lee, J. F., Padilla Dalmau, Y. C., Kopelman, T. G., Lindgren, S. D., Kuhle, J., & Waldron, D. B. (2013b). Conducting functional analyses of problem behavior via telehealth. *Journal of Applied Behavior Analysis, 46,* 31−46. Available from http://dx.doi.org/10.1002/jaba.29.

Wacker, D.P., Schieltz, K.M., Berg, W.K., Harding, J.W., Padilla Dalmau, Y.C., & Lee, J.F. (2017). The long-term effects of functional communication training conducted in young children's home settings. *Education & Treatment of Children, 40,* 43−56.

Wacker, D. P., Schieltz, K. M., & Romani, P. W. (2015). Brief experimental analyses of problem behavior in a pediatric outpatient clinic. In H. S. Roane, J. E. Ringdahl, & T. S. Falcomata (Eds.), *Clinical and organizational applications of applied behavior analysis* (pp. 151−177). Amsterdam: Elsevier Inc.

Wacker, D. P., Schieltz, K. M., Suess, A. N., Romani, P. W., Padilla Dalmau, Y. C., Kopelman, T. G., & Lindgren, S. D. (2016). Telehealth. In N. N. Singh (Ed.), *Handbook of evidence-based practices in intellectual and developmental disabilities* (pp. 585−613). Switzerland: Springer International Publishing.

Wacker, D. P., & Steege, M. W. (1993). Providing outclinic services: Evaluating treatment and social validity. In R. Van Houten, & S. Axelrod (Eds.), *Behavior analysis and treatment* (pp. 297−319). New York: Plenum Publishing.

Consultation Practices: Organizations

11

Heather M. McGee
Western Michigan University, Kalamazoo, MI, United States

Introduction to organizational behavior management and relevance for behavioral practitioners

Applied behavior analysis (ABA) is concerned with the prediction and control of behaviors that are considered *socially important* (Bailey & Burch, 2002). As ABA is concerned with socially important behaviors, each individual subfield of ABA, or area of application, strives to improve socially important behaviors *relevant to the context of that subfield*. Practitioners of ABA, then, have experience and expertise in the science of behavior as applied to specific types of clients and settings. In fact, many ABA practitioners are even certified or licensed as experts in their area (s) of application. The science of behavior is consistent across areas of application. When viewed this way, the various subfields of ABA are more similar than dissimilar. We all strive toward the same goal: Improving performance by altering environmental variables that affect socially important behaviors.

While the science is consistent across application areas, the tools and techniques used to change behavior vary area to area, as do the specific career-related skills or competencies required to be successful. For example, the skills required to implement an intervention with a child diagnosed on the autism spectrum are not the same as those required to analyze and improve workplace safety, though both sets of skills require an understanding of the science of behavior to be performed successfully. Even within the same area, different jobs require different knowledge and skill sets. Behavior analysts in academia know that teaching content courses requires knowledge and skills in both the content (e.g., behavior analysis and developmental disabilities) and teaching (behavior analytic instructional design). When an ABA practitioner moves from a role that is primarily client-facing (e.g., behavior technician) to a role that is primarily staff-facing (e.g., supervisor, director), different tools, techniques, and skills are required for successful performance. These skills fall under the area of organizational behavior management (OBM).

OBM is the field of study concerned with the performance of people at work. Hall (1980) defined the field of OBM as consisting of "the development and evaluation of performance improvement procedures which are based on the principles of behavior discovered through the science of behavior analysis" (p. 145). Hall further stated that the goal of the field of OBM is to "establish a technology of broad-scale performance improvement and organizational change so that employees will be more productive and happy, and so that our organizations and institutions

Applied Behavior Analysis Advanced Guidebook. DOI: http://dx.doi.org/10.1016/B978-0-12-811122-2.00011-5

will be more effective and efficient in achieving their goals" (p. 145). Sometimes, these performance improvement initiatives involve identifying and manipulating the antecedents and consequences directly associated with the targeted behaviors. This aspect of OBM is referred to as performance management (PM). PM interventions may involve setting goals, providing feedback and reinforcement, employing the use of job aids, etc. (Daniels & Bailey, 2014).

While PM interventions alone can (and do) impact individual and group workplace performance, it is often necessary to additionally analyze and subsequently implement more molar changes within the organization. This aspect of OBM is referred to as behavioral systems analysis (BSA). BSA involves analyzing organizational performance at multiple levels. The most common BSA models involve analyzing performance at three levels (organization, process, performer), though some practitioners have proposed as many as six levels of analysis (Gilbert, 1978; Malott, 2003; Rummler & Brache, 1995; Rummler, 2004). The goals of each level of analysis and improvement in a three-level approach are depicted in Table 11.1.

Organizational success is a function of the performance of individuals within that organization. That said, employees are only as good as the systems within which they work. As Rummler and Brache (1995) stated, "If you pit a good performer against a bad system, the system will win almost every time" (p. 13). The combination of contingency and system design differentiates BSA from PM, though it should be noted that the performer/job level of BSA *is* PM.

Behavior analysts from all ABA subfields could benefit from having at least a basic OBM repertoire. Whether you work for a private or public, for profit or not-for-profit organization, understanding how organizations work and how they can be improved is a desirable skill. For example, as the number of individuals diagnosed on the autism spectrum increases, so does the demand for services, particularly ABA. As a result, the number and size of ABA organizations has and continues to increase rather rapidly. Organizational leaders need to know how to adapt their organizations to the changing demands and needs of its consumers and employees.

Table 11.1 **The three-level approach and goals**

Performance level	Goal (understand and improve)
Organization	• Environment in which the organization operates • Necessary organizational strategies to adapt to changes in that environment • How the organization is structured to support the strategies employed
Process	• Inputs and outputs between the various departments or functions of the organization • Workflow through which inputs are converted into outputs
Job/Performer	• Job characteristics • Antecedents, behaviors, and consequences of the individuals who work within the system

Concerns for capacity, training, and customer satisfaction should be addressed early and often. Many of these same organizations are either currently providing or planning to provide Board Certified Behavior Analyst (BCBA) supervision for their employees. The most common way that organizations implement this is to add supervision to a current certified employee's job responsibilities (often without removing any other responsibilities or reducing caseload). This can result in a decrease in employee satisfaction, a decrease in quality of service (if the employee is now working over capacity), and low-quality supervision. Low-quality supervision is especially likely if the employee does not have the required instructional design/training skill set, as training is an essential component of supervision as laid out in the Behavior Analyst Certification Board® (2012). A working knowledge of OBM can help practitioners identify potential negative effects like these before they become problems (before major changes are implemented within the organization).

Past and current status of practitioner training in OBM

The level of OBM training you need as a practitioner is dependent upon the work you intend to do once the training is complete. For example, if you would like to be an OBM consultant, you would need much more comprehensive training than if you would like to be a clinical director managing the performance of your employees. The consultant needs to be well versed in evidence-based performance analysis and improvement areas across levels of the organization. The director, however, should know enough OBM to provide excellent PM (supervision) and training, as well as to analyze and improve minor organizational issues. For larger organizational issues, the director should know to bring in an OBM professional.

If you are interested in developing OBM knowledge and/or skills, you have more options now than ever before. This is thanks, in part, to the advancement of online training, but also to the increase in the demand for OBM learning opportunities for practitioners without a formal OBM education (mostly other behavior analysts), and increasing need for performance improvement in behavior analytic organizations and agencies. Academically speaking, the current options are as follows: ABA graduate programs that include some OBM coursework, OBM certificate programs, OBM master's programs, or OBM doctorate programs. As stated earlier, the level of training sought should be aligned with career goals. Academically, the lowest level of training would likely be through an ABA graduate program that includes some OBM coursework. Of course, the more OBM courses offered, the higher the level of OBM training. A review of the Association for Behavior Analysis International (ABAI)-accredited graduate programs shows that out of 22 accredited master's degree programs, 9 offer zero OBM courses as either requirements or electives, 8 offer one OBM course, 2 offer 2 courses, and 1 offers 5 courses. It should be pointed out that two schools—Florida Institute of Technology (FIT) and Western Michigan University (WMU)—offer standalone OBM programs. Both schools' programs are "true" OBM—not a blend of behavioral and nonbehavioral approaches to performance improvement, but only FIT's OBM and ABA/OBM programs are accredited by ABAI. The ABA program at FIT is one of the two programs that offers two OBM courses as either requirements or electives and the ABA program at WMU is the program that offers five OBM courses as either requirements or electives. This is important to note because the existence of the standalone OBM programs provide the non-OBM programs at these schools with the opportunity to offer higher numbers of OBM courses. At the doctoral level, of the 11 ABAI accredited degree programs, 5 offer zero OBM courses as either requirements or electives, 3 offer 1 OBM course, and 1 offers 2 courses. The ABA doctoral program at FIT offers three courses, and again it is worth pointing out that FIT also has standalone OBM programs at the master's level, so it is possible that students would be allowed take additional OBM courses as electives, if desired. Finally, the ABA doctoral program at WMU offers seven courses, but WMU also offers a standalone OBM doctoral program (not accredited by ABAI) which provides the ABA program with OBM course choices for its students.

   If you are interested in working primarily in OBM, whether as an academic, an internal or external consultant, an instructional designer or training expert, a behavior-based safety expert, or any other practice that focuses on workplace performance improvement, a graduate-level OBM program is recommended. There are fewer graduate programs in OBM than there are in behavior analysis. WMU and FIT each offer master's degrees in OBM (FIT also offers a joint ABA/OBM master's degree) WMU also offers a doctoral OBM program. In addition, some traditional Industrial/Organizational (I/O) Psychology programs offer courses in OBM. For example, the I/O Psychology Track of the Master of Arts in Psychological Science program at University of Minnesota, Duluth; the I/O Psychology and Human Resource Management program at Appalachian State University; and the I/O Psychology program at Central Michigan University offer OBM courses, taught by OBM professionals, in addition to more traditional I/O coursework.

   Not all practitioners need or want to develop OBM skills in a traditional academic setting. If you fall into this category, a certificate program offers an opportunity to develop a basic OBM repertoire, and typically involve hands-on practice. Aubrey Daniels International (consulting firm) and FIT (university) both offer OBM certificate programs. In addition, the OBM Network has recently developed an OBM Mentorship Program. Current OBM Network members can volunteer to serve as mentors to practitioners and students interested in learning how to apply OBM in their current or future practice.

   Finally, you can find a variety of OBM knowledge and skill building opportunities through conferences and workshops. The annual ABAI conference, the biennial OBM Network conference, as well as a variety of performance improvement-related nonbehavioral conferences (e.g., the International Society for Performance Improvement, the Association for Talent Development) offer OBM talks and workshops covering recent OBM research, current best practices, and tools for experts and novices alike.

OBM research base and implications for practice

There is a wealth of research supporting OBM tools and techniques. In fact, there is a journal dedicated exclusively to research in OBM—the *Journal of Organizational Behavior Management* (*JOBM*). First published in 1977, *JOBM* has primarily published research falling under the umbrella of PM. Feedback, goal setting, monetary and nonmonetary incentives, clarification of performance expectations, performance-based training, BBS, and more have been empirically validated in a wide variety of settings. Readers are encouraged to read Dickinson's (2001) paper, *The Historical Roots of OBM in the Private Sector*, Redmon and Agnew's (1991) book chapter, *Organizational Behavioral Analysis in the United States: A View from the Private Sector*, and Redmon and Wilk's (1991) book chapter, *Organizational Behavioral Analysis in The United States: Public Sector Organizations*, for thorough reviews of OBM research in both public and private sector organizations.

While BSA research is less common, there have been several studies at each of the three levels of performance. At the organization level, Frederiksen, Riley, and Myers (1985) implemented change in the organizational structure of an insurance agency in addition to forming self-managed work teams in order to address challenges in automating key business functions and creating new products for a changing marketplace. In addition, Strouse, Carrol-Hernandez, Sherman, and Sheldon (2004) used a systems-based approach to improving the scheduling system of a human service (HS) program. Multiple studies have demonstrated improved performance through changes at the process level. These changes have included reducing product preparation error rates in a retail furniture distribution warehouse (Berglund & Ludwig, 2009), implementing an automation process change that resulted in savings of $220,000 for two auto parts distribution centers (Goomas, 2010), implementing a district-wide process change for submission of Medicaid billing forms for services rendered by school psychologists that resulted in increases of approximately $3000 in billing per 2 weeks (Hybza, Stokes, Hayman, & Schatzberg; 2013), and others. Readers are encouraged to read Sigurdsson and McGee's (2015) book chapter, *Organizational Behavior Management: Systems Analysis*, for detailed reviews of these studies. As the performer level involves PM changes, readers are encouraged to review the materials described earlier.

There have been considerably fewer research studies demonstrating the effectiveness of OBM assessment tools. While the previously described studies demonstrate the efficacy of PM and BSA interventions, little research has attempted to validate the OBM assessment tools and approaches used to indicate the most appropriate intervention or interventions for a given problem or set of problems. Johnson, Casella, McGee, and Lee (2014) reviewed *JOBM*, the flagship journal of OBM, to determine whether validation research exists for two common assessment approaches: Austin's (2000) Performance Diagnostic Checklist (PDC) and its related HS version, the PDC-HSs; and BSA. It should be noted that in the context of this review, BSA was investigated from an assessment perspective—studies involving systems-level interventions, but without explicit comparison of the preintervention assessment to either a control or alternative condition, were not considered to provide empirical validation of BSA. Their results identified eight *JOBM* publications that examined the PDC or PDC-HS, and 31 that examined BSA. Of these, one PDC and 22 BSA articles were theoretical or conceptual in nature, meaning they "were based purely at the level of discussion or theory" (p. 107). Seven PDC and eight BSA publications provided minimal empirical data, meaning they "presented empirical evidence (i.e., actually used BSA or the PDC) but utilized designs that prevented the establishment of cause-and-effect relations regarding enhancements to the interventions resulting from a particular preintervention diagnostic tool" (p. 109). Only one BSA and zero PDC publications provided more than minimal empirical data. Sasson, Alvero, and Austin (2006) utilized a 2×2 experimental design to compare two different types of process variables and intervention and no intervention conditions, thus resulting in Johnson et al. (2014) labeling this as both a comparison with a control (compared interventions selected through BSA to a no intervention condition) and a comparison with an alternative (compared interventions selected through BSA to active interventions) selected by another type of analysis (or no prior analysis) research study.

Johnson et al. (2014) discussed several reasons for the lack of empirical research on assessment in OBM. One such reason is that these assessments are being employed in complex workplace environments, where tight experimental control is often difficult if not impossible. Laboratory studies would provide the experimental control, but most likely at the expense of ecological validity. In other words, once you remove the ongoing environmental changes inherent to the workplace, you have removed a core aspect of what makes a workplace a workplace. This simplification of the environment, which provides experimental control, might lead to results that are not representative of the results you would achieve in the field.

Another issue that researchers face when trying to compare or validate OBM assessment tools is that the implementation of an assessment itself alters the environment. As OBM assessments involve informant assessment, if a researcher wanted to compare the effects of two different types of assessments (e.g., the PDC vs BSA), the researcher–employee interactions during the first assessment could influence the results of the second assessment, if the same employees are involved in both. Interviewing different individuals within the same organizational site, or using different sites altogether would ameliorate this issue. However, there is no guarantee that the different individuals would have the same level of knowledge or skill, even if they operate at the same level in the organizational hierarchy. Similarly, different sites might experience different performance issues, even if they produce the same products or services.

Finally, cost and time involvement, combined with the previously mentioned control concerns, may deter researchers and organizational clients from experimentally evaluating performance assessments. This is especially likely for BSA, which can take weeks or months to conduct (Rummler, 2004). Organizations are not likely to allow for a complete assessment prior to the implementation of at least one intervention targeting performance improvement. In addition, BSA practitioners are unlikely to risk upsetting and potentially losing a client for the sake of science.

It is not all bad news for OBM assessment, however. Researchers at WMU are currently conducting two different assessment validation studies. One is a comparison of two different PM-based assessments, Austin's (2000) PDC and Mager's (1997) Performance Flowchart, using simulated performance scenarios. The other is a comparison of the PDC and BSA in two similar applied settings. It is hoped that these studies will not only provide insight into the validity of various OBM assessments, but also that they will provide a roadmap for other researchers interested in this topic.

OBM consultation practice guidelines, procedures, and implementation recommendations

As previously stated, practitioners can employ OBM within a wide range of jobs (supervisor, academic, consultant, trainer, etc.). This section will focus on the OBM consultant, and will describe a process for providing that consultation. But first, it is important to differentiate two different types of consultant: the internal consultant and the external consultant.

Internal versus external consultants

The internal consultant holds a performance-improvement-related position within an organization and is charged with responding to requests for performance analysis and improvement from throughout that organization. The external consultant provides contracted services to external organizational clients. In other words, organizational clients hire external consultants to come into their organizations to provide performance analysis and improvement services, but the consultants are not internal employees of the organization.

These differences have practical implications. Rummler (2004) identified several unique challenges faced by internal consultants. One of these challenges is that, because internal consultants are typically housed within functions named for specific solutions (e.g., training, organizational development, process improvement), their services are often requested when the internal client seeking help has already decided that this specific solution is warranted. Unfortunately, this determination is sometimes made without any formal (or even informal) assessment of the perceived issue. The external consultant is usually seen as providing a broader range of services, though marketing specific solutions could result in similar pigeon-holing.

Compounding the solution-specific issue for the internal consultant is the fact that she may face push back if she suggests the requestor allow her to conduct a performance assessment before providing recommendations for a solution. In some cases, the organizational politics may even result in the internal consultant perceiving that she must provide the requested solution, *or else*. At best, the *or else* might mean loss of an internal client, at worst loss of the internal consultant's job. In addition, internal consultants often face time and budget constraints that prevent them from conducting thorough performance assessments prior to the implementation of a performance improvement solution.

These issues and others may prevent the internal consultant from conducting formal or informal performance assessments prior to identifying and implementing solutions, at least some of the time. Rummler's (2004) recommendations for addressing these concerns involve continually educating internal clients on the value of understanding the causes of a problem before implementing solutions, picking your battles (i.e., do not try to make every request into a full systems analysis and improvement project), and testing requests for solutions by gently but firmly asking requestors to back up solution requests with data that demonstrates a problem actually exists and the requested solution would likely have a positive impact. This advice is valuable for external consultants as well, but external consultants are also in a much better position to avoid these issues altogether in that they can simply refuse a request for services as long as they haven't already signed a contract.

The consultation process

Specific practices in consultation will differ organization to organization, consultant to consultant. That said that most OBM consultants follow some variation of a standard consultation process based in a general performance analysis and improvement model. For example, Malott's (1974) analyze, specify, design, implement, evaluate, and recycle (ASDIER) process is similar to Rummler's (2004) four-phase Results Improvement Process (desired results determined and project defined; barriers determined and changes specified; changes designed, developed, and implemented; and results evaluated and maintained or improved). Both of these models are similar to the analyze, design, develop, implement, evaluate (ADDIE) model (Molenda, Pershing, & Reigeluth, 1996) used in instructional design—both from a behavioral and nonbehavioral perspective, as well as the behavioral-consultative problem solving model (problem identification, problem analysis, intervention, and evaluation) used in school psychology (Kratochwill & Bergan, 1978). If you take on the role of internal or external OBM consultant in your career, be sure that the model you choose includes defining and analyzing the performance issue(s); designing and developing solutions based on the results of your analysis; implementing those solutions, and evaluating whether the solutions were, in fact, effective. Skipping steps can result in nondata-driven decisions around causes of and solutions for performance problems.

Table 11.2 presents a basic OBM consultation process, along with the specific phases and phase outputs of the process. It should be noted that the number of phases in which the consultant will be directly involved may vary. For example, one client might ask a consultant to take an active role in all five phases, while another might ask the consultant to complete the first two phases, ending with a list of recommendations that the client can then use to internally design and develop solutions, implement solutions, and program for maintenance. In addition, the level of consultant direct involvement, referred to by Rummler (2004) as engagement models, in any consultation project may vary. For example, the client may ask the

Table 11.2 **OBM consultation phases and outputs**

Consultation phase	Outputs
1. Respond to request for services	• Project defined and scoped • Results to be Impacted determined • Project goals and deliverables outlined • Project proposal developed • Project approved/contract signed
2. Analyze performance	• Data collected • Assessment tools completed • Diagnostics conducted • Findings validated • Initial recommendations made
3. Design and develop solutions	• Design team established/resources secured • Solutions designed • Solutions developed/built • Solutions piloted • Performance change evaluated • Revisions made as necessary
4. Implement solutions	• Organization prepared • Solutions implemented • Performance change evaluated • Revisions made as necessary
5. Program for maintenance	• Maintenance team established • Performance supports implemented

consultant to conduct the majority of work throughout the phases, with input from individuals within the organization (i.e., do it for us); or to work hand-in-hand with an internal team or teams (i.e., do it with us); or to serve only as facilitator or coach for an internal team or teams completing the process (i.e., let us do it). The engagement model can even vary across phases of a consultation project. For example, the first two phases might take a "do it with us" approach, while the remaining three phases might take a "let us do it" approach.

Phase 1: Respond to requests for services

In the first phase, the consultant works with the organizational client to define and scope the project, determine the results to be impacted, outline project goals and deliverables, develop a project proposal, and obtain project approval/sign the contract. These steps set the stage for the remaining phases, so clarity and agreement are paramount. For external consultants, the outputs produced in the first four steps may determine whether you agree to work with the client (sign the contract). For example, clients may insist that deliverables include interventions that are not evidence based, or that the project be scoped larger or smaller than you are comfortable with. As an external consultant, you can walk away from such a project provided you have not already signed the contract. Internal consultants might not have this luxury, so one of your goals should be to ensure that the outputs of the first four steps do not outline a project that would violate your professional ethics (providing interventions that are not evidence-based) or that may harm your professional reputation in the long run (scoping a project in a way that you are confident will not solve the issues that resulted in the request for service). This can require a fair amount of discussion and delicacy, especially in politically charged organizations.

Step 1: Define and scope the project

The first step of consultation is to define and scope the project. To do this, you will need to determine what is driving the request for services. Understanding the driver (s) of the request will help you and the client determine the appropriate project scope. It can be helpful to categorize requests into the following three categories: (1) the client wants to understand something, (2) the client wants to fix something, or (3) the client wants to initiate something.

Sometimes clients will request services because they believe there are likely opportunities to improve performance within their organization, but they are not sure where those opportunities lie. Or they may have experienced recent large-scale change (accelerated growth, merger, acquisition, addition of new product or service line, etc.) and they are not sure how those changes impact performance throughout the organization. In these situations, the requests fall under the category of "the client wants to understand something." Depending on how broad the "something" is that the organizational client wants to understand, your project might involve all three levels of analysis (organization, process, performer), or just one or two levels of analysis. Imagine a scenario in which a client requests your services because of a recent merger with another organization. This is a major organizational change, with far reaching impacts, so a full, three-level analysis would be warranted. Now imagine a scenario where a client requests your services because he is unsure whether his supervisees' performance expectations are clear. This would require a performer-level analysis, and possibly a process-level analysis, but it would be unlikely that an organization-level analysis would be warranted. A benefit of "understand something" requests is that they typically are not solution-specific, giving you the opportunity to conduct a proper analysis. Depending on the nature of an "understand" request, you will either conduct a general systems analysis, where you are analyzing the organization to achieve a general understanding of system, or a specific systems analysis, where you are analyzing the organization through the lens of a recent change to achieve a specific understanding of the impact of that change on the system.

Other times, clients will request your services because they believe that something is "broken" within the system. These requests fall under the category of "the client wants to fix something." These requests can come after a large-scale change such as those mentioned previously if performance is suffering (or perceived to be suffering) postchange. They can also come when systems are not properly monitored and managed over time, so that performance is not sufficiently supported. As with the previous category, depending on how broad the "something" is that the organizational client wants to fix, your project might involve all three levels of analysis, or just one or two. The analysis itself should be conducted through the lens of the performance issue that prompted the request (once the issue has been validated).

Requests that fall under this category need to be handled carefully in order to avoid potential traps of steering the project in the wrong direction. One of those traps presents itself when the "something" the clients believe to be broken is an employee or group of employees. Behavior analysts understand that behavior is a function of its environment, so this should be an easy pitfall to avoid, but it is important to realize that the clients will almost never use language as simple as "we believe our employees are broken." Instead, they will describe the employees' perceived lack of professionalism, difficulties in interpersonal communications, or personality conflicts. The key to avoiding falling into this trap is to ask plenty of questions such as:

- What leads you to say that?
- How is that impacting productivity/results?
- What are they doing that you do not want them to do?
- What would you like them to do that they are not doing?

The answers to these questions can help to steer the conversation away from person blaming and toward the need to understand the environmental/system variables that are negatively impacting performance.

Another potential trap is that clients might tell you that they already know what is broken and what they think should be done to fix it. Here your biggest challenge will be to work with the client to develop a project plan or proposal that allows for an analysis to either validate the clients' beliefs about the root causes of the problem or, if it turns out the clients were wrong, identify the true root causes. The same questions posed previously can help with this, along with some additional questions:

- How would the solution you are suggesting address the issue?
- What would you measure to be sure performance improved?
- Would you be okay with me conducting an analysis to validate what you have shared with me today/see the problem for myself so I can better understand it?

A third category of request is "the client wants to initiate something." Requests that fall under this category can appear similar to those discussed in the "understand something" category (accelerated growth, merger, acquisition, addition of new product or service line, etc.), but in this case the large-scale change has not yet occurred. Though these requests can come for small-scale changes, it is less common and, therefore, you should plan to conduct a full, three-level analysis through the lens of the initiative.

Once you have defined the project, you will have partially determined scope. But you will still need to determine which phases of the consultation process the clients would like you to be directly involved with, as well as which engagement model or combination of engagement models they (and you) are comfortable with.

Step 2: Determine the results to be impacted

With the overall project defined and scoped, your next step is to determine the specific results to be impacted. Create an initial project proposal based on the information gathered in first step (it is likely that you will have already identified some potential results to be impacted). Meet with the clients and ask them to validate the information in that proposal. Make changes as necessary until both parties agree. For each performance level you will analyze, ask the clients how they measure success. For example, imagine you are going to conduct an analysis on an ABA autism service agency's proposed initiative to accept 10 more clients in the next year. The agency currently has a total of 12 clients. This request falls under the category of "the client wants to initiate something" and would be a large-scale change (almost doubling the number of clients served). Therefore, this would require a three-level analysis. Your goal in this step is to work with the clients to determine which overall business results, functional performance results (for both clinical and administrative functions), relevant process performance results (clinical service, intake, billing, etc.), and job results are most likely to be impacted by the change, in which direction (get better or worse) the impact is likely to be seen, and how the systems analysis project is expected to either bolster or mitigate those results.

Step 3: Outline project goals and deliverables

At this point, you will have defined and scoped the project and determined the specific results to be impacted by the project. Your next step is to use that information to set project goals and identify your deliverables. Include what you will produce for the client, milestones and deadlines to be achieved, and specific goals for the results identified in the previous step. When determining goals, remember that there are multiple measurement dimensions that can be employed to determine whether performance is successful or not. The four most common are quality, quantity, timeliness, and cost. Be aware that focusing on only one dimension can result in performance deteriorating along the other dimensions. Table 11.3 provides a list of deliverables for each level of analysis and each phase of the consultation process.

Step 4: Develop a project proposal

The fourth step is to develop a project proposal. Essentially, you are pulling the information gathered in the previous steps together into a single document, with a couple of additions, to provide to the final decision maker at the organization. Your project plan should also include (1) who will be involved in the project and in what roles, (2) the resources (people, materials, money, technology, access) required for a successful project, and (3) the budget for the project. For the budget, you will need to determine your own consulting fees in addition to any other direct and indirect costs associated with the project.

When determining your consulting fees, you should consider several factors: (1) whether you will charge by analysis levels involved, scope of project, engagement model, deliverables, or by hourly or daily rate; (2) your level of experience and reputation in the field (the more experienced and the better your reputation, the more you can reasonably charge); (3) travel costs; and (4) billable versus nonbillable

Table 11.3 OBM consultation phases and deliverables

Consultation phase	Deliverables
1. Respond to request for services	• Project proposal • Signed contract
2a. Analyze performance— organization level	• Organizational system map—current state • Relationship map—current state • Summary report of organization-level analysis results and recommendations
2b. Analyze performance—process level	• Process map(s)—current state • Summary report of process-level analysis results and recommendations
2c. Analyze performance—job/ performer level	• Job design, performance support, and contingency analysis—current state • Summary report job/performer-level analysis results and recommendations
3. Design and develop solutions	• Design team charter and budget • Solution design documents • Organizational system map—future state • Relationship map—future state • Process map(s)—future state • job design, performance support, and contingency analysis—future state • Pilot data and analysis • Summary report of solutions revisions
4. Implement solutions	• Roll-out performance data and analysis • Summary report of solutions revisions
5. Program for maintenance	• Maintenance team charter and budget • Maintenance performance support design documents

hours (e.g., work directly related to the project is billable, but attending training to build your consulting skills is not).

Step 5: Obtain project approval/sign the contract

The final step in responding to a request for services is to obtain project approval and/or sign the contract. Once you have created your project proposal, you should submit it to whoever is responsible for making a final decision on whether the project will move forward. If the individual or individuals responsible for making this decision are different from the individual(s) you previously met with, be prepared to provide explanations or justifications, and potentially to make some revisions to the proposal, as necessary. Once the proposal is reviewed, a contract should be drafted and signed by both parties. The party responsible for drafting the contract will depend on the size and previous experiences of both parties. If you find yourself in a position where you are responsible for writing the contract, you would be amazed at how much information you can find through a simple internet search.

Phase 2: Analyze performance

The levels and content of your analysis will be determined by the outputs of the first phase of the consulting process, but the analysis process will remain consistent across levels and content and involves (1) identifying system components, (2) identifying issues or performance gaps within and across those components, and (3) creating a prioritized list of recommended actions to close the identified gaps. Several BSA tools are available to complete the analysis process at each level of performance.

Organization-level tools and analysis

Organization-level analysis involves looking at both the external variables and internal strategies and structures that impact organizational performance. One of the original BSA tools is Brethower's (1972) total performance system (TPS). It should be noted that the TPS can be used at any level of performance, but is typically described as an organization-level tool (Sigurdsson & McGee, 2015). The TPS consists of seven components: mission/goal, products/services, customers/stakeholders, external feedback (customer measures), processing system, inputs, and internal feedback (processing system measures). In 1995, Rummler and Brache introduced another organization-level tool, the Super-System, which added two additional external elements to the TPS: external variables (e.g., government regulations, economy) and competition (for inputs and customers). When using either of these tools, practitioners are encouraged to refer to available resources (Brethower, 1982, 2000, 2001, 2002; Brethower & Dams, 1999; Rummler, 2001, 2004, 2008; Rummler & Brache, 1995; Rummler, Ramias, & Rummler, 2006a, 2006b, 2009) for instruction and guidance around completing the steps of the BSA analysis process.

Ludwig, McGee, and Ludwig (2016) introduced the Performance Analysis Toolkit, which includes tools for each level of analysis. The Toolkit represents an evolution of Diener, McGee, and Miguel's (2009) BSA Questionnaire, which sought to incorporate what the authors had learned from exemplars in the field of BSA and through their own professional experiences to create a guided approach that integrated the concepts, tools and various approaches of BSA. The current Performance Analysis Toolkit includes step-by-step instructions for following the BSA analysis process. The organizational analysis tool provides guided questions to help the practitioner (1) collect organizational information on the nine system components previously described; (2) identify measures and goals around components; (3) collect baseline data (gather data if you already have it or observe and collect data if you do not); (4) analyze the components and identify disconnects; (5) create an organizational system map that provides a visual depiction of the system and disconnects; (6) analyze the overall functioning of the system; (7) organize opportunities for improvement based on root cause analysis; (8) analyze impact of performance improvement opportunities; and (9) make initial recommendations for solutions, determine individuals who must be involved in design and implementation of changes, and set deadlines for action items. Fig. 11.1 shows a generic example of organizational system map (or TPS or Super-System Map).

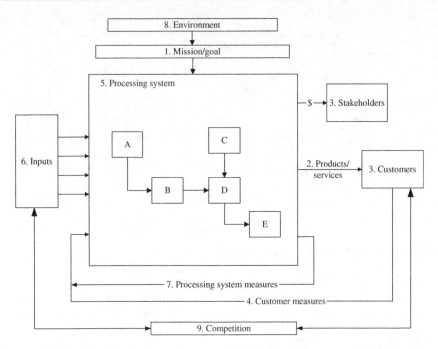

Figure 11.1 Organizational system map.

Two tools exist for analyzing the internal structures of the organization. Rummler and Brache's (1995) Relationship Map illustrates the various functions of the organization, the input-output relationships between them (i.e., who produces what for whom), and where goals, standards, and feedback loops exist between the suppliers and customers (internal or external). Once the functional components are mapped, missing, unnecessary, confusing or misdirected inputs and outputs are identified. Once again, when using this tool, practitioners are encouraged to refer to available resources (Rummler, 2001, 2004, 2008; Rummler & Brache, 1995; Rummler et al. 2006a, 2006b, 2009) for instruction and guidance around completing the steps of the BSA analysis process.

Ludwig et al.'s (2016) functional relationships tool provides guided questions to help the practitioner (1) collect crossfunctional information (see Relationship Map description); (2) identify measures and goals around crossfunctional components; (3) collect baseline data (gather data if you already have it or observe and collect data if you do not); (4) analyze the components and identify disconnects; (5) create a functional relationships map that provides a visual depiction of the relationships and disconnects between the organization's suppliers, departments/functions, and customers; (6) analyze the overall functioning of the organization's departments or functions; (7) organize opportunities for improvement based on root cause analysis; (8) analyze impact of performance improvement opportunities; and (9) make initial recommendations for solutions, determine individuals who must be involved in

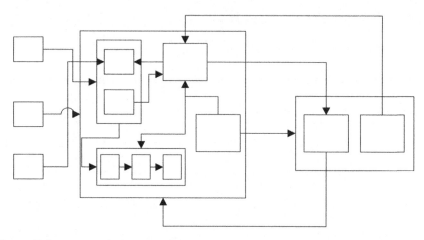

Figure 11.2 Functional relationships map.

design and implementation of changes, and set deadlines for action items. Fig. 11.2 shows a generic example of functional relationships map (or Relationship Map).

Process-level tools and analysis

A process is a series of steps designed to produce a product or service. Breaking one down into its component steps is similar to conducting a task analysis and, in fact, is referred to as a task analysis by Malott (2003). In the workplace, processes that involve more than one function are referred to as crossfunctional processes (Rummler & Brache, 1995). Those processes that only involve one function should be considered subprocesses and should be analyzed in context of a larger crossfunctional process. This is because changing a process within one function will likely impact other functions upstream or downstream. The crossfunctional process map, or task analysis map, provides a visual depiction of a process from beginning to end and is the primary tool used at the process level of analysis. Creating a process map allows practitioners to identify the scope of process being analyzed (where it starts and stops); the performers/functions involved in the process; the steps or tasks involved; and the inputs, outputs, and standards of each step. Once the process is mapped, disconnects are identified with respect to missing, redundant, or convoluted steps; standards; time; and resources involved. As previously stated, when using this tool, practitioners are encouraged to refer to available resources (Malott, 2003; Rummler, 2001, 2004, 2008; Rummler & Brache, 1995; Rummler et al. 2006a, 2006b, 2009) for instruction and guidance around completing the steps of the BSA analysis process.

Ludwig et al.'s (2016) process mapping tool provides guided questions to help the practitioner (1) define the process; (2) identify process phases and steps; (3) identify measures and goals around phases and steps; (4) collect baseline data (gather data if you already have it or observe and collect data if you do not); (5) analyze the components and identify disconnects; (6) create a crossfunctional

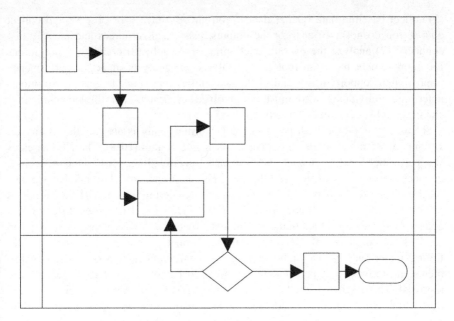

Figure 11.3 Crossfunctional process map.

process map that provides a visual depiction of the phases and steps, along with any identified disconnects within or between steps; (7) analyze the overall functioning of the process; (8) organize opportunities for improvement based on root cause analysis; (9) analyze impact of performance improvement opportunities; and (10) make initial recommendations for solutions, determine individuals who must be involved in design and implementation of changes, and set deadlines for action items. Fig. 11.3 shows a generic example of process map (or Task Analysis Map).

Job/Performer-level tools and analysis

A multitude of tools are available for analyzing performance at the job/performer level, both within OBM as well as the larger I/O and human resource management fields. This level of analysis involves understanding and analyzing (1) the design of the jobs in which people work, along with the broader performance support mechanisms that impact performance and (2) the behavioral contingencies that impact worker performance. Some tools combine, to a greater or lesser extent, both types of job/performer analysis, while others are designed to analyze only one or the other.

One tool designed to help practitioners analyze job design and performance support mechanisms is Ludwig et al.'s (2016) Job Management Tool, which provides guided questions to help the practitioner (1) define the job outputs; (2) determine the critical tasks that produce those outputs; (3) determine the resources required to complete the tasks (time, tools/equipment/materials, foundational skills and knowledge, training, and information); (4) identify measures and goals around outputs and tasks, along with how performers receive feedback on their performance;

(5) collect baseline data (gather data if you already have it or observe and collect data if you do not); (6) analyze the outputs, tasks, and resources and identify disconnects; (7) analyze the overall functioning of the job; (8) organize opportunities for improvement based on root cause analysis; (9) analyze impact of performance improvement opportunities; and (10) make initial recommendations for solutions, determine individuals who must be involved in design and implementation of changes, and set deadlines for action items.

Tools that combine both types of job/performer analysis are, for the most part, variants of Rummler's (1972) human performance system (HPS). The HPS assesses six performer-level variables: performance specifications, task support, consequences, feedback, knowledge/skill, and individual capacity. The notable variants of the HPS are Gilbert's (1978) behavior engineering model (BEM), Binder's (1998) Six Boxes model, and Austin's (2000) PDC. The BEM uses different language for the six variables (data, instruments, incentives, knowledge, capacity, and motives) and organizes the HPS into a matrix format, with each of the six variables falling under one of two main categories: environmental supports (data, instruments, incentives) and person's repertoire of behavior (knowledge, capacity and motives). The Six Boxes model translated the BEM into a more user-friendly diagnostic tool, while the PDC condensed the six categories of the HPS, BEM, and Six Boxes into four (antecedents and information, equipment and processes, knowledge and skills, and consequences) and turned it into a checklist. When using these tools, practitioners should refer to available resources (Austin, 2000; Binder, 1998; Gilbert, 1978; Rummler, 2001, 2004, 2008; Rummler & Brache, 1995; Rummler et al., 2006a, 2006b, 2009) for instruction and guidance around completing the steps of the BSA analysis process.

Tools for practitioners interested in analyzing specific behavioral contingencies that impact worker performance include Daniels and Bailey's (2014) PIC/NIC Analysis and Braksick's (2007) E-TIP Analysis. To conduct a PIC/NIC Analysis, first identify both the desired behavior as well as the undesired (or currently occurring) behavior. Next, identify the antecedents and consequences associated with each behavior. Finally, categorize the consequences as either positive or negative (from the performer's perspective), immediate or future, and certain or uncertain. Once completed, identify which consequences (whether programmed or naturally occurring) suppress desired behavior and/or support undesired behavior and how antecedents and consequences could be added, modified, or removed to increase the likelihood of the desired behavior occurring and decrease the likelihood of the undesired behavior occurring. The E-TIP Analysis follows a similar process, but adds an analysis of the importance of the consequence, from the performer's perspective. As always, when using these tools, practitioners are encouraged to refer to available resources (Braksick, 2007; Daniels & Bailey, 2014) for instruction and guidance around completing the steps of the BSA analysis process.

A final contingency analysis tool is Ludwig et al. (2016) Behavior Change Tool. This tool provides guided questions to help the practitioner (1) define an essential task to be analyzed; (2) determine the essential behaviors that must be performed to consider the task complete; (3) determine whether the essential behaviors occur at the right time, every time they are supposed to occur, accurately, and completely; (4) identify the antecedents associated with the essential behaviors, along with the competing behaviors, and determine probability of those antecedents occurring; (5) identify the positive, negative, immediate, and delayed consequences (for both the performer and the organization) for the essential behaviors, along with the competing behaviors, and determine probability of those consequences occurring; (6) develop rule statements using the information gathered; (7) analyze the rule statements and identify disconnects; and (8) make initial recommendations for solutions, determine individuals who must be involved in design and implementation of changes, and set deadlines for action items.

Phase 3: Design and develop solutions

Once you have completed the appropriate analyses, you will need to turn your initial recommendations into pilot tested solutions. This phase of consultation involves four steps: (1) establish a design team and secure resources, (2) design solutions, (3) develop (build) any materials necessary for the effective implementation of those solutions, and (4) pilot test the solutions. As previously stated, various engagement models can be employed throughout the consultation process. That said, for the remaining phases it is strongly recommended that you work hand-in-hand with an internal team or teams (i.e., do it with us) or serve as facilitator or coach for an internal team or teams completing these phases (i.e., let us do it). As it is the organizational members who will eventually need to work within the system, they should be actively involved in its design, development, implementation, and maintenance.

Step 1: Establish design team and secure resources

The first step is to work with the organization to identify individuals who will make up the design team or teams for your recommended solutions. Once teams are established, review the analysis results, maps, and recommendations created to date. The maps represent the current system—what each of the levels looks like right now. These are referred to as the "Is" or "Current State" maps. The analysis results (along with the maps) document where performance gaps exist. The recommendations provide a broad view of what needs to occur to close the gaps. Use this information to create a Team Charter, a document that outlines who the team members are, what aspect(s) of the solution design they are responsible for, resources required for success (including a budget), milestones/deadlines, and deliverables. A variety of Team Charter templates are available online for free. The charter should be submitted to whoever is responsible for making a final decision on whether the team and project can move forward as outlined in the charter. If the individual or individuals responsible for making this decision are different from the individual(s) you previously met with, be prepared to provide explanations or justifications, and potentially to make some revisions to the charter, as necessary.

Step 2: Design solutions

Once approval is obtained, your design team is ready to develop "Should" or "Future State" maps and supporting documents. These maps and documents will serve as your design documents and will detail what each of the levels will look like once the gaps have been closed. This will likely take several team meetings or workshops—your role as consultant should be to lead or facilitate the team(s) as they brainstorm potential solutions, analyze those solutions by identifying constraints that might prevent or limit their successful implementation and maintenance, and refine their solutions based on the results of the analysis until they have a solution or solution set that is likely to be successful (though remember that the solution will need to be piloted and then fully implemented before you will know for sure that it is successful). Finally, you should lead or facilitate the team(s) in creating the actual "Should" or "Future State" maps and documents. The maps should be similar to those created in the analysis phase, but represent the system as is will look once the solutions are implemented. The "Should" or "Future State" documents should detail exactly what needs to be done (including any materials to be built), by whom and by when, in order to pilot test the solutions, evaluate and revise based on pilot data, and eventually implement the solutions on a larger scale.

Step 3: Develop (build) materials necessary
for effective implementation of solutions

Once the final design documents are complete, your role as consultant will be to lead or facilitate the team(s) in the development of any and all materials that are required for pilot testing the solution. These materials might include trainings, job aids, manuals, policies, procedures, etc. All materials should be reviewed and revised by the team as necessary until they are ready to be used.

Step 4: Pilot test solutions

While you and the design team will have put considerable effort into designing and developing an effective solution or solution set, it is possible (even likely) that you will not have thought of everything. This is why it is always a good idea to pilot test your solutions (just like you would if you were conducting research). Whenever possible, find a small group of individuals or function of the organization in which you can test your newly developed solutions. Implement within this microsystem and evaluate the effects of your solutions. Based on the results, determine what needs to be revised and make the revisions. If possible, pilot test the revised solutions (repeat as necessary or as is feasible/practical). Be sure to record any changes made, along with the rationale for the changes, for future reference in a summary report.

Phase 4: Implement solutions

The fourth phase of the consultation process involves the following steps: (1) prepare the organization, (2) implement solutions, and (3) evaluate and revise as necessary. This phase will look very similar to the pilot testing, but will occur on a much larger scale.

Step 1: Prepare the organization

While your design team has been actively involved in designing and developing (and even implementing on a small scale) the solutions, it is important to remember that the rest of the organization has not. Failure to prepare the remaining members of the organization for the coming changes can have disastrous effects and effectively kill the project. In addition, failure to involve the appropriate people in the preparation can have the same effects. Organizational leaders must be involved in the communication and implementation of the changes. In addition, any individuals who will be responsible for providing performance support (e.g., training) should be brought onto the team at this point and provided with all information, materials, and training they might need to help ensure successful implementation. Once the "stage is set," leaders should communicate the coming changes throughout the organization and identify/introduce the design team, along with any additional pre and postimplementation performance support personnel. These individuals should be made available to discuss the changes should anyone have questions or concerns.

Step 2: Implement solutions

The organization should now be ready for the implementation of solutions. Any training, coaching, or performance support requirements should be implemented before, during, and after the solution implementation, as appropriate. Do not underestimate the amount of training and performance clarification that will be required and do not rush this part of implementation. Doing so will result in the changes having a punishing effect on desired behavior which will potentially result in eventual failure of the solutions. In addition, your team, the organizational leaders, and the performance support personnel should provide ample reinforcement for solution-adoption-related behaviors, even if the solutions are not being implemented perfectly. Implementation fidelity can be shaped over time and you should expect a learning curve—the key is to continue to reinforce successive approximations.

Step 3: Evaluate and revise as necessary

Evaluate performance postimplementation to determine where revisions are necessary. Based on the results of your evaluation, determine what needs to be revised, where the revisions should be made (it won't always make sense to implement changes in the exact same way across the board—Sometimes, revisions will need to be made in certain parts of the organization, but not others), and then make the revisions. If possible, pilot test the revised solutions before implementing on a large scale (repeat as necessary or as is feasible/practical). Be sure to record any changes made, along with the rationale for the changes, for future reference in a summary report.

Phase 5: Program for maintenance

The final phase of the consultation process involves determining what actions need to be taken in order to institutionalize or systematize the changes. Consultants must eventually end their involvement in a project, and without programming for maintenance, this often means the solutions end as well. Before leaving the project, work with your design team (or form a new team for maintenance) to determine what changes, if any, need to be made within the organization to increase the likelihood of the solutions maintaining. The team should identify who will be responsible for ongoing monitoring of the solutions, reviewing data to determine when and where additional changes are required, and making the changes. The team will also need to seek authorization for those individuals to engage in the actions. For external consultants, it is also a good idea to train one or more internal individuals to continue to use the performance analysis tools and process after you are gone. The same can be said for internal consultants, but it might also be possible for internal consultants to continue on in some lesser role moving forward.

Summary

The process and tools presented here are designed to help OBM and other ABA professionals within a wide range of jobs (supervisor, academic, consultant, trainer, etc.) to employ a systematic and systemic approach to workplace performance analysis and improvement. Practitioners wishing to take this approach should not assume that it involves a one-time effort. As organizations and the environments they operate within change, the systems that make up the organization must also change. Organizations must revisit their goals and strategies, structures, processes, and jobs. In other words, BSA is an ongoing approach to organizational improvement.

Practice guidelines checklist

- Organizational success is a function of the performance of individuals within that organization, but individual performance is only as good as the systems within which it occurs. While PM interventions alone can (and do) impact individual and group workplace performance, it is often necessary to additionally analyze and subsequently implement systems changes within the organization.
- The BSA three levels approach provides a framework for understanding and improving performance throughout the organization.
  - Organization level
  - Process level
  - Job/Performer level
- OBM consultants and practitioners charged with improving organizational performance should follow a standard consultation process that is based in a performance analysis and improvement model.
  - Respond to request for services
  - Analyze performance
  - Design and develop solutions
  - Implement solutions
  - Program for maintenance

- OBM consultants and practitioners should take advantage of the multitude of tools available to them when analyzing and improving performance across the three levels of the organization.
- Systems analysis is an ongoing effort that should be encouraged as part of everyday strategic and tactical operations within any organization.

References

Austin, J. (2000). Performance analysis and performance diagnostics. In J. Austin, & J. E. Carr (Eds.), *Handbook of applied behavior analysis*. Reno, NV: Context Press, pp. 321−349.

Bailey, J. S., & Burch, M. R. (2002). *Research methods in applied behavior analysis*. Thousand Oaks, CA: Sage Publications, Inc.

Behavior Analyst Certification Board®. (2012). Supervisor training curriculum outline. Retrieved from http://bacb.com/wp-content/uploads/2015/05/supervisor_curriculum.pdf.

Berglund, K. M., & Ludwig, T. D. (2009). Approaching error-free customer satisfaction through process change and feedback systems. *Journal of Organizational Behavior Management, 29*(1), 19−46.

Binder, C. (1998). The Six Boxes™: A descendent of Gilbert's behavior engineering model. *Performance Improvement, 37*(6), 48−52.

Braksick, L. W. (2007). *Unlock behavior, unleash profits: Developing leadership behavior that drives profitability in your organization*. New York: McGraw Hill Professional.

Brethower, D. M. (1972). *Behavioral analysis in business and industry: A total performance system*. Kalamazoo, MI: Behaviordelia, Inc.

Brethower, D. M. (1982). The total performance system. In R. M. O'Brien, A. M. Dickinson, & M. P. Rosow (Eds.), *Industrial behavior modification: A management handbook* (pp. 350−369). New York: Pergamon Press.

Brethower, D. M. (2000). A systematic view of enterprise: Adding value to performance. *Journal of Organizational Behavior Management, 20*(3/4), 165−190.

Brethower, D. M. (2001). Managing a person as a system. In L. J. Hayes, J. Austin, R. Houmanfar, & M. C. Clayton (Eds.), *Organizational change* (pp. 89−105). Reno, NV: Context Press.

Brethower, D.M. (2002). *Behavioral systems analysis: Fundamental concepts and cutting edge applications*. Retrieved February 28, 2003, from http://www.behavior.org/performancemgmt.

Brethower, D. M., & Dams, P. C. (1999). Systems thinking (and systems doing). *Performance Improvement, 38*(1), 37−52.

Daniels, A. C., & Bailey, J. S. (2014). *Performance management: Changing behavior that drives organizational effectiveness*. Atlanta, GA: Performance Management Publications.

Dickinson, A. M. (2001). The historical roots of organizational behavior management in the private sector: The 1950s−1980s. *Journal of Organizational Behavior Management, 20* (3−4), 9−58.

Diener, L. H., McGee, H. M., & Miguel, C. F. (2009). An integrated approach for conducting a behavioral systems analysis. *Journal of Organizational Behavior Management, 29*(2), 108−135.

Frederiksen, L. W., Riley, A. W., & Myers, J. B. (1985). Matching technology and organizational structure: A case study in white collar productivity improvement. *Journal of Organizational Behavior Management, 6*(3), 59–80.

Gilbert, T. F. (1978). *Human competence: Engineering worthy performance.* New York: McGraw-Hill.

Goomas, D. T. (2010). Replacing voice input with technology that provided immediate visual and audio feedback to reduce employee errors. *Journal of Organizational Behavior Management, 30*(1), 26–37.

Hall, B. L. (1980). Editorial. *Journal of Organizational Behavior Management, 2*(3), 145–150.

Hybza, M. M., Stokes, T. F., Hayman, M., & Schatzberg, T. (2013). Increasing medicaid revenue generation for services by school psychologists. *Journal of Organizational Behavior Management, 33*(1), 55–67.

Johnson, D. A., Casella, S. E., McGee, H. M., & Lee, S. C. (2014). The use and validation of pre-intervention diagnostic tools in organizational behavior management. *Journal of Organizational Behavior Management, 34*(2), 104–121.

Kratochwill, T. R., & Bergan, J. R. (1978). Training school psychologists: Some perspectives on a competency-based behavioral consultation model. *Professional Psychology, 9*(1), 71.

Ludwig, L. H., McGee, H. M., & Ludwig, T. D. (2016). *Performance analysis toolkit [electronic toolkit].* Blowing Rock, NC: Performance Blueprints.

Mager, R. F. (1997). *Making instruction work: A step-by-step guide to designing and developing instruction that works.* Atlanta, GA: CEP Press.

Malott, M. E. (2003). *Paradox of organizational change.* Reno, NV: Context Press.

Malott, R. W. (1974). A behavioral systems approach to the design of human services. In D. Harshbarger, & R. F. Maley (Eds.), *Behavior analysis and systems analysis: An integrative approach to mental health programs.* Kalamazoo, MI: Behaviordelia.

Molenda, M., Pershing, J. A., & Reigeluth, C. M. (1996). Designing instructional systems. In Robert L. In Craig (Ed.), *The ASTD training and development handbook* (4th ed., pp. 266–293). New York: McGraw-Hill.

Redmon, W. K., & Agnew, J. L. (1991). Organizational behavioral analysis in the United States: A view from the private sector. In P. A. Lamal (Ed.), *Behavioral analysis of societies and cultural practices* (pp. 125–139).

Redmon, W. K., & Wilk, L. A. (1991). Organizational behavioral analysis in the United States: Public sector organizations. In P. A. Lamal (Ed.), *Behavioral analysis of societies and cultural practices* (pp. 107–123).

Rummler, G. A. (1972). Human performance problems and their solutions. *Human Resource Management, 11*(4), 1–10.

Rummler, G. A. (2001). Performance logic: The organization performance Rosetta stone. In L. J. Hayes, J. Austin, R. Houmanfar, & M. C. Clayton (Eds.), *Organizational change* (pp. 111–132). Reno, NV: Context Press.

Rummler, G. A. (2004). *Serious performance consulting according to Rummler.* Silver Spring, MD: International Society for Performance Improvement.

Rummler, G. A. (2008). *Rummler process methodology: Reference manual.* Tucson, AZ: Performance Design Lab.

Rummler, G. A., & Brache, A. P. (1995). *Improving performance: How to manage the white space on the organization chart* (2nd ed.). San Francisco: Jossey-Bass.

Rummler, G.A., Ramais, A.J., & Rummler, R.A. (2006a, November). Potential pitfalls on the road to a PMO (Part 1). *BPTrends, 4*(10). Retrieved February 10, 2007,

from   http://www.bptrends.com/resources_publications.cfm?publicationtypeID =
DFFB9D1C-1031-D522-3AAF1211DDD4AD95.

Rummler, G.A., Ramais, A.J., & Rummler, R.A. (2006b, December). Potential pitfalls on the
road to a PMO (Part 2). *BPTrends, 4*(11). Retrieved February 10, 2007, from http://
www.bptrends.com/resources_publications.cfm?publicationtypeID = DFFB9D1C-1031-
D522-3AAF1211DDD4AD95.

Rummler, G. A., Ramias, A. J., & Rummler, R. A. (2009). *White space revisited: Creating
value through process.* San Francisco: Jossey-Bass.

Sasson, J. R., Alvero, A. M., & Austin, J. (2006). Effects of process and human performance
improvement strategies. *Journal of Organizational Behavior Management, 26*(3),
43−78.

Sigurdsson, S. O., & McGee, H. M. (2015). Organizational behavior management: Systems
analysis. In H. S. Roane, J. E. Ringdahl, & T. S. Falcomata (Eds.), *Clinical and organizational applications of applied behavior analysis* (pp. 627−648). Waltham, MA:
Elsevier.

Strouse, M. C., Carroll-Hernandez, T. A., Sherman, J. A., & Sheldon, J. B. (2004). Turning
over turnover: The evaluation of a staff scheduling system in a community-based program for adults with developmental disabilities. *Journal of Organizational Behavior
Management, 23*(2/3), 45−63.

Consultation Practices: Multidisciplinary Settings

12

Claire C. St. Peter[1], Sacha T. Pence[2] and Kathryn M. Kestner[1]
[1]West Virginia University, Morgantown, WV, United States,
[2]Auburn University, Auburn, AL, United States

Introduction

As behavior analysts, we attempt to change socially significant behavioral issues by making changes to people's environments. In this way, we can provide a unique perspective on presenting problems. Despite the wide array of behavioral problems to which we could assist with solutions, there are a limited number of behavior analysts in the world, and our knowledge of the complex interplays that lead to socially significant problems is incomplete. In this chapter, we will describe some potential roles for behavior analysts to contribute to multidisciplinary teams. We highlight examples of how behavior analysts can work with individuals from other professionals in ways that benefit the client, the behavior analyst, and the other team members. Our aim is to convince readers, particularly those who are behavior-analytic practitioners, that collaboration as a part of multidisciplinary teams is a worthwhile endeavor.

For applied behavior analysts, the goal of identifying and intervening on socially significant behavior has been paramount since the inception of the field (Baer, Wolf, & Risley, 1968). It is not the behavior analyst who determines what behavior should be considered socially significant, but rather the consumers of our services (Wolf, 1978). Collaboration on multidisciplinary teams may provide opportunities for us to identify forms of behavior with social significance to broader consumers. In addition, although behavior analysis can address an enormous array of issues, other disciplines have also accrued significant information about problems of behavior. For example, the medical field has identified many behavioral excesses and deficits that can lead to, or stem from, a variety of health concerns. We would be remiss to ignore the insight that can be provided from other literatures.

In some cases, it may be critical for behavior analysts to seek collaboration with professionals from other disciplines, even when we are the primary service provider. Behavior analysts have worked collaboratively with a variety of professionals, including nurses, pediatricians, dentists, neurologists, psychiatrists, speech-language pathologists, occupational therapists, clinical psychologists, mental health counselors, and social workers toward mutually beneficial outcomes. For example, medical issues (e.g., swallowing difficulties) must be considered before we implement feeding programs like escape extinction (e.g., nonremoval of the spoon; Cornwell, Kelly, & Austin, 2010; LaRue et al., 2011). Because of possible safety

Applied Behavior Analysis Advanced Guidebook. DOI: http://dx.doi.org/10.1016/B978-0-12-811122-2.00012-7

concerns and unique motor deficits, behavior analysts working with feeding interventions commonly collaborate with professionals such as dietitians, medical doctors, occupational therapists, and speech-language pathologists (e.g., Piazza, et al., 2003; Piazza, Patel, Gulotta, Sevin, & Layer, 2003; Shore, Babbit, Williams, Coe, & Snyder, 1998). For example, a speech-language pathologist may conduct an assessment to identify oral motor deficits or difficulties (e.g., masticating, swallowing) and a dietitian could select an appropriate texture level and foods that meet the nutritional needs of the individual. In more severe cases, a physician can rule out medical causes and determine if the client requires feeding support (e.g., a G-Tube). Cornwell et al. (2010) provide an example of a team made up of multidisciplinary members each conducting an assessment and contributing to the treatment plan for G-Tube dependent children.

Behavior analysts must consider medical issues when attempting to change behavior such as serious self-injury or enuresis (Carr & Owen-DeSchryver, 2007; Friman, 2010; Harvey, Luiselli, & Wong, 2009). For example, pain and pressure from an ear infection may be an establishing operation contributing to the maintenance of head hitting. In these instances, collaboration with medical professionals is not only desirable, it is also mandated by the Behavior Analyst Certification Board (2016), whose compliance code states, "Behavior analysts recommend seeking a medical consultation if there is any reasonable possibility that a referred behavior is influenced by medical or biological variables" (p. 11). Medical providers may provide prescriptions for protective equipment for self-injury (Braga-Kenyon, Kenyon, & Guilhardi, 2015), including helmets, arm limiters, and Posey Mitts to be used for safety in addition to (or until development of) an effective behavioral intervention. Physicians, nurses, and physical therapists have the specific training to the ensure proper fit of protective equipment to reduce unintended injuries such as those resulting from blocked circulation or skin irritation. Medical professionals can also assist in establishing safety protocols and session-termination criteria during assessment of severe behavior.

Behavior analysts can share information to assist medical professionals with their treatments and assessments. For example, behavioral data can be used to assess seizures, including the frequency and type of seizures and the effects of medication on seizures (Braga-Kenyon et al., 2015). Similarly, behavior-analytic methods of data collection can assist in objective assessments of the efficacy, side effects, and social validity of psychotropic medication (Poling & Ehrhardt, 1999). As a specific example, I (St. Peter) collaborate with a pediatric psychiatrist in my clinical work with children who engage in chronic and severe problem behavior. Many of these children come to us on a wide array of medications, and we typically do not have extensive knowledge about the direct effects, side effects, and possible interactions among the medications. With parental permission, we share our data with the psychiatrist and meet with her at least once a month to discuss behavioral issues that may be related to medication. The psychiatrist adjusts medications based on child behavior, and then follows up with us to determine the behavioral effects of the changes. Fig. 12.1 diagrams a collaborative interaction between a medical professional and a behavior-analytic practitioner. This type of collaboration is important

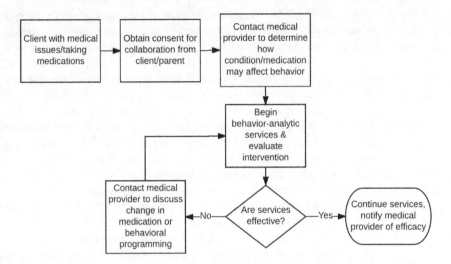

Figure 12.1 Collaborative arrangement between medical professional and behavior-analytic practitioner.

because of known interactions between behavioral interventions and medication regimens (e.g., Northup et al., 1999).

The benefit of collaboration with practitioners from other disciplines is not unidirectional; we gain valuable insight from other professionals. When done well, multidisciplinary collaboration benefits all involved. Clients benefit from having a team of professionals with diverse knowledge and skillsets that they can apply to address the behavioral concern. For example, behavior analysts seeking to increase client's vocal communication might benefit from working on a multidisciplinary team with a speech-language pathologist. As part of the team, the behavior analyst can contribute an array of sophisticated behavior-change procedures to increase communicative skills and target verbal operants (e.g., mands, tacts, intraverbals) because she is likely to have a deeper knowledge of the function of verbal operants than the speech-language pathologist. The speech-language pathologist is likely to have more extensive training in language development, including areas in which the behavior analyst may have had little previous exposure, such as articulation, language position, and formation of the mouth palate (e.g., Braga-Kenyon et al., 2015). These features of speech production may have important implications for the initially reinforced response and targeted terminal behavior selected for a shaping program increasing vocal language production. For example, a speech-language pathologist can provide valuable insight on sequencing developmentally appropriate sounds to teach during an echoic program. Without collaboration with another trained professional, a behavior analyst may inadvertently set behavioral goals that would be difficult for the client to obtain.

Behavior analysts have developed a wide array of effective, empirically based approaches to address problems of behavioral excess or deficit. A behavior-analytic approach targets observable and measurable responses, allowing for quantification of behavior change. Although we often take for granted the importance of behavior quantification, individuals with different theoretical or philosophical backgrounds may assume that complex behaviors are too difficult to measure accurately or may not consider such measurement as worthwhile (Montee et al., 1995). Behavior analysts are often well-trained in the development of measurement systems that are sensitive to subtle changes in behavior and that can be used across settings. Such measurement systems may be a critical step to the identification of treatment goals for a client. The first step in having a treatment goal is to define the target response so that an intervention can be designed to address that behavior. For example, if a team is working to decrease awkward social behavior (e.g., standing too close to other people when talking, failing to have meaningful conversations, and having odd reactions to humor), the behavior analyst can contribute by defining the appropriate social behavior and helping to create sensitive measurement systems. We can write operational definitions that clearly outline a target response. Such definitions help establish objective guidelines by which to measure a response targeted to increase or decrease. Behavior analysts are uniquely qualified to operationalize responses that can be difficult to quantify, such as social skills. As in the previous example, it can be difficult to define what constitutes an appropriate conversation or the steps to respond appropriately to humor. Behavior analysts can bring experience to a multidisciplinary team to help define such skills and identify the best measurement and data collection procedure for the situation, which can help a team to teach and reinforce these skills.

Behavior analysts focus on "malleable factors" rather than static traits. We identify variables in an individual's environment that can be modified to lead to significant improvements in responding, rather than assuming that behavior is a function solely of the individual's traits or genetic makeup. The focus on malleable factors leads us to adopt a change-oriented approach in which every individual has the possibility of improving behavior for the better, regardless of previous patterns of behavior. The focus on behavior change of an individual allows us to evaluate individualized interventions that address the specific needs of that person. By systematically observing and measuring the behavior, a behavior analyst can determine if an intervention is effective or not and make changes accordingly.

When examining problems at the level of the individual, behavior analysts can identify individual differences that contribute to positive or negative outcomes. As a classic example in the applied behavior analysis literature, the function of behavior (i.e., why a particular behavior occurs) differs dramatically across individuals even when the form of the behavior (e.g., self-injury) is nearly identical. This outcome was demonstrated clearly by Iwata, Dorsey, Slifer, Bauman, and Richman (1994) and has been subsequently replicated hundreds of times (Beavers, Iwata, & Lerman, 2013). This functional, individualized approach to the causes of behavior differs from the traditional approach in psychology that focuses on the form of behavior classified into diagnostic categories (e.g., *Diagnostic and Statistical Manual of Mental Disorders-Fifth Edition*; American Psychiatric Association, 2013).

Behavior analysts largely use single-subject designs to evaluate research and clinical questions. Single-subject methodology includes experimental designs that allow for the examination of problems without random assignment or the need for no-treatment control groups. Teams can use single-subject designs to evaluate a question with each individual as his or her own control. As these designs rely on repeated observations of behavior over time, the experimental design permits clear identification of changes in behavior, including positive gains achieved or undesirable trends or levels indicating that the intervention needs to be modified to better serve that individual. Behavior analysts can contribute to multidisciplinary teams by providing this individualized, scientific approach to problem solving. Approaches based on single-subject design may permit us to assist other professionals in evaluating the efficacy of their procedures.

Relevance for behavioral practitioners

In addition to working with a variety of collaborators, behavior analysts can work with a variety of populations, including children, adults, typically developing individuals, the elderly, individuals with gambling and drug addictions, individuals with traumatic brain injury, parents of children with disabilities, teachers, and direct-care staff. Although we have the skills to work with a range of populations, at present, most behavior analysts work with individuals with autism spectrum disorder (ASD) and intellectual disabilities (Johnston, 2009). Participating in multidisciplinary teams provides opportunities for us to develop new skills and to expand expertise to new and diverse populations. LeBlanc, Heinicke, and Baker (2012) discuss rationales for diversification of consumer bases, including personal (e.g., spousal job change or need to support an aging parent), practical (e.g., increased financial stability), and professional (e.g., intellectual challenges) benefits. In particular, LeBlanc et al. discuss that the elderly and individuals with traumatic brain injury are two populations currently underserved by behavior analysts. For example, we could work with teams involving doctors, nurses, physical therapists, caregivers, and nutritionists to improve the care and quality of life for elderly individuals. We could play a vital role to help increase physical activity, involvement in leisure and social activities, compliance with medical procedures and medicine regiments, and independence with health-related tasks.

In addition to working with diverse populations, behavior analysts could consider expanding their skillsets to new areas of inquiry. Normand and Kohn (2013) outlined a range of areas in which behavior analysts could receive additional training to expand their expertise. These areas include health and fitness, health care, child care, education, animal behavior, and management and business. Expanding the domains in which a behavior analyst has substantial expertise may naturally put us in touch with other professionals. In the domains listed above, we may be able to collaborate with personal trainers, occupational therapists, alcohol and drug counselors, child-care program owners, special-education teachers, animal trainers, and human-resource specialists. Working collaboratively with individuals from other disciplines may help to inform what behaviors are of interest in their respective fields. In this way, multidisciplinary collaboration can inform responses that would be socially valid targets for intervention by a broader population.

Behavior-analytic practitioners, clients of those practitioners, and the field of behavior analysis may all benefit from behavior-analytic participation on multidisciplinary teams. Practitioners may benefit by acquiring the new skills associated with finding a common language and working in collaborative teams. Collaboration in areas such as pharmacology, economics, neuroscience, medicine, and education leads to a better understanding of such areas and the development of new methodological skills (St. Peter, 2013). Those broader skill sets may allow us to better communicate with individuals from other disciplines, furthering the extent to which behavioral technologies are seen as acceptable and are widely adopted. Behavior analysts who are well-versed on collaboration and multiple areas of service provision may have more flexibility in job location, more variability in their careers and daily responsibilities, and more marketability as a professional than those who have limited training or collaborative expertise (LeBlanc et al., 2012; Normand & Kohn, 2013).

Clients of behavior analysts may benefit from increased safety and better communication between an array of service providers. As noted above, collaboration with medical professionals can increase clients' safety, particularly with assessments (e.g., functional analysis) or interventions (e.g., extinction) that carry a risk of temporarily increased rates or intensities of challenging behavior. Clients may also benefit from increased communication among providers who have different types of expertise with a specific problem. For example, LeBlanc et al. (2012) discuss that individuals with traumatic brain injury often have diffuse residual pain and sensory impairments, including light sensitivity and auditory sensitivity. These biological factors could increase the likelihood of escape-maintained problem behavior (e.g., an individual may engage in problem behavior to be removed from an environment with certain tones or lights). Sleep can also play a role in the occurrence of problem behavior (e.g., Kennedy & Meyer, 1996; O'Reilly, 1995) and influence treatment effects (e.g., Reed, Dolezai, Cooper-Brown, & Wacker, 2005). For example, O'Reilly (1995) observed that aggression occurred at higher levels in demand conditions following nights with less than 5 hours of sleep compared to nights in which the participant got more than 5 hours of sleep. By understanding the biology behind sleep patterns, we can better communicate with other professionals and may be better able to predict when problem behavior will occur, allowing for the development of more effective interventions.

Finally, collaborations on multidisciplinary teams may benefit the field of behavior analysis by increasing the visibility of behavior-analytic approaches to problems (Dillenburger et al., 2014; LeBlanc et al., 2012) and the scope of our research. Through collaboration, we can link our work to other fields and with scientists using other methods. Such work could result in publications in journals in which behavior analysis currently has little or no representation. In addition, collaborations could result in other professionals gaining a greater appreciation for within-subject research designs and a better understanding of how those designs can be integrated into group studies so behavior can be examined at the levels of individual and group (St. Peter, 2013). Addressing issues like overpopulation, global warming, obesity, famine and disease in poor countries, and genocide from a behavior-analytic perspective would almost certainly require a multidisciplinary approach (Poling, 2010). Working on these broader issues may result in the diversification of behavior-analytic research in a way that increases the number of professionals who find our work interesting and useful to their related professions. By diversifying the consumer base, we are more likely to attract public attention and awareness to the strengths and contributions of the field of behavior analysis (LeBlanc et al., 2012; Normand & Kohn, 2013).

Past and current practitioner training

Applied behavior analysis emerged as a recognized area of research and practice in the 1960s. At that time, behavior analysts were almost necessarily collaborating with individuals from other disciplines because the field was too new and small for us to work primarily in isolation. Perhaps for this reason, early research and training programs in applied behavior analysis occurred in settings like hospitals and schools that would be considered multidisciplinary by today's standards. For example, one of the first research studies in applied behavior analysis taught nurses to structure psychiatric wards to improve patient behavior (Ayllon & Michael, 1959).

As applied behavior analysis emerged as a field in its own right, there seemed to be a shift away from explicit consideration of multidisciplinary settings and practices in the training of behavior-analytic practitioners. For example, there is only one item on the Behavior Analyst Certification Board's 4th edition task list explicitly covering work in multidisciplinary settings or with professionals from other areas of practice: "provide behavior-analytic services in collaboration with others who support and/or provide services to one's clients" (item G-06, p. 6). Perhaps understandably, most areas of the task list related to multidisciplinary work are broader, including domains like "explain behavioral concepts using nontechnical language" (G-04, p. 6), "establish support for behavior-analytic services from direct and indirect consumers" (item K-08, p. 8), and "secure the support of others to maintain the client's behavioral repertoires in their natural environments" (item K-09, p. 8). Although not explicitly stated as such, these repertoires are necessary for behavior analysts to be successful in multidisciplinary settings. The Behavior Analyst Certification Board suggests that supervisees working toward certification should demonstrate "appropriate sensitivity to nonbehavioral providers" (BACB, 2016, p. 7) in their supervised experiences, but the definition or experiences that should be used for this skill are not specified clearly.

Despite behavior analysts' seemingly implicit recognition of the importance of multidisciplinary collaboration, few current training programs in behavior analysis highlight multidisciplinary training as part of the experience in that program. For example, none of the 11 doctoral programs accredited by the Behavior Analysis Accreditation Board (BAAB) in 2016 included the words "interdisciplinary" or "multidisciplinary," or references to multidisciplinary training, as part of their posted mission statements (ABAI website retrieved September 14, 2016). The 20 BAAB-accredited Master's programs included only slightly more emphasis on multidisciplinary training. For example, a few programs referenced settings that might be multidisciplinary. Caldwell University, Simmons College, and Western Michigan University included references to "developmental services, special education, and mental health," "multiple education and human service settings," and "developmental disabilities, business and industry, mental health, substance abuse, education, and government" in their mission statements, respectively. Other programs alluded to graduates' preparation to work with others. The mission statements of the Oslo and Akershus University and University of South Florida mentioned "...graduates who can meet challenges in a number of fields..." and "...prepares graduates to work in a variety of fields...," respectively. Only one accredited Master's program included explicit reference to interdisciplinary or multidisciplinary training; St. Cloud State University included a program goal "to develop interdisciplinary skills for students in behavior analysis through interaction with other programs and agencies."

Thus, although behavior analysts seem to value multidisciplinary collaboration, contemporary training practices in such collaboration seems weak overall, at least in the extent to which such training raises to the importance of the mission statement. For many practitioners, training in multidisciplinary collaboration may occur incidentally through practicum or on-the-job experiences. It is also possible that many practitioners build the skills necessary to participate successfully in multidisciplinary teams without such skill building being labeled explicitly as preparation for multidisciplinary collaboration. We describe specific examples of skills that might contribute to successful collaboration in the next section.

Research base and implications for practice

Bringing behavior analysis to other disciplines

The many examples referenced so far should be taken as evidence that behavior analysts work in multidisciplinary settings and collaborate with those in other fields. The behavior-analytic research literature shows us that behavior analysts in practice work with other professionals in settings such as schools (Boyce & Hineline, 2002), businesses and organizations (Wilder, Austin, & Casella, 2009), nursing homes and geriatric day-service providers (LeBlanc, 2010), mental health facilities (Harvey et al., 2009), and medical facilities (Friman, 2010). Despite the evidence that behavior analysts are bringing aspects of our science to other disciplines, there is currently a limited research base within the field of behavior analysis to inform the development of those collaborations. Given this relatively limited literature within the field, behavior analysts who wish to further the discipline through collaborations should consider reading broadly about ways to improve impact. For example, we should consider strategies for dissemination that have been developed through implementation science, which has developed systematic frameworks (e.g., Damschroder et al., 2009) that provide recommendations for effective dissemination.

Behavior analysts may be able to foster multidisciplinary collaboration by learning about other fields. We discuss details about how practitioners might learn about other fields in the sections on Relevance for Behavioral Practitioners (above) and Practice Guidelines (below). Regardless of the specific avenues that practitioners pursue, it will probably be necessary to talk openly with professionals from those other disciplines. Becirevic, Critchfield, and Reed (2016) propose, "interacting mainly with like-minded individuals has left behavior analysts unproductively isolated both topically (by addressing too few of the problems that concern the broader population) and linguistically (by discussing important problems with language that fails to inspire, inform, or motivate nonbehavior analysts)" (p. 306). There appear to be few behavior-analytic research studies or descriptions on the establishment of effective multidisciplinary collaborations in which behavior analysts begin working in other established areas (Braga-Kenyon et al., 2015). Specifically, we have not yet published studies about how to create multidisciplinary teams or how to train practitioners to work on them effectively. In the last few years, some prominent thinkers in the field have commented on the tendency of behavior analysts to distance ourselves from other disciplines, particularly when it comes to publication and dissemination practices (Friman, 2014; Morris, 2014; Normand, 2014; Reed, 2014; Schlinger, 2014; St. Peter, 2013; Vyse, 2013).

We have adopted a technical language and research methodology that are relatively unique to the field, and have primarily shared the fruits of our labor within our own dedicated journals and conferences (Normand, 2014). To be successful on multidisciplinary teams and when collaboration with other professionals, we must be cognizant of our audience and purpose when choosing our language and how we implement our methodologies. Clearly, technical language, systematic single-subject evaluations, and publication in behavior-analytic journals are important activities for the long-term development of behavior analysis as a discipline. However, behavior analysts may find additional verbal repertoires helpful for maximizing our ability to collaborate with others and increase the reach of our field. For example, the field of applied behavior analysis will benefit from the repertoires of behavior analysts who can effectively convey information to parents, medical professionals, CEOs of corporations, and the general public and who are able to write in such a way as to publish research in nonbehavior-analytic journals. We provide recommendations in the section on Practice Guidelines for behavior analysts interested in expanding their practice repertoires, establishing collaborations, and helping to widely disseminate multidisciplinary research and practice.

Bringing others to behavior analysis

Other fields may benefit from learning about behavior-analytic research and practice. As noted in the sections above, behavior analysts might be able to contribute to other professions in at least three ways. First, behavior analysts might be able to create measurement systems that capture behavioral change. For example, behavior analysts have been able to evaluate the extent to which types of measurement and data displays impact performance of workers (Alvero, Bucklin, & Austin, 2001) and students (Sigurdsson & Ring, 2013). Second, behavior analysts might be able to focus others on the importance of measuring behavior at the level of the individual rather than of groups as a whole. For example, I (St. Peter) introduced single-subject designs to a prominent sleep researcher who had previously used primarily group-level analyses in her research (St. Peter, Montgomery-Downs, & Massullo, 2012). Working collaboratively, we evaluated correspondence between participants' self-reports of how much sleep they received and their actual measured sleep (using actigraphy as direct measurement) as a baseline. Participants generally reported getting much more sleep than they actually did during baseline. We used correspondence training to establish better do-say correspondence, which may be a necessary prerequisite for individuals to seek help for poor sleep habits, or for interventions based on sleep knowledge to be effective. In this example, we were able to demonstrate to a professional in another field (sleep psychopathology) that behavior was lawful and should be changed at the level of the individual.

Using behavior-analytic language

The creation of multidisciplinary collaborations may require that collaborators use a common language. Behavior-analytic jargon is unfamiliar to most laypeople; Hineline (1980) went as far as to suggest it is a distinct English dialect. Practices that makes our field seem unapproachable compared to other human services may put behavior analysis at a disadvantage in multidisciplinary settings (Becirevic et al., 2016; Lindsley, 1991). Lindsley (1991) cautioned that behavior-analytic jargon may be interpreted as "abrasive," and pointed out some terms are misleading to consumers. Specifically, he gave the examples of "negative reinforcement," and "radical behaviorism." For these reasons, some behavior analysts shy away from using jargon.

In an effort to make data-driven recommendations about the use of jargon, some researchers have proposed an evaluation of effects of behavioral jargon on listeners untrained in behavior analysis. In these studies, behavior-analytic jargon was compared to possible replacement terms. Becirevic et al. (2016) assessed the reactions of members of the public to jargon and common terms, and found their common (nontechnical) terms were rated as more acceptable than the behavior-analytic jargon (examples of terms can be found in Table 12.1). There may be other advantages to avoiding jargon: the general public prefers behavior plans written in nontechnical language (Rolider, Axelrod, & Van Houten 1998; Rolider & Axelrod, 2005), and caregivers implement interventions with higher treatment integrity when those interventions were written in conversational language (Jarmolowicz et al., 2008). Although these studies suggest that there may be negative outcomes associated with the use of jargon, this line of research is still in its infancy. In addition, effects of behavioral jargon on nonbehavioral professionals working on multidisciplinary teams are still unknown.

Table 12.1 **Comparison of behavior-analytic and lay terms from Becirevic et al. (2016)**

Behavior-analytic term	Synonym/substitute lay term
Escape extinction	Follow-through training
Negative reinforcement	Relieving consequence
Negative punishment	Penalty
Chaining	Teaching a sequence of responses
Operant conditioning	Learning from consequences
Reinforcement	Incentivizing

Until empirical data are collected, recommendations for multidisciplinary collaborators may need to be generalized from research on the general public, and perhaps derived from the experience of those who have excelled in working with other professionals. For example, Friman (2014) recommends colloquial explanations of behavioral interventions with medical providers as well as with the direct consumers. On the other hand, Lattal (n.d.) is skeptical of categorical recommendations of this nature. He posits the idea that physicians gauge their language based on the person with whom they are conversing and proposes our task should be no different. He cautions that the attitude of, "dumbing down our language to communicate with other practitioners, clients, or caregivers [. . .] has more problems than does using overly technical language, though both approaches may convey equal disrespect for the listener" (para. 5). Lattal suggests that we allow the listener to shape our verbal behavior. Perhaps rather than always or never using jargon, another option is to intersperse behavior-analytic jargon paired with the use of synonyms and less technical explanations. The extent to which, and manner in which, this is done should depend on the effect we are having on our listener.

Practice guidelines

Behavior analysts who hope to work collaboratively with individuals from other fields should first make contact with the research and practices of the other discipline, as well as behavior-analytic work previously done with that population or problem area. Behavior analysts interested in multidisciplinary work should consider how their skills could be used with novel (1) populations, (2) age groups, (3) areas of research, and (4) settings. Initial interests in other areas might be a catalyst to expand one's areas of expertise. For example, a behavior analyst with a history working with individuals with developmental and intellectual disabilities to increase leisure and vocational skills could collaborate with others to expand such work to help promote engagement with elderly persons with dementia.

Those who are interested in developing expertise with another population, age, area, or setting should engage in training opportunities to help develop skills. We can attend conferences, participate in focused workshops, or take courses. For example, a behavior analyst interested in obesity could enroll in a college course on nutrition. Training can also include seeking specific internships that would allow for focused experiences with that population, age, area, or respective setting. We can seek mentors who are currently experts in the area of interest and work directly with that mentor. Such mentors can be found by joining national and international groups for specific populations (e.g., Alzheimer's Association of America, the American Society on Aging, American Brain Injury Society). In addition, collaborations with other professionals can help provide opportunities for networking and specialized training.

Behavior analysts striving to increase competence with a new population should initially review the existing literature. LeBlanc et al. (2012) discuss procedures to conduct a literature search in the *Journal of Applied Behavior Analysis* and general database search engines (e.g., PsycINFO, PubMed, Google Scholar) by pairing key terms to capture papers related to the area. Once we make initial contact with the literature, it is important to keep up-to-date on trends in other fields and current collaborations between fields. In addition, reading research from other fields can facilitate ideas about collaborative research projects or application of behavior analysis to practical issues in other areas such as health care, environmental sustainability, or education.

Behavior analysts involved in collaborations should engage in professional development opportunities (e.g., workshops, attend conferences) that will help develop knowledge related to the collaboration. This will help the behavior analyst contribute to the collaborative relationship and can lead to the development of the collaboration. In addition to developing knowledge, professional development can include skills such as grant writing, leadership, teaching, and technology that could contribute to the collaboration. Within a multidisciplinary team, behavior analysts and other professionals can arrange for regular meetings to help disseminate knowledge. For example, Braga-Kenyon et al. (2015) suggest that peer-reviewed articles can be shared with collaborators and behavior analysts can establish reading groups with people from multiple disciplines. Meetings may include more formal presentations to help develop knowledge related to the project. For example, as part of a collaboration with the director of a school for children with ASD and developmental disabilities, I (Pence) developed and presented two focused workshops for the teachers and paraprofessionals at the director's school to help train behavior-analytic skills (e.g., preference assessments, discrete-trial instruction, prompting procedures, and error-correction procedures). In addition to the training, the teachers and paraprofessionals had time to ask me questions and interact less formally, which helped to build a working relationship between the staff and myself. The staff had positive feedback on the training and our interactions, which may increase the likelihood that the new collaboration will be successful.

Collaboration can be difficult and involves establishing and maintaining a healthy, professional, productive relationship with colleagues from other fields. To effectively collaborate, professionals (including behavior analysts) need to have good communication and social skills, and need to be practical and realistic about the goals of the collaboration. Perhaps a brief example from my personal collaborations will help to underscore the importance of communication. I (St. Peter) am currently involved in a multidisciplinary team in an elementary school whose primary purpose is to decrease escape-maintained aggression of a student with an ASD. We decided to try demand fading as a potential intervention for this student (Geiger, Carr, & LeBlanc, 2010). In an attempt to reduce the burden on the teacher, my doctoral student and I decided to test the efficacy of the intervention by having the doctoral student implement during one of three instructional blocks during the school day. We figured that starting with implementation by the doctoral student would allow us to assess the efficacy of demand fading as an intervention before we arranged for teacher training and full-day implementation. After 10 days of our testing the intervention, the teacher emailed me with a desperate plea to stop the intervention. I was astounded. The data from our 10 instructional blocks suggested that demand fading was a highly effective intervention, and that the efficacy persisted across days. I asked the teacher for more details. That email string illuminated a previous failure to communicate clearly. As the multidisciplinary team had not made an overall change to the student's Individualized Education Plan, the teacher felt that she needed to address all of his educational goals during the remaining two instructional blocks on days that we tested demand fading during one of the blocks. This resulted in increased rates of demands during the other two instructional blocks in the day, as well as a more significant transition between blocks (from essentially no demands to a higher-than-typical rate of demands). Her data, which appear in Fig. 12.2, clearly showed that aggression actually got *worse* across the day on days that we tested demand fading in her classroom, even though aggression

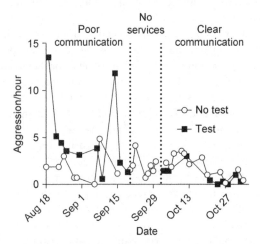

Figure 12.2 Data from a collaboration in which poor communication resulted in increased rates of aggression on days in which a behavior analyst worked with the student. Improving the communication among team members helped to improve student outcomes.

was near-zero during the block with demand fading. We suggested the multidisciplinary team hold a meeting, which occurred about a week and a half later. During that meeting, we showed our demand-fading data (just during the single instructional block) and explained the procedure. Together with the teacher and the rest of the team, we wrote a modified demand-fading protocol that the teacher could follow throughout the day. Implementation of this protocol resulted in reduced aggression throughout the day.

To us, this example highlights several important issues regarding communication during multidisciplinary collaboration. First, we should not assume that individuals from other disciplines share our assumptions or have our training. We never thought to tell the teacher *not* to change what she was doing in the other instructional blocks, in part because we did not approach the collaboration and our suggestions from her perspective. Second, we need to ensure that we are doing everything we can to keep our collaborators comfortable regarding approaching us with problems or concerns. In the case of the client described above, the teacher waited several weeks to approach us about the problem, even though it was probably an apparent issue to her from the very first day of our intervention. When our collaborators are uncomfortable approaching us about concerns, we are likely to find ourselves with fewer collaborators rather than with more successful collaborations. Finally, we need to be open to working together with our collaborators to solve problems. In the case of our client, this problem solving was relatively painless (apart from the logistics of getting a team meeting scheduled). In other cases, however, collaborations may need to involve contracts that outline expectations and agreements between parties to be successful. Behavior analysts new to multidisciplinary work may need to develop new skills and practices to help them be successful in collaborative relationships. We can benefit from meeting with other professionals who are successfully collaborating with others to help identify a mentor who can provide advice and guidance.

Behavior analysts working with individuals unfamiliar with technical jargon should use approachable language and explanations. This may mean the using more user-friendly terms as synonyms or replacements for behavior-analytic jargon. Behavior analysts engaged in long-term collaborations may be able to include more jargon as others on the team become more familiar with commonly used terms. We encourage behavior analysts to pay careful attention to how their verbal behavior is affecting the listener, and gauge their behavior based on context. Behavior analysts should prepare practical and relatable examples to illustrate the work they do and the methodology they use (e.g., single-subject designs). For example, I (Pence) recently began a collaboration with a colleague from Special Education to evaluate a manualized intervention designed to teach social skills to adolescents. The manualized intervention relied on indirect measures of behavior, including parental report and indirect assessments. I talked to my collaborator about how we could take data directly on the behavior of interest (in addition to the parental reports and indirect assessments) as a way to evaluate if our intervention successfully taught the target skills. I explained that we would have objective, repeated measurements across time during the 15-week intervention that could allow us to look at acquisition and maintenance at the level of the individual. We also discussed how we could use a multiple-probe across-participants experimental design as a way to demonstrate experimental control and to help us make decisions about modifying the intervention if our adolescents were not acquiring the skill. As we directly measured behavior, we have observed that some of our adolescents are not performing skills (e.g., two-way conversations) at consistently high levels, which has resulted in the decision to add extra training and practice to the manualized intervention.

A more nuanced aspect of communication is the way we frame information. Behavior analysts should be sensitive to the values of the professionals we would like to work with, and highlight where we can help contribute to outcomes that are important to them. For example, Bailey (1991) points out behavior analysts often value the demonstration of "functional relationships" and "control over behavior." However, not all potential partners from other fields will share these sentiments. For example, a teacher may value an intervention that will help a student, "become more independent, mature, and self-confident" and feel put off by selling points rooted in determinism (Bailey, p. 447). One way to foster collaborative relationships is to take time to learn about the values of those we might have the opportunity to work with, and determine whether and how we can contribute in a meaningful way.

We urge behavior analysts who engage in collaborative projects to take systematic data and consider contributing to the research base on multidisciplinary work. We see benefits to sharing this information with both behavior analysts and other professionals. Increasing the dissemination of diverse applications of behavior analysis within our field may help encourage other researchers and practitioners to branch out into multidisciplinary settings. Sharing successful collaborations in the journals, and at conferences, of the other fields involved can help to garner interest of those working in diverse settings. It is important to note that solely "preaching to the choir" may be of limited utility (Normand, 2014). *The Behavior Analyst* published a special issue in 2014 on the topic of publishing outside of behavior-analytic journals. The recommendations from the articles in this issue may be helpful to those interested in widening their scope of dissemination.

Behavior analysts have called for the field to increase our presence in the general media and public light. Participation in successful multidisciplinary collaborations may generate new interest in the field and result in media attention. Such positive attention increases the reputation of behavior analysis and the public's general knowledge of the field. Behavior analysts involved in new and interesting collaborations should consider determining ways to help increase our media and general population presence or to take advantage of resources obtained through the collaboration that help to publicly disseminate our work. For example, some agencies have personnel whose job is to promote the agency and could write an article on the collaboration that could be shared with the public through newsletters, social media, or emails.

Behavior analysts should not be afraid to branch out, try something new, and potentially fail. Collaborations offer several advances professionally, personally, and intellectually. They allow us to develop new relationships with colleagues and to grow in our professions. However, not all collaborations are successful and it is important that we understand that sometimes collaborations fail for reasons outside of our control. In addition, even if a collaboration is unsuccessful we can still learn and grow from the experience.

Practice guidelines checklist

I want to learn about a new area of interest:

1. Clearly articulate to yourself the new population, age, setting, or research area about which you would like to increase your expertise.
2. Read books or review articles that focus on the area of interest to provide an overview and more general information.
3. Read journal articles that are applicable to the population, age, setting, or research area.
4. Attend presentations by experts in the area of interest.
5. Attend workshops or conferences in the area of interest.
6. Join national or international groups related to the area of interest
7. Talk to experts in the area of interest to receive guidance about training and networking opportunities, important research articles, and to answer questions.
8. Consider attending an intensive training or taking a class to help develop additional knowledge.
9. Identify a mentor in the new area of interest to help guide your pursuit for knowledge and training.

I want to start a new collaboration:

1. Outline initial ideas for expanding your current expertise in a new population, age group, area of research, or setting and what kinds of collaborations would facilitate the success of your idea.
2. Give consideration to additional knowledge and training you need to be successful in the collaboration.
3. Participate in trainings (e.g., course, workshop, conference) or read articles to increase your knowledge and to learn new skills that would benefit you in the collaboration.
4. Participate in networking opportunities to meet new colleagues and to help form new working relationships.
5. Identify colleagues that would be good partners in the area of interest. Some suggestions for good partners are outlined below:
   a. Colleagues who have published peer-reviewed articles in the area of interest.
   b. Colleagues who have extensive experience working in the area of interest.
   c. Colleagues who have received specialized training in the area of interest.
   d. Colleagues who are actively involved (e.g., training others, working with the target population) in the area of interest.
   e. Colleagues who are willing to commit to the time necessary to work with you and who are willing to provide training and constructive feedback.
6. Approach colleagues to discuss area of interest and to share ideas for working with the population, age group, area of research, or setting.
7. Work with colleagues to identify goals for the project. Discuss the procedures to answer the research question or the steps to expand your expertise into the new clinician population, age, or setting.

8. Make agreements with colleagues about roles, responsibilities, and timelines. You may decide to complete a contract to outline these agreements.
9. Set goals to advance the collaboration and meet with collaborators regularly to discuss progress toward those goals.

My collaboration is not going well:

1. Seek guidance from a trusted mentor (or mentors) to identify the challenges in the collaboration and why those challenges are occurring. Challenges to collaborations can occur for several reasons. Although not an exhaustive list, some challenges include miscommunication, time constraints, differing professional priorities, staffing or resource issues, and administrative pressures.
2. Determine what next steps you would like to take with the collaboration.
3. If you want the collaboration to continue:
    a. Have an open discussion with the collaborator. Talk about your concerns and your ideas to address the challenge and to move forward.
    b. Seek feedback from the collaborator to confirm that he or she would like to continue with the collaboration. Ask the collaborator what challenges he or she is facing and his or her ideas to move forward.
    c. Create an action plan that outlines the steps each individual needs to complete to address the concerns and to strengthen and move forward with the collaboration.
    d. If a contract was not signed at the onset of the collaboration, then consider writing a contract that outlines roles, responsibilities, timelines, and other relevant information and having all parties sign the contract.
    e. Schedule frequent, regular meetings to check-in on progress, discuss concerns, and to ask questions.
4. If you decide to terminate the collaboration:
    a. Create an exit strategy that outlines when and how the relationship will end.
    b. Determine how the collaboration can be dissolved with minimal disruption and without negatively impacting services to consumers.
    c. Have an open discussion with the collaborator. Talk about your concerns and your plan to move forward in a professional manner. Refrain from placing any blame or having negative interactions with the collaborator.
    d. Discuss who will be responsible for resuming responsibility for any clients or responsibilities that were part of the collaboration. Discuss who is responsible for any data collected and the storage of those data. If the collaboration could result in a publication or presentation, discuss authorship and who will coordinate the publication or presentation and what roles each collaborator will have to finalize those products.
    e. Aim to maintain a professional relationship even though you are ending the collaboration.
5. Use the lessons you learned from this collaboration to help you navigate future collaborations to increase the likelihood of having a successful, mutually productive collaborative relationship.

Acknowledgment

The authors would like to thank Cory Whirtley for her contribution to examples on the importance of communication.

References

Alvero, A. M., Bucklin, B. R., & Austin, J. (2001). An objective review of the effectiveness and essential characteristics of performance feedback in organizational settings (1985−1998). *Journal of Organizational Behavior Management, 21*(1), 3−29.

American Psychiatric Association (2013). *Diagnostic and statistical manual of mental disorders* (5th ed.). Washington, DC: American Psychiatric Association.

Ayllon, T., & Michael, J. (1959). The psychiatric nurse as a behavioral engineer. *Journal of the Experimental Analysis of Behavior, 2*, 323−334. Available from http://dx.doi.org/10.1901/jeab.1959.2-323.

Behavior Analysis Certification Board. (2016). Professional and ethical compliance code for behavior analysts. Retrieved from: https://bacb.com/wp-content/uploads/2017/05/170525-compliance-code-english.pdf >.

BACB Experience Supervision Form. (2016). *Behavior analyst certification board—Experience standards.* Retrieved from: http://bacb.com/experience-standards/.

Baer, D. M., Wolf, M. M., & Risley, T. R. (1968). Some current dimensions of applied behavior analysis. *Journal of Applied Behavior Analysis, 1*, 91−97. Available from http://dx.doi.org/10.1901/jaba.1968.1-91.

Bailey, J. S. (1991). Marketing behavior analysis requires different talk. *Journal of Applied Behavior Analysis, 24*, 445−448. Available from http://dx.doi.org/10.1901/jaba.1991.24-445.

Beavers, G. A., Iwata, B. A., & Lerman, D. C. (2013). Thirty years of research on the functional analysis of problem behavior. *Journal of Applied Behavior Analysis, 46*, 1−21. Available from http://dx.doi.org/10.1002/jaba.30.

Becirevic, A., Critchfield, T. S., & Reed, D. D. (2016). On the social acceptability of behavior-analytic terms: Crowdsourced comparisons of lay and technical language. *The Behavior Analyst, 36*, 305−317. Available from http://dx.doi.org/10.1007/s40614-016-0067-4.

Braga-Kenyon, P., Kenyon, S., & Guilhardi, P. (2015). The behavior analyst as a team member: Toward a cohesive multidisciplinary approach to individuals diagnosed with autism spectrum disorder (ASD). *International Journal of Behavior Analysis & Autism Spectrum Disorders, 1*(2), 18−29.

Boyce, T. E., & Hineline, P. N. (2002). Interteaching: A strategy for enhancing the user-friendliness of behavioral arrangements in the college classroom. *The Behavior Analyst, 25*(2), 215−226.

Carr, E. G., & Owen-DeSchryver, J. S. (2007). Physical illness, pain, and problem behavior in minimally verbal people with developmental disabilities. *Journal of Autism and Developmental Disabilities, 73*, 413−424. Available from http://dx.doi.org/10.1007/s10803-006-0176-0.

Cornwell, S. L., Kelly, K., & Austin, L. (2010). Pediatric feeding disorders: Effectiveness of multidisciplinary inpatient treatment of gastrostomy-tube dependent children. *Children's Health Care, 39*, 214−231. Available from http://dx.doi.org/10.1080/02739615.2010.493770.

Damschroder, L. J., Aron, D. C., Keith, R. E., Kirsh, S. R., Alexander, J. A., & Lowery, J. C. (2009). Fostering implementation of health services research findings into practice: A consolidated framework for advancing implementation science. *Implementation Science: IS, 4*, 50. http://dx.doi.org/10.1186/1748-5908-4-50.

Dillenburger, K., Röttgers, H., Dounavi, K., Sparkman, C., Keenan, M., Thyer, B., & Nikopoulos, C. (2014). Multidisciplinary teamwork in autism: Can one size fit all? *The*

Australian Educational and Developmental Psychologist, 31, 97−112. Available from http://dx.doi.org/10.1017/edp.2014.13.

Friman, P. C. (2010). Come on in, the water is fine: Achieving mainstream relevance through integration with primary medical care. *The Behavior Analyst, 33*(1), 19−36.

Friman, P. C. (2014). Publishing in journals outside the box: Attaining mainstream prominence requires demonstrations of mainstream relevance. *Behavior Analyst, 37,* 73−76. Available from http://dx.doi.org/10.1007/s40614-014-0014-1.

Geiger, K. B., Carr, J. E., & LeBlanc, L. (2010). Function-based treatments for escape-maintained problem behavior: A treatment-selection model for practicing behavior analysts. *Behavior Analysis In Practice, 3*(1), 22−32.

Harvey, M. T., Luiselli, J. K., & Wong, S. E. (2009). Application of applied behavior analysis to mental health issues. *Psychological Services, 6,* 212−222. Available from http://dx.doi.org/10.1037/a0016495.

Hineline, P. (1980). The language of behavior analysis: Its community, its functions, and its limitations. *Behaviorism, 8*(1), 67−86.

Iwata, B. A., Dorsey, M. F., Slifer, K. J., Bauman, K. E., & Richman, G. S. (1994). Toward a functional analysis of self-injury. *Journal of Applied Behavior Analysis, 27,* 197−209. Available from http://dx.doi.org/10.1901/jaba.1994.27-197.

Jarmolowicz, D. P., Kahng, S., Ingvarsson, E. T., Goysovich, R., Heggemeyer, R., & Gregory, M. K. (2008). Effects of conversational versus technical language on treatment preference and integrity. *Intellectual and Developmental Disabilities, 46,* 190−199. Available from http://dx.doi.org/10.1352/2008.46:190-199.

Johnston J. (2009). APBA 2009 Professional employment survey results (survey results published by the Association of Professional Behavior Analysts). Archived resource for Association of Professional Behavior Analysts members. Retrieved from: http://www.apbahome.net/index.php APBA Survey Results section.

Kennedy, C. H., & Meyer, K. A. (1996). Sleep deprivation, allergy symptoms, and negatively reinforced problem behavior. *Journal of Applied Behavior Analysis, 29,* 133−135. Available from http://dx.doi.org/10.1901/jaba.1996.29-133.

LaRue, R. H., Stewart, V., Piazza, C. C., Volkert, V. M., Patel, M. R., & Zeleny, J. (2011). Escape as reinforcement and escape extinction in the treatment of feeding problems. *Journal of Applied Behavior Analysis, 44,* 719−735. Available from http://dx.doi.org/10.1901/jaba.44-719.

Lattal (n.d.). *The Sweet Spot in Communicating Behavior Analysis to the Lay Public.* Retrieved from: http://aubreydaniels.com/institute/from-the-field/the-sweet-spot-communicating-behavior-analysis-the-lay-public.

LeBlanc, L. A. (2010). Integrating behavioral psychology services into adult day programming for individuals with dementia. *Behavior Modification, 34,* 443−458.

LeBlanc, L. A., Heinicke, M. R., & Baker, J. C. (2012). Expanding the consumer base for behavior-analytic services: Meeting the needs of consumers in the 21st century. *Behavior Analysis in Practice, 5*(1), 4−14.

Lindsley, O. R. (1991). From technical jargon to plain English for application. *Journal of Applied Behavior Analysis, 24,* 449−458. Available from http://dx.doi.org/10.1901/jaba.1991.24-449.

Montee, B. B., Miltenberger, R. G., Wittrock, D., Watkins, N., Rheinberger, A., & Stackhaus, J. (1995). An experimental analysis of facilitated communication. *Journal of Applied Behavior Analysis, 28,* 189−200. Available from http://dx.doi.org/10.1901/jaba.1995.28-189.

Morris, E. K. (2014). Stop preaching to the choir, publish outside the box: A discussion. *Behavior Analyst, 37,* 87−94. Available from http://dx.doi.org/10.1007/s40614-014-0011-4.

Normand, M. P. (2014). Opening Skinner's box: An introduction. *Behavior Analyst, 37,* 67−68. Available from http://dx.doi.org/10.1007/s40614-014-0016-z.

Normand, M. P., & Kohn, C. S. (2013). Don't wag the dog: Extending the reach of applied behavior analysis. *The Behavior Analyst, 36*(1), 109−122.

Northup, J., Fusilier, I., Swanson, V., Huete, J., Bruce, T., Freeland, J., Gulley, V., & Edwards, S. (1999). Further analysis of the separate and interactive effects of methylphenidate and common classroom contingencies. *Journal of Applied Behavior Analysis, 32,* 35−50. Available from http://dx.doi.org/10.1901/jaba.1999.32-35.

O'Reilly, M. F. (1995). Functional analysis and treatment of escape-maintained aggression correlated with sleep deprivation. *Journal of Applied Behavior Analysis, 28,* 225−226. Available from http://dx.doi.org/10.1901/jaba.1995.28-225.

Piazza, C. C., Fisher, W. W., Brown, K. A., Shore, B. A., Patel, M. R., Katz, R. M., … Blakely-Smith, A. (2003). Functional analysis of inappropriate mealtime behaviors. *Journal of Applied Behavior Analysis, 36,* 187−204. Available from http://dx.doi.org/10.1901/jaba.2003.36-187.

Piazza, C. C., Patel, M. R., Gulotta, C. S., Sevin, B. M., & Layer, S. A. (2003). On the relative contributions of positive reinforcement and escape extinction in the treatment of food refusal. *Journal of Applied Behavior Analysis, 36,* 309−324. Available from http://dx.doi.org/10.1901/jaba.2003.36-187.

Poling, A. (2010). Looking to the future: Will behavior analysis survive and prosper? *The Behavior Analyst, 33*(1), 7−17.

Poling, A., & Ehrhardt, K. (1999). Applied behavior analysis, social validation, and the psychopharmacology of mental retardation. *Mental Retardation & Developmental Disabilities Research Reviews, 5,* 342−347. http://dx.doi.org/10.1002/(SICI)1098-2779 (1999)5:4%3c342::AID-MRDD12%3e3.0.CO;2-7

Reed, D. D. (2014). Determining how, when, and whether you should publish outside the box: sober advice for early career behavior analysts. *Behavior Analyst, 37,* 83−86. Available from http://dx.doi.org/10.1007/s40614-014-0012-3.

Reed, G. K., Dolezai, D. N., Cooper-Brown, L. J., & Wacker, D. P. (2005). The effects of sleep disruption on the treatment of a feeding disorder. *Journal of Applied Behavior Analysis, 38,* 243−245. Available from http://dx.doi.org/10.1901/jaba.2005.42-04.

Rolider, A., & Axelrod, S. (2005). The effects of ''behavior-speak'' on public attitudes toward behavioral interventions. A cross-cultural argument for using conversational language to describe behavioral interventions. In W. L. Heward, T. E. Heron, N. A. Neef, S. M. Peterson, D. M. Sainto, G. Cartledge, …, & J. C. Dardig (Eds.), *Focus on behavior analysis in education* (pp. 283−293). Upper Saddle River, NJ: Pearson/Merrill Prentice Hall.

Rolider, A., Axelrod, S., & Van Houten, R. (1998). Don't speak behaviorism to me: How to clearly and effectively communicate behavioral interventions to the general public. *Child & Family Behavior Therapy, 20,* 39−56. Available from http://dx.doi.org/10.1300/J019v20n02_03.

Schlinger, H. D. (2014). Publishing outside the box: Unforeseen dividends of talking to strangers. *The Behavior Analyst, 37,* 77−81.

Shore, B. A., Babbit, R. L., Williams, K. E., Coe, D. A., & Synder, A. (1998). Use of texture fading in the treatment of food selectivity. *Journal of Applied Behavior Analysis, 31,* 621−633. Available from http://dx.doi.org/10.1901/jaba.1998.31-621.

Sigurdsson, S. O., & Ring, B. M. (2013). Evaluating preference for graphic feedback on correct versus incorrect performance. *Journal of Organizational Behavior Management, 33,* 128−136. Available from http://dx.doi.org/10.1080/01608061.2013.785889.

St. Peter, C. C. (2013). Changing course through collaboration. *The Behavior Analyst, 36*(1), 155−160.

St. Peter, C. C., Montgomery-Downs, H. E., & Massullo, J. P. (2012). Improving accuracy of sleep self-reports through correspondence training. *The Psychological Record, 62*(4), 623−630.

Vyse, S. (2013). Changing course. *The Behavior Analyst, 36*(1), 123−135.

Wilder, D. A., Austin, J., & Casella, S. (2009). Applying behavior analysis in organizations: Organizational behavior management. *Psychological Services, 6,* 202−211. Available from http://dx.doi.org/10.1037/10015393.

Wolf, M. M. (1978). Social validity: The case for subjective measurement or how applied behavior analysis is finding its heart. *Journal of Applied Behavior Analysis, 11,* 203−214. Available from http://dx.doi.org/10.1901/jaba.1978.11-203.

Further reading

BACB Fourth Edition Task List. (2012). *Behavior analyst certification board.* Retrieved from: http://bacb.com/fourth-edition-task-list/.

BACB Professional and Ethical Compliance Code for Behavior Analysts. (2016). *Behavior analyst certification board.* Retrieved from: http://bacb.com/ethics-code/.

Section III

Professional Development

Continuing Education: Accessing the Peer-Reviewed Literature

Jennifer Gillis Mattson
Binghamton University, Binghamton, NY, United States

Introduction to the topic and relevance for behavioral practitioners

In the first chapter of *Science and Human Behavior*, Skinner (1965) states, "...not everyone is willing to defend a position of stubborn 'not knowing.' There is no virtue in ignorance for its own sake." (p. 5). As scientific research continues, behavior analysts' knowledge will increase and change for the benefit of consumers and society. Hence, it is critical that behavior analysts consistently stay in contact with contemporary scholarly literature.

Maintaining contact with the current scientific literature to inform multiple areas of one's practice (e.g., assessment, intervention, staff training, etc.) is a key component in an evidence-based practice (EBP) model. Over the past two decades, several health-related fields, including medicine and psychology, have adopted an EBP model. According to the Institute of Medicine (2001), EBP is defined as "the integration of best research evidence with clinical expertise and patient values." (p. 147). The American Psychological Association (2005) defined EBP in psychology as "the integration of the best available research with clinical expertise in the context of patient characteristics, culture, and preferences." (p. 5). An EBP model clearly requires the practitioner (in at least medicine and psychology) to maintain contact with the current scholarly literature. Using the term "evidence-based practice" to label how behavior analysts approach their practice might be appropriate. Indeed, a closer examination of the items within the BACB's Fourth Edition Task List and the codes of *The Professional and Ethical Compliance Code for Behavior Analysts*, commonly referred to as the "Compliance Code" (BACB, 2014), reveals several items and codes that are particularly relevant to practicing behavior analysts and are also in alignment with the definition of EBP.

With respect to the Task List, under the "Intervention" section, item J-02 "Identify potential interventions based on assessment results and the best available scientific evidence," is mostly in alignment with the definitions of EBP. Slightly different but still relevant to EBP includes item J-04, "Select intervention strategies based on client preferences," as well as under the Task List section, "Identification of Problem," item G-07 "Practice within one's limits of professional competence in ABA and obtain consultation, supervision, and training or make referrals as necessary." This latter item emphasizes that behavior analysts are aware of their expertise

Applied Behavior Analysis Advanced Guidebook. DOI: http://dx.doi.org/10.1016/B978-0-12-811122-2.00013-9

and therefore can make decisions within the identified area of expertise. These three Task List items together meet the definitional criteria of EBP.

Some relevant codes within the BACB's Compliance Code to the EBP model fall under the first code, "Responsible Conduct of Behavior Analysts" and more specifically include the following codes:

1.01 Reliance on scientific knowledge

Behavior analysts rely on professionally derived knowledge based on science and behavior analysis when making scientific or professional judgments in human service provision, or when engaging in scholarly or professional endeavors.

1.02 Boundaries of competence

1. All behavior analysts provide services, teach, and conduct research only within the boundaries of their education, training, and supervised experience.
2. Behavior analysts provide services, teach, or conduct research in new areas (e.g., populations, techniques, behaviors) only after first undertaking appropriate study, training, supervision, and/or consultation from persons who are competent in those areas.

1.03 Maintaining competence through professional development.

Behavior analysts maintain knowledge of current scientific and professional information in their areas of practice and undertake ongoing efforts to maintain competence in the skills they use by reading the appropriate literature, attending conferences and conventions, participating in workshops, obtaining additional coursework, and/or obtaining and maintaining appropriate professional credentials.

Another relevant code to staying in contact with the literature is under Code 2, "Behavior Analysts' Responsibility to Clients":

2.09 Treatment/intervention efficacy.

1. Clients have a right to effective treatment (i.e., based on the research literature and adapted to the individual client). Behavior analysts always have the obligation to advocate for and educate the client about scientifically supported, most effective treatment procedures. Effective treatment procedures have been validated as having both long-term and short-term benefits to clients and society.
2. Behavior analysts have the responsibility to advocate for the appropriate amount and level of service provision and oversight required to meet the need behavior-change program goals.
3. In those instances where more than one scientifically supported treatment has been established, additional factors may be considered in selecting interventions, including, but not limited to, efficiency and cost-effectiveness, risks and side-effects of the interventions, client preference, and practitioner experience and training.
4. Behavior analysts review and appraise the effects of any treatments about which they are aware that might impact the goals of the behavior-change program, and their possible impact on the behavior- change program, to the extent possible.

In addition to the above codes, Code 3.0 "Assessing Behavior" states, "Behavior analysts using behavior-analytic assessment techniques do so for purposes that are appropriate given current research." The description of this code fits within the definition of EBP. Taken together, practicing behavior analysts are likely trained to utilize an EBP model and compelled to continue doing so throughout their careers.

Recall that an EBP model requires that a practitioner is knowledgeable of the best, current research regarding the assessment and treatment of a client's needs.

Maintaining contact with the literature is emphasized in the Compliance Code and the Task List. The code, "Maintain Competence through Professional Development" (Code 1.03) requires that the behavior analyst maintain competence "by reading the appropriate literature, attending conferences and conventions, participating in workshops, obtaining additional coursework, and/or obtaining and maintaining appropriate professional credentials." Also referenced within the Task List is the emphasis on identifying interventions based on the "the best available scientific evidence" (J-02), contact with the current peer-reviewed literature is a necessity and is, therefore, a major component of training programs. Thus, remaining in contact with the literature is clearly an important endeavor and is one component of remaining an informed, ethical, and competent professional.

Training in maintaining contact with the scholarly literature often begins in one's graduate (or undergraduate) studies when contact with the literature is frequent and usually includes recently published scholarly readings due to coursework, supervision, and/or research demands and activities. However, upon graduation, the response effort required to maintain contact with the literature might change and increase for several reasons. For example, no short-term contingencies are necessarily in place, such as receiving a poor score on an exam due to neglecting to read the literature. In addition, there may be competing responsibilities or demands depending on the nature of one's job responsibilities, and personal needs. Other examples of barriers include easy access to the literature and increased costs to attend conferences, which provide exposure to new research and other scholarly topics. For example, once a student graduates, they may no longer have access to the university/college library system. Moreover, the cost of attending a conference as a professional, as opposed to a student, is sometimes substantially greater and might be difficult to manage given other potential financial responsibilities (e.g., mortgage, education loans, daycare expense, saving for retirement). Despite these potential challenges or barriers, behavior analysts remain charged with the task of identifying ways to remain active in the pursuit of new scholarly literature.

Although the BACB's Compliance Code provides guidance to behavior analysts in the professional behaviors that are important and necessary, the Compliance Code does not state "how to" effectively maintain contact with the peer-reviewed literature. There are contingencies in place by the BACB to promote increased contact with the literature by way of continuing education (CE) requirements. Specifically, at present time, the BACB requires behavior analysts to obtain a certain number of CE units (CEUs) every 2 years in order to maintain certification. There are, of course, other strategies for maintaining contact with the literature not only for professional development but also to be consistent with an EBP model (i.e., remaining aware of the best available research regarding any number of important professional and practice areas).

The goal of this chapter is to review ways in which practitioners are trained to access and review the literature, identify strategies for maintaining contact with literature based on available research and scholarly contributions within the behavior-analytic field, and to provide a set of practice guidelines for behavior analysts' consideration.

Status of practitioner training

It is not surprising that there are no publications ascertaining how behavior analysts receive training prior to certification (as students or supervisees) on the specific topic of contacting the peer-reviewed, scholarly literature. Graduate and undergraduate programs in behavior analysis most likely include a high frequency of contact with the contemporary scholarly literature. Despite the lack of specific information on this topic, it is commonplace for a student to read journal articles or other behavior-analytic scholarly content identified by an instructor, fieldwork supervisor, or lab director on a weekly basis throughout the semester. Given that several codes of the BACB Compliance Code reference needing to be aware of the best available research or evidence for specific purposes, the topic of maintaining contact with the literature in professional practice is likely covered in a course on ethics and professional behavior, at least to varying degrees. Specific skills relevant to maintaining contact with the literature might be taught during practitioner training include learning how to use search engines or databases, how to evaluate the scholarly literature, and learning about CE requirements.

Accessing the literature

Training on how to access and use search engines and databases, such as PsychInfo or ERIC, is typically offered or available during the course of graduate or undergraduate studies. There might be opportunities as part of a course requirement, within the context of a lecture in a course, during supervision, or as part of research-related activities. College or university libraries offer these types of trainings either as a formal workshop scheduled throughout the semester for any interested student, as a guest lecture in a course, or on an individual basis at the library (sometimes, appointments are needed for the latter). Science librarians are experts in the efficient and effective use of search engines for a variety of purposes. It is strongly recommended that students consult with a science librarian if he/she is unfamiliar with search databases or how to search for and retrieve the relevant scholarly literature. As science librarians keep up to date with this information, often they are aware of new features and/or search tools. Interestingly, science librarians are astutely aware of the importance and challenge facing scientists, practitioners, and students in maintaining contact with the growing literature. As such, many libraries' websites post tutorials, written or video, on how to maintain contact with the literature. For example, Binghamton University libraries offer to the public, a 15-minute video tutorial entitled, "Monitoring Information and Keeping in Current" which covers how to use Google Reader, RSS Feeds, and Table of Contents alerts (http://www.binghamton. edu/libraries/research/tutorials/index.html, September, 7, 2016).

Evaluation of the scholarly literature

Throughout one's academic training, learning how to evaluate the available literature is usually a standard component of at least graduate education and sometimes is introduced at the undergraduate level. Maintaining one's fluency of research evaluation terms, such as those associated with evaluating the validity of information presented in a range of scholarly literature (e.g., empirical studies, review papers, chapters and books), is necessary to be able to determine its relevance to one's practice or to a specific clinical or professional issue. Graduate programs typically require a research methods course where one learns to critically read and evaluate the peer-reviewed literature, as well as other sources. At a minimum, students are taught to identify (1) threats to validity, (2) methodological issues, and (3) potential bias (e.g., author, source, etc.).

Linking the activity of reading scholarly literature to clinical or applied decision-making in EBP is likely a common and necessary component of practitioner training. As supervisors, this activity is frequent and ongoing. In fact, the BACB Supervision Form provides prompts for supervisors to do this activity! Another activity sometimes offered in graduate programs is a weekly case conference or "brown bag" wherein students, faculty, or invited guests present a clinical case to other students and faculty. This activity allows for contact with recent literature that might not have been covered in courses.

Continuing education

A final point on practitioner training in contacting the peer-reviewed literature is the topic of continuing education. The importance of continuing education is incorporated in practitioner training as a course or part of a course, such as within the topic of ethics or professional development as it is a required ongoing activity for all levels of certified behavior analysts. Another common way that students learn to obtain CEUs is through conference attendance. Many graduate programs encourage or require students to attend state/regional, national and/or international behavior-analytic conferences, not only to provide exposure to CE events but also to reinforce the numerous important professional behaviors, including networking, public speaking skills, exposure to the professional context and purpose of board meetings, staying abreast of local and global issues affecting behavior analysts.

In sum, there are likely numerous opportunities throughout the course of one's behavior-analytic training to achieve the goal of learning the value in contacting the literature and how to achieve this goal likely varies across training experiences and may or may not be formally summarized.

Research base and implications for practice

Although there is clear agreement that maintaining contact with the scholarly literature is an important and necessary task for behavior analysts, and likely is introduced to practitioners prior to certification, there is limited empirical research on this topic in the field of behavior analysis. Specifically, it is unclear how often or

for which professional, ethical, or clinical issues behavior analysts consult the contemporary literature, nor is there ample research on the specific barriers faced by
practitioners in accessing the literature. At the time, this chapter was written there
was only one empirical study on the positive effects of a journal club on knowledge
acquisition (Parsons & Reid, 2011) and two additional articles describing common
barriers, solutions to those barriers, and other considerations for staying in contact
with the literature (Carr & Briggs, 2010; Gillis & Carr, 2014). Interestingly, there
has been increased attention in describing how to engage in this important practice
amongst behavior analysts at professional conferences. For example, the article by
Gillis and Carr resulted from several conference presentations over the course of a
few years wherein the authors shared with the audience "Top Ten" articles for
behavior analysts to read. Future research is needed in this area and given increased
attention, there will hopefully be more scholarly work available in the near future.
A summary of the three published articles mentioned above is provided followed
by implications for practice based on these articles. At the end of this section an
analysis of CE events offered at different conferences will be discussed.

Carr and Briggs (2010) identified three key tasks in order to maintain contact
with the literature, associated barriers with each task and provided possible solutions to the barriers. The three major tasks included searching the literature for relevant content, accessing content (e.g., articles), and remaining current with new
literature. Searching for relevant content is a first important step but not always an
easy or straightforward one. One barrier in identifying pertinent literature is only
searching a familiar journal's database, for example, searching for articles within
the *Journal of Applied Behavior Analysis (JABA)*. Although *JABA* is an excellent
journal publishing relevant and high-quality articles, behavior analysts publish in
other quality journals as well and articles of interest and relevance might be missed
if only a narrow search amongst literature sources (e.g., journals) is conducted. One
potential reason for limiting the search for behavior-analytic literature to a select
number of journals might be limited awareness of the range of journals that
routinely publish behavior-analytic research. To increase awareness of these other
journals, the authors included a table with 17 journals that publish behavioral
research in the area of autism and developmental disabilities.

The second task, accessing the literature, also presents with challenges. Two of
these include having access to databases such as PsycINFO (includes journals in
the behavioral and psychological sciences), which is not free to the public, and
navigating through the range of found content using an open-access search engine
such as Google. Possible solutions offered include gaining access to PsycINFO,
either through an employer (agency) or subscribing as an individual, accessing
archived articles via PubMed, and contacting authors of journal articles.

The third important task identified by Carr and Briggs is maintaining contact
with the literature on a routine basis. The authors offer several strategies to accomplish this task, including a step-by-step guide for setting up RSS feeds, and signing
up for email alerts from journals or publishers for notifications of new content such
as a new issue. Carr and Briggs also suggest bookmarking relevant journal websites
as many "in press" articles are available on the journal's website for free. The

authors further recommended self-management strategies and as well as cultivating a social or work community, such as negotiating time to read the literature.

With respect to allowing behavior analysts to access the relevant literature in the work setting, Parsons and Reid (2011) conducted an empirical study demonstrating an effective approach in conducting reading groups that improved staff knowledge within a human service setting. In their study, eight employees participated in a monthly reading group. First supervisors generated a list of topics and then employees who participated in the group identified three topics of interest from that list. From these topics, a set of readings was selected for the group meetings. Given that the participants were not behavior analysts or individuals with a background in reading journal articles, chapters instead of journal articles were selected. The authors generated several study questions for each chapter that participants completed before the group meeting. To assess whether the assigned readings improved knowledge, pre and postreading group quizzes were administered to participants. The results showed staff knowledge improved and also that staff was satisfied with the reading group, attended consistently, and the reading group continued after the study was completed. Parsons and Reid recommended (1) obtaining agency approval to conduct scheduled reading groups, (2) addressing barriers to allow the maximum number of staff interested in the reading groups to participate, (3) keeping a consistent and structured group format that includes active participation of the members of the group, (4) continuously assessing the acceptability of the reading group by its participants, and (5) allowing participants to be part of the decision process in selecting topics.

Recognizing that it can be difficult to know where to start with staying current with the literature, Gillis and Carr (2014) provided an annotated bibliography of 15 peer-reviewed articles and shared their process of reviewing and selecting the article set. To identify articles to include in the bibliography the authors first identified the theme or topic of interest. For their article, the focus was on topics of interest to practicing behavior analysts and mostly within the area of developmental disabilities. The next step was to select a date range for the review. The authors reviewed articles from the last 3−5 years, in an effort to read the most current research on the identified topic. While using search engines such as PsycINFO or ERIC is helpful in finding a range of articles on this topic, the authors chose to use the set of 17 journals included in Carr and Briggs (2010) as these journals frequently published behavior-analytic articles within the topic area of developmental disabilities. The criteria used to search the journals included identifying articles that covered a range of specific topics and article types (excluding replication studies, but including empirical studies, reviews, etc.). Each author identified 50 articles and through a consensus process narrowed the list to 15 articles. The authors indicated that 15 articles seemed to be an appropriate number of articles for review over a short period of time. One of the interesting findings from this article was that the majority of the 15 selected articles were in the journals, *Behavior Analysis in Practice* and *Journal of Applied Behavior Analysis*.

Implications for practice

Maintaining ongoing contact with the current literature can require considerable effort and is often associated with several barriers. Carr and Briggs (2010) suggest consideration of the following strategies: "(a) generating a core list of journals to follow, (b) securing access to journal content, and (c) developing a system and contingencies for making contact with the newly published literature." (p. 18). Note that the core journals might differ depending on the area within behavior analysis that one wishes to maintain frequent contact. Behavior analysts should consider developing a list of journals that routinely publish behavior-analytic content generally and also within different specialty areas of interest such as autism, traumatic brain injury, aging, and organizational behavior management.

With respect to securing access to journal content, the authors recommend using PsycINFO. Another commonly used database is ERIC, which includes education journals. These are two relevant databases that practitioners likely accessed during graduate school; unfortunately, these databases are rarely accessible by individuals not affiliated with a higher education institution (though some allow continued access for alumni). However, all levels of certified behavior analysts have access to the ERIC database through the BACB. In addition, the BACB offers access to the *Journal of Applied Behavior Analysis, Journal of the Experimental Analysis of Behavior*, and *Behavioral Interventions*.

While accessing PsycINFO or ERIC databases might present with certain barriers, it is important to not default to open-access databases, such as Google, Bing, Yahoo, or other major Internet search engines, as well as GoogleScholar. These search engines might produce a large number of "hits," not all of which are peer-reviewed or contain accurate content, and therefore, one's response effort immediately increases as a more careful review of the results is required to discriminate between relevant and irrelevant results.

To examine this issue more closely, the author of the chapter conducted a search based on the terms "self-injurious behavior" and "autism." First, using the ERIC database, a Basic Search (which will search for the specified terms in the title, keywords, abstract or text), limited to peer-reviewed scholarly journals for the year 2015, yielded six results. This search in PsycINFO yielded 33 results, which included all six articles from the ERIC search results. Using the same criteria and restricting the results to articles using Google Scholar yielded 795 results (in .04 seconds!). The same criteria in Google, yielded 131 results (cannot specify peer-reviewed journals). From this example, behavior analysts are encouraged to use either ERIC or PsycINFO (or both).

One advantage of Google Scholar is the availability of full-text access by authors of published articles, usually via ResearchGate (www.researchgate.net) or from a researcher's own website. [ResearchGate is a social networking site for researchers to share their research with others, including members or nonmembers of ResearchGate. You can follow a researcher and be informed of new publications uploaded to ResearchGate. Similar social networking sites for researchers include Mendeley (www.mendeley.com), Scirus (www.scirus.com), Academia.edu (www.academia.edu), among dozens of others. Not all researchers will be members of these sites as it is too cumbersome a task for most. It is also important to know that individuals on these various sites can upload unpublished data or papers so it is important to verify the documents or material that you review.] However, a disadvantage of using open-access Internet search engines, including Google Scholar, is that the algorithms these search engines use might be biased in the display of the order of the results. It is also important to remember that most open-access Internet search engines, such as Google or Bing, are not intended for the user who is searching for scholarly literature and, as a result, sifting through the results can be overwhelming.

Regarding access to new publications, all of the reviewed articles offer helpful strategies for developing a system or strategies for maintaining contact with the literature. Carr and Briggs outline a step-by-step process for setting up RSS feeds. It is also important to remember that most science librarians can provide assistance with these procedures and librarians do remain current in the new ways to access the literature important to the user. Gillis and Carr (2014) demonstrated that conducting a careful review of recent scholarly work within a topic area (e.g., developmental disabilities) allows for dissemination of this information to other behavior analysts, decreasing other behavior analysts' response effort for reviewing the literature but also allowing others to use a similar procedure to identify relevant literature across a range of topics within behavior analysis and to share with colleagues or students. However, some behavior analysts might find that they do not have a significant amount of time to review multiple journals over a 3−5-year period in order to identify 15 articles for review. Based on the recommendation from Gillis and Carr, it might be reasonable to limit the search to the two identified journals that contained the majority of the 15 articles: *Journal of Applied Behavior Analysis* and *Behavior Analysis in Practice*. Parsons and Reid also provided a procedure for setting up a reading club as a way to keep current with the literature. The authors' procedure certainly could be applied to a journal club format or a reading group for behavior analysts within an agency as well. The important take home message from all of these articles is to decide on a plan for staying current that will be effective and endure over time.

Continuing education at conventions

One activity to maintain contact with the literature is participating in continuing education events. According to the BACB, continuing education is required in order "to ensure that all certificants engage in activities that will expand and maintain their behavior-analytic skills." (retrieved from bacb.com/continuing-education/ retrieved on September 14, 2016). There are different requirements for the different certificant levels with the BCBA (with our without the "D" distinction) requiring 32 CEUs every 2 years and the BCaBA certificants are required to obtain 20 CEUs every 2 years. At the present time, behavior analysts are also required to obtain a specific number of CEUs within the area of Ethics and, if providing supervision, CEUs in that area are also required. There are seven different types of continuing education approved by the BACB (for detailed and current information please visit the BACB website: www.bacb.com). Continuing education units must be provided by a BACB-approved ACE provider (see bacb.com for a current listing and more information on this topic). There are plentiful opportunities and formats to obtain CEUs, including online, through journal clubs, and participation in professional activities with the BACB. However, a mainstay and recommended method to obtain CEUs and to contact the current literature is attending behavior-analytic conferences.

To more carefully examine this recommendation, the percentage of CE-eligible events offered were examined from a sample of three 2016 regional conventions (state associations) and the Association for Behavior Analysis International (ABAI) 42nd Annual Convention. The regional associations were selected at random and included Georgia Association for Behavior Analysis (ABA), South Carolina ABA, and Arizona ABA. Each convention offered between 8 and 9 CEUs for a 1.5-to-2-day conference. Thus, the majority of the events offered at the state association conferences are eligible for CEs. It is notable that for these and most other state/regional association-sponsored conferences, the cost of the CEUs is included in either the registration fee or as a one-time fee. The review of the events offered at the 2016 ABAI 42nd Annual Convention was completed using the app developed by DataFinch Technologies. Interestingly, all ABAI workshops, B. F. Skinner lectures and Invited Presentations offered CEUs across all specialty tracks. Examination of the number of CEUs offered at other convention events (i.e., symposia, paper presentations, or panel discussions) across tracks revealed more variability, though the majority of events offered CEUs. In fact, all of the events offered by the Ethics and Supervision tracks offered CEUs. Similarly, the majority of tracks offered more than 50% CEU-bearing events. Clearly, there are ample opportunities to obtain numerous CEUs across a number of specialty areas within behavior analysis at conventions or conferences (many of which were not listed here) and conferences can be venues for consumers to learn about novel empirical findings from researchers, updates from the BACB and important discussions about relevant issues for behavior analysts.

In summary, the amount and types of CEUs required for certified behavior analysts have changed and will likely continue to change in order to assist the professional behavior analyst, at least to some extent, in staying current with the literature within the areas of research, policy, and practice with the intent to uphold high standards of professionalism and competence of behavior analysts worldwide.

Practice guidelines

Maintaining contact with the literature is a necessary activity within an empirically based practice approach and is emphasized within practitioner training, guided by the BACB Task List, and Compliance Code, and of course, the latter also applies to posttraining (and certification). Ideally, all behavior analysts frequently read relevant literature on an ongoing basis as it is a critical professional activity to maintaining or improving one's competence, leads to positive outcomes for clients, and is a cornerstone of our professional identity. Although no data exist to suggest that behavior analysts fail to engage in this activity, it may be somewhat challenging to some behavior analysts. In addition, the rate at which one should contact the literature in order to benefit one's professional growth, level of expertise, and ultimately to benefit the range of one's consumers (client, staff, agencies, etc.) is unknown. Thus, for the newly minted behavior analysts or those who find it challenging to routinely contact the literature, it is important to consider some strategies and guidelines. Below, four major guidelines are provided for the reader to consider in one's practice of maintaining contact with the literature.

Guideline 1: Periodically, do a self-assessment on one's contact with the literature and identify any barriers

This requires a consideration of a large number of factors given the different roles and responsibilities of a behavior analyst. To begin, consider conducting a brief assessment of your own practice in maintaining contact with the peer-reviewed literature. A starting point might be to examine how often and for what purposes you are contacting the literature, and what type of literature, for the range of clinical and organizational issues that are in your practice. Are your clients doing well? In what areas are clients not doing as well? Are there areas of clinical or professional practice that you might not have attended to for a while and could benefit from an update on the current status? If you are in a new position as a supervisor or staff trainer, are you reading the recent literature in these areas? What would be the results of an outside evaluation of your knowledge and contact with the current literature? These questions are only a starting point for one to consider. Answers to these questions, and other questions not included here, allow one to begin to identify potential barriers as well as to identify potential solutions to improve one's contact with the literature.

There are numerous barriers that might compete with consistently contacting the literature. One example might be poor time management. Some individuals might state that there is "simply no time in the day" to search, find, and read relevant literature. Others set aside time for this activity but might forgo completing (or starting) it when competing demands receive greater prioritization. A functional assessment might help to identify why one is not routinely contacting the literature. Perhaps it is due to avoidance as no adverse consequences (e.g., reduced number of referrals, lawsuit, ethical violation, loss of certification, etc.) have occurred and the reinforcers in place for contacting the literature simply are not powerful. For example, if one does come into contact with an aversive consequence such as a family firing a behavior analyst for a failed intervention, it might not be the case that the behavior analyst considers that not maintaining contact with the literature might have been a contributing factor leading to the failed intervention. The act of making a list of potential barriers is an important step that will hopefully lead to consideration of possible areas that one could change to improve contacting the literature on a regular basis.

Using a problem solving approach can be helpful in addressing a range of identified barriers. Make a list of barriers (e.g., interfering behaviors or activities, organizational constraints, access to the literature), then for each barrier generate a number of possible solutions. Determine which solution might best address the barrier(s) and implement that solution. It will be important to identify a date to review the impact (positive or negative) of the chosen solution to determine if a new one if needed, if other factors are identified that need to be addressed, and/or some level of modification is required to achieve your goals.

One possible solution might be to alter the environment to occasion your review of the literature. This is a broad or general solution that requires brainstorming of several different potential solutions. For example, in supervision meetings, aim to bring an article on a topic you plan to discuss with your supervisor or supervisee (note: this could be part of a supervisory contract). Another example is to place the current issue of a relevant journal in the same magazine basket as other sources one enjoys reading. Consider designing client records or periodic reviews to include the citation for recent or relevant research related to the intervention, assessment, or target behavior(s). Finding specific solutions to address identified barriers can be a time consuming process but it is an important one that might yield positive long-term effects on your engagement in this important professional behavior.

If you find from your self-assessment that you do routinely contact the literature and have a practical and effective system in place for doing so, consider sharing with colleagues, students, and supervisees. The next few guidelines provide different recommendations to assist in the development of strategies to improve to improve this set of skills.

Guideline 2: Improve awareness of and access to the contemporary scholarly literature

Sometimes, it might be difficult to identify a good starting point for increasing contact with the literature. It is recommended to identify peer-reviewed journals within one's specific field of practice (e.g., traumatic brain injury, OBM, behavioral health, ASD). Select journals that routinely publish on professional topics of interest to behavior-analytic practitioners (e.g., *The Behavior Analyst, Behavior Analysis in Practice*) and sign up to be notified of new issues. To assist with how to efficiently use of search engines, journal alerts, and RSS feeds, consult with a science librarian or read Carr and Briggs (2010). Do you find it difficult to know where to start in selecting articles to read? If so, consider reading Gillis and Carr (2014). The authors offer a systematic process for identifying a short list of relevant articles for behavior-analytic practitioners to read. One can also review the procedure used by Parsons and Reid (2011) to identify chapters (or other scholarly work) for a reading group of not only behavior analysts but other practitioners within the same agency. Another consideration is to subscribe to a journal that you read often or that publishes articles of interest to you. At least a few times a year, you will receive the electronic or print version of the journal to occasion your reading of the literature. If you are a certified behavior analyst, consider the resources available from the BACB, such as free access to peer-reviewed journals that publish behavioranalytic literature.

Although using the Internet as a search engine or Internet sites might be, at first glance, a low response effort strategy, it typically requires a careful review of the sites that you visit to determine the accuracy of the information provided. It is imperative that one considers the source of the information provided to the reader on all sites. To facilitate efficient use of the Internet, you will need to put the work in upfront (e.g., bookmark websites that are maintained by scientific organizations or societies). One could also identify scientific blogs or social media pages that contain scientific and relevant information. For example, consider following ABAI or the Association for Professional Behavior Analysts' (APBA) Facebook page. Identify researchers who frequently publish on behavior-analytic topics of interest and follow them on Research Gate, Google Scholar, or other science communication sites to receive updates on their recent scholarly work from articles, chapters, and books.

Routine attendance to professional conferences offers opportunities to increase awareness of current literature and science in the field. Typically, there are continuing education events offered as well. Attending these events exposes one to current science and areas within behavior analysts that might not be frequently contacted in the course of one's professional practice but might be relevant to learn about, such as policy updates from the BACB, new strategies for improving staff training, and information relevant to psychopharmacology and related topics. Similarly, maintaining contact with fellow behavior analysts within one's local region or even with other behavior analysts throughout the world allows one to stay abreast about important issues within the field.

Guideline 3: Consider organizational factors to promote a work environment that values contacting the literature

Although maintaining contact with the literature is an important professional activity, employers might vary in the value placed on this activity. Information regarding whether reading the literature is included in one's job responsibilities and/or contract is important. Employment settings that do not routinely hire behavior analysts might simply not be aware of the ethical and professional importance of maintaining contact with the literature. If that is the case, providing supporting documentation (e.g., from the Compliance Code) might help. Consider negotiating protected time to do so. This protected time can take many forms, one of which might be a group activity similar to staff training. Some organizations might host a weekly or monthly "case conference" wherein a professional staff presents a case and discusses relevant literature. Other considerations would be to develop a journal or reading club for interested colleagues (Parsons & Reid, 2011) and negotiating for time to attend behavior-analytic conferences, on at least an annual basis.

Many organizations, from higher education to human service agencies, are involved in the training of behavior analysts. If you are a supervisor of behavior analysts-in training, assess whether supervisees and site supervisors maintain contact with the literature and the value placed on doing so. In supervision consider providing the reason for assigning an article to read, such as how the article is relevant to a specific practice or professional issue. One can model and share how you successfully maintain contact with the literature as well as the challenges or barriers you might encounter and how you implement a problem solving process to address those challenges or barriers.

Another organizational factor to consider is the "density" of behavior analysts at an organization. The lone behavior-analytic practitioner might find it more difficult to frequently discuss literature with colleagues compared to a behavior analytic-rich environment. Consider recruiting others within the agency to continue to learn and contact the literature with you. This shared activity could lead to more open and effective communication between colleagues, especially in multidisciplinary settings, and even lead to collaborative activities that benefit client and organizational outcomes.

Guideline 4: Think outside the box by considering other valued outcomes

Some behavior analysts might find that the previous guidelines are not applicable to them, or the suggestions within those guidelines have not been successful in increasing contact with the literature. There are other strategies for some behavior analysts to consider that might result in increasing contact with the literature that also result in increased contact with other reinforcing outcomes, such as dissemination of behavior analysis to colleagues or the public. For example, consider developing or contributing to a column in a newsletter, which can be within our outside the field of behavior analysis, where a critical review of an article or other literature (chapter, book, etc.) is provided. Consider replicating Gillis & Carr and present your findings at a professional conference. If you are an ACE provider, consider offering CEs to others (for a small fee) by developing reading guides (or using other active responding strategies) and quizzes for a set of articles. To increase public relations with important agencies or organizations, consider offering a lunch presentation on a topic. If one opts to use strategies within this guideline or similar strategies, it is imperative that one is, at a minimum, selecting literature that relates to their specialty area within the field, consumers, or relevant professional issues. This brings us back to the EBP approach and that the literature read should ultimately be improving the outcomes for the consumers and society for whom behavior analysts serve.

Practice guidelines checklist

There are four main points to take home in the area of maintaining contact with peer-reviewed literature that has more recently captured the attention of the practicing behavior analysts. Future work in this area might include assisting practitioners in elaboration of the agreed upon value of maintaining contact with the literature, identifying effective methods for doing so, and considerations for practitioner training and posttraining opportunities to refine and improve one's expertise in this important area.

1. **Claiming one is conducting evidence-based practice requires routine contact with the literature.**

   Evidence-based practice involves incorporating one's clinical expertise, the client's values (including preferences), and the empirical literature in making decisions regarding the provision of services for each client. Our ethical and professional compliance code falls in alignment with the EBP approach and requires that practitioners remain in contact with the current research to guide assessment and intervention for clients, in addition to client preferences.

2. **Continuing education provides opportunities for maintaining contact with the literature, but should not be the only option selected.**

   It is likely that many certified behavior analysts (at all certification levels) maintain contact with the literature, to varying degrees, through continuing education events, such as those offered at regional or national conferences as well as CE online modules. Although many of these might offer dissemination of recent research findings or expose practitioners to the peer-reviewed literature, it is not equivalent to reading the primary sources (the literature) cited in presentations or online modules. The review and approval process for CE events might not be as rigorous as it typically is for the peer-review process to publish articles in scholarly journal articles. Journal articles can also offer the reader a breadth of topics within behavior analysis. Although this can be obtained through CE events, one-day conferences will be limited in the range and number of topics addressed. Thus, it is recommended that behavior analysts consider a multimethod approach to obtaining CEUs as well as contacting the scholarly literature.

3. **Critically assess peer-reviewed literature as well as its source.**

   Behavior analysts should critically assess the published work to evaluate its relevancy to a particular client or group of clients, the validity of the results and how those results were obtained and reported, and the peer-review process (or lack thereof) utilized in approving published work. Not all literature one reads is considered "equal" in that the quality of the information provided to the reader might vary depending on the source (e.g., specific journal, the Internet, books) and in the content of the published work. Following some of the suggestions from previous sections of this chapter to identify a list of peer-reviewed journals and researchers (or experts in the field) to follow is important. It might also be helpful to consider using a checklist or guideline for evaluating the validity of research articles (e.g., see Horner et al., 2005).

4. **Start your plan to make maintaining contact a routine activity and find others to join you!**

   Behavior analysts understand how to change behavior, including their own. Use problem solving and self-management procedures to increase your contact with the literature. Include others, within or outside of the field and/or employment setting, to participate with you in this activity. Including others might increase accountability as well as the level of social reinforcement for engaging in this important professional behavior.

References

American Psychological Association Task Force Report. (2005). *Report of the 2005 presidential task force on evidence based practice*. Retrieved from http://www.apa.org/practice/resources/evidence/evidence-based-report.pdf.

Behavior Analyst Certification Board (2014). *Professional and ethical compliance code for behavior analysts*. Retrieved from http://bacb.com/ethics-code/.

Carr, J. E., & Briggs, A. M. (2010). Strategies for making regular contact with the scholarly literature. *Behavior Analysis in Practice, 3*, 13–18.

Gillis, J. M., & Carr, J. E. (2014). Keeping current with the applied behavior-analytic literature in developmental disabilities: Noteworthy articles for the practicing behavior analyst. *Behavior Analysis in Practice, 7*(1), 10–14.

Horner, R. H., Carr, E. G., Halle, J., McGee, G., Odom, S., & Wolery, M. (2005). The use of single-subject research to identify evidence-based practice in special education. *Exceptional children, 71*(2), 165–179.

Institute of Medicine (2001). *Crossing the quality chasm: A new health system for the 21st century*. Washington, DC: National Academy Press.

Parsons, M. B., & Reid, D. H. (2011). Reading groups: A practical means of enhancing professional knowledge among human service practitioners. *Behavior analysis in Practice, 4*(2), 53.

Skinner, B. F. (1965). Science and human behavior *(First Free Press Paperback edition)*. New York, NY: The Free Press.

Further reading

Behavior Analyst Certification Board (2012). *Fourth edition task list* (for BCBA/BCaBA). Retrieved from http://bacb.com/fourth-edition-task-list/.

Practice Dissemination: Writing for Publication

14

James K. Luiselli[1,2]
[1]Clinical Solutions, Inc., Beverly, MA, United States, [2]North East Educational and Developmental Support Center, NEEDS Center, Tewksbury, MA, United States

Writing for publication is a critical activity for disseminating information and research findings that advance knowledge and professional practice standards. Recall, for example, about how many books, book chapters, and journal articles you have read in acquiring the skills necessary to function as a competent applied-behavior-analysis (ABA) practitioner. Furthermore, accessing the published literature is a necessary activity for continuing education and career development (Gillis & Carr, 2014). Put succinctly, it is imperative that we read the published literature in order to practice effectively, refine our skills, and help the people we serve (see, e.g., the *Professional and Ethical Compliance Code for Behavior Analysts*: BCBA, 2014).

Unfortunately, very few practitioners write for publication. Among clinical psychologists in general practice, the reported modal number of publications is zero (Eke, Holttum, & Hayward, 2012). More specifically, not many ABA practitioners contribute research publications (Kelley et al., 2015). This situation is perplexing because working in applied settings such as schools, homes, human services organizations, and similar locations enables ABA practitioners to describe and report the results of intervention within the most natural conditions. In effect, this work has high external validity beyond the constraints imposed by simulated and traditional academic research. What better way to learn about the most effective behavioral practices than from the professionals who design, implement, supervise, and evaluate them?

Another consideration pertinent to practitioner-generated publication dissemination is the increasing demand for and availability of credentialed behavior analysts within education, psychological, counseling, and administrative occupations (http://bacb.com/wp-content/uploads/2015/10/151009-burning-glass-report.pdf). Notably, the number of ABA doctoral programs and doctoral-level researchers has remained relatively constant over the years (Critchfield, 2011). Kelley et al. (2015) advised that the steady rise in credentialed behavior analysts "has increased the number and variety of applied topics that need investigation by researchers and has created a gap between what practitioners are expected to undertake in practice and the available research literature on which to base their work" (p. 299). Once again, best practices in ABA will be informed by research and publications that "real-world" practitioners produce.

Applied Behavior Analysis Advanced Guidebook. DOI: http://dx.doi.org/10.1016/B978-0-12-811122-2.00014-0

This chapter is intended as a procedural guide for ABA practitioners interested in writing for publication. I begin by reviewing the appeal of writing for publication, then consideration of obstacles that get in the way. Next, the chapter covers practice elements of building a writing repertoire, including the choice of publication targets, prerequisites to writing successfully, and integrating writing for publication within a typical schedule of practitioner activities. There follows a performance guide specifying writing tactics consistent with ABA methodology and advice from professional authors. This guide is subsequently recounted in a task checklist of easy-to-follow steps.

The appeal of writing for publication

Motivational influences have a lot to do with writing for publication. In colleges and universities, faculty members are required to demonstrate a record of scholarly publications. Among several reinforcing contingencies operating in academia, successful publishing is tied to promotion, salary increases, tenure-track advancement, and grant funding. Of course, none of these arrangements exist in common practice venues. On the other hand, there are other positive consequences which should appeal to practitioners and motivate writing for publication.

Contribution to professional practice

I mentioned previously how reading the published literature informs practice. By publishing your work, you contribute to the development of other professionals, particular areas of practice (e.g., instructional methodology, behavior support, function-based intervention), and nonbehavioral disciplines that can benefit from ABA expertise. Think of your writing the same way you would deliver an oral presentation at a training workshop, seminar, or conference. These and similar events are required activities for professional continuing education certification by the BACB and other credentialing agencies. Having your work represented in print serves the same educational function as these face-to-face interactions with colleagues, students, trainees, and other aspiring professionals.

Writing as learning

Writing aficionado, Zinsser (2006), advised that the best way to learn about a subject is to write about it. If you take writing for publication seriously, keep an eye on the relevant literature, scouring books and journals for the latest research findings and commentary by respected authorities. Routinely accessing the literature is the only way you can stay current with trends and new developments which, in turn, guide your work and publication objectives. This reading-in-order-to-write successfully is a powerful forum for learning and intellectual pursuit.

Improving expository skills

Beyond technical knowledge, training, and expertise, ABA practitioners must have exemplary communication skills. Verbal communication comes into play within myriad activities such as conducting meetings, providing supervision, delivering consultation, and training care-providers. Written communication is equally prescient in the form of case notes, reports, intervention plans, and project proposals. By writing for publication you are honing your expository skills on multiple levels: addressing key points in a meeting, speaking clearly, anticipating listener reactions, and so on. I cannot emphasize enough how putting words on the page, with the intent of publication, and doing so routinely, builds fluent communication competencies.

Professional development

In addition to learning by writing, the feedback you receive from editors and reviewers through the process of publication peer review is a vital source of professional development. As I describe later in the chapter, submitting a manuscript for publication leads to written feedback about your work from accomplished professionals who are sought out for their respective expertise and editorial guidance. In effect, you as a writer are taught by other writers toward improving your work, skills, and expression. Though the quality of publication reviews varies widely, in most cases the critical scrutiny from knowledgeable experts almost always enhances a practitioner's professional development.

Further professional development occurs by writing for publication when your name is recognized among the large community of readers. For example, many times in my career I received telephone calls or email inquiries starting with, "Dr. Luiselli, I read an article of yours about—and would like to consider your services." Whether intended or not, name visibility is a marketing strategy that practitioners should not overlook for expanding practice opportunities. Recognition through high-quality publications will also garner other worthwhile activities such as speaking engagements, conference presentations, consultations, and invitations to write more! Consider, too, that practitioners who are familiar with your publications will refer you to their colleagues.

Obstacles to writing for publication

If writing for publication offers many positive outcomes, why do so few practitioners write? The answer rests with identifying and then overcoming real and presumed obstacles.

Publication knowledge

On several occasions, I have listened to practitioners present an impressive clinical case or systems project at a conference or similar professional event. When asked,

"Have you considered writing that up for publication?", many of them respond reluctantly, stating that they are unfamiliar with the mechanics of preparing and submitting a manuscript. This lack of knowledge is easily remedied by referring to the "Instructions for Authors" section that accompanies virtually every peer reviewed journal and other publication sources. The instructions specify the format for manuscript preparation, including page length, style, section headings, word count, and in some cases, font type and size. These preparation guidelines further define the steps for submitting a manuscript, corresponding with the editorial office, and providing ancillary documentation (transfer of copyright authorization, author consent, declaration of conflict of interest). Therefore, knowledge about preparing and submitting a manuscript for publication is easily acquired and not at all a burden for novice and less experienced writers.

Publication options

Practitioners sometimes opine that not knowing about different publication options is another obstacle to writing for publication. Journal articles include letters-to-the-editor, case reports, literature reviews, single-case studies, and group-design experiments. Other options are also available. For example, most professional organizations publish newsletters that are always seeking contributions from members and nonmembers alike. Behavioral practitioners have many of these outlets available— the Association of Behavior Analysis International (*Inside Behavior Analysis*), the Association of Behavioral and Cognitive Therapies (*the Behavior Therapist*), and the Association of Professional Behavior Analysts (*APBA Reporter*). Book reviews are another source for your writing. Although editors usually solicit book reviews, other outlets actively recruit reviewers, including online platforms (see, e.g., www.metapsychologyonlinereviews.com). You may also be affiliated with a state licensing or credentialing entity which makes publishing possible through member-distributed periodicals. In illustration, I have been a contributing writer to a newsletter that is sent ten times per year to all licensed psychologists within the New England states. With these many sources for publication, there should be no excuse for not making your work visible to a wide readership both within and outside the professional behavioral community (Reed, 2014).

Practice demands

One very legitimate obstacle to writing for publication is the time-activity demands of practitioners and other constraints within typical service settings. Kelley et al. (2015) captured this matter accurately with regard to research-driven publications: "Individuals attempting to conduct research in applied settings may have few resources available to them," they "are very busy and may have little time to devote to research," and "many employers may see little value in research and may not additionally compensate employees for time spent conducting research" (p. 22). Indeed, finding time to write in a busy schedule can be daunting, whether or not it is devoted to research publications, review articles, case reports, or descriptive papers. The upcoming sections of this chapter consider methods to plan publication objectives, address the issue of time management, and make writing routine among other requisite activities.

Keep in mind that as practitioners, we write all the time in the form of client reports, case summaries, consultation notes, and instructional and behavior support plans. Truly, you could not function as a competent practitioner if you were not able to produce written product in the conduct of service delivery. My advice is to view writing for publication as shaping an already existing skills repertoire.

As another tactic, you can approach an employer to request that conducting research and writing for publication be integrated within your job description and work performance standards. This strategy assumes that the administrators in charge value these activities. Of course, you may have to pursued them by articulating several appealing benefits. First, developing a program of research and publishing findings improves service delivery and program effectiveness. These activities also serve as a valuable facet of staff training (Luiselli, 2013, 2015). Writing for publication establishes a public record which can enhance an organization's reputation among professionals, referral agencies, and stakeholders. In turn, the visibility achieved through publication will attract desirable employees and individuals seeking training and supervision at the highest level.

Writing is hard work

In his book, *Overdrive*, the late and prolific writer William F. Buckley, Jr. had this to say about writing: "I do not like to write, for the simple reason that writing is extremely hard work, and I do not 'like' extremely hard work" (Buckley, 1984, p. 77). Yes, writing for publication is not easy, especially when it is subjected to the critical eyes of peer review. Some other factors contributing to the "aversiveness" of writing are when a writer (1) questions her/his ability, (2) does not have adequate research material, (3) demands perfection, (4) is exhausted, stressed-out, and overwhelmed, and (5) lacks interest in what is being written (McCutcheon, 2006). But like exercising, playing a musical instrument, or delivering presentations, writing becomes more facile with repetition and implementation of performance improvement tactics. And please, do not attribute writing difficulty to "writer's block," two words that incorrectly label negatively reinforced nonwriting. Designing, applying, and evaluating a writing plan is the key to success.

Publication targets

Practitioners many times overlook already existing writing projects that can be turned into publication submissions. Consider that you and one or more colleagues may have a graduate school practicum study, thesis, or dissertation which is journal worthy. Similarly, you can turn conference and poster session presentations into manuscripts on their way to publication. The information you and others provide in a grant proposal lends itself to a literature review. It makes sense to capitalize on this previously completed work as potential publications.

Writing projects also evolve from service descriptions with accompanying process and outcome data. With one organization I worked in, educational and home-care providers had developed "wrap around" support services for families of students in residential treatment. We wrote and eventually published a detailed description of the program, linking it to prior research and illustrating effectiveness with case results (Luiselli et al., 1999). Another publication described a behaviorally oriented partial hospitalization program for adults with intellectual and developmental disabilities based on effectiveness data from a standardized rating scale that was administered upon admission and discharge (Luiselli, Benner, Stoddard, Weiss, & Lisowski, 2001). Yet another example was a descriptive analysis of protective holding (physical restraint) utilization among community-living adults with learning and behavior challenges (Luiselli, Sperry, & MaGee, 2011). None of these writing projects represented prospective studies but they proved to be informative and well received by journal reviewers.

Writing projects also emerge by putting a "publication lens" to your clinical and applied work. As a skilled ABA practitioner you collect data, conduct functional behavioral assessments, formulate intervention plans, train care-providers, and evaluate outcome effects. With not much more formality you can select an experimental design, assess interobserver agreement (IOA), measure procedural fidelity, and consider other methodological controls that will meet publication standards. That is, you should approach every practice situation as an opportunity to conduct meaningful research leading to publication. Notably, the most productive ABA practitioner-authors identify research topics from issues that arise in practice, institute research to improve their service delivery, and recruit natural care-providers as research implementers (Kelley et al., 2015).

Concerning research skills, Codd (2016) proposed that most clinical practitioners "fail to build a successful repertoire because they do not arrange conditions that afford repeated reinforced practice" (p. 118). Failures are most common when the effort to start a research project is too great, the steps toward completion are too long, and contact with reinforcement is too delayed. A more effective path, guided by the principle of successive approximation, is to (1) target easy-to-solve problems, (2) incorporate basic experimental designs, (3) simplify measurement procedures, (4) plan for large intervention effects, and (5) conduct "research that matters" (Codd, 2016).

I would add that getting involved with collaborative research projects and sharing responsibilities among practitioners can promote productivity. In one of my studies, several colleagues were interested in identifying the types of assessment protocols applied with children who had autism. We convened a project team and assigned specific tasks to individual members such as reviewing the relevant literature, preparing documents for data entry, and designing a survey that we sent to national educational and treatment centers (Luiselli et al., 2001). As discussed later in the chapter, collaborative efforts also contribute efficiently to jointly-authored publication submissions.

Performance improvement guide to writing for publication

No less of an authority than Skinner (1981) examined the writing process in a publication titled "How to Discover What You Have to Say." Skinner adhered to a rigorous writing schedule, starting early in the morning, at a particular desk in his home office (see, also, Epstein, 1997). He monitored the time devoted to writing and his progress. Skinner advised keeping notes as a way to accumulate ideas that could be put on paper. He also concluded that productivity could be enhanced by having high-quality writing materials and maintaining a healthy lifestyle.

Although few in number, some studies have evaluated the effects of ABA methods on writing skills and productivity. Boice (1983) documented the number of pages written daily by two groups of college faculty. One group scheduled weekly writing sessions but only wrote when "inspired." The second group also planned weekly writing sessions, had to write when scheduled, and were required to send money to nonpreferred organizations if they were not productive. The latter group wrote significantly more pages than the inspiration-only group.

McDougall (2006) studied how much time one writer committed to preparing manuscripts for publication submission. Following a baseline phase, the writer implemented a self-management protocol to increase writing preparation activities. This was a multicomponent plan in which the writer allocated a predetermined amount of time to individual manuscripts, self-recorded his performance, and evaluated results with reference to graphed data. This combination of procedures was associated with more time spent working on manuscripts.

Porritt, Burt, and Poling (2006) recorded the cumulative words submitted by fiction writers who participated in an online community. An internet-based intervention that was introduced across groups of writers featured graphic performance feedback, praise contingent of goal completion, and evaluative comments from writing colleagues. Compared to baseline conditions, both groups wrote more words during intervention.

A study reported by Johnson, Perris, Salo, Deschaine, and Johnson (2016) arranged contingencies to reduce avoidance of writing assignments by university students. There were four assignments the students had to complete on or before predetermined deadlines and leading to submission of a final paper. Control group conditions explained the assignments, course credit, and consequence for not meeting the final deadline. The treatment condition was the same except the students were informed that if they missed earlier assignment deadlines, the due date for the final paper would be two days sooner. On average, the students completed more of the assignments on time and also had higher quality writing during treatment.

The preceding ABA research suggests several methods for improving different aspects of writing. One impression is that writing is sensitive to both negative reinforcement (Boice, 1983; Johnson et al., 2016) and positive consequences elicited through praise, acknowledgment, performance feedback, and collegial support (Porritt et al., 2006). These studies also weighed heavily on self-management of the conditions and outcomes associated with writing.

The habits of professional writers further inform some of the steps practitioners can take in writing for publication. My strongest recommendations are the books *Bird by Bird* (1995) by Anne Lamont (Lamont, 1995), *On Writing* (2010) by Stephen King (King, 2010), *On Writing Well* (2006) by William Zinsser (Zinsser, 2006), and *The Sense of Style: A Thinking Person's Guide to Writing in the 21st Century* (2015) by Steven Pinker (Pinker, 2015). Among many ABA concepts, these books illustrate how professional authors establish stimulus control over their work by writing in particular locations, quantifying output (e.g., number of words and pages), favoring certain media (e.g., writing in longhand or on a computer), and employing organizational guides. Many professional authors require "writing first" before they allow themselves to enjoy pleasurable activities. And as you read about the habits of these authors, it is striking how the principle of delay discounting (Madden & Johnson, 2010) emerges in their work—they are motivated by "large-later" versus "small-shorter" rewards. Good and productive writing takes time!

Practitioners can refer to several other books for sound writing advice. *How to Write a Lot: A Practical Guide to Productive Academic Writing* (2007) by Paul J. Silvia (Silvia, 2007) concentrates on college and university faculty but many of his suggestions apply equally well to nonacademic professionals. Similarly, in *How to Write for a General Audience* (2007), Kathryn Kendall-Tackett counsels academics about writing for the lay public, with strategies that practitioners can likewise adopt (Kendall-Tackett, 2007).

The following performance guide to writing for publication integrates several methods that should resonate with most ABA practitioners. I have presented the gist of this writing plan elsewhere (Luiselli, 2010). As well, Kelley et al. (2015) reported some of the writing methods the most productive ABA practitioners use in getting their work published. These methods are also represented in the performance guide.

Reading

Purposeful reading of the professional literature is a prerequisite to writing for publication. Staying current with the literature reveals publication trends, topics of contemporary interest, and the types of articles featured in different publication outlets. Having this information functions as a roadmap for selecting research projects and writing manuscripts that are timely and will appeal to other practitioners.

The peer review process further shapes the required content of publications. For example, current convention dictates that a clinical case study has sufficient follow-up data to warrant publication. Single-case intervention studies in most behavioral journals generally demand a well-executed functional analysis preceding treatment evaluation. A topical review, in journal or book-chapter format, must be grounded in evidence-based practices. Reading the professional literature keeps you abreast of publication requisites, current contents, and prevailing themes.

I suggest another benefit derived from active reading: sampling the writing style of successful authors. Some of the characteristics of good composition I noticed early in my writing career were clarity of prose, sentence structure, word selection, and what can best be described as the element of "turning a phrase." Keep in mind that in addition to the methodology, results, and implications of your work, *how* you communicate in the written medium strongly influences probability of success. By reading the professional literature, you will come in contact with some exemplary writing models.

Reading opportunities present themselves in different ways but it is most desirable to schedule time in the same manner you would plan a meeting, supervision session, interview, or similar activity. Dedicated reading time can be arranged in your office early in the day, at home during the evening, or on a lunch break. To be most effective, have your reading materials preselected and one or more objectives you want to accomplish such as reviewing particular journal articles or summarizing a book chapter that addresses a topic of interest. The setting for your reading should be carefully chosen so that there are no distractions or interruptions. On many occasions, I have scheduled time in a library because it was the most conducive setting for concentrated reading.

Carr and Briggs (2010) commented about some of the obstacles practitioners face in trying to access the professional literature, notably the financial costs of books and journal subscriptions. Some reasonable alternatives are (1) registering with email publication alerting services, (2) making use of open-access journals online, (3) securing library privileges, and (4) requesting publications directly from authors. Practitioners should also look to colleagues and supervisors for sharing reading materials.

One more collaborative effort is to participate in reading groups. Parsons and Reid (2011) found that ABA practitioners enjoyed and gained new knowledge by meeting in a monthly group devoted to reading a specific journal article or book chapter. The practitioners described what they read, answered questions about content, and summarized key conclusions. Reading groups enable practitioners to discuss topics of mutual interest, often leading to group-shared research, review, and writing projects.

Establishing a writing schedule

I have heard colleagues and students say that they can only write when "inspired." Another person told me his writing depended on "feeling creative." In graduate school, a professor of mine waited until a last-minute deadline approached, fired-up a 10-cup pot of coffee, and started writing around midnight into the early morning hours. Expecting inspiration to strike, ruminating on creative ideas, and engaging in "binge writing" will not make you a productive writer and produce publications.

Instead, you must establish a dedicated writing schedule. The schedule establishes times and days of the week that are *devoted exclusively* to writing for publication. The scheduled writing time should not be different from any other activity that you plan in a typical week. You need to take out your weekly calendar, put in the days and times of scheduled writing sessions, and write during those sessions no matter how you feel! I know, all of this sounds overbearing, compulsive, and oddly neurotic until you try it and experience the effects.

To get started and familiar with a writing schedule, I recommend a 60-minute writing session one time per week. Experience tells me that most practitioners can easily follow this schedule without overlooking time needed for other activities. This one time per week, 60-minute writing session can easily produce 1−2 pages of text and eventually a first-draft manuscript 2−3 months later. With success, you can increase productivity by scheduling and devoting more days and times to writing.

There are a few things you can do in constructing a writing schedule:

1. Take a week or two to complete a time study of your usual activities and responsibilities. The task is to find out when, where, and how you spend your time. In most cases, you will discover gaps in your weekly schedule that can accommodate a planned 60-minute writing session.
2. Pick a 60-minute writing session on a day and time that is reliable and best fits your daily rhythm. For example, you may be more energetic and attentive during early morning hours. Or, writing later in the day may be more suitable because you are able to get other things accomplished beforehand. Whether it is "Tuesday: 8:00−9:00 am" or "Thursday: 5:00−6:00 pm, establish a writing schedule and follow it without compromise.
3. Of course, there are going to be weeks when your scheduled writing time is disrupted by a crisis event or unanticipated request that demands immediate attention. In such situations, find an alternative day and time in the week. Do not give up your scheduled writing session without making it up. Performance monitoring, discussed later in the chapter, will help you adjust and maintain a writing schedule.
4. The location for your weekly writing session must be carefully considered. Optimal performance will be promoted if you are comfortable in your surroundings, there are no distractions (or you can effectively control them), necessary materials are at hand, and you do not have to relocate. For many of us, our offices on the job and at home meet these criteria. But as noted previously, you may perform more efficiently at other locations such as a library or pleasant community setting.

Writing opportunistically

So, you have routinized your weekly writing schedule, made adjustments as warranted, and found a location that supports performance. This foundation to writing for publication can be supplemented by also writing whenever opportunities arise. In illustration, you may be in your office waiting for a meeting to begin but at the last moment, the meeting is canceled. Why not use that time to work on a writing project? Or, you may have arrived early at a consultation appointment, giving you 30−45 minutes of "free" writing time. Remember, many practitioners complain about busy schedules and not being able to find the time for writing. Opportunistic writing addresses this matter and will quickly build productivity.

Nonscheduled writing opportunities also appear outside of the work setting. I have written waiting to pick up my children from school, having a cup of coffee at a local shop, watching hockey and lacrosse practices, and reclining at the beach. These opportunities usually arise spontaneously but can also be planned by carefully scrutinizing your weekly schedule. A few minutes of opportunistic writing add up and should be sought out whenever possible.

To make the most of opportunistic writing you have to be a "mobile writer." If you write in longhand, carry manuscripts and composition pads with you in a brief-case or folders. Certainly, laptop computers and tablet devices support writing at any time and in any location. More than ever, you should be able to expand the stimulus control over writing, perhaps discovering conditions that actually accelerate productivity. For example, a colleague of mine told me that he writes most fluently in coffee shops and restaurant cafes because the community forum forces him to concentrate more dutifully to the work at hand. Disciplining yourself to write opportunistically is a potent generalization-promoting strategy to publication success.

Completing prewriting tasks

Assume you have decided to write a program description manuscript that will contain illustrative data and suggestions for care-providers. Before writing, you should identify several publication targets with the following question in mind: Does the journal, newsletter, or periodical routinely publish this type of article? Having what appears to be a worthy writing project will be unsuccessful unless there is a match between manuscript content and publication outlet. At the same time, rank order your selections so that there are back-up options in case earlier submissions of the manuscript are reviewed unfavorably.

Publication outlets can be further differentiated by their behavioral and nonbe-havioral orientation. Within the ABA community, writing about "concurrent oper-ants," "transfer of stimulus control," or "function-based treatment" will not be off-putting to editors, reviewers, and readers. The same terminology will potentially alienate professionals less familiar with ABA. And yet, publishing "outside the box" (Reed, 2014) promotes wider dissemination of behavioral practices. Personally, I have made it a special point to publish in multidisciplinary journals that embraced data-based studies. On other occasions, I received requests to write chapters for books that were not solely ABA focused. If you decide on a nonbehavioral publica-tion outlet, choose your words accordingly and expect a more challenging path to success than if you were "preaching to the choir" (Reed, 2014).

A second prewriting task, which I cited earlier, is being thoroughly acquainted with and adhering to the style requirements for manuscript preparation. Failing to follow the Instructions-to-Authors guidelines will result in a manuscript being returned without editorial review. The most common preparation errors are submit-ting a manuscript that exceeds the limits on number of words and pages, does not fol-low the progression of section headings, and inserts tables and figures incorrectly.

Organizing your materials is another additional and valuable prewriting task. A good strategy is to prepare a file folder for each manuscript you are writing. The folder can accommodate hardcopy documents or be formatted as an electronic file. Use the folder to house the manuscript outline, composition notes, copies of publi-cations, and editorial correspondence. Keeping a file folder facilitates quick access to necessary documents and saves time throughout the writing process.

Finally, use goal-setting (Rouillard, 2002) to set timeline objectives such as a deadline date for completing a first-draft manuscript. Other goals are targeting dates for publication submission and revising a manuscript in response to editorial reviews. Evaluating your achievement of goal-setting objectives is another example of effective performance monitoring.

Putting words on the page

When you sit down to write, your objective is to put words on the page. Silvia (2007) said it well: "Writing is a set of concrete behaviors such as sitting on a bench, chair, stool, toilet, or patch of grass and slapping your flippers against the keyboard to generate paragraphs" (p. 7). From an ABA perspective, writing is behavior that can be promoted, shaped, and maintained according to the same learning principles that influence other actions.

Find a writing medium

I mentioned earlier that most professional authors have distinct writing preferences. You should write in the medium that is both comfortable and productive. In my case, I always write a first-draft manuscript in longhand, on a particular brand of writing pad, using a Bic0.7 mm, #2 pencil. Why? Because writing longhand slows down my thinking, the pencil-to-paper writing texture makes my script legible, and I can erase entries that I want to change. For me, writing a first-draft manuscript directly on a computer takes more time than composing in longhand. When I assess that the first-draft longhand manuscript is about 90% complete, I then convert it to word processing, creating an electronic file that I can print, edit, and revise as a near-final product. I do not suggest that you follow my manner of writing but I do advise that you find a medium that provides the same comfort and outcome.

Write from an outline

Writing from an outline is a great organizational tool. An outline offers a sequence of small steps you can complete in moving toward a final manuscript. The outline does not have to be extensive—a single page is sufficient. Your outline should have primary headings that correspond to the required sections of a manuscript and sub-headings that add more detail. For example, in the Introduction heading of my outlines, I list the publication citations I expect to include and describe. In the subheadings of the Discussion heading in an outline, you can set the order of summary points, implications, relevance to prior research, limitations, and recommendations.

Write for time

Some professional authors document the number of words and pages they produce during writing sessions. King (2010), for example, sets a goal of writing 10 pages of text each day. The quantity of words and pages is a reasonable metric but my preference is to focus on time spent writing and not output per se. In effect, concentrate on sitting down during your scheduled, unplanned, and opportunistic writing sessions, spending time putting words on the page, but not worrying about how many words and pages. I have found that this strategy is an effective method for generating content because it is "low demand" and consistent with my uncompromising recommendation of achieving writing proficiency by spending more time writing.

Write first drafts

However much you intend to write, a publication-worthy manuscript will be the result of writing a first draft and many subsequent drafts thereafter. The bottom line to writing first drafts is that they do not have to be perfect. More precisely, they are a beginning, typically crude, uneven, and in need of editing. Nobody but you reads your first draft, there is no evaluator looking critically over your shoulder, and these initial efforts will have to be finely shaped into a complete manuscript. Therefore, do not expect the first words you write to be the final words in a publication submission. Instead, get something on the page that can be molded and refined later. Trying to write the perfect sentence or craft the most resolute paragraph at the earliest stages will severely hamper productivity.

There are a few strategies to start and complete a first draft manuscript. With regard to preparing an outline, you can easily write out of order. As an example, the Methods section of a manuscript is often easiest to write because you report descriptive information about participants, settings, behavior definitions, and implementation methodology. In the same vein, writing the Results section is usually a straightforward process. Finishing these sections first gives you and reinforces a permanent product before moving on to the more expansive Introduction and Discussion sections. The same can be said of the usual sections that comprise literature reviews and other nonempirical publications.

Behavioral momentum (Nevin & Shahan, 2011) is another strategy to kick-start and sustain your writing. When starring for too long at the blank page or computer screen, begin writing key words, descriptive phrases, possible manuscript titles, or any text that comes effortlessly. Then expand on what you have written, adding detail, related information, whatever comes to mind. Gradually, you will be putting more words on the page, whereas the text becomes more fluid and complete. Over several writing sessions you can produce a substantive manuscript.

Here is another example of behavioral momentum applied to writing for publication. Picture that you are working on the first-draft of a manuscript dealing with an intervention study for several children who had feeding problems. Despite having an idea about the content for that writing session, the words are slow to come. You could get started by writing the following text:

I am sitting here trying to describe the study we conducted that combined several antecedent intervention procedures to treat food refusal. We combined procedures similar to Smith and Jones (2011) and added an escape extinction component reported in several recent studies (add references). One notable feature of our study was a pre-treatment functional analysis with each child. In the manuscript

we can emphasize the relatively few studies that have incorporated functional
analysis.. ..

In the preceding example, you are able to put words on the page by "writing about what you intend to write about." Through behavioral momentum you construct text which can be worked into a first-draft manuscript.

Editing and rewriting

When you complete a first draft manuscript, put it away for a week or two (not much longer) and then bring it out to review with fresh eyes. With this perspective you are ready to begin a critical stage of writing for publication: *editing and rewriting*. Without qualification, there is not a professional author I have read about or solid academic-practitioner writer I know who does not emphasize editing and rewriting as a key to publication success. First-draft manuscripts must be cleaned up and shaped into form, leading to second, third, and as many drafts as needed to reach the level required for publication submission.

1. Good editing should find typographical, grammatical, and composition errors that alert you to careless writing. Editors and reviewers will think negatively about your work if they encounter a manuscript containing misspelled words, incomplete sentences, and incoherent prose.
2. Rewrite sections of the manuscript to improve clarity and comprehension. Clean, simple, and concise language is best—see *Writing Mechanics, Style, and Grammar*, later in the chapter.
3. Is the manuscript consistent with the style and formatting guidelines specified in the journal, periodical, newsletter, or book you have targeted? Recall a previous admonition: know and follow all of the manuscript preparation requirements for your publication choices.
4. Be sure that in-text publication citations appear fully in the Reference section of the manuscript. Omissions either way are another indication of sloppy preparation.
5. Attentive editing and rewriting will eventually produce a manuscript you deem ready for publication submission. However, you should consider the additional step of asking one or more trusted colleagues to read the final version and give you feedback. Whenever possible look to readers who have previously published and you view as being skilled writers. Ask to have a quick turnaround so that the manuscript does not languish. Use the feedback you receive to edit and correct the manuscript further.

Writing mechanics, style, and grammar

Much academic writing is abstract, difficult to understand, imprecise, and obtuse (Hartley, 2008; Hartley, Pennebaker, & Fox, 2003). The following excerpt from a peer-reviewed journal article is such an example:

At its most basic level, a metacognitive system can be seen as a feedback loop between an internally perceived and experienced external object, person, activity, experience, or event, and the mental model an individual constructs of it.

The preceding passage cannot be understood no matter how many times you read it. Although this passage is an extreme illustration, many publications are similarly deficient. Silvia (2007) proposed that "bad writing" often results from authors trying to show off their intelligence. He added that most people seeking publication were never taught basic writing skills. Not spending enough time writing also contributes to poorly constructed prose.

It is beyond the scope of this chapter to present a tutorial on writing mechanics, style, and grammar, but a few points are noteworthy. In *Verbal Behavior*, Skinner (1957) wrote that we should select words for their effects on the listener and not the effects on the speaker. It is equally true that our writing should be devoted to the reader—write words, sentences, and paragraphs that clarify and do not confuse. Lindsley (1991), a colleague of Skinner and an ABA pioneer, was dedicated to writing in *plain English*, which he defined as "one- or two-syllable words in active voice and present tense" (p. 450). He concluded that basic plain English words have more accurate meaning because most people are familiar with them from an early age. "We instantly know their meanings without having to think about them. And, being old friends, we are comfortable with them" (Lindsley, 1991, p. 450).

Table 14.1 lists some of the writing books I previously cited and a few more I recommend for improving style, grammar, composition, and expression. Some of the best writing advice gleaned from these books is to keep written language simple and concise. Strunk and White (1979) famously warned writers to "omit needless words." Lindsley (1991) opined that writing for practitioners is most easy to understand by avoiding technical jargon. Kendall-Tackett (2007) suggested, "To make your work readable, keep an eye on how many nouns you use in a sentence,

Table 14.1 Recommended writing books

Kathleen A. Kendall-Tackett, *How to Write for a General Audience* (2007). Washington, DC: American Psychological Association
Steven King, *On Writing* (2010). New York: Scribner
Anne Lamott, *Bird by Bird: Some Instructions About Writing and Life* (1995). New York: Knopf Doubleday Publishing Group
Steven Pinker, *The Sense of Style: The Thinking Person's Guide to Writing in the 21st Century* (2015). New York: penguin Publishing Group
Bruce Holland Rogers, *Word Work: Surviving and Thriving as a Writer* (2002). Invisible Cities Press
Paul J. Silvia, *How to Write a Lot: A Practical Guide to Productive Academic Writing* (2007). Washington, DC: American Psychological Association
William Strunk & E. B. White, *The Elements of Style* (1979). New York: Macmillan Publishing Company
William Zinsser, *On Writing Well* (2006). New York: Harper Collins Publishers

especially those with abstract meanings" (p. 66). The succinct guidance from Zinsser (2009) best summarizes the topic of writing mechanics, style, and grammar:

> *The secret of good writing is to strip every sentence to its cleanest components. Every word that serves no function, every long word that could be a short word, every adverb that carries the same meaning that's already in the verb, every passive constriction that leaves the reader unsure of who is doing what—these are the thousand and one adulterants that weaken the strength of a sentence (p. 64).*

Positive reinforcement

It usually takes 9–12 months to complete and publish a writing project. Seeing your work in print is a potent reinforcer but delayed. The time from conception through publication is even longer when a rejected manuscript is reviewed and submitted several times before being accepted. Writing efficiency and productivity are strengthened when more immediate reinforcement is programmed and contacted.

1. Achieving your writing goals and completing sections of a manuscript are frequent reinforcers. Display these data visually as graphic performance feedback.
2. Arrange writing-contingent positive consequences such as treating yourself to a special lunch following a productive morning writing session, purchasing a new CD when you complete a first draft manuscript, and sharing approval from writing partners during collaborative meetings.
3. Working on several writing projects increases exposure to immediate and delayed reinforcers.
4. I have displayed on the walls of my office the first peer-reviewed article I published, an article that won an award, and covers of several of my books. These stimuli are not arrogant gestures, rather conspicuous cues which remind me about and reinforce the hard work that goes into writing for publication.
5. Never permit *nonwriting* as a consequence for adhering to your writing schedule and achieving your writing objectives.

Monitoring performance

Tracking your writing progress is high on the list of performance improvement tactics. A simple monitoring system shows if you are achieving writing goals or where problems arise such as maintaining scheduled writing sessions. With the time it takes writing, submitting, and revising a manuscript, performance monitoring is also a source of positive reinforcement bridging the gap before publication.

Choose a method of performance monitoring that is practical. Fig. 14.1 is a graph depicting the number of minutes writing each week—These data are plotted as the combined duration of writing recorded from scheduled weekly sessions and nonscheduled opportunities. The horizontal line represents the targeted writing objective, in this case a minimum of 60 minutes each week. With positive results,

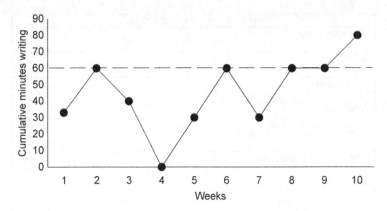

Figure 14.1 Example of performance monitoring.

this practitioner could plan for more writing time in the context of a changing criterion design. Other performance monitoring measures are the number of words and pages written or percentage of weekly writing sessions achieved each month. Of course, the ultimate measure of writing progress and success is manuscripts completed, submitted, and published!

A second performance monitoring tool, presented in Fig. 14.2, is a form that tracks pertinent details of manuscript submission, editorial reviews, and publication decisions. This type of monitoring helps greatly when you have more than one manuscript being reviewed or revised. If you are the corresponding author on a multiauthored manuscript, such a form also helps organize shared information and the sometimes surprising amount of correspondence that can accumulate.

Dealing with manuscript reviews

Whether you are writing a journal article, have been invited to write a book chapter, or are preparing a piece for a newsletter, your manuscript is going to be reviewed to determine if it is acceptable for publication. Reviewers may be members of an editorial board, a book editor, section editors from an organization periodical, or professionals solicited by a publisher. The written feedback you receive, anywhere from 2 to 5 reviews, details the reasons why your manuscript should or should not be accepted for publication. You cannot write for publication successfully unless you strategically prepare for and respond to these reviews.

Decisions about publication fall within three categories. "Reject," the most dreaded decision, means that the consensus opinion among reviewers was recommending against publication. Rejections are common and should be expected, especially with journals whose acceptance rates typically hover between 20% and 25% or lower. The second type of decision is "revise and resubmit." Although seemingly disappointing, this decision is promising because you have the opportunity to repair the manuscript and submit it again for further consideration. Most of the time a

Manuscript submission form
Manuscript title:
Author(s):
Corresponding author:
Target publication outlet:
Date of manuscript submission:
Date of acknowledgment:
Date of editorial decision:
Editorial decision: □ Reject □ Revise-resubmit □ Accept-pending revision
Date revised and submitted:
Outcome of resubmission
Further action:

Figure 14.2 Manuscript submission form.

"revise and resubmit" manuscript will be sent to a new group of reviewers but occasionally may be evaluated by the reviewers who read the original manuscript. If you receive an "accept pending revision" decision, the manuscript will be published as long as you satisfactorily address critical questions, comments, and suggestions contained in the reviews. There is actually a fourth type of decision, "accept without revision," but it is rare, reserved for luminaries in the field, and an event I have never experienced!

The quality of editorial reviews varies considerably. Some reviewers appear to have barely read the manuscript. Their reviews have little substance and are often inaccurate, presented in a negative tone, and not instructive. Thankfully, many reviewers thoughtfully appraise the manuscript and independent of their publication decision, offer constructive feedback that builds your skills as a practitioner, researcher, and writer.

You should also expect delays in receiving reviews and editorial correspondence for your publication submissions. The usual time-span is 2−3 months but not infrequently, twice that duration. On one occasion, it was more than 12 months before a decision was made on a manuscript I had submitted to a journal. Lengthy delays occur because most reviewers have busy academic and practice schedules, many of them assume multiple editorial roles, and they are active writers themselves. Having editors systematically prompt reviewers to meet requested deadlines is one method to reduce delays (Caruso & Kennedy, 2004). As an author, you should not hesitate to inquire about tardy reviews.

1. After you have decided on a writing project and selected a publication outlet, prepare the manuscript with reviewers in mind. Try to anticipate what the reviewers will be looking for in their critical appraisal. Remember, the task for reviewers is to evaluate both the strengths and weaknesses of the manuscript relative to purpose, content, conclusions, and contribution. If you intend to submit a research study, do not ignore obvious methodological, experimental design, and interpretive limitations. With literature review articles, be sure you have included seminal and contemporary publications, the implications you draw from them, and directions for future research. Your task before submission is to evaluate the manuscript as if you had been assigned to review it.

2. When you receive an editorial decision, consider every reviewer comment and recommendation. Some reviewers will have similar conclusions about publication and the reasons for their decisions. There will also be different opinions between and among reviewers. Read the reviews several times until you are able to clearly summarize every point that is reasonable.

3. If the manuscript is not accepted for publication do not reflexively submit it to another publication outlet in its present form. Instead, incorporate issues presented in the reviews that will improve quality of the manuscript and increase probability of publication elsewhere.

4. With "revise and resubmit" and "accept pending revision" decisions, you should try to incorporate every reviewer's concerns and recommendations. You do not have to accept every suggestion from reviewers but you do not want to overlook essential and mandatory points of revision, even if you disagree with them.

5. Set a timetable for completing and returning the revised manuscript. You will be asked to submit-resubmit the manuscript on or before a due date. Although having a firm deadline is a source of motivation for most writers, I advise getting the work done as promptly as possible. Rapid responding can be facilitated by harnessing the momentum of publication from an "accept pending revision" decision and potential publication from a "revise and resubmit" decision.

6. You will be required to list and explain how you handled inquiries and requests from reviewers for a manuscript that was resubmitted for publication or was accepted for publication pending revision. Convention calls for a cover letter which spells out how the author(s) responded to the reviews. Prepare the cover letter without confronting or challenging the opinions of reviewers. Your purpose should be to convey the conscientious care and effort you demonstrated in revising the manuscript.

Writing collaboratively

Most publications have more than one author. Several practitioners may have contributed to a study or prepared a review paper stemming from mutual interests. Writing collaboratively shares responsibilities among several people and in consequence, reduces response effort from a single author. Nonetheless, special considerations govern joint-writing projects.

1. Decide authorship before writing. The *Publication Manual of the American Psychological Association* (American Psychological Association, 2009) specifies that "Authorship is reserved for persons who make a primary contribution to and hold primary responsibility for the data, concepts, and interpretation of results for a published work" (p. 43). Substantial contributions to a study independent of writing also qualify for authorship (e.g., designing a research protocol, statistical analyses, interpretation of findings). Determining authorship is a serious matter and demands early attention (Arthur et al, 2004; Bridgewater, Bornstein, & Walkenbach, 1981; Winston, 1985).

2. One person should fulfill the role of coordinating author. Skilled coordination entails assigning writing tasks, setting deadlines, distributing materials, corresponding with authors, and mediating decision making. Essentially, the coordinating author is in charge of putting together the manuscript from conception through publication submission and beyond.

3. Forming a writing group helps organize collaborative writing projects (Drotar, 2000). Group members set a mutually agreeable meeting schedule in order to review work in progress, share their writing sections, and plan next steps. A public commitment to collaborative writing usually motivates participants to complete their assignments.

4. Schaumberg et al. (2015) described an unusual approach to collaborative writing which they labeled "The Paper Chase." Interns at a graduate training center formed two groups with the goal of writing two scientific manuscripts in a 24-hour period. On the day of the paper chase, both teams started in the morning in expectation "that the manuscripts would be written, formatted for a specific journal, and submitted to the faculty supervisors and other team members within 24 hours" (p. 44). I doubt that this approach will resonate with most practitioners nor will it serve productivity in the manner of routinized writing practices.

√ Dedicate time for reading and summarizing the published literature

√ Identify publication objectives, outlets, and submission requirements

√ Organize materials into a hardcopy or electronic manuscript folder

√ Look for collaborative writing projects

√ Schedule weekly 60-minute writing session

√ Make up any missed weekly writing session

√ Seek out and be prepared to write during unscheduled opportunities

√ Write from an outline

√ Write a rough, approximate, and less-than-perfect first-draft manuscript

√ Edit and rewrite a first-draft manuscript into an approved publication submission

√ Complete final proof-reading and obtain author consent before publication submission

√ Anticipate reviewer reactions and appraisal before publication submission

√ Monitor performance

Figure 14.3 Performance guide checklist.

Summary

I learned a long time ago about the joys and fulfillment that come from writing for publication. For me, writing is integral to clinical practice, training, consultation, and just about every other activity I perform as an ABA practitioner. Hopefully, this chapter has persuaded you to approach writing for publication in the same way.

Fig. 14.3 is a performance guide checklist condensing the narrative descriptions found in the chapter. I propose that you follow these steps to develop a personalized and dedicated writing plan. You should also read the writing books I recommended —they are instructive and will further inform good writing habits.

Remember, if you wait for inspiration, you will not be a productive writer. And publications do not appear from bouts of creativity. Deep and tortured introspection is also unrelated to writing process and outcome. As an ABA practitioner, apply the learning principles you know so well to build a writing repertoire, produce gratifying results, contribute to the welfare of the people you serve, and educate professionals within and outside of the ABA community.

References

American Psychological Association (2009). *Publication manual of the American Psychological Association* (6th ed.). Washington, DC: Author.

Arthur, A., Anchan, J. P., Este, D., Khanlou, N., Kwok, S. M., & Mawani, F. (2004). Managing faculty-student collaborations in research and authorship. *Canadian Journal of Counselling, 38*, 177–192.

Behavior Analyst Certification Board (2014). *Professional and ethical compliance code for behavior analysts*. Retrieved from http://bacb.com/ethics-code/.

Boice, R. (1983). Contingency management in writing and the appearance of creative ideas: Implications for the treatment of writing blocks. *Behavior Research and Therapy, 5*, 537–543.

Bridgewater, C. A., Bornstein, P. H., & Walkenbach, J. (1981). Ethical issues in the assignment of publication credit. *American Psychologist, 36*, 524–525.

Buckley, W. F. (1984). *Overdrive: A personal documentary*. Boston, MA: Little, Brown, and Company.

Carr, J. E., & Briggs, A. M. (2010). Strategies for making regular contact with the scholarly literature. *Behavior Analysis in Practice, 3*, 13–20.

Caruso, M., & Kennedy, C. H. (2004). Effects of a reviewer prompting strategy on timely manuscript reviews. *Journal of Applied Behavior Analysis, 37*, 523–526.

Codd, R. T., III (2016). How to develop a robust practice-based research repertoire. *The Behavior Therapist, 39*, 118–120.

Critchfield, T. (2011). Interesting times: Practice, science, and professional associations in behavior analysis. *The Behavior Analyst, 34*, 297–310.

Drotar, D. (2000). Training professional psychologists to write and publish: The utility of a writer's workshop seminar. *Professional Psychology: Research and Practice, 31*, 453–457.

Eke, G., Holttum, S., & Hayward, M. (2012). Testing a model of research intention among U.K. clinical psychologists: A logistic regression analysis. *Journal of Clinical Psychology, 68*, 263−278.

Epstein, R. (1997). Skinner as self-manager. *Journal of Applied Behavior Analysis, 30*, 545−568.

Gillis, J. M., & Carr, J. E. (2014). Keeping current with the applied behavior analytic literature in developmental disabilities: Noteworthy articles for the practicing behavior analyst. *Behavior Analysis in Practice, 7*, 10−14.

Hartley, J. (2008). *Academic writing and publishing: A practical handbook*. London: Routledge.

Hartley, J., Pennebaker, J. W., & Fox, C. (2003). Abstracts, introductions, and discussions: How far do they differ in style? *Scientometrics, 57*, 389−398.

Johnson, P. E., Perris, C. J., Salo, A., Deschaine, E., & Johnson, B. (2016). Use of an explicit rule decreases procrastination in university students. *Journal of Applied Behavior Analysis, 49*, 1−13.

Kelley, D. P., III, Wilder, D. A., Carr, J. E., Rey, C., Green, N., & Lipschultz, J. (2015). Research productivity among practitioners in behavior analysis: Recommendations from the prolific. *Behavior Analysis in Practice, 8*, 201−206.

Kendall-Tackett, K. A. (2007). *How to write for a general audience: A guide for academics who wants to share their knowledge with the world and have fun doing it*. Washington, DC: American Psychological Association.

King, S. (2010). *On writing*. New York: Demco Media.

Lamott, A. (1995). *Bid by bird: Some instructions on writing and life*. New York: Knopf Doubleday Publishing Group.

Lindsley, O. R. (1991). From technical jargon to plain English for application. *Journal of Applied Behavior Analysis, 24*, 449−458.

Luiselli, J. K. (2010). Writing for publication: A performance enhancement guide for the human services professional. *Behavior Modification, 34*, 459−473.

Luiselli, J. K. (2013). Peer review. In D. D. Reed, F. DiGennaro Reed, & J. K. Luiselli (Eds.), *Handbook of Crisis Intervention and Developmental Disabilities* (pp. 27−48). New York: Springer.

Luiselli, J. K. (2015). Performance management and staff preparation. In F. D. Reed, & D. D. Reed (Eds.), *Autism service delivery: Bridging the gap between science and practice in autism service delivery*. New York: Springer.

Luiselli, J. K., Wolongevicz, J., Egan, P., Amirault, D., Sciaraffa, N., & Treml, T. (1999). The family support program: Description of a preventive, community-based behavioral intervention for children with pervasive developmental disorders. *Child & Family Behavior Therapy, 21*, 1−18.

Luiselli, J. K., Benner, S., Stoddard, T., Weiss, R., & Lisowski, K. (2001). Evaluating the efficacy of partial hospitalization services for adults with mental retardation and psychiatric disorders: A pilot study using the Aberrant Behavior Checklist (ABC). *Mental Health Aspects of Developmental Disabilities, 4*, 61−67.

Luiselli, J. K., Campbell, S., O'Malley-Cannon, B., DiPietro, E., Ellis, J. T., Taras, M., & Lifter, K. (2001). Assessment instruments used in the education and treatment of persons with autism: Brief report of a survey of national service centers. *Research in Developmental Disabilities, 22*, 389−398.

Luiselli, J. K., Sperry, J. M., & MaGee, C. (2011). Descriptive analysis of physical restraint (protective holding) among community living adults with intellectual disability. *Journal of Intellectual Disabilities, 15*, 93−99.

Madden, G. J., & Johnson, P. S. (2010). A delay discounting primer. In G. J. Madden, & W. K. Bickel (Eds.), *Impulsivity: The behavioral and neurological science of discounting* (pp. 1−37). Washington, DC: American Psychological Association.

McCutcheon, M. (2006). *Damn, why didn't I write that?* New York: Linden Publishing.

McDougall, D. (2006). The distributed changing criterion design. *Journal of Behavioral Education, 15*, 237−247.

Nevin, J. A., & Shahan, T. A. (2011). Behavioral momentum theory: Equations and applications. *Journal of Applied Behavior Analysis, 44*, 877−895.

Parsons, M. B., & Reid, D. H. (2011). A practical means of enhancing professional knowledge among human services practitioners. *Behavior Analysis in Practice, 4*, 53.

Pinker, S. (2015). *The sense of style: The thinking person's guide to writing in the 21st century.* New York: Penguin Publishing Group.

Porritt, M., Burt, A., & Poling, A. (2006). Increasing fiction writer's productivity through an Internet based intervention. *Journal of Applied Behavior Analysis, 39*, 393−397.

Reed, D. D. (2014). Determining how, when, and whether you should publish outside the box: Sober advice for early career behavior analysts. *Behavior Analysis in Practice, 37*, 83−86.

Rouillard, L. (2002). *Goals and goal setting.* Rochester, NY: Axzo Press.

Schaumberg, K., Mota, N., Dixon, L., Sippel, L., Jackson, M., Vinci, C., ... Coffey, S. F. (2015). The paper chase: Reflections on an exercise in collaborative scientific writing. *The Behavior Analyst, .*

Silvia, P. J. (2007). *How to write a lot: A practical guide to productive academic writing.* Washington, DC: American Psychological Association.

Skinner, B. F. (1957). *Verbal behavior.* New York: Macmillan Publishing Company.

Skinner, B. F. (1981). How to discover what you have to say: Talk to students. *Behavior Analyst, 4*, 1−7.

Strunk, W., & White, E. B. (1979). *The elements of style.* New York: Macmillan Publishing Company.

Winston, R. B. (1985). A suggested procedure for determining order of authorship in research publications. *Journal of Counseling and Development, 63*, 515−518.

Zinsser, W. (2006). *On writing well: The classic guide to writing nonfiction.* New York: Harper Collins.

Practice Dissemination: Public Speaking

15

Patrick C. Friman
Boys Town, NE, USA and The University of Nebraska School of Medicine

The action is at the front of the room. By front I mean the location in a room (or other setting) toward which people assembled focus their attention. Thus, it is possible to turn the back of a room into the functional front by standing in back and speaking. Occupying the front of the room with authority and influence is essential, regardless of the task at hand, and front of the room tasks vary greatly ranging from toasts and eulogies to lectures and addresses. Some of the greatest moments in human history occurred at the front. Remember, for example, the words spoken by Winston Churchill as he sought to inform Great Britain and the world about what was needed to safeguard freedom: "We shall go on to the end, we shall fight in France, we shall fight on the seas and oceans, we shall fight with growing confidence and growing strength in the air, we shall defend our island, whatever the cost may be, we shall fight on the beaches, we shall fight on the landing grounds, we shall fight in the fields and in the streets, we shall fight in the hills; we shall never surrender..." Some of the greatest moments in the arts also occurred at the front. Remember, for example, the words spoken by Shakespeare's Mark Antony in Julius Caesar: "Friends, Romans, countrymen, lend me your ears. I come to bury Caesar, not praise him..." Some of the greatest human beings in history had their finest moments at the front. Lincoln's Gettysburg address, Chief Joseph's surrender, and Martin Luther King's "I have a dream" all come to mind. So too do Elizabeth I's speech to the troops at Tilbury, Emmeline Pankhurst's "Freedom or death" response to the death of fellow Suffragette Emily Davison, and Sojourner Truth's "Ain't I a woman." My aims in this paper are threefold. The first is to inform you that there is always room at the front for another speaker and invite you to be one. The second is to inform you that once you are at the front you are in a position of power. And the third is to admonish you not to waste the opportunity.

Let me begin by explaining why there is always room at the front. The obvious answer is that there are more occasions requiring a speaker than there are speakers. This is undoubtedly true but it does not address the reason for the disparity. I submit that the reason, very simply put, is fear. We, and I mean the all-inclusive we, are afraid of the front of the room. The power available there is volatile and can work for or against the speaker. Successful speeches educate, entertain, motivate, and/or inspire audiences and all of these outcomes help fulfill the speaker's goals. Unsuccessful speeches, however, bore, confuse, disturb, and/or anger audiences and all of these outcomes thwart the speaker's goals. An implicit goal, presumably for all speakers, is that the audience will accept them and even find them attractive

Applied Behavior Analysis Advanced Guidebook. DOI: http://dx.doi.org/10.1016/B978-0-12-811122-2.00015-2

along a number of dimensions (e.g., physical, intellectual, spiritual). And indeed, successful speeches produce these outcomes. Unfortunately, unsuccessful speeches often do just the opposite and most speakers (e.g., me), fear, or are terrified by the possibility of those.

And therein resides the challenge. People are afraid of public speaking because of the real (but actually rare) possibility that their speech will fail, positions will be ignored or rebutted, and one's reputation will be damaged. The aversive possibilities seem to magnify with the size of the audience. In the early days of my own career as speaker, the cutoff was three. When speaking to three or fewer people, my anxiety levels were virtually undetectable. When speaking to more than three, they were off the charts. This fear actually put me in good company because most people fear public speaking. In the first edition of the *Book of Lists* (Wallace, Wallace, & Wallechinsky, 1977) it was the number one fear—above death and it has hovered near the top of lists of fears ever since (e.g., Kangas-Dwyer & Davidson, 2012).

My fear may have been a little stronger than most. I remember trying to design a life where public speaking (speaking to more than three people at a time) would never happen. The first challenge to this plan was the scheduled defense of my Master's Thesis at the University of Kansas. I had only three faculty members on the committee but four of my fellow students decided to sit in. Uh oh! A crowd is forming. As I drove from Kansas City to Lawrence on the day of the defense, I came very close to driving my truck off the road so that it would roll and I would be injured and thus be allowed to phone in my defense from my hospital bed. I am not making this up. But it was this plainly psychotic plan that made me realize I needed to address my fear of public speaking.

The remainder of this paper summarizes in 25 suggestions what I have learned over the years as I have made the fearsome journey to the front of the room. These suggestions are drawn from my own experiences, an earlier abbreviated version of this paper (Friman, 2014a) and numerous commercially available books, videos, tutorials, seminars, and workshops whose aim is to help people master public speaking (e.g., Atkinson, 2005; Carnegie, 2014; Goodman, 2006; Reynolds, 2008; Long, 2015; Sarnoff, 1972; Silvia & Feldman, 2012). The 25 suggestions are divided into three sections, two general suggestions, eight for preparation, and fifteen for delivery. Let's get started.

General suggestions

1. *Plain speaking please.* This is a point relevant for most talks but one that would come later if this paper were being written for a general audience. I make it here first because the ostensible purpose of this book is to supply information for behavior analysts. That purpose notwithstanding, I am aiming for broader readership and therefore will use mostly colloquial expression. I am not going to twist the paper into a technical pretzel in order to achieve behavior analytic precision and avoid mentalism. Said differently, I know the behavior analysts reading this will understand it easily. I want non behavior analysts to be

able to understand it too. If I write in "behavior-analytic-ese" not only will non behavior analysts not understand it, it is unlikely they will even try.

And therein lies an essential lesson for you speakers. Speak to be understood by the majority of your audience. If half of the audience understands French and English and the other half only English, speak English. Everyone who reads this book will understand colloquial writing. Most, but not all, of these readers will be also be fluent in "behavior-analytic-ese." Therefore I am writing this paper with colloquial and not technical language. The theme of this book is dissemination. And the dissemination of an idea is dependent on the ease of the means of its transmission. Technical language does not disseminate widely because it is not easy to understand and use. Colloquial language transmits readily because it is easy to understand and use. This is not the first time I have made this point (cf., Friman, 2004, 2006, 2010; 2014a). It will not be the last, and I am not alone in making it. Some of the most influential behavior analysts in the history of the field have made a similar point (e.g., Bailey, 1991; Foxx, 1996; Lindsley, 1991). So from here forward I will eschew obfuscation and embrace clear communication. That does not mean I will stoop to "ain't," "shoulda," and "woulda" but I will also not be reaching for "tact," "mand," and "autoclitic."

Nonetheless, many speeches will necessarily include some technical material. It is still important to make it easy for the audience to understand and follow your message. If your talk necessarily includes abstract or technical material, I recommend starting with concrete (i.e., readily accessible points) and introducing the abstract or technical stuff during the middle or toward the end.

2. *Feel the fear and do it anyway.* With a nonbehavior analytic audience, this would have been the first recommendation because it is the most important for all but a few speakers and it is the advice that finally led me away from my own psychotic-level notions about public speaking (e.g., "wreck your truck"). My initial attempts to learn to speak to more than three people involved getting over my fear. That is, I believed that I had to learn to not be afraid. I got nowhere with that goal. Truth to tell, I am still afraid of public speaking. What does that mean? It means that prior to any speaking engagement, whether it be giving a toast at a dinner party in my home, a presentation to staff working for me, or a keynote address at a major conference, I always have the same reaction. If you are afraid of public speaking you have this reaction too.

It is called a threat-based stress response. The sympathetic nervous system releases stress hormones (e.g., cortisol, epinephrine) which recruit glucose, which is essentially fuel—glucose in the body is like gasoline in a car. Turning this fuel into energy requires that it be metabolized and, thus, the body increases its demand for oxygen. This is why anxious speakers sometimes seem to run out of air as they speak. Their bodies are taxing their oxygen stores in order to metabolize glucose and they need to breathe more regularly and deeply to complete their comments (but they often don't). To distribute the energy thus created, heart rate and blood pressure go up. And now the engine is running, so to speak. Unfortunately, the sympathetic nervous system supplies only two options for using this energy—attack and kill everyone in the audience or run away. Obviously, these are unworkable options. Yet I, like most anxious speakers, find this aroused state highly aversive, especially because the two ways to relieve it supplied by the sympathetic nervous system are off limits for speakers. As indicated above, my alternative attempts to contend with it by waiting for it to not occur were futile. What I have learned to do instead is to override the dictates of my sympathetic nervous system and just start speaking. As the late, great Lonnie Phillips, primary architect of the Teaching Family Model (Phillips, Phillips, Fixsen & Wolf, 1971) claimed, the best thing to do in the presence of paralyzing fear or stupefying depression is to exhibit behavior. Speaking is behavior. So in the presence of my own fear of speaking, I now just speak. And to make it easier, I now think of the aroused state that inevitably occurs as excitement rather than fear and I use it to invigorate my speaking. There is actually substantial research supporting this strategy (e.g., Brooks, 2013). So I am recommending against attempts at getting over fear of public speaking and for learning to speak while afraid (cf., Friman, 2014a). I have gotten quite good at this, so good in fact that I have a hard time convincing people that I still fear public speaking.

However, there are some methods that actually do reduce fearful arousal. One involves medication which I will discuss below. Another involves the reductive effect exposure to aversive stimuli has on arousal (Friman, 2007; 2014a). For most speakers, arousal reduces within talks themselves; it is high at the beginning and reduces as the talk progresses. Arousal also reduces across talks; the more talks one gives, the less arousing they tend to be. But for many speakers (e.g., me) arousal will never actually be completely avoided or eliminated. Another option involves various types of relaxation procedures ranging from deep muscle relaxation to focused breathing. One example used by navy SEALs, a group whose job periodically generates substantial arousal, involves slowly breathing in through the nose to a count of four, holding the breath for a count of four, breathing out to a count of four, and continuing this process for 4 minutes. This method countermands the threat-based stress response described above and allows better access to the central nervous system. In other words, using it allows Navy SEALs to shoot straighter and speakers to speak more effectively.

Suggestions for preparation

1. *As a last resort, consider medication.* Rather than employing behavioral methods for reducing fear of public speaking, some people attempt to control it by using medications whose purpose is to interfere with or mask the biology of fear (e.g., Ativan, Xanax). This strategy has its detriments, the most notable of which are side effects such as slowed thought processes, speech, and reaction time, all of which affect functions critical to effective speaking. However, there is one group of medications that reduce arousal with virtually no performance altering side effects. These are beta blockers, the most notable example of which is Propranolol (brand name Inderal). Its primary medical use is to control heart beat and reduce blood pressure but it has also become known for reducing performance anxiety in numerous domains, ranging from precision activities that require hand/arm steadiness (e.g., golf, billiards, surgery) to musical performances and public speaking (e.g., Kelly & Saveanu, 2005). I learned of it when assisting two pediatric residents to prepare for Grand Rounds presentations in which I played a part. During practice sessions they were very nervous but on the day of the presentation they appeared quite relaxed. When I inquired, they informed me that they had taken 10 mg of Propranolol. It is available only by prescription and is accompanied by some risks so if you decide to try it be sure and ask your physician for the complete risk profile.
2. *If you feel no fear seek feedback.* There is a widely held, yet patently false belief, that fear of public speaking is abnormal. The primary meanings of the word normal are expected, typical, or most likely to occur (Soukhanov, 1992). Given the widespread fear of public speaking, it seems safe to say that not being afraid may actually be abnormal. Nonetheless there are some people who are simply unafraid of public speaking. Rather

than fearing and avoiding it, they relish and pursue it. You may think they are the lucky few and indeed, there may be some lucky members among their group, but most are unlucky in my opinion. They are so assured of their appeal as speakers that they do not seek and thus do not benefit from the corrective influence of feedback. Anxious performers actively seek feedback, sometimes to a fault, but fearless performers usually do not. Rather than anxiety, these speakers suffer from what might be called overconfidence. They may proclaim proudly that they never practice a presentation and do little to prepare. Thus, they routinely expose audiences to presentations that are raw and unburnished by preparation, rehearsal, and the incorporation of feedback. If you are in this group please, do your future audiences a favor and ask some people on whom you can depend for honesty to give you feedback on previous and planned talks.

3. *Look for and emulate models.* I am a thief. And in my thieving I am reminded of something said by T. S. Elliott and repeated in various forms so often as that it has achieved the status of cliché: "Immature poets imitate; mature poets steal." I am not a poet, mature or otherwise, but I am a mature speaker and I steal from good speakers. I am particularly likely to purloin style (and material) from Sunday morning televangelists. They are routinely terrific at the front of the room. They have no slides, notes, or props (other than a bible) and yet they hold audiences in thrall, sometimes for hours. One that comes to mind (quite often actually) is David Ring, He has cerebral palsy and his speech is significantly impaired by his condition. As just one example, during one of his sermons he stated "I can't even say Jesus plain." Yet his effect on audiences is virtually hypnotic. He is a vivid example of how important speaking style is as reflected in the Delivery Suggestions below especially suggestions 2–4, 6–7, and 9–11. To see what I am saying merely go to youtube.com and type David Ring into the search window. Watch any clips that are listed. As an aside, I'll bet you can't watch just one. They are habit forming.

I can also refer you to people I admire in our field. One of the best speakers ever was Ogden Lindsley but he has passed on and I do not know if any of his presentations are available in recorded form. But there are some contemporaries. Among my favorites are Scott Geller, Greg Hanley, Jonathan Tarbox, Jim Carr, Bill Heward, Derek Reed, Dermot Barnes, Kelly Wilson, Lori Unumb, and Gina Green. There are several others and I am sure I am slighting some by listing these but they came quickly to mind. I recommend watching them and emulating (i.e., stealing) anything you like and can reproduce. I worked with Edward Christophersen as a graduate student and I taped all of his public presentations and then listened to them repeatedly, "stealing" any lines, concepts, and logical progressions I could reproduce. Initially I sounded like him when I talked (although I could never reproduce the celerity of his wit or perfection of his timing) but I gradually developed my own distinctive style. Note here that I am crediting him for the influence he had on me and have done so continuously throughout my career. I recommend you do the same. When you borrow (i.e., steal) from those whose speaking you admire, acknowledge them frequently and publicly.

4. *Proactively create the presentation.* I recommend you begin this process immediately after you have accepted an invitation to speak. Presumably your hosts or you will have decided on a topic. Ask yourself what you would like to say about this topic. Do this multiple times after the invitation and then regularly afterwards. Doing this heightens the salience of relevant material available in your environment. I call this the "red Volkswagen" effect. You never see them—unless you own one and then they show up regularly. Once you "own" the topic for your talk, so to speak, then you will begin seeing relevant material regularly. On the front end of this task, be noncritical. Write down every idea that occurs to you. Also be on the alert for any relevant content (e.g., research,

pictures, media-based content, etc.) and file it with your presentation information. Once you have a substantial amount of material (I usually start this about a month before a major talk) create an outline.

5. *Over-practice the presentation.* Once you have a draft of the slide presentation make a photocopy of it and have it at hand. Then practice out loud. Doing so will produce material substantially different from material produced by practicing silently (i.e., in your head). Said differently, we don't really know what we have to say about something until we hear ourselves saying it. As the new material is generated, scribble it onto the copy of the pertinent slide(s). When you are done practicing, revise the slides accordingly. Once you have an acceptable draft, begin rehearsing in earnest at least occasionally in front of a mirror. Excellence is born of practice, not talent. Alternatively, it takes a lot of practice to be truly talented (cf., Gladwell, 2009; Lindsley, 1992). So practice your presentation over and over. Note that I did not say memorize, I said practice. With practice you will likely notice that although you make the points you intend, each time they occur just a little differently. And these slight differences expand your flexibility in front of your audience. If you memorize your talk, you lose flexibility. Forget one small segment and you may lose the ability to present the larger message.

Furthermore, I recommend repetitive practice with special emphasis on the first and last 5 minutes of your talk (Friman, 2014a). The first 5 minutes are when the speaker is most nervous, and fluency born of repeated practice is a tonic for nervousness. The last 5 minutes are when a speaker's most important points are made (or when they should be made). This is when the talk moves from the particular (e.g., "This case reflects the results of repetitive practice.") to the universal (e.g., "Ultimately all masterful performances rest upon the incremental and ultimately synergistic contributions of simple repetitive practice."). All great performers practice (although some try to hide that fact). For example, Ernest Hemmingway rewrote the ending of *A Farewell to Arms* 39 times. Roald Dahl, author of *Charlie and the Chocolate Factory,* rewrote his stories more than 100 times before he published them. Jerry Seinfeld is well known to revise and practice a single joke for years (Weiner, 2012). An effective method for practice is a version of crosstraining first used by Demosthenes, a prominent statesman of ancient Athens. As a young man he stammered, was easily winded, and had a weak voice. But he badly wanted some of the power available at the front of the room. So he practiced speeches with pebbles in his mouth (to overcome his stammer), in competition with waves pounding on the shore (to increase his volume) and while running up and down sand dunes (to expand his lung capacity). The result of his practice is that he became one of the most effective orators in his day and remains one of the most famous in recorded history.

6. *Prepare the room the way you want it.* Hotel, program, or convention staff will set up the room. But you will be giving the presentation, not them. So go to the room well before your talk and either set it up or have it set up the way you want it. As just one example to consider, if the podium is to be on one side of the room make sure it is to the audience's left. Most of your audience will be right handed (unless you are speaking to a convention for left handed people) and right handed people have an easier time looking to their left than their right. Check the lighting (make sure it will not wash out your slides). Test the microphone (e.g., volume, batteries, etc.), projector, and computer you will be using. Do not be shy about this, be assertive. If active or passive resistance on the part of support staff results in a breakdown in your presentation, the audience will hold you accountable, not them.

7. *Prepare yourself.* Start with your psychological response system. Although eliminating fear altogether has proven impossible for me and will likely be for you as well, it can be

reduced through known behavioral processes most notably respondent and operant extinction. To accomplish this spend time in the room where you will present. Visit every part. Then ascend the stage (if there is one) and imagine the audience looking at you and then, if you are alone in the room, give the imaginary audience a portion of your talk (e.g., first and last 5 minutes). Doing all this will likely reduce the aversive qualities of the room through extinction, desensitization, or to use the acronym from my favorite book on managing anxiety in childhood *GUTI* (getting used to it) (Chanksy, 2004).

Then move to your body. Relaxation can also help as suggested above and master presenters and performers use a variety of methods that go beyond reducing arousal (e.g., focused breathing) to generally preparing the body for flexible performance (e.g., neck rolls, hip swings, stretching). See Long (2015) for descriptions and exhibitions.

Then prepare your voice. Vocal performances benefit from increasing the range of motion in the face and vocal apparatus. There are numerous exercises for accomplishing this ranging from stretching the mouth wide and then narrowing it to pronouncing tongue twisters and extending the lips to make vowel sounds. See Long (2015) for descriptions and exhibitions of these as well.

8. *Dress for the occasion.* The audience will notice your clothing so dress with that in mind. I recommend aiming for a level of dress slightly better than the average audience member. Do this not to show your superiority but to show your respect: you dressed up for them. Your clothing should attract some but not too much attention. It should underscore your role in the room. If you dress way down, you convey disrespect for the audience (you didn't care enough about them to dress up) and you draw attention but the wrong kind. You appear to not belong in the room or at least not anywhere near the front (e.g., "Is that guy the janitor or the speaker"). Conversely if you dress up too much you risk drawing attention to your clothes rather than your message. You do not want the audience to remember more about what you wore than about what you said. The basic goal is to have your clothing communicate respect and convey that you have an important role in the room. Ideally, audience members should identify you as the speaker when you enter the room, and the clothing you select should help them do so.

Suggestions for delivery of your talk

1. *Make an entrance.* Having captured your audience's attention with your clothing, keep it by making a captivating entrance. It does not matter from where you come—first row of the arranged chairs, side stage, or back of the room. It does matter that you make something happen. As an exaggerated example, watch a clip of Will Smith acting as Mohammad Ali entering George Foreman's training room before their boxing match in Zaire (https://www.youtube.com/watch?v = wjkoBMS3bmM) or actual footage of Mohammad Ali entering the weigh-in room for his first championship fight with Sonny Liston (https://www.youtube.com/watch?v = zaTbr5TrnHA). He made something happen when he entered a room and that is something I recommend you do. Perhaps not as dramatic as Ali but distinguish yourself from those assembled to hear you talk.

There are two major options for making an entrance, creating power or relationship and the main goal is to have all of your attention on achieving one or the other and no attention on your worries or concerns about your appearance or incipient presentation. I usually choose the power option. I enter the room with dignity and purpose. I do not make eye contact until I am on stage. If I enter from the back I walk steadily to the front with my eyes on the stage. I am not self-conscious. I am conscious of only one thing, having the audience notice something is happening—The speaker has entered the room and is heading toward the stage. I attempt to make something similar happen, although smaller in scale and shorter in time when I enter from the front row or side stage but, I prefer to enter from the back. It is easier to make something happen from there. I recommend reminding yourself that these people are assembled to hear you speak and it is important that you to give them something for the investment of their time and attention. You are the show and the show begins when you enter the room.

The other way to enter the room is to create friendly (nonthreatening) relationships as you make your way to the stage. If you enter from the back you can issue greetings and shake hands all along the way. Politicians seem to favor this approach. It can also be a balm for nervous speakers. The more friends they make or contact, the less threat the audience seems to pose. If you approach the stage from the front row or from the side, you can extend greetings to people you know or want to know who are seated in front.

2. *Stand up straight and smile.* The nonverbal parts of your presentation are almost always as important as the verbal parts (Mehrabian & Ferris, 1968). For example, your posture has stimulus functions; make them work for rather than against you. Standing up straight will improve your confidence and sense of purpose. To test what I claim, stand up and introduce yourself to an imaginary person first while slouching and then while standing straight. A significant difference in how you feel about the introduction should be apparent. To judge what I am saying from a scientific perspective consult evidence well summarized thoroughly in book form (Cuddy, 2015) or in an abbreviated video form (Cuddy, 2012). Strong posture produces multiple beneficial effects on the person assuming the posture. At the physiological level, it decreases the presence of stress hormones underlying the threat-based stress response discussed in General Suggestion #2 while increasing the presence of hormones associated with confident performance (e.g., testosterone). At the level of performance it improves such things as self-expression, negotiating skills, job seeking, and managing difficult social situations.

Your posture also has an effect on the audience. It is composed of persons, most of whom have been admonished, at least occasionally and probably frequently, to stand up straight. If the person in front of them is slouching, then on some level, possibly beneath awareness, they will sense that person is doing something wrong. Conversely, if the person is standing up straight, they will sense the person is doing something right. It is important for these stimulus functions to work in support of what you are saying because they will influence how the audience judges your talk. In addition, an erect posture seems to suggest confidence and strength—qualities that could increase the confidence the audience has in you.

Your face has stimulus functions too. As with the functions of posture, make face functions work for you rather than against you. Consider the timeless quote "Smile and the world smiles with you, frown and the world looks down." There are actually several benefits of smiling, many of which pertain to you the speaker. For example, smiling reduces the experience and biological markers of stress. It also releases pleasure hormones such as endorphins and serotonin. Stress is a correlate of fear and pleasure hormones exert a reductive influence on fear. Recall that public speaking is one of the things people fear most. Smiling also has beneficial effects on the audience. In fact, the positive effects smiling has on others (i.e., the audience) are as well documented as the positive effects it has on the speaker. Smiling makes one appear more physically attractive and likeable, recruits more helping behavior from others, generates more trust, and increases cooperation. It even enhances memory retrieval of your name by the recipients of your smile (cf., Kraft & Pressman, 2012; Jaffe, 2010; Lewis & Bowler, 2009). At the risk of stating the obvious, each and every one of these salutary effects of smiling would enhance your presentation.

3. *Be present.* In the previous iteration of this paper (Friman, 2014a), this segment was titled "Show Up" but after reading an article titled *"The Importance of Being"* (Verghese, 2016) and portions of *Being and Time* (Heidegger, 2008) I changed it because, although *show up* works well, *be present* works better. Verghese exhorted physicians to be more present with their patients and warned of the distractions posed by electronic medical records and the compelling desire to do rather than just be. Heidegger spent much of his career attempting to delineate being—which reflects how tricky the concept of being actually is. I will use examples to bring it forth because an actual definition would likely be little help. As a first example, when a hospitalized person is near death the most important thing for loved ones in the person's room is to be present. But that can be difficult. It would be much easier to confer with staff, pray, cry, lean on each other, or engage in other distracting activities. But the dying person is all alone quite possibly with at least a vestige of consciousness left and the best thing for him or her would be to have a least one person physically close and vividly present as he or she makes the lonely transition from here and alive to dead and gone.

But being present under stressful conditions is challenging. It is much easier to focus on the conditions, the emotional experience of them (e.g., "I hate this," "this is awful" etc.) and the thoughts they evoke (e.g., "why is this happening" "I can't do this"). But that focus diminishes presence. The clearest examples of not being present involve persons who seem distracted, self-conscious, or preoccupied. True, they are right there in front of you but in a certain sense they are elsewhere. I had a powerful experience of the difference between being present and not being present years ago during a karate match.

It was my first match and I was terrified. As I stood across from my formidable opponent my thoughts were not on the fight, they were on the pain and shame I was likely to experience when he was done with me. I was not at all present; I was preoccupied with fear and thoughts of failure. Being preoccupied rather than present is truly dangerous when we are confronted by someone intent on harming us. Then, for reasons I will never understand, my pants fell down, all by themselves. It was as if they thought "We will go down before he goes down." I stood there for what seemed like an eternity. The large audience laughed. Teammates and opponents laughed. The announcer made fun of me ("Ladies, if you would like this man's phone number it will be available after the match."). No one seemed to notice how helpless I was. I had fighting gloves on and I could neither pull up nor tie my own pants. Finally, the referee and my coach simultaneously recognized my plight and pulled them up and tied them for me. The effect of this was remarkable. I left my mournful reverie and became fully present in the room just as the referee started the match. I swiftly crossed the mat and struck my opponent in the chest with a strong front punch and knocked the wind out of him. He never recovered and I won the match. I won no others. I was not very good at karate. I am persuaded I won the match with my first opponent simply because the pants episode set the occasion for me to become fully present. (In retrospect, it may have had the opposite effect on him).

So I recommend that you conduct exercises that produce being present prior to taking the stage. When I conduct trainings for speakers I use such exercises. For example, I recently did a "front of the room training" with eight of the junior staff in our program. I did body and voice exercises with them as described in Preparation Suggestion #7. And I also had them do a getting present exercise. I had each of them repeat something outrageous ("Do not let me catch you brushing that dog's teeth with my toothbrush!") and had those observing rate the intensity of the utterance until it was at least 8 on a 10 scale (one being low intensity and presence and 10 no reservation, full expression, full presence). Their subsequent performances were extraordinary especially insofar as their being present was concerned. My supervisory staff subsequently observed that the increased presence seen in the practice talks appeared to generalize to day-to-day performance. This exercise is merely one option for helping others (or yourself) to be fully present for a presentation. The general strategy is to do anything to move your (or their) attention away from the debilitating self-evaluations that diminish presence and compromise performance toward the material to be delivered and the audience.

4. *Quiet the room.* If you have followed my advice so far, many or most of the people in the room will have their attention on you already and know you are about to speak. So some quieting will have occurred as a function of your entrance. But probably not all, so someone will have to quiet the rest. For those presentations where you will be introduced, this is your introducer's job. But if you follow the advice I offer in Delivery Suggestion #5 it will be yours. Here are a few options. One is just start talking. The downside of this option is that it may take a few moments for listening to occur and thus some of your opening remarks may be missed. Another is to ask for the audiences' attention and wait till you receive it to begin. This is probably the easiest and the most conventional. I actually pursue a third option, one consistent with my power entrance strategy. I stand at center stage quietly and essentially "will" the audience to notice I am standing there waiting to begin. This is a little nerve wracking because it takes a few moments and time does seem to slow down during uncomfortable silences. But the audience does take notice and inexorably quiets.

5. *Introduce yourself.* In my first paper on the front of the room (Friman, 2014a) I rather strongly recommended that speakers take control of the introduction by doing it themselves. Since making that point I have paid close attention to how my hosts handle my introductions when they are aware of the position I have taken. At times it seems awkward for them because the person whose job it is to introduce speakers has to tell the audience that I will be introducing myself and it can almost seem as if they are avoiding the task for their own reasons rather than mine. I hate to put hosts in that position. Nonetheless, I still favor managing the introduction myself if it can be easily and comfortably arranged. However, I am also quite willing to surrender the task to my hosts if that is their wish. As just one example, the introduction of an invited speaker is often one of the first opportunities a graduate student has to speak at a major formal event. Although nervous, they are always well prepared and eager to conduct the task. Depriving them of such a formative experience is grossly inconsistent with my interest in helping people master the front of the room. But I still maintain that a self-introduction is preferable for reasons I will discuss below.

First, the audience has assembled to hear from, not about, you. Second, the material to be included in the formal introduction is usually readily available elsewhere (e.g., the program booklet). Third, a formal introduction can put you in a potentially embarrassing position. For example, if you are keynote speaker, your sponsors will likely have requested a bio sketch and your introduction will usually merely involve someone reading it or parts of it. You are then in a position that requires you to thank your introducer for saying such nice things about you even though you wrote them yourself. Fourth, formal introductions sometimes contain inaccuracies which can be distracting for you and the audience. Fifth, if there is a mismatch between the tone of the introduction and the tone planned for the presentation you have to either adjust the tone or let the disparity stand. Sixth, formal introductions take time. Presentations are rarely open-ended; the schedule assigns a set beginning and end. If you prepare remarks to fill an assigned interval that is subsequently shortened by a lengthy introduction you must either shorten your prepared remarks or go over your allotted time.

My advice is to take charge of the introduction and make it work for your presentation. One way to do this is to ask your sponsors for permission to introduce yourself. I prefer this option over all others because it solves virtually all of the problems mentioned above. Most importantly, perhaps, is that this strategy allows the audience to get to know you quickly and in the way you want to be known. For example, most introductions exaggerate the speaker's accomplishments, reputation, and influence, thereby elevating audience expectations. Unfortunately for the speaker, the higher the expectations, the harder they are to meet. By taking control of your introduction, you have a greater chance of setting audience expectation at a level you can actually meet. You can also emphasize qualities you seek to embody. You may prefer to be thought of as friendly and well informed rather than as highly accomplished and really important.

6. *Exploit your voice.* Another powerful source of nonverbal communication is your voice. It has three qualities, volume, tempo, and tone that can be exploited to draw attention and convey a message. Raising your voice does both. It draws attention and suggests something really important is being said. Lowering your voice can also do both. It draws attention and suggests what you are saying is confidential, just between you and the audience. Tempo affects attention and conveys messages too. Up-tempo can suggest the speaker is moving rapidly toward an important point that he or she is really excited for the audience to hear. Down tempo can suggest that each word is important, and the point the words are leading to is not to be missed. Stopping cold and saying nothing for a moment will typically draw every eye to the speaker. If you employ this tactic to produce that result, however, it is important to reward the attention with something significant (e.g., funny, enlightening, conclusive, etc.). Finally, tone can transform the meaning of almost any word or phrase. As an example, think of the various meanings that can be drawn from the phrase "nice job." A down inflection would produce an affirmative tone that suggests the speaker was actually impressed with job. An up inflection would produce an interrogative tone that suggests the speaker is uncertain about the quality of the job. A derisive tone produces the experience of derision and would be hard to misinterpret.

7. *Use your hands purposefully.* Your audience's attention will inevitably travel where your body tells it to go. So remember your hands. If left unattended they can take on a life of their own. Where they go and how they are positioned will affect audience attention. If they head to your pockets as so many do, the audience may wonder what is going on in there. If they stiffen statically by your sides you will begin to look wooden and possibly uncomfortable. This could distract the audience away from your message. So I recommend you use them purposely to produce a broad range of influences such as emphasis, direction of attention, expanding or diminishing a point, and a variety other possibilities. Regardless of their politics, most people believe Barack Obama is an excellent public speaker and one of his several strengths is how well he uses his hands.

8. *Move intentionally.* Some speakers prowl the stage for no apparent purpose. They walk back and forth almost like a zoo animal stereotypically moving from one side of its cage to the other. This kind of nonpurposeful movement generates a nervous energy that can be distracting to the audience. Staying stationary is not necessarily the best alternative although many great speakers typically remained in the same position when they spoke (e.g., Martin Luther King, John F. Kennedy). I recommend occasional movement to

connect with as much of the audience as possible. My own strategy is to think of the room as the outfield in baseball and try to spend a similar amount of time with each field. So for a 60-minute talk I would aim to spend 20 minutes each on the right, center, and left parts of the stage.

9. *Start powerfully and foreshadow your conclusion.* Strive to ignite audience interest and maintain it with your first sentence. I remember reading a paper on medical noncompliance in graduate school. I no longer have the reference nor do I remember the author. But I remember very well the first sentence of the paper: "Colonialism has discredited history." I also remember that the only reason I read the full paper was because of that sentence. I just had to know how colonialism had discredited history and, more importantly, what it had to do with medical compliance. The author drew me all the way in with just one sentence. Seek something similar with your first remarks. Give the audience a reason to listen. I often start my presentations with a variation of the following: "Behavioral analysis is founded on the most powerful idea ever invented by mankind for understanding, knowing, and approaching human behavior" I used that sentence recently to begin a talk on 10 reasons why behavior analysts should study thumb sucking (Friman, 2014b). Reason # 10 was to save the world. How I got there from thumb sucking is too much to explain in this paper. The point is that I obtained audience interest with my first sentence and gave them a reason to keep listening.

10. *Make it relevant to them.* There are many reasons why people attend talks, and some have little to do with the speaker or the content. For example, they may attend simply because they are at a conference and nothing else is going on at that time. Maybe they are earning easy CEUs. Or perhaps they wanted to accompany a friend. There are others. By making the content of your talk relevant to the audience members, however, you create a new purpose for these individuals. Specifically, the purpose of hearing what you have to say and listening with interest. To do that, make your talk relevant to audience members on as many levels as possible. For example, I am frequently asked to do keynote addresses for theme oriented conferences (e.g., autism, precision teaching, parenting). I always address the main theme of the conference, but I also always show how what I am saying is relevant, not just to the theme, but to behavior analysts, psychologists, people (or any classification that fits the entire room) in general. By doing that I provide all the audience members a reason to listen, not just those that came to hear about the assigned topic.

11. *Tell stories.* Remember that the primary purpose of your talk is to persuade the audience to adopt your point of view on your chosen subject. One of the lessons of the recent presidential election is that the candidate who tells the best story, not the one with the best facts, is likely to be the one elected. This is true in most domains in human intercourse. Freud had a much greater influence over the culture at large than Skinner because he told a better story. Skinner had more and better facts, by a wide margin, but the story he told about those facts was not as compelling as the story Freud told about the few facts he was able to assemble. Einstein is the most influential, recognized, and beloved physicist of all times, not because he was the best physicist but because he was the physicist who told the best stories. Presumably your talk will have a few facts, perhaps many, but those facts will not come to life for the audience until you supply a story that gives them meaning. When I visit graduate programs, advisors often have their students present their research to me. The students usually describe a dizzying array of facts and how they obtained them, and I usually get lost early in the mix. At that point I usually stop them and ask them to simply tell me a story about their work, one that their

mother would readily understand. After they do so, the facts in their presentation become much more interesting and apprehensible.

More generally, people love stories so give them what they love. The audience's attention is fragile and fickle. Maintaining it for more than 10 minutes at a time is a challenge (Goodman, 2006). There are many ways to regain attention that has drifted. A moment of silence might do it. Shifting topics can work. Asking if there are any questions can perk people up. But the moment a speaker says "For example..." eyes that have wandered away from the speaker quickly find their way back. *That* this occurs has been documented well (Atkinson, 2005; Goodman, 2006). *Why* this occurs is a matter for speculation. It seems plausible that the material following those words is much more likely to reinforce listening with understanding than the material that preceded the example. Producing or expanding understanding is the *raison d'etre* for the example. Good speakers intuitively recognize when the material they have just delivered is challenging for the audience for any of a number of reasons (e.g., having been very abstract, complex) and offer an example to make the material more clear and comprehensible (e.g., Horn, 1996). One of the most effective ways to do this is to use a pertinent story.

12. *Do not obsess over the data or the slides.* The audience is perfectly capable of reading your slides. You do not need to do it for them. This is never truer than when you use a humor slide. Do not (ever) explain the joke; merely make the point the joke is intended to support. For example, I sometimes show a humor slide depicting a therapist saying to a patient "your therapy will be a combination of drugs and clowns," whereas a clown on a unicycle rides around the therapy room and the horrified client looks on. As the audience looks at it I say that one of the reasons people are reluctant to see a therapist is that they have no way of knowing what is going to happen. I do not explain the slide. If there is no point to support and you want to include the slide merely because you think it is funny, don't. All your materials should flow to your themes. The purpose of slides is to augment your presentation, but augment is the key word here. You and your message are the show, not the slides. You want the audience's attention on you and most importantly on your message. The slides cue your narrative flow and give the audience a place to focus when they are not focused on you. In order to limit their focus on the slides, use few words and rely more on pictures. If you have a very wordy slide the audience will be inclined to read it. Meanwhile, you will have been talking and they will have missed what you said.

When it comes to data, the most important function of a data slide is to let the audience know you have it. If you spend time going over all the data on your slide you will lose your narrative flow and a lot of the audience along with it. The only times I recommend spending more time on your data slides is when there is really something interesting depicted there (e.g., a significant spike in the baseline data) or if an audience member asks a question about them. In the latter case, the audience will blame the questioner for bothering you and boring them.

13. *Make your point, early and often.* Recall the time honored speaker triptych purportedly passed down from Aristotle: (1) Tell them what you are going to tell them; (2) Tell them; (3) Tell them what you told them. You have a fundamental purpose for being in front of a group. Specifically it is to deliver a message. Make sure you serve that purpose throughout your talk. To do so effectively, it is critical that you know your that message is. This should be worked out well in advance. For example, defense lawyers have a message they have worked out with their client: My client is innocent. During the court proceedings, the attorney never loses sight of that message and continuously presents it until it is at least plausible and, possibly, until it is undeniable. Then during the closing arguments they virtually always follow the triptych. For example, "I am going to recap

what we have learned over the past five days of testimony. Specifically, that my client is innocent. He had no motive. He had no means. And he has an iron clad alibi. After deliberating, I am convinced you will conclude as I have that this man could not have committed this crime." As another example, watch video footage of Martin Luther King's *I Have a Dream* speech (one of the most moving speeches of all time) and notice how many times he tells the audience he has a dream and how many different ways he tells them what it is.

14. *Do not go over your time limit.* What you have to say will certainly be important, especially to you. And if your talk is successful, it will also be important to your audience. But no matter how important your message is, entertaining you are, or enraptured the audience seems, it is still essential, mandatory, critically important (you choose) that you end your talk on time. Some speakers seem to believe that what they have to say is *so* important that they use up all of their time and then some of the next speaker's time to get it all said. Nothing, save possibly directions about how to exit the building if it is on fire, is that important, so do not do it. The only justification for going past your time limit I'd be willing to entertain with equanimity would be the appearance of an emergency (e.g., active shooter in the building, fire in the next wing). Under emergency circumstances you may be called upon to stay at the microphone and keep your listeners calm. Your failure to wrap up in a timely fashion does not qualify as an emergency. If you go over your time limit, you are implicitly communicating that you consider what you have to say as more important than what the next speaker has to say and you are explicitly taking some of their time. So be organized enough to fill your time and respectful enough to end on time. If you happen to end early, more power to you. You may think it wise to use the time saved for questions. If so, see the next suggestion.

15. *Kill em and leave.* This is the title to the very well-received biography of James Brown by McBride (2016). Its message, wow the audience and leave the stage, is one I want to convey to you. Too many powerful endings to presentations are disempowered by the following: "Does anyone have any questions?" School is not in. There will be no test. Thus there is no need to ask for and answer questions. Although you may be in a classroom (some presentations take place in them) this is not class. This is a presentation. Frankly, the word I like better is performance. This is an intellectual performance. And if done well, it ends on an inspiring, universal point. If you allow questions, your interrogators will ask you to make uninspiring, specific points. Don't let them steal your show. Your presentation was for the entire audience. Their questions are for themselves. If you answer their questions you are basically ignoring the audience to take care of individual questioners. I realize I am going against a strong, longstanding intellectual current flowing the other way, especially in the field of behavior analysis. But I believe that current needs to be dammed and redirected. I am not suggesting there should not be questions; they are inevitable. I am just saying that the stage is not the best place to answer them. You and the questioner(s) will be better served if you ask them to hold their question(s) for after you have left the stage. Doing so also serves the next speaker because questions take time and answering them well can take you over your time limit.

Concluding remarks

My last piece of advice is to talk to groups—every chance you get. Start right away. We would all like to get ahead, distinguish ourselves, develop as a person, have more influence, confidence and power, be better known, and make a bigger difference. Mastering the front of the room contributes to all of these goals. Opportunities abound. The world perpetually needs public speakers. The need ranges from the small, such as dinner parties needing someone to give a toast, to the large, such as plenary sessions at major conferences needing a keynote speaker. If elected public office is among your loftier aspirations, there is virtually no chance of obtaining office without first standing at the podium, on the stage, or in front a microphone. Elected offices are often gained or lost as a result of successful or failed public presentations. Perhaps something less ambitious, but nonetheless important, is among your ambitions, such as a wedding toast, eulogy, or a talk to your elementary school child's class. Opportunities such as these arise frequently and I recommend pursuing them to expand your role in your general day to day life.

In closing, the importance of your development as a speaker notwithstanding, I have something larger in mind: the influence of behavior analysis on the turbulent world in which we live. Please recall my claim about the power of the core idea of behavior analysis in the Abstract and in Delivery Suggestion #9. Going even further, I also claim that everything that idea touches improves, from the lives of persons with disabilities to the performance of institutions. Yet this idea is little known and even less understood. In order for people in everyday life to become more acquainted with it, someone will have to explain it to them—effectively. This can be done in lots of ways and one of the most powerful is to stand in front of them, at the front of the room as it were, and tell them. My aim is to have large numbers of behavior analysts, especially students and junior members of the field, see that mastering the front of the room not only benefits them personally and professionally, but also benefits behavior analysis itself by virtue of an enhanced capacity to explain it to groups. The world may indeed be a stage as Shakespeare argued but the stage to which he referred was metaphorical. In this world, there are countless actual stages. Find one. No, strike that, find many, ascend them and start talking. Then tell the people assembled in front of you about our field. Speaking for the field, we need you.

References

Atkinson, M. (2005). *Lend me your ears*. New York, NY: Oxford University Press.
Bailey, J. S. (1991). Marketing behavior analysis requires different talk. *Journal of Applied Behavior Analysis, 24*, 445–448.
Brooks, A. W. (2013). Get excited: Reappraising pre-performance anxiety as excitement. *Journal of Experimental Psychology: General, 14*, 1144–1158.
Carnegie, D. (2014). *Secrets of sales success by Dale Carnegie and Jeffrey Gitomer*. New York, NY: Dale Carnegie & Associates.
Chanksy, T. E. (2004). *Freeing your child from anxiety*. New York, NY: Broadway Books.
Cuddy, A. (2012). *Your body shapes who you are*. TED.com. <https://www.ted.com/talks/amy_cuddy_your_body_language_shapes_who_you_are>.
Cuddy, A. (2015). *Presence*. New York, NY: Little Brown.

Foxx, R. M. (1996). Translating the covenant: The behavior analyst as ambassador and translator. *The Behavior Analyst, 19*, 146–161.

Friman, P. C. (2004). Up with this I shall not put: 10 reasons why I disagree with Branch and Vollmer on "behavior" used as a count noun. *The Behavior Analyst, 27*, 99–106.

Friman, P. C. (2006). Eschew obfuscation: A colloquial description of contingent reinforcement. *European Journal of Behavior Analysis, 7*, 107–110.

Friman, P. C. (2007). The fear factor: A functional approach to anxiety. In P. Sturmey (Ed.), *Treatment and intervention in clinical psychology: Functional analytic approaches* (pp. 335–355). San Diego, CA: Elsevier.

Friman, P. C. (2010). *Presidential address: Steps to take and Missteps to Avoid on the Quest for Mainstream Relevance.* Paper presented at 36th annual convention of the Association for Behavioral Analysis International, San Antonio, TX.

Friman, P. C. (2014a). Behavior analysts to the front! A 15-step tutorial on public speaking. *The Behavior Analyst, 37*, 109–118.

Friman, P. C. (2014b). *Thumb sucking: A love story.* Paper presented at the 35th annual conference of the Berkshire Association for Behavior Analysis and Therapy. Amherst, MA.

Gladwell, M. (2009). *Outliers: The story of success.* New York, NY: Little, Brown and Company.

Goodman, A. (2006). *Why bad presentations happen to good causes.* Los Angeles, CA: Cause Communications.

Heidegger, M. (2008). *Being and time.* New York, NY: Harper Perennial.

Horn, S. (1996). *Tongue Fu!* New York, NY: St. Martin's Press.

Jaffe, E. (2010). The psychological study of smiling. *The Observer, 23*(10). Retrieved March 2, 2014 from <http://www.psychologicalscience.org/index.php/publications/observer/2010/december-10/the-psychological-study-of-smiling.html>.

Kangas-Dwyer, K., & Davidson, M. M. (2012). Is public speaking really feared more than death. *Communication Research Reports, 29*, 99–107.

Kelly, V. C., & Saveanu, R. V. (2005). Performance anxiety: How to ease stage fright. *Current Psychiatry, 4*, 25–34.

Kraft, T. L., & Pressman, S. D. (2012). Grin and bear it: The influence of manipulated facial expression on the stress response. *Psychological Science, 23*, 1372–1378.

Lewis, M. B., & Bowler, P. J. (2009). Botulinum toxin cosmetic therapy correlates with a more positive mood. *Journal of Cosmetic Dermatology, 8*, 24–26.

Lindsley, O. R. (1991). From technical jargon to plain English for application. *The Behavior Analyst, 24*, 445–448.

Lindsley, O. R. (1992). Precision teaching: Discoveries and effects. *Journal of Applied Behavior Analysis, 25*, 51–57.

Long, M. M. (2015). *Mastering stage presence: How to present to any audience.* Chantilly, VA: The Teaching Company.

McBride, J. (2016). *Kill em and leave: Searching for the real James Brown.* New York, NY: Penguin Random House.

Mehrabian, A., & Ferris, S. (1968). Inference of attitudes from nonverbal communication in two channels. *Journal of Consulting Psychology, 31*, 605–611.

Phillips, E. L., Phillips, E. A., Fixsen, D. L., & Wolf, M. M. (1971). Achievement place: Modification of the behavior of pre-delinquent boys within a token economy. *Journal of Applied Behavior Analysis, 4*, 45–59.

Reynolds, G. (2008). *Presentation Zen: Simple ideas on presentation design and delivery.* Berkley, CA: New Riders.

Sarnoff, D. (1972). *Speech can change your life.* New York, NY: Dell.

Silvia, P., & Feldman, D. B. (2012). *Public speaking for psychologists: A lighthearted guide to research presentations, job talk, and other opportunities to embarrass yourself.* Washington, DC: American Psychological Association.

Soukhanov, A. H. (1992). *American heritage dictionary.* Boston, MA: Houghton Mifflin.

Verghese, A. (2016). The importance of being. *Health Affairs, 35,* 1924–1927.

Wallace, D., Wallace, A., & Wallechinsky, I. (1977). *The book of lists.* New York, NY: Bantam Books.

Weiner, J. (2012). Jerry Seinfeld intends to die standing up. *New York Times Magazine* Retrieved January 12, 2014 from <http://www.nytimes.com/2012/12/23/magazine/jerry-seinfeld-intends-to-die-standing-up.html?_r = 0>.

Further reading

Carlson, N. R. (1994). *Physiology and behavior.* Needham Heights, MA: Allyn & Bacon.

Endress, P. (2009). *Communication University.* Harrisburg, PA: Maximum Advantage.

Gleick, J. (2008). *Chaos: The making of a new science.* New York, NY: Penguin.

O'Connor, J., & Seymour, J. (1990). *Introducing NLP: Psychological skills for understanding and influencing people.* London: Harper Collins.

Licensure and Certification

16

William H. Ahearn
New England Center for Children, Southborough, MA, United States

Certification and licensure of the practice of applied behavior analysis

The practice of applied behavior analysis (ABA) has received extensive exposure in the healthcare and lay communities given the increased recognition of the efficacy of ABA as an intervention for autism spectrum disorders (ASDs; e.g., American Academy of Pediatrics, 2001; Eldevik et al., 2009, 2010). ABA as a treatment strategy is not limited to any specific population, having been shown to be effective with individuals with atypical and typical development across a broad range of treatment targets including skill deficits (e.g., reading, writing, math, and other academic skills as well as communication and social skills) and behavioral excesses (e.g., challenging behavior such as self-injury and aggression, smoking, anxiety, phobia, exercise, and weight control; see Austin & Carr, 2000). However, the most extensive application of ABA has been with individuals with ASDs and intellectual and developmental disabilities (IDD). ASDs in particular have been increasingly recognized as a complex set of neurobehavioral developmental disorders that are diagnosed at least once in every 68 live births (1 in 42 boys and 1 in 189 girls; Centers for Disease Control and Prevention, 2014). The rise in autism prevalence, though slightly controversial, is primarily due to improved recognition, surveillance, and the expansion of diagnostic criteria (e.g., Shattuck, 2006; Whitehouse et al., 2017; Wing & Potter, 2002).

Due to there being extensive and growing demand for ABA services for persons with ASDs and beyond, this chapter's purpose is to discuss the landscape relative to this emerging practice discipline and to specifically focus on how one becomes a member of the professional practice of ABA. The goal is to serve as a roadmap for prospective applied behavior analysts and as a source of information relative to the current state of mechanisms by which ABA services have been recognized and regulated for established ABA clinicians. It must be noted that these developments have happened quite rapidly and it is likely that there will be many additional developments that cannot at this time be anticipated. That said, the current trends reflect a likely path for the regulation of ABA for at least the near future.

The untreated prognosis for individuals with ASDs varies based upon the severity of the disorder, but one thing is clear—individual's outcomes are optimized by structured behavioral interventions, such as ABA, targeted at addressing the core, and associated deficits of autism (e.g., Eldevik et al., 2010). Moreover, given the prevalence of ASDs, there are substantial societal costs for caring for individuals who cannot function independently as adults. Teaching those with ASDs the skills

Applied Behavior Analysis Advanced Guidebook. DOI: http://dx.doi.org/10.1016/B978-0-12-811122-2.00016-4

to become as independent as possible and to be productive members of society represents a wise long-term investment (Ganz, 2007; Jacobson, Mulick, & Green, 1998).

History of ABA treatment for ASD

ABA intervention has about a 50-year history where behavior analytic interventions have shown good efficacy for treating autism spectrum and intellectual and developmental disorders, specifically problem behavior and learning deficits (Lerman, Iwata, & Hanley, 2013). Early intensive ABA for children with autism is the most widely known ABA treatment, and it is geared toward directly teaching developmentally appropriate skills (i.e., those that same-aged typically developing peers are exhibiting) and designing clinical interventions for the problem behavior of children with ASDs that interfere with their daily lives based upon the environmental function that problem behavior serves.

The most well-known studies of ABA for treating ASDs were conducted by Lovaas and his colleagues (Lovaas, 1987; McEachin, Smith, & Lovaas, 1993; Sallows, & Graupner, 2005; Smith, Groen, & Wynn, 2000). The initial studies (1987; McEachin et al.) showed that 47% of the young children who received approximately 40 hours per week of intensive ABA for 2−3 years were successfully transitioned into a typical school setting with minimal to no support (i.e., were functioning independently). Only 2% of the comparison group of those who did not receive ABA services achieved this outcome. Subsequent findings suggest that the percentage of children who successfully integrated into the public school setting may be slightly lower than those achieved in the initial Lovaas study. For example, Smith et al. provided intensive ABA for 25 hours a week for approximately 33 months but only 4 of 15 children were successfully transitioned to a typical school setting. It should be noted, however, that 13 of the 15 children in this study were mute (i.e., did not vocally communicate) at the start of intervention, a much higher percentage than in the initial Lovaas study. In addition, the intensity of service was also lower. On the other hand, MacDonald, Parry-Cruwys, Dupere, and Ahearn (2014) studied the effects of ABA services on children 3 years of age and younger and found that all children aged 18−23 months, regardless of the severity of their impairment prior to intervention, performed at the highest cognitive skill level (i.e., on par with their typically developing peers) following ABA treatment. The other two age groups benefitted significantly also but the implication of this study is that age at which ABA intervention begins is a critical variable. More research is necessary to better predict which individuals are more likely to maximally benefit from treatment.

Another recent study by Sallows and Graupner (2005) replicated the initial results of the Lovaas studies by randomly assigning subjects to a group that received clinic-directed services similar to those provided in the original study or to a group where services were as intense but were parent-directed (i.e., parents were trained to implement services with support from applied behavior analysts). Children in both groups had comparable gains in intelligence test scores and adaptive function with 48% of children across groups being successfully integrated into the public schools by age 7. The authors also found that, though most children benefitted from ABA treatment, success was best predicted by a child's pretreatment language, imitation, and social skills (i.e., children presenting with higher skills tended to be the most sensitive to the effects of ABA treatment).

Notably, ABA has become accepted as an effective treatment for autism (e.g., AAP, 2001; NIMH, 2007; NYSDH, 1999a, 1999b, 1999c; Surgeon General, 1999); no other intervention strategy can claim to be more effective. There have been at least 10 controlled (with about 25 other systematic comparisons with lesser control) group-design treatment comparisons supporting the efficacy of early intensive behavioral intervention for autism (for a thorough description of the components of the ABA intervention strategy see, Green, Brennan, & Fein, 2002). These studies of ABA as a treatment modality have received some criticism on a number of variables that could affect the implications of that research. One such variable is sample size (e.g., Kasari, 2002). To address this concern, Eldevik et al. (2009) conducted a metaanalysis of nine of these controlled studies (one controlled treatment comparison was not published prior to the metaanalysis). There were 297 children with an ASD in an intensive ABA treatment group, 105 children with an ASD in a control group, and 39 children with an ASD in a comparison treatment (i.e., not intensive ABA) group. The metaanalysis suggested that intensive ABA produced a large positive effect on full-scale intelligence scores, with an effect size of 1.1, and a positive moderate effect, an effect size of .66, on adaptive behavior.

An important caveat should be noted when comparing ABA intervention to standard early intervention services or "eclectic" treatment that may include behavioral intervention. The available evidence suggests that eclectic intervention does not produce a positive impact (Eldevik et al., 2009; Howard, Sparkman, Cohen, Green, & Stanislaw, 2005). Howard et al. found that after over a year of service delivery, children in the intensive ABA group had gained substantially more skills than either of the two comparison groups, one of which consisted of eclectic treatment including behavioral intervention. In a follow-up study, Howard, Stanislaw, Green, Sparkman, and Cohen (2014) found that children who received just ABA services were more than twice as likely to have achieved a typical range on measures of cognitive, language, and adaptive functioning than were children who received eclectic treatment intervention. Also, significantly more children receiving ABA services had cognitive, language, and adaptive behavior increases of at least one standard deviation from intake to final assessment. These findings suggest that ABA alone is superior to an eclectic intervention with unproven treatments even when these are combined with ABA services. This may be due to the time allocated to the unproven treatments reducing the amount of time allocated to ABA. Therefore, the efficacy of ABA services for treating ASDs has been firmly established.

The socially significant outcomes produced by applying the principles of behavior analysis, in combination with the recognition of these outcomes, have led to a new societal perspective on the importance of a behavioral approach to understanding and treating human behavior. From this perspective, one implication has been that disorders of development and delays in learning are viewed as treatable. Though this chapter focuses on the application of behavior analysis for treating persons with ASDs, as mentioned previously, behavior analysis has been applied to nearly every population including other intellectual/developmental disabilities, learning disabilities, traumatic brain injury, other neurologically based problems, and to problem behavior and skill deficits of typically developing persons (see Austin & Carr, 2000).

Autism insurance reform

A number of large companies, such as Microsoft, have self-insured their employees' health benefits such that their insurance coverage provides reimbursement for behavioral services rendered by a BCBA for children with autism (Stuebing, 2009). Microsoft has provided this benefit since 2001 and a number of other large companies such as Eli Lilly, Home Depot, Halliburton, IBM, Intel, Michelin, and Symantec have also covered ABA services. In addition, TRICARE, the US military's health plan, provides a similar benefit. However, the most significant impact on insurance coverage for ABA services has been due to work spearheaded by Autism Speaks. The Autism Speaks initiative Autism Votes (Autism Speaks, 2017a; https://www.autismspeaks.org/advocacy) has successfully advocated for insurance reimbursement for treating autism on a broad scale. As of the writing of this chapter, the work of Autism Votes has led to autism insurance reform wherein insurance coverage is mandated by law to cover treatment in 45 states that specifically includes reimbursement for ABA intervention (Autism Speaks, 2017b; https://www.autismspeaks.org/advocacy/insurance).

These laws vary from state to state but in each state, in some manner, the law identifies Board Certified Behavior Analysts (BCBAs) as qualified providers. The BCBA is a credential developed and overseen by the Behavior Analyst Certification Board, Inc. (BACB). The BACB credentials will be discussed further below. The first effective autism insurance law was enacted in Indiana and provided coverage in 2001 (Unumb & Unumb, 2011). This law mandated that insurers offer coverage for, among other things, treatment provided by applied behavior analytic health care providers. This mandate resulted in all group plans covering ABA services when prescribed by a physician. There were no age or dollar limits imposed for services and licensure of qualified providers was not included in the insurance reform law. The Indiana law was a significant step for ABA services being recognized and reimbursed via insurance coverage, but it was not until 2006 that state-mandated autism insurance coverage moved beyond Indiana.

Autism insurance reform then swept across the country and in many state legislatures a number of topics were being raised and debated. Some of these included whether there was sound evidence for ABA services as a treatment; is treatment educational or "medically necessary"; should all health plans cover treatment; should all ages receive coverage for services; as well as many other questions. One of the early states that passed insurance reform was South Carolina (Unumb & Unumb, 2011). "Ryan's Law" was enacted in June of 2007 and requires state employee health plans and fully insured group plans to cover treatment prescribed by a physician for individuals up to 16 years of age with an annual cap of $50,000/year for ABA services. The bill had been introduced in 2005 and faced many obstacles including a Governor's veto which was overridden by the South Carolina state legislature.

Some states were willing to move forward with insurance reform to cover treatment but only for younger children diagnosed with autism. Maine, for example, only mandated coverage for children through 5-year old. Although there are no age or monetary limits in some states (e.g., Massachusetts), other states like Alaska cap autism treatment coverage at 21 years of age, beyond the age cap in South Carolina. The annual amount of treatment covered can also vary by age such as in Arizona where reimbursed ABA treatment is subject to annual caps for those under the age of 9 at $50,000/year with less reimbursement for those between the ages of 9 and 16 at $25,000/year. Though the amount of treatment covered varies by states, all 45 autism insurance laws provide coverage for ABA services and for this reason the demand for ABA treatment is producing great growth in the field. One aspect of the laws that is not always clearly stipulated in statute or regulation is who is and, just as importantly, is not qualified to provide ABA services. For those seeking to enter the profession, it is very important to be aware of the requirements for practicing and how to meet them.

Identifying competent ABA providers

Due to the recognition of ABA as a mandated treatment option, one of the questions that become particularly important is what minimal competencies are expected of a practitioner of ABA. Insurance companies, consumers, and regulatory authorities will typically require that clear criteria exist for the purpose of determining competent practitioners. Green and Johnston (2009) describe the professional credentialing and licensure processes as they specifically relate to the practice of behavior analysis. They duly note that credentialing and licensure have much in common but have differing implications. Credentialing typically emanates from the field and is guided by the established history of practice in the field and the empirical evidence of the best practices that have been revealed through research. Many practice professions initially develop credentials that are intended to align with the expected duties of the practitioner and are used to describe how one learns about and is supervised while learning to perform these duties. Credentials typically start off as voluntary and are managed by the profession in some manner. How this is achieved, whether by established and recognized means of developing practice credentials, or less systematically, likely has a strong impact on the significance and durability of the professions' credentials.

Licensure involves an authority outside of (though, hopefully, in conjunction with) the profession providing rules and regulation for practitioners. Licensure is overseen by, in the United States, state governments through the mechanism that each state establishes for recognizing the profession in law. However, as delineated by Green and Johnston (2009), both credentialing and licensure establish the coursework and/or degree requirements in addition to the supervised experience necessary for demonstrating minimal competency. This is why, it is important for licensure and certification to closely align because these criteria then determine whether an individual is eligible to sit for an exam that qualifies one for a certification or license (although passing a licensing exam is not always a requirement for licensure especially in the initial stages of establishing a licensure mechanism) and whether there is consistency in how the profession is practiced from one state to the next. Passage of an exam is often the means for determining that the individual meets the final criterion for a credential or license. There are usually additional steps to obtain the credential/license such as paying a fee and passing a criminal background check. Maintaining the credential/license also requires meeting criteria following certification/licensure such as obtaining relevant continuing education (CE).

Credentialing

For ABA, credentialing of practitioners was established long before licensure initiatives were started as is typically the case for a professional practice. Bailey and Burch (2016) describe some of the historical events that led to the development of an ABA credential. In the 1960s and 1970s, the term "behavior modification" was used to generically describe the loosely defined practices of many clinicians providing behavioral treatment services. There were no minimal competencies or supervision requirements for practicing behavior modification and many of these behavior modification practitioners worked with individuals with what we would today refer to as having an ASD or IDD. In Florida in 1972, an investigation by the Dade County Attorney General's Office found that abuse of residents served at the Sunland Training Center in Miami occurred on a large scale under the supervision of a psychologist who claimed expertise in behavior modification. A committee was commissioned by the Florida State Health and Rehabilitative Services that further investigated these events and recommended, among other things, that more regular review of providers of behavioral services to persons with IDD occur. Eventually the state of Florida supported developing a Certified Behavior Analyst credential under the Florida Department of Professional Regulation and Florida Department of Health and Rehabilitative Services (1991; see also, FL, 1987; 1989; 1992). Other states started to establish their own programs for identifying minimal competencies for ABA professionals and eventually these were all folded into one entity, the Behavior Analyst Certification Board (BACB, 2017a; www.BACB.com/about-the-bacb).

The BACB developed specific guidelines for qualifying for certification with coursework requirements, specific criteria for supervised experience, and a psychometrically validated examination. The BACB also developed guidelines for responsible conduct, mechanisms and criteria for CE, and disciplinary standards. These will be described in more detail below. There are three nationally accredited levels of behavior analyst practitioners. The primary certification level is the Board Certified Behavior Analyst or BCBA (BACB, 2017d; https://bacb.com/bcba/). Clinicians with this certification have obtained, at least, a Master's degree with a minimum of 270 graduate-level coursework hours in behavior analysis with specific course content (see Table 16.1), have met a substantial supervision requirement, and passed a certification exam (there is also a Doctoral-level BCBA with the same core requirements along with a Ph.D., which itself meets certain criteria, referred to as BCBA-D®; BACB, 2017e; https://bacb.com/bcba-d/). CE is required to maintain certification and the current CE requirement is 32 CEs every 2 years (with a minimum of 4 CEs in ethics; and 3 CEs in supervision for supervisors; supervision will be elaborated on below).

A lower level certification, Board Certified Associate Behavior Analysts or BCaBA, is offered for behavioral therapists with a Bachelor's degree with a minimum of 180 undergraduate or graduate-level coursework hours in behavior analysis with specific course content (see Table 16.1), have met a supervision requirement, and passed a BCaBA certification exam (BCBA, 2017c; https://bacb.com/bcaba/). CE is required to maintain certification and the current CE requirement is 20 CEs every 2 years (with a minimum of 4 CEs in ethics; and 3 CEs in supervision for supervisors). The most recently established credential introduced by the BACB is the Registered Behavior Technician (RBT; BACB, 2017l; https://bacb.com/rbt/). The RBT is offered for those with at least a high school diploma or its equivalent and 40 hours of training implementing ABA services, the passage of competency

Table 16.1 BACB credentials (option 1)

Credential	Degree	ABA coursework	Additional requirements
BCBA	Masters degree or higher in Behavior Analysis, Psychology, or Education	45 h Ethics 45 h Behavior Analysis 45 h Research Methods 30 h Discretionary 105 h ABA	Supervised experience by a BACB-approved supervisor Passing the BCBA exam
BCaBA	Bachelors degree or higher in any discipline	15 h Ethics 45 h Behavior Analysis 15 h Research Methods 15 h Discretionary 90 h ABA	Supervised experience by a BACB-approved supervisor Passing the BCaBA exam
RBT	High School degree or equivalent	No specific coursework	40 h of training by a BACB certificant Passing the RBT competency assessment posttraining Passing a criminal background check Passing RBT exam

checks related to the training on implementing ABA procedures, having a criminal history evaluation, and the passage of the RBT exam.

RBTs have the lowest level of ABA competency and work under the direct supervision of a more established ABA provider. As will be described below, the RBT credential is not required for those providing ABA services directly to clients (i.e., implementing procedures) in all states. Some have not adopted standards of training for direct care staff but many state entities (e.g., State Departments of Public Health) have and it is likely that this credential will be adopted on a wider scale as time goes by. BCaBAs and BCBAs are the professionals who supervise, train, and support direct care services with BCBAs supervising, training and supporting BCaBAs when BCaBAs are employed. There are many fewer BCaBAs than RBTs and BCBAs. BCBAs are independently practicing professionals and supervise and train staff who provide direct care services.

Licensing

For ABA, licensure has been established in 26 states at the writing of this chapter (Carr & Nosik, 2017). The licensure laws differ in each state, have different implications for ABA services and service providers, and vary in the breadth with which ABA services are regulated. One kind of licensure law is a *title act*, which identifies those professionals that can use the title *Behavior Analyst* or *Applied Behavior Analyst* (the term "licensed" is sometimes part of the title; Green & Johnston, 2009). Wisconsin's licensure law is a title act that currently requires professionals seeking a license to meet the BACB requirements for obtaining the BCBA certification, be verified by the BACB as remaining in good standing, to pass a criminal background check, properly fill out the licensure application, and to pay the associated fees. Persons meeting these requirements are legally authorized to use the title *Behavior Analyst*. However, title acts do not necessarily mandate the recognition of services a profession provides but title acts provide a state-approved definition of the minimal competencies for those practitioners. Indiana also has a title act that prohibits any person for referring to themselves as a BCBA unless they are a BCBA in good standing with the BACB.

Title acts are often combined with *practice acts*. A practice act more specifically delineates the practices a licensee is qualified to provide and prohibits those who do not hold the license/credential from providing those services with certain exceptions (Green & Johnston, 2009). Most licensure laws include both title and practice criteria for the profession and provide some form of oversight (e.g., a licensing board) for practice. This will also be described further below. One example of a state with a title and practice component to their licensing law is Massachusetts (MA). In addition to criteria relative to obtaining and using the state-approved title for practicing ABA, the MA law (in combination with regulations for carrying out the law) identifies the scope of practice of providers, when they can practice, the types of intervention they provide, how they design and oversee services, how they are to establish and manage their professional relationships with clients, and ethical guidelines. When a practice component of a law has been developed by a state, there is typically an entity, such as a licensing board, that serves to regulate the profession. This entity varies in the 26 states that have established a regulatory authority (i.e., Board). In some states, the Board is an independent behavior analysis board whereas other states have combined professions and the Board consists of persons that are not behavior analysts (e.g., physicians, psychologists, mental health counselors, etc.) as well as practicing behavior analysts. Member of the public are commonly included on all types of state Boards to represent the consumers of services.

As mentioned previously, autism insurance reform in the majority of the United States has established a means of insurance coverage for the treatment of autism by ABA service providers. In some of those insurance laws, the BACB's BCBA credential is used specifically to denote that this credential qualifies a practitioner to provide ABA treatment. However, some states require a license for certain professionals, like health care providers, to practice and licensure is a natural next step for identifying competent services providers that the state will provide some form of oversight for their professional practice. For anyone interested in becoming a professional it is critically important for them to be well informed about the current and projected landscape for obtaining the relevant experiences necessary to become a practitioner. For ABA providers, the current status of certification converges with the licensing mechanisms that have been established in states with licensure. The Association of Professional Behavior Analysts (APBA) maintains a clearinghouse of information about laws and regulations for the practice of behavior analysis (APBA, 2017; http://www.apbahome.net/APBALicensure.php) that is available to APBA members. Professional associations will be discussed briefly below. In the 26 states with licensure, the BACB credential is currently either wholly or in part linked to the licensing standards. So for the prospective ABA provider, obtaining credentials in accordance with the procedures and standards developed by the BACB is a logical first step.

The essential components of the BACB credentials

The BACB, a 501(c) (3) nonprofit corporation whose primary focus was to develop professional ABA credentials, was founded in 1998 (Johnston, Carr, & Mellichamp, 2017). The professional practice of behavior analysis, as represented by the BACB's credentials, reflects a similar process by which other behavioral health care professions have developed into licensed professions. ABA as a practice oriented around the principles of behavior analysis has been around since the late 1960s. Thus, regulation of ABA practitioners became more pertinent both inside and outside of behavior analysis as time has lapsed. As suggested by Carr and Nosik (2017) regulation of a profession has two main functions. The first is consumer protection by identifying minimal competencies for practice and practice standards, whereas the other is protecting the professional practice by enforcing practice standards. Kazemi and Shapiro (2013) compare the history of the BACB's credentials with the development of similar credentials for other professions (e.g., Educational Psychologists, Social Workers, and Psychologists). They suggest that the degree and educational requirements for certification of behavior analysts are commensurate to board standards for licensure of other behavioral health professionals but that the experience requirements for BACB certification were not in line with other behavioral health professionals. That was as of 2013 and the BACB's standards were scheduled to change (and have) in 2015 and are now more in line with those professions' experience requirements (supervision will be discussed specifically below).

Mimicking the paths followed by other professions is one indicator of the BACB's status as the most valid source for identifying the competencies of ABA providers. More importantly, there are national accreditation agencies that have established how professions should develop professional credentials. In the United States, there are two accreditation entities: The National Commission for Certifying Agencies (NCCA) of the Institute for Credentialing Excellence and the American National Standards Institute (ANSI). These agencies provide accreditation standards for establishing credentialing programs that offer professional credentials. Both of these accreditation programs require that a professional credentialing program follow rigorous standards for developing, maintaining, and managing a professional credential. This includes how the credentialing body evaluates knowledge and skills, how it relates those to coursework requirements, how individuals are trained, and how it develops and validates its examination. The BACB is accredited by the NCCA, the accrediting arm of the National Organization for Competency Assurance. In accordance with NCCA accreditation standards, the BACB has also established supervised experience requirements, ethical guidelines, disciplinary standards, and CE requirements.

To date, the BACB has credentialed over 22,274 BCBAs, 2439 BCaBAs, and 26,429 RBTs worldwide with the projected total number of BACB certificants and RBTs well exceeding 300,000 within about 10 years (Carr & Nosik, 2017). With the demand for ABA services and growth of the number of ABA practitioners, there is a great need for programs to provide coursework, training, and experience for prospective clinicians. Toward this end, the BACB has approved course sequences for certification eligibility at 301 institutions worldwide with 219 of those in the United States (BACB, 2017m; http://info.bacb.com/o.php?page = 100358). For the prospective ABA clinician, there is a clear choice when it comes to identifying the training programs that will provide them with the experience and support necessary to attain the qualifications to be eligible to sit for the BACB's certification exam.

Coursework

The BACB has established eligibility criteria for obtaining the BCBA. There are currently three options (BACB, 2017a–o; http://bacb.com/bcba-requirements/). The first, and most commonly used, requires that an applicant have an acceptable graduate degree (i.e., Masters or Ph.D. in either behavior analysis, education, or psychology or a degree from a program that is a BACB-approved course sequence) from an accredited university, completion of acceptable graduate coursework in behavior analysis (i.e., a BACB-approved course sequence), and a defined period of supervised practical experience to apply to sit for the BCBA exam. A second option requires an acceptable graduate degree (as in option 1), a full-time faculty position in behavior analysis that includes research and teaching, and supervised practical experience also as with option 1. The last option requires an acceptable doctoral degree (as in options 1 and 2) that was conferred at least 10 years ago and at least 10 years' postdoctoral practical experience.

Given that option 1 is the most common and that there is some overlap between required coursework for the BCBA and the BCaBA and RBT, that coursework will be briefly reviewed here. The current coursework requirements are based upon the BACB's Fourth Edition Task List. The Task List outlines basic behavior analytic skills, client-centered responsibilities, and foundational knowledge in behavior analysis. This task list has been in place since 2010, replaced the Third Edition Task List, and was developed according to NCCA accreditation standards which included expert oversight and a thorough job analysis of the current practice of behavior analysis. A job analysis is, as noted by the NCCA, an essential component of credentialing and is stipulated by the NCCA to consist of several steps. Job analyses consist of convening panels of subject matter experts to, initially develop and to subsequently review, descriptions of the knowledge and skills necessary for practicing the profession. These subject matter expert reviews are converted into an extensive survey by a psychometrician that is then sent to a large number of members of the profession who rate the importance of each component identified by the subject matter experts. The results of the survey are then analyzed by a psychometrician and are converted into eligibility requirements to qualify for the certification exam as well as the examination items that are on the exam.

With the Fourth Edition of the task list, the BACB also introduced an increase in coursework requirements from 225 to 270 hours for the BCBA (and from 135 to 180 hours for the BCaBA credential; Johnston et al., 2017). The first examinations for the BCBA and BCaBA under the Fourth Edition Task List were delivered in February 2015 (BACB, 2017j). A job analysis process for updating the Fourth Edition of task list started at about the same time and another increase in educational standards and coursework requirements from 270 to 315 hours for the BCBA credential and from 180 to 225 hours for the BCaBA credential are scheduled to occur for examinations that will be administered in 2022 (BACB, 2017o; http://bacb.com/newsletter/).

The course content, linked to the Fourth Edition task and/or the BACB Professional Disciplinary and Ethical Standards, requires 45 hours of instruction in ethical and professional conduct; requires 45 hours of instruction in courses devoted to concepts and principles of behavior analysis; requires 45 hours of instruction in research methods in behavior analysis (25 in measurement and 20 in experimental design); requires 105 hours of instruction in ABA (45 in behavior change, 30 in assessment, 10 in treatment, 10 in behavior change systems, and 10 in implementation and supervision); and 30 hours of instruction in discretionary related to behavior analysis. The BCaBA and RBT coursework requirements consist of a smaller subset of this core coursework requirement for BCBAs. The Fifth Edition of the task list will add core coursework in organizational behavior management and theory (BACB, 2017i).

Supervised experience

Prospective BCBAs need to accrue supervised experience by a professional who meets the BACB's criteria for an acceptable supervisor (BACB 2017n; http://bacb. com/supervision-requirements/). The supervisor must complete a free BACB-mandated supervisor training intended to inform the supervisor of the essential components of providing supervision to prospective professionals related to the knowledge and skills indicated in the BACB's task list. The supervisee must also complete a parallel training designed to inform the prospective ABA professional on what is required in the supervised experience before they can accrue supervised experience. The supervisor must be a BCBA or BCBA-D in good standing with the BACB or be an approved instructor in a BACB-approved course sequence, or be a licensed or registered psychologist certified by the American Board of Professional Psychology in Behavioral and Cognitive Psychology who was tested in ABA as part of obtaining their credential.

There are three routes to completing acceptable supervised experience, completing either Supervised Independent Fieldwork, a Practicum, or an Intensive Practicum (some combination of these three routes can also be used to meet the supervised experience requirement to qualify to sit for the BCBA exam). Supervised fieldwork consists of accruing 1500 hours of experience with the supervisor providing supervision direct contact with supervisee once every two week supervisory period. Across the fieldwork the supervisor has a total of 75 contact hours during the 1500 hours of experience. A practicum involves more intensive contact relative to experience hours with, again 75 contact hours for a total of 1000 hours of experience. Contacts occur weekly with the practicum and the supervisee must obtain a passing grade (i.e., at least a C). An intensive practicum is the most intensive contact relative to experience hours with 75 contact hours across 750 experience hours with two contacts per week and obtaining a passing grade in the class.

The supervisor plays a crucial role in guiding the prospective ABA professional by providing training and support while conducting ABA service delivery. It is required that the supervisor observe and provide feedback on the implementation of the ABA procedures with clients. This is best achieved with regular, in person, one-to-one, real-time contact with the supervisee. The BACB does, however, allow supervision conducted via videoconferencing, videotape, or similar observation with real-time observation being strongly encouraged. Some supervision will likely consist of some training that will be similar for all supervisees (e.g., conducting discrete-trial instruction with clients) and may be conducted in small groups but this is allowed for no more than 50% of the total supervised hours in each supervisory period (which varies by the type of experience being accrued, see above).

Supervisors should ensure that the prospective ABA professional is exposed to as many different behavior analytic activities as possible to provide a well-rounded experience. Working with different supervisors who work with different clients, different presenting problems, and implement different types of ABA assessments and interventions is highly desirable. It is also helpful to accrue experience observing others implement ABA services, assessing staff performance/providing feedback while implementing ABA procedures, and developing new ABA programs to implement with clients. The BACB requires that only ABA activities be counted toward supervised experience (e.g., first aid or mandated reporter training, though important, are not ABA activities) and that at least 50% of the total accrued experience hours must be spent in activities other than direct implementation of ABA-procedures with clients (e.g., designing ABA assessments or programs, summarizing and interpreting data, developing data collection systems). Licensure laws in the states with them may have additional requirements for supervision (APBA, 2017; http://www.apbahome.net/APBALicensure.php).

Exam

The BACB requires that prospective BCBAs meet their coursework and supervision requirements prior to allowing them to take the BCBA exam (BACB, 2017h; https://bacb.com/examination-information/). The exam is administered using a computer-based testing format by Pearson VUE, Inc. consisting of 150 multiple-choice questions. As noted above the exam content is currently based on the Fourth Edition Task List with this changing to the Fifth Edition task list for exams administered in 2020. Questions come from each content area and in addition to the 150-graded questions, exams typically include up to 10 ungraded pilot questions, and candidates have 4 hours to complete the exam. The BACB exams are professionally developed to meet the standards developed by the NCCA accrediting agency. The exam results are reviewed after each administration by a psychometrician and subject matter experts with the goal of having a well-designed valid, instrument for determining whether or not candidates meet the minimal competencies for referring to themselves as a BCBA. Over the last 3 years of exam administration between 58% and 65% of first time test takers have passed the exam (see below).

Requirements for ABA professionals

Continuing education

Once a practitioner acquires a certification or a license to practice there are additional aspects of professional practice that are relevant. One is CE. The purpose of CE is to maintain and extend knowledge and skills acquired during training for the professional practice. CE is a common requirement for maintaining a professional certification and/or license. The BACB's current requirements for maintaining the BCBA credential (again the BCaBA and RBT have similar but lower requirements) consists of obtaining 32 units (CE hours or CE units) of acceptable CE with at least 4 hours covering ethics and 3 hours covering supervision practices for supervisors overseeing supervised experience for prospective ABA service providers (BACB, 2017f; http://bacb.com/continuing-education/). There are a number of categories for earning CEs such as taking a novel graduate course, delivering an approved CE event to others, publishing research in a peer-reviewed ABA journal, and retaking the certification exam but the most common means is to attend an approved CE event. These events are referred to by the BACB as Type 2 CEs and many local, state, regional, national, and international ABA organizations (which will be discussed briefly below) offer them either at a professional conference or to be viewed interactively online. Conferences are excellent opportunities for professionals to interact with each other and many of the states with licensure laws (and some without) have an organization that hosts meetings that typically also offer CEs. One advantage of attending a state organization's meetings is that the most up-to-date information on regulations and other relevant matters for practitioners is likely to come from the state organization.

Some states with licensure may have requirements that differ from the BACB's CE standards/requirements but most of them converge with the BACB's requirements (APBA, 2017). In Alaska, the licensed behavior analyst or licensed assistant behavior analyst must submit a copy of their BACB certificate showing that they remain in good standing when they apply to renew their license. This means that they have obtained acceptable CE according to the BACB criteria and have maintained/renewed their certification. Alaska licensees must also attest to whether or not they have had disciplinary action taken against them as professionals in Alaska or elsewhere, whether they have been subject to any criminal charges, whether they have had mental health or substance abuse events that impair their ability to practice behavior analysis. Mental health and substance abuse histories require that Alaskan licensee seek and provide fitness to practice evaluations as part of their renewal application.

Massachusetts is one state with rules that vary from the BACB's guidelines for CE. The licensed practitioners of behavior analysis in MA (called "Applied behavior analysts") are overseen by an omnibus board consisting of several mental health professions and the CE requirement is for 30 CE hours for the 2-year license. This requirement applies to all of the professions overseen by the board and the 2 years of CE is aligned with the date the license was acquired and not when the licensee obtained, if they have one, a certification from the BACB. There are also no content requirements such as the 4 ethics CEs and 3 CEs on supervisory practices for supervisors. In Arizona the license renewal requirements relative to CE, like in MA, require 30 CEs for a 2-year period, but they explicitly note that BACB standards for CE are adhered to in the licensees qualifying CE.

Disciplinary standards

One of the functions of certification and licensure, as discussed earlier in this chapter, is the protection of the public. One of the most critical aspects of practicing within a professional practice is to behave ethically but what does that mean? Ethical standards have been developed by many professions and ABA is no different. The BACB's current ethical guidelines are referred to as the Professional and Ethical Compliance Code for Behavior Analysts (BACB, 2017k; http://bacb.com/wp-content/uploads/2016/03/160321-compliance-code-english.pdf). This "Compliance Code" first outlines and then details the responsible conduct of behavior analysis, the behavior analyst's responsibility to clients, and many other issues related to behavior analysis including training and supervision. BACB-credentialed practitioners are expected to be fluent in and to adhere to these ethical guidelines. Failing to do so can result in a complaint being filed against the ABA practitioner and discipline being meted out relative to the ethical lapse.

The BACB has established a Disciplinary Review Committee (DRC) and Disciplinary Appeals Committee (DAC) to field complaints filed with the BACB (BACB, 2017g; http://bacb.com/disciplinary-and-appeals-process/). When a complaint is lodged with the BACB against a credentialed individual, a process is initiated that includes notifying the credentialed person that is the subject of the complaint and providing them an opportunity to respond to it. As long as the complaint was submitted within 6 months of the alleged violation and evidence was submitted in the complaint that a violation may have occurred, the written notice and reply of the complainant will be reviewed by the DRC. The DRC is charged with determining the validity of the complaint and whether this alleged violation merits sanctions (e.g., credential revocation, suspension, or some other discipline) or not. Once that final decision is made by the DRC the complainant has an opportunity to appeal the DRC decision to a DAC which may modify, uphold, or overturn the DRC's decision.

If the final determination includes sanctions those will be reported with the name of the complainant, the section of the Compliance Code violated, the sanction, date, and location of the violation on the BACB website and will be reported directly to applicable regulatory authorities (e.g., state licensing board). The disciplinary process typically takes between 4 months and 1 year to resolve (BACB, 2017g; http://bacb.com/disciplinary-and-appeals-process/). The timeline is increased in cases involving legal representation of the credential-holder or candidate, third party determinations, evidence and disclosure issues, appeals, and translation.

State licensing boards follow similar processes but the disciplinary standards and practices of licensing boards vary from state to state. Complaints are typically handled in a somewhat analogous manner to the BACB's disciplinary process. Once a complaint has been filed with a state licensing board, the complainant is notified and given an opportunity to respond. An investigation follows if the complaint meets the criteria (e.g., is not obviously false, claims a violation of the profession's ethical standards, there is reasonable evidence) for an investigation and the licensing board hears the matter once the investigation has been conducted. State licensing board's disciplinary actions can also involve revocation, suspension, or other sanctions as stipulated in state law relative to that licensing board's scope of oversight. Actions taken by a state's licensing board are also typically available to the public and can have a substantial impact on the practitioner's ability and authority to engage in professional practice. It is incumbent upon both licensed and credentialed individuals to protect their rights to practice. Practicing in an ethical manner is every practitioner's obligation to themselves, the consuming public, and to their profession.

A roadmap to entering the professional practice of ABA

The most daunting challenge for the field of ABA is meeting the demand for behavior analytic services with competent clinicians. As this chapter has outlined, determining who is qualified to implement behavior analytic services is a priority recognized by behavior analysts for quite some time and has also garnered substantial notice by consumers and governmental agencies. Toward this end, the BACB was formed, and specific guidelines for qualifying for certification, guidelines for professional and ethical conduct, disciplinary standards and for identifying necessary components of training programs for ABA providers were developed as noted above. The BACB's standards have been effectively incorporated into the 26 states' licensing laws that currently exist and serve as the foundational requirements for qualifying for a license to practice ABA. The two most commonly recognized levels of professional behavior analysts are the BCBA and BCaBA. The BCBA is the more common credential and requires a Master's degree in behavior analysis, psychology, or education and specific coursework in behavior analysis, substantial supervised experience, and passing a psychometrically validated certification exam. With the BCBA credential in the 45 states with autism insurance reform and with a license in the 26 states with an ABA licensing law, an ABA provider can practice independently whereas the BCaBA practices under the supervision of a BCBA.

Therefore, if one's goal is to practice ABA as a provider qualified to independently practice the logical starting point is entering a BACB-approved course sequence. Not all BACB-approved course sequences, however, are created equally. Some behavior analytic graduate programs have been training practitioners for decades (like the University of Florida and Western Michigan University), whereas many others have only started providing training within the last few years. Some states in the United States have an abundance of graduate programs that have a BACB-approved course sequence (California and Massachusetts both have 17 though Massachusetts has many fewer residents), whereas others may have none (such as South Dakota and Wyoming) or one (e.g., North Dakota and Montana). In places where there are few to no choices and the prospective ABA provider is geographically tied to their home state, there are distance learning programs that are available (BACB, 2017a−o; http://info.bacb. com/o.php?page=100358).

One program that offers distance learning is the Florida Institute of Technology (Florida Tech). Florida Tech is by far the largest training program in ABA when combining their graduate programs (or by just counting their distance learning program) and they offer an on campus program as well as a distance learning program and a hybrid course (i.e., one that includes both in-person and distance learning). Given that Florida Tech offers multiple programs it provides an interesting means of comparing them. The on campus program, over the last 4 years, has had between 15 and 29 graduates take the BCBA exam for the first time with between 74% and 100% passing the exam with an annual average of 88% passing the exam. The distance program has had many more enrollees over the last 4 years with between 566 and 932 graduates taking the exam for the first time and between 66% and 76% passing the BCBA exam with an annual average of 70.5% passing. Florida Tech trains a large number of ABA practitioners and there is a disparity in how well those trained on campus fare on the BCBA exam relative to their distance learning counterparts. It should be noted that graduates of other on campus BACB-approved course sequence programs do not fare as well in passing the BCBA exam as the Florida Tech distance learning peers so it is probably very important for prospective ABA practitioners to carefully choose where they apply to receive training. If one were to set a stringent criterion for graduates passing the BCBA exam, such as a minimum of 80% first time test takers passing, then there are a number of schools that meet this criterion across the 4 years for which data are available on graduates passing (BACB; 2017b; http://bacb.com/wp-content/uploads/2016/06/2015-ACS-pass-rate-BCBA-percent.pdf). One such school is Auburn University where between 9 and 12 graduates have taken the BCBA exam and the lowest percentage of first time test takers passing was 90% over the past 4 years with 100% passing in two of those years. For 2016 data on BCBA-exam passage shows that of the 81 programs with a BACB-approved course sequence who had candidates taking the exam, 28% of program had 80% or greater first time test takers pass, whereas 72% of schools did not meet this mark. Certainly the number of individuals taking the exam can vastly skew the passing percentages in either direction and a program's longer term history is most relevant when compared to any single year, but the better informed the prospective ABA provider is the more likely they will choose the best training program for them.

Experience

Another important consideration for the prospective ABA provider is to seek experiences that will best prepare them to provide the types of services they envision themselves providing as independent practitioners. For example, providing early intensive behavioral intervention and treating severe self-injurious behavior consist of different, yet related, skill sets. If a prospective clinician's goal is to work with young children with ASD in their home setting it is best to be trained by professionals providing those services. Having a variety of experiences, however, broadens an individual's foundation skill set. Therefore, working with clinicians providing services to both young children with ASDs and with others performing functional analyses and function-based treatments with self-injurious behavior would also be a productive training goal. One way of learning about the types of services provided by supervisors is to visit the graduate programs and training sites the prospective supervisor works in. Another option to more broadly expose oneself to a variety of supervisors is to attend local, state, regional, national, and/or international meetings of behavior analytic professionals. At professional meetings there are generally a broad range of topics available to attendees and there are opportunities to network with other ABA providers and other behavior analysts. In fact, it is in the best interest of everyone in the behavior analytic practice and scientific communities to be actively involved in professional organizations.

Professional organizations

The behavior analytic community has long supported a number of professional organizations, many of which regularly hold conferences. As mentioned above, the most important professional organization for a practicing behavior analyst to be involved in is their state's behavior analytic organization. Every state that currently has a licensing law has a state-based behavior analysis organization except North Dakota. These organizations generally hold meetings of elected officers and members but not all of them hold professional conferences. In Massachusetts there are two state-based organizations, the Berkshire Association for Behavior Analysis and Therapy and Massachusetts Association for Behavior Analysis (MassABA). Both organizations host annual professional conferences and meetings of elected officers and members. The state organization is going to have the most up-to-date information on the state laws, rules and regulations for practicing ABA. If there are proposals for establishing, changing, or eliminating state laws, rules and regulations relative to practicing behavior analysis the state organization is and needs to serve as the voice of the ABA community. It is in the best interest of all ABA providers to be a member of their state's behavior analysis organization.

There are also two main national/international behavior analytic organizations. The APBA was founded to promote and advance the science and practice of ABA. APBA has consistently advocated for the recognition of the BACB's credentials and representing the interests of professional and paraprofessional practitioners of ABA. APBA has also provided support and resources to state behavior analytic organizations and has worked with federal, state, and third-party entities to enhance recognition of professional and paraprofessional practitioners of ABA services. APBA is an excellent organization for prospective and practicing behavior analysts to join and support. The Association for Behavior Analysis International is the largest behavior analytic organization and represents the broad range of interests of behavior analysts covering the philosophy, science, application, and teaching of behavior analysis. Both organizations hold annual professional meetings.

Concluding remarks

Behavior analysis is broad community and there is no question that the professional practice of behavior analysis is a rapidly growing and healthy field. Becoming a part of the ABA service industry is quite a viable career choice and the demand for

ABA services is much greater than the current capacity of the field to meet that demand. The purpose of this chapter was to provide a summary of the qualifications for becoming a professional practitioner in ABA. Additional information can be obtained through the BACB on the most current qualifications for obtaining the relevant qualifications for becoming a member of the ABA service field.

References

American Academy of Pediatrics (2001). The pediatrician's role in the diagnosis and management of autistic spectrum disorder in children. *Pediatrics, 107,* 1221−1226. Available from http://dx.doi.org/10.1542/peds.107.5.1221.

Association of Professional Behavior Analysts. (2017). *Licensure and other regulation of ABA practitioners.* Retrieved from http://www.apbahome.net/APBALicensure.php.

Austin, J., & Carr, J. E. (2000). *Handbook of applied behavior analysis.* Reno, NV: Context Press.

Autism Speaks. (2017a). *Autism votes: Advocacy.* Retrieved from https://www.autismspeaks.org/advocacy.

Autism Speaks. (2017b). *Autism votes: Insurance.* Retrieved from https://www.autismspeaks.org/advocacy/insurance.

Bailey, J., & Burch, M. (2016). *Ethics for behavior analysts.* London: Routledge.

Behavior Analyst Certification Board. (2017a). *Behavior Analyst Certification Board® about the BACB.* Retrieved from http://bacb.com/about-the-bacb.

Behavior Analyst Certification Board. (2017b). *Behavior Analyst Certification Board® approved course sequence passing rates.* Retrieved from http://bacb.com/wp-content/uploads/2016/06/2015-ACS-pass-rate-BCBA-percent.pdf.

Behavior Analyst Certification Board. (2017c). *Behavior Analyst Certification Board® board certified assistant behavior analyst.* Retrieved from https://bacb.com/bcaba/.

Behavior Analyst Certification Board. (2017d). *Behavior Analyst Certification Board® board certified behavior analyst.* Retrieved from https://bacb.com/bcba/.

Behavior Analyst Certification Board. (2017e). *Behavior Analyst Certification Board® board certified behavior analyst-doctoral designation.* Retrieved from https://bacb.com/bcba-d/.

Behavior Analyst Certification Board. (2017f). *Behavior Analyst Certification Board® continuing education.* Retrieved from http://bacb.com/continuing-education/.

Behavior Analyst Certification Board. (2017g). *Behavior Analyst Certification Board® disciplinary procedures.* Retrieved from http://bacb.com/disciplinary-and-appeals-process/.

Behavior Analyst Certification Board. (2017h). *Behavior Analyst Certification Board® examinations.* Retrieved from http://bacb.com/examination-information/.

Behavior Analyst Certification Board. (2017i). *Behavior Analyst Certification Board® fifth edition task list-English.* Retrieved from https://bacb.com/wp-content/uploads/2017/01/170113-BCBA-BCaBA-task-list-5th-ed-english.pdf.

Behavior Analyst Certification Board. (2017j). *Behavior Analyst Certification Board® fourth edition task list-English.* Retrieved from https://bacb.com/wp-content/uploads/2016/03/160101-BCBA-BCaBA-task-list-fourth-edition-english.pdf.

Behavior Analyst Certification Board. (2017k). *Behavior Analyst Certification Board® professional and ethics compliance code.* Retrieved from http://bacb.com/wp-content/uploads/2016/03/160321-compliance-code-english.pdf.

Behavior Analyst Certification Board. (2017l). *Behavior Analyst Certification Board*[R] *registered behavior technician*. Retrieved from https://bacb.com/rbt/.

Behavior Analyst Certification Board. (2017m). *Behavior Analyst Certification Board*[R] *approved course sequences*. Retrieved from http://info.bacb.com/o.php?page=100358.

Behavior Analyst Certification Board. (2017n). *Behavior Analyst Certification Board*[R] *supervision standards*. Retrieved from http://bacb.com/supervision-requirements/.

Behavior Analyst Certification Board. (2017o). *Behavior Analyst Certification Board*[R] *January 2017 newsletter*. Retrieved from https://bacb.com/wp-content/uploads/2017/01/170113-newsletter.pdf.

Carr, J. E., & Nosik, M. R. (2017). Professional credentialing of practicing behavior analysts. *Policy Insights from the Behavioral and Brain Sciences*, 1—6. Available from http://dx.doi.org/10.1177/2372732216685861.

Centers for Disease Control and Prevention (2014). Prevalence of autism spectrum disorders—Autism and developmental disabilities monitoring network, 11 sites, United States, 2010. *MMWR Surveillance Summaries*, 63(2), 1—22.

Eldevik, S., Hastings, R. P., Hughes, J. C., Jahr, E., Eikeseth, S., & Cross, S. (2009). Meta-analysis of early intensive behavioral intervention for children with autism. *Journal of Clinical Child & Adolescent Psychology*, 38(3), 439—450.

Eldevik, S., Hastings, R. P., Hughes, J. C., Jahr, E., Eikeseth, S., & Cross, S. (2010). Using participant data to extend the evidence base for intensive behavioral intervention for children with autism. *American Journal on Intellectual and Developmental Disabilities*, 115, 381—405.

Florida Administrative Code. Chapter 1 OF-4. (1992).

Florida Department of Health and Rehabilitative Services (1987). *Behavioral analysis curriculum and evaluation guide* (3rd ed). Tallahassee, FL: Author.

Florida Department of Health and Rehabilitative Services (1989). *Behavioral programming manual*. Tallahassee, FL: Author.

Florida Department of Professional Regulation and Florida Department of Health and Rehabilitative Services (1991). *Information and registration booklet for the behavior analysis certification examination*. Tallahassee, FL: Author.

Ganz, M. L. (2007). The lifetime distribution of incremental societal costs of autism. *Archives of Pediatric Adolescent Medicine*, 161, 343—349.

Green, G., Brennan, L. C., & Fein, D. (2002). Intensive behavioral treatment for a toddler at high risk for autism. *Behavior Modification*, 26, 69—102.

Green, G., & Johnston, J. M. (2009). Licensing behavior analysts: Risks and alternatives. *Behavior Analysis in Practice*, 2, 59.

Howard, J., Sparkman, C., Cohen, H., Green, G., & Stanislaw, H. (2005). A comparison of intensive behavior analytic and eclectic treatments for young children with autism. *Research in Developmental Disabilities*, 26, 359—383.

Howard, J. S., Stanislaw, H., Green, G., Sparkman, C. R., & Cohen, H. G. (2014). Comparison of behavior analytic and eclectic early interventions for young children with autism after three years. *Research in Developmental Disabilities*, 35, 3326—3344.

Jacobson, J. W., Mulick, J. A., & Green, G. (1998). Cost-benefit estimates for early intensive behavioral intervention for young children with autism: General model and single state case. *Behavioral Interventions*, 13, 201—226.

Johnston, J. M., Carr, J. E., & Mellichamp, F. H. (2017). A history of professional credentialing of Applied Behavior Analysts. *The Behavior Analyst*, doi: 10.1007/s40614-017-0106-9.

Kasari, C. (2002). Assessing change in early intervention programs for children with autism. *Journal of Autism and Developmental Disorders*, 32, 447—461.

Kazemi, E., & Shapiro, M. (2013). A review of board standards across behavioral health professions: Where does the BCBA credential stand? *Behavior Analysis in Practice, 6,* 18–29.

Lerman, D. C., Iwata, B. A., & Hanley, G. P. (2013). Applied behavior analysisIn G. J. Madden, W. V. Dube, T. D. Hackenburg, G. P. Hanley, & K. A. Lattal (Eds.), *APA handbook of behavior analysis* (Vol. 1, pp. 81–104). Washington, DC: American Psychological Association.

Lovaas, O. I. (1987). Behavioral treatment and normal educational and intellectual functioning in young autistic children. *Journal of Consulting and Clinical Psychology, 55,* 3–9.

MacDonald, R., Parry-Cruwys, D., Dupere, S., & Ahearn, W. (2014). Assessing progress and outcome of early intensive behavioral intervention for toddlers with autism. *Research in Developmental Disabilities, 35,* 3632–3644.

McEachin, J. J., Smith, T., & Lovaas, O. I. (1993). Long-term outcome for children with autism who received early intensive behavioral treatment. *American Journal on Mental Retardation, 97,* 359–372.

National Institute of Mental Health (2007). *Autism spectrum disorders.* Bethesda, MD: Author.

New York. State Department of Health, Early Intervention Program (1999a). *Clinical practice guideline: The guideline technical report. Autism/pervasive developmental disorders, assessment and intervention for young children (age 0–3 years).* Albany, NY: Author.

New York. State Department of Health, Early Intervention Program (1999b). *Clinical practice guideline: Quick reference guide. Autism/pervasive developmental disorders, assessment and intervention for young children (age 0–3 years).* Albany, NY: Author.

New York. State Department of Health, Early Intervention Program (1999c). *Clinical practice guideline: Report of the recommendations. Autism/pervasive developmental disorders, assessment and intervention for young children (age 0–3 years).* Albany, NY: Author.

Sallows, G. O., & Graupner, T. D. (2005). Intensive behavioral treatment for children with autism: Four-year outcome and predictors. *American Journal on Mental Retardation, 110,* 417–438.

Shattuck, P. (2006). The contribution of diagnostic substitution to the growing administrative prevalence of autism in US special education. *Pediatrics, 117,* 1028–1037.

Smith, T., Groen, A. D., & Wynn, J. W. (2000). Randomized trial of intensive early intervention for children with pervasive developmental disorder. *American Journal on Mental Retardation, 105,* 269–285.

Stuebing, L. (2009). Self-insured employers cover ABA intervention for autism and other special needs. *APBA Reporter, 3.* <http://www.apbahome.net/newsletter.php?nid=3>.

United States Department of Health and Human Services. Surgeon General (1999). *Mental health: A report of the Surgeon General.* Washington, DC: Author.

Unumb, L. S., & Unumb, D. R. (2011). *Autism and the law: Cases, statutes, and materials.* Durham, NC: Carolina Academic Press.

Whitehouse, A. J. O., Cooper, M. N., Bebbington, K., Alvares, G., Lin, A., Wray, J., & Glasson, E. J. (2017). Evidence of a reduction over time in the behavioral severity of autistic disorder diagnoses. *Autism Research, 10,* 179–187. Available from http://dx.doi.org/10.1002/aur.1740.

Wing, L., & Potter, D. (2002). The epidemiology of autistic spectrum disorders: Is the prevalence rising? *Mental Retardation and Developmental Disabilities Research Reviews, 8,* 151–161.

Further reading

American Psychiatric Association (2000). *Pervasive developmental disorders. Diagnostic and statistical manual of mental disorders* (4th ed.-text revision DSM-IV-TR Washington, DC: American Psychiatric Association.

Autism Speaks. (2017). *State initiatives.* Retrieved from https://www.autismspeaks.org/stateinitiatives.

Florida Association for Behavior Analysis (1989). *Code of ethics.* Tallahassee, FL: Author.

Florida Statutes. Chapter 393. (1989).

Ethical and Competent Practice in Applied Behavior Analysis: Perspective, Requirements, and Dilemmas

17

Raymond G. Romanczyk
State University of New York at Binghamton, Binghamton, NY, United States

Terminology

The concept of ethical and competent practice might seem straightforward and would seem to apply to all "helping" professions. If there is ethical and competent practice, it would be reasonable to conclude that both client (In the context of this chapter, "client" is used in the broadest sense to encompass individuals participating in service delivery, or supervisees, students taking coursework, and individuals within and outside the profession of applied behavior analysis.) and practitioner (In the context of this chapter, "practitioner" is used in the broadest sense to encompass individuals who provide humans services, conduct research, teach, and supervise.) would benefit. But achieving ethical and competent practice is complex, as the reality of the nature of human interaction, and the extant systems of providing services, provide significant hurdles for the practitioner, researcher, teacher, and student. A core factor in this complexity is that ethical practice is defined by each given profession and competent practice of a given profession is defined both by the profession and any controlling laws and regulations. This presents a complex mix. It is thus possible to behave ethically and competently yet still provide no benefit to the client, or even harm the client. Thus, all of these elements must be examined and evaluated.

The first definitional issue concerns the use of the terms moral, legal, and ethical. These concepts are often confused. For example, when referring to someone's behavior as unethical, often the speaker actually means immoral. Morality is a sense of right and wrong that a person adheres to. It typically arises from family and cultural influences and is acquired in childhood, modified over time by life experiences. Legality is simpler. It involves violating a law or regulation. Finally, ethics is the code of conduct that a profession or group requires of its members. It only applies to members of that profession or group, and thus only members can behave in an unethical manner with respect to the group's specific ethical code. It is possible for two individuals to behave in exactly the same manner, one of whom has violated the ethical code of their profession and the other not, simply because they belong to two different professions, each with its own ethical code.

Applied Behavior Analysis Advanced Guidebook. DOI: http://dx.doi.org/10.1016/B978-0-12-811122-2.00017-6

Such differences in ethical codes can cause substantial challenge when participating in a multi-profession environment, such as is the case for most human services delivery and higher education settings. Thus, perspective on ethical codes of conduct and competent practice is a necessity.

Historical perspective

Because human interaction in general, and therapeutic interaction in specific, is extremely complex and diverse, behaving in an ethical manner requires utilizing principles of conduct in complex and dynamic situations rather than simple rule following. The principles of competent practice (along with its inverse, deception, and fraud), and ethical practice have long and diverse roots across many cultures. For our purposes a few examples will highlight this intertwined history.

Competence

The concept of competence has at its base the provision of useful/effective goods or services as promised by a provider. The process of consumers seeking to insure quality of goods and services has a very long and colorful history. A classic example of a consumer seeking corroboration of a provider's claim of quality comes from the 3rd century BC. A request was made to Archimedes, the philosopher/scientist, by Hiero II, the King of Syracuse in Sicily, to ascertain if a gold crown was indeed all gold as claimed by the goldsmith. By using an analytical approach based in objective observation, Archimedes was able to prove that indeed the crown was not of the quality claimed.

Because of the universal problem of determining accuracy in representation, typified by the warning "caveat emptor" (let the buyer beware), complex moral and legal systems have evolved around this issue. Historically, very wealthy individuals employed crude quality assurance by using, for example, their servants as tasters to sample food to protect them from contaminants, placed either intentionally or unintentionally, in the food supply. Over time, a quality control approach was adopted by designating certified providers, such as purveyors to the czar, or purveyors to the queen. This designation recognized proven quality and provided clear lines of responsibility if quality should falter. Typically very harsh penalties were enacted for those who attempted to deceive such high ranking, powerful, individuals.

At the individual provider level, the hallmark was developed by gold and silver smiths to provide proof of quality and source of production. Consumers were then able to seek out goods that had specific hallmarks that could be used for acquisition decisions. Over time these designations became more elaborate to include the smith's trademark, standard mark, town mark, date mark, and duty mark. These provided the consumer with expanding information as to quality and value.

Contrary to this perspective of benign self-promotion through the standards developed within a profession in concert with government regulation, an interesting method of influence arose and became an "art form"—the snake oil purveyor. Today the term "snake oil" is a pejorative term for unproven treatment that is purported to cure problems and/or disorders. In the 17th and 18th century, innumerable products were offered for sale with claims of extraordinarily wide medical application that had roots in the belief that extracts from certain snakes had medicinal effect. These claims and manufacturing procedures far exceeded the limited application that was in use in China, of extracting the "oil" of specific snake species. However, as popularized in the United States, such "snake oil remedies" were worthless and often had high alcohol content and at times very dangerous ingredients. Such product sales tended to be localized, based upon individual distribution. However, in the late 19th and early 20th century, the rapid growth of formal advertising in mass media produced a radical change.

There were a few "patent medicines" at that time that might have had a useful effect, such as Lydia E. Pinkham's Vegetable Compound. Lydia Pinkham, in response to financial hard times and also a genuine interest in women's health, developed the compound in the late 1800s, soon to be followed by Lydia E. Pinkham's Liver Pills, Lydia E. Pinkham's Blood Purifier, and Lydia E. Pinkham's Sanative Wash. Her Vegetable Compound (which was about one fifth alcohol) was very widely advertised using flyers, postcards, newspaper ads, and numerous testimonials, and even immortalized as a popular song (http://thebards.net/tales/2004/10/download-lily-pink-free.shtml). One advertisement (http://www.mc.vanderbilt.edu/biolib/hc/nostrums/lydia2.html) read in part:

Lydia E. Pinkham's Vegetable Compound Is a positive cure for all those painful complaints and weaknesses so common to our best female population.

It will cure entirely all Ovarian troubles, Inflammation and Ulceration, Falling and Displacements, and the consequent Spinal Weakness, and is particularly adapted to the Change of Life. It removes Faintness and Flatulency, destroys the craving for stimulants, and relieves weakness of the stomach. It cures Bloating, Headaches, Nervous Prostration, General Debility, Sleeplessness, Depression, and Indigestion.

Variations on this product are still available today and debate continues as to the efficacy of the compound (http://womenshistory.about.com/gi/dynamic/offsite.htm? zi = 1/XJ&sdn = womenshistory&zu = http%3A%2F%2Fwww.mum.org%2FMrs Pink1.htm).

Another product of the times, Pond's Extract, also claimed broad use along with expert testimonial. One of the advertisements claimed:

Invaluable for sprains, Burns, Scalds, Bruises, Soreness, Rheumatism, Boils, Ulcers, Old Sores, Toothache, Headache, Sorethroat, Asthma, Hoarseness, Neuralgia, Catarrh, &., &.

The Learned and Eminent Scholar, Andrew D, White, President of Cornell University, Ithica, N.Y., writes under date Dec 2, 1884: "Long experience has taught my family to prize Pond's Extract very highly and to regard it as one of the absolute necessities of housekeeping".

This product also can be traced to a current beauty product under the Pond's brand, albeit without the extraordinary claims of diverse benefit. However, other products of the time were not benign, but actively dangerous (http://wings.buffalo. edu/aru/preprohibition.htm). To alleviate the discomfort of children's teething, there were clearly harmful products, such as "Cocaine Toothache Drops", which were in contrast to products that did not emphasize ingredients, such as "Mrs. Winslow's Soothing Syrup" (http://www.heroin.org/images/soothingsyrup.html). It was advertised as:

For children teething. Greatly facilitates the process of Teething, by softening the gums, reducing all inflammation; will allay ALL PAIN and spasmodic action, and is SURE TO REGULATE THE BOWELS. Depend on it, Mothers, it will give rest to yourselves and RELIEF AND HEALTH TO YOUR INFANTS.

This product contained morphine and, along with many other similar products, was widely marketed using a variety of methods.

With the growth of rapid and widespread communication early in the 20th century, the abuses and dangers of contaminated food products and the use of harmful metals and chemicals in "remedies," created an atmosphere that challenged caveat emptor. The publication of *The Jungle* in 1906 by Upton Sinclair is often credited with providing a strong impetus for the Pure Food and Drug Act of 1906. A marked shift, albeit limited, began to embrace the principle of "caveat venditor" (let the seller beware), to reflect the responsibility of the seller, especially as applied to food, additives, medicines, and medical procedures, to provide both safe and effective products and procedures.

Much later in the 20th century a conceptually linked proposal was made by Cochrane (1972). With a background in epidemiology, he argued that the ever changing balance in society of health care needs and resources required an empirical approach to rational allocation of resources. That is, resources should be allocated to those interventions that had demonstrated objective efficacy. He argued persuasively for controlled evaluation of medical procedures, particularly evaluations using randomized controlled trials. His efforts resulted in the establishment of centers to conduct and promulgate research that would directly influence service delivery. While the recognition of the need for, and the systematization of, the formal evaluation of clinical interventions had been described in the literature for decades, interestingly the term "evidence-based medicine" appeared comparatively recently in 1992 (Guyatt, Cairns, Churchill & Evidence-Based Medicine Working Group, 1992).

This short, abbreviated history describes the basis of establishment of government regulation of practices as well as the basis for evidence based approaches to determining efficacy of an approach and in turn setting standards for professional competency. That is, at its core, a competent professional should utilize evidence based procedures. While it may seem amusing in a "black humor" manner that people would believe such claims in the above examples, sadly the situation has not substantially changed when one examines contemporary patterns of belief in similarly ineffective and harmful interventions (Romanczyk, Turner, Sevlever, & Gillis, 2014).

Ethical conduct

As stated above, ethical conduct requires the presence of an ethical code of conduct. Absent a code, one relies on the law and morality to judge conduct. The development of ethical codes has a very long history, but some brief examples illustrate the core principles. In order to properly adhere to a complex ethical code, such as the one adopted by the Behavior Analyst Certification Board (BACB), it is essential to understand the core underpinnings of human services ethical codes.

Perhaps the most commonly known and cited example of an ethical code is the Hippocratic Oath, and the admonition "to do no harm." Interestingly Hippocrates spoke of honoring those who taught the profession, the teaching of successors, not engaging in euthanasia, adhering to boundaries of competency, and protecting privacy. The latter two were insightful and it would be many centuries before becoming generally accepted. It was actually in later writings he used the phrase "to do good or to do no harm" which can be seen as emphasizing that when one chooses to intervene in the well-being of another, it is incumbent on the provider to be aware of and prevent iatrogenic effects.

While many there were many admonitions by philosophers, religious leaders, and members of professions over the centuries since Hippocrates, modern history beginning in the 1940s was the functional birth of current professional ethics. Below are some of the important events in chronological order:

1940s Nuremberg Code
1953 APA Code of Ethics (recent changes in 2002, 2010)
1964 Declaration of Helsinki
1966 NIH Office for Protection of Research Subjects
1974 Congress passes National Research Act Public Law 93-348 requires that all universities that receive federal funding must establish an IRB
1979 Belmont Report
1988 FABA Code of Ethics
1991 Code of Federal Regulations
1998 Office for Human Research Protections (OHRP)
1998 BACB established—Guidelines for Responsible Conduct came soon afterwards.

In this approximately 50 year time period, the dual nature of responsibility for ethical conduct was articulated, emphasizing that governments/professions had responsibilities to establish protections but also that the individual had responsibilities as well, and that these responsibilities cannot be abrogated to government, nor "authority." This was the outcome of the Nuremburg Trials, wherein individuals, particularly physicians, were held responsible for human experimentation that violated the core of "do no harm." These trials established the imperative that an individual cannot hold as a defense that an authority or government ordered the actions. At the trial Adolf Eichman famously declared "I never did anything, great or small, without obtaining in advance express instructions from Adolf Hitler or any of my superiors" as his defense for why he should not be accountable. The Tribunal affirmed the principle that ethical, and moral, standards were responsibility of the individual to uphold.

The trial resulted in the Nuremburg Code. It stated, in the context of experiments involving human participants, that:

> The voluntary consent of the human subject is absolutely essential
> The experiment should be such as to yield fruitful results for the good of society.
> The experiment should be so designed and based on the results of animal experimentation and a knowledge of the natural history of the disease or other problem under study, that the anticipated results will justify the performance of the experiment.
> The experiment should be so conducted as to avoid all unnecessary physical and mental suffering and injury.
> No experiment should be conducted, where there is an a priori reason to believe that death or disabling injury will occur; except, perhaps, in those experiments where the experimental physicians also serve as subjects.
> The degree of risk to be taken should never exceed that determined by the humanitarian importance of the problem to be solved by the experiment.
> Proper preparations should be made and adequate facilities provided to protect the experimental subject against even remote possibilities of injury, disability, or death.
> The experiment should be conducted only by scientifically qualified persons.
> The human subject should be at liberty to bring the experiment to an end.
> The scientist in charge must be prepared to terminate the experiment at any stage if it is likely to result in injury, disability, or death to the experimental subject.
> "Trials of War Criminals before the Nuremberg Military Tribunals under Control Council Law No. 10", Vol. 2, pp 181–182. Washington, DC: U.S. Government Printing Office, 1949.

Later, to also specify the duty of governments, in a speech to Congress in 1961 on the topic of "Conflict-of-Interest Legislation and on Problems of Ethics in Government", President John F. Kennedy said "No responsibility of government is more fundamental than the responsibility of maintaining the highest standards of ethical behavior by those who conduct the public business" (http://www.presidency.ucsb.edu/ws/?pid = 8092). Of note, one of the primary methods for government to fulfill this responsibility is through state licensing laws for professions, which provide government oversight as well as consumer protection procedures.

Clearly influenced by the Nuremburg Trials, the American Psychological Association began its creation of a comprehensive ethics code, and the federal government began a series of initiatives to establish clear ethical guidelines for human-subjects research. However, the infamous Tuskegee Syphilis Experiment, conducted contemporaneously with these efforts (1932–72), illustrated the need for greater emphasis and priority. The Tuskegee Syphilis Experiment was conducted by the US Public Health Service in rural Alabama and involved the tracking of the effects of syphilis on 600 African American males. Informed consent was not provided, and although participants thought they were being offered medical care, in fact they were simply being monitored to study the course of the disease, even though during the course of the experiment penicillin discovered known to be an effective treatment. Participants were not provided this established effective treatment. Remarkably, the experiment spanned different administrators and the study teams were composed of Caucasian and African American researchers.

The exposure of the Tuskegee Syphilis Experiment in the media occurred in 1972 and led to the Belmont Report, the next major influence on ethics codes after the Nuremburg Trials. The Belmont Report was commissioned by the National Commission for the Protection of Human Subjects of Biomedical and Behavioral Research, and was entitled *Belmont Report: Ethical Principles and Guidelines for the Protection of Human Subjects of Research, Report of the National Commission for the Protection of Human Subjects of Biomedical and Behavioral Research*. Now simply referred to as the "Belmont Report," it was published in the Federal Register in 1979. Importantly, the Report focused on the basic affirmative values that should underlie the treatment of human participants, and also greatly influenced the concept of informed consent both for research participation as well as for those in a "patient" role with respect to a provider of services.

The Belmont Report stated three key principles:

Respect for Persons
Respect for persons incorporates at least two ethical convictions: first, that individuals should be treated as autonomous agents, and second, that persons with diminished autonomy are entitled to protection.

Beneficence
Two general rules have been formulated as complementary expressions of beneficent actions in this sense: (1) do not harm and (2) maximize possible benefits and minimize possible harms.

Justice
An injustice occurs when some benefit to which a person is entitled is denied without good reason or when some burden is imposed unduly...

Many current comprehensive ethics codes were substantially influenced by the Belmont Report and these three principles.

Evidence-based practice

The Agency for Health Care Policy and Research (AHCPR) was established in 1997, and is currently designated as the Agency for Healthcare Research and Quality (AHRQ). The AHRQ is part of the United States Public Health Service and is the primary federal agency involved with health services research. In order to promote evidence-based practice, Evidence-based Practice Centers (EPCs) were established. These Centers "... develop evidence reports and technology assessments on topics relevant to clinical, social science/behavioral, economic, and other health care organization and delivery issues—specifically those that are common, expensive, and/or significant." (http://www.ahrq.gov/clinic/epc/)

The AHCPR clinical practice guideline methodology uses principles for developing practice guidelines recommended by the US Institute of Medicine (IOM, 1992). This AHCPR methodology is considered to be the standard for developing evidence-based clinical practice guidelines (Eddy & Hasselblad, 1994; Holland, 1995; Schriger, 1995; Woolf, 1991, 1994).

Essentially in parallel to the AHCPR efforts, in 1995 the American Psychological Association's (APA) Division 12 (Clinical Psychology) Task Force developed criteria for Empirically Supported Therapies (EST) in order to provide guidelines for researchers, practitioners, and consumers to evaluate psychological treatments or interventions. They established three categories to describe degrees of evidence available: well established, probably efficacious, and experimental. Chambless and Ollendick (2001) reviewed eight other groups that subsequently developed criteria and guidelines for evaluating psychological treatments. Specific criteria for each category were mostly similar to the Task Force's criteria, but there was more variability across groups when defining criteria for category III. The following table is adapted from Chambless and Ollendick (2001) and displays the Task Force's criteria for empirically supported treatments.

Category I. Well-established treatments
    At least two good between-group design experiments must demonstrate efficacy in one or more of the following ways:
        Superiority to pill or psychotherapy placebo, or to other treatments
        Equivalence to already established treatment with adequate sample sizes
        OR
    A large series of single-case design experiments must demonstrate efficacy with:
        Use of good experimental design
        Comparison of intervention to another treatment
        OR
    Experiments must be conducted with treatment manuals or equivalent clear description of treatment.
    Characteristics of samples must be specified.
    Effects must be demonstrated by at least two different investigators or teams.
Category II. Probably efficacious treatments
    Two experiments must show that the treatment is superior to waiting-list control group
        OR
    One or more experiments must meet well-established criteria Ia, Ib, III, and IV above but V is not met
        OR
    A small series of single-case design experiments must meet well-established treatment criteria
Category III. Experimental treatments
    Treatment not yet tested in trials meeting task force criteria for methodology

As an example, Eikeseith (2009) evaluated 25 studies that utilized a comprehensive psycho-educational approach for early intervention for autism. Twenty studies evaluated behavioral intervention, and five studies evaluated broad educational programs. Using the guidelines established by Chambless, only Applied Behavior Analysis (ABA) was determined to be "Well Established," the highest level of scientific merit under this system.

In addition to such numerous scholarly reviews, such as Odom et al. (2003) there are many government empaneled reviews that use the general methodology of the AHCPR that have arrived at the same conclusion concerning the efficacy of ABA in the treatment of autism. Examples of such large-scale reviews include:

New York State Department of Health, Early Intervention Program (1999a,b). Clinical Practice Guideline: Guideline Technical Report. Autism/Pervasive Developmental Disorders, Assessment and Intervention for Young Children (Ages 0–3 Years), no. 4217, NYS Department of Health, Albany, NY.

National Research Council (2001). Educating Children with Autism. Washington DC: National Academy Press.

National Autism Center (2009). National Standards Report: National Standards Project— Addressing the need for evidence-based practice guidelines for autism spectrum disorders. Randolph, MA: National Autism Center, Inc.

Missouri Department of Mental Health (2012). Autism Spectrum Disorders: Guide to Evidence-based Interventions. http://www.autismguidelines.dmh.mo.gov/.

The research base for the efficacy of ABA for autism is an essential component for the establishment of a sound ethics code. It is particularly important that the evaluation of efficacy is not simply an insular evaluation from within the profession, but rather is robust enough to withstand scrutiny using broadly accepted methodologies and standards. Such objective, independent evaluation is a key component with respect to providing informed consent to consumers. In parallel, it is also important to keep apprised of the efficacy of treatments outside one's own profession, through reviews of nonbehavioral approaches such as Smith (1996).

Specific ethics code for behavior analysts

The primary organizations associated with applied behavior analysis consist of the Association for Behavior Analysis International (ABAI), the Association of Professional Behavior Analysts (APBA), and the BACB.

The Association for Behavior Analysis International (ABAI) is a membership organization that provides the typical membership benefits of a professional organization, including the accreditation of university training programs. Interestingly, unlike most professional membership organizations, it does not have its own standalone ethics code. In recognition of the historical multiple professions a given behavior analyst may belong to, the ABAI provides the following statement:

Code of Ethics: The Association for Behavior Analysis International expects its members to uphold the highest standards of personal and professional behavior in the conduct of their work and the advancement of behavior analysis. ABAI embraces the diversity of professions within its membership; thus each ABAI member should adhere to the ethical standards that have been defined for his or her profession. Examples include, but are not limited to:

The American Psychological Association's Ethical Principles of Psychologists and Code of Conduct
The Association for Clinical Researchers' Code of Ethics
The Association for Institutional Research's Code of Ethics
The Behavior Analyst Certification Board's Professional and Ethical Compliance Code
The National Association of School Psychologists' Professional Conduct Manual
The National Association of Social Workers' Code of Ethics
The National Education Association's Code of Ethics of the Education Profession
(https://www.abainternational.org/about-us/policies-and-positions.aspx)

In a similar, but more limited, manner, the Association of Professional Behavior Analysts (APBA), also a member organization, directs its members to follow the ethical code of the BACB. The APBA, as a member organization, also offers the typical professional organization benefits, but in this context, it is important to note that it's member newsletter offers a continuing "Ethics Challenge" section to serve as a mechanism for member ongoing ethics analysis enhancement.

The BACB

The BACB, established in 1998, is not a member organization, but rather a credentialing organization and is a nonprofit 501©(3) corporation. The BACB is in turn accredited by the National Commission for Certifying Agencies, a division of the Institute for Credentialing Excellence. This accreditation requires the BACB to follow specific methodological and procedural practices in constructing, implementing, and evaluating the BACB certification exam for behavior analysts. In the context of this chapter, being certified by the BACB is the equivalent of the profession's hallmark/trademark. One is not required to have it, but it signifies to the public a level of competency and quality. At the time of this writing, the BACB had four categories of certificants with the approximate number of certificants in each category in parenthesis:

BCBA-D (2000): board certified behavior analyst at the doctoral level
BCBA(20,000): board certified behavior analyst
BCaBA(2400): board certified assistant behavior analyst
RBT(24,000): registered behavior technician

Prior to obtaining certification or registration in the case of RBT, for each category, an individual must complete specific coursework on the ethics code of the BACB. Further, as a component of maintaining BACB certification, an individual must engage in sanctioned continuing education activities, and of those activities, a specific proportion must be specific to ethics training. (The annual requirements for the RBT have a different format, but the emphasis on continued development and ethics competency is similar.) As the ethical code of conduct by the BACB is the standard for the profession of applied behavior analysis, the preamble and table of contents (http://bacb.com/ethics-code/) are presented here, by permission, in it's entirety.

Professional and ethical compliance code for behavior analysts

The BACB's Professional and Ethical Compliance Code for Behavior Analysts (the "Compliance Code") consolidates, updates, and replaces the BACB's Professional Disciplinary and Ethical Standards and Guidelines for Responsible Conduct for Behavior Analysts. The Compliance Code includes 10 sections relevant to professional and ethical behavior of behavior analysts, along with a glossary of terms. Effective January 1, 2016, all BACB applicants, certificants, and registrants will be required to adhere to the Compliance Code.

In the original version of the Guidelines for Professional Conduct for Behavior Analysts, the authors acknowledged ethics codes from the following organizations: American Anthropological Association, American Educational Research Association, American Psychological Association, American Sociological Association, California Association for Behavior Analysis, Florida Association for Behavior Analysis, National Association of Social Workers, National Association of School Psychologists, and Texas Association for Behavior Analysis. We acknowledge and thank these professional organizations that have provided substantial guidance and clear models from which the Compliance Code has evolved.

Approved by the BACB's Board of Directors on August 7, 2014. © 2014 Behavior Analyst Certification Board, Inc. (BACB), all rights reserved. Ver. 09/10/2014d.

1.0 Responsible Conduct of Behavior Analysts
    1.01 Reliance on Scientific Knowledge RBT
    1.02 Boundaries of Competence RBT
    1.03 Maintaining Competence through Professional Development RBT
    1.04 Integrity RBT
    1.05 Professional and Scientific Relationships RBT
    1.06 Multiple Relationships and Conflicts of Interest RBT
    1.07 Exploitative Relationships RBT
2.0 Behavior Analysts' Responsibility to Clients
    2.01 Accepting Clients
    2.02 Responsibility RBT
    2.03 Consultation
    2.04 Third-Party Involvement in Services
    2.05 Rights and Prerogatives of Clients RBT
    2.06 Maintaining Confidentiality RBT
    2.07 Maintaining Records RBT
    2.08 Disclosures RBT
    2.09 Treatment/Intervention Efficacy

2.10 Documenting Professional Work and Research RBT
2.11 Records and Data RBT
2.12 Contracts, Fees, and Financial Arrangements
2.13 Accuracy in Billing Reports
2.14 Referrals and Fees
2.15 Interrupting or Discontinuing Services
3.0 Assessing Behavior
  3.01 Behavior-Analytic Assessment RBT
  3.02 Medical Consultation
  3.03 Behavior-Analytic Assessment Consent
  3.04 Explaining Assessment Results
  3.05 Consent-Client Records
4.0 Behavior Analysts and the Behavior-Change Program
  4.01 Conceptual Consistency
  4.02 Involving Clients in Planning and Consent
  4.03 Individualized Behavior-Change Programs
  4.04 Approving Behavior-Change Programs
  4.05 Describing Behavior-Change Program Objectives
  4.06 Describing Conditions for Behavior-Change Program Success
  4.07 Environmental Conditions that Interfere with Implementation
  4.08 Considerations Regarding Punishment Procedures
  4.09 Least Restrictive Procedures
  4.10 Avoiding Harmful Reinforcers RBT
  4.11 Discontinuing Behavior-Change Programs and Behavior-Analytic Services
5.0 Behavior Analysts as Supervisors
  5.01 Supervisory Competence
  5.02 Supervisory Volume
  5.03 Supervisory Delegation
  5.04 Designing Effective Supervision and Training
  5.05 Communication of Supervision Conditions
  5.06 Providing Feedback to Supervisees
  5.07 Evaluating the Effects of Supervision
6.0 Behavior Analysts' Ethical Responsibility to the Profession of Behavior Analysts
  6.01 Affirming Principles RBT
  6.02 Disseminating Behavior Analysis RBT
7.0 Behavior Analysts' Ethical Responsibility to Colleagues
  7.01 Promoting an Ethical Culture RBT
  7.02 Ethical Violations by Others and Risk of Harm RBT
8.0 Public Statements
  8.01 Public Statements
  8.02 Avoiding False or Deceptive Statements RBT
  8.03 Intellectual Property RBT
  8.04 Statements by Others RBT
  8.05 Media Presentations and Media-Based Services
  8.06 Testimonials and Advertising RBT
  8.07 In-Person Solicitation RBT
9.0 Behavior Analysts and Research
  9.01 Conforming with Laws and Regulations RBT
  9.02 Characteristics of Responsible Research

9.03 Informed Consent
9.04 Using Confidential Information for Didactic or Instructive Purposes
9.05 Debriefing
9.06 Grant and Journal Reviews
9.07 Plagiarism
9.08 Acknowledging Contributions
9.09 Accuracy and Use of Data RBT
10.0 Behavior Analysts' Ethical Responsibility to the BACB
10.01 Truthful and Accurate Information Provided to the BACB RBT
10.02 Timely Responding, Reporting, and Updating of Information Provided to the BACB RBT
10.03 Confidentiality and BACB Intellectual Property RBT
10.04 Examination Honesty and Irregularities RBT
10.05 Compliance with BACB Supervision and Coursework Standards RBT
10.06 Being Familiar with This Code
10.07 Discouraging Misrepresentation by Non-Certified Individuals RBT

Many aspects of the BACB ethics code can be linked to the principles of the Belmont Report. "Responsible Conduct of Behavior Analysts," "Behavior Analysts' Responsibility to Clients," "Assessing Behavior," "Behavior Analysts and the Behavior-Change Program," and "Behavior Analysts and Research," all fall directly under Respect for Persons, Beneficence, and Justice. However, topics such as "Behavior Analysts' Ethical Responsibility to the Profession of Behavior Analysts," "Behavior Analysts' Ethical Responsibility to Colleagues," and "Behavior Analysts' Ethical Responsibility to the BACB," fall more under the category of profession specific rules concerning its members interactions with each other and the profession. Last, parts of "Responsible Conduct of Behavior Analysts" relating to scientific evidence and maintaining professional competence and "Public Statements" relate directly to the principle of Evidence-Based Practice.

Thus the BACB code is on solid ground with respect to the key principles reviewed here as well as with respect to similarity and the comprehensiveness of preexisting, well respected ethical codes, such as for the American Psychological Association. Comprehensive is a critical attribute. Although an imperfect measure of comprehensive, it is interesting to compare the length of the ethics codes of different professions. The length for the National Association of Special Education Teachers (NASET) ethics code is approximately 800 words, approximately 3700 words for the American Occupational Therapy Association, approximately 11,000 words for the APA ethics code, and approximately 8000 words for the BACB.

Having such a solid ethics code for behavior analysts is, however, just a first step. It is a straight-forward task to train certificants of a professional organization, such as the BACB, in the specific items in their specific ethics code. The challenge for the members of a profession that adhere to an ethics code is that the world of professional practice, teaching, research, and impacting public policy is complex and dynamic. The application of specific rules is but a starting point.

Regulatory influences and an ethics code

Human services as well as education and research activities are typically conducted under numerous government regulations that vary from country to country, and often also vary with more local governing bodies (e.g., state, province, regions, etc.). The ethics code of the BACB, as for most ethics codes, explicitly requires adherence to such regulatory oversight and can be found in:

2.0 Behavior Analysts' Responsibility to Clients
  2.07 Maintaining Records
  2.11 Records and Data
7.0 Behavior Analysts' Ethical Responsibility to Colleagues
  7.02 Ethical Violations by Others and Risk of Harm
9.0 Behavior Analysts and Research
  9.01 Conforming with Laws and Regulations

One example of a pervasive regulation affecting human services is the P.L. 104-191, Health Insurance Portability and Accountability Act of 1996 of the 104th Congress. Two primary, and often confused, sections of HIPAA are the Privacy Rule and the Security Rule. The privacy rule governs the collection, use, and storage of an individual's information in the context of providing services or conducting research, as well as indirectly, such as supervision of students in training. More technically, it specifies procedures needed for handling "Protected health information" (PHI), which is defined as follows:

1. Name;
2. All geographic subdivisions smaller than a State, including street address, city, county, precinct, zip code, and their equivalent geocodes, except for the initial three digits of a zip code;
3. All elements of dates (except year) for dates directly related to an individual, including birth date, admission or service date, discharge date, date of death; and all ages over 89 and all elements of dates (including year) indicative of such age, except that such ages and elements may be aggregated into a single category of age 90 or older;
4. Telephone numbers;
5. Fax numbers;
6. Email addresses;
7. Social security numbers;
8. Medical record numbers;
9. Health plan beneficiary numbers;
10. Account numbers;
11. Certificate and license numbers;
12. Vehicle identifiers and serial numbers, including license plate numbers;
13. Device identifiers and serial numbers;
14. URL addresses;
15. IP addresses;
16. Biometric identifiers (i.e., fingerprints or voice prints);
17. Full photographic images or any comparable images; and
18. Any other unique identifying number, characteristic, or code, except as permitted by an assigned code or other means of record identification to allow information deidentified

under this section to be reidentified by the covered entity that is not derived from some means of prohibited identifying information.
(HIPAA Privacy Rule (45 CFR Part 160 and Subparts A and E of Part 164))

At the risk of overgeneralization, often it is the Security Rule that is compromised by behavior analysts in service provision, teaching, and research activities. That is, the Security Rule specifies the methods by which PHI can be shared and transmitted. The Security Rule is of particular importance with the growing reliance, both personally and professionally, on electronic transmission of information, and the reality that many individuals tend to blur the lines of what they consider personal vs professional with respect to their devices such as cell phones and computers. Violations of the Security Rule have substantial sanctions.

It is critical for all behavior analysts, whether engaged in service provision, teaching, or research, to be familiar with HIPAA's Privacy Rule (45 CFR Part 160 and Subparts A and E of Part 164) and HIPAA's Security Rule (45 CFR Part 160 and Subparts A and C of Part 164). The specific regulations may be found at: Privacy rule—https://www.hhs.gov/hipaa/for-professionals/privacy/ and Security Rule—http://www.hhs.gov/hipaa/for-professionals/security/.

There are numerous procedural and technical aspects to HIPAA regulations, and it is wise to follow the regulations even if in one's setting it is not a requirement. From an ethics perspective, one would always simply ask "Why not follow federal regulations for protection of clients?" Doing so reflects a commitment to standard of care over provider convenience. A more in depth discussion of HIPAA and related regulations is beyond the scope of this chapter. For a more complete discussion of HIPAA and its relation to applied behavior analysis, see Cavalari, Gillis, Kruser, and Romanczyk (2015).

Ethical dilemmas

While the application of BACB code is rather straightforward in the majority of situations that involve simple discrete behaviors, such as record keeping, establishing initial service fees, maintain confidentiality, etc., other aspects are more challenging. For instance, 5.0 Behavior Analysts as Supervisors, has the complexity of application across very different settings, e.g., the workplace vs university courses, and the complexity of balancing protecting clients and offering the most effective services when training behavior analysts as clients interact with precompetent trainees. While much has been written about what skills should be taught to supervisees, much less has been written about the critical process of conducting supervision, although that is beginning to change, e.g. Turner, Fischer, and Luiselli (2016).

The true challenge of ethical practice lies in the complexity of ethical dilemmas—the balance of competing principles. There are numerous philosophical positions that have impacted discussions of ethical decision making. Consequentialism (related to Teleology) is perhaps the simplest, stating that it is only the consequence of actions that determine whether the action was ethical. Thus intent is irrelevant. Critique of this position often occurs in the form of "the ends justify the means" not being defensible if the means are themselves not ethical. In contrast, deontology emphasizes a social system approach in which the individual has an obligation or duty to follow the specific codified ethical rules of the group. The nexus for conflict between these conceptualizations lies in the ethical dilemma.

An ethical dilemma exists when there is a conflict between two (or more) ethical mandates. As there is a conflict, it implies a complex situation, and thus ethical dilemmas present the greatest hazard to ethical conduct. Ethical dilemmas also include balancing the risk and benefits to the client of an action, and conflicts between interests of the client versus interests of the profession and practitioner. It is because of the reality of ethical dilemmas that ethics codes are typically viewed as aspirational rather than simply "what is the correct answer" in an "item violation" context.

Lee (1999) described various forms of ethical dilemmas as follows:

"What is an ethical dilemma?" It is a Conflict between...
One's personal *and* professional ***values***
*Two values/ethical **principles***
*Two **possible actions**, each with reasons strongly* favorable *and* unfavorable
Two unsatisfactory alternatives
One's values/principles *and one's* perceived role
The need to **act** *and the need to* **reflect**.
https://www.google.com/url?sa = t&rct = j&q = &esrc = s&source = web&cd = 2&ved
= 0ahUKEwiLwcnF3vjPAhVMPD4KHRS6BQUQFgglMAE&url = http%3A%2F%2F
www7.cityu.edu.hk%2Fsspltr%2Fp1%2Fpreparation%2Fpowerpoint%2FField6_code.
PPT&usg = AFQjCNF9ncJay0NCyJSUAqqqYwlOVUV-Gg

One example of an ethical dilemma that faces every profession and thus every individual within the profession is the conflict between establishing competency standards for practitioners through certification/licensing and the mandate to provide services to those in need of services. All certification/licensing systems set the minimum standards for competency. Even in professions that have systems such as the Diplomate status, that signifies having achieved a very high standard of competency, nevertheless, the examination process sets the minimum standards for that level of recognition. Within applied behavior analysis, there has been criticism of certification standards, such as Leaf et al. (2016), as well as proposals for additional standards, such as Eikeseth (2010). The setting of minimum standards involves not only debate within a profession and relevant research, but also the applicable laws and regulations external to the profession that control establishing standards for any profession.

The essence of this dilemma is how does one balance setting the required minimum standards for competency with the large number of underserved individuals in need? As an example, arguably applied behavior analysis is the treatment of choice for autism and also the number of individuals requesting services exceeds the number of certified practitioners. It is certainly an ethical principle to set high standards of training and certification. It is also an ethical principle to not restrict services to those in need. It is the classic debate as to whether no service is better than suboptimum service. There are complex, substantial negative consequences for choices made on both sides of this ethical debate, some affecting the profession and some affecting the client. This is an ongoing debate in all helping professions and a necessary one for applied behavior analysis.

Ethical and competent practice

Given the complexity of balancing many ethical principles and perspectives, engaging in ethical conduct is a process, not an act. While ethical and competent conduct can be difficult, it is absolutely essential to benefitting the client and the success of a profession. Central to ethical conduct is the utilization of broad principles that can be stated as:

- First, "do no harm"
- Deciding who to serve
- Deciding when not to serve
- Deciding when to stop serving

Because human services, research, and teaching roles and interactions are complex, in turn ethical dilemmas are complex. An important principle with respect to interactions among members of a profession is that there can be disagreement as to the resolution of ethical dilemmas, and thus it does not mean that in such situations one of the individuals is necessarily "unethical". As ethical and competent practice is an on-going process, it's important to understand history and guidelines as a whole, these can be applied to any given situation or ethical dilemma.

We have limited tools to answer important ethical dilemma questions empirically. But, as a process, there are steps than can be articulated that assist in aspiring to the highest ethical and competency standards:

1. Obtain fluency with the ethics code of the BACB.
2. Understand the BACB code in the context of the history of competency and ethics.
3. Emphasize the primacy of the client in deliberations.
4. Beneficence and Nonmaleficence are the imperatives.
5. Identify the risk/benefits of action versus nonaction.
6. Identify what personal/professional behaviors are being reinforced.
7. Identify and list the risks and benefits to the client of intervention.
8. Identify the controlling agency—is it a matter that falls under BACB guidelines or regulatory guidelines, or both.
9. Emphasize engaging in active ethics and competency continuing education where responding is required and feedback provided.
10. Develop and utilize consultative relationships to discuss your analysis. Such relationships should not be limited to behavior analysts, and especially useful are relationships with individuals who don't always agree with you.

Of this list, arguably the most important is number 10. Behaving in a competent and ethical manner derives from the generalized application of specific principles as well as specific ethics code items and utilization of the extant research base.

Real world application is always more complex that the controlled research setting. Ethical dilemmas arise from competing complex and dynamic variables within the broad professional and interpersonal aspects of service provision. With recognition of this complexity, analysis and judgment of ethical, as well as legal, problem situations hinges on the process the individual uses to determine their course of action. From and ethics and legal perspective, great weight is placed on the process of consultation that was used. It is understood that perfect decisions rarely exist, and that the next best alternative is a reasoned decision. Part of an operational definition of reasoned decision in the present context would be consultation to help assess the parameters of the situation that requires a decision. It is because of this that consultation can include those from other professions as well as those within applied behavior analysis, as long as their profession has a comprehensive ethics code. As comprehensive ethics codes share the same "lineage," much of the process of resolving ethical dilemmas is very similar.

It is important to state that ethics, competency, and morality are not about risk aversion nor income enhancement. There can be negative consequences, particularly with respect to interaction with other professionals within and outside of applied behavior analysis, when resolving ethics and competency issues. While one strives to resolve such conflicts through positive interaction, consequences can include very uncomfortable interactions. In colloquial terms, the advice is "big deal—get over it." That is, by choosing to engage in specific activities in, and associated with, applied behavior analysis, one in like manner agrees to specific standards of professional behavior. It is thus critical to arrange establishing operations, such as choice of colleagues one consults with on ethics, to maximize reinforcement for ethical and competent behavior. The central reinforcement for behavior as a professional must not be the avoidance of unpleasant interactions with other professionals, avoidance of professional (clinical, teaching, or research) productivity decrease because of the demands of regulatory compliance, nor avoidance of income attenuation. The central reinforcement for professional behavior must be the wellbeing of the client evaluated using the principles of Respect for Persons, Beneficence, and Justice, followed by reinforcement by one's professional colleagues who share this ethics and values system.

Our on-going responsibility is to assess our own competency and ethics behavioral repertoire. That assessment should result in a list of acquired and needed repertoires. New behavioral repertoires required can be established through focused and selective training and continuing education. The assessment should also identify and critically evaluate current sources of reinforcement for our own professional behavior repertoire. This is complex as there are many discrete repertoires, each with its own cluster of reinforcement variables. In order to increase and sustain a repertoire of competent and ethical professional behavior, management of sources of differential reinforcement is critical. A key to management of sources of differential reinforcement lies in the differential selection of colleagues with whom to consult about issues of competency and ethics, and the selection of individuals both within and outside the profession who can assist in the development of new competency skills.

References

Cavalari, R. N. S., Gillis, J. M., Kruser, N., & Romanczyk, R. G. (2015). Digital communication and records in service provision and supervision: Regulation and practice. *Behavior Analysis in Practice, 8*(2), 176−189. Available from http://dx.doi.org/10.1007/s40617-014-0030-3.

Chambless, D., & Ollendick, T. (2001). Empirically supported psychological interventions: Controversies and evidence. *Annual Review of Psychology, 52,* 685−716.

Cochrane, A. L. (1972). *Effectiveness and efficiency. Random reflections on health services.* London, UK: Nuffield Provincial Hospitals Trust.

Eddy, D. M., & Hasselblad, V. (1994). Analyzing evidence by the confidence and profile method. In K. A. McCormick, S. R. Moore, & R. A. Siegel (Eds.), *Clinical practice guideline development: Methodology perspectives.* Rockville, MD: Agency for Health Care Policy and Research, Public Health Service, US Department of Health and Human Services, (AHCPR Publication No. 95-0009).

Eikeseth, S. (2009). Outcome of comprehensive psycho-educational interventions for young children with autism. *Research in Developmental Disabilities, 30,* 158−178. Available from http://dx.doi.org/10.1016/j.ridd.2008.02.003.

Eikeseth, S. (2010). Examination of qualifications required of an EIBI professional. *European Journal of Behavior Analysis, 11*(2), 239−246.

Guyatt, G., Cairns, J., Churchill, D., Evidence-Based Medicine Working Group, et al. (1992). Evidence-based medicine. A new approach to teaching the practice of medicine. *Journal of the American Medical Association, 268,* 2420−2425.

Institute of Medicine. Committee on Clinical Practice Guidelines (1992). Guidelines for clinical practice: From development to use. Washington, DC: National Academy Press.

Holland, J. P. (1995). Development of a clinical practice guideline for acute low back pain. *Current Opinion in Orthopedics, 6,* 63−69.

Leaf, J. B., Leaf, R., McEachin, J., Taubman, M., Smith, T., Harris, S. L., ... Waks, A. (2016). Concerns about the registered behavior Technician™ in relation to effective autism intervention. *Behavior Analysis in Practice.* Available from http://dx.doi.org/10.1007/s40617-016-0145-9.

Lee, T.Y. (1999). Code of Practice and Ethical Dilemmas. < www7.cityu.edu.hk/sspltr/p1/preparation/powerpoint/Field6_code.PPT > .

Missouri Department of Mental Health (2012). *Autism Spectrum Disorders: Guide to Evidence-based Interventions.* < http://www.autismguidelines.dmh.mo.gov/ > .

National Autism Center. (2009). National Standards Report: National Standards Project-Addressing the need for evidence-based practice guidelines for autism spectrum disorders. Randolph, MA: National Autism Center, Inc.

National Research Council. (2001). *Educating children with autism. Committee on educational interventions for children with autism. Division of behavioral and social sciences and education.* Washington, DC: National Academy Press.

New York State Department of Health Early Intervention Program. (1999a). Clinical practice guideline quick reference guide: Autism/pervasive developmental disorders—Assessment and intervention for young children (age 0−3 years). Health Education Services, P.O. Box 7126, Albany, NY 12224 (1999 Publication No. 4216).

New York State Department of Health Early Intervention Program. (1999b). New York State Department of Health Clinical Practice Guideline: The guideline technical report.

Autism/pervasive developmental disorders, assessment, and intervention for young children (age 0—3 years). Publication No. 4217.

Odom, S. L., Brown, W. H., Frey, T., Karasu, N., Smith-Canter, L. L., & Strain, P. S. (2003). Evidence-based practices for young children with autism: Contributions for single-subject design research. *Focus on Autism & Other Developmental Disabilities, 18*, 166—175.

Romanczyk, R. G., Turner, L. B., Sevlever, M., & Gillis, J. (2014). The status of treatment for autism spectrum disorders: the weak relationship of science to interventions. In S. O. Lilienfeld, J. M. Lohr, & S. J. Lynn (Eds.), *Science and pseudoscience in contemporary clinical psychology*. New York, NY: Guilford.

Schriger, D. L. (1995). Training panels in methodology. In K. A. McCormick, S. R. Moore, & R. A. Siegel (Eds.), *Clinical practice guideline development: Methodology perspectives*. Rockville, MD: Agency for Health Care Policy and Research, Public Health Service, US Department of Health and Human Services, (AHCPR Publication No. 95-0009).

Smith, T. (1996). Are other treatments effective? In C. Maurice, G. Green, & S. Luce (Eds.), *Behavioral intervention for young children with autism: A manual for parents and professionals* (pp. 45—59). Austin, TX: PRO-ED.

Turner, L. B., Fischer, A. J., & Luiselli, J. K. (2016). Towards a competency-based, ethical, and socially valid approach to the supervision of applied behavior analytic trainees. *Behavior Analysis in Practice, 9*, 287. Available from http://dx.doi.org/10.1007/s40617-016-0121-4.

Woolf, S. H. (1991). *AHCPR interim manual for clinical practice guideline development*. Rockville, MD: Agency for Health Care Policy and Research, Public Health Service, US Department of Health and Human Services, (AHCPR Publication No. 91-0018).

Woolf, S. H. (1994). An organized analytic framework for practice guideline development: using the analytic logic as a guide for reviewing evidence, developing recommendations, and explaining the rationale. In K. A. McCormick, S. R. Moore, & R. A. Siegel (Eds.), *Clinical practice guideline development: Methodology perspectives*. Rockville, MD: Agency for Health Care Policy and Research, Public Health Service, US Department of Health and Human Services, (AHCPR Publication No. 95-0009).

Further reading

Holland, J. P., Noyes-Grosser, D., Holland, C. L., Romanczyk, R. G., Gillis, J. M., & Lyons, D. (2005). New York State clinical practice guidelines I: Rationale and methodology for developing guidelines for early intervention services for young children with developmental disabilities evidence-based clinical practice guidelines for infants and toddlers with disabilities and their families: Recommendations for finding children early and supporting parents in the intervention process. *Infants and Young Children, 18*(2), 119—135.

Romanczyk, R. G., Callahan, E. H., Turner, L. B., & Cavalari, R. N. S. (2014). Efficacy of behavioral interventions for young children with autism spectrum disorders: Public policy, the evidence base, and implementation parameters. *Review Journal of Autism and Developmental Disorders, 1*(4), 276—326.

U.S. Department of Health and Human Services (1999). *Mental health: A report of the surgeon general—Executive summary*. Rockville, MD: U.S. Department of Health and Human Services, Substance Abuse and Mental Health Services Administration, Center for Mental Health Services, National Institutes of Health, National Institute of Mental Health.

Index

Note: page numbers followed by "*f*" and "*t*" refer to figures and tables, respectively.

A

ABA. *See* Applied behavior analysis (ABA); Association for Behavior Analysis (ABA)

ABAI. *See* Association for Behavior Analysis International (ABAI)

ABC data. *See* Antecedent–behavior–consequence data (ABC data)

Abolishing operation (AO), 199–200

Academic responding, 172–174

Acquisition, 176–177, 241
acquisition-level training, 185
decisions, 390
response, 231
of training in FBA methods, 43–44

ADDIE model. *See* Analyze, design, develop, implement, evaluate model (ADDIE model)

Adult Risk Version, 97

Agency for Health Care Policy and Research (AHCPR), 395–396

Agency for Healthcare Research and Quality (AHRQ), 395–396

Aggression, 93, 97–98

AHCPR. *See* Agency for Health Care Policy and Research (AHCPR)

AHRQ. *See* Agency for Healthcare Research and Quality (AHRQ)

AIMSweb Technical Manual, 174

Alaska licensees, 380

Alternative parent and family training options, 241–251
Day Treatment service, 241–246
in-home service, 246–251

American National Standards Institute (ANSI), 376

American Psychological Association (APA), 309, 396

American Telemedicine Association (ATA), 156

Analytical approach, 201, 390

Analyze, design, develop, implement, evaluate model (ADDIE model), 266

Analyze, specify, design, implement, evaluate, and recycle process (ASDIER process), 266

ANSI. *See* American National Standards Institute (ANSI)

Antecedent strategies for escape-maintained problem behavior, 207–208

Antecedent–behavior–consequence data (ABC data), 51, 235

AO. *See* Abolishing operation (AO)

APA. *See* American Psychological Association (APA)

APBA. *See* Association for Professional Behavior Analysts (APBA)

Applied behavior analysis (ABA), 3, 21–22, 73, 93–94, 171–172, 259, 325, 367, 389, 396–397
autism insurance reform, 370–371
in evaluation of risk, 93–96
identification of multiple topographies, 95
identification of secondary consequences, 96
identification of settings, 95
specialist involvement, 96
historical perspective, 390–397
competence, 390–393
ethical conduct, 393–395
evidence-based practice, 395–397
history of ABA treatment for ASD, 368–370
identifying competent ABA providers, 371–375
credentialing, 372–374
licensing, 374–375
of practice, 367–371
principles and procedures, 172
priority in field of, 73–77

Applied behavior analysis (ABA)
  (*Continued*)
  Professional and Ethical Compliance
    Code for Behavior Analysts,
    399–406
  requirements for ABA professionals
    CE, 379–380
    disciplinary standards, 380–382
    roadmap to entering professional practice
      of, 382–384
    experience, 383–384
    professional organizations, 384
    specific ethics code for behavior analysts,
      397–399
    terminology, 389–390
Applied behavior analysts, 285, 291, 374, 380
Aptitude–treatment interaction (ATI), 169
ASD. *See* Autism spectrum disorder (ASD)
ASDIER process. *See* Analyze, specify,
  design, implement, evaluate, and
  recycle process (ASDIER process)
"Assessing Behavior" states, 310, 400
Assessment of skills, 9–11
Association for Behavior Analysis (ABA),
  318
Association for Behavior Analysis
  International (ABAI), 136, 261–262,
  318, 328, 384, 397–398
Association for Professional Behavior
  Analysts (APBA), 321, 328, 375,
  384, 397–398
Association of Behavioral and Cognitive
  Therapies, 328
ATA. *See* American Telemedicine
  Association (ATA)
ATI. *See* Aptitude–treatment interaction
  (ATI)
Audience, 215, 351–352, 354, 359, 362
Authorship, 344
Autism, 316
  ABA for, 397
  insurance reform, 370–371, 375
Autism Speaks initiative Autism Votes, 370
Autism spectrum disorder (ASD), 289, 367
  history of ABA treatment for, 368–370
  untreated prognosis for individuals with,
    367–368
Automatic reinforcement, 41–42, 56, 62,
  197

B
BAAB. *See* Behavior Analysis Accreditation
  Board (BAAB)
BACB. *See* Behavior Analyst Certification
  Board (BACB)
BBS. *See* Biobehavioral Service (BBS)
BCaBA. *See* Board Certified Associate
  Behavior Analysts (BCaBA)
BCBA. *See* Board Certified Behavior
  Analysts (BCBA)
Behavior analysis, 136, 285, 290–291, 312
  using behavior-analytic language,
    294–295, 295*t*
  bringing behavior analysis to other
    disciplines, 292–293
  bringing others to behavior analysis,
    293–294
Behavior Analysis Accreditation Board
  (BAAB), 291–292
Behavior Analyst Certification Board
  (BACB), 3–4, 6, 22, 43, 77, 155,
  198, 260–261, 286, 291, 370,
  372–373, 393, 398–401
  BACB-credentialed practitioners,
    380–381
  behavior analysts ethical responsibility to,
    401
  code, 401
  Compliance Code, 312
  essential components of BACB
    credentials, 375–379
    coursework, 376–378
    exam, 379
    supervised experience, 378–379
    standards, 382
  Supervision Training Curriculum, 12–13
Behavior analyst(s), 8, 285, 299, 323,
  350–351, 374
  and behavior-change program, 400
  ethical responsibility
    to BACB, 401
    to colleagues, 400
    to profession of behavior analysts, 400
  Professional and Ethical Compliance
    Code for Behavior Analysts,
    399–406
  and research, 400–401
  responsibility to clients, 399–400
  responsible conduct of, 399

specific ethics code for, 397—399
  BACB, 398—399
as supervisors, 400
telehealth training, 135—138, 139*t*
  need for formal, 136—137
  recommendations, 137—138
Behavior analytic
  approaches, 290—291
  assessment and treatment evaluations, 229
  assessment techniques, 310
  "behavior-analytic-ese", 350—351
  community, 384
  jargon, 294
  language, 294—295, 295*t*
  literature, 314
  methods, 286—287
Behavior analytic supervision
  behavior analytic practice model for, 7*f*
  behavioral practitioners, 3
  continuously monitoring supervisory
    behaviors, 15—16
  past and current status of practitioner
    training, 4
  practice guidelines, procedures, and
    implementation recommendations,
    7—15
    assessment of skills, 9—11
    using behavioral skills training, 13—15
    deciding to supervising, 7—8
    developing clearly defined and
      measurable behavioral objectives,
      12—13
    selecting target skills, 11—12
    setting stage for positive supervision
      experience, 8—9
  procedural checklist for first supervision
    meeting, 19—20
  research base and implications for
    practice, 4—6
Behavior Change Tool, 276—277
Behavior disorder, 94, 97
Behavior engineering model (BEM), 276
Behavior Intervention Plan (BIP), 12
Behavior Interventions Rating Scale-Revised
  (BIRS-R), 217—218
Behavior modification, 372
Behavior problems, 168—169
  differences with children's academic
    problems and, 168—169

Behavior-change program, 400
Behavioral
  analysis, 360
  assessment, technology and telehealth
    applications in, 144—146
    using telehealth in clinical, school, and
      residential settings, 145—146
  deficits, 168
  momentum, 337
  orientation, 335
  Pediatrics Clinic, 233
  practitioners, 3, 21, 328
    preparing, 21—22
    relevance for, 309—311
  processes, 354—355
  research, 23
Behavioral rehearsal. *See* Performance
  practice
Behavioral risk assessment
  ABA in evaluation of risk, 93—96
    clinical-behavioral risk in individuals with
      IDD, 93
  conceptualizing risk and developing
    mitigation plan, 104—108
  practice guidelines, procedures, and
    implementation recommendations,
    96—104
    administering screening tool,
      102
    appropriateness for admission to
      setting, 98
    avoiding tangents, 103
    building rapport, 102—103
    comprehensive record review,
      99—100
    general-to-specific strategy, 103—104
    informants, 100—101
    other considerations, 101—102
    preparation, 99
    preparing for safer entry into program,
      98—99
    reassessment of chronic complexities,
      99
    screening tool for behaviors of concern,
      98
    using understandable language, 103
  screening tool for behavior of
    concern—adult risk version,
    113—112

Behavioral skills training (BST), 5–6,
     13–15, 25–26, 210, 212–213
   guidelines and recommendations for
     implementing steps of, 26–30
     behaviors, 26
     demonstrating skill, 28–29
     example of performance checklist, 27t
     providing performance feedback,
        29–30
     providing rationale, 26
     providing written description of skill,
        26–28
     staff practice performing skill, 29
     training session, 30
   on-the-job component of, 30–31
Behavioral systems analysis (BSA), 260
Belmont Report, 395
BEM. See Behavior engineering model
     (BEM)
Beneficence, Belmont Report principle, 395
BFA. See Brief functional analysis (BFA)
Bing, 316
Biobehavioral Service (BBS), 145
BIP. See Behavior Intervention Plan (BIP)
BIRS-R. See Behavior Interventions Rating
     Scale-Revised (BIRS-R)
"Black humor" manner, 392–393
Blind raters, 87
Board, 374–375
Board Certified Associate Behavior Analysts
     (BCaBA), 3, 373–374, 377–378
Board Certified Behavior Analysts (BCBA),
     3, 370, 372–373, 382
   BCBA-D®, 372–373
   Task List, 43
"Bobby's" problem behavior, 232
Brief functional analysis (BFA), 57
BSA. See Behavioral systems analysis (BSA)
BST. See Behavioral skills training (BST)
Building rapport, 102–103

C
Caregiver(s), 80–81, 107
   caregiver-conducted FAs, 57
   preparation, 105–106
"Caveat emptor", 390, 392
"Caveat venditor" principle, 392
CBM. See Curriculum-based measurement
     (CBM)

CBM reading probes (CBM-R probes), 173,
     180, 181f
CBM-M. See Curriculum-based measures in
     mathematics (CBM-M)
CBM-WE. See Curriculum-based measures
     in written expression (CBM-WE)
CE. See Continuing education (CE)
CE units (CEUs), 311
Central reinforcement for behavior, 406
Certification
   essential components of BACB
     credentials, 375–379
   identifying competent ABA providers,
     371–375
   of practice of ABA, 367–371
   requirements for ABA professionals,
     379–382
   roadmap to entering professional practice
     of ABA, 382–384
CEUs. See CE units (CEUs)
Challenging behavior(s), 93–95, 197
   individualizing training, 210–211, 211t
   preventing, 210–211
   target socially significant, 216
Child behavior, 229–230, 286–287
Children's academic problems, differences
     with behavior problems and,
     168–169
Ci3T models. See Comprehensive,
     integrated, three-tiered models
     (Ci3T models)
Clients, 29, 81, 265–266, 389
   behavior analysts' responsibility to,
     399–400
   records, 100
   variables, 101
Clinical competence, 137–138
Clinical-behavioral risk in individuals with
     IDD, 93
"Cocaine Toothache Drops", 392
Code of Ethics, 397
Collaboration, 285–287, 290–292,
     296–300
Collateral effects, 76–77
Colleagues, 34, 79
   behavior analysts' ethical responsibility
     to, 400
   face-to-face interactions with,
     326

Colloquial expression, 350–351
Colonialism, 360
Competence, 296, 390–393
  global indicators of reading, 180
  technological and clinical, 137
  trainee, 31
Competency-based approach, 4, 7, 25
Competency-based staff training, 25, 25*t*
  ABA, 21
  behavioral practitioners, 21
  behavioral research developing evidence-
    based staff training procedures, 23
  critical but qualified role of staff training,
    35–36
  guidelines and recommendations
    for implementing steps of BST, 26–30
    for practice, 26
  informal staff training, 31–32, 32*t*
  making staff training more time efficient
    for practitioners, 32–35
  pyramidal staff training, 33–34, 34*t*
  using visual media and technology in
    staff training, 34–35
  on-the-job component of behavioral skills
    training, 30–31
  practice checklist for, 36–37, 36*f*
  preparing behavioral practitioners, 21–22
  research on singular staff training
    procedures, 23–24
  research on staff training programs, 25
Competent practice, 405–406
Complaints, 381–382
"Compliance Code", 309, 399
Composite skills, 175–177
Comprehensive, integrated, three-tiered
    models (Ci3T models), 78–79
Comprehensive assessment of risk, 95
Conceptualization of treatment intensity,
    188–189
Conferences, 15, 262, 293, 379–380, 384
Confidentiality, 155
Consequence(s)
  events, 230–231
  manipulation, 214–215
Consequentialism, 403–404
Consultation practice guidelines, procedures,
    and implementation
    recommendations, 265–280
  analyze performance, 272–277

job/Performer-level tools and analysis,
    275–277
  organization-level tools and analysis,
    272–274
  process-level tools and analysis,
    274–275, 275*f*
consultation process, 266–280
design and develop solutions, 277–278
  design solutions, 278
  developing materials for effective
    implementation of solutions, 278
  establishing design team and secure
    resources, 277
  pilot test solutions, 278
implement solutions, 278–279
  evaluating and revising performance,
    279
  preparing organization, 279
  solutions implementation, 279
internal *vs.* external consultants, 265–266
program for maintenance, 279–280
Consultation process, 197–198, 266–280
  evaluating acceptability of, 217–218
  OBM consultation phases and outputs,
    267*t*
  responding to requests for services,
    267–271
    defining and scope of project,
      268–269
    determining results, 270
    developing project proposal, 270–271
    obtaining project approval/sign
      contract, 271
    outline project goals and deliverables,
      270
Consumers, 309, 390
Contact with literature, 311
"Contingency space", 53–54
Contingent response protocols, 107
Continuing education (CE), 311, 313, 325,
    371–373, 379–380
  at conventions, 317–318
  practice guidelines, 318–322
    checklist, 322–323
  relevance for behavioral practitioners,
    309–311
  research base and implications for
    practice, 313–318
  status of practitioner training, 312–313

Core ethical responsibility of behavior
    analysts, 10
Correlational information, 198
Coursework, 136, 187, 371–372, 376–378,
    389
  BCaBA and RBT, 377–378
  OBM, 261–262
  requirements, 376
Credentialed behavior analysts, 325
Credentialing, 372–374, 373*t*, 398
  agencies, 326
  entity, 328
  professional, 371
Crossfunctional processes, 274, 275*f*
"Current State" maps, 277
Curriculum-based measurement (CBM), 170,
    173–174
Curriculum-based measures in mathematics
    (CBM-M), 173
Curriculum-based measures in written
    expression (CBM-WE), 173–174

D
DAC. *See* Disciplinary Appeals Committee
    (DAC)
DAs. *See* Descriptive assessments (DAs)
Database search engines, 296
Day Treatment service, 241–246. *See also*
    In-home service
  case illustration and benefits of, 243–246
  during evaluation, 242–243
  follow-up after evaluation, 243
  limitations of, 246
  referral process and preparation prior to
    evaluation, 242
DCPM. *See* Digits correct per minute (DCPM)
Deductive approach, 170–171
Demand fading, 106
Deontology, 403–404
Descriptive assessments (DAs), 43, 51–55,
    63, 198. *See also* Indirect
    assessments (IAs)
  implications for practice, 55
  research base, 54–55
*Diagnostic and Statistical Manual of Mental
    Disorders-Fifth Edition*, 288
Diagnostic-prescriptive approach, 169
DIBELS. *See* Dynamic Indicators of Basic
    Early Literacy Skills (DIBELS)

Differential reinforcement (DR), 174–175,
    199–200
Differential reinforcement of alternative
    behavior (DRA), 200
Differential reinforcement of other behavior
    (DRO), 200
Digits correct per minute (DCPM), 173
Direct measures, 47
Direct techniques, 86–87
  normative comparison, 86
  participant preference assessment, 86–87
  sustained use, 87
Disciplinary Appeals Committee (DAC), 381
Disciplinary Review Committee (DRC), 381
Disciplinary standards, 380–382
Dissemination, 292–293, 299
Distal effects of treatment, 76–77
DR. *See* Differential reinforcement (DR)
DRA. *See* Differential reinforcement of
    alternative behavior (DRA)
DRC. *See* Disciplinary Review Committee
    (DRC)
DRO. *See* Differential reinforcement of
    other behavior (DRO)
Dynamic Indicators of Basic Early Literacy
    Skills (DIBELS), 173

E
"Earn-back" component, 122
EBP model. *See* Evidence-based practice
    model (EBP model)
"Eclectic" treatment, 369
Editing and rewriting, 338
Effective staff training approaches, 212–214
Emphasis, 4, 359
Empirically Supported Therapies (EST), 396
Employee behavior, 117
Employee-of the-month (EOM), 120
Employing behavioral methods, 352
Endorphins, 356–357
EO. *See* Establishing operation (EO)
EOM. *See* Employee-of the-month (EOM)
EPCs. *See* Evidence-based Practice Centers
    (EPCs)
ERIC database, 316
Escape-maintained problem behavior,
    antecedent strategies for, 207–208
EST. *See* Empirically Supported Therapies
    (EST)

Establishing operation (EO), 55–56, 202,
    212, 406
Ethical codes, 390, 393
    specific ethics code for behavior analysts,
        397–399
Ethical conduct, 393–395
Ethical dilemma, 403–405
Ethical practice, 389, 405–406
Ethical responsibility, behavior analysts
    to BACB, 401
    to colleagues, 400
    to profession of behavior analysts, 400
Ethics, 389
    challenge, 398
    code, 402–403
E-TIP analysis, 276
Evidence-based approach, 4, 392–393
Evidence-based medicine, 392
Evidence-based Practice Centers (EPCs),
    395–396
Evidence-based practice model (EBP
    model), 309, 323, 395–397
Evidence-based staff training procedures,
    behavioral research developing, 23
Experimental control, 45
EXT. See Extinction (EXT)
External
    consultants, 265–266
    evaluation, 87
Extinction (EXT), 199, 206–207

F
FA. See Functional analysis (FA)
Factor structures, 82
Family Educational Rights and Privacy Act
    (FERPA), 154
FAST. See Functional Assessment Screening
    Tool (FAST)
FBA. See Functional behavior assessment
    (FBA)
FCR. See Functional communicative
    response (FCR)
FCT. See Functional communication training
    (FCT)
Fear, 349–350, 352
FERPA. See Family Educational Rights and
    Privacy Act (FERPA)
Florida Institute of Technology (FIT),
    261–262, 382–383

Fluency, 175–177, 179–181, 185, 312–313
Function-based treatment, 199–200
    DR, 200
    employing, 206
    EXT, 199
    NCR, 199–200
Functional analysis (FA), 41–42, 44,
    55–63, 145, 229–232
    clarifying undifferentiated responding in,
        203
    employing skill-and function-based
        treatments
        antecedent strategies for escape-
            maintained problem behavior,
            207–208
        conducting treatment analysis,
            208–209, 209t
        creating practical treatment via
            reinforcement schedule thinning,
            207
        EXT, 206–207
        FCT, 206
    implications for practice, 61–62
    open-ended indirect and direct
        assessments to informing, 201
    potential barriers to conducting FA, and
        selecting FA format, 201–203
    research base, 59–61
    synthesized contingency analysis,
        203–205, 205t
Functional Assessment Screening Tool
    (FAST), 47
Functional behavior assessment (FBA),
    9–10, 41–42, 145, 198–199.
    See also Social validity assessment
    DAs, 51–55
    FA, 55–62
    IA, 45–51
    implications for practice
        DA, 55
        FA, 61–62
        IA, 50–51
    potential decision-making process for
        selecting, 52f
    practice guidelines checklist, 62–63
    recommendations for practitioner training,
        44
    research base
        DA, 54–55

Functional behavior assessment (FBA)
(*Continued*)
FA, 59–61
IA, 47–50
status of practitioner training, 43–44
types, 45
Functional communication training (FCT),
146, 200, 206–209, 230–231
Functional communicative response (FCR),
206
Functional relationships tool, 273–274, 274*f*
"Future State" maps, 278

G
General-to-specific strategy, 103–104
Generalization, 231, 241
plan for, 214
Generalized oral-reading fluency, 180
Getting used to it (GUTI), 354–355
Gold standard, 199
Google, 314, 316–317
Google Scholar, 296, 316–317
Graduate programs, 313
Group videoconferencing, 157–158
Group-design treatment, 369

H
Habilitative validity, 76
Health Information Technology for
Economic and Clinical Health Act
(HITECH Act), 154
Health Insurance Portability and
Accountability Act (HIPAA),
153–154, 402–403
Privacy Rule, 393, 403
High-risk behaviors, 107–108
Hippocratic Oath, 393
Human performance system (HPS), 276
Human service program (HS program), 263

I
IAs. *See* Indirect assessments (IAs)
IDD. *See* Intellectual and developmental
disabilities (IDD)
IDEA. *See* Individuals with Disabilities
Education Act (IDEA)
IH. *See* Instructional hierarchy (IH)
IISCA. *See* Interview informed structured
contingency analysis (IISCA)

Implementation science, 292–293
In vivo and via telehealth, 246–251
In-home service, 231–232, 241, 246–251.
See also Day Treatment service
case illustration and benefits, 248–251
during evaluation, 247–248
follow-up after evaluation, 248
limitations of, 251
preparation prior to evaluation, 247
referral process, 247
In-person Day Treatment service, 231–232
Incentive programs, 121
Incentive-based performance improvement,
117–119
group incentive plan, 121
individual incentive system, 120–121
intervention targeted safety behavior,
123
lotteries, 124
PFP system, 122
practice recommendations, 125–131
Independent evaluation, 397
Index of learning, 172–174
Indiana law, 370
Indirect assessments (IAs), 43, 45–51,
62–63, 198. *See also* Descriptive
assessments (DAs)
implications for practice, 50–51
process, 145
psychometric properties, 49*t*
research base, 47–50
Individual incentive system, 120–121
Individual provider level, 390
Individuals with Disabilities Education Act
(IDEA), 148, 167–168, 170–171,
198
Inductive approach, 170–171
Industrial/Organizational Psychology
programs (I/O Psychology programs),
262
Informal staff training, 31–32, 32*t*
Informants, 100–101
Information dissemination, 34–35
Instant messaging, 157–158
Instruction/Instructional, 23
consultation in schools, 167–168
intervention, 168–169
designing instructional sessions,
184–186

providing implementation support to
  teachers, 186—189
selecting instructional intervention,
  183—184
student skills and skill deficits,
  179—183
session designing, 184—186
training strategy, 26—27
Instructional hierarchy (IH), 172, 175—179,
  177f
Insurance laws, 375
Intangibles, 118, 126
Intellectual
  disability, 94
  performance, 362
Intellectual and developmental disabilities
  (IDD), 93, 367
  clinical-behavioral risk in individuals
    with, 93
Internal
  consistency, 82
  consultants, 265—266
Internet, 321
  internet-based intervention, 331
  search engines, 316
Interobserver agreement (IOA), 330
Intervention, 309—310
  agent, 80
  and consultation, 147—152
    in clinical settings, 151—152
    in home settings, 147—148
    in school settings, 148—151
Intervention Rating Profile-15 (IRP-15),
  217
Intervention Rating Profile-20 (IRP-20), 82
Intervention targeted safety behavior,
  123
Interview informed structured contingency
  analysis (IISCA), 58—59, 203—204
Interviews, 45, 47, 82—85
IOA. See Interobserver agreement (IOA)
IOM. See US Institute of Medicine (IOM)
I/O Psychology programs. See Industrial/
  Organizational Psychology programs
  (I/O Psychology programs)
IRP-15. See Intervention Rating Profile-15
  (IRP-15)
IRP-20. See Intervention Rating Profile-20
  (IRP-20)

J
Job analysis, 377
Job Management Tool, 275—276
Job/Performer-level tools and analysis,
  275—277
Journal of Applied Behavior Analysis
  (JABA), 73, 198—199, 296, 314
*Journal of Organizational Behavior
  Management* (*JOBM*), 263
Jungle, The (1906), 392
Justice, Belmont Report principle, 395

K
Knowledge-based assessment, 10

L
Latency-based FAs, 202
Learning. *See also* Writing for publication
  hierarchy, 172, 175—179, 177f
  packages, 5
  trial, 174
Legal and ethical considerations, 153—156
  assessment and intervention, 155—156
  confidentiality, 155
  initiation of services, 155
Licensing, 374—375
Licensure
  essential components of BACB
    credentials, 375—379
  identifying competent ABA providers,
    371—375
  laws, 379
  of practice of ABA, 367—371
  requirements for ABA professionals,
    379—382
  roadmap to entering professional practice
    of ABA, 382—384
Listening passage preview (LPP), 182—183
Lotteries, 123—125, 131—132
Lydia E. Pinkham's Vegetable Compound,
  391

M
MA law. *See* Massachusetts law (MA law)
"Maintain Competence through Professional
  Development" code, 310—311
"Malleable factors", 288
Manuscript reviews, 341—343, 342f

MAS. *See* Motivation Assessment Scale (MAS)
Massachusetts Association for Behavior Analysis (MassABA), 384
Massachusetts law (MA law), 374−375
Mobile telepresence robots, 149−151
"Mobile writer", 335
Modeling, 23−24
  training strategy, 28
Monitoring performance, 340−341, 341*f*
Morality, 389
MOs. *See* Motivating operations (MOs)
Motivating operations (MOs), 230
Motivation Assessment Scale (MAS), 47
Multidisciplinary collaboration, 287, 291−294, 299
Multidisciplinary settings, consultation practices
  past and current practitioner training, 291−292
  practice guidelines, 295−300, 297*f*
    checklist, 300−301
  relevance for behavioral practitioners, 289−291
  research base and implications for practice
    using behavior-analytic language, 294−295, 295*t*
    bringing behavior analysis to other disciplines, 292−293
    bringing others to behavior analysis, 293−294

N
National Association of Special Education Teachers (NASET), 401
National Center for Education Statistics (NCES), 167
National Commission for Certifying Agencies (NCCA), 376
National/international behavior analytic organizations, 384
NCES. *See* National Center for Education Statistics (NCES)
NCLB. *See* No Child Left Behind (NCLB)
NCR. *See* Noncontingent reinforcement (NCR)
"Negative reinforcement", 294
No Child Left Behind (NCLB), 170−171

Nonbehavior
  analytic audience, 351−352
  nonbehavioral orientation, 335
Noncontingent reinforcement (NCR), 199−200
Nonverbal communication, 359
Normative comparison, 86
Nuremburg Code, 394

O
OBM. *See* Organizational Behavior Management (OBM)
Office for Human Research Protections (OHRP), 393
On-going responsibility, 406
On-the-job component of behavioral skills training, 30−31
Onscreen document sharing, 157−158
Open-access Internet search engines, 316−317
Open-ended
  functional assessment interview, 204
  indirect and direct assessments to informing functional analysis, 201
Organization-level tools and analysis, 272−274
  functional relationships map, 274*f*
  organizational system map, 273*f*
Organizational Behavior Management (OBM), 117, 259
  consultation practice guidelines, procedures, and implementation recommendations, 265−280
  past and current status of practitioner training in, 261−262
  and relevance for behavioral practitioners, 259−261
    three-level approach and goals, 260*t*
  research base and implications for practice, 263−265
Organizational success, 260
Outpatient clinics, 232−241, 234*t*
  case illustration and benefits of, 239−241
  during evaluation, 235−239
  follow-up after evaluation, 239
  limitations of, 241
  preparation prior to evaluation, 235
  referral process, 233−235, 236*f*
Over-practice presentation, 354

P

Parent(s), 80–81
  attention, 230
  behavior, 212
  and family training approach, 233–241
    alternative parent and family training
      options, 241–251
    guidelines and recommendations for,
      251–254, 252*t*, 253*t*
    outpatient clinics, 232–241
Participant, 75
  preference assessment, 86–87
"Patent medicines", 391
Pay-for-performance (PFP), 119, 122, 126
Pay-for-time (PFT), 118–119
PD. *See* Phrase drill error correction (PD)
PDA. *See* Performance-deficit analysis
      (PDA)
PDC. *See* Performance Diagnostic Checklist
      (PDC)
PDC-human services (PDC-HS), 129
Peer review process, 332
Peer training. *See* Pyramidal staff training
Peer-reviewed journals, 320–321
Peer-reviewed literature, 310–311, 322–324
Performance Analysis Toolkit, 272
Performance Diagnostic Checklist (PDC),
      129, 263–264
Performance feedback, 24, 187–188
Performance Flowchart, 265
Performance improvement guide to writing
      for publication, 331–344
  completing prewriting tasks, 335–336
  establishing writing schedule, 333–334
  putting words on page, 336–338
    dealing with manuscript reviews,
      341–343
    editing and rewriting, 338
    monitoring performance, 340–341
    positive reinforcement, 340
    write first drafts, 337–338
    write for time, 336–337
    write from outline, 336
    writing collaboratively, 343–344
    writing mechanics, style, and grammar,
      338–340
    writing medium, 336
  reading, 332–333
  writing opportunistically, 334–335

Performance management (PM), 117,
      259–260
Performance matrix for employees,
      126–127
Performance practice, 24, 29
Performance staff training, 25, 25*t*
Performance-based assessment, 10
Performance-deficit analysis (PDA),
      181–182, 182*f*
Peter Principle, 118
PFP. *See* Pay-for-performance (PFP)
PFT. *See* Pay-for-time (PFT)
PHI. *See* Protected health information (PHI)
Phrase drill error correction (PD), 182–183
PIC/NIC Analysis, 276
Pilot test solutions, 278
PIRS. *See* Primary Intervention Rating Scale
      (PIRS)
PLS. *See* Preschool life skills (PLS)
PM. *See* Performance management (PM)
Point system, 126–128
Positive reinforcement, 340
Practice act, licensure law, 374–375
Practice guidelines
  CE, 318–322
    checklist, 322–323
    improving awareness of and access to
      contemporary scholarly literature,
      320–321
    organizational factors, 321–322
    outcomes for consumers and society,
      322
    self-assessment, 319–320
  checklist, 62–63
    descriptive assessments, 63
    functional analyses, 63
    indirect assessments, 62–63
Practice/practicing
  behavior analysts, 10
  CE at conventions, 317–318
  clinicians, 117
  research base and implications for,
      313–318
Practitioner, 329–330, 389
  practitioner-generated publication
      dissemination, 325
  training, 312–313
    accessing literature, 312
    CE, 313

Practitioner (*Continued*)
  evaluation of scholarly literature,
    312–313
  recommendations for, 44
  status of, 43–44
Preference assessment technology, 86–87
Preschool life skills (PLS), 210
Primary Intervention Rating Scale (PIRS),
    79
Primary prevention, 78–79
Prioritization, 11
Privacy Rule, 154, 402–403
Problem behavior, 41–42, 57–58, 231
Problem solving, 6–7
Process mapping tool, 274–275
Process-level tools and analysis, 274–275,
    275*f*
Professional and Ethical Compliance Code
    for Behavior Analysts, 309,
    380–381, 399–406
  ethical and competent practice, 405–406
  ethical dilemmas, 403–405
  regulatory influences and ethics code,
    402–403
Professional contribution to professional
    practice, 326
Professional development, 327
Professional literature, 332
Professional organizations, 384
Protected health information (PHI),
    402–403
Proximal effects, 76–77
PsycINFO, 296
PSYCInfo database, 316
"Publiation lens", 330
Public speaking, 350
  general suggestions, 350–352
  suggestions for delivery of talk, 355–362
  suggestions for preparation, 352–355
Public statements, 400
Publication
  knowledge, 327–328
  options, 328
  peer review process, 327
Published literature, 325
Publishing, 326, 329
PubMed, 296
Putative reinforce, 202
Pyramidal staff training, 33–34, 34*t*

Q
Quality control approach, 390
Quantitative methods, 53–54
Questions About Behavioral Function
    (QABF), 47

R
Radical behaviorism, 294
Raffles. *See* Lotteries
Rapport, 8
Reading, 332–333
"Red Volkswagen" effect, 353–354
Reductive techniques, 80
Refer–test–place model, 169–170
Registered Behavior Technician (RBT),
    373–374, 377–378
Regulatory influences, 402–403
Reinforcement schedule thinning, creating
    practical treatment via,
    207
Relationship Map, 273
Reliance on scientific knowledge,
    310
Repeated readings (RRs), 181–182
RESAA. *See* Retention, endurance, stability,
    application, and adduction (RESAA)
ResearchGate, 316–317
Respect for Persons, Belmont Report
    principle, 395
Response acquisition, 231, 234*t*, 250
Response to intervention (RtI), 167
Responsible Conduct of Behavior Analysts,
    310
Retention, endurance, stability, application,
    and adduction (RESAA), 176
Risk assessment, 104–105
Risk mitigation plan, 104–108
  contingent response protocols,
    107
  documentation, 108
  preparation of caregivers, 105–106
  preventive approaches, 106
  protecting people and settings, 107
  seeking consultation, 107–108
  treatment planning considerations, 108
Risk reduction plan, 105
RRs. *See* Repeated readings (RRs)
RtI. *See* Response to intervention (RtI)
"Ryan's Law", 370–371

S

Scatterplot, 52–53
Scholarly literature, 311
    contemporary scholarly literature,
        320–321
    evaluation, 312–313
School staff behavior, 197–198, 212
School-based behavior support, 197–198
    FBA, 198–199
    function-based treatment, 199–200
    practice recommendations
        analytical approach, 201
        employ skill-and function-based
            treatments, 206–209
        employing functional analysis,
            201–205
        preventing challenging behavior
            development, 210–211
        social validity assessment, 215–218
        training and supervising staff, 211–215
School-based consulting teams, 172
School-based instructional intervention,
        169–171
School-based instructional support
    applied behavior analysis, 171–172
    differences between children's academic
        and behavior problems, 168–169
    foundations of effective instruction
        academic responding, 172–174
        learning/instructional hierarchy,
            175–179, 177f
        stimulus control, 174–175
    instructional consultation in schools,
        167–168
    instructional intervention, 179–189
    past and present of school-based
        instructional intervention, 169–171
School-wide positive behavior support
    system (SWPBS system), 167
Screening tool, 99
    administering, 102
    for behavior of concern–adult risk
        version, 113–112
    for behaviors of concern, 98
Secondary prevention, 78–79
Secondary recommendation, 44
Security Rule, 154, 403
Self-directed process, 6
Self-harm, 99

Self-injurious behavior (SIB), 96, 316,
        383–384
Self-report rating scales, 82, 83t
Serotonin, 356–357
Service-delivery documents, 100
SIB. *See* Self-injurious behavior (SIB)
Single-function test, 57
Single-subject methodology, 288–289
Singular staff training procedures
    instructions, 23
    modeling, 23–24
    performance feedback, 24
    performance practice, 24
    research on, 23–24
Singular strategies, 23
Skill-based treatments, employing, 206
Sleep role in problem behavior, 290
"Snake oil", 390–391
Social acceptability of intervention
    procedures, 75–76
Social importance of effects, 76–77
Social positive reinforcement, 199
Social significance of goals, 74–75
Social validity assessment, 73, 215–218.
    See also Functional behavior
        assessment (FBA)
    direct techniques, 86–87
    at each level of prevention, 78–80
    essential learnings, 87–88
    evaluating acceptability
        of assessment and treatment procedures,
            217
        of consultation process, 217–218, 218t
    evaluating practical significance of
        behavior change, 216–217
    external evaluation, 87
    interviews, 82–85
    practical applications of social validity,
        78–87
    priority in field of ABA, 73–77
    using range of methods, 81
    relevance for practicing professional,
        77–78
    self-report rating scales, 82, 83t
    social acceptability of intervention
        procedures, 75–76
    social importance of effects, 76–77
    social significance of goals, 74–75
    from stakeholders involvement, 80–81

Social validity assessment (*Continued*)
    intervention agent, 80
    parents and caregivers, 80–81
    students or clients, 81
    student preferences, 217
    target socially significant challenging
        behavior, 216
Staff training. *See also* Competency-based
        staff training
    effective approaches, 212–214
    informal, 31–32, 32*t*
    performance, 25, 25*t*
    programs, 25, 25*t*
    pyramidal, 33–34, 34*t*
    singular staff training procedures, 23–24
    training and supervising staff, 211–215,
        216*t*
        consequences manipulation, 214–215
        effective staff training approaches,
            212–214
        establishing operations, 212
        plan for generalization, 214
        variables influencing integrity, 212–215
    visual media and technology in, 34–35
Stimulus, 174–175
    functions, 356–357
    learning/instructional hierarchy as model
        for control, 175–179
Structured interviews, 45
Student(s), 81
    preferences, 217
    skills and skill deficits, 179–183
Super-System, 272
Supervised experience, 378–379
Supervised Independent Fieldwork, 11
Supervision, 3–4
SWPBS system. *See* School-wide positive
        behavior support system (SWPBS
        system)
Sympathetic nervous system, 351–352
Synthesized contingency analysis, 203–205,
        205*t*
Systematic formative evaluation, 170–171,
        180

T
Tangents, avoiding, 103
Tangibles, 118, 125–126, 129–130
Task analysis, 27, 250–251, 250*t*, 274

Task Analysis Map, 274–275, 275*f*
Task Force, 396
Task List, 13, 43, 309–311
    BACB's Fourth Edition Task List, 309,
        377, 379
    Third Edition Task List, 377
Team Charter templates, 277
Technological competence, 137–138
TEI. *See* Treatment Evaluation Inventory (TEI)
Telecommunication, 135
Teleconferencing, 156–158
Teleconsultation, 139*t*, 149–151
Telehealth
    behavior analyst telehealth training,
        135–138, 139*t*
    practice guidelines, procedures, and
        implementation recommendations,
        153–158
    features important for behavior
        analysts, 157–158
    implementation recommendations,
        156–157
    legal and ethical considerations,
        153–156
    research base and implications for
        practice, 138–153
    implications and future directions,
        152–153
    intervention and consultation, 147–152
    technology and telehealth applications
        in behavioral assessment, 144–146
    technology and telehealth applications,
        135
Telepresence robots, 149–151
Therapist-led behavioral evaluations, 229
Threat-based stress response, 351–352
Three-level approach, 260, 260*t*
Time consuming process, 320
Title act, licensure law, 374–375
"To do no harm", 393
Topography-based assessment approach,
        104–105
Total performance system (TPS), 272
"Train and hope" approach, 214
Treatment
    acceptability, 75
    adherence, 230–231
    analysis, 208–209, 209*t*
    components, 230

fidelity, 230−231
integrity, 186−187
intensity, 186−187
Treatment Evaluation Inventory (TEI), 82
Trial-based FAs, 202
Trial-by-trial format of FA, 60
Tuskegee Syphilis Experiment, 394−395

U
Unstructured formats, 45
US Institute of Medicine (IOM), 396

V
Verbal behavior, 339
Verbal communication, 327
Verbal statement, 12−13
Video modeling (VM), 212−213
Videoconferencing, 135, 145, 147−149,
    157, 378
Visual media
    and technology in staff training, 34−35
    written instructions, 23
Vocal
    client's vocal communication, 287
    description, 27
    instructions, 23, 251
    performances, 354−355
    utterances, 206

W
"Wait-to-fail" model, 170
Western Michigan University (WMU),
    261−262

Words read correctly per minute (WRCM),
    173−174, 179−180, 185, 188−189
Write
    first drafts, 337−338
    from outline, 336
    for time, 336−337
Writing, 336
    collaboratively, 343−344
    hard work, 329
    as learning, 326
    mechanics, style, and grammar, 338−340,
        339t
    opportunistically, 334−335
    schedule, 333−334
Writing for publication, 325
    appeal of, 326−327
        contribution to professional practice,
            326
        improving expository skills, 327
        professional development, 327
        writing as learning, 326
    obstacles to, 327−329
        practice demands, 328−329
        publication knowledge, 327−328
        publication options, 328
    performance guide checklist, 344f
    performance improvement guide to,
        331−344
    publication targets, 329−330
Written communication, 327

Y
Yahoo, 316

Made in United States
North Haven, CT
10 May 2024

52380974R00239